OXFORD WORLD'S CLASSICS

MY LIFE

BENVENUTO CELLINI was born in Florence in 1500. Apprenticed at the age of 13 to a goldsmith, Cellini entered the fascinating world of the Italian workshop, the focal point of artistic production in Renaissance Italy. During his long distinguished career, he created some of the period's most famous jewellery and objets d'art (such as the famous salt-cellar for the King of France). His masterpiece, the statue of *Perseus* with the head of the Medusa, was returned to the Piazza della Signoria of Florence after its successful restoration in 2000. Cellini died in 1571 and was buried in the Chapel of St Luke in the Church of the Santissima Annunziata in Florence, the chapel sacred to artists of the city.

Cellini's autobiography grows out of a long tradition of Florentine writing about art and family memoirs, but no single prose work in Italian during the period captures the colour, the intrigue, and the personalities of sixteenth-century Renaissance Italy better than Cellini's *My Life*. In it the artist becomes the embodiment of the hero who succeeds against all odds. Although today it stands as a monumental accomplishment along-side the statue of Perseus, Cellini's manuscript was not published until 1728 in Italy; the first English translation appeared in 1771; Goethe produced a German translation in 1798. As a result of the discovery of his life story, Cellini became famous during the Romantic revolution not only for his artistic production but also for the adventuresome quality of his life, inspiring Hector Berlioz's Romantic opera, *Benvenuto Cellini* (1838). Cellini has thus come to embody the heroic qualities of the artist in both the Renaissance and the Romantic periods.

JULIA CONAWAY BONDANELLA is Professor of French & Italian and Associate Dean of the Honors College at Indiana University. She is the author of *Petrarch's Visions and Their Renaissance Analogues*; co-editor of *The Cassell Dictionary of Italian Literature*; and the translator of many literary classics, including *Rousseau's Political Works: A Norton Critical Edition*, Giorgio Vasari's *Lives of the Most Famous Artists*, Carlo Ridolfi's *The Life of Titian*, and Niccolò Machiavelli's *Discourses on Livy*. She is a Past President of the National Collegiate Honors Council.

PETER BONDANELLA is Distinguished Professor of Comparative Litera-ture, Film Studies, Italian, and West European Studies and Chairman of the Department of West European Studies at Indiana University. He is the author of critical works on Machiavelli, Guicciardini, Umberto Eco, Fellini, Rossellini, and a history of Italian cinema. His translations include Machiavelli's *Discourses on Livy* and *The Prince*, Giovanni Boc-caccio's *The Decameron*, Giorgio Vasari's *Lives of the Most Famous Artists*, and Carlo Ridolfi's *The Life of Titian*. He is a Past President of the American Association for Italian Studies.

OXFORD WORLD'S CLASSICS

BENVENUTO CELLINI

My Life

Translated with an Introduction and Notes by
JULIA CONAWAY BONDANELLA
and PETER BONDANELLA

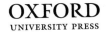

OXFORD
UNIVERSITY PRESS

OXFORD
UNIVERSITY PRESS

Great Clarendon Street, Oxford OX2 6DP

Oxford University Press is a department of the University of Oxford.
It furthers the University's objective of excellence in research, scholarship,
and education by publishing worldwide in

Oxford New York

Athens Auckland Bangkok Bogotá Buenos Aires Cape Town
Chennai Dar es Salaam Delhi Florence Hong Kong Istanbul Karachi
Kolkata Kuala Lumpur Madrid Melbourne Mexico City Mumbai Nairobi
Paris São Paulo Shanghai Singapore Taipei Tokyo Toronto Warsaw

with associated companies in Berlin Ibadan

Oxford is a registered trade mark of Oxford University Press
in the UK and in certain other countries

Published in the United States
by Oxford University Press Inc., New York

First published as an Oxford World's Classics paperback 2002
Reissued 2009

British Library Cataloguing in Publication Data

Data available

Library of Congress Cataloging in Publication Data

Data available

ISBN 978–0–19–955531–4

4

Typeset in Ehrhardt
by RefineCatch Limited, Bungay, Suffolk
Printed in Great Britain by
Clays Ltd, St Ives plc

For family and friends
and especially for two of that greatest generation
Russell Raymond Rohlff
John Gilbert Conaway

CONTENTS

INTRODUCTION

Benvenuto Cellini's autobiography remained in manuscript from the
time of its composition (between 1558 and 1566) until 1728, when
the first Italian edition appeared, followed by the influential English
translations of Thomas Nugent (1771) and Thomas Rosco (1822).
No less a literary figure than Goethe made the first German translation, which appeared in book form in 1798. Nineteenth-century
writers such as Stendhal were enthusiastic about the work, and
the artist's life became the basis of a major opera, *Benvenuto Cellini*,
by Hector Berlioz (1838). Cellini became famous in the age of
Romanticism because that period worshipped the figure of the solitary, defiant artist with the same passion that Cellini himself
embodied. Romantic readers of *My Life* saw Cellini as a kindred
spirit, and although this elective affinity falsified, in many respects,
not only the historical facts but the real artistic culture of Cellini's
times, the popularity of Cellini's autobiography during the nineteenth century guaranteed his subsequent reputation as one of the
High Renaissance's greatest artists.

Literary Precedents

Many precedents existed for a work of this kind, although in the
history of Italian literature nothing quite like Cellini's autobiography
exists before his fascinating account of sixteenth-century Italy and
France, populated by colourful Renaissance popes, kings, and dukes,
as well as some of the greatest artists Europe has ever produced.
While its author was no university graduate, Cellini's autobiography,
as well as his art, reflected a very substantial education acquired from
a variety of literary, artistic, and historical sources.

It would be impossible to mention the genre of autobiography
without citing the formative model of St Augustine's *Confessions*.
Certainly, Cellini's account of his spiritual transformation while
imprisoned in Rome shows evidence of the influence of both Augustine and Boethius. Augustine, or any of the many saints' lives that a
practising Catholic such as Cellini must have known, would certainly
have suggested the major division of the autobiography into two

sections, divided between the portion of his life that took place before his miraculous religious experience in prison and the second, mature portion of his life that included his triumph with the casting of the *Perseus*. In fact, one of the most important themes in the autobiography is Cellini's belief that he has been saved by the intervention of divine grace from the influence of malevolent stars to accomplish great things in his chosen profession.

Literary influences from Cellini's place of birth, sixteenth-century Florence, probably play a more important role in the author's intellectual formation than any perceptible antecedents in classical or humanist literature. It had long been customary for Florentine merchants and businessmen, as well as more learned intellectuals, to write their memoirs (*ricordanze*) or at least to jot down important events of note (*ricordi*) for their family and posterity. In fact, besides his autobiography, a number of such *ricordi* by Cellini himself are extant. We know that Cellini was an avid reader of both the Bible and the *Chronicle* of Giovanni Villani (*c.*1275–1348). Villani's account of early Florentine history was published during Cellini's lifetime (between 1537 and 1554), but the work had enjoyed a wide manuscript circulation in Florence for many years before this. Like most Florentines, Cellini also knew Dante's *Divine Comedy* extremely well. In fact, while giving an account of his experiences in France, he offers a novel interpretation of one of the most vexing passages in Dante's epic poem based upon his own experiences in the Parisian courts and a hypothetical visit by both Dante and Giotto to the same city.

As an artist, Cellini was clearly conversant with classical mythology, since many of his artistic subjects depended upon sometimes extremely complex allegorical references to the past, or equally sophisticated parallels between classical history and events in Cellini's own world. Based upon a number of his own poetic compositions (sonnets and longer poems), it is clear that he knew something of the Petrarchan lyric tradition. Cellini's prose may well be said to equal or surpass the greatest Italian writers of his century, but his poetic ability is far less substantial, as a reading of the poems included in *My Life* will easily demonstrate.

The most colourful and humorous elements of *My Life* owe an obvious debt to the only contemporary tradition of fiction available to Cellini: the collections of Florentine short stories or *novelle* best exemplified by Giovanni Boccaccio's masterpiece, *The Decameron* (1349–50), which by Cellini's day had become the acknowledged model for Italian Renaissance prose, just as Petrarch's *Canzoniere* or *Songbook* was accepted as the model for Renaissance lyric poetry. A number of the most memorable episodes Cellini describes in *My Life* might well be lifted from the pages of such a collection of period *novelle*. One of Cellini's closest friends and a fellow member of the Accademia delle Arti del Disegno was Anton Francesco Grazzini, known as Il Lasca (1503–84). Grazzini produced an important collection of some thirty *novelle*, heavily indebted to Boccaccio's example, which were published as *Le cene* (*The Suppers*, 1549), one of which received an English translation by no less a figure than D. H. Lawrence. Undoubtedly Cellini and most of his contemporaries considered such fictional literature far more important than the learned treatises of humanist intellectuals associated with the Medici court, like Benedetto Varchi (1503–63), although he did seek the latter's advice on the literary language employed in *My Life*.

Much of Cellini's autobiography discusses his adventures while travelling in both Italy and France. Renaissance Spain had only a short time before given birth to the picaresque genre with the novel *Lazarillo de Tormes* (1554). While the literary form of the autobiography differs from that of the picaresque novel, there is definitely something of the *picaro* in Cellini's personality, for he is not merely an artist: he is also a man of action, an individual quite capable of committing criminal acts ranging from brawling and sodomy to theft and murder. Like the Spanish *picaro*, the literary figure Benvenuto Cellini created by the author Benvenuto Cellini represents a character constantly in search of economic betterment. There is also something Spanish (or at least Southern Italian) about Cellini's violent temper and his instant jump from words to weapons when he feels his honour, courage, or artistic abilities have been called into question. But such anger and a propensity to violence are also exquisitely Florentine traits, if we are to believe Dante, who placed many of his compatriots in Hell for precisely such violent behaviour.

Cellini's Character

The artistic milieu of Renaissance Florence was itself an important centre of literary activity. Many of the artists of the period wrote works that are today acknowledged literary classics. Michelangelo was the period's most original and inspired lyric poet, but other artists (Cellini, Bronzino) also produced lyrics. Leonardo da Vinci's notebooks are masterpieces of inventiveness, intelligence, and wit. Like Cellini, both Pontormo and his arch-rival, Baccio Bandinelli, produced works about their activities and daily lives in the *ricordanze* tradition. Of course, the most important precedent that Cellini could have known was Giorgio Vasari's masterful collection of artists' biographies celebrating the greatness of Florentine art from Giotto to his own day. The first version of his *Lives of the Artists* appeared in 1549–50, some years before Cellini settled down to write his own autobiography. The fact that Vasari virtually ignores Cellini in both the first and the final, definitive (1568) edition of his highly influential work certainly explains, to some extent, why Cellini felt compelled to set the record straight with *My Life*. No love was lost between the two men: both idolized Michelangelo and tried to emulate his style in a number of ways. Cellini could never forgive Vasari (whom he calls 'Little George'—Giorgetto or Giorgino—in his autobiography) for his support of a rival (Bartolomeo Ammannati) in a contest to decide who would construct the Neptune fountain in the Piazza della Signoria. When Ammannati received the commission, Cellini placed much of the blame for his loss upon Vasari. Unlike Vasari, Cellini was not a proper courtier and never learned to control either his tongue or his temper around his superiors, who frequently expected that his opinion should conform with their own. Much of Cellini's appeal to modern readers lies precisely in his refusal to become a 'yes man', in his rebellious stance in the face of what was very often niggardly, patronizing, ignorant, and arbitrary power. Vasari probably did not provide a separate biography of Cellini in his *Lives of the Artists* for the obvious reason that, by 1568, Cellini had written both his autobiography (which circulated widely in manuscript) as well as two extensive treatises on goldsmithing and sculpture in which there are lengthy discussions of his life and works. Vasari nevertheless felt obliged to note that Cellini was 'a person who unfortunately knew all too well how to express his opinions with princes.'[1] Cellini's unwillingness to remain in his proper 'place', the

---

[1] Giorgio Vasari, *Le vite de' più eccellenti pittori, scultori e architettori*, ed. Paola della Pergola, Luigi Grassi, and Giovanni Previtali (Novara: Istituto Geografico de Agostini, 1967), viii. 46 (editors' translation).

rank society would have imposed upon him if he had obeyed its strictly hierarchical rules, naturally caused him problems with his patrons, including popes, kings, dukes, and wealthy private citizens. None of these individuals particularly enjoyed being told they were mistaken, misguided, or incorrect, something Cellini never hesitated to point out.

Cellini's belief in the superiority of his artistic talent often caused him to disagree with his patrons or to denigrate his inferior artistic competitors. But his personal temperament also frequently caused him to fly into fits of rage with all sorts of other classes of people, from soldiers and bureaucrats to doctors, innkeepers, and peasants. His talents as a swordsman were almost as renowned as his abilities as an artist and writer, and Cellini frequently called upon these bellicose skills to defend his life, his honour, and his property. If a historically accurate film were made of *My Life* today, the script would require an action-hero actor such as Errol Flynn, Arnold Schwarzenegger, or Russell Crowe to portray this swashbuckling artist unafraid to measure himself with emperors, kings, dukes, and popes (not to mention men of baser station).

Cellini's life story reads as if it were created from the pages of a Hollywood screenplay. Nevertheless, for the most part, Cellini's description of his life and times is basically accurate. True, we cannot prove that his miraculously accurate and lengthy shot from the Castel Sant'Angelo killed the leader of the army besieging the pope there during the Sack of Rome, but there is no doubt that Cellini performed prodigious feats of bravery at the time. Only a small fraction of the artistic work Cellini produced during his lifetime has survived. Unfortunately, jewellery and works containing valuable metals and precious jewels were frequently melted down in hard times or political emergencies. But the extant work is truly marvellous. His coins and medals are beautifully wrought, small masterpieces. His brilliant salt-cellar is a Mannerist triumph of sculpture in miniature. His masterpiece, the complex project of the *Perseus*—for it includes many works, not merely a single sculpture—is truly as astounding an achievement as Cellini makes it out to be in the dramatic pages of *My Life*, where the artist narrates its almost supernatural moment of creation and its miraculous casting in the midst of overwhelming personal, artistic, and technical difficulties. Cellini had a very high opinion of himself and his works, but scholars such as John Pope-Hennessy remind us that Cellini's talents were as awe-inspiring as his claims. Furthermore, the account of his life is corroborated by a great deal of archival evidence. It is difficult, therefore, to interpret *My Life* as merely an imaginary story full of fictitious events designed solely to embellish a posthumous reputation. Of course, Cellini wrote *My Life* to establish the pre-eminence of his artistic talent. But with some few exceptions (his sex life, for example), Cellini's autobiography is far more accurate and has far more historical buttressing in extant documents than many other such autobiographic works of the period. No other Renaissance autobiography, with the possible exception of Montaigne's *Essays*, creates such a sympathetic and complex protagonist.

The Perseus *and How It Was Created*

The central event of Cellini's narrative, after the spiritual awakening in prison which confirms his artistic vocation by signs of divine favour, is the casting of the *Perseus*. Cellini was always plagued by an inferiority complex, since his first profession (goldsmith) was considered much less exalted a craft than painting, sculpture, or architecture. Back in his native city of Florence, which boasted the greatest sculpture and bronze casting since classical antiquity, Cellini needed to measure himself against such titanic figures as Donatello, Verrocchio, and Michelangelo if he were to be taken seriously. Cellini needed the *Perseus* project to catapult him into the ranks of major artistic talents. It did so, even if Duke Cosimo I, the despotic and niggardly patron who commissioned the work, never truly appreciated Cellini's achievement, paying him the final instalments of his fee some thirteen years after the work was triumphantly unveiled in the Loggia de' Lanzi in 1554. It has remained for centuries the second most-popular work of Italian Renaissance sculpture, after Michelangelo's *David*. In some respects, it may well be an even greater achievement.

The casting of *Perseus* is the crucial event in *My Life*. Consequently, a detailed explanation of how Cellini worked in bronze may be useful.[2] Initially, Cellini constructed a framework (*armature*),

---

[2] The website provided during the restoration of the *Perseus* (www.perseo.org) contains the most thorough explanation of Cellini's technique in casting the *Perseus*, and our discussion here is greatly indebted to it. The website also provides information

essentially a skeleton made of iron rods fixed into a base. This framework resembled a stick figure with arms, legs, trunk, and head. Then he placed a rough version of the figure, slightly smaller than the final product, over the frame. This rough version was known as the casting core (*anima*) and was made from a mixture of clay and other materials. In Italian, this clay was called *luto*. As Cellini noted, such a casting core should be about a finger's width in thickness. Parts of the core were carbonized when it was fired so that the core became porous and could absorb the gases given off during the casting of the molten bronze. After Cellini fired the core, he covered it with a thick coat of wax, which he then sculpted into the image he aimed to produce with the bronze.

At this point, Cellini removed the core (although many bronze castings leave the core intact) by placing openings he called *morse* or clamps in the wax. They were designed to keep the hollow spaces between the core and the jacket separate during the melting of the wax. Then Cellini created casting channels (*getti*) and air vents (*arie*) to channel the molten bronze and to allow air to escape. These channels were constructed by applying a system of wax sticks to the wax model, sealing them so that the mould filled completely while the air was completely expelled. After these channels were set up, Cellini covered the wax and all the channels with clay. The first layer (about a finger's width in thickness) was called the jacket (*camicia*). Subsequent applications produced a mantel or hood (*mantello*, *cappa*) strengthened with rags, wire, and rings.

Next, Cellini subjected the bulky mass, covered with several layers of various materials surrounded by wire and held up by iron, to a very slow fire to melt the wax. The wax flowed out of the holes and was 'lost' as it left empty spaces between the casting core and the jacket. This is why the process has traditionally been known as the 'lost wax' method of casting bronze. This 'lost wax' process was one employed in ancient times—another reason why it was esteemed by Renaissance artists mesmerized by the artistic masterpieces of

---

about the discoveries made during the restoration. For an important discussion of Cellini's casting process, see John Pope-Hennessy, *Cellini* (London: Macmillan, 1985). For the theory guiding the restoration work, see Lorenzo Morigi, 'Cellini's Splendor: The Reversible Theory of Restoration', *Sculpture Review*, 48: 3 (1999), 16–19.

classical antiquity. Cellini then placed the mould, in which the clay was fired and dried, into a pit (*fossa*) in the floor of the workshop. He mixed earth removed from the pit with sand and pressed it around the mould so that the earth would be able to support the bronze when it was cast. He employed terracotta tubes to connect the vent holes in the mould with the surface. He then poured the molten metal during the casting into a casting mouth or opening (*bocca di colata*). Two channels (*canali di colata*) were built to carry the molten bronze from the furnace to the casting mouth and were constructed of unfired bricks covered with clay, which were then fired.

Finally, the moment of casting arrived. Cellini placed bronze ingots in the furnace so that the flames melted them easily. It was precisely at this stage in the casting process that Cellini's work encountered a technical crisis, for the bronze began to solidify because the furnace was not functioning properly. This artistic crisis also provided Cellini with the literary excuse to portray his artistic solution to the crisis as something almost superhuman, the ultimate proof of his artistic genius and his Godlike creativity. As he recounted the tale in *My Life*, Cellini's assistants frantically awakened the artist from a deep sleep when the casting began to go badly. Cellini immediately added oak wood that had been dried thoroughly to increase the fire's temperature. Since he had no tin at hand, he threw a number of tin household plates (*piatti di stagno*) from his kitchen into the fire, which reduced the melting point of the bronze low enough so that the metal flowed freely and went into the mould, completely filling it up. Cellini's salvation of his masterpiece by literally throwing into the fire most of his kitchenware has a dramatic, almost incredible quality. Most readers of *My Life* assume that his description of his casting of the statue was provided to embellish the tale with literary, dramatic, and therefore false touches. Yet, his emergency solution would have been unsuccessful had Cellini not understood, as few of his contemporaries did, all the intricate details of the technology involved in casting bronze statues. Had Cellini not grasped totally the various scientific principles involved in the casting, and if he had not cleverly arranged the vents and channels so that the mould filled as quickly as it did, his *Perseus* would have become only one more of a long line of unsuccessful public statues, another victim of too much ambition and too little scientific knowledge.

After the casting, Cellini removed the mould from the pit and allowed it to cool down. Then the statue was dug out of the mould. At this point, the results left him completely satisfied, since only the right foot of *Perseus* was defective, as the artist had earlier predicted to his incredulous patron, the duke. The recent restoration of the statue confirms Cellini's claim in *My Life*.[3] It substantiates the artist's explanation that the statue was definitely poured in one piece, with only a defective right ankle. This defect was removed by cutting away the faulty section and recasting it with a seamless patch. The most difficult parts of the casting—the head of the Medusa, the arm and head of Perseus—were brilliant successes. At this stage, air or gas bubbles that appeared had to be removed, part of the cleaning and retouching process (*rinettatura*) that was a far more laborious part of sculpture than one might imagine from reading Cellini's account. This involved serious manual labour and required chiselling, beating small pieces of bronze into holes, even recasting and remelting. In fact, Cellini spent some seven years after the casting thoroughly closing the pores on the metal's surface with hammers and chisels, thereby protecting the internal parts of the metal from corrosion. The complexity of Cellini's chasing his statue after it had been cast has also been confirmed by the scientific evidence obtained during the recent restoration. The fact that the *Perseus* has survived for so many centuries standing uncovered in the centre of Florence is no accident. Cellini's own refined method of refinishing the cast statue, and the original patina he provided for the work, saved it from destruction by water, pigeons, and acid rain.

After employing abrasives to smooth and polish the surface, Cellini gave his masterpiece a patina with mixtures of alkaline sulfides. The original patina he applied was darker than contemporary tastes might select and was closer to the dark patina that he and other metal sculptors applied to the small bronze works that may be found in great number in the National Sculpture Museum in Florence, the Bargello. On certain parts of the statue Cellini applied thin gold foil, most of which has been worn off in the passage of time. Some pieces

---

[3] For details on the discoveries about Cellini's working methods made during the restoration, see Morigi, 'Cellini's Splendor'. Basically, the recent restoration work confirmed Cellini's description of his working methods and his extraordinary success in casting the statue with a single pouring of the metal.

of the work (the sandals worn by Perseus or the wings on his helmet) were welded to the figure. The Medusa's body was anchored to the figure of Perseus by an iron ring attached with an iron rod encased in lead. Rings and an anchor held the figures of both Perseus and Medusa to the statue's base, devices also created by Cellini. Finally, the blood of Medusa was fastened to the statue by another iron rod and rivets.

The Medici Commission

My Life never provides a satisfactory explanation for Cosimo's reason for wanting to commission an image of Perseus to be placed in the Loggia de' Lanzi. As an artist, Cellini was far more interested in the implicit competition which pitted his talents against those of Donatello and Michelangelo, whose masterful statues stood in the square facing the Loggia de' Lanzi where his Perseus would be placed. When the first expulsion of the Medici family from Florence took place in 1494, not only was a radical republican form of government instituted but Donatello's famous statues, *David* and *Judith and Holofernes*, originally private commissions for the interior of the Medici palace, were removed and set up in public view in front of the Palazzo della Signoria (eventually known as the Palazzo Vecchio) to signal the end of Medici tyranny. David and Judith were seen by Florentine republicans as archetypal Old Testament tyrannicides, Hebrew counterparts to Livy's first Brutus, who freed Rome of the Tarquin tyrants. Anti-Medici republicans further defined the public space there in a political and ideological context when Michelangelo's *David* was erected in the square in 1504. Michelangelo's political leanings were definitely republican, even though he worked on many projects commissioned by the Medici family, a stance clearly embodied in another republican work, his great bust of Brutus, and by the fact that during the time Florence was besieged by Medici forces before it capitulated to their army in 1530, Michelangelo was actively engaged in building the city's fortifications. Moreover, when the Medici entered the city, he was forced to save his life from angry Medici partisans by hiding in the Church of San Lorenzo, the very church for which he had created so many works for his Medici patrons.

The story of Perseus is a complex mythological tale.[4] Perseus was the offspring of the union between Danaë and Jupiter, who impregnated her after transforming himself into a shower of gold. Perseus' most heroic exploit involved the killing of Medusa, one of the snake-haired Gorgons, a monster whose face turned whoever set eyes upon it into stone. Aided by a mirror-like shield from Minerva (his protectress) and a curved sword from Mercury, Perseus killed Medusa by looking at the monster's reflection in his shield, rather than staring directly at her. Upon Medusa's death, the winged horse Pegasus sprang from her body. After his return home on Pegasus, Perseus rescued the beautiful maiden Andromeda, with whom he fell in love, by killing a sea monster which was about to devour her. When he finally reached home and married Andromeda, a disappointed suitor led a mob against him, but by using Medusa's head, Perseus turned them all into stone. After that, Perseus became a great mercenary leader and the founder of royal dynasties in Greece. In short, he was a brave warrior, he slew monsters, he fought evil, and he established order where once there existed only chaos.

Cosimo de' Medici belonged to a minor branch of the Medici family, and only became ruler of Florence because another Medici, Duke Alessandro, was murdered by Lorenzaccio de' Medici in 1537. The Medici had returned to Florence with the assistance of outside forces (imperial troops), and despite extremely hostile opposition to them from many sectors of the city. Cosimo, the son of the mercenary leader Giovanni delle Bande Nere, and not part of the original line that could be traced back to Cosimo de' Medici Il Vecchio or Lorenzo il Magnifico (the two greatest members of the family from the preceding century), was a mere boy of 18. The Florentine patricians who opposed both Medici absolutism and the radical republicanism of the government that had just been overthrown, led by the distinguished diplomat and historian, Francesco Guicciardini (1483–1540), basically gave the title of ruler of Florence to Cosimo because they felt they could control this youthful and inexperienced boy. They were sadly mistaken, for Cosimo proved to be one of the cleverest political rulers of his century.

Cosimo not only succeeded in defeating the armies of the

---

[4] A beautiful explanation of the myth's interesting complexities may be found in Italo Calvino's *Six Memos for the Next Millennium*, trans. Patrick Creagh (New York: Vintage, 1993).

expatriates sent against him, but he also managed to use the conflict between Habsburg emperors and French monarchs to his
advantage by allying himself with the imperial forces and becoming, in effect, an important buffer state and ally of the most powerful political force in Europe. By clever marriages, Cosimo increased
his personal power and reduced his real rivals, the Florentine
patricians who wanted to prevent the creation of a hereditary Medici
dynasty, to a state of impotence. After 1557, Cosimo's military
victory over Siena enlarged the duchy of Tuscany, and his hegemony in the province was confirmed by the title of Grand Duke,
which he received from his foreign allies. When he died in 1574 at
the age of 55, Cosimo left behind a stable, durable government that
would last for two centuries. When his dynasty died out in the
mid-eighteenth century Tuscany became part of the Austrian
empire, until it joined the new nation state of Italy formed in the
nineteenth century.

Cosimo's legacy represented an important political achievement.
But the image we have of him from Cellini's autobiography represents something less than a heroic figure. In Cellini's experience
Cosimo was capricious, suspicious, tyrannical, and difficult to please.
In this, he resembled the popes for whom Cellini had worked, and,
on occasion, the king of France. However, there was a cheap,
ungenerous, petty streak in Cosimo's character that the French
monarch never exhibited. And, in some respects, Cosimo's artistic
tastes may well have been less refined than those of Francis I.
Cosimo clearly favoured such artists as Baccio Bandinelli, Giorgio
Vasari, and Bartolomeo Ammannati over Cellini, while his treatment
of Cellini seems shabby, ungrateful, and essentially unfair. But posterity, with a little assistance from Cellini's autobiography, has
reversed Cosimo's judgement. Today, Cellini ranks as one of the
most popular of all Renaissance artists, while few visitors to Florence
remember Vasari as the architect of the Uffizi and fewer still admire
his painting. And thanks in good measure to Cellini's scathing comments about Bandinelli's style, few onlookers in the Piazza della
Signoria regard his *Hercules and Cacus*, standing near the copies of
Michelangelo's *David* and Donatello's *Judith and Holofernes*, with
anything but amusement. In life, Cellini always sought to have the
last word, even with popes, kings, and dukes. In death, thanks to his
talent and his autobiography, he may well have enjoyed the last word

in his competition with his rivals, through the legacy of his *Perseus* and the exciting tale of its creation.

For Cosimo, who faced serious opposition during the first two decades of his rule, political legitimacy was a paramount concern. Faced with so many republican images directly in front of the major government offices and his own residence, it is not surprising that he desired to set his own stamp upon the public space of Florentine civic life. The selection of the subject of Cellini's commission as Perseus slaying Medusa could easily be linked to Cosimo's own achievements. Like Perseus, he was a notable military leader. Like Perseus (at least from the Medici perspective), Cosimo had liberated Florence from the Medusa of political turmoil. A new dispensation could be seen at work in the square: Judith and David (republican images of freedom from tyranny) gave way to a tyrant's self image that promoted order over disorder, stability over chaos.

Contemporary admirers of Cellini's *Perseus* need not understand the iconographical and ideological overtones of his great bronze work to appreciate its stunning beauty and monumental technical achievements, any more than they must be partisans of an ancient republican cause to praise the works of Donatello and Michelangelo that once contended ideologically with Cellini's work in the Piazza della Signoria. Cellini, who was constantly vexed by his relationship with Duke Cosimo, would turn to the composition of *My Life* at precisely the lowest moment of his career: after he was released from a prison term for sodomy and had obviously fallen out of the duke's good graces as far as future work was concerned, despite the astounding success and popular acclaim of the *Perseus*.[5] Cellini did very little important artistic work after he began

[5] For details about how the charge of sodomy late in life affected Cellini and his composition of *My Life*, see Paolo L. Rossi, 'The Writer and the Man: Real Crimes and Mitigating Circumstances: *Il caso Cellini*', in Trevor Dean and K. J. P. Lowe (eds.), *Crime, Society and the Law in Renaissance Italy* (Cambridge: Cambridge University Press, 1994), 157–83; or '*Sprezzatura*, Patronage, and Fate: Benvenuto Cellini and the World of Words', in Philip Jacks (ed.), *Vasari's Florence: Artists and Literati at the Medicean Court* (Cambridge: Cambridge University Press, 1998), 55–69, 263–5. Rossi argues that Cellini's accusation of sodomy in 1557 (when he escaped the death penalty but was fined, imprisoned, and deprived of the right to hold public office) moved him to write *My Life* in order to justify his life to that period of time. In fact, as Rossi notes, the first part of the book is dominated by astrology. In that section, Cellini presents himself as an innocent man controlled by the stars. The second part of the autobiography shifts the focus away from an astrological explanation of his chronic misfortunes and disagreements with colleagues and patrons, and concentrates more upon his *virtù* as an

dictating and composing his life story. Apparently, his literary muse received direct inspiration from his artistic energy. When hope of completing a further great work seemed to have vanished entirely, the author Cellini set aside the composition of his autobiography as well, abandoning his literary creation, the artist Cellini, almost in mid-sentence of his manuscript, as he sets off for Pisa.

Although Cellini received less from Duke Cosimo for the *Perseus* than he was promised, the posthumous fame he achieved with the eventual publication of *My Life* would have more than compensated the artist for his excursion into the literary field. For perhaps the first and only time in his career, Cellini created an artistic masterpiece without owing the slightest debt to miserly, disagreeable, tasteless, or ungrateful patrons. His self-portrait was entirely of his own making, and it may rightly be said to rank, in literary terms, alongside the heroic statue of Perseus and Medusa that remains as Cellini's legacy, long after the memory of his unworthy patrons has faded.

---

artist, with the apotheosis in his description of the casting of the *Perseus*. In this section of the autobiography, the protagonist seems to have triumphed over the evil influence of the stars as a result of his close relationship with God (a change in his life that took place while imprisoned in the Castel Sant'Angelo).

NOTE ON THE TEXT AND TRANSLATION

Not unlike the adventurous life of its author, the history of the actual manuscript of Cellini's autobiography and its publication history are extremely complex.[1] Cellini probably composed his autobiography between 1558 and 1567: the contents of *My Life* cover events from the author's birth in 1500 until 1562, some nine years before his death in 1571. Even though Cellini published several treatises on sculpture and goldsmithing during his lifetime (1568), for a number of personal reasons he decided not to send the manuscript of his autobiography to the publisher, even though it seems that he had prepared what one scholar has called a 'bella copia', or a manuscript destined for the printer, that contains a number of autograph sections.[2] This manuscript is extant and is known to scholars as manuscript A: the Codice Mediceo–Palatino 2342 in Florence's Biblioteca Laurenziana. Antonio Cocchi was responsible for the first Italian edition in 1728, a publication that apparently was not based upon this particular autograph manuscript but, rather, upon another that was in circulation. During Cellini's lifetime, his friend Benedetto Varchi (1503–65), a Florentine academician, historian, and linguistic theorist, examined the text around 1559 and suggested revisions in the language. The author of the most famous book on art during Cellini's lifetime, Giorgio Vasari (1511–74), was certainly aware of

[1] The basis of the present edition and translation is the fundamental critical edition prepared by Lorenzo Bellotto: Benvenuto Cellini, *La vita* (Parma: Fondazione Pietro Bembo, 1996). Bellotto's notes and commentaries should be supplemented by what still remains the most impressive commentary on Cellini's writing, the English translation in two volumes by Robert H. Hobart Cust, *The Life of Benvenuto Cellini* (London: G. Bell, 1910). Cust's work represents a unique instance in the history of Renaissance scholarship in which an English translation of a classic text contains a more erudite and useful scholarly apparatus than many of the Italian critical editions subsequently published. Much of the critical literature after 1910 relies upon Cust's commentary, often without acknowledging this source. While the Symonds translation has traditionally been the edition of choice for decades, followed years later by the Bull version, no edition of Cellini in *any* language (including our own) would be possible without Cust's work.

[2] The phrase is Paolo L. Rossi's in his fundamental essay '*Sprezzatura*, Patronage, and Fate: Benvenuto Cellini and the World of Words', in Philip Jacks (ed.), *Vasari's Florence: Artists and Literati at the Medicean Court* (Cambridge: Cambridge University Press, 1998), 57. We are very much in Professor Rossi's debt for his lucid discussion of the manuscript tradition of *My Life* and its method of composition.

the existence of Cellini's autobiography in manuscript form. In the definitive edition of his *Lives of the Most Famous Artists* (1568), Vasari notes that he will not include a detailed biography of Cellini in his work, since the artist himself has treated the subject in both an autobiography and in two treatises on sculpture and goldsmithing, large sections of which are autobiographical.

The actual composition of *My Life* followed a complex itinerary. The original manuscript A—Codice Mediceo-Palatino 234² in Florence's Biblioteca Laurenziana—is composed of 520 leaves or 1,019 pages, numbered only on the recto. Of these, 114 pages are autograph, including the opening sonnet, a brief section of prose following the poem, and pp. 464b–520a. Several pages are blank (69–80), one is repeated (112), and one is missing (113).³ Most of the other pages of the manuscript are written by the hand of copyist Michele di Goro Vestri, except for pp. 461a–464b, which were composed by an as-yet unidentified second copyist. The manuscript contains a number of corrections and additions by Cellini and others (including Varchi), as well as erasures in several places. In particular, sections critical of Cellini's patron, Duke Cosimo I of Tuscany, have been changed, erased, or toned down. The current condition of this autograph manuscript is extremely fragile, but an examination of it underscores the fact that it was hardly dictated to a scribe from memory but was, instead, the product of several previous revisions. It is simply too polished a document to have been produced by dictation to a scribe while its author was engaged in other activities (particularly the strenuous physical labours associated with sculpture and goldsmithing).

In addition to this fundamental autograph manuscript, there are others of importance currently preserved in Florence. The Biblioteca Laurenziana also holds two manuscripts that seem to be based upon manuscript A: manuscript B, the Palatino 234, in a seventeenth-century hand; and manuscript C, the Laurenziano Antinori 229, in an eighteenth-century hand. The Biblioteca Nazionale Centrale of Florence holds a third manuscript, D, known as the Magliabechiano XVII, v, 29 (probably the source of the first printed Italian edition in 1728). And the Accademia di Belle Arti in Florence

---

³ Detailed discussions of the manuscript tradition of *My Life* are to be found in the Cust translation, the Bellotto edition, and in Rossi, '*Sprezzatura*, Patronage, and Fate', 55–69, 263–5.

holds a fourth manuscript, E, identified as Codice 101, S. In short, even though Cellini never decided to send his 'bella copia' to the publisher, the manuscript obviously circulated among his friends and fellow artisans sufficiently widely to generate a number of copies or versions.

While the details are unclear, the original Mediceo–Palatino 2342 manuscript A apparently became the property of the Cavalcanti family around the end of the seventeenth century, and was jealously preserved by Andrea Cavalcanti (1610–73), a member of the Accademia della Crusca. Subsequently, it was given to the Florentine poet Francesco Redi (1626–98), who cited it in the Accademia della Crusca's Italian dictionary (1729), a year after *My Life* appeared in Italian. Somehow, manuscript A then migrated to a monastery library in Florence. In 1805 it was acquired by the director of the Biblioteca Laurenziana from a Florentine bookseller. Upon his death in 1825, it was bequeathed to the library, where it remains today.

Our translation has attempted to retain the freshness and clear quality of Cellini's language, which is not that of the learned academic treatise but, rather, the beautiful Tuscan tongue spoken by Cellini's contemporaries and the basis of contemporary Italian. According to Cellini's own account, the manuscript was primarily dictated by the author to a copyist, and not actually written out by his hand as a literary document. But the most recent scholarship[4] rejects the somewhat incredible notion that Cellini was a carefree artisan-biographer who smoothly produced a literary masterpiece through dictation, assisted by a prodigious memory and a single copyist. On the contrary, manuscript A itself argues against such a romantic theory of composition, for it is one of the most polished literary works of Italian Renaissance prose in existence, clearly the result of earlier revisions, corrections, and deletions. Cellini's literary language possesses all the quotidian characteristics of the vigorous Florentine speech of his era: a pleasant, conversational tone; great wit and humour; dramatic figures of speech; unusual metaphors; and passionate outbursts of anger. There is nothing of the academic or the pedantic in his prose. On the contrary, we may consider *My Life* as an accurate reflection of language in the various

[4] In particular, see Rossi, '*Sprezzatura*, Patronage, and Fate', 56–7.

milieux in which Cellini travelled, not only the most refined salons and courts of the day but also the inns, workshops, brothels, and post-houses that he frequented.

As other editors and translators have done in the past, we have provided readers with chapter numbers and, occasionally, paragraphs, following those in the Bellotto edition, in order to facilitate the use of our edition. Cellini did not provide such assistance. One further explanation is also in order. We have decided to entitle our translation and edition *My Life*, and have rejected the traditional title chosen by other previous translations and actually invented by their editors or translators: *The Autobiography of Benvenuto Cellini*. We believe *My Life* reflects not only the spirit but the letter of the autograph manuscript. Neither Cellini nor his contemporaries employed the somewhat scholarly term 'autobiography'. Even today, the term has a dry, professorial ring to it; it is a label rather than a title. For such an egocentric author as Benvenuto Cellini, only the much bolder and expressive term, *My Life*, does justice to its talented creator.

In recognition of their varied and valuable contributions to this new edition and translation of Cellini's *My Life*, we would like to express our appreciation to Bruce Cole, our colleague and friend of a quarter-century; Rachel Johnson, an honours student at Indiana University, who has savoured Cellini's writing and his art; Ronald Conaway, prize-winning biochemist; and Don Glass, from 'A Moment of Science', produced by WFIU, the public radio station at Indiana University. We are grateful to the research support we received from the Indiana University College of Arts and Sciences, especially to former Dean Mort Lowengrub. Last and most especially, we owe a great debt to our fine editor, Jeff New, who helped us polish and refine our translation and critical materials with his wise advice, creative guidance, and skilful editing.

SELECT BIBLIOGRAPHY

Italian Critical Editions of Cellini's Writings

I trattati dell'oreficeria e della scultura di Benvenuto Cellini, ed. Carlo Milanesi (Florence: Felice Le Monnier, 1857; repr. 1994).

La vita, ed. Lorenzo Bellotto (Parma: Fondazione Pietro Bembo, 1996).

La vita, ed. Guido Davico Bonino (Turin: Einaudi, 1973).

Vita, ed. Ettore Camesasca (Milan: Rizzoli, 1985).

English Translations of Cellini's Writings

Autobiography, trans. George Bull (Harmondsworth: Penguin, 1956; rev. edn., 1998).

The Autobiography of Benvenuto Cellini, ed. Charles Hope, trans. John Addington Symonds (New York: St Martin's Press, 1983; abridged edn. with illustrations).

The Life of Benvenuto Cellini, trans. Robert H. Hobart Cust, 2 vols. (London: G. Bell, 1910).

The Life of Benvenuto Cellini Written by Himself, trans. John Addington Symonds, with an Introduction and Notes by John Pope-Hennessy (London: Phaidon, 1951).

The Treatises of Benvenuto Cellini on Goldsmithing and Sculpture, trans. C. R. Ashbee (New York: Dover, 1967).

Studies of Cellini's Art and Writings

Avery, Charles and Susanna Barbaglia (eds.), *L'opera completa del Cellini* (Milan: Rizzoli, 1981).

Morigi, Lorenzo, 'Cellini's Splendor: The Reversible Theory of Restoration', *Sculpture Review*, 48: 3 (1999), 16–19.

Pope-Hennessy, Sir John, *Cellini* (London: Macmillan, 1985).

Rossi, Paolo L., 'The Writer and the Man: Real Crimes and Mitigating Circumstances: *Il caso Cellini*', in Trevor Dean and K. J. P. Lowe (eds.), *Crime, Society and the Law in Renaissance Italy* (Cambridge: Cambridge University Press, 1994), 157–83.

—— 'Sprezzatura, Patronage, and Fate: Benvenuto Cellini and the World of Words', in Philip Jacks, (ed.), *Vasari's Florence: Artists and Literati at the Medicean Court* (Cambridge: Cambridge University Press, 1998), 55–69, 263–5.

Historical and Cultural Background to Cellini's Times

Alberti, Leon Battista, *On Painting*, trans. John R. Spencer (New Haven: Yale University Press, 1970).

Bondanella, Julia, and Mark Musa (eds. and trans.), *The Italian Renaissance Reader* (New York: New American Library, 1987).

Bondanella, Peter, and Julia Bondanella (eds.), and Jody Shiffman (associate ed.), *Cassell Dictionary of Italian Literature* (London: Cassell, 1996).

Brucker, Gene, *Renaissance Florence* (Berkeley: University of California Press, 1983).

—— (ed.), *The Society of Renaissance Florence: A Documentary Study* (New York: Harper, 1971).

Burckhardt, Jacob, *The Civilization of the Renaissance in Italy*, 2 vols. (New York: Harper, 1975).

Cennini, Cennino d'Andrea, *The Craftman's Handbook: The Italian 'Il Libro dell'Arte'*, trans. Daniel V. Thompson (New Haven: Yale University Press, 1933; repr. New York: Dover, 1960).

Chastel, André, *The Sack of Rome*, trans. Beth Archer (Princeton: Princeton University Press, 1983).

Cole, Alison, *Virtue and Magnificence: Art of the Italian Renaissance Courts* (New York: Abrams, 1995).

Cole, Bruce, *Italian Art 1250–1550: The Relation of Renaissance Art to Life and Society* (New York: Harper, 1987).

—— *The Renaissance Artist at Work: From Pisano to Titian* (New York: Harper, 1983).

Guicciardini, Luigi, *The Sack of Rome*, trans. James H. McGregor (New York: Italica Press, 1993).

Hale, J. R. (ed.), *A Concise Encyclopaedia of the Italian Renaissance* (New York: Oxford University Press, 1981).

Hall, James, *Dictionary of Subjects and Symbols in Art*, rev. edn. (London: John Murray, 1984).

—— *A History of Ideas and Images in Italian Art* (New York: Harper, 1983).

Hartt, Frederick, *History of Renaissance Art: Painting, Sculpture, Architecture* (New York: Abrams, 1969).

Hibbert, Christopher, *The House of Medici: Its Rise and Fall* (New York: Morrow, 1975).

Jacks, Philip (ed.), *Vasari's Florence: Artists and Literati at the Medicean Court* (Cambridge: Cambridge University Press, 1998).

Kempers, Bram, *Painting, Power and Patronage: The Rise of the Professional Artist in Renaissance Italy* (Harmondsworth: Penguin, 1994).

McHam, Sarah Blake (ed.), *Looking at Italian Renaissance Sculpture* (Cambridge: Cambridge University Press, 1998).

Mirollo, James V., *Mannerism and Renaissance Poetry: Concept, Mode, Inner Design* (New Haven: Yale University Press, 1984).

Muir, Edward, *Mad Blood Stirring: Vendetta in Renaissance Italy* (Baltimore: Johns Hopkins University Press, 1998).

Murray, Peter, *The Architecture of the Italian Renaissance* (London: Thames and Hudson, 1986).

Partner, Peter *Renaissance Rome 1500–1559: A Portrait of a Society* (Berkeley: University of California Press, 1976).

Partridge, Loren, *The Art of Renaissance Rome 1400–1600* (New York: Abrams, 1996).

—— *Introduction to Italian Sculpture*, 3 vols. (London: Phaidon, 1986).

Rocke, Michael, *Forbidden Friendships: Homosexuality and Male Culture in Renaissance Florence* (Oxford: Oxford University Press, 1996).

Saslow, James M., *Ganymede in the Renaissance: Homosexuality in Art and Society* (New Haven: Yale University Press, 1986).

Schlosser, Julius, *La letteratura artistica*. 3rd rev. edn., ed. Otto Kurz (Florence: La Nuova Italia, 1964).

Shearman, John, *Mannerism* (Harmondsworth: Penguin, 1967).

Stinger, Charles L., *The Renaissance in Rome* (Bloomington: Indiana University Press, 1985).

Thompson, Daniel V., *The Materials and Techniques of Medieval Painting* (New York: Dover, 1956).

Turner, A. Richard, *Renaissance Florence: The Invention of a New Art* (New York: Abrams, 1997).

Vasari, Giorgio, *Vasari on Technique*, ed. Louisa Maclehose and G. Baldwin Brown. (London: Dent, 1907; repr. New York: Dover, 1960).

Wackernagel, Martin, *The World of the Florentine Renaissance Artist: Projects and Patrons, Workshop and Art Market*, trans. Alison Luchs (Princeton: Princeton University Press, 1981).

Woods-Marsden, Joanna, *Renaissance Self-Portraiture: The Visual Construction of Identity and the Social Status of the Artist* (New Haven: Yale University Press, 1998).

Further Reading in Oxford World's Classics

Ariosto, Ludovico, *Orlando furioso*, trans. and ed. Guido Waldman.

Leonardo da Vinci, *Selections from the Notebooks*, ed. Irma A. Richter.

Machiavelli, Niccolò, *The Prince*, trans. and ed. Peter Bondanella and Mark Musa.

Michelangelo Buonarroti, *Life, Letters, and Poetry*, trans. and ed. George Bull with Peter Porter.

Vasari, Giorgio, *The Lives of the Artists*, trans. and ed. Julia Conaway Bondanella and Peter Bondanella.

A CHRONOLOGY OF BENVENUTO CELLINI

In order to assist the reader, the editors have linked this chronology to the text of *My Life* by book and chapter numbers in parenthesis. (Book and chapter divisions were added by later editors of Cellini's manuscript.) Some dates listed here are still a matter of dispute among art historians and scholars. Because Cellini omits some events from his life and breaks off the composition of the autobiography some years before his death, this chronology naturally covers some events that have no relevant textual referents.

1500	Born in Florence on 3 November in the Cellini family home on Via Chiara (I, 1–5).
1513	Obtains father's permission to enter the workshop of Michelangelo Brandini, a goldsmith and armour maker and the father of Baccio Bandinelli, Cellini's future rival (I, 6–7).
1515	Enters the workshop of the goldsmith Antonio di Sandro, known as Marcone (I, 7).
1516	After a duel, Cellini is exiled with his younger brother from Florence for six months; works in Siena with the goldsmith Francesco Castoro; sent by his father to study music in Bologna and works in several workshops with goldsmiths (I, 9).
1517	Leaves Florence for Pisa, where he works in the workshop of Ulivieri della Chiostra (I, 10–11).
1518	Back in Florence, Cellini works for Antonio di Sandro, Francesco Salimbene, and executes a silver belt-buckle that gains him admission into the goldsmiths' guild (I, 13).
1519	Moving to Rome with his friend Giovanbattista Tasso, he works for the goldsmith Giovanni de Giorgis, called Firenzuola, is invited to work in England by the sculptor Pietro Torrigiani, and executes a silver salt-cellar for a cardinal (I, 14).
1522	After the plague breaks out in Rome, he returns to Florence and to Salimbene's workshop; the goldsmith Giambattista Sogliano gives Cellini a part of his workshop (I, 15).
1523	Cellini is fined for sexual misconduct with a certain Domenico di Giuliano da Ripa and provokes a fight with the Guasconti family, for which he receives a fine; subsequently he wounds Gherardo Guasconti (I, 16–17) and is condemned to death *in absentia* after

he flees to Rome. Among his commissions are two candlesticks for the Bishop of Salamanca and jewellery for the wife of Sigismondo Chigi (I, 19–21).

1524   Cellini works in the workshop of Giovanpiero della Tacca and plays in the papal band (I, 23); he eventually opens his own workshop. Has numerous disputes and duels with various people, interrupting his work (I, 24–5), and makes ewers, vases, medallions, and seals for important churchmen (I, 25–31). Also encounters such artists as Giulio Romano and others in the circle around Raphael.

1525   Cellini convalesces in Cerveteri, where he meets Rosso Fiorentino.

1527   He ends his quarrel with the Guasconti family. On 6 May imperial troops enter Rome and the Sack of Rome continues for most of the year. During the siege, Cellini takes refuge in the Castel Sant'Angelo with Pope Clement VII and performs, by his own testimony, prodigious feats of bravery (I, 34–7). The Pope orders Cellini to melt down quantities of gold and unset many of the papal jewels (I, 38). After the sack ends Cellini leaves Rome for Florence (I, 39). Meanwhile, in Florence, the Pope's problems with the Emperor allow republican forces to drive out the Medici and to install another republican government.

1528   Cellini is in Mantua working on seals and a reliquary for the Gonzaga court (I, 40).

1529   Cellini returns to Florence, where the plague has killed his father. He is recalled to Rome by Clement VII and begins to work at the Papal Mint designing coins, as well as ornaments for the papal garments (I, 41–5). His brother Cecchino is killed, and Cellini buries him in San Giovanni dei Fiorentini in Rome (I, 48–50). The Pope and the Emperor make peace, and the republicans in Florence are besieged.

1530   Cellini avenges his brother by killing his assassin, escaping serious punishment because of the Pope (I, 51). He opens a shop in what is today the Via dei Banchi Nuovi. The Medici re-enter Florence.

1531   Clement VII names Cellini *mazziere* (mace-bearer), a post he will lose in 1533 because of the Milanese goldsmith Pompeo de' Capitaneis (I, 55). Alessandro de' Medici becomes head of a new government backed by Emperor Charles V, ending Florentine republican government forever and beginning the dynastic rule of the Medici family that will last until the eighteenth century.

1532–3   Cellini works with Tobia da Camerino on jewellery for Clement VII, as well as on medals (I, 60–3). He attributes his eye trouble to a contagion of a young serving girl. He performs acts of necromancy in the Roman Colosseum (I, 64) and loses his position as *mazziere*.

1534   After wounding a notary, he flees to Naples (I, 66–7). Returning to Rome, he presents to Clement VII a bronze medal (I, 70–1). On 26 September he kills Pompeo (I, 73) and is absolved by the new pope, Paul III (I, 74), who commissions him to make his coins.

1535   Worried by the opposition of the Pope's son, Pier Luigi Farnese, Cellini goes to Florence (I, 75), then to Venice, accompanied by Tribolo, where he meets Sansovino (I, 76–7). Back in Florence he executes some coins for Duke Alessandro de' Medici (I, 80), falls ill in Rome after returning there on the Pope's invitation, and almost dies (I, 84–5). Still sick, Cellini goes back to Florence. Paul III gives him several commissions, including one for a jewelled book cover.

1536   Emperor Charles V comes to Rome and Cellini presents him with the still-unfinished book cover (I, 90–3).

1537   Cellini goes to France with his young pupil Ascanio de' Mari (I, 93–4). Not warmly welcomed by Rosso Fiorentino, Cellini meets King Francis I at Fontainebleau (I, 98) and accompanies him to Lyons, where the artist falls ill. He meets Ippolito d'Este, soon to become cardinal. Alessandro de' Medici is assassinated and replaced by Cosimo de' Medici from a different branch of the family. Cellini leaves for Italy (I, 99) and returns to Rome (I, 100).

1538   Pier Luigi Farnese manages to have Cellini imprisoned in the Castel Sant'Angelo (I, 101–3) on charges of stealing jewels during the Sack of Rome, an accusation lodged by his former apprentice Girolamo Pasucci. Cellini escapes and finds refuge in the home of Cardinal Cornaro (I, 108–10).

1539   After being returned to the Pope by the Cardinal, Cellini is placed in the Prison of Tor di Nona (I, 114) and then returned to the Castel Sant'Angelo (I, 116), where he experiences a vision (I, 122) before being liberated on 24 November through the intercession of the now Cardinal Ippolito d'Este (I, 127).

1540   Cellini works for Cardinal Ippolito d'Este, making a wax model for what will eventually be the famous golden salt-cellar of King Francis I (II, 1–2). On his journey to France he kills a man in

Siena (II, 4) and stops in Ferrara (II, 3–8), where he executes a medal and other works for Duke Ercole II d'Este. King Francis welcomes him (II, 8) and he goes to Paris, where he is assigned the same stipend that was given to Leonardo da Vinci and the castle of Le Petit Nesle. Cellini begins work on large statues with classical themes (II, 12–15) and numerous other projects.

1542   Cellini receives naturalization papers from the King (II, 19), as well as the commission for a large fountain at Fontainebleau; he works on the famous salt-cellar (II, 16, 18) and the model for the portal and fountain of Fontainebleau (II, 20).

1543   Probably completes the salt-cellar, plus work on the Nymph of Fontainebleau, a model for the portal, and a model for the statue of Mars (II, 22).

1544   On 7 June his daughter Costanza is born (the mother is one of his models: II, 37). He works on a statue of Jupiter, the first of the large silver statues (II, 41). During the year Cellini probably executes the bas-relief of the Saluki hound.

1545   Returning to Italy because of problems with the King's mistress (II, 49), Cellini travels via Lyons (II, 50–1) before stopping at Piacenza and then Florence (II, 51–2), where Duke Cosimo gives him the commission for the *Perseus*, for which he executes a wax model (II, 53, 57). He begins the bronze bust of Cosimo I and receives a house from the Duke on Via del Rosario, where he goes to live with his sister Liperata and her six daughters. He has arguments with the Duke's majordomo Pier Francesco Riccio (II, 54–5), and does various small projects for the Duchess, Eleonora di Toledo (II, 58, 64).

1546   After being accused of sodomy, Cellini flees for a few months to Venice, where he encounters Titian and Sansovino (II, 62). Back in Florence, he works on Cosimo's bust, on the head of the Medusa, and on *Perseus* (II, 63), as well as works in marble (II, 71–2) and other items for the Duchess (II, 65, 68). During some time in this year the banker Bindo Altoviti, must have posed in Florence for his bronze bust that is delivered several years later.

1547   In Cosimo's presence Cellini argues with Baccio Bandinelli over a block of marble (II, 70–1); Cellini restores the Greek statue of Ganymede (II, 69) and works on a marble figure of Narcissus (II, 72), during which he is injured in his eye by a splinter of steel. He completes the bronze bust of Cosimo I (II, 73). King Francis dies and is succeeded by Henry II, who had married Catherine de' Medici in 1533.

1548   Cellini buys farms in Trespiano and in Fiesole; the body of Medusa is cast.

1549   The casting of the main part of the *Perseus* takes place (II, 73, 75–8). Pope Paul III dies.

1550   Bindo Altoviti's bust is completed (II, 79); small figures for the base of the *Perseus* are executed.

1551   Cellini goes to Rome and stays with Bindo Altoviti (II, 79–80). He meets Michelangelo (II, 81), but fails to convince him to return to Florence.

1552   Completes a number of the smaller works to be included in the structure around the base of the *Perseus*.

1553   Refinishing work takes place on various parts of the *Perseus* project (the date 1553 on the actual statue refers to this phase and not to the casting). A son is born on 27 November, the offspring of another model named Dorotea. Cellini works on the fortification of two of the gates of Florence (II, 85–6).

1554   *Perseus* is unveiled to an astonished public in the Loggia de' Lanzi on 27 April (II, 89–92). The final touches to the work will require some seven years of additional work. Cellini makes a pilgrimage to give thanks for his success (II, 93–4). Upon his return, his relations with the Duke deteriorate, and the artist requests permission to leave Florence (II, 93–4). Cellini recognizes his son Jacopo Giovanni and provides a dowry for his mother Dorotea, who subsequently married a certain Sputasenni, with whom Cellini has many quarrels.

1555   Cellini's son Jacopo dies after being included in his will. Cellini begins receiving a stipend from the Duke that will continue until 1558.

1556   Cellini spends time in prison for an assault on the goldsmith Giovanni di Lorenzo Papi before being reprieved by the Duke on 26 October. He buys half of a farm in Trespiano.

1557   An Arno River flood damages Cellini's workshop and his statue of Narcissus. Cellini is condemned for sodomy, fined, and condemned to imprisonment for four years on 27 February, but is released to house arrest by the Duke's intervention so that he can complete his Crucifix. The disfavour into which he has fallen with the Duke is reflected by the fact that his bronze bust of Duke Cosimo is banished to an obscure spot in Portoferrario.

1558   Begins the composition or the dictation of *My Life*, covering his autobiography to November 1562 (I, 1). He decides to take religious vows, and receives minor orders on 2 June (he will renounce them two years later).

1559   Exhibits models for a statue of Neptune (II, 99, 100–6) in the Loggia de' Lanzi, a competition he will lose to Ammannati, perhaps as a result of Giorgio Vasari's influence.

1560   Cellini begins his unlucky dealings with the peasant Sbietta, giving birth to arguments, attempted poisonings, and legal disputes that last until his death (II, 104–5). Cellini's arch-rival, Baccio Bandinelli, dies.

1561   On 22 March one of Cellini's domestics gives birth to another son (Giovanni), whom Cellini recognizes in his will. Cellini goes to Livorno to ask Cosimo's permission to leave Florence, but is unsuccessful (II, 108).

1562   Completes his marble Crucifix (II, 100–1). He petitions the Duke for permission to wear armour and carry a sword in Florence. He has a daughter, Elisabetta, and secretly marries her mother, Piera. Caterina de' Medici asks Cellini if he wants to return to France, but the Duke opposes the move (II, 112). Three members of the ducal family die after Cellini goes to Pisa, and here *My Life* abruptly ends without following the rest of the author's life. The manuscript is not published during Cellini's lifetime.

1563   Joins the newly created Accademia delle Arti del Disegno, for which he does designs for the seal. His son Giovanni dies.

1564   Cellini is delegated by the Accademia to put together the apparatus for the magnificent funeral for Michelangelo, and argues with Vasari over the allegories representing the various arts. Because of an illness, Cellini cannot attend the funeral. Another daughter, Reparata, is born.

1565   The marble Crucifix is brought to the Palazzo Pitti, a work for which Cellini asked 1,500 ducats (in 1570 he will be paid half that sum). During the year he is cancelled from the ducal payroll.

1566   On 3 September Cellini has another daughter, Maddalena. He buys a house in Via Benedetta and rents it to a nobleman from Ferrara, with whom he has many disputes.

1567   Receives 3,500 scudi instead of the 10,000 he had requested for the *Perseus*. He begins his treatises on goldsmithing and sculpture (the only works he published during his lifetime), hoping to dedicate them to Francesco I. He officially marries Piera de' Parigi.

1568   Cellini's treatises on goldsmithing and sculpture are published in Florence.

1569   On 24 March a third son, Andrea Simone, is born.

1570   Cosimo I receives the official title of Grand Duke of Tuscany. Cellini is elected Consul of the Accademia delle Arti del Disegno.

1571   Cellini dies on 13 February. After official ceremonies by the Accademia, he is buried in the Chapel of St Luke in the Church of the Santissima Annunziata in Florence, near the tomb of Pontormo.

1728   Antonio Cocchi publishes the first Italian edition of *My Life*.

1771   Thomas Nugent publishes the first English translation of *My Life* (*The Life of Benvenuto Cellini*); subsequent translations by Thomas Rosco (*Memoirs of Benvenuto Cellini*, 1822) and John Addington Symonds (*The Life of Benvenuto Cellini*, 1888) spread Cellini's fame throughout the English-speaking world.

1796   Goethe begins publishing the first German translation of *My Life* in magazine instalments, with a complete translation appearing in 1798; because of Goethe's reputation, interest in Cellini and his work increases all over Europe.

1838   Hector Berlioz writes his opera, *Benvenuto Cellini*.

1898   *The Treatises on Goldsmithing and Sculpture* are first translated into English by C. R. Ashbee.

1910   Robert H. Hobart Cust publishes a two-volume translation, *The Life of Benvenuto Cellini*, which includes a fundamental scholarly commentary.

1998–2000 After a lengthy and successful restoration completed in public view at the Uffizi Museum in Florence, on 24 June 2000 the resplendent *Perseus* returns to its original place in the Loggia dei Lanzi.

MY LIFE

THE LIFE OF BENVENUTO
SON OF MASTER GIOVANNI CELLINI

WRITTEN BY HIMSELF IN FLORENCE

I write* of this troubled life of mine
to thank the God of Nature,
who gave me my soul and then cared for it;
I have achieved many noble exploits, and still I live.

God has rendered harmless this cruel destiny of mine;
now He makes my life and my ability grand beyond all measure;
in me He exemplifies grace, valour, and beauty so that
I surpass many others and reach even those who surpass me.

It pains me intensely only now that I realize
how much precious time I lost in vanities
as our fragile thoughts are carried away by the wind.

Since repentance is of no avail, I shall be content
to rise as high as I fell as Benvenuto
in the flower of this worthy Tuscan land.*

I had begun to write this life of mine in my own hand, as can be seen
in certain of the pages assembled here, but just when I thought I was
losing too much time and it seemed an utterly futile effort, a son of
Michele Goro from Pieve a Groppine* showed up, a young fellow of
around fourteen who was rather sickly. I began to have him do the
writing, and while I was working, I dictated* the story of my life to
him; and since I actually took some pleasure in it, I worked much
more diligently and produced many more works of art. Thus, I left
the burden of writing to this boy, and I hope to continue on as long as
my memory serves me.

BOOK ONE

1. All men of any condition who have done something of special worth or something that may truly resemble those things of special merit,* should, if they are truthful and good people, write in their own hands the story of their lives, but they should not begin such a fine undertaking* until they have passed the age of forty. I have finally realized this, now that I am over the age of fifty-eight, and finding myself in Florence, my native city, I recall the many adversities that befall anyone who lives; being now freer from such adversities than I have ever been to this point in my life, it seems to me that I enjoy greater happiness of mind and health of body than I ever did in previous years; and I can recall both delightful blessings and immeasurable afflictions, which, when I think back upon them, make me utterly astonished that I have reached the age of fifty-eight and, through the grace of God, continue to grow older.*

2. Although men who have toiled with some measure of exceptional skill have made themselves known to the world, this skill alone should suffice to make them regarded as men of renown, but since it is necessary to live in such a way that one discovers how others live, a bit of pride enters into the account, which may take on many different aspects. The first thing to be done is to make it known to others that one is descended from persons of special abilities and ancient origins. My name is Benvenuto Cellini, son of Master Giovanni, son of Andrea, the son of Cristofano Cellini; my mother was Madonna Elisabetta, daughter of Stefano Granacci; and both were Florentine citizens. We find in the chronicles written by our Florentines of ancient times, who were all trustworthy men, according to what Giovanni Villani writes,* that the city of Florence was evidently built in imitation of the fair city of Rome, and certain vestiges of the Colosseum and Baths can still be seen.* These ruins are near Santa Croce; the Capitol was where the Old Market is now located; the Rotunda* made for the Temple of Mars is still standing; today it is our Baptistery dedicated to St John. The truth of this can easily be seen and cannot be denied, but these buildings are much smaller than those in Rome. It is said that the man who had them built was Julius Caesar, along with some Roman noblemen, who, once Fiesole had been conquered and taken, raised a city in this spot, and each of them took the responsibility for erecting one of these notable edifices. Julius Caesar had a captain of the highest rank and courage by the name of Fiorino of Cellino, which is a small town about two miles from Montefiascone.* Once Fiorino had made camp under the hills of Fiesole, where Florence now stands, in order to be near the Arno river for the convenience of his troops, all the soldiers and those who had anything to do with this captain used to say: 'Let us go to Fiorenze,'* both because this captain's name was Fiorino and because there was a natural abundance of flowers in the place where he had made his camp. Thus, in founding the city this name struck Julius Caesar as being most beautiful and appropriate, and, since flowers bring good fortune, he gave the name of Florence to this town. And Caesar also wanted to show this great favour to his valiant captain, whom he loved all the more since he had raised him from a very humble rank and transformed him into a man of exceptional abilities. The learned and inventive etymologists declare that the name Florence is derived from the fact that the city is located on the flowing Arno;* this does not appear to be the case, because Rome is on the flowing Tiber, Ferrara on the flowing Po, Lyons on the flowing Saône, and Paris is on the flowing Seine, and yet the names of all these towns are different, having arisen in other ways. This is the truth of the matter, and we believe, therefore, that we are descended from a man of exceptional ability. Moreover, there are Cellinis of our family in Ravenna, the most ancient city in Italy, where there are many noble families; there are also Cellinis in Pisa, and I have discovered them in many parts of Christendom; and in this state,* some parts of the family have remained, who are still devoted to the profession of arms; not long ago, a beardless youth named Luca Cellini fought with an experienced soldier and an extremely courageous man, who had often before fought in the ring,* by the name of Francesco da Vicorati. Through his own special ability and with sword in hand, this Luca overcame and killed that man with such bravery and skill that he amazed everyone, for all were expecting completely the opposite outcome, so that I take enormous pride in tracing my origin back to men of exceptional ability.*

Now, as for how I myself have gained honour for my family, con-tributing to its present status both through well-known events and through my own art, which is not yet a subject of great importance,* I shall discuss these things in the proper place. I take far more pride in having been humbly born and having laid down the beginnings of fame for my family than if I had been born into an aristocratic lineage and stained or sullied it by my defects. I will begin, then, by telling how, as it pleased God, I came to be born.

3. My ancestors used to live in Val d'Ambra,* where they had a great deal of property, and having taken refuge there on account of the strife between political factions, they lived like little lords: they were all devoted to soldiering and were extremely brave. At that time, a younger son of theirs, who was called Cristofano, started a great quarrel with friends of theirs and neighbours, and the heads of the families on both sides became involved in it and considered the fire Cristofano had kindled to be of such importance that it placed both families in danger of being destroyed. Once the older family members had considered this prospect, they agreed that my ancestors would send Cristofano away and the other side would send away the other young man who was at the origin of the quarrel. The other family sent their young man to Siena, while our family sent Cristofano to Florence, where they bought him a little house in Via Chiara* near the convent of Santa Orsola, as well as some very good property near Ponte a Rifredi. This Cristofano took a wife in Florence and had a family of sons and daughters, and the daughters were all provided for; then, after their father's death, all the sons divided what remained of his property. The house in Via Chiara, along with a few other things, went to one of these sons who bore the name of Andrea. Andrea also took a wife and had four male children. The first was named Girolamo; the second Bartolomeo; the third Giovanni, who became my father; and the fourth Francesco. This Andrea Cellini had a good knowledge of architecture as it was practised in those times, and he made a living through this craft;* Giovanni, who was my father, dedicated himself to this craft more than any of his brothers. And since, as Vitruvius declares, anyone who wants to practise that art well must have, among others things, a good deal of experience in music and good design,* once Giovanni had made himself into a good draughtsman he began to work at the study of music, and at the same time learned to play the viola and flute very well; and being a very studious person, he rarely went out. As a next-door neighbour they had a man named Stefano Granacci,

interesting who he starts with

who had several daughters, all of whom were very beautiful. As it pleased God, Giovanni saw one of these young women, whose name was Elisabetta, and she pleased him so much that he asked if he could have her as his wife. Since both of the fathers were extremely well acquainted, through living in such close proximity, this marriage was easily arranged, and each of them felt that he had organized his affairs very well indeed. First of all, those two worthy old men concluded the match, after which they began to discuss the dowry, and since at this point there was some friendly disagreement between them, Andrea said to Stefano: 'My son Giovanni is the most worthy youth in Florence and in all of Italy, and had I wanted to give him a wife before now, I would have had one of the largest dowries bestowed in Florence upon people like us.' But Stefano answered: 'You have a thousand good reasons, but since I have five daughters as well as many sons, given my calculations, this is as high as I can go.' Giovanni had been listening for a while, hidden away from them, and he suddenly came up and declared: 'O Father, this is the young woman I have desired and loved, not their money: woe to anyone who wants to better himself through his wife's dowry. In fact, since you have always boasted about my abilities, won't I know how to support my wife and to satisfy her needs with a lesser sum of money than what you wish? Now I want to make you understand that the lady is mine, and, as for the dowry, I want it to be yours.' Andrea Cellini, who was a bit irascible,* was rather annoyed by this, but in a few days Giovanni married his beloved and never requested any additional dowry. They enjoyed their youth and their holy love for eighteen years, always with a great longing for children. Then, in the eighteenth year of their marriage, Giovanni's wife miscarried two sons because of the doctors' incompetence; soon after, she again became pregnant and gave birth to a girl, whom they named Cosa after my father's mother.* Then two years later she again became pregnant, and since those little problems that in pregnant women require a good deal of attention were exactly like those she had with the last child, they were absolutely certain she would give birth to a girl as before, and they had agreed to give her the name of Reparata after my mother's mother. It happened that she gave birth on the night of All Saints' Day at exactly half past four in the year 1500.* The midwife, who knew my parents were expecting a girl, cleaned the little creature, wrapped it in beautiful white linens, and very

He was thought a girl.

quietly approached Giovanni, my father, saying: 'I am bringing you a fine gift, one you did not expect.' My father, a truly wise man, was pacing back and forth, and he replied: 'What God gives me is always dear to me', and drawing back the linens, he saw with his own eyes the son who was entirely unexpected. Joining the palms of his old hands, he raised them, along with his eyes, to God, and exclaimed: 'Lord, I thank you with all my heart: this gift is very dear to me: and let him be welcome [*benvenuto*].'* Everyone there was happily asking him what the child would be called. Giovanni never responded to them, except to say: 'And let him be welcome.' And so they decided to baptize me with that name, and I go on living with it by the grace of God.

4. When I was already about three years old, Andrea Cellini, my grandfather, was still living and had passed the age of one hundred. One day they had changed a pipe on a kitchen sink when out of it emerged a large scorpion they had not seen, and it dropped to the ground from the pipe and disappeared under a bench: I saw it, and having run over to it, I took it in my hand. It was so big that, in my small hand, its tail hung out from one side and both its claws from the other. They say that I ran to my grandfather with great joy, crying out: 'Grandfather, look at my nice crab!' Realizing it was a scorpion,* my grandfather almost dropped dead out of great fear and concern for me, and while he asked me for it in the kindest way, I grasped it even more tightly, crying that I did not want to give it to anyone. My father, who was still at home, came running when he heard my cries and, dumbfounded, he did not know how to find a way to prevent that poisonous creature from killing me. At that moment he happened to spy a pair of scissors, and so he coaxed me into letting him cut off the tail and the claws. Once he felt the great danger was over, he took this as a good omen.

When I was around the age of five, Giovanni, my father, was in one of our small rooms where some washing had been done and there was a good oak-wood fire burning, and he was playing with his viola in his arms and singing all alone near the fire. It was extremely cold: gazing at the fire, in the midst of the brightest flames, he happened to catch sight of a little animal like a lizard which delighted in that intense blaze. Immediately realizing what the little animal was, he called my sister and me, and, while showing it to us children, he gave me such a hard slap that I immediately broke out crying. Then he gently consoled me and spoke to me in this fashion: 'My dearest little boy, I did not slap you because of something you did wrong but only so that you will remember that this lizard you have seen in the fire is a salamander,* which has never before been seen by anyone else as far as we know.' And then he kissed me and gave me a few *quattrini*.

5. My father began to teach me to play the flute and to sing; and although I was at the very tender age when young children usually take pleasure in whistles and other similar playthings, I found it exceedingly displeasing and would play only to be obedient. In those days my father fabricated marvellous organs with wooden pipes, and harpsichords—the best and most beautiful that could be seen at that time—as well as extremely beautiful and excellent viols, lutes, and wonderful harps. He was a skilled artisan, and in making musical instruments, as well as in constructing bridges, making equipment to work cloth, or other kinds of machines, he worked wonders; he was the first to execute fine work in ivory. But since he fell in love with music, which became my mother as he was my father, perhaps because of that little recorder he played rather more than he should have, the flautists of the Signoria* asked him to play with them. Thus, he did so for a time, first to amuse himself, and then because his fellow flautists urged him so insistently to become a member of their company. Lorenzo de' Medici and his son Piero,* who were very fond of him, then saw that he was spending all his time on the recorder and was neglecting his fine talent and craftsmanship: they therefore took this position away from him. My father took this very badly, since he felt that they had done him a serious affront. Immediately he returned to his craft and created a looking-glass of bone and ivory about an armslength in diameter, which contained both figures and foliage, executed with great finesse and strong design. The looking-glass represented a wheel: in its centre was the mirror itself; surrounding it were seven circles in which the seven virtues* were carved in ivory and black bone and joined together; the entire mirror and the seven virtues were balanced in such a fashion that when the wheel was turned the virtues revolved with it; and the counterweight at the base held the virtues upright. And because my father had some familiarity with the Latin tongue, he inscribed a Latin verse around this mirror which read as follows: 'Through all the turns of Fortune's wheel, virtue remains upright.'

Rota sum; semper, quoquo me verto stat virtus.*

Shortly thereafter, his position as flautist was restored. And even though some of these events occurred before I was born, recalling that I had heard about them, I did not want to leave them out. In those days such musicians were all very highly esteemed artisans, and some of them were even members of the major guilds of the silk and wool trade;* and this was the reason why my father felt no disgrace in following such a profession. The greatest desire he had in the world, in my regard, was for me to become a great musician, and the greatest displeasure I ever experienced in the world was when he discussed it with me, saying that if I wished, he thought I was so adept at such things that I would be the best of all.

6. As I said, my father was a very devoted servant and friend of the House of Medici, and when Piero was sent into exile,* he relied upon my father for numerous extremely important matters. Then, when the magnificent Piero Soderini* came to power and my father still held his post as a musician, Soderini, who knew of my father's marvellous talents, began to employ him in many important projects as an engineer, and as long as Soderini remained in power in Florence, he treated my father as well as can possibly be imagined. In those days, while I was still at a tender age, my father had me carried on someone's shoulders and had me play the flute; I played the soprano flute along with the palace musicians in front of the Palazzo della Signoria, and I played from the musical score while a page carried me on his shoulders. Then the Standard-bearer, who was the previously mentioned Soderini, took great pleasure in having me chatter away, and he gave me sweets and said to my father: 'Master Giovanni, along with the craft of music, you must teach him those other most beautiful crafts of yours,' to which my father replied: 'I don't want him to learn any other crafts except those of playing and composing, for in this profession I hope to make him the greatest man in the world if God will give him long life.' To these words some of the old priors* answered, saying to Master Giovanni: 'Do what the Standard-bearer is telling you to do; why should he never be anything but a good musician?' Thus, some time passed until the Medici returned.* Immediately after their return, the Cardinal, who later became Pope Leo,* did many kind favours for my father. While the Medici had been in exile, the balls on their coat of arms at the

Medici Palace had been removed and in their place had been painted a giant red cross, which was the coat of arms and insignia of the city government: when they returned, they immediately scraped off the red cross and on the shield they placed their red balls on a field of gold and decorated it very beautifully.* My father, who possessed a bit of natural poetic talent, as well as a touch of the prophetic, a gift that was certainly divinely inspired, placed these four verses under the Medici coat of arms as soon as it was uncovered; and they went like this:

> These arms, buried for so long
> Under the gentle and holy cross
> Now show their joyful and glorious face
> Awaiting St Peter's holy mantle.

This epigram was read by all Florence. A few days later Pope Julius II died. Upon going to Rome, and against every expectation in the world, Cardinal de' Medici was elected pope, becoming the generous and magnanimous Pope Leo X. My father sent him his four prophetic verses. The Pope sent him a message, telling him to come to Rome and that it would be worth his while. He did not want to go: indeed, instead of a reward, Iacopo Salviati* took his position in the palace away from him* as soon as he was elected Standard-bearer. This was the reason why I dedicated myself to the goldsmith's trade; part of the time I spent learning that craft and part of the time I played, though much against my will.

7. When my father spoke to me about this, I begged him to allow me to draw for so many hours of the day, while during all the rest I would devote myself to playing music for the sole purpose of making him happy. To this request, he replied: 'So, you don't like playing the flute?' To this I answered that I did not, because the art of music seemed to me far too contemptible compared to what I had in mind. My good father, in despair over this, placed me in a workshop with the father of Cavaliere Bandinello, whose name was Michelangelo, a goldsmith from Pinzi di Monte* and very good at his craft; he lacked the honour of a noble name, but was the son of a charcoal vendor: this would not be to Bandinello's discredit, who was the first to make his own family famous, had he done so with good reason. Whatever the case may be, I need not speak further of him. Although I had only been there for a few days, my father took me away from the

previously mentioned Michelangelo, since he could not bear to live without seeing me continuously. Thus, discontented, I continued playing the flute until the age of fifteen. If I wanted to describe all the important events that occurred in my life up to this time, including dangers to my own life, I would amaze anyone who would read about them, but since I want to avoid being long-winded and have a great deal to say, I shall leave them out.

At the age of fifteen, contrary to my father's desires, I became an apprentice in a goldsmith's shop, with a man called Antonio di Sandro, nicknamed Marcone the goldsmith.* He was a real expert and a fine man, proud and generous in his every action. My father did not want him to give me a salary as he usually did with the other apprentices, so that, since I had voluntarily chosen this craft, I could satisfy my wish to spend as much time as I liked on the art of design. And thus I did so most willingly and my excellent master took the greatest pleasure in my work. He had his only natural son, to whom he often gave orders so that he could spare me. Whether it was my great desire or true natural inclination, or both one and the other, in only a few months I reached the level of the good apprentices— actually the best young apprentices in the craft—and I began to profit from my labours. For all that, I did not fail in bringing pleasure to my good father on several occasions, now playing the flute and then the cornett; every time he heard me, the tears always streamed down his face, accompanied by heavy sighs; and often out of compassion I made him happy by showing him that I still derived some pleasure from playing my instrument.

8. At that time, I had a brother* two years younger than I who was extremely high-spirited and proud: he later became one of the great soldiers in the school of that marvellous Lord Giovannino de' Medici, the father of Duke Cosimo.* This young fellow was then about fourteen and I was two years older than he. One Sunday around two hours before sunset he became involved in a fight between the San Gallo and the Borgo Pinti gates with a young man of about twenty; they both had swords and my brother pressed him so bravely that, after severely wounding him, he was closing in on him. A great many people were present, among whom were quite a few of the young man's male relatives; when they saw things going badly for him, they took their many slingshots in hand, and one of the stones hit my poor young brother on the head: he immediately

fell down unconscious on the ground as if he were dead. By chance I was nearby, and without friends or arms, I was yelling at my brother as loudly as I could to withdraw, since what he had done was enough, when he fell down like a dead man, as I described. I immediately ran over and seized his sword and stood in front of him against a host of swords and many stones, but I never moved away from my brother until several very brave soldiers appeared at the San Gallo gate and rescued me from that furious mob, expressing their amazement that such great bravery could be seen in such a youth. Thus, I carried my brother home for dead, and when I reached home he came to his senses only with great difficulty. Once he was healed, the Eight,* who had already condemned our adversaries and banished them for several years, then banished us for six months to remain at least ten miles outside the city. I said to my brother: 'Come with me,' and so we departed from our poor father, and instead of giving us a small sum of money, since he had none, he gave us his blessing. I went off to Siena to find a certain gentleman by the name of Master Francesco Castoro;* and since on another occasion, when I had run away from my father, I had gone to this worthy man and stayed with him for several days until my father sent for me, always working at the goldsmith's trade, once I found this previously mentioned Francesco he immediately recognized me and set me to work. Once I began working for him, this Francesco gave me one of his houses to live in free of rent, for as long as I wished to stay in Siena; and there I brought my brother and myself, intent upon working for many months. My brother had begun to study Latin, but he was so young that he had not yet acquired the taste for developing his abilities, and he went around amusing himself.

9. At that time Cardinal de' Medici, who later became Pope Clement,* had us called back to Florence at my father's entreaties. A certain pupil of my father, moved by his own bad nature, told the Cardinal to send me to Bologna to learn to play well from a great music teacher who lived there, by the name of Antonio, truly a worthy man in the profession of playing an instrument. The Cardinal said to my father that if he sent me to Bologna, he himself would provide me with letters of introduction and assistance. My father, who was dying to see such a thing, sent me off and, eager to see the world, I willingly went. Once I had arrived in Bologna, I set to work with a man who called himself Master Ercole the Flautist,

and I began to earn my living; meanwhile I went every day for
music lessons, and in a few weeks I made great gains in playing that
cursed instrument, but I made even greater gains in the craft of
goldsmithing, for since I received no assistance whatsoever from the
Cardinal, I set myself up in the house of a Bolognese miniaturist
named Scipione Cavalletti, who lived on the street of Our Lady of
Baraccan;* and there I began to draw and to work for a Jew named
Graziadio, with whom I earned a good deal of money. At the end of
six months I returned to Florence, where that Piero the fife player,
who had been a student of my father's, took it rather badly, and in
order to please my father, I would go to Piero in his house and play
the cornett and the flute together with a brother of his by the name
of Girolamo, who was several years younger than this Piero, and who
was a good and worthy young man, completely the opposite of his
brother. On one such day my father came to this Piero's home to
hear us play, and since he took the greatest pleasure from my playing,
he declared: 'I shall make a wonderful musician out of him against
the wishes of those who have tried to stop me.' To this Piero replied
(and he spoke the truth): 'Your Benvenuto will derive much more
honour and profit if he applies himself to the craft of goldsmithing
instead of this fifing business.' My father took such great offence at
these words, since I held exactly the same opinion as Piero, that he
said in a rage: 'I knew very well you were the one who was hindering
the outcome I so greatly desired, and you were the one who had me
removed from my position at the palace, repaying me with the
enormous ingratitude that is too often the reward for great favour. I
had the post given to you, and you took mine away from me; I taught
you to play with all of the skill that you have, and you prevent my son
from fulfilling my wishes. But bear in mind these prophetic words: I
don't say that years or months will pass, but in just a few weeks you
will come to ruin for your shameful ingratitude!' To these words
Piero responded, saying: 'Master Giovanni, most men, when they
grow old, go a little mad at the same time, as you have; I'm not
surprised by this, since you have most generously given away all your
possessions, not having considered that your children might need
them, whereas I have thought of doing exactly the opposite—of
leaving so much to my children that they can help yours out.' To this
my father replied: 'No bad tree ever bore good fruit, but just the
opposite. Furthermore, let me say to you that you are evil, and your

children will all be foolish and poor, and they will come to beg from my exceptionally talented and wealthy children.' And so he left Piero's home, both men muttering the craziest things to each other. At this, I, who had taken my father's side, left along with him, and I told him I wanted to avenge the insults that ruffian had paid him on condition, I said, that 'you allow me to study the art of design'. My father answered: 'My dear son, I, too, was a good draughtsman in my day, but as a means of refreshment after such marvellous undertakings and for my sake, since I am your father who gave you life, raised you, and gave a beginning to your most honourable skills, will you promise me that on occasion, in order to relax, you will take your flute and your seductive cornett and play, amusing yourself and finding some real pleasure in it?' I replied that I would do so, and most willingly out of love for him. Then my good father said that these abilities of mine would be the best revenge I could contrive for the insults he had received from his enemies. Not a month after these words were spoken, the previously mentioned Piero, while having a vaulted cellar built in a home which he owned in the Via dello Studio, was standing on the ground floor one day right over the vault he was having built, along with some friends; the subject came up of his own master, who had been my father, and repeating the words my father had uttered to him about his downfall, no sooner had he uttered those words than the room in which he was standing—either because the vault had been poorly constructed or by the true power of God, Who does not wait until Saturday to pay what He owes—collapsed; and some of the stones and bricks of the vault that fell along with him broke his two legs, while the people standing with him, who remained on the edges of the vault, suffered no harm, although they stood dumbfounded and astonished, especially those who just a moment earlier had heard him speak with such contempt. Once my father learned of this, he armed himself and went to find Piero, and in the presence of Piero's father, a trumpeter of the Palazzo della Signoria named Niccolaio da Volterra, he announced: 'Piero, my dearest disciple, I deeply regret your misfortune, but, if you remember correctly, only a short time ago I warned you about this, and what I told you about the relationship between your children and mine will likewise come true.' Shortly thereafter, the ungrateful Piero died from his injuries. He left behind a loose wife with a son, who several years soon after came begging me for alms in Rome. I gave him some money, because it was my nature to give generously, and straightaway I recalled with tears the happy state in which Piero once lived, when my father pronounced those words—that is, that the children of that very Piero would someday go begging for mercy from his own talented children. I have said enough on this subject, and no one should ever make light of the prophecies of a good man who has been unjustly insulted, because he is not the one who speaks, but rather it is the voice of God Himself.

10. Meanwhile I was applying myself to the craft of goldsmithing and assisting, in that way, my good father. His other son—my brother who was named Cecchino, as I mentioned above—had been taught the rudiments of Latin, because my father wanted to make me, the elder son, a great performer and musician and to make him, the younger, a great and learned lawyer, but he could not thwart our natural inclinations, which made me apply myself to the art of design, while my brother, who was well proportioned and graceful, was completely devoted to arms. He was still very young when, after his first lesson in the school of that marvellous Signor Giovannino de' Medici,* he arrived home while I was not there, and since he had fewer clothes than I, he found our sisters, who, keeping it a secret from my father, gave him my new and beautiful hooded cloak and robe; these fine garments I had had made for myself from what remained of my earnings beyond the assistance I gave my father and my good and honest sisters. Finding that I had been cheated and that my clothes had been taken from me, and unable to find my brother from whom I wished to take them back, I asked my father why he had allowed them to wrong me so badly, seeing that I had willingly worked so hard to help him. To this question, he answered that I was his good son, and that he had found again my brother who he thought was lost;* that it was necessary, following even one of the commands of God Himself, that he who had something good should give some of it to him who possessed nothing; that I should bear up under this insult for his sake; and that God would increase my own possessions. Like a young man without experience, I spoke back to my poor, afflicted father, and after I had gathered up what remained of my wretched clothes and few coins, I went off toward one of the city gates; and not knowing which gate would lead me to Rome, I found myself in Lucca, and from Lucca I went to Pisa. After I

reached Pisa—this was approximately in my sixteenth year—I stopped by the middle bridge near a spot they call the Fish Stone, at a goldsmith's shop, looking with attention at what that master was creating, and the master asked me who I was and what my profession was, to which I declared that I worked a bit in the same craft that he practised. This good man told me to enter his shop, and he immediately gave me some work to do, saying these words: 'Your kind face makes me believe that you are a good and worthy young man.' Thus, he placed before me some gold, silver, and jewels, and that evening, after the first day had passed, he took me to his home, where he lived honourably with his beautiful wife and children. When I recalled the unhappiness my good father must be feeling because of me, I wrote to him that I was in the home of a very good and most worthy man, who called himself Master Ulivieri della Chiostra,* and that along with him I was creating many beautiful and important works; I also wrote that he should be of good cheer since I was making every effort to learn, and that I hoped, with these skills, shortly to bring back to him both profit and honour. My good father immediately replied to my letter, writing these words: 'My son, the love I bear for you is so great that were it not against my honour, which I value above all else, I would have set out to come to you, since it certainly seems to me like living without the light of my eyes not to see you every day, as I was accustomed to do. But I shall devote myself to leading my family toward useful honour, while you devote yourself to learning some skills; I only wish that you would remember these few simple words; follow them and never forget them:

> In whatever house you take your meal,
> Live in honesty and never steal.

11. This letter fell into the hands of my master Ulivieri, and without my knowing he read it; later, he revealed that he had done so and spoke these words: 'So, my dear Benvenuto, your kind face didn't fool me; that much is affirmed by a letter that came into my hands from your father; it shows that he is a very good and worthy man; and so, act as if you are in your own home and living with your own father.' Since I was living in Pisa, I went to see the Campo Santo,* and there I discovered many beautiful ancient works of art, that is, marble sarcophagi, and in many other places in Pisa I saw many other ancient works, which I used to examine

with great care whenever I made good progress on my work in the shop. And since my master with great affection came to visit me in the little room he had given me, when he saw that I spent all my time industriously, he bore a love for me as if he were my father. During the year I stayed there, I earned a great deal and worked on many important and beautiful things in both gold and silver, which made me extremely anxious to make even more progress. In the meantime, my father wrote me in a very piteous way, saying that I should return to him, and in his every letter he reminded me not to neglect the musical skills he had worked so hard to teach me. At this point I would immediately lose the desire ever to return home to him, because I hated that damned playing so much, and it truly seemed like being in Paradise the entire year I stayed in Pisa, where I never played at all. At the end of the year, my master Ulivieri had occasion to go to Florence to sell some of his gold and silver sweepings,* and because that unhealthy Pisan air had given me a bit of a fever, I returned with that and with my master to Florence, where my father gave him an extremely warm welcome, kindly informing my master behind my back that it would make him happy if he did not take me back to Pisa. Remaining, I stayed there for nearly two months, and my father had me treated and healed with the greatest affection, continuously saying that it seemed like a thousand years before I would be cured and he could hear me play a little; and while he discussed this business of playing, holding his fingers on my pulse, since he had some knowledge of medicine and of Latin letters, as soon as he mentioned playing he would feel such a great change in my pulse that often, terrified and in tears, he would leave me. Thus, realizing how unhappy he was, I told one of my sisters to bring me a flute, since even though I continued to have a fever, the flute was an effortless instrument and playing it would not cause my pulse to jump, and I played it with such beautiful fingering and tonguing that when my father came upon me unexpectedly, he blessed me a thousand times, telling me that in the time I had been away it seemed to him that I had made great progress, and he begged me to go on with my playing, so that I should not lose such a beautiful talent.

12. Once I was well I returned to my Marcone, a worthy man and a goldsmith, who helped me to earn money with which I helped my father and my family. During this period a sculptor named Piero

Torrigiani* came to Florence, who returned from England where he had been for many years. Because he was a great friend of my master I went to visit him every day, and having seen my drawings and my works, he said: 'I came to Florence to hire as many young men as possible, for since I must execute a great work for my king, I want some of my fellow Florentines as my assistants, and because your methods of working and your drawings are more like those of a sculptor than those of a goldsmith, and I must execute a large work in bronze, I shall at the same time make you both skilled and rich.' This man cut a handsome figure and was quite audacious; he had more the air of a great soldier than a sculptor, especially because of his admirable gestures, his booming voice, and his way of raising his eyebrows in a manner that would terrify even the bravest man; and every day he spoke of his brave deeds with those beasts of Englishmen. In the same way, he one day fell to speaking about Michelangelo Buonarroti;* the occasion was a drawing I had done, sketched from a cartoon of the most divine Michelangelo.* This cartoon was the first beautiful work* in which Michelangelo demonstrated those marvellous abilities of his, and he executed it in competition with another who was working there, Leonardo da Vinci: the two cartoons were meant to be suitable for the Council Chamber of the Palazzo della Signoria. They represented scenes from the capture of Pisa by the Florentines, and the admirable Leonardo da Vinci had elected to represent a battle between horsemen involving the capture of certain standards that was as divinely executed as one could possibly imagine.* In his own, Michelangelo Buonarroti showed a number of soldiers who, because it was summer, had begun to bathe in the Arno river; he shows them at the very moment the alarm has been sounded and the naked soldiers rush for their weapons, doing so with so many beautiful gestures that neither the ancients nor other moderns ever saw a work that reached such a high mark; and as I said, Leonardo's was extremely beautiful and admirable. One of these two cartoons was in the Medici Palace, and the other in the rooms of the Pope.* While they remained in place, they served as the school for the entire world. Even though the divine Michelangelo executed the great chapel for Pope Julius later on,* his skill never again reached such a level of perfection even by half; his skill never again equalled the power of those first studies.

13. Now let us return to Piero Torrigiani who, with my drawing in his hand, spoke in this way: 'This Buonarroti and I went along together when we were children to learn in the Church of the Carmine from Masaccio's chapel,* and because Buonarroti had the habit of making fun of everyone who sketched there, one day in particular when he was bothering me, I became much more irritated than usual and, clenching my fist, I gave him such a punch in his nose that I felt the bone and cartilage in the nose crumble under my fist like a wafer: he will remain marked by me in that way as long as he lives.'* These words generated so much hatred in me, since I was looking at the works of the divine Michelangelo every day, that not only did I not have any desire to go to England with him but I could not even bear to look at him.

All the while I was in Florence, I applied myself to learning Michelangelo's beautiful style,* and from that style I have never strayed. At this time I met and became close friends with a fine young man of my own age who was also working in the goldsmith's trade. He bore the name of Francesco, the son of Filippo di Fra Filippo, a most excellent painter.* Working together generated such a strong sense of friendship between us that neither day nor night were we ever out of each other's company. Since his home was still full of those beautiful studies that his splendid father had executed, which were in several books drawn in his own hand, depicting some of the beautiful antiquities of Rome, when I saw these things, I fell completely in love with them, and we worked together for around two years. During this period, I executed in low relief a work in silver as large as the hand of a small child. This piece was used for the buckle of a man's belt, since in those days they wore them that large. Carved on it was a bunch of foliage in the ancient style, with many cherubs and some extremely beautiful masks. I completed the work in the shop of a man called Francesco Salinbene. When it was seen by members of the goldsmith's guild, they praised me as the most talented young man in the trade. And because a certain Giambattista,* known as Tasso, a woodcarver and a youth of exactly my age, started telling me that if I wanted to go to Rome, he would most gladly come with me—this topic we discussed together just after our midday meal—and since, for the usual reason, that is, playing music, I was angry with my father, I said to Tasso: 'You're the kind of person who talks but doesn't do anything.' To this Tasso answered:

'Since I'm angry with my mother, too, if I had enough money to get myself to Rome, I would never turn back even to lock up that sorry shop of mine.' To these words I added that, if money were all that was keeping him in Florence, I had set aside so much money that it would suffice to take us both to Rome. Thus, talking this over together while we were walking, we found ourselves without realizing it at the San Piero Gattolini Gate.* I said to him: 'Tasso, my friend, this is God's work, arriving at this gate, since neither you nor I realized that we were here; now that I am here, it seems to me as if we have already made half the trip.' And so we both agreed, and while we continued on our way, we said to each other: 'Oh, what will our parents say this evening?' And so we made a bargain not to give them another thought until we had arrived in Rome. Thus, we tied our aprons behind our backs and, almost without speaking, we went off as far as Siena. When we had reached Siena, Tasso said that he had hurt his feet and that he did not want to go any further, and he asked me to loan him some money to go back home; to this request I replied: 'I wouldn't have enough left to go on, and you should have thought about this before leaving Florence; if you don't want to come on account of your feet, we will find a horse that is making a return journey* to Rome, and then you won't have any excuse for not coming.' And so we hired a horse and, seeing that he did not reply, I took the road toward the gate for Rome. When he saw my resolve, never ceasing to complain, and hobbling along behind me as best he could, he followed along slowly and some distance back. Once I reached the gate, feeling sorry for my companion, I waited for him and put him behind the saddle, saying: 'What the devil will our friends say about us if after leaving to go to Rome, we didn't even have the guts to reach Siena?' Then the good Tasso declared that I spoke the truth: on account of the fact that he was a happy person, he began to laugh and sing, and in this fashion, always singing and laughing, we went on our way to Rome. This occurred at the exact moment I was nineteen years old, the same age as the century.* Once we had arrived in Rome, I immediately set to work in a shop with a master who was called Firenzuola. This man had the name of Giovanni and he came from Firenzuola in Lombardy;* he was a very accomplished goldsmith in working on large trays or dishes and other large objects. After I had showed him something of the model for that belt buckle I had executed in Florence with Salinbene, this pleased him tremendously, and, turning to an apprentice he kept on, who was a Florentine named Giannotto Giannotti* and who had been with him for a fair number of years, he said these words: 'This is one of the Florentines who knows something, while you are one of the Florentines who knows nothing.' When I recognized Giannotto I turned to say a word to him, because before he had left for Rome we had often gone drawing together, and we had been very close companions. He took such offence at the words spoken to him by his master that he said he was not acquainted with me and did not know who I was; whereupon, angered by his remarks, I said: 'O, Giannotto, once my close friend, we often were in this place and that, both to draw and to eat and drink or sleep in your country home; I don't care whether you vouch for me to this honest master of yours, since I hope that my own hands will be sufficient to declare what kind of a man I am without your help.'

14. Once I had finished speaking, Firenzuola, who was an extremely bold and decent person, turned to Giannotto and said to him: 'You vile rascal, aren't you ashamed of using such language and behaving like that to somebody who has been such a good companion of yours?' And in the same bold fashion, he turned to me and said: 'Come into the shop and do as you have said, and let your hands declare what sort of man you are.' And he set me to work on an extremely beautiful silver object for a cardinal. This was a small vessel copied from the porphyry urn standing in front of the door of the Rotunda.* Besides what I copied, I embellished it with so many beautiful little masks that my master went about bragging and showing it off as an example to the other guild members of the high-quality work his shop produced. In size it was about half an armslength, and it was made in such a way that it served as a salt-cellar to place on the table. This provided the first earnings that I had a taste of in Rome; a part of what I earned I sent to help out my good father; the other part I put aside for my own living expenses, and with it I went about studying the antiquities until I ran out of money and had to return to the shop to work. This companion of mine, Giovanbattista del Tasso, did not stay for long in Rome, and he went back to Florence. But after taking up new work, once I had completed it, I decided to change my master, strongly encouraged by a certain Milanese named Master Pagolo Arsago.* My own master Firenzuola first had a tremendous argument with this Arsago,

speaking insulting words to him in my presence, whereupon I spoke in defence of my new master. I said that I had been born free and that I therefore wished to live free, and that he could not complain of Arsago, and even less of me, since he still owed me a few coins; as a free worker, I wished to go wherever I liked, knowing that I was harming no one. That new master of mine also employed similar words, saying that he had not called me and that he would be delighted if I returned to Firenzuola. To this I responded that I was not aware of doing harm to anyone, that having completed the works I had begun, I wanted to be my own man and not beholden to others, and that whoever wanted my services should ask me for them. To this Firenzuola replied: 'I no longer want to request your services, and don't you ever come my way again.' I reminded him of my money: he scoffed at me; to this I said that, just as I had used tools to create the works that he had seen, I could use a sword no less well to recoup the fruit of my labours. When these words had been uttered, by chance a certain old man, who was called Master Antonio da San Marino,* stopped by. He was the most outstanding goldsmith in Rome and had been the master of this Firenzuola. After he had heard my argument, which I stated in a way that he could very easily understand it, quickly taking my side, he told Firenzuola to pay me. A big altercation arose, since this Firenzuola was a marvellous swordsman, even better than he was at the gold-smith's craft; yet reason had its way, and with my own talents I served my craft so that I was finally paid; and in time the same Firenzuola and I became friends again, and at his request I served as godfather to his son.

15. Continuing to work with this Master Pagolo Arsago, I earned a great deal of money, always sending the largest part of it to my good father. By the end of two years, following my father's entreaties, I returned to Florence, and once again I went to work with Francesco Salinbene, with whom I earned a good deal and worked very hard at learning. I started going around with Francesco di Filippo again, given that I was intent upon the pursuit of some pleasure, thanks to practising that damned music, and I always saved certain hours of the day or night which I gave over to my studies. In that period I created a silver 'heart-key', which is what these objects were called at that time. This was a belt three fingers in width that new brides were in the custom of wearing, and it was made in low

relief with some little figures in the round among the others. I made
it for a man who was called Raffaello Lapaccini. Although I was very
poorly paid, I gained so much honour from it that it was worth much
more than the recompense I justly earned. During this period I had
worked with many different people in Florence, where I had made
the acquaintance of some very worthy men among the goldsmiths,
such as that Marcone who was my first master, as well as others who
had very good reputations but who did me down in my work and
blatantly robbed me whenever they could. Once I saw this, I kept
away from them and considered them wicked men and thieves. One
goldsmith among them, named Giovanbattista Sogliani, kindly set
aside for me a section of his shop, which was on the corner of the
Mercato Nuovo near the bank belonging to the Landi family. There
I made many beautiful little objects and earned a great deal of
money: I was easily able to help my family. This aroused the jealousy of these wretched masters for whom I had first worked, who
were called Salvadore and Michele Guasconti.* They owned three
large workshops in the goldsmiths' guild and did a great deal of
business, and as a result, when I saw that they were attacking me,
I complained to several honest men, saying that it should have
been sufficient for them to rob me under the cloak of their falsely
demonstrated goodness. When this remark reached their ears they
boasted that they would make me very sorry for my words, but
since I did not know the colour of fear, I gave little or no thought to
them.

16. One day it happened that as I was leaning against the shop of
one of these goldsmiths he called out to me, partly reproaching and
partly threatening me; to his remarks I responded that if they had
done their duty towards me, I would have said of them what one says
about honest and worthy men. But, since they had done the contrary,
they should complain about themselves and not about me. While I
was standing there talking, one of them, their cousin, who was called
Gherardo Guasconti, perhaps compelled by all of them together,
waited until a pack-animal with a load passed by. This was a load of
bricks. When the load was near me, this Gherardo pushed it against
me so forcefully that he hurt me very badly. I immediately turned on
him, and when I saw that he was laughing I gave him such a hard
blow with my fist on his temple that he fell down unconscious, like a
dead man; then I turned to his cousins and announced: 'This is how

to treat thieving cowards like you!' And because they were about to make some move, since there were several of them, incensed, I put my hand on a small knife that I had and said: 'Whichever one of you leaves his shop, the other will go fetch his confessor, because there'll be no use for a doctor.' These words so terrified them that no one went to the assistance of his cousin. Immediately after I had left, their fathers and children ran to the Eight and claimed that I had assaulted them with a weapon in their own shops, something which was unheard of in Florence. The Eight had me summoned before them, whereupon I appeared; they gave me a severe reprimand and scolding, since they saw me dressed in a cloak, while the Guascontis wore the mantle and hood of well-bred people,* but they did so also because while my adversaries had gone to speak with all these magistrates at their homes in private, I, lacking experience, had not spoken to any of them, since I relied upon being entirely in the right; and I declared that for the enormous offence and injury that Gherardo had done to me, I had, in my deep anger, given him nothing more than a slap and did not think I deserved such a strong reprimand. No sooner had Prinzivalle della Stufa,* who was one of the Eight, allowed me to utter the word 'slap' than he declared: 'You gave him a punch, not a slap!' When the bell rang and we were all sent outside the court, Prinzivalle said to his colleagues in my defence: 'Consider, my lords, the ingenuousness of this poor young man, who accuses himself of having given a slap, thinking that this is less serious than giving a punch; the penalty for a slap in the Mercato Nuovo is twenty-five scudi, while that for a punch is little or nothing at all. This is a very talented young man, and he maintains his poor family with his many labours extremely well; I wish to God that our city had an abundance of such young men rather than a shortage.'

17. Among the magistrates were some of those followers of Savonarola with their crooked cowls who, swayed by the entreaties and evil information from my adversaries, and by the fact that they were part of Fra Girolamo's faction,* would have gladly put me in prison and punished me as harshly as possible,* but the good Prinzivalle put everything aright. And so they imposed upon me a small fine of four bushels of flour,* which were to be donated to the Convent of the Murate.* When I was quickly summoned back inside, Prinzivalle ordered me not to utter a word under pain of their

displeasure and to obey the terms of my sentence. Thus, after they gave me a vigorous scolding, they sent me to the Chancellor: I continued to mutter to myself 'it was a slap, not a punch', so that the Eight remained there laughing. The Chancellor ordered us on behalf of the magistracy to give our assurances, and they sentenced me alone to pay those four bushels of flour. I felt as if I had been totally discredited, and it was not long before I sent for my cousin, who was called Master Annibale the surgeon, the father of Messer Librodoro Librodori,* wanting him to serve as my guarantee. Annibale refused to come: for this reason, I became very indignant and, puffing myself up like an asp, decided to do something desperate. In all of this it is obvious how much the stars not so much influence us as force us into certain courses of action. Knowing how much this Annibale owed my family, my anger became so great that it turned toward a harmful course of action—being also somewhat hot-blooded by nature—and I stood waiting until the members of the Eight had gone out to dinner, then, while I remained there alone, seeing that the guards of the Eight were no longer keeping an eye on me, and inflamed with anger, I left the Palazzo, ran to my workshop, where I seized a large dagger, and bounded into the home of my adversaries, which served as both home and workplace. I found them at table, and that young Gherardo, who had been the main cause of my interrogation, threw himself upon me: I responded by stabbing him in the chest, piercing his tunic and vest through to the shirt without touching his flesh or doing him even the slightest harm. I thought, by the way in which my hand entered his garments and by the sound his clothes made, that I had hurt him very seriously, and when he fell terrified onto the floor, I shouted: 'You traitor, today is the day I kill you all.' Believing that the Day of Judgement had arrived, his father, mother, and sisters threw themselves down on their knees, and at the top of their lungs they called out for mercy; once I saw that they had no defence against me and that Gherardo was stretched out on the floor like a dead man, I thought it too cowardly an act to attack them, but still furious, I ran down the stairs, and when I reached the street I came upon the rest of the clan, more than twelve of them: one of them held an iron shovel, another a huge iron pipe, while others carried hammers, anvils, and cudgels. I attacked them, like an enraged bull, throwing four or five to the ground, and I fell along with them, always striking out with my dagger, now at one, now at another.

Those who had remained standing hastened as best they could to deal me some blows with both hands, with their hammers, cudgels, and anvils, and because God in His mercy sometimes intervenes in such matters, He kept us from doing each other any harm whatsoever.* All I left there was my hat, captured by my adversaries although previously they had fled from it, which each one struck with his weapon; then they looked around them for their dead and wounded, but nobody had been harmed.

18. I went off in the direction of Santa Maria Novella, where I immediately ran into Friar Alesso Strozzi whom I did not know; I implored this good friar for the love of God to save my life, since I had made a serious mistake. The good friar told me not to be afraid of anything, since regardless of all the sins in the world I had committed, I would be completely safe in his little cell. In the space of about an hour the Eight, having gathered together for an extraordinary session, pronounced against me one of the most terrifying edicts ever heard, threatening severe penalties against anyone who knew my whereabouts or gave me shelter without regard for my circumstances or for my actions.* My good father, poor and distressed, went in to the Eight, and throwing himself down upon his knees, he begged clemency for his poor young son, whereupon one of these infuriated magistrates, shaking the top of his crooked cowl, rose to his feet, and with insulting words said to my father: 'Get up from there and leave immediately, for tomorrow morning we shall send your son to the country with the lancers.'* My poor father still dared to reply: 'You will do what God has ordained and nothing more.' At this the same magistrate answered that God had certainly ordained it so. And my father said to him: 'I take comfort in the fact that you certainly don't know that.' After leaving the magistrates he came to find me, along with a certain young man of my age whose name was Piero di Giovanni Landi:* we loved each other more than if we had been brothers. This young man was holding under his mantle a splendid sword and a beautiful coat of mail, and once he found me, my courageous father explained the situation and what the Eight had said to him. Then he kissed me on the forehead and on both my eyes; he blessed me in a heartfelt way, exclaiming: 'The power of God will be what helps you,' and giving me the sword and armour, he helped me put them on with his own hands. Then he said: 'My good son, with these in hand you will either live or die.' Pier Landi, who was

standing there in my presence, did not stop crying, and he gave me ten gold scudi; I asked him to pull out some small hairs from my chin, the first fine hairs of my beard. Friar Alesso dressed me like a friar and gave me a lay brother for a companion. Leaving the monastery, I left by the Prato Gate, and went along the walls as far as Piazza San Gallo; then I climbed up the slope of Montughi, where in one of the first houses I came upon a man called Grasuccio, the brother of Messer Benedetto da Monte Varchi.* I immediately defrocked myself and, once again a man, I and Grasuccio mounted two horses there for us, and rode that night to Siena. Grasuccio was sent back to Florence, where he greeted my father, and reported that I had reached safety. My father was greatly cheered by this, and it seemed a thousand years before he came across the magistrate of the Eight who had been so insulting, and once he found him, he said: 'Antonio, do you see now that it was God who knew what was to become of my son and not you?' To this Antonio answered: 'Just let us get our hands on him again!' And my father concluded: 'I shall go to thank God that he has escaped from that danger.'

19. Since I was in Siena, I waited for the courier to Rome and travelled with him. When we had passed over the Paglia river* we encountered the courier who was bringing news about the new pope, who called himself Pope Clement.* After I reached Rome I began to work in the workshop of Master Santi, a goldsmith:* even though Santi had died, one of his sons owned the workshop. This son did not work there, but he had all the shop's affairs run by a young man from Jesi called Luca Agnolo.* This Luca Agnolo was a peasant, and as a small child he had come to work with Master Santi. He was small but well proportioned. This young man worked better than any man I had ever seen up to that time, with great ease and a great sense of design: he worked only on large objects, such as extremely handsome vases, bowls, and the like. Once I set to work in this kind of shop, I took on the task of executing some candlesticks for the Spanish Bishop of Salamanca.* These candlesticks were richly decorated as such objects should be. A disciple of Raphael of Urbino, called Gianfrancesco and nicknamed 'Il Fattore',* was a very talented painter, and because he was a friend of the previously mentioned Bishop, he put me in his good graces, so that I was commissioned to do many works by this Bishop and earned a great deal of money. During this period I went to sketch sometimes in Michelangelo's

chapel,* sometimes in the home of Agostino Chigi from Siena,* in whose residence were many extremely beautiful paintings from the hand of the most excellent Raphael of Urbino, and it was a feast day when I went to that same house, where Messer Gismondo Chigi,* the brother of the previously mentioned Agostino, lived. They were very proud when they saw young artisans like me who came to learn inside their dwellings. The wife of Messer Gismondo, seeing me frequently in her home—and this lady was as kind as could be and beautiful beyond all measure—came up to me one day and, looking at my sketches, asked me whether I was a sculptor or a painter, and to the lady I answered that I was a goldsmith. She said that I sketched far too well to be a goldsmith;* she had one of her chambermaids bring out a lily created from the most beautiful diamonds set in gold; and showing them to me, she wished me to appraise them. I appraised them at eight hundred scudi. Then she said that I had appraised the object very accurately indeed. Subsequently, she asked if I thought I might be capable of setting it better: I declared I was most willing to do so, and in her presence I sketched out a little design for it, and the design was all the more beautiful because I took pleasure from passing the time with this extremely beautiful and delightful noblewoman. Once I finished my sketch, another very beautiful Roman noblewoman who had been upstairs arrived, and when she came downstairs, this lady asked Madonna Porzia* what she was doing, and with a smile Porzia answered: 'I am taking pleasure in watching this worthy young man sketch, for he is both good and handsome.' Moved by a bit of boldness that was still mixed with a bit of modesty, I blushed red and said: 'Whatever I may be, my lady, I shall always be more than ready to serve you.' The noble lady, also blushing a little herself, replied: 'You know very well that I wish you to serve me.' Bringing me the lily, she told me to take it away with me, and moreover, she gave me twenty gold scudi, which she had in her pocket, and she remarked: 'Set it for me in the way you sketched it out for me, and save the old gold in which it is now set.' The Roman noblewoman then remarked: 'If I were in that young man's shoes, I would willingly abscond with it.' Madonna Porzia added that virtues rarely coinhabit with vices, and that if I were to do such a thing I would strongly belie the handsome appearance that I gave as a worthy young man, and she turned, took the Roman noblewoman by the hand, and with the most delightful laugh, said:

'Goodbye, Benvenuto.' I lingered a bit over the sketch that I was drawing, tracing certain figures of Jupiter from the hand of Raphael of Urbino. When I had finished it I left, and began creating a little wax model, showing how it was to look once I had executed the work, and when I took it to show to Madonna Porzia, she was with the Roman noblewoman I mentioned previously, and both of them were greatly satisfied with my labours and treated me with such kindness that, moved by some slight bit of boldness, I promised them that the finished work would be better by one half than the model.* Thus I set to work, and in twelve days I finished this jewel in the form of a lily, as I said above, adorning it with little masks, cherubs, animals, all most beautifully enamelled, so that the diamonds, which made up the lily, were enhanced by more than half.

20. While I was working on this piece the worthy Luca Agnolo, whom I mentioned above, showed his annoyance, telling me on more than one occasion that I would earn greater profits and a greater reputation if only I would help him to work on large silver vases as I had done in the beginning. To this I replied that I would be able, whenever I liked, to work on large silver vases, but that works such as this one did not come one's way every day, and that in such works as these there was no less reputation to be gained than from large silver vases but, rather, a great deal more profit. This Luca Agnolo scoffed at me, saying: 'You'll see, Benvenuto, for in the same moment you have completed that work, I shall make haste to complete this vase, which I began when you started the jewel; experience will show what profit I shall make with my vase and what you will earn from your jewel.' I answered him that I would gladly put this to the test with such a fine man as he was, for in the completion of such works, we would see who of the two of us was mistaken. Thus, with a bit of scornful laughter, we both bowed our heads proudly, each one anxious to complete the objects we had begun; in this way, in the space of roughly ten days each of us had completed his work with great polish and craftsmanship. Luca Agnolo's vase was a very large piece to be used at Pope Clement's table, into which he would toss, while at the dinner table, small bones from meat and the skins of various fruits; it was created more for luxurious display than for real need. The vase was decorated with two beautiful handles, many masks, both large and small, and many lovely clusters of leaves, and as much grace and beauty of design as could be imagined; and to Luca

Agnolo I declared that it was the most beautiful vase I had ever seen.
To this remark, thinking that he had made me see sense, Luca
Agnolo said: 'Your work seems no less beautiful to me, but soon we
shall see the difference between the two.' Thus, he took his vase and
carried it to the Pope, who was extremely satisfied with it and
immediately had him paid according to the custom of the trade in
such large works. Meanwhile, I took my jewel to the noble lady
Madonna Porzia, who in great astonishment told me that I had in
large measure surpassed the promise I had made to her, and she then
added that I could request for my labours whatever I liked, since she
thought I deserved so much that if she gave me a castle, it would
scarcely seem enough to satisfy me, but since she could not do that,
she told me with a laugh to ask for something she could do. To this I
answered that the best reward I desired for my labours was to have
satisfied Her Ladyship. And thus, laughing myself, I bowed to her
and began to leave, declaring that I wanted no other reward than this.
Then Madonna Porzia turned to that Roman noblewoman and
remarked: 'Do you see that the company of those virtues we judged
to be in him are indeed virtues and are not vices?' Both were astonished, and then Madonna Porzia said: 'My dear Benvenuto, have you
ever heard the saying that when the poor give to the rich, the devil
laughs?' To this question, I replied: 'And still, in the midst of his
many vexations, this time I want to see him laugh,' and as I departed,
she remarked that she did not want the devil to be treated with such
kindness this time. When I returned to my workshop, Luca Agnolo
had in a paper pouch the money he received for his vase; he came
over to me and said: 'Come over a little closer and let's compare the
reward for your jewel to the reward for my vase.' I replied to him that
this should be put off until the following day, because I hoped that,
even as my work had not been any less beautiful in its way than his
own, just so I would look forward to showing him its reward.

21. When the next day came, Madonna Porzia sent her steward to
my workshop, who called me outside, and placing in my hand a paper
pouch full of money from that lady, he told me that she did not want
the devil to laugh at all, indicating that what she was sending me was
not the entire payment my labours deserved, along with many other
courteous remarks worthy of such a noble woman. Luca Agnolo,
who thought it would be an eternity before he could place his packet
next to mine, immediately ran into the workshop, and in the

presence of twelve workers and other neighbours who had come forward and who were anxious to witness the outcome of the contest, he took hold of his pouch, laughing scornfully, and saying 'Oh, oh!' three or four times while he poured his money on the bench with a great racket. He had twenty-five scudi di giuli,* thinking that I had received four or five scudi in coins, while I, although I felt stifled by his shouting and by the looks and laughter of the crowd around me, upon glancing inside my own pouch, saw that it was completely filled with gold; then, keeping my eyes down, from one side of the counter and without the slightest noise in the world, with both my two hands held high, I raised up my pouch and emptied it out as if it were the hopper of a mill. My money was at least half again as much as his,* so that all those eyes which had been fixed upon me with some scorn suddenly turned toward him, as they all said: 'Luca Agnolo, Benvenuto's money is in gold, and since it is half again as much, his is much finer to look at than yours!' I felt sure that Luca Agnolo would instantly drop dead from envy coupled with the scorn he had endured, and although a third of my money went to him—that was the custom, two-thirds went to the workman and the other third went to owners of the shops—his foolhardy envy overcame his greed, which should have been the other way around, since this Luca Agnolo was the son of a peasant from Jesi. He cursed his craft and those who had taught it to him, declaring that from that time forward he no longer wished to work on large objects and only wanted to concentrate upon making such little whorish trifles, since they were well-paying. No less indignant, I said that every bird whistles its own tune and that he spoke in the manner of the hovels from which he came, but I said in no uncertain terms that I could succeed perfectly well in producing his crappy nonsense and that he would never be able to succeed in producing my kind of whorish trifles. Thus, leaving in a rage, I told him that I would soon show him what was what. Those present loudly told him that he was in the wrong, holding him to be the peasant he was, as they held me to be the man I had shown myself to be.

22. The following day I went to thank Madonna Porzia, and I told her that Her Ladyship had done the opposite of what the proverb said, and that while I had wanted to make the devil laugh, she had once again made him renounce God. Both of us laughed pleasantly, and she told me to create other beautiful and fine works. Meanwhile,

through one of the disciples of Raphael from Urbino,* the Bishop of
Salamanca commissioned me to do a large water vase, called a ewer,
which was used on sideboards as a form of decoration. And since the
Bishop wished to have two made of equal size, one was commissioned to Luca Agnolo, while the other was to be executed by me,
and the design for the form of these vases was provided by the
previously mentioned painter, Gianfrancesco. Thus, I set to work on
this vase with amazing eagerness, and I was given a small space in the
workshop of a Milanese named Master Giovanpiero della Tacca.*
Once I had organized myself, I made my calculations of the money
that I might need for some of my affairs, and all the rest I sent to
support my poor, good father who, while he was being paid in Florence, by chance ran into one of those angry men who were members
of the Eight at the time when I caused that bit of trouble, the man
who had insulted him and said he would send me away to my execution no matter what. Since this choleric individual had certain
worthless sons of his own, my father replied in a suitable fashion:
'Anyone can suffer misfortune, especially quick-tempered men who
are in the right, as happened to my son, but it is easy to see from the
rest of his life how virtuously I knew how to raise him. Would to
God in your case that your sons do neither worse nor better than
mine have done for me, because, as God made me able to understand
how to bring them up, when my own ability failed, He Himself
rescued them, despite what you thought, from your very own violent
hands.' And after he left, he wrote all of this to me, begging me for
the love of God to play on occasion, so that I would not lose that
admirable skill he had taught me with such great effort. His letter
was filled with the most loving paternal words ever heard, and they
moved me to tears of piety in the hope that, before his death, I could
make him happy in good measure as far as my playing was concerned, since God grants to us the lawful favours we devoutly ask of
Him.

23. While I was working diligently on the beautiful vase for the
Bishop of Salamanca, I had only a young boy as an assistant, who,
half against my will, because of the special entreaties of my friends, I
had hired as my shop-boy. This boy was about fourteen years of age;
he was called Paulino and was the son of a Roman citizen who lived
on his own private revenues. This Paulino was the most well edu-
cated, the most honest, and the most handsome young fellow I had

ever seen in my life, and because of his honest actions and habits, his enormous beauty, and the great love he bore for me, it happened that for these reasons I bore as much affection for him as it would be possible for the breast of a man to contain. This tender love was the reason why I wished to see his marvellous face, which was by his nature virtuous and melancholic, brighten up; especially, whenever I took up my cornett, there immediately arose a smile, so honest and so beautiful, that I am not at all surprised by those foolish remarks that the Greeks write about the gods in the heavens.* If he had been alive in those times, he might have pushed them further off the deep end.* This young fellow had a sister called Faustina, who was even more beautiful, in my opinion, than the Faustina about whom the ancient books are always rattling on.* Sometimes they took me to their vineyard, and as far as I could judge, it seemed that this worthy man, the father of the previously mentioned Paulino, would have liked me as a son-in-law. This circumstance made me play my music more than I had previously. It happened at this time that a certain Gianiacomo,* a fifer from Cesena and a most admirable musician who was in the Pope's service, let me know through Lorenzo, a trombonist from Lucca who today is in the service of our Duke,* that if I wanted to I could help them by playing on my cornett that same day the soprano part of some beautiful motets they had chosen for the Pope's celebration of Ferragosto.* Although I was extremely anxious to complete that beautiful vase I had begun, since music is something marvellous in and of itself and since I was satisfying my old father's wishes, I was happy to keep them company, and eight days before Ferragosto we spent two hours a day together practising, so that on the first of August we went to the Belvedere,* and while Pope Clement dined, we played these motets with such precision that the Pope had to admit he had never heard music played more delicately or harmoniously. He called this Gianiacomo over and asked him how and where he had found such a fine soprano cornet-tist, and asked him in detail who I was. Gianiacomo told him my name. At this the Pope said: 'So this is Master Giovanni's son?' And then he said that this was so. The Pope said that he wanted me in his service along with his other musicians. Gianiacomo then replied: 'Holy Father, I can't claim that you may have him, because his profession, at which he constantly strives, is the craft of goldsmithing, and in this craft he executes marvellous work and earns much more than he would by playing.' To this the Pope said: 'I want him all the more, since he has this skill in addition that I was not expecting. Give him the same compensation that you all receive, and tell him on my behalf that he should work for me and that I shall very soon give him plenty to do in that other profession;' and holding out his hand, he gave Gianiacomo one hundred gold scudi di Camera* in a hand-kerchief as he said: 'Divide it so that he receives his share.' After taking the Pope's leave, Gianiacomo came over to us and repeated everything exactly as the Pope had told him, and he divided the money among the eight of us, giving me my share, and he said to me: 'I am going to have you enrolled as one of our company.' To this I replied: 'Let it go for today, and I shall give you my answer tomorrow.' When I left them, I went off pondering whether I should accept the offer, considering how much this might lead me astray from the beautiful studies of my craft. The following night my father appeared to me in a dream, and with loving tears he begged me for the love of God and himself to be content to undertake this enter-prise, and I seemed to reply I had no wish whatsoever to do so. Suddenly he appeared to me in a horrible shape that terrified me, and he said: 'If you don't do it, you will receive a father's curse, while if you do it, you will always receive my blessing.' Out of fear, I awoke and ran to enrol myself; then I wrote about it to my aged father, who was so overjoyed that he suffered an attack which brought him near death; and he immediately wrote to me that he had also dreamed almost the same thing that I had dreamed.

24. Once I had satisfied my good father's honest wishes, I thought that everything would come to an honourable and glorious conclu-sion. And so I set to work with the greatest care to finish the vase that I had begun for the Bishop of Salamanca. This Bishop was a very admirable man, extremely wealthy but difficult to please: every day he sent someone to see what I was doing; and every time his messenger did not find me, the Bishop became absolutely furious, declaring that he wanted to take my commission away from me and give it to others to complete. This all came about because of the time I spent with that damned music. Still, I set to work with the greatest diligence day and night until, having brought the work to the point where I could show it to this Bishop, I let him see it: as a result, his desire to see it completed grew so powerful that I regretted having shown it to him. In the space of three months I finished the work,

with as many beautiful little animals, leaves, and masks as is possible
to imagine. Immediately I sent it with my shop-boy Paulino to that
splendid man, Luca Agnolo, mentioned above, and with his boundless grace and handsome features, Paulino spoke in this manner:
'Messer Luca Agnolo, Benvenuto says that he is sending this to
demonstrate his promises and your crappy nonsense, while he is
waiting to see those whorish trifles from you.' When these words
were spoken, Luca Agnolo took the vase in his hands and examined
it closely; he then replied to Paulino: 'My handsome young fellow,
tell your master that he is a most talented man, that I beg him to
accept me as a friend, and let's leave it at that.' Most happily, this
honest and wonderful young man brought me the message. The vase
was taken to the Bishop, who wanted it to be appraised. Luca Agnolo
took part in this appraisal, and he quite honestly assessed its value
and praised it at much greater length than I would have done. After
he had taken the vase, the Bishop, just like a Spaniard, said: 'I swear
to God that I shall take as long to pay him as he took to execute it.'
When I heard this I was extremely disgruntled, cursing all of Spain
and anyone who loved that country. Among the other beautiful decorations on this vase, there was a handle made in one piece, most
subtly wrought, which was placed directly over the mouth of the
vase by means of a spring. One day, when the Bishop was showing
off this vase of mine to some Spanish gentlemen, it happened that
one of them, after the Bishop had left the room, treated the beautiful
vase handle too carelessly, and as the fragile spring could not resist
his clumsy force, it broke in his hand, and realizing the harm he had
done, he begged the steward who was in charge of it to take it
immediately to the master who had made it so he might repair it on
the spot, promising any reward the craftsman might ask, so long as it
was quickly fixed up. Thus, the vase fell into my hands once again,
and I promised to fix it very quickly and did so. The vase was
brought to me before dinner: about two hours before sunset the man
who had brought it to me arrived all in a sweat, because he had run
the entire way, since the Bishop happened to ask once again to show
the vase to certain other gentlemen. For that reason, this steward did
not allow me to get a word in edgewise as he said: 'Hurry, hurry,
bring the vase!' Whereupon, eager to take my time and to avoid
giving it to him, I declared that I did not wish to do so right away.
The servant then became angry and motioned as if to put his hand to

his sword, while with the other he threatened to force his way into the shop; I barred his way immediately with my weapon, a gesture accompanied by many spirited words, telling him: 'I don't wish to give it to you; go to my lord your master and tell him that I want the money for my labours before the vase leaves my shop.' Once this man saw that he could not obtain the vase by making threats, he began to beg me just as if he were praying to the Holy Cross, saying that if I gave it to him, he would make sure I was paid. These words in no way moved me from my objective, and I always replied to him in the same fashion. Finally, growing desperate over the enterprise, he swore to come back with so many Spaniards that they would cut me to pieces; once he ran off, giving some credence to his offensive remarks, I swore to defend myself bravely; and after I had armed and loaded a superb little musket of mine which I used for going hunting, I said to myself: 'Can I allow somebody who has taken my property along with my labours to take away my life as well?' While I was debating this issue, a large number of Spaniards appeared along with the steward, who, in his reckless manner, ordered them to enter the shop, seize the vase, and beat me up. At these words, I showed them the mouth of my musket, cocked ready to fire, and I cried out loud: 'You *Marrani*,* you traitors, is this how you despoil the houses and workshops of a city like Rome? You thieves, I'll shoot dead with this gun of mine as many of you as approach these shutters.' After pointing the mouth of my gun toward the steward, making a motion as if to fire, I said: 'And as for you, you thief and instigator, I want you to be the first to die.' Immediately he spurred the jennet* on which he was mounted and fled quickly away. At the sound of this racket, all the neighbours came out of their homes, while in addition, some Roman noblemen were passing by, and they said: 'Kill these *Marrani*, and we'll give you a hand.' These words were spoken with such force that the Spaniards, who were terrified of me, left, so that, forced by necessity, they were obliged to relate the entire affair to their master, who was extremely arrogant, and he yelled at all his servants and ministers, both because they had gone to commit such an abuse of power and also because, once begun, they had not finished the job. Then the painter* who had become involved in the affair arrived on the scene, and the Bishop told him to go and tell me on his behalf that if I did not bring the vase immediately, the best part left of me would be my ears, and that if I did bring it, he would pay me for it right away. This event did not scare me in the least, and I let him know that I would go tell the Pope right then. And so, when his anger and my fear passed, under the guarantee of certain important Roman noblemen that the Bishop would not harm me, and with the reliable assurance that he would pay me for my labours, I provided myself with a large dagger and my good coat of mail and went to the home of the Bishop, who had armed his entire household staff. As I entered, I had my Paulino by my side with the silver vase. It was more or less like passing through the middle of the Zodiac: one looked like Leo, another like Scorpio, a third like Cancer,* and so on until we reached the presence of this rascal of a priest, who blathered the most priest-like Spanish words one could imagine. I never raised my head to look at him nor answered a single word. This made him look even angrier, and after he had some writing materials offered to me, he ordered me to write in my own hand the declaration that I was very content and had been paid by him. To this I raised my head and said that I would gladly do so if first I had my money. The Bishop's anger grew, and his threatening and quarrelsome remarks were loud. In the end I first received my money, then I wrote, and pleased and delighted, I took myself off.

25. Later the Pope, who had earlier seen the vase but was not told it was the work of my hand, learned about this affair. He took great delight in it, praised me a great deal, and in public declared that he was extremely fond of me, to such an extent that my lord the Bishop of Salamanca regretted his threatening words, and in order to patch things up, he sent me a message through the same painter that he wanted to commission me to execute many great works; to this I answered that I would gladly do so, but first I wanted the payment before I began them. These words also reached the ears of Pope Clement, moving him to hearty laughter. It was in the presence of Cardinal Cibo* that the Pope recounted the entire disagreement I had had with this Bishop; later, he turned to one of his ministers and ordered him to keep me constantly employed with work for the palace. This same Cardinal Cibo sent for me, and after many very pleasant discussions, he commissioned me to make a large vase, even larger than the one for the Bishop of Salamanca; and so Cardinal Cornaro and many other cardinals, especially Cardinals Ridolfi and Salviati,* all gave me commissions, so that I earned a great deal of money. The previously mentioned Madonna Porzia told me that I

ought to open a workshop that would be mine alone, and I did just that, and I never ceased to work for that worthy noble lady, who always paid me handsomely, for it was practically because of her alone that I had shown myself to the world as a man of some merit. I struck up a great friendship with Signor Gabbriello Ceserino,* who was the Standard-bearer of Rome, and for this gentleman I executed many works. One among others was worthy of note, a large golden medallion to be worn on a hat: on it were engraved the figures of Leda and the swan;* he was very pleased with my efforts and said that he wanted to have it appraised in order to pay me a fair price. But since the medallion was executed with great precision, the appraisers of the guild valued it much higher than he had imagined. Thus, since it remained in my hands, I gained nothing for my labours. The same fate befell this medallion as befell the vase for the Bishop of Salamanca. But in order not to let these matters take up too much room at the expense of affairs of greater importance, I shall only recount them briefly.

26. Although I depart somewhat from the subject of my profession in wishing to describe my life, some of these events constrain me from describing them in detail but not from noting them in passing. One morning during the Feast of St John,* I was eating with many other citizens of our city, including members of various professions: painters, sculptors, goldsmiths; among the other noteworthy men was one called Rosso the painter,* Gianfrancesco, a pupil of Raphael of Urbino,* and many others. And because I had brought them together in that place by common agreement, they were all laughing and joking, as usually occurs when a number of men are gathered together, rejoicing at such a marvellous feast. Passing by chance and hearing the noise, a careless, swaggering young man, one of Rienzo da Ceri's soldiers,* mockingly said many offensive things about the Florentine nation. Since I was the leader of these talented and worthy men and felt that I was the offended party, quietly and without anybody seeing me, I came up to this fellow, who was there with one of his whores, still going on with his rude mockery in order to make her laugh. Confronting him, I asked if he was that impertinent man who was speaking ill of Florentines. He immediately replied: 'I am that man.' Upon hearing his words, I raised my hand and gave him a slap in the face, saying: 'And I am this man!' Immediately we both boldly reached for our weapons, but no sooner had we started to

fight than many people separated us, more readily taking my side rather than his because they had heard and seen that I was in the right. The very next day I was given a challenge to fight him, which I accepted most gladly, declaring that I thought this affair was an undertaking I could finish off much more quickly than those involved in my other craft, and I immediately went to speak to an old man called Bevilacqua, who had the reputation of being the first swordsman in Italy, because he had personally fought more than twenty duels and always came out of them with honour. This worthy man was a very good friend of mine, who knew me through my profession and had also intervened in serious conflicts between me and others. Because of this, he said quite cheerfully to me: 'Benvenuto, my friend, if you had to fight a duel with Mars, I am confident that you would come out of it with honour, because for as many years as I've known you, I've never seen you fight when you were in the wrong.' And so Bevilacqua took on my undertaking, and after we had proceeded with weapons in hand to the place agreed on, without shedding any blood and delivered from my opponent,* I came out of this affair with much honour. I shall provide no further details, for although of their kind they would be very pleasant to hear, I wish to reserve these words for a discussion of my profession, which is the thing that has moved me to write this narrative; and even about my profession I shall have too much to tell. Although I was truly moved by an honest spirit of competition, eager to create some other work that would reach and even surpass those of the previously mentioned and talented man, Luca Agnolo, nonetheless I never strayed from my own beautiful craft of goldsmithing, so that between one kind of work and the other, they brought me a great deal of profit and even greater honour, and in both one and the other trade I continually executed objects different from those of other artisans. During this time in Rome there lived a very talented man from Perugia by the name of Lautizio,* who worked only at one craft and in that craft he was unique in the world. It happened that in Rome every cardinal had a seal upon which was engraved his coat of arms;* these seals were about the size of the hand of a twelve-year-old boy; and as I mentioned above, on them was engraved the coat of arms of the cardinal, in which numerous figures were interposed: a well-made seal sold for one hundred scudi or even more. I bore an honest spirit of competition toward this talented man, although this craft is very different from others that are employed in goldsmithing, and this Lautizio, engaging in this craft of minting seals, did not know how to do anything else. Setting myself to the study of this craft as well, even though it is found to be extremely difficult, I never tired on account of the labour it involved as I continued to earn and to learn. At that time in Rome there lived another most talented man, who was from Milan and went by the name of Messer Caradosso.* This man worked solely on small medals chiselled on metal plate and many other objects; he executed some 'Pace' tabernacles,* in half-relief, and figures of Christ about a palm's length in height that were made of the thinnest gold plate and so well finished that I judged him to be the most talented master in such objects I had ever seen, and I was more envious of him than of anybody else. There were also other masters who worked on medals cut out of steel, and such medals are the source and true guide of those who wish to know how to stamp fine coins. I took the greatest pains in learning all these different crafts. Besides this, there was the most beautiful craft of enamelling, which I never saw done better than by one of our fellow Florentines named Amerigo,* whom I never knew, but I had an excellent knowledge of his marvellous works, for in no part of the world did I ever see any man who could even begin to approach their divine quality. Although this craft is extremely difficult because of the fire, which in the great labours of the finishing process frequently spoils and destroys the work completely, I set myself with all my power to learning this skill as well, and if I did find it difficult, the pleasure I derived from it was so great that these difficulties seemed to me as if they were moments of repose; this feeling came to me through a special gift from the God of nature, a constitution so sound and well balanced that I could freely allow myself to move forward with whatever came into my mind to accomplish. The previously mentioned professions are numerous and very different from one another, so that if a man does one of them well and wishes to work in the others, he is almost never as successful as in the craft in which he already excels; but I strove with all my strength to do my best equally well in all these crafts; and in the proper place I shall show (as I have said) that I have achieved this goal.

27. During this time, while I was still only a young man of about twenty-three years of age, a deadly plague broke out again in Rome of such unexpected severity that many thousands died from it every

day. Rather frightened by this, I began to take up certain pleasures, as the spirit led me, for a reason that I shall explain. On feast days I used to visit the ancient ruins, sketching them either in wax or on paper, and since these same buildings are all in ruins, and among them a great number of pigeons take shelter, I felt the urge to use my musket against them. In order to avoid contact with people, and terrified by the plague, I would place a musket on the shoulder of my Paulino, and he and I alone would go off to the ancient ruins. As a result of this, on numerous occasions I returned loaded down with the plumpest pigeons. I did not like to load my musket with more than one ball, and so it was through a true talent in this craft that I bagged such a large catch. I had an upright musket that I had made with my own hands, and inside and out, there was never a mirror with the same polish. I also made with my own hands the finest gunpowder, discovering the most wonderful secrets that no one else has discovered even to this very day, and of these secrets, since I do not wish to discuss this at great length, I shall give only one instance which should amaze all those who are skilled in this profession. That is the fact that with a quantity of powder equal to one-fifth the weight of the projectile, the ball would reach over two hundred paces in a straight shot. If the great pleasure I derived from this musket of mine seemed to divert me from my craft and my studies, and in truth it did so, in another way it gave me back much more than it had taken away: the reason for this was that every time I went on these hunting expeditions of mine, my health improved greatly because the air did me a great deal of good. As I was by nature melancholy,* when I found myself at these pleasant pastimes, my heart was immediately lifted up, and it was possible to work much better and with more skill than when I continually kept to my studies and activities, so that when all is said and done, my musket was more of a profit than a loss. Also, through this pleasurable pastime of mine, I became friends with certain collectors who kept watch over certain Lombard peasants who came at the proper season to Rome to hoe the vineyards. In hoeing the soil, these peasants always found ancient medals, agates, chrysopases, cornelians, and cameos; they also found jewels, such as emeralds, sapphires, diamonds, and rubies. These collectors sometimes obtained such things for very little money from the peasants; sometimes—and actually quite often—I would come upon the collectors and give them many times more in gold scudi than what they had just paid in silver 'giulios'. This business, notwithstanding the great profit I derived from it, which was tenfold or more, also made me welcome to almost all the cardinals of Rome. I shall only speak of one of the most noteworthy and rare of such transactions. There came into my hands the head of a dolphin equal in size to one of those large beans used in political ballots.* Among other things, regardless of the fact that the head was extremely beautiful, in this object Nature had far outdone skill, for this emerald was of such a good colour that the man who purchased it from me for tens of scudi had it reset like an ordinary stone to be worn on a ring: reset in this fashion, he sold it for hundreds. There was yet another kind of stone: this was a head carved from the most beautiful topaz ever seen in the world; in this one, skill equalled nature. It was as large as a huge hazelnut, and the head was as well formed as could be imagined; it represented Minerva. There was yet another stone different from these: this one was a cameo: and on it was carved a Hercules who was tying up the three-faced Cerberus.* It was so beautiful and executed so well with such great skill that our great Michelangelo had to declare that he had never seen anything so marvellous. Also, among the many bronze medals, one came into my hands which showed the head of Jupiter. This medal was larger than any other medal I had ever seen: the head was so well executed that such a medal had never been seen. It had an extremely handsome reverse side with some little figures that were just as beautifully executed. I could say a great deal about these things, but I do not want to take too much time with a drawn-out discussion.

28. As I said above, the plague had broken out in Rome: although I want to go back a bit, I will not stray from my subject. There was a most skilful surgeon who came to Rome who was called Master Iacomo da Carpi.* This worthy man, among his other remedies, took on certain desperate cases of the French disease.* And since these diseases were very fond of priests in Rome, especially the richest among them, this worthy man, having become well known, proved he could, amazingly enough, cure such infirmities by means of certain vapours, but he wanted an agreement before he initiated his cure, and his prices ran into the hundreds, and not just the tens. This talented man also had a good understanding of the art of design. While he was passing my workshop one day by chance, he happened to see certain drawings that I had begun, among which were some

whimsical little vases I had sketched for my own delight. These vases were very different and dissimilar from all those that had ever been seen before until that time. This Master Iacomo wanted me to execute some of them in silver, and I was extremely willing to do so, since they followed my own whim. Although this worthy man paid me very well for them, the distinction they earned me was worth a hundred times more, because among the guild of those talented goldsmiths they said that they had never seen anything more beautiful or more perfectly executed. I had no sooner given them to him than this man showed them to the Pope, and then the next day he departed. He was a very learned man and could speak in a wonderful way about medicine. The Pope wanted him to remain in his service, and this man declared that he did not want to be in the service of anyone and that whoever needed him could follow after him. He was a very astute character, and he wisely brought himself to leave Rome, because not many months later all those he had treated became so ill that they were a hundred times worse, so that if he had remained he would have been murdered. Master Iacomo showed my little vases to many gentlemen, including, among them, His Excellency the Duke of Ferrara,* claiming that he had received the vases from a great lord in Rome by telling this nobleman that if he wished to be cured of his illness, he wanted those vases;* and that this gentleman had replied to him that they were classical vases, and that if he would be so good as to request anything else he liked, there would be no difficulties about giving it to him, but that he did not wish to let them go; the doctor then said that he had pretended not to want to provide the medication, and he had therefore obtained the vases. This was recounted to me by Messer Alberto Bendedio* in Ferrara, who with great pomp showed me some reproductions of them in clay which caused me to laugh, and when I said nothing more, Messer Alberto Benedio, who was a very proud man, indignantly said to me: 'So, you are laughing at them, are you? And I am telling you that there hasn't been a man born in the last thousand years who would even know how to copy them!' And I, in order not to rob them of their reputation, remained silent, admiring them with astonishment. In Rome I was told about these works by many noblemen, for to them the works seemed miraculous and ancient, and some of these noblemen were friends of mine; emboldened by this affair, I confessed to having made them myself. Meeting with their disbelief and wishing to remain trustworthy in their eyes, I had to provide proof and to produce new drawings of them; my own testimony was not sufficient, because Iacomo had cleverly carried off the original drawings with him. In this little operation I made quite a bit.

29. The plague continued for many months, but I had managed to defend myself, although many of my companions had died while I remained healthy and free. One evening among others it happened that a fellow goldsmith brought a Bolognese whore called Faustina to my home for dinner. This woman was very beautiful, but she was about thirty years of age and had with her a maidservant of about thirteen or fourteen. Since this Faustina belonged to my friend, I would not have touched her for all the gold in the world. Although she said that she was madly in love with me, I never failed to keep faith with my friend, but when they were in bed, I stole the little maidservant, who was a fresh virgin, and it would have meant trouble for her had her mistress known about it. Thus, I enjoyed myself pleasantly that night with much more satisfaction than I would have had with her mistress Faustina. When mealtime approached I was tired, because I had journeyed many miles,* and when I tried to take some food a terrible headache overpowered me, accompanied by a large number of swellings in my left arm, as I discovered a small tumour on the outside surface of the wrist-bone of my left hand. Everyone in the house was terrified—my friend, the fat cow, and the little one*—and fleeing, they left me alone with a poor shop-boy of mine who refused to abandon me, and feeling my heart being smothered, I knew that I was a dead man for certain. At that moment, the father of this shop-boy of mine passed by in the street; he was the doctor of Cardinal Iacoacci* and worked in his employ, and this shop-boy said to his father: 'Come, my father, look at Benvenuto, who is in bed, feeling slightly indisposed.' Not considering what the malaise might be, the doctor immediately came to see me, and after he had taken my pulse, he saw and felt what he would have preferred not to know. Immediately he turned to his son and said: 'Oh, my treacherous son, you have ruined me: how can I go back to the Cardinal again?'* To this the son replied: 'Father, this master of mine is worth much more than all the cardinals in Rome.' Then the doctor turned to me and said: 'Since I'm already here, I want to treat you. I will warn you of only one thing, that is, if you engaged in coitus, then you are in danger of death.' I replied: 'I did

so this evening.' To this the doctor said: 'With what kind of creature and when?' And I said: 'Last night—and with a very young girl.' Feeling that he had spoken rashly, the doctor quickly said: 'Since the swellings are recent in their own way and don't smell yet, and since the remedy is timely, don't be so afraid, for I hope in any case to cure you.' Once he had treated me and left, one of my very dear friends named Giovanni Rigogli* appeared immediately, and displeased that I had fallen ill and had been abandoned that way by my companion, said: 'Don't worry, Benvenuto my friend—I shall never leave you until I see that you're well.' I told my friend that he should not come near me, since I was done for. I only begged him to be willing to take a certain good number of scudi that were in a drawer near my bed and, when God had taken me from the world, to send them as a gift to my poor father, writing to him in a kindly fashion that I had done as well as this desperate season allowed. My dear friend told me that he would not leave me for any reason, and that however things went, in one way or another he knew very well how friends ought to act. Thus, with God's assistance we went on, and with the marvellous remedies I began to become much better and soon I happily escaped from that terrible infirmity. Still keeping the sore open, with a small dressing inside it and a plaster bandage on top, I rode out on the wild pony that I owned. This pony was covered with hair longer than four fingers; he was about the size of a large bear, and he truly looked like a bear. On this pony I went to find Rosso the painter, who was outside Rome near Civitavecchia, in a place owned by the Count dell'Anguillara called Cervetera,* and when I had found my friend Rosso, who was extremely delighted to see me, I said to him: 'I've come to do to you what you did to me so many months ago.'* He immediately burst into laughter, embraced and kissed me, and next told me to remain silent for the sake of the Count. And so, gladly and happily, I stayed there nearly a month with good wines and excellent vittles, welcomed by the Count; and every day I went out alone on the seashore, where I would dismount and load myself down with the most diverse stones, little snails, and rare and extremely beautiful shells. The last time, after which I went there no more, I was attacked by a group of men in disguise who came ashore from a Moorish galley; when they thought they had me cornered in a certain spot and it seemed impossible to escape from their clutches, I quickly mounted my little pony, resolved to die in one way or another in this dangerous position, since I saw little hope of escaping being either shot or drowned, but as God would have it, the pony I described above jumped clear in an unbelievable way: thus finding myself saved, I gave thanks to God. I told the Count; he sounded the alarm: we saw the galleys at sea. The next day, healthy and happy, I returned to Rome.

30. The plague had already almost died out, so that those who remained alive were greeting each other in the most affectionate fashion. From this practice was born a company of painters, sculptors, goldsmiths, the best who were in Rome, and the founder of this company was a sculptor named Michelangelo.* This Michelangelo was a Sienese, and he was a man so very talented that he stood out among all others in that profession, but above all else, he was the most delightful and pleasant man that the world had ever known. In this previously mentioned company he was the eldest, but he was actually the youngest in physical vigour. We were very frequently together, at least twice a week. I cannot fail to mention that this company of ours included the painter Giulio Romano and Gian Francesco,* both marvellous pupils of the great Raphael of Urbino. As we found ourselves together more and more frequently, our honourable leader thought that on the following Sunday we should all meet for supper at his home, and that each one of us would be obliged to bring along his 'crow',* which was the name this Michelangelo gave to them; and anyone who did not bring his along would be obliged to offer a supper to the entire group. Those of us who had no dealings with such women of ill-repute were forced to procure one with no little expense and inconvenience, in order not to be disgraced at this respectable supper. I had thought myself well provided for in the person of a beautiful young girl named Pantasilea, who was deeply in love with me, but I was forced to concede her to a very dear friend of mine called Il Bachiacca,* who had been, and still was, deeply in love with her. This situation stirred up a bit of lover's indignation, since when she saw that at the first request I conceded her to Il Bachiacca, Pantasilea felt that I took little account of the great love she bore me; an enormous quarrel arose over this in time, since she wanted to take revenge for the injury she had received from me, a matter I shall explain in its proper place. It came about that the time for us all to appear before our virtuous company, each man with his 'crow', was beginning to grow near and I was still

without one, but I thought it would be a mistake to fail at such a crazy thing as this, and what concerned me the most was that I did not want to bring there under my protection and among all those talented friends some broken-down old 'crow'; I thought of a pleasant prank to add more laughter to the merriment. Thus, with my mind made up, I called a young boy of sixteen years of age, who lived next door to me: he was the son of a Spanish brass-worker. This young man was studying Latin literature and was very studious. His name was Diego; he was handsome in appearance with a marvellous complexion; the profile of his head was much more beautiful than the ancient one of Antinous,* and I had sketched him on numerous occasions; he had been greatly honoured through his depiction in my works. This young fellow never went around with anyone, so that he was unknown; he dressed badly and carelessly: he was only in love with his marvellous studies. After calling him to my home, I begged him to let me dress him up in the women's garments gathered together there. He was willing and soon put them on, and I enhanced the great beauties of his handsome face with the most beautiful hairstyle: I put two little rings in his ears which contained two large and beautiful pearls—the rings were broken and only clasped the ears, which appeared to have been pierced; then I placed extremely beautiful necklaces of gold and rich jewels around his neck; then I adorned his beautiful hands with rings. Afterwards, I pleasantly took him by the ear and pulled him over to my large mirror. When this young boy saw himself, he said with great feeling: 'Alas, is this Diego?' Then I replied: 'This is Diego, from whom I have never asked any kind of favour: only now am I begging this Diego to grant me this one honourable favour.' And the favour was that I wanted him to come to supper in that very costume with that talented company about whom I had spoken on so many occasions. This young man who was so honest, virtuous, and wise, having screwed up his courage, turned his eyes to the floor and stood there a while without saying a word; then, in a moment, he looked up and said: 'With Benvenuto I will go; now let's be off.' I put a large wrap on his head, the kind that is called a 'summer cloth' in Rome, and when we reached the meeting-place everyone was already there and all of them came to greet us: Michelangelo was standing between Giulio and Gian Francesco. When I took the wrap off the head of my beautiful young creature this Michelangelo—as I have said before, he was the most humorous and delightful man you could ever imagine—catching hold of Giulio with one hand and Gian Francesco with the other, as best he could in this position forced them to bow down, while he, with his knees upon the ground, cried out 'Mercy' and called everyone, saying: 'Look, look at what the angels of Paradise are like, for even though they are called angels, you can see that some of them are also women.'* And shouting, he said:

> Oh angel of beauty, oh angel of grace,
> Bless me and guard me with the sign of the cross.

Upon hearing these words, the charming creature raised his right hand with a smile and gave them a solemn blessing along with a good many delightful words. Then as he arose, Michelangelo said that while one kissed the feet of the Pope, one kissed the cheeks of angels; as he did so, the young man blushed intensely, and because of this, he looked even more beautiful. And so we went forward, finding the room was filled with sonnets which each of us had written and sent to Michelangelo. This young boy began to read them, and he read them all: this increased his infinite beauty to such an extent that it would be impossible to describe. Then many discussions and marvels followed, which I do not wish to set down in writing, since that is not my purpose: I shall only call to mind a single remark by that marvellous painter Giulio, who turned his eyes around knowingly on everyone in the room, fixing them more on the women than the men, and then, turning to Michelangelo, he said: 'My dear Michelangelo, this name of yours, of "crows", seems to fit these ladies very well today, although they are somewhat less beautiful than crows next to one of the most beautiful peacocks that might possibly be imagined.' Since the food was ready, arranged and prepared, and since we wished to sit down to eat, Giulio asked our leave to be the one who placed us around the table. After everyone agreed on this, he took the ladies by the hand and set them all down on the inside of the table, with my creature in the middle; then he placed all the men around the outside, with me in the middle, saying that I deserved every high honour. Behind the ladies there was a hanging of beautiful painted jasmines, which provided such a beautiful backdrop for those women, and especially for mine, that it would be impossible to describe in words. And so each of us with the greatest good will partook of this magnificent dinner, which was wonderfully abundant. After we had eaten, there was a bit of marvellous vocal music accompanied by some instruments; as we sang and played with the songbooks in front of us, my lovely model asked to sing her part; and since this boy's singing was better than all the other women, he caused such astonishment that the remarks Giulio and Michelangelo made about him were no longer merely pleasantries as they had been at first, but were composed of serious, sober words, full of utter amazement. After the music, a certain Aurelio Ascolano,* who was marvellous at poetic improvisation, began to praise the ladies with divine and beautiful words, and while he was declaiming, the two ladies who had my model between them never stopped chattering: one of them explained how she happened to end up badly, while the other asked my model how she had started out, who were her friends, how long it had been since she had arrived in Rome, and other such questions. It is the simple truth that if I only wanted to describe such delightful details, I would recount many unforeseen events that took place there, caused by that Pantasilea, who was passionately in love with me, but since this is not my subject, I shall pass over them briefly. Now, the talk of these beastly women began to annoy my model to whom we had given the name Pomona, and this Pomona, wishing to free herself from these foolish topics of theirs, turned now to one side and now to another. She was asked by the woman Giulio had brought if there was something bothering her. She said that there was, that she thought she was several months pregnant, and that she felt some discomfort in her uterus. The two women sitting on either side of her, moved to compassion by Pomona, immediately placed their hands on her body and discovered that she was a male. Quickly drawing away their hands, with offensive remarks, the kind usually used against pretty young men, they rose from the table and immediately the cries spread through the company, along with great laughter and amazement; the stern Michelangelo asked them all for permission to give me a penance he thought suitable. When this request was granted, amid the loudest cries he lifted me up, saying: 'Long live the Lord, long live the Lord!', and he declared that this was the condemnation I deserved, since I had played such a wonderful joke on them. And so this most pleasant supper and the day ended, and each of us returned to his home.

31. If I wished to provide a detailed account of the identity and quantity of my many works and the various kinds of men for whom I executed them, my description would be far too long. For the time being, all I need to say is that with great care and diligence I applied myself to gaining experience in every different facet of my craft, as I have explained above. Thus, I worked continually on all of them, and since I have not yet taken the opportunity to describe some of my most noteworthy works, I shall wait to put them in their proper place, which will come about soon enough. In this period, this same Michelangelo, the Sienese sculptor, did the tomb for the dead Pope Adrian.* Giulio Romano, the painter already mentioned, went off to work for the Marquis of Mantua.* The other members of our company all went back to their own business, some here and some there, so that our virtuous company was almost disbanded. During this time I came upon some small daggers in the Turkish style, the handles of which, as well as the blades, were made of iron; likewise, even the sheaths were of iron. These daggers had been engraved, using iron tools, with the most beautiful leaf clusters in the Turkish style, and they were inlaid with gold with great precision; they inspired me with a strong desire to try my hand and labour at this craft, which was so different from the others; and when I discovered that I could do very well at it, I made several such things. These were much more beautiful and much more durable than the Turkish ones for a variety of reasons. One was that, in my steel, I cut much deeper and at a more acute angle than was customary in Turkish craftsmanship. Another reason was that the Turkish leaf-clusters were only arum leaves with some small sunflowers which, though quite pretty, eventually lose their charm, unlike our foliage. In Italy we have various methods of creating foliage: the Lombards make extremely beautiful foliage, copying the leaves of ivy and clematis with extremely beautiful spirals that are delightful to look at; the Tuscans and the Romans make a much better choice in this kind of work, because they imitate the leaves of the acanthus, also known as bear's claw, with its stems and flowers, curling them in various ways; and among these leaves some little birds or various animals are nicely placed, which reveals who has good taste. Some such figures are naturally found in wild flowers, like those called snapdragons, and so can be seen in some of the engraved flowers, accompanied by other beautiful conceits of these talented craftsmen: these things are called 'grotesques'* by those without much knowledge. These grotesques have acquired this name among the moderns, since they were found in certain underground caverns in Rome by scholars, and these caverns were, in ancient times, rooms, baths, studies, halls, and other such structures. These learned men discovered them in such cavernous sites, since the ancients had erected them on the ground level, where they remained while the ground rose, and because in Rome such underground sites are called 'grottos', from this is derived the name 'grotesques'. This is not their proper name, because just as the ancients took delight in composing monsters by the copulation of goats, cows, and horses, from which were born those sorry mixtures they called monsters, so in like manner their artisans created with their foliage this same kind of monster: and 'monsters' is their true name and not 'grotesques'. When I made this kind of foliage and inlaid it in the manner described above, it was far more beautiful to see than the Turkish kind. At this time it happened that in some vases, ancient funeral urns full of ashes, a number of iron rings inlaid with gold by the ancients were found in the ashes, and in each of these rings was fastened a tiny shell. Making enquiries among the learned, I was told that such rings were worn by those who preferred to remain sound of mind, no matter what extravagant events befell them in good times as well as bad. At the request of certain gentlemen who were very good friends of mine, I set myself to work and made some of these rings, but I made them with well-tempered steel; later, when they were finely engraved and inlaid with gold, they were extremely beautiful to look at; and it happened on some occasions that one of these rings would earn me, just for my craftsmanship alone, more than forty scudi. In those days it was the custom to wear golden medallions on which every nobleman or gentleman liked to have engraved his own capricious design or coat of arms, and they wore them on their hats. I made a good number of such medallions, and they were very difficult to make. And because the great and worthy man who I mentioned earlier, named Caradosso, also made some of them, he never wanted less than one hundred gold scudi apiece, since they contained more than one figure; for this reason—not so much due to his price as to his slowness in working—I was presented to certain of these noblemen for whom, among other things, I made a medallion in competition with this great and talented man; and in this medallion there were four figures, upon which I had worked very hard. It happened that these same gentlemen and noblemen, placing my medallion beside the one made by the marvellous Cara-dosso, said that mine was much better executed and more beautiful, and that I should ask whatever I wished for my labours, because I had pleased them so well and they wanted to reward me in the same measure. To them I answered that the greatest reward for my labours and the one I most desired was that I had nearly reached the level of the works of such a great and talented man, and that if their lord-ships thought I had done so, I considered myself extremely well paid. Thus, I left immediately, and they subsequently sent me a very generous gift, at which I was pleased, and my disposition to do well grew so strong that it was the cause of what you will hear about in what follows.

32. Although I shall be digressing a bit from the topic of my profession, I wish to recount a few trying incidents that occurred in this troubled life of mine,* for I have already recounted stories about that talented company and the delightful pranks that were played on account of Pantasilea, that woman I mentioned, who bore me that false and bothersome love; extremely angry with me on account of that prank when the Spanish boy named Diego had participated in the supper I described earlier, she had sworn to take revenge upon me, and an occasion arose, which I shall describe, that put my life in the greatest peril. This occurred when a young man named Luigi Pulci* came to Rome; he was the son of one of the Pulci family who had been beheaded for abusing his daughter; this young man pos-sessed the most marvellous poetic genius and a sound knowledge of good Latin literature; he wrote well, and was graceful and extremely handsome. He had just left some bishop or other, and he was full of the French pox.* When he was a young boy in Florence, on summer nights in some places in the city groups would gather in neighbour-hood streets, where this young man was among the best at improvis-ing a song; it was so beautiful to hear his singing voice that the divine Michelangelo Buonarroti, that most excellent sculptor and painter, would always go to hear Luigi when he knew that he was there, with the greatest desire and pleasure; and a certain person named Piloto,* a most talented man and a goldsmith, and I would keep him company. In this manner came about the acquaintance between Luigi Pulci and me, whence, after many years had passed and in that sorry state, he sought me out in Rome, begging me to help him for the love of God.

I was moved to compassion by his great talents, for the love of our
native city, and because I am like that by nature, and I took him into
my home and had him treated so that, since he was still a young man,
he was soon restored to health. Meanwhile, as he was working to
regain his health he studied continuously, and I helped him to procure many books insofar as I was able to do so, so that as this Luigi
recognized the enormous kindness I had showed to him, on numerous occasions with words and tears he thanked me, saying that if
God ever placed some good fortune in his path he would recompense
me for all the favours I had done for him. To this I replied that I had
not done for him what I would have liked, but only what little good I
was able to do, and that it was the duty of human beings to help one
another; I only reminded him that he should render the help I had
shown him to another person who needed him, just as he needed me,
and that he should love me as a friend and consider me as such. This
young man began to frequent the court of Rome, in which he quickly
found hospitality, and he found a place for himself in the service of a
bishop, a man of some eighty years of age, who was called Bishop
Gurgensis.* This bishop had a nephew called Messer Giovanni, a
Venetian gentleman. This Messer Giovanni proved to be enamoured
of the talents of this Luigi Pulci, and with the excuse of these talents
he had come to be on such intimate terms with him that he treated
Luigi as himself. Since Luigi had spoken of me and of the great
obligation he bore me with the said Messer Giovanni, it came about
that this Messer Giovanni wanted to meet me. Thus it happened
that, one evening when I had made a little meal for the previously
mentioned Pantasilea and had invited many of my talented friends to
it, just as we were about to eat, this Messer Giovanni arrived with
Luigi Pulci, after having taken part in some nearby ceremony, and
remained to eat with us. When this shameless whore saw the handsome young man, she immediately had designs on him; for this
reason, after the delightful dinner was over, I called Luigi Pulci aside
and told him that, inasmuch as he had boasted about the obligation
he owed me, he should not in any way seek out the company of that
whore. To my words he replied: 'Alas, my dear Benvenuto, have you
taken me, then, for somebody with no sense?' To this I answered:
'Not without sense, but for someone who is young, and I swear to
God that I have no interest in her at all, but I'd be very sorry if
you broke your neck over her.' To my remarks Luigi swore that he

prayed to God that if he ever spoke to her, he might immediately break his neck. This poor young man must have sworn to God with all his heart, because he did break his neck, as will soon be recounted. This same Messer Giovanni revealed himself to have a filthy and immoral love for him, because the young man was seen to change his velvet and silk garments every day, and it was evident that he had given himself over to wickedness and had neglected his marvellous and beautiful talents; he pretended not to see me or to recognize me, because I had reproached him, telling him that he had given himself up to the ugly vices that would cause him to break his neck as I had predicted.

33. That Messer Giovanni of his bought him a very handsome black horse, for which he had spent one hundred and fifty scudi. This horse was wonderfully easy to handle, so that Luigi went every day to trot and jump with this horse in front of this whore Pantasilea. When I became aware of it, I did not pay attention to it, declaring that everything turned out according to nature, and I applied myself to my studies. One Sunday evening it happened that we were invited by that Sienese sculptor Michelangelo for supper at his home; and it was during the summer. At this supper there was Bachiacca of whom I have previously spoken, who had brought along that same Pantasilea, his first lover. So, after we were all seated at the dinner table, she was sitting between me and Bachiacca, and at the high point of the meal she stood up and said she had to relieve herself, for she felt a pain, and would return directly. And while we were talking and eating in the most pleasant fashion, she had stayed away rather longer than was required. It happened that, pricking up my ears, I thought I heard quiet snickering in the street. I held a knife in my hand, which I was using at the table. The window was so near the table that, by raising myself up a bit, I saw in the street that Luigi Pulci together with Pantasilea, and I heard Luigi say: 'Oh, if that devil of a Benvenuto saw us, we would be in real trouble!' And she replied: 'Don't be afraid: listen to the noise they're making; they're thinking about everything but us.' At those words, and after having recognized them, I threw myself to the ground from the window and, having seized Luigi by the cloak, I surely would have murdered him with the knife I held in my hand, but since he was mounted on a little white horse, which he spurred on, he left his cloak in my hand to save his life. Pantasilea fled to take shelter in a nearby church.

Those who were at the table immediately arose and came in my direction, begging me not to disturb either myself or them on account of a prostitute; I told them that I would never have bestirred myself for her but rather for that young scoundrel, who had showed how little respect he had for me; and so I did not allow myself to yield to any of the entreaties of those talented and virtuous men, but, on the contrary, I took my sword and, on my own, went to the Prati district,* for the house where we were drinking was near the gate to the Castello which leads to the Prati. So, as I headed for the Prati, it was not long before the sun set, and at a slow pace I returned to Rome. It was already night and dark, and the gates of Rome were not yet closed. Nearly two hours after sunset I passed by the home of this Pantasilea, determined that if Luigi Pulci were there I would do them both a bad turn. When I had seen and learned that there was no one at home except a wretched servant girl named Canida,* I left to put on my cloak and my scabbard and then came back to the house, which was behind the Banchi* on the Tiber river. Opposite the house there was the garden of an innkeeper named Romolo: this garden was enclosed by a thick hedge of thorny shrubs, inside which I hid myself standing up, waiting for the woman to come home together with Luigi. After I had remained there for a while, the friend of mine called Bachiacca happened by, who either guessed I was there or had been told where I was. Softly, he called me 'pal'* (which is what we used to call each other as a joke), and he begged me for the love of God, saying these words, almost in tears: 'My dear pal, I beg you not to cause any harm to the poor girl, since she isn't the slightest bit guilty.' To this I replied: 'If you don't get up and leave immediately, I shall give you a blow on the head with this sword.' This poor pal of mine was so frightened that his bowels began moving and he had to go off a little way to relieve himself. It was a starry night and there was a great deal of light: all of a sudden I heard the sound of a number of horses, which were advancing from both directions; it was Luigi and Pantasilea, accompanied by a certain Messer Benvegnato,* a Perugian who was Pope Clement's chamberlain, and they had with them four quite fearless Perugian captains, along with other extremely brave young soldiers—all told, they numbered more than twelve swordsmen. When I saw this, having considered that I did not know by which street to get away, I sought to hide in that hedge, and because the sharp thorns were hurting me and goading me on as one does to a bull, I had almost resolved to leap out and flee; at this moment Luigi had his arm around Pantasilea's neck, and he was saying: 'Let me give you a good long kiss to show our contempt for that traitor Benvenuto.' Hearing this, being aggravated by the thorns and driven on by the words of the young man, I leaped into the open and raised my sword, saying in a loud voice: 'You are all dead men!' The stroke of the sword fell at that instant upon Luigi's shoulder; and although these lascivious men had dressed this wretched youth in coats of armour and other such things, the blow was extremely powerful; and as the sword turned, it struck Pantasilea on the nose and the mouth. They both fell down to the ground, while Bachiacca screamed and fled with his pants halfway down his legs. I boldly turned upon those other valiant men with my sword, who, hearing a great commotion inside the inn, thought that they were attacked by an army of one hundred men, and even though they bravely put their hands to their swords, two of their horses became so terrified that it threw them into such confusion that two of their best men were thrown off, and the others took to flight, and when I saw that I had come out of this very well, I took off at top speed, having come out of the affair with my honour intact, but not wanting to tempt Fortune more than necessary. During this immense confusion, some of the soldiers and their captains wounded themselves with their own swords, and the same Messer Benvegnato, the chamberlain of the Pope, was thrown off and trampled by his mule, while one of his servants, after drawing his sword, fell with him and wounded him badly in one of his hands. This misfortune caused that Messer Benvegnato to swear more than all the others in that Perugian fashion, saying: 'By God's arsehole,* I want Benvegnato to teach this Benvenuto how to behave;' and he entrusted the job to one of his captains, perhaps one braver than the others but with less sense. This fellow came looking for me at the place where I had retreated, the home of a grand Neapolitan nobleman, who had seen and understood some of the objects of my profession and who was also of a disposition and physical size appropriate to soldiering, which was the profession to which the gentlemen was inclined; and so, seeing how well I was treated there and finding myself quite at home, I had given this captain such a reply that I believe he must have deeply regretted having come to find me. A few days later, when the wounds of Luigi, his whore, and those others had healed a bit, this grand Messer Benvegnato, whose anger had subsided, sought out this grand Neapolitan gentleman to induce me to make peace with young Luigi and those brave soldiers, who had nothing against me and only wanted to make my acquaintance. That gentleman told them all that he would bring me wherever they liked and that he would gladly prompt me to make peace, but that no one on either side should resume arguing, since this would be far too dishonourable; it was sufficient to go through the motions of drinking and embracing each other, and that he would make all the speeches, by which he would most willingly deliver them all. And so it was done. One Thursday evening this nobleman took me to the home of Messer Benvegnato, where all the soldiers who had participated in that defeat were still sitting at the table. With my nobleman were more than thirty brave men, all well armed, something that Messer Benvegnato did not expect. Once we entered the hall, the gentleman first and myself nearby, he pronounced these words: 'God save you, my lords! Benvenuto, whom I love like a brother, and I have come here, and we are here most ready to do everything that you want to do.' When Messer Benvegnato saw the hall fill up with so many men, he said: 'All we ask from you is to make peace, and nothing else.' So, Messer Benvegnato promised that the police agents of the Roman governor would not bother me. We made the peace: whereupon I immediately returned to my workshop, unable to remain alone an hour without the company of that Neapolitan nobleman, who either came to visit me or sent for me. Meanwhile, after Luigi had recovered, he was out every day on that black horse of his, the one that was so easy to ride. One day or another, when it was raining, he was showing off on his horse near Pantasilea's door, and slipping, fell with the horse on top; having broken his right leg at the thigh, he died a few days later in the home of this same Pantasilea, and he fulfilled the vow he had made so ardently to God. And so we see that God takes account of both the good and the evil, and He gives each man what he deserves.

34. The whole world was already at war.* Pope Clement had sent word to Giovanni de' Medici* asking for certain troops who came, and did such bad things in Rome that it was dangerous to remain in the public workshops. This was the reason why I withdrew to a nice little house behind the Banchi; and there I worked for all those friends I had made. My works during this period were not of great

importance, and so it is not necessary for me to discuss them. At this time I took great pleasure in playing music and in other such small pleasures. After Pope Clement, on the advice of Messer Jacopo Salviati, had disbanded the five companies sent to him by Lord Giovanni, who had already died in Lombardy,* Borbone,* knowing there were no soldiers in Rome, very promptly pushed his army in that direction. On this occasion all of Rome took up arms: and so, since I was a great friend of Alessandro,* the son of Piero del Bene, and since at the time when the Colonna came back to Rome* he had requested that I guard his home, so on this crucial occasion, he asked me to gather together fifty men to guard his house, and to act as their leader, just as I had done when the Colonna had attacked Rome; on this occasion I selected fifty brave young men and, both well paid and well treated, we took up quarters in his home. Borbone's army had already appeared outside the walls of Rome* when Alessandro del Bene begged me to go with him to keep him company: so I went along with him, accompanied by one of my best men, and on the way we were joined by a young man named Cechino della Casa. We reached the walls of the Campo Santo,* and there we saw that amazing army already making every effort to break into the city. At the part of the city walls where we drew near, a great many young soldiers had been killed by the attackers, and the fighting was extremely bitter, while the fog was as thick as you could imagine. I turned to Alessandro and said: 'Let's return home as soon as possible, because there's nothing we can do here: you can see them climbing up the walls and our own men are in flight.' Terrified, Alessandro replied: 'I wish to God we had never come here!', and so he turned around in the greatest haste to leave, for which I reproached him, saying: 'Since you brought me here, we've got to perform some manly action.' And so I pointed my arquebus toward where I spotted a very dense, tightly grouped formation of soldiers, and I took aim at the middle, specifically at a man whom I noticed standing out from the others, although the fog prevented me from seeing whether he was mounted on horseback or on foot. I quickly turned toward Alessandro and Cechino, told them to fire their arquebuses, and showed them how to do so in a way that would prevent them from being hit by an arquebus from the other side. We each fired like this two times in a row, and then I cautiously went toward the wall and saw the most extraordinary uproar arise among the enemy, because one of our shots had killed Borbone,* and, from what I learned later, he was the leader I first saw standing out from the others. After we got out of the way, we went off through the Campo Santo, entering through St Peter's, and then, coming out behind the church of Sant' Angelo, we reached the gate of the Castello only with great difficulty, because Signor Renzo da Ceri and Signor Orazio Baglioni* were wounding or killing all those soldiers trying to escape from the fighting near the walls. When we reached this gate, part of the enemy had already entered Rome and they were right on our heels. Since the Castello wanted to drop the portcullis of the gate, a small space was left so that the four of us got inside. As soon as I entered, Captain Pallone de' Medici* took charge of me, and since I was part of the retinue of the Castello* he forced me to leave Alessandro behind, which I did very unwillingly. Thus, I climbed up the main tower at the same time that Pope Clement had entered the Castello through the corridors,* for earlier he had not wanted to leave the palace of St Peter, unable to believe that the enemy might enter the city. When I found myself inside the fortress I drew near to some of the artillery pieces which were guarded by an artilleryman named Giuliano the Florentine. This Giuliano, standing there near the battlements of the Castello, saw his own poor house being sacked and his wife and children tortured, so that in order to avoid hitting his own family he did not dare to fire his artillery pieces; once he threw the fuse down on the ground, weeping copiously, he tore at his face, and a number of other artillerymen were doing the same thing. Because of this I seized one of the fuses, and with the assistance of some of the men standing there who did not have such personal sentiments, I turned some pieces of heavy and light artillery towards where I saw the need, and with them I killed many of the enemy's men; and if I had not done so, the part of the invading army that had entered Rome that morning would have come directly to the Castello, and it would have been possible for them to enter it easily, since the artillery did not get in their way. I continued to fire, and because of this some cardinals and noblemen blessed me and gave me the greatest encouragement. Through boldness I forced myself to do what was impossible; enough to say that I was the reason why the Castello was saved that morning and that those other artillerymen went back to fulfil their duties. I continued all that day, and when evening fell, while the army entered Rome through the Trastevere district, Pope Clement named as head of all the artillerymen a grand Roman nobleman named Messer Antonio Santa Croce;* the first thing this grand nobleman did was to come to me and embrace me: he set me up with five marvellous artillery pieces on the most prominent spot of the Castello, which is called the Angel;* this area runs right around the Castello and looks toward the Prati district and toward Rome. And so he gave me as many men as I could command to assist me in turning my artillery pieces, paid me in advance, consigned to me some bread and a bit of wine, and then begged me to continue in the manner in which I had begun. Because I was perhaps more inclined to this profession than to the one I considered my own, I did so quite willingly, and I did a better job of firing artillery than of being a goldsmith. When night fell and the enemy entered Rome, we in the Castello, and most particularly myself, who has always delighted in seeing new things, stood there contemplating this unbelievable spectacle and conflagration, which was of a magnitude that those who were situated in any other spot but the Castello could neither see nor imagine. Nonetheless I do not wish to set myself to describing such a thing; I shall only continue to describe this life of mine that I have begun and the matters that pertain specifically to it.

35. For an entire month* I went on constantly using my artillery pieces while we were besieged in the Castello, and because of this a great many important things, all worthy of being recounted, happened to me, but in order not to be too long-winded, as well as not wishing to stray too far beyond the topic of my own profession, I shall leave most of them aside, speaking only of those that oblige me to do so, which will be fewer and only the most noteworthy. Here is the first one. After this Messer Antonio Santa Croce had made me come down from the Angel so that I could fire on some houses near the Castello where some enemy troops had been seen to enter, while I was firing, a cannon-ball came toward me, struck a corner of the battlements, and took off a part, which was the reason it did me no harm; a large quantity of the masonry hit me in the chest and knocked the wind out of me, and as I was lying prostrate on the ground like a dead man, I heard all those around me talking, among whom was this Messer Antonio Santa Croce, who was loudly lamenting and saying: 'Alas, we have lost the best help we had.' At the sound of this uproar a certain companion of mine, called

Gianfrancesco the Fifer, arrived—this man was more inclined to medicine than to playing the fife—and he quickly ran off in tears for a carafe of excellent Greek wine. After he had made a tile red-hot and placed a good handful of wormwood on it, he then sprinkled that good Greek wine over it; when the wormwood had absorbed the wine, he quickly placed it upon my chest where the mark of the blow could plainly be seen. The strength of that wormwood was such that it immediately restored to me my lost powers. When I wanted to start speaking I could not, because some foolish soldiers had filled my mouth with earth, thinking that they had given me communion, but in fact nearly excommunicating me, since I was unable to regain my senses, the earth doing me more harm than the blow. Once I had escaped from this situation I returned to the fury of the artillery, executing that task with all the skill and care I could imagine. And since Pope Clement had sent for help from the Duke of Urbino,* who was with the Venetian army, telling his ambassador to inform His Excellency that as long as the Castello continued to light three beacons on its summit every night, accompanied by three artillery shots repeated three times in succession—as long as these signs continued, they would show that the Castello had not surrendered—I had the task of lighting these beacons and firing these artillery rounds: during the day, I always happened to direct them towards those places where they would do the most harm. For this reason the Pope liked me even better, because he saw that I was pursuing the art of artillery with the care that such a thing required. The help from the Duke never came;* I shall not recount anything else about this matter, since I am not writing for that purpose.

36. While I was engaged in this diabolical business of mine,* some of the cardinals in the Castello came to see me, most frequently Cardinal Ravenna and Cardinal de' Gaddi,* both of whom I told on numerous occasions not to come near me, because their awful red hats could be spotted from far away, which placed them and me in grave danger from the nearby palaces, such as the Torre de' Bini,* so that I finally had them locked out and thereby incurred their bitter enmity. Besides this, Signor Orazio Baglioni came around quite often and was very fond of me. One day while he was talking with me, he saw some movement in a particular inn which was outside the gate of the Castello in a place called Baccanello. For a sign, this inn had a red sun painted between two of the windows. The windows

were closed, but Signor Orazio judged that behind that sun and between those two windows there might be a table full of soldiers carousing, and he therefore said to me: 'Benvenuto, if you were of a mind to fire about one armslength from that sun with your small cannon, I believe you would do some fine work, because a great commotion can be heard from there, and they must be men of great importance.' To the nobleman's words I replied: 'I think I can hit that sun right in the middle', but I told him that there was a barrel full of stones near the mouth of the cannon, and that the explosion and blast would have hurled it to the ground. To this objection the nobleman answered: 'Don't waste time, Benvenuto! To begin with, it's not possible, given the way it's placed, that the blast of the cannon will make it fall, but even if it fell and the Pope were standing underneath it, the result would be less bad than you think, so fire away, fire away.' Not giving the matter any more thought, I fired and struck the sun in the middle just as I had promised. The barrel, as I predicted, fell down midway between Cardinal Farnese* and Messer Jacopo Salviati, and it might well have crushed them both: Cardinal Farnese had just reproached Messer Jacopo for causing the Sack of Rome,* and they were exchanging insults, drawing apart to give room for the most offensive words, which was the reason my barrel did not crush them both. When he heard the great noise in the lower court-yard, my good Lord Orazio went down there with great haste, while I leaned out from where the barrel had fallen and heard some people say: 'That artilleryman ought to be killed.' Because of this, I turned two falconets toward the stairway that led up there and resolved to discharge one of the falconets at the first person who came up. The servants of Cardinal Farnese must have received orders from the Cardinal himself to do me a bad turn; I stepped forward with the lighted fuse in my hand. Since I knew some of them, I said: 'You scoundrels, if you don't get out of here, and if one of you dares to climb up these stairs, I have here two loaded falconets with which I shall blow you to bits; now go and tell the Cardinal that I was carry-ing out the orders of my superiors, orders which were and are being carried out for the defence of these priests and not to injure them.' They left, and the said Signor Orazio Baglione came running up, but I told him to stay back or I would kill him, although I knew exactly who he was. This nobleman paused a bit, not without fear, and he said to me: 'Benvenuto, I'm your friend.' To this I said: 'My lord, so long as you come up alone, come by all means, as you wish.' This nobleman, who was a very proud man, stood still a moment, and he angrily declared: 'I have a mind not to come any further and to do exactly the contrary of what I had intended to do for you.' To this I retorted that, although I had taken on this office for the defence of others, I was equally skilled at defending myself. He answered that he would come up alone, and once he had done so his expression had changed more than normal, which caused me to keep my hand on my sword, and I stood there scowling at him. At this he began to laugh, and the colour returned to his cheeks, and he told me in the most pleasant way: 'My dear Benvenuto, I'm extremely fond of you, and when God wills it, I shall demonstrate that to you. [Would to God you had killed those two scoundrels, for one of them is the cause of this enormous disaster, while the other will perhaps be the cause of even worse.'* Then he told me that if I were interrogated, I should not say that he was here with me when I fired the artillery pieces, and for the rest, I should not worry about it. The commotion from this was enormous, and the affair lasted for a good long while. I do not wish to prolong this any further: it is sufficient to declare that I very nearly avenged my father on Jacopo Salviati, who had done him a thousand bad turns (so many that my father used to complain about them). Still, I inadvertently gave him an enormous scare. About Farnese I shall say nothing, for it will be evident in the proper place that it would have been better if I had killed him.]*

37. I applied myself to firing my artillery pieces, and every day I accomplished something most noteworthy with them, so that I had acquired inestimable credit and favour with the Pope. Hardly a day passed without my killing some of the enemies outside the walls. One day the Pope was walking around the keep and spotted a Spanish colonel in the Prati whom he recognized by certain tokens, seeing that he had once been in the Pope's service; and while he stared at him he began to talk about him. I was up above on the Angel and knew nothing about all this, but I spied a man who was standing out there, directing the preparation of trenches, holding a lance in his hand and dressed in a rose-coloured uniform, and considering what I might do to harm him, I took a falconet that I had with me which was larger and longer than a normal small artillery piece, something close to a half-culverin: I turned this piece, then loaded it with a good charge of fine gunpowder mixed with the coarser variety; then

I aimed it carefully at the man dressed in red, giving the shot an astonishing arc, since the target was very far away and the artilleryman's craft did not permit a direct aim with artillery of this type from such a distance. I fired it and hit the man in red right in the middle; he was wearing his sword pretentiously across his front, following a particular Spanish fashion, and when the shot of my cannon reached him it struck that sword, and we saw the man cut into two pieces. The Pope, who had not expected such a feat, was very pleased and amazed, because he thought it was impossible for a cannon to reach such a distance with accuracy, and although the man was sliced in two he could not understand how this could happen; he sent for me and asked for my explanation. I told him how very carefully I had taken aim, but as for how the man was sliced in half, neither he nor I knew the cause. Falling on my knees, I begged him to absolve me of this murder and of others I had committed in that Castello in the service of the Church. At my request, the Pope raised his hands and made an enormous sign of the cross above my head, declaring to me that I had his blessing and that he had pardoned all the murders I had ever committed and all those I would ever commit in the service of the Apostolic Church. After I left him I climbed back up the tower and, taking great care, I never stopped firing, and my shots almost never went astray. My drawings, my wonderful studies, and the beauty of playing music were all drowned in the music of those artillery pieces, and if I recounted in any detail the daring deeds I performed in that cruel, hellish place,* I would amaze the world, but in order not to linger, I shall pass over them. I shall only recount some of the most noteworthy events which are necessary to my story, and this is one of them. And so, as I thought day and night about what I could do for my part in the defence of the Church, I considered that when the enemy changed the guard they passed through the Santo Spirito gate,* which was a shot within reasonable range, but since I had to fire crosswise I did not manage to do the great damage that I had hoped to do, but still, every day a large number were killed, so that when the enemy saw this passage blocked they placed more than thirty barrels on the top of a roof one night which blocked my view. I began to think a bit more carefully about the matter than I had before, and I turned all five of my artillery pieces, pointing them at those barrels; then I waited for two hours before sunset just in the middle of the changing of the guard;

and when the enemy, thinking themselves to be safe, came by more slowly and in more crowded formations than was their usual practice, I fired my artillery pieces, and I not only tossed the barrels that blocked my view to the ground, but in that single volley I killed more than thirty men. In this way, following up with two more volleys, I threw the enemy troops into such disarray that, seeing that they were well stocked with the booty from the great Sack and that some were most anxious to enjoy the fruit of their labours, they started becoming mutinous in the hope of getting away. They were, however, restrained by their brave captain, whose name was Gian di Urbino,* and they were forced, to their very great inconvenience, to follow another path for the changing of the guard, which took more than three miles rather than the first path of less than half a mile. After I had accomplished this feat, all the noblemen in the Castello did me the most astonishing favours. I have wished to recount this particular incident, which had such important consequences, in order to bring to an end such stories, for they have nothing to do with the profession which inspires me to write, and if I wished to embellish the story of my life with such events, I would have far too much to say. But there is one other anecdote that I shall recount in the proper place.

38. Skipping over a few things, I shall describe how Pope Clement, in order to save the papal tiaras, with all of the numerous large jewels belonging to the Apostolic Chamber, had me summoned, and he shut himself up alone in a room with me and Cavalierino.* This Cavalierino had once worked in the stable of Filippo Strozzi:* he was a Frenchman, a person of very humble origins, and since he was a very faithful servant, Pope Clement had made him an extremely rich man and trusted him as he did himself. Thus, with the Pope, Cavalierino, and me locked inside this room, they placed before me the tiaras with that large number of jewels belonging to the Apostolic Chamber, and I was given the commission of extracting them all from the gold in which they were set. And I did so: then I wrapped each of them up in small pieces of paper and sewed them up in the linings of some garments worn by the Pope and this Cavalierino. Then they gave me all the gold, which was around two hundred pounds, and they told me to melt it down in as much secrecy as I could. I went to the Angel where my own room was located, and where I could lock the door so that no one would disturb me, and

once I had built a small brick blast-furnace in the bottom of which I set a fairly large ash-tray shaped like a dish, I tossed the gold on the charcoal, which little by little dripped down into the dish. While this furnace was in operation, I constantly studied on how I could do our enemies harm, and since we had the enemy's trenches beneath us less than a stone's throw away, I did them a great deal of damage in those trenches using some bits of old scrap, of which there were several piles, formerly used in the Castello as ammunition. Taking a saker and a falconet, both of which were broken a bit at the muzzle, I filled them with this scrap metal, and then as I opened fire with these weapons my shots flew down like mad, causing many unexpected injuries in the trenches. And so, keeping these weapons constantly loaded while I melted down that gold, a short time before the hour of vespers I saw a man mounted on a mule riding on the edge of the trench. This mule was moving along very swiftly, and the man was speaking to the men in the trenches. I stood ready to fire my artillery before he arrived in front of me. So, with good judgement, I commenced firing and hit him, knocking him directly in the face with one of those scraps of metal, while the rest hit the mule which fell down dead; I heard a tremendous uproar from the trench, and I fired another piece, not without doing them great damage. This man was the Prince of Orange,* who was carried along the trenches to a certain inn nearby, where all the noblemen in the army quickly gathered. When Pope Clement learned what I had done, he immediately sent for me and asked me about the affair, and I explained everything to him and, moreover, I told him that he must have been a man of very great importance, since all the leaders of the army, as far as one could determine, immediately gathered at the inn to which they had carried him. The Pope, with great presence of mind, called for Messer Antonio Santa Croce, the gentleman who was the leader in charge of all the artillerymen, as I mentioned before: the Pope told him to order us all to point all of our cannons, of which there was a vast number, at that particular house, and that at the shot of an arquebus everyone should commence firing, so that by killing all their leaders the enemy army, which was on its last legs, would be completely routed; he added that on this occasion, God might have heard the prayers that they constantly addressed to him, and that in this way they might be liberated from these ungodly scoundrels. We set up our artillery in order, according to the directions of Santa

Croce, and waited for the signal, but when Cardinal Orsino* learned about this he began screaming at the Pope, saying that nothing of the sort should be done, since they were about to conclude an agreement, and that if the enemy leaders were killed their army, without leadership, would enter the Castello by force and would destroy everything; they did not, therefore, want anything like this to happen. In desperation, the poor Pope, seeing himself murderously attacked from without and within, declared that he would leave the decision to them. So the order was revoked, and since I could not contain myself, when I learned that they were coming to give me the order not to shoot I fired a small cannon that I had, hitting one of the columns in the courtyard of that house where I had seen so many people gather. This shot caused such great damage to the enemy that they were about to abandon the house. This Cardinal Orsino wanted to have me either hanged or killed in any other way, but the Pope boldly defended me. The angry words that passed between the two men, even though I know them, I do not feel it necessary to recount here, since it is not my profession to write history: I shall only attend to my own doings.

39. After I had melted down the gold I carried it to the Pope, who thanked me profusely for what I had done and entrusted to Cavalierino the task of giving me twenty-five scudi, begging my pardon that he was unable to give me more. A few days later the peace accord was signed.* I went with Signor Orazio Baglioni and three hundred soldiers toward Perugia, and when there, Signor Orazio wanted to give me command of the company, something I did not wish for at that time, telling him that I wanted to go and see my father first and have the ban lifted that had been placed on me in Florence.* Baglioni told me that he had been made a captain of the Florentines; and Messer Pier Maria di Lotto was there, sent by the Florentines, to whom Signor Orazio recommended me very highly as one of his own men. So I came to Florence with several other companions. The plague was causing incalculable damage. Reaching Florence, I found my good father, who thought that I had either died during the Sack of Rome or would return to him penniless. But everything was quite the contrary: I was alive, and I had lots of money, a servant, and a fine mount. Meeting my old father, the rejoicing was so great when I saw him, I certainly thought, while he hugged and kissed me, that he would drop dead on the spot because of it. After I had recounted to

him all the devilish events of the Sack of Rome and had placed a goodly quantity of scudi in his hand, which I had earned as a soldier, we embraced each other once again, my good father and I, and he immediately went to the Eight to pay for lifting the ban; and it happened that among those serving as a member of the Eight was one of those who had banned me, and it was the one who had imprudently declared at that time to my father that he wanted to send me off to my execution; because of this, given the favour Signor Orazio Baglioni had shown to me, my father employed some very sharp words in retaliation. That was how matters stood when I told my father that Signor Orazio had named me his captain, and that I ought to begin thinking about how to recruit the company. At these words my poor father immediately became very upset, and begged me for the love of God not to get involved in such an enterprise, although he recognized that I was capable of this or something even greater, saying that he had another son, my brother, who was an extremely brave soldier, and that I ought to concentrate upon that marvellous craft in which I had laboured for so many years and with such great study. Although I promised to obey him, he, reasoning like a wise man, saw that if Signor Orazio arrived I could not avoid pursuing the affairs of the war, since I had given him my word and for other reasons; and so he thought of a good way of getting me out of Florence, saying: 'My dear son, the plague here is causing incalculable damage, and I am in constant dread of seeing you come home with it; I remember going to Mantua when I was young, a city in which I was treated very kindly, and I remained there for several years. I beg and command you for the love of me, today rather than tomorrow, that you get out of Florence and go to Mantua.'

40. Because I had always taken great pleasure in seeing the world and had never been to Mantua, I went there most willingly, taking the money I had brought, the largest portion of which I left for my good father, promising that I would always help him wherever I was, and leaving my older sister to take care of the poor man. She was called Cosa,* and never having wanted to marry, she had been accepted as a nun at Santa Orsola, and so she remained to help and care for my old father and to give guidance to my other, younger sister,* who was married to a sculptor named Bartolomeo.* So I departed with my father's blessing, mounted my fine horse, and rode on him to Mantua. I would have far too many extraordinary events to

recount if I wanted to describe this brief journey in great detail.
Since the world was under the clouds of pestilence and war, I travelled to Mantua with the greatest difficulty; when I had arrived I
sought to begin working; then I was put to work by a certain Milanese master named Niccolò, who was the goldsmith of the Duke of
Mantua.* About two days after I had begun work I went to visit
Messer Giulio Romano, that truly excellent painter, who I already
mentioned was my very good friend, and Messer Giulio treated me
in the kindest possible way and took it very badly that I had not taken
up lodgings at his home; he was living like a nobleman and was doing
a project for the Duke outside the walls of Mantua at a place called
Tè.* This project was grand and wonderful, as perhaps can still be
seen. Immediately Messer Giulio spoke about me to the Duke in the
most praiseworthy terms, and the Duke commissioned me to make a
model of a reliquary for the blood of Christ which the Mantuans
declare was brought to the city by Longinus;* and then he turned to
Messer Giulio, telling him to make me a drawing for the reliquary.
To this request Messer Giulio replied: 'My lord, Benvenuto is a man
who has no need for drawings done by others, and Your Excellency
will judge this very well for yourself when you see his model.' I set to
work executing this model and sketched a design for a reliquary that
could easily contain the vial; then from my design I made a little
model in wax. This was a seated figure of Christ: in His left hand
raised up high He held His great cross, against which He was leaning; with His right hand He made a gesture as if to open the wound
in His side with His fingers. After this model was finished it pleased
the Duke so much that his favours were endless, and he made me
understand that he would keep me in his service on terms that would
allow me to live there lavishly. Meanwhile, after I had paid my
respects to the Cardinal, his brother,* I begged the Duke to agree to
allow me to make His Most Reverential Eminence's pontifical seal,*
which I had begun. While I was working on this project I was overcome by the quartan fever;* and when this illness overtook me it
completely exhausted and overpowered me, whereupon I cursed
Mantua, its ruler, and anybody who lived there by choice. My words
were reported to the Duke by that Milanese goldsmith of his, who
saw very well that the Duke wished to have me in his service. Upon
hearing my feverish words the Duke became very angry with me,
and since I had become very angry with Mantua, we were equal in

our irritation. After I had completed my seal over a period of four months, along with some other minor commissions that I did for the Duke on behalf of the Cardinal, I was very well paid by the Cardinal, and he begged me to return to the wonderful city of Rome, where we had met each other. I departed with a good sum of scudi from Mantua and reached Governo, the place where that most valorous Lord Giovanni was killed.* There I had another mild bout of fever, which did not at all hinder my journey, and once it vanished in that city I never had another attack. Then I reached Florence, thinking that I would find my dear father, and while I was knocking at his door an angry, hunchbacked old woman looked out of the window and chased me away with the most vile insults, telling me that I was bothering her. To this hunchback I said: 'O tell me, you twisted hunchback, is there no other face in the house except yours?' 'No, damn you.' To this response I shouted: 'Well, may that face last no more than two hours!'* During this argument a neighbour came out, and she informed me that my father and everyone in my household had died of the plague; I had already partly suspected this, and for that reason my sorrow was lessened. Then she told me that the only one left alive was my younger sister, the one named Liperata, who had been taken in by a holy woman named Mona Andrea de' Bellacci.* I left the house to go to an inn. By chance I ran into a very close friend called Giovanni Rigogli.* I dismounted at his house and we went into the piazza, where I had news that my brother was alive, and I went to find him at the home of one of his friends named Bertino Aldobrandi.* After I found my brother and we had exchanged embraces and countless words of welcome—an extraordinary situation, since we had both been given news of each other's deaths—we then roared with laughter, and he took me by the hand in amazement and said to me: 'Let's go, brother, and I shall lead you to a place you'll never imagine; I married off our sister Liperata again, and she certainly thinks you are dead.' While we went to that spot we recounted to each other all the wonderful things that had happened to us; when we reached the house where our sister was living, she was so astounded by the unexpected news that she fell into my arms in a swoon; and if it had not been for the presence of my brother, her fainting without murmuring a word would have made her husband believe right away that I was not her brother. While my brother Cecchino was speaking and helping her, she quickly revived from her faint. After shedding a few tears for our father, my other sister, her husband, and their son, supper was set out, and during that delightful wedding meal* we spoke no more of the dead for the entire evening, but rather discussed weddings. Thus, cheerfully and with great pleasure we finished our supper.

41. Compelled by the entreaties of my brother and sister, I remained in Florence, although my wish was to return to Rome. Also, that dear friend of mine—the one I described earlier who gave me so much help in my difficulties, Piero di Giovanni Landi*—told me that I should remain for a time in Florence; since the Medici had been chased out of Florence (that is, Signor Ippolito and Signor Alessandro,* who were respectively a cardinal and the Duke of Florence), this Piero told me that I should stay a while to see how things developed. So I began to work in the Mercato Nuovo, where I set a great quantity of jewels and earned quite a bit of money. Around that time, a man from Siena named Girolamo Marretti* arrived in Florence: he had spent a great deal of time in Turkey and was a man of lively intellect. He came to my shop and gave me an order for a gold medal to be worn on a hat, and he wanted me to engrave on the medal a figure of Hercules prising open the lion's mouth.* So I set about making the medal, and while I was working on it Michelangelo Buonarroti came on more than one occasion to see it; and because I had worked very hard on the medal, the action of the figure and the fierce aspect of the animal were very different from anything of the sort that had been made up to that time. Since my method of working was completely unfamiliar to that divine Michelangelo, he praised this work of mine so highly that my desire to do well greatly increased; this praise was invaluable.* As I had nothing else to do but to set jewels, even though this was the work from which I could make the most profit, I was not happy, because I wanted to create works of greater complexity than jewel-settings, and at that moment a certain Federigo Ginori* arrived, a young man of highly refined spirit. He had been in Naples for many years, and since he was very handsome and had a striking presence, he had had a love-affair with a princess while in Naples. Now, wishing to create a medal which represented Atlas holding the world on his shoulders, he asked the great Michelangelo to draw up a little sketch for him. Michelangelo replied to this Federigo: 'Go and find a certain young goldsmith by the name of Benvenuto; he will serve you very well, and he certainly

has no need of any drawing of mine, but just so you don't think that I am trying to avoid the bother of such a small thing, I shall willingly draw a little sketch for you. Meanwhile, speak with this Benvenuto and have him make a small model as well; then you can execute whichever design is the best.' This Federigo Ginori came to find me and told me his wishes, as well as how highly that amazing Michelangelo had praised me; I was to produce a small model in wax while that astonishing man had promised to draw him a little sketch. The words of that great man gave me such encouragement that I immediately set to work with the greatest care to make this model, and after I had completed it, a painter named Giuliano Bugiardini,* who was a good friend of Michelangelo, brought me the sketch of Atlas. At the same time I showed Giuliano my little wax model, which was very different from the sketch of Michelangelo, so different that Federigo and also Bugiardini concluded that I should execute the work following my wax model. So I began work on it, and when that most excellent Michelangelo saw it, he praised me so highly that it was beyond belief. There was a figure of Atlas, as I said, engraved on a thin plate; on his back he bore the heavens, represented by a crystal ball, engraved with the zodiac against a background of lapis-lazuli: all this was so beautiful to see that it was indescribable. Underneath, there was a motto written out which said: *Summa tulisse juvat**. Satisfied, Federigo paid me most generously. At that time Messer Luigi Alamanni* was then in Florence; he was a friend of this Federigo Ginori, who brought him to my workshop on numerous occasions, and thanks to him Luigi and I became very close friends.

42. Pope Clement declared war on the city of Florence,* and when the city prepared its defences by creating in each quarter a people's militia, I was ordered to do my part. I equipped myself elaborately and kept company with the greatest nobles of Florence, who seemed most willing to fight in the city's defence, while the usual speeches were delivered in every district. Moreover, the young men gathered together more than usual and never spoke of anything except the war. One day around noon, when a group of important people and young men, the first citizens of the city, was in my workshop, I received a letter from Rome which came from a certain individual called Master Iacopino della Barca.* His real name was Iacopo dello Sciorina, but he was called della Barca in Rome because he had a

boat that passed between the Sisto Bridge and the Santo Agnolo Bridge on the Tiber. This Master Iacopo was a very clever person and carried on fine and delightful conversations: he had formerly been a designer for the tapestry weavers in Florence. He was a close friend of Pope Clement, who took great delight in hearing him speak. One day, while they were engaged in such conversation, they fell to talking about the Sack of Rome and the fighting at the Castello, and because of this the Pope remembered me and spoke as well of me as could possibly be imagined, adding that if Iacopo knew where I was, he would be delighted to see me again. This Master Iacopo said that I was in Florence; for this reason, the Pope ordered him to write to me, saying that I should return to his service. This letter contained the order that I should return to Pope Clement's service, and that it would be to my benefit. The young men who were standing there in my presence wanted to know what my letter contained, but I hid it as best I could; then I wrote to Master Jacopo, begging him not to write to me under any circumstances, either good or bad. Master Iacopo, becoming even more determined, sent me another letter, which contained so many compromising things that, had it been seen, I would have ended up very badly.* The second letter said, on behalf of the Pope, that I should come immediately, for he wanted me to work on projects of the greatest importance, and that, if I wanted to do well by myself, I should abandon everything immediately and not remain to fight against the Pope along with those desperate madmen. After I had seen this letter, which terrified me, I went to see my dear friend Piero Landi, who upon seeing me immediately asked me what was going on, since I looked so upset. I told my friend that what was upsetting me so much could not be told to anyone; I only begged him to keep some keys I gave him and return the jewels and the gold to all those he would find listed in a little book of mine, then to take my belongings from my home and to look after them with his usual kindness; and I told him that within a few days he would know where I was. This wise young man, perhaps imagining more or less what was the matter, said to me: 'My dear brother, leave at once, then write to me, and don't give a thought to your things.' I did just that. He was the most faithful, the wisest, the most honourable, the most discreet, and the kindest friend I had ever known. After I left Florence I went to Rome, and I wrote to him from there.

43. As soon as I reached Rome I looked up some of my friends, who saw and greeted me affectionately, and I immediately went to work on projects designed to earn money and not unworthy of description. There was a certain old goldsmith called Raffaello del Moro,* who was a man of great reputation in the profession, and he was, moreover, a very honourable person. He asked me if I would like to go to work in his shop, for he had to execute some works of importance which would bring a very nice profit, and so I went there willingly. More than ten days passed before I encountered that Master Iacopino della Barca, who, seeing me by chance, gave me the warmest welcome, and when he asked when I had arrived I told him, about fifteen days ago. He took this very badly and told me that I took very little account of a Pope who with great insistence had already made him write to me three times, and I, who had already taken this even more badly than he, made no reply, but rather swallowed my anger. This man, who was a great talker, entered into an endless discussion, and talked so much that, when I saw he was exhausted, I did not say anything at all except that he could take me to see the Pope any time he wished; he said that any time was fine with him, and so I replied: 'And I, too, am always ready.' He began to head toward the palace, and I with him (this was Maundy Thursday),* and upon reaching the Pope's chambers he, who was known there, and I, who was expected, were immediately shown inside. The Pope was in bed slightly indisposed, and with him was Messer Iacopo Salviati and the Archbishop of Capua.* When the Pope saw me he cheered up in the most extraordinary fashion, and I, kissing his feet, with as much modesty as I could muster came up close and indicated that I wished to say something of importance to him. He immediately made a sign with his hand, and both Messer Iacopo and the Archbishop drew some distance away from us. I immediately began, saying: 'Most Blessed Father, from the Sack of Rome until the present I have been unable either to make confession or take communion, for no one will grant me absolution. The situation is this—that is, when I melted the gold down and did the work to remove the jewels from their settings, Your Holiness gave an order to Cavalierino that I was to receive some small reward for my labours, but I never received anything; instead he gave me a good deal of abuse. When I went up to my room where I had melted down the gold, I washed the ashes and discovered about a pound and a half of gold in so many tiny grains, the size of millet seed, and since I did not have enough money to travel in a decent manner to my home I thought I would use this gold and return it to you later when I had the opportunity. Now I am here at the feet of Your Holiness, who is the true confessor: if Your Holiness would do me the favour of allowing me to make my confession and take communion, through Your Holiness's grace, I may be restored to the grace of Our Lord God.' Then the Pope, after a small, modest sigh, perhaps thinking of all his tribulations, said these words: 'Benvenuto, I am very certain of all that you say—I can absolve you of every sin that you have committed, and I should like to do more. You may most freely tell me everything in your heart for, even if you took what one of those papal tiaras was worth, I am more than ready to pardon you.' Then I replied: 'Most Blessed Father, I took no more than the amount I told you, and this did not exceed the value of one hundred and forty ducats, which is the amount I received from the Mint in Perugia, and with it I went home to give comfort to my poor old father.' The Pope then said: 'Your father was as virtuous, as good, and as honest a man as was ever born, and you haven't deviated one iota from his path: it bothers me a great deal that the money was so little, but that money, in the amount that you have specified, I give you as a present, and I forgive you everything. Tell that to your confessor, if there is nothing else that concerns me; then, once you have taken confession and communion, come back to see me again, for it will be worth your while.' Once I had left the Pope's side Messer Iacopo and the Archbishop drew near to him, and the Pope spoke more highly of me than could be spoken of anyone in the world, and he declared that he had taken my confession and had absolved me; then he told the Archbishop of Capua that he should send for me, ask me if anything else was required in this matter, and then absolve me completely, giving him total authority to do so, and that he was, moreover, to treat me as kindly as he could. While I was walking away with Master Iacopino he asked me with great curiosity what secrets and long discussions I had had with the Pope. After he had asked me about this more than twice, I told him I did not wish to tell him, since they were matters that did not concern him, and that he should therefore not ask me again. I went to do everything that had been agreed upon with the Pope; then, after the two holidays* were over, I returned to see him; he welcomed me even more graciously than before, and said to me:

'If you had come to Rome a bit sooner, I would have commissioned you to remake those two tiaras of mine that we ruined in the Castello, but since they are of little value, apart from their jewels, I shall employ you in a work of the greatest importance, where you can demonstrate what you know how to do. And this is the button for my cope (which should be round like a plate and as large as a small plate, about a third of an armslength): I want you to engrave on it a God the Father in half relief, and in the centre of the figure I want you to accommodate this large, beautifully cut diamond with many other jewels of great value. A man named Caradosso has already begun the work, but he never finished it; I want it completed quickly, for I wish to enjoy it if only for a little while; now go and make a fine little model.' And he had all the jewels shown to me, whereupon I went off like a shot.*

44. While the siege had surrounded Florence, the Federigo Ginori for whom I had made the medal of Atlas died of consumption, and that medal fell into the hands of Messer Luigi Alamanni, who in the space of a short time carried it himself as a gift to Francis, King of France, along with some of his beautiful writings. Since this medal pleased the King beyond all measure, this most virtuous Messer Luigi Alamanni spoke of me to His Majesty, saying a few words about my personal qualities, not to mention my professional talents, doing so with so much good will that the King made it known that he would like to meet me. With all the care that I could muster I was pressing forward with this little model, which I made in exactly the same size that the work was to be, and many of the members of the goldsmiths' guild became resentful over it, since they believed they were capable of executing such a work. A certain Micheletto* had come to Rome. He was very talented at engraving cornelians, a most intelligent jeweller, and an old man with a good reputation, who had undertaken the job of repairing the Pope's two tiaras, and as I executed this model he was amazed that I had not relied upon him, since he was a very intelligent man and in good relations with the Pope. Finally, seeing that I was not going to come to him, he came to me, asking me what I was doing: 'What the Pope commissioned me to do', I replied. Then he said: 'The Pope has commissioned me to oversee all these projects that are being done for His Holiness.' To this I declared that I would first ask the Pope about it, and that I would then know what kind of answer I would have to

give him. He told me I would be sorry, and having left me in anger, he got together with all the other members of the guild and, discussing the matter, they put Michele in charge of the entire affair. With his great ingenuity, he had more than thirty drawings of this button made by a number of talented draughtsmen, all of them different from one another. Since he had the Pope's ear at his disposal, he struck a deal with another jeweller from Milan, named Pompeo* (who was a great favourite of the Pope and a relative of Messer Traiano,* the first papal chamberlain); these two (that is, Michele and Pompeo) began telling the Pope that they had seen my model and that they thought I was not an apt instrument for such a marvellous undertaking. To this the Pope said that he wanted to see the model for himself; then, if I was not up to it, he would search for someone who was. Both of them declared that they had several wonderful drawings for this subject. To this the Pope said that he was very pleased to hear it, but that he did not want to see them before I had finished my model; then he would look at them all together. Within a few days I had finished the model, and I brought it to the Pope one morning, when this Messer Traiano made me wait while he took great care to send for Micheletto and Pompeo, telling them to bring their drawings. When they arrived we were all shown inside; Michele and Pompeo immediately began to hand over their designs, and the Pope looked at them. Because draughtsmen who are not jewellers do not understand the setting of jewels, and those who were jewellers had not instructed the draughtsmen (a jeweller must know how to draw when he sets his gems among figures, otherwise nothing good will come of his work), all of their drawings had placed that marvellous diamond in the middle of the chest of that figure of God the Father. Once the Pope, who had very good judgement, saw the drawings, he was not entirely pleased, and after he had seen about ten of them he tossed the rest on the floor and said to me, who was standing there beside him: 'Benvenuto, show me a bit of your model so that I can see if you have made the same mistake as the others.' After I stepped forward and opened a little round box, it seemed as if the Pope's eyes lit up, and he declared in a loud voice: 'If you had been in my place, you wouldn't have done it any other way than what I see here; the others couldn't have thought of a better method of disgracing themselves.' A great number of important noblemen drew near, and the Pope showed them the difference between my

model and their drawings.* When he had given it great praise, and
the other goldsmiths were cowed and dumbfounded, he turned to
me and said: 'I recognize only one thing that may go wrong, but it is
of the greatest importance. My dear Benvenuto, wax is easy to work,
but the challenge is to do it in gold.' To these words I boldly
answered: 'Most Holy Father, if I do not do it ten times better than
this model of mine, let it be agreed that you will not pay me for it.'
At the sound of these words a great commotion arose among the
noblemen, who said that I was promising too much. One of these
noblemen, a very distinguished philosopher, spoke in my favour:
'From the physiognomy and the symmetry I see in this young man's
body, I expect he will do everything he says and even more.' The
Pope then said: 'And that's why I think so, too.' After the Pope
summoned that chamberlain of his, Messer Traiano, he told him to
fetch five hundred papal golden ducats.* While we waited for the
money the Pope once again, but more slowly, considered the beautiful way in which I had combined the diamond with the figure of God
the Father. I had placed this diamond exactly in the middle of the
work, and above it I had arranged God the Father in a beautiful
sitting position turned to one side, that produced a beautiful balance
but did not hide the jewel at all: raising His right hand, He delivered
a benediction. Under the diamond I had arranged three cherubs
with their arms raised high to support it. One of these cherubs in the
middle was in full relief; the other two were in half relief. Around
them a great number of different little cherubs were arranged in
harmony with the other beautiful jewels. The rest of God the Father
was covered in a flowing mantle from which emerged a number of
cherubs, with many other beautiful decorations, making the work
most beautiful to see. The model was made with white stucco on a
black stone. When the money arrived the Pope gave it to me with his
own hand, and with the greatest delight he begged me to work in
such a way that he would have it while he was still alive, and said it
would be very profitable to me.

45. I carried off the money and my model, but it seemed like a
thousand years before I could put my hands to the task. I immediately began to work with great diligence, and in the space of eight
days the Pope sent his chamberlain, a very important nobleman
from Bologna, to tell me that I had to go to him and bring him what I
had done. While I was going to him this chamberlain, who was the

kindest person at the court, informed me that the Pope did not want so much to see my work but that he wished to give me another commission of the greatest importance, which was to create the designs for the coins of the Mint of Rome, and that he had warned me about this so that I could prepare myself to respond to His Holiness. When we reached the Pope, I set in front of him the layer of gold upon which I had as yet only sculpted the figure of God the Father, which, although roughed out in this fashion, displayed far more talent than the little wax model: the Pope was so astonished that he said: 'From now on I shall believe everything you say.' Having paid me endless compliments, he said: 'I want to give you another project, which is as dear to me as this other one, and even more so, if you have the confidence to do it.' After telling me that he would like me to make the dies for his coins, he asked me if I had ever made any, and if I had the confidence to do so. I declared that I most certainly had the confidence, that I had seen how they were produced, but that I had never made any of them myself. Also present there was a certain Messer Tommaso from Prato,* who was His Holiness's datary, and since he was a close friend of those enemies of mine, he said: 'Most Holy Father, the favours Your Holiness has shown to this young man, since he is by nature most bold, are the reason why he will promise you an endless number of new things; adding a greater project to the other one now will cause one project to get in the way of the other.' Growing angry, the Pope turned to him and told him to mind his own business; he ordered me to produce a model for a gold doubloon,* on which he wanted the nude figure of a Christ with his hands bound and with the inscription 'Ecce Homo';* the reverse would contain figures of the Pope and the Emperor, who would together hold upright a cross looking as if it was about to fall, with the inscription *Unus spiritus et una fides erat in eis*.* After the Pope commissioned me to make this beautiful coin, the sculptor Bandinello,* who had not yet been knighted, arrived, and with his usual presumption adorned by ignorance, he said: 'These goldsmiths need to have drawings of such beautiful objects done for them.' I quickly turned to him and declared that I had no need of his designs for my craft, but that I certainly hoped before long to give his craft* something troublesome to think about with my own designs. The Pope showed that he prized these words more than could be imagined, and turning to me he said: 'Go now, my

Benvenuto, and put all your energy into working for me, and don't lend your ear to the words of these madmen.' So I left, and with great speed made two steel dies: I stamped a coin in gold, and one Sunday after dinner I brought the coin and the dies to the Pope who, upon seeing the coin, was amazed and delighted, not so much by the beautiful work, that pleased him beyond all measure, but more so by the speed I had employed. To increase his satisfaction and amazement, I brought with me all the old coins that had been minted in the past by those talented men who had served Pope Julius and Pope Leo, and when I saw that my coin gave him much greater satisfaction, I took from my breast pocket a *motto proprio** in which I requested the office of Master of the Dies of the Mint,* which paid six gold scudi of provisions per month, not counting the fact that the dies were then paid for by the superintendent of the Mint, who paid a ducat for every three dies. The Pope took my *motto proprio*, turned, and gave it to his datary, ordering him to draw it up immediately. The datary took the *motto proprio*, and while trying to slip it into his pocket he said: 'Most Blessed Father, Your Holiness should not move in such haste: these are matters that deserve some consideration.' Then the Pope said: 'I have heard you; now give me the *motto proprio*.' He took it, quickly signed it in his own hand, and then he said to the datary: 'Now there's nothing more to say: expedite this, because this is my wish, for Benvenuto's shoes are worth more than the eyes of all these other simpletons.' And so I thanked His Holiness and, happy beyond all measure, I went off to work.

46. I was still working in the shop belonging to Raffaello del Moro, whom I mentioned previously. This worthy man had a beautiful little daughter for whom he had set his eyes on me, and once I became partly aware of his plan I desired it too, but even though I felt this desire, I showed no sign of it at all; on the contrary, I was so well behaved that I amazed him. It happened that this poor little girl had a disease in her right hand which had caused the two bones of her little finger and the one next to it to deteriorate. And because the poor girl was being treated, through her father's carelessness, by an ignorant charlatan, who declared that the poor girl might be crippled in her entire right arm, if worse did not happen to her, when I saw how terrified her poor father was I told him not to believe everything that ignorant quack said. As a result, he told me that he was not acquainted with any surgeons and begged me, if I knew of any, to have him sent for. I immediately summoned a certain Master Iacomo from Perugia,* a most excellent surgeon, and after he had seen this poor little girl, who was terrified, since she must have surmised what that ignorant charlatan had said, this intelligent surgeon declared that she would not suffer the slightest harm; that she would perfectly well make use of her right hand even though those two last fingers would be a little weaker than the others; and that this would not bother her at all. And once he began his cure, in the space of a few days he wanted to cut away a bit of the diseased bone; her father called me in so that I might see the pain the poor daughter would have to endure. For the operation Master Iacopo took certain crude iron instruments, but when I realized that with these he would do little good and cause a great deal of pain to the young girl, I told him to stop and wait for me for a few minutes. After running to my workshop, I made a very delicate little steel instrument that was extremely sharp and curved, and it cut like a razor. After I returned to the surgeon, he began to work with such gentleness that she felt no pain at all, and in a short time he had finished. For this reason, among others, this worthy doctor had more affection for me than he had for his two male children; and thus he attended to curing the beautiful little girl. I was great friends with a certain Messer Giovanni Gaddi,* who was the surgeon of the Chamber; this Messer Giovanni took great pleasure in true talent even though he had none himself. He lived with a certain Messer Giovanni, a Greek and a very distinguished scholar;* a Messer Lodovico da Fano,* like him, a scholar; Messer Antonio Allegretti;* and Messer Annibal Caro,* then a young man. Messer Bastiano the Venetian,* that most talented painter, and I were from other cities, and almost every day we saw each other at least once in the company of this Messer Giovanni. Because of this friendship, that worthy goldsmith Raffaello said to Messer Giovanni: 'My dear Messer Giovanni, you know me, and since I should like to give my little daughter to Benvenuto, and finding no better means than Your Lordship, I beg you to help me, and I should like you to decide, based on my means, whatever dowry she should have.' This man of little intelligence hardly allowed that poor, worthy father to finish speaking before, without any motive at all, he told him: 'Don't speak about this any longer, Raffaello, you are further away from this goal than blackberries are from January.'* The poor man, beaten down, soon sought to marry her off, and the girl's mother and all her sulking relatives were very angry at me without my understanding the cause. Believing that they were paying me back in bad money for all the kindness I had shown them, I sought to open a workshop near them. Messer Giovanni did not say anything until the daughter was married, which occurred in the space of a few months. I was working with the greatest diligence on completing my work* and serving the Mint, where once again the Pope had commissioned me to make a coin in the value of two carlini, upon which were represented the portrait of His Holiness and on the reverse a figure of Christ walking on the sea while offering his hand to St Peter, and with the inscription that read: *Quare dubitasti?** This coin brought him such pleasure that a certain secretary of the Pope, a man of the greatest talent, named Sanga,* declared: 'Your Holiness can glory in the fact that you have a type of coin that was never seen among the ancients in all their splendour.' To this the Pope responded: 'Benvenuto, too, can glory in the fact that he serves an emperor like me who appreciates him.' While I continued the great work in gold, I often showed it to the Pope, who importuned me to see it, every day being more amazed.

47. My brother was in Rome in the service of Duke Alessandro, for whom at that time the Pope had procured the Duchy of Penna;* numerous soldiers were serving the Duke, worthy, brave men of the school of that great Lord Giovanni de' Medici,* and my brother was among them, considered by the Duke as one of his most courageous soldiers. One day after supper, this brother of mine was in the Via dei Banchi Nuovi inside the shop of a certain Baccino della Croce,*- where all the mercenary soldiers stayed: he was seated on a chair and was sleeping. At that very moment the constable's patrol passed by, taking to prison a certain Captain Cisti, a Lombard who was also from the same school as that great Lord Giovanni but who was no longer in the Duke's service. Captain Cattivanza degli Strozzi* was inside the workshop of this Baccino della Croce. When Captain Cisti saw Captain Cattivanza degli Strozzi, he said to him: 'I was bringing you those scudi I owed you; if you want them, come get them before they take me off to prison!' Strozzi was the kind of man who gladly stirred up others, taking care not to risk his own neck, and when he found himself among a number of the most courageous young men who were more willing than capable of such a serious undertaking, he told them to approach Captain Cisti and to make him give that

money of his to them, and that if the constable's patrol offered any resistance they should employ force, if they were bold enough. There were only four of these young men, all four adolescents: the first was named Bertino Aldobrandi, the next Anguillotto from Lucca; and as for the others, I don't remember their names. This Bertino had been trained by my brother and was his true apprentice, and my brother loved him as much as could possibly be imagined. These four brave young men drew near the constable's patrol, which numbered more than fifty police agents carrying pikes, arquebuses, and two-handed swords. To be brief about it, they drew their swords and those four young men attacked the patrol in such an astonishing way that, if Captain Cattivanza had only shown his face without even drawing his sword, those young men would have put the patrol to flight, but having stayed at it too long, Bertino suffered some serious wounds and was thrown to the ground; at the same moment, Anguillotto also suffered a wound in his right arm so that he could no longer hold his sword, and he retreated as best he could; the others did the same; and Bertino Aldobrandi was lifted from the ground badly wounded.

48. While these things were happening we were all at the dinner table, for the morning meal had been served over an hour later than was our usual custom. Hearing the commotion, one of those children, the eldest son, got up from the table to go and see the fight. His name was Giovanni, and I said to him: 'Please don't go, because in such affairs there is always something to be lost but nothing to be gained.' And his father said much the same thing: 'Ah, my son, don't go out there.' This young man, without listening to anyone, ran down the stairs. He reached the Banchi, where the great brawl was taking place, and he saw Bertino being picked up, and running back he encountered my brother Cecchino, who asked him what was going on. Although Giovanni had been warned by some that he should not say anything about this affair to Cecchino, like a thoughtless madman he told Giovanni how Bertino Aldobrandi had been murdered by the patrol. My poor brother let out such a loud cry that it could have been heard for ten miles; then he said to Giovanni: 'Alas, could you tell me which one of them killed him?' Giovanni said that he could, and that it was one of the men who held a two-handed sword, with a blue feather in his cap. My poor brother pushed forward and, having recognized the murderer by that mark, he threw himself with all his

marvellous quickness and courage into the midst of the entire patrol, and without giving them time to react, he stabbed that fellow in the gut and ran him through, shoving him to the ground with the hilt of his sword, and rounding on the others with so much skill and bravery that he would have put them all to flight if he had not turned and given to a man carrying an arquebus, who fired his weapon in self-defence, the chance to strike the brave but unfortunate young man under the knee of the right leg. And as he lay on the ground, the patrol, put to flight, hastened to run away, so that they would not be attacked by another soldier like this one. Hearing this uproar continue, I too got up from the table and strapped my sword on my side, since everyone at that time wore one, and I reached the Sant'Agnolo gate where I saw a group of many men. As I was going forward I was recognized by some of them, and they made way for me and showed me what I would never have wished to see, even though I was very curious to see what was going on. At first I did not recognize my brother, for he was dressed in different clothes than those I had recently seen him wearing, so he recognized me first and said: 'My dearest brother, don't let my great misfortune bother you, because my profession promised me such a fate; have me carried away from here quickly, for I have few hours to live.' While the affair was recounted to me as he spoke, with the brevity that such tragedies require I replied: 'Brother, this is the greatest pain and sorrow that I shall ever experience in the course of my entire life, but be of good will, for before you close your eyes the man who wounded you will see your revenge carried out by my own hand.' His words, as well as mine, were to this effect, though very brief.

49. The patrol was some fifty paces away from us, for Maffio,* who was the constable, had made some of them return to pick up the body of the corporal my brother had killed, so that after walking those few paces briskly, with my cloak wrapped about me and closed, I came right to Maffio's side and would certainly have murdered him, since there were a great many people and I had mingled with them. Already, and as quickly as it is possible to imagine, I had half drawn my sword when Berlinghier Berlinghieri, an extremely brave young man and my close friend, grabbed my arms from behind, and with him were four other young men like himself, who shouted at Maffio: 'Get out of here, for this man will kill you by himself!' Maffio asked: 'Who is this fellow?' And they replied: 'He is the

brother of the man you see over there.' Not wishing to hear anything further, Maffio retreated to the Torre di Nona* with dispatch, and to me they said: 'Benvenuto, holding you back against your will was done for a good reason: now let us go give comfort to your brother, who is on the point of death.' So we turned about and went to my brother, whom I had told them to carry inside a house. A group of doctors quickly met together and treated him, but they could not resolve the problem of whether or not to amputate his leg, which might have saved him. As soon as he was treated, Duke Alessandro appeared and spoke very affectionately to Cecchino (my brother had not yet lost consciousness), and Cecchino said to the Duke: 'My lord, I do not grieve over anything except that Your Excellency has lost a servant who might not be the bravest in this profession, but who has loved and served you more faithfully than any other.' The Duke told him to do everything to survive, and as for the rest, he clearly recognized him as a worthy and brave man. Then he turned to some of his men, telling them that this brave young man should want for nothing. After the Duke had left, the heavy flow of blood, which could not be stopped, caused my brother to lose his senses, so that he was delirious the entire night except when they wanted to give him communion, and then he said: 'You should have given me confession earlier; now it's impossible for me to receive this divine sacrament in this already ruined body; only be content that I am tasting it through the divinity of my eyes, through which it will be received by my immortal soul, which alone asks God for mercy and forgiveness.' After he said these words the sacrament was taken away, and he returned at once to the same delirious state as before, which brought on even greater ravings and the most horrible words that men could ever possibly imagine, nor did he once cease the whole night through until the next day. As the sun was rising over the horizon he turned to me and said: 'My dear brother, I don't want to stay here any longer, for they will force me to do something serious for which they will repent of having bothered me.' Then, flinging out both legs, he lifted the one we had placed in a very heavy cast as if he were mounting a horse; turning his face toward mine, he said three times: 'Goodbye, goodbye', and with his last word that most courageous soul passed away. At the proper hour, which was late in the evening, around ten o'clock, I had him buried with the greatest honour in the Florentine church,* and then I had an extremely beautiful marble tombstone made for him, upon which were engraved some trophies and banners. I should not fail to relate that, when he was asked by one of his friends if he could describe the soldier who shot him, and if he would recognize him, he said he could and described him in detail, and although my brother tried to prevent me from hearing this, I heard it very well, and in the proper place I shall describe the outcome.

50. Returning to the subject of the marble tombstone, certain brilliant men of letters who knew my brother dictated an epitaph to me, saying that this amazing young man deserved one, which read as follows:

Francisco Cellino Florentino, qui quod in teneris annis ad Joannem Medicem ducem plures victorias retulit et signifer fuit, facile documentum dedit quantae fortitudinis et consilii vir futurus erat, ni crudelis fati archibuso transfossus, quincto aetatis lustro iaceret, Benvenutus frater posuit. Obiit die XXVII Maii MDXXIX.*

He was twenty-five years old,* and because among the soldiers he was called Cecchino del Piffero,* whereas his true name was Giovanfrancesco Cellini, I wanted to inscribe the name by which he was known under our coat of arms. I had this name carved in extremely beautiful antique lettering which I had done in entirely broken characters except for the first and the last letter. I was asked about these broken characters I had ordered by the men of letters who had written that beautiful epitaph. I told them that the letters were broken because that marvellous instrument, his body, was broken and dead, and that the two whole letters, the first and the last, were, in the case of the first letter, a reminder of the great gift bestowed upon us by God of our soul which is kindled with His divinity (and which will never be broken), and in the case of the last letter, to recall the glorious renown of his brave talents. This pleased them a great deal, and since then some other people have used this same idea. Afterwards I had the Cellini coat of arms carved on the tombstone, which I modified from its normal shape, for in Ravenna, which is a most ancient city, members of our Cellini family are highly honoured gentlemen who have for their coat of arms a rampant lion the colour of gold on an azure field, with a red lily placed in his right paw and a heraldic label over it containing three small golden lilies. This is the true coat of arms of the Cellini family.* My father showed me one in which there was only the paw* with all the other details, but I liked best the one that can be seen in the coat of arms of the Cellini from Ravenna. Returning to what I had carved on my brother's tomb, I included the lion's paw, and rather than a lily I placed a battle-axe in the lion's paw, with the field divided in quarters; I put the battle-axe there only so that I would not forget to avenge him.

51. I worked with the greatest diligence to finish the work in gold for Pope Clement, who was extremely eager to have it, and he had me summoned two and three times a week, wishing to see it, and the pleasure it gave him always increased. On numerous occasions he reproached me, almost yelling at me for the great sadness I felt over the death of my brother, and on one occasion, after he saw that I was dejected and paler than was fitting, he said: 'O, Benvenuto, I didn't know that you were crazy; didn't you know before this that for death there is no remedy. You go about trying to follow him.' After I left the Pope, I kept on working on my button and the dies at the Mint, and I had begun pursuing this soldier with the arquebus who killed my brother as if he were my mistress. This fellow had once been a light cavalryman, but then he became a arquebusier with the constable's corporals, and the thing that most aroused my anger was the fact that he bragged about the killing in this way, saying: 'If I had not killed that brave young man, with every moment that passed he alone would have put us all to flight with great losses.' Realizing that this passion for seeing him so often was depriving me of sleep and my appetite, and was leading me down an evil path, since I no longer worried about committing a base and unpraiseworthy deed, I decided one evening to rid myself of this torment. The fellow was staying in a house near a place called Torre Sanguigna,* beside a house where one of the most popular courtesans of Rome had her lodgings, a woman who called herself Signora Antea. The clock had just struck the hour of nightfall, and this arquebusier was standing in his doorway, his sword in hand, and he had eaten. With great dexterity, I approached him with a large dagger of the type made in Pistoia* and spun him around with a back-stroke, hoping to cut off his head cleanly, but he turned quickly and my blow hit him on the edge of his left shoulder and broke the entire bone; he got up, leaving his sword behind, and confused by the intense pain, he began to run, but I followed him and caught up with him in four steps. After I raised my dagger above his head, he lowered it as far as he could and

took the blow at a point right on the neckbone and halfway down the nape of the neck, and the whole blade of the dagger went in so deeply that although I applied tremendous force to extract it, I could not do so, because four soldiers issued forth from Antea's house with their swords drawn in their hands, so that I was forced to draw my own weapon to defend myself from them. Leaving the dagger behind, I got out of there, and for fear of being recognized I went to the home of Duke Alessandro, who lived between Piazza Navona and the Rotonda.* After I reached the palace I asked someone to speak to the Duke, who gave me to understand that if I was alone I should keep quiet and not worry about anything, that I should go to work on the project for the Pope, which he was very eager to have, and that for eight days I should work inside his home, especially since the soldiers who had interrupted me came by holding the dagger and recounting how the affair had transpired and what hard work it had been to extract that dagger from the collarbone and head of the victim, and how they did not know to whom the dagger belonged. At this moment Giovan Bandini* arrived, and told them: 'This dagger is mine, and I loaned it to Benvenuto who wanted to avenge his brother.' The reactions of the soldiers were many, and they all were sorry to have interrupted me, even though my revenge was taken to excess. More than eight days passed: the Pope did not send for me as he usually did. Then he sent for me through that Bolognese gentleman who was his chamberlain, whom I have already mentioned, and with great tact he indicated to me that the Pope knew everything and that His Holiness held me in such great affection that I should apply myself to my work and remain silent. When I went to the Pope he scowled at me, and his glance alone seemed both menacing and terrifying, but when he turned to observe my work his face began to brighten up, and he praised me beyond measure, telling me that I had done a great deal in a very short time. Then, looking me in the eye, he said: 'Now that you are cured,* Benvenuto, take care of the way you live.' And I, who understood him, said that I would do just that. I immediately opened a fine workshop in the Via dei Banchi Nuovi, across from Raffaello's,* and there I brought the Pope's morse to completion in just a few months.

52. The Pope sent me all the jewels, except for the diamond, which he had pawned with some Genoese bankers for some of his needs, and I had possession of all the other jewels with only a cast of

this diamond. I had five good workmen, and besides this particular project I was working on many commissions, so that the workshop was filled with many valuable works, jewels, gold, and silver. In the house I kept a very large, handsome, shaggy dog that Duke Alessandro had given me, and although the dog was good for hunting, because he brought me every sort of bird or animal that I had killed with my arquebus, as a guard dog he was absolutely astonishing. During this period it happened that, as was suitable for someone at my age of twenty-nine years, I had taken as my servant a young woman of great beauty and grace; I employed her as a model in my professional work, and I also enjoyed her in my youth to satisfy my carnal desires. For this reason I had my own room set apart at some distance from those where my workmen slept, and very far away from the workshop, but connected to a miserable cubbyhole of a room for my young serving girl, and I very often went there to enjoy her (but although I am the lightest sleeper in the world, on these occasions of working the flesh my sleep sometimes became very heavy and deep). As it happened, one night, after my shop was cased by a thief who, under the pretext of claiming to be a goldsmith, set his eyes on those jewels, he made plans to steal them from me. To do so, he broke into my workshop and discovered many small minor pieces in gold and silver, and while he was busy trying to pick the locks on some of the drawers to find the jewels that he had seen, that dog of mine sprang on him, and he clumsily defended himself with a sword; so that the dog ran through the house several times, going into the bedrooms of my workmen, which were open, since it was summertime. When they refused to listen to his loud barking he pulled the covers off them, but when they still did not listen, he seized first one and then another by the arms and woke them by force, and by barking in his horrendous fashion he tried to show them where to go by running in front of them. But they had no intention of following him, and when these traitors became annoyed with him, they threw stones and sticks at the dog (they could easily do this, since I had ordered them to keep a fire burning all night), and finally they locked the bedrooms tightly, and the dog, having lost all hope of any help from these rascals, set out to do the job alone. He ran downstairs, but no longer finding the thief in the workshop, he ran after him, and struggling with him, he had already ripped off his cloak and would have taken it had the thief not called for the assistance of some tailors, telling them for God's sake to help him defend himself from a rabid dog; these men, believing this to be the truth, drove the dog away with a great deal of effort. When day broke these workmen went down into the workshop, and they saw it ransacked and open with all the drawers broken. They began to cry 'Alas, alas' at the top of their voices, whereupon I awoke, alarmed by those noises, and came out. When I appeared they came to me and said: 'Oh, what a misfortune, we have been robbed by somebody who has broken in and taken everything!' Their words struck me with such force that I could not run to my chest to see if the Pope's jewels were still inside, but having almost lost the power of vision through anxiety, I ordered them to open the chest to see which of the Pope's jewels were missing. These young men were still all in their night-shirts; and when they opened the chest they saw all the jewels and the golden morse with them, and rejoicing, they declared: 'Nothing's really wrong, since the golden morse and the jewels are all here, but this thief has left us all in our nightshirts, because last night in the great heat we took all our clothes off in the workshop and left them there.' My strength quickly returned, and giving thanks to God, I replied: 'All of you go buy new clothes and I'll pay for everything, once I've had time to understand how this has happened.' The thing that grieved me most and which was the cause of my confusion, and a fear quite uncommon to my nature, was the fact that people might possibly have thought that I had invented the fiction of this thief solely for the purpose of stealing the jewels myself, and Pope Clement was, indeed, told by one of his most trusted servants, as well as by others, such as Francesco del Nero,* Zana de' Biliotti his bookkeeper, the Bishop of Vasona,* and many other similar people: 'How can you, Most Blessed Father, entrust such a great fortune in jewels to a young man who is a complete tearaway, more interested in fighting than in his profession, and who still isn't even thirty years old?' To this the Pope replied by asking if any of them had any knowledge of my doing anything to arouse their suspicion. Francesco del Nero, his treasurer, immediately replied and said: 'No, Most Blessed Father, because he has never had the proper opportunity.' To this the Pope said: 'I consider him a thoroughly honourable man, and even if I saw him do something wrong, I would not believe it.' This was what immediately came to mind and worried me most. After I had ordered the young workmen to purchase new clothes, I took the gold morse along with the jewels, arranging them as best I could in their proper places, and with them I immediately went to see the Pope, who had already been told some of the rumours going round about my workshop by Francesco Del Nero; and the Pope's suspicions were immediately aroused. The Pope quickly assumed the worst and gave me a terrible glare as he said in a haughty voice: 'What are you doing here? What's the matter?' I answered: 'Here are all your jewels and gold—nothing is missing.' Then the Pope, his face clearing up, declared: 'Well, then you are truly welcome.'* I showed him the gold morse, and while he was examining it I gave him an account of the whole incident of the thief, my anxieties, and what had worried me the most. Hearing my words, he turned to look me straight in the eye several times, and in his presence was this Francesco Del Nero, and for that reason the Pope seemed half annoyed at not having guessed the truth. Finally, the Pope burst out laughing at all the things I told him, and said to me: 'Go, and continue to be the honourable man I knew you to be.'

53. As I worked diligently on the morse and toiled continuously for the Mint, some counterfeit coins stamped with my own dies began to appear in Rome. They were immediately brought to the Pope, and suspicion was cast on me; the Pope said to Iacopo Balducci,* the head of the Mint: 'Do everything possible to discover the malefactor, because we know that Benvenuto is an honourable man.' This treacherous fellow, who was my enemy, replied: 'God willing, Most Blessed Father, that it should turn out just as you say, although we have some evidence.' In response to this, the Pope turned to the Governor of Rome and ordered him to get to work and find this criminal. At this time the Pope sent for me, and then with a clever turn of the conversation began discussing coins, and right at this point he said to me: 'Benvenuto, would you be bold enough to make counterfeit coins?' To this question, I answered that I believed I could surely make them more skilfully than other men who would apply themselves to something so vile, for people who would work in such a lazy fashion are not men who know how to earn money, nor are they men of great ingenuity; with my meagre talent I earned enough to keep me going, and when I made dies for the Mint, every morning before I ate I received at least three scudi (which had always been the customary payment for the dies of the coins, and that fool of a Mint superintendent was my enemy, because he would have

liked to purchase them for less); what I earned with God's grace and the favour of the world was more than sufficient for me; by making counterfeit coins I would not earn as much as this. The Pope understood my words very well, and while he had earlier given orders to take care that I should not leave Rome, he now ordered his men to search for the criminal very diligently and to pay no attention to me, because he would not wish to offend me, thus risking the loss of my collaboration. This task was assigned, with rigorous instructions, to some of the clerics in the Chamber, who after carrying out a careful investigation, which was their duty, immediately uncovered the thief. He was a coinmaker at the Mint named Ceseri Macheroni, a citizen of Rome, and along with him was arrested one of the coin-finishers.*

54. On that very same day, as I was walking through Piazza Navona with that handsome poodle of mine, when I arrived before the gate of the constable's palace, my dog began barking ferociously and hurled himself through the gate at a young man who had been held for a short time on the accusation of a goldsmith from Parma named Donnino,* once a student of Caradosso, who had a suspicion that this man had robbed him. This dog of mine made such an effort to tear the young man to pieces that, once the police were moved to take pity on him, the young man audaciously presented his own defence to good effect, and since this Donnino could not provide enough evidence to have him arrested, especially since one of the police corporals was from Genoa and knew the young man's father, what with the dog and these other circumstances they wanted to release the young man straightaway. As soon as I approached, the dog, having no fear either of sword or club, threw himself once again upon this young man, and the police told me that if I did not get my dog under control they would kill him. I grabbed the dog as best I could, but while the young man was drawing back his cloak some paper bundles fell from his hood, which this Donnino recognized as being his property. And then I recognized a tiny little ring of mine, so I immediately said: 'This is the thief who broke in and robbed my workshop, and this is why my dog recognizes him.' When I'd released the dog, he once again flung himself upon the young man; whereupon the thief implored me for mercy, telling me he would return everything he had of mine. After I grabbed the dog once more he returned my gold and silver, some little rings of mine he had

taken, and some twenty-five scudi; then he begged for mercy once more. Hearing his pleas, I said that he should beg God for mercy, since I would do him neither good nor ill. And after I returned to my business this Ceseri Macherone, the counterfeiter of coins, was hanged a few days later in Via dei Banchi Nuovi right in front of the door to the Mint; his companion was sentenced to the galleys; the thief from Genoa was hanged in the Campo de' Fiori; and I was left with a greater reputation for honesty than I had enjoyed before.

55. Just as I was finishing the golden morse, that disastrous flood occurred that engulfed all of Rome in water.* As I stood waiting to see what was going to happen, the day was almost over and the clock had already struck two hours before sunset while the waters rose to an exceedingly high level. Since the front of my home and workshop were in Via dei Banchi Nuovi, and the back part rose up several armslengths as it looked out toward Monte Giordano, thinking first to save my life and then my honour, I placed all those jewels on my person and left the gold morse with my workmen standing guard, and barefoot as I was I climbed out of the back windows and, as best I could, made my way through the waters until I reached Monte Cavallo,* where I came upon Messer Giovanni Gaddi, a clerk at the Chamber and Bastiano Veniziano, the painter.* Approaching Messer Giovanni, I gave him all the jewels that I had saved; he used to consider me as if I was his own brother. A few days later, when the fury of the waters had subsided, I returned to my workshop and finished the golden morse so successfully, through the grace of God and my own great labours, that it was considered the most beautiful work ever seen in Rome, and when I brought it to the Pope he could not give me enough praise for it, and he said: 'If I were a rich emperor I would give my Benvenuto as much land as his eye could survey, but though We are impoverished and bankrupt emperors at the moment, We shall, in any case, give him enough bread to satisfy his meagre needs.' After allowing the Pope to end this flood of words, I asked him for a vacant position as mace-bearer.* In answer to my request, the Pope said he wanted to give me something of much greater importance. I answered His Holiness that he could, in the meanwhile, give me this as a down-payment. Bursting out laughing, he said he was happy to do so but that he did not want me actually to do the work, and that I should strike a deal with the mace-bearers so that I did not serve; and he granted them the favour they

had already asked the Pope for, the authority to recover their income. And this was done. This post as a mace-bearer earned me a little less than two hundred scudi a year in income.

56. I continued to serve the Pope, now doing one little task, now another, and he gave me the task of making a drawing for a magnificent chalice,* for which I made both a drawing and a model. This model was of wood and wax. At the place where the stem of the chalice bulges, I had made three figures of good size in full relief, which represented Faith, Hope, and Charity;* on the base, to match the other figures, I had done three scenes in low relief within medallions: inside the first was Christ's Nativity; inside the second was Christ's Resurrection; and inside the third was St Peter crucified upside down; I did exactly what I was commissioned to do. While I was moving ahead with this work the Pope very often wanted to see it; so that, seeing that His Holiness had still not remembered to give me anything, and since there was a vacant position for a friar in the Piombo,* I asked him for it one evening. No longer recalling that enthusiasm that he had shown when I completed the other work for him, the good Pope said: 'The post in the Piombo brings in more than eight hundred scudi a year, and if I gave it to you, you would spend your time scratching your stomach, and that beautiful talent you possess in your hands would be lost, and I would bear the blame.' I instantly replied that pure-bred cats kill birds better when they are fat than when they are lean: 'Thus, the kind of honourable men who have talent put it to much better use when they have abundant resources to live on; Your Holiness should realize that those rulers who provide such talented men with plenty of everything are nurturing their abilities; when the contrary is done, their talents are born emaciated and unhealthy; and Your Holiness should also know that I did not request the position with the intention of receiving it. It's lucky enough that I should be a miserable mace-bearer! I only dreamed about having this post. Your Holiness will do well, since you do not wish to give it to me, to give it to some talented man who deserves it and not to some big ignoramus who spends his time scratching, as Your Holiness said. Follow the example of Pope Julius of blessed memory, who bestowed such a position upon Bramante, that most excellent architect.'* I bowed abruptly and left in a furious rage. Bastiano Veniziano stepped forward and said: 'Most Blessed Father, Your Holiness should be happy to give the

position to another man who toils on works that require skill, and since, as Your Holiness knows, I most willingly toil on such projects, I beg you to consider me worthy of such a position.' The Pope answered: 'This devil of a Benvenuto never listens to any criticism. I was inclined to give him the job, but it is not good to act so arrogantly with a pope, and therefore I don't know what I shall do.' Immediately the Bishop of Vasona stepped forward and begged on Bastiano's behalf, saying: 'Most Blessed Father, Benvenuto is a young man, and a sword by his side suits him much better than a monk's habit: Your Holiness should be happy to give the position to this talented man Bastiano, while to Benvenuto you can give something else good at another time, something which will perhaps be more appropriate than this post.' Then the Pope, turning to Messer Bartolomeo Valori,* said to him: 'When you see Benvenuto, tell him on my behalf that he himself caused the post at the Piombo to go to Bastiano the painter, and that he can rest assured that the first of the better positions to fall vacant will be his, and that in the meanwhile he should apply himself to doing well and complete my work.' The following evening, two hours after nightfall, I ran into Messer Bartolomeo Valori at the corner near the Mint: there were two torch-bearers walking in front of him and he was in a great hurry, having been summoned by the Pope; I bowed to him, and he stopped and called me over, and he told me with the greatest affection all that the Pope had told him to tell me. To his words I replied that I would complete my work with even greater diligence and study than anyone else, but that I would do so without the slightest hope of ever receiving anything from the Pope. Messer Bartolomeo reproached me, saying that one did not reply to the offers of a pope in such a manner. To this I said that even if I placed my hopes in such words, since I knew that I would never receive anything in any case, I would be crazy to respond in any other way, and after I departed I went off to attend to my own affairs. Messer Bartolomeo must have repeated my impertinent remarks to the Pope, perhaps making them a bit more impertinent than those I actually spoke, for the Pope went more than two months before summoning me, and in that period I had no wish to go to the palace for anything. Since the Pope was anxious to see the work, he ordered Messer Ruberto Pucci* to check on what I was doing. This very distinguished and honourable man came to see me every day and constantly spoke affectionately to me, as I did to him. As the time for the Pope's departure for Bologna was drawing near, when he finally saw that I would not come to the palace he made me understand, through Messer Ruberto, that I should bring my work to him, because he wanted to see how far along I was. So I brought it, showing that the most important parts of the chalice had been completed, and I begged him to give me five hundred scudi, partly as an advance payment and partly because I lacked enough gold to finish the work. The Pope said to me: 'Keep working, keep working to finish it.' I replied, as I departed, that I would finish it if he gave me some money. And so I left.

57. After the Pope went off to Bologna,* he left Cardinal Salviati* as his legate in Rome, and he also left him orders to keep after me about this chalice, and said to him: 'Benvenuto is a man who values his talents very little and Ourself even less; see to it that you keep after him so that I find it finished when I return.' This stupid Cardinal sent for me after a week, telling me to bring the work with me, and I went to him without it. When I arrived, the Cardinal immediately said to me: 'Where is your little onion omelette? Have you finished it?' To this I replied: 'O, Most Reverend Monsignor, I haven't completed my onion omelette yet, and I won't finish it if you don't give me the onions to do so.' At these words, this Cardinal, who had more the face of an ass than a man, became half as ugly again, and quickly coming to the point he said: 'I shall send you to the galleys, and then you'll be happy to finish the chalice.' Then I flew into a rage with this beast, and I replied to him: 'Monsignor, when I shall have sinned enough to deserve the galleys, then you can send me there, but for my sins up to now I have no fear of your galley, and in addition let me tell you that because of Your Lordship, I don't ever want to finish it, so don't send for me ever again, because I shall never come here again even if you try to force me to come with your policemen.' The good Cardinal tried on several occasions, in a more amicable fashion, to make me understand that I ought to set to work and that I should bring the chalice to show him; with the result that to these requests I would say: 'Tell the Monsignor that he should send me some onions if he wants me to finish the onion omelette.' I never responded to him with any other words, so that he finally abandoned the task as hopeless.

58. The Pope returned from Bologna,* and he immediately sent for me, for the Cardinal had already written the worst he could about

my case. Since the Pope was in the worst possible temper that could
be imagined, he gave me to understand that I should come with my
work. And so I did. During the time that the Pope was in Bologna I
experienced an extremely excruciating inflammation of my eyes that
caused me so much pain I could hardly live, and this was the first
reason why I had not made progress on the work; the pain was so
great I was certain I would remain blind, and had already worked out
how much I would need to live as a blind man. While I was going to
see the Pope, I thought about how I was going to excuse myself for
not having been able to make progress on the chalice. I was thinking
that while the Pope was looking at it and examining it, I would tell
him the facts. I was unable to do so because, when I reached him, he
immediately said, rudely: 'Give that chalice here; is it finished?' I
uncovered it: instantly, with even greater anger, he said: 'In God's
truth, I tell you that you make a profession of considering no one but
yourself, and if it were not for the honour of my position in the
world I would have you and your chalice thrown out of these windows to the ground below.' When I saw that the Pope was in an even
greater rage I hastened to get away from him. While he continued to
threaten me I put my work under my cloak and, grumbling, I said:
'Nothing in the world can force a blind man to work on such projects.' Raising his voice even higher, the Pope replied: 'Come here,
what is it you're saying?' I was of two minds about whether to make a
run for it down the stairs: then I made a decision, and falling to my
knees, I cried out loudly, since he had not ceased to shout himself:
'And if an illness has made me blind, am I still bound to work?' To
this, he answered: 'You were able to see the light in coming here; I
don't believe anything you have said is true.' To this I said, hearing
him lower his voice a bit: 'Your Holiness should consult His doctor,
and He will discover the truth.' The Pope said: 'We shall find out if
things are as you say in Our own good time.' Then, when I saw he
was giving me a hearing, I explained: 'I don't believe that this great
illness of mine has any other cause than Cardinal Salviati, because he
sent for me immediately after Your Holiness left, and when I came to
him he called my chalice an onion omelette and told me that he
would make sure I ended up in the galleys; and the power of these
ungracious words was so great that I immediately felt my face
become inflamed from my extreme anger, and an unbelievably strong
burning sensation came into my eyes, so that I could not find my way

back home; then, a few days later, two cataracts developed in my eyes; because of these I could not see any light at all, and so since Your Holiness's departure I have not been able to work on anything.' Rising to my feet, I left with God's grace, and it was recounted to me that the Pope had said: 'You can give someone a position but you can't provide discretion along with it. I didn't tell the Cardinal to be so heavy-handed: if it's true he has an infection of the eyes, something I shall learn from my physician, we must show him some compassion.' In the Pope's presence was a great gentleman who was an intimate friend of his and an extremely talented man. He asked the Pope what kind of a person I was, saying: 'Blessed Father, I ask You this because it seems to me that You have just passed in an instant from the greatest anger I have ever seen to the greatest compassion; it is for this reason that I ask Your Holiness who he is, for if he is a person who deserves help, I will show him a secret that will cure him of this infirmity.' The Pope replied with these words: 'This is the greatest man who was ever born into his profession, and one day when we are together I shall show you some of his marvellous works, along with the man himself; it will give me pleasure to see if any help can be found for him.' Three days later the Pope sent for me after dinner, and this same gentleman was in his presence. As soon as I arrived, the Pope sent for the morse of his cope. Meanwhile I had taken out that chalice of mine, with the result that the Pope's friend declared that he had never seen such a marvellous work. When the morse arrived he was even more astonished; looking me in the eye, he said: 'He is rather young to know so much, and he is still quite capable of learning more.' Then he asked me my name. To this I answered: 'Benvenuto is my name.' And he replied: '*Benvenuto* shall I be for you on this occasion;* take some irises with their stems, their flowers, and their roots all together, then distil them over a low fire, and wash out your eyes with this liquid several times each day, and you will most certainly be cured of this illness, but purge yourself first and then continue with the liquid.' The Pope addressed some affectionate words to me: and so I went away half content.

59. It was true that I had the disease, but I think I caught it from the beautiful young serving girl I had at the time I was robbed. Put off for more than four full months, that French pox* then covered me all at once all over my entire body; it did not show up in the usual way but it looked as if I were covered by a kind of blister, the size of

pennies and red. The physicians never wanted to call it the French disease, and I continued to cite the reasons why I thought it was. They kept on treating me in their fashion and nothing helped me; then at last I decided to take *lignum vitae*,* against the wishes of the best doctors in Rome. I took this with all the discipline and restraint that might be imagined, and in the space of a few days I felt very much better, so that at the end of fifty days I was cured and as healthy as a fish. Then, to gain some relief after the great strain I had endured, as winter was coming on I started to enjoy myself by going out hunting with my musket, which had me going through wind and water and standing in swamps, with the result that in a few days I became a hundred times as ill as I had been before. I put myself back in the doctors' hands, but while they continued to treat me I continued to get worse. A fever attacked me, and I resolved to take the *lignum vitae* again: the doctors did not wish me to do so, telling me that if I started taking that while running a fever, I would be dead in eight days. I decided to go against their wishes, and following the same regimen that I had followed the first time, drinking as I had this holy water of *lignum vitae* for four days, that fever in fact went away. I began to feel greatly improved, and while I took the *lignum vitae* I continued to move ahead with my models for the chalice; in this period of abstinence I produced the most beautiful and rarest things I had ever created in my life. At the end of fifty days I was completely cured, and then with the greatest care I set out to build up my health. After I had abandoned that long fast I found myself freed from my illnesses as if I had been reborn. Even if I took pleasure in securing my desired state of health, I no longer neglected my work, so that I gave as much of my time as was appropriate both to the chalice and to the Mint.

60. It happened that Cardinal Salviati, who as I have mentioned above had always harboured great hatred for me, was made legate of Parma. In Parma a certain Milanese goldsmith, a counterfeiter of coins who went by the name of Tobbia,* was arrested. After he had been condemned to be hanged and burned, the case was mentioned to the legate, presenting him as a man of great talent. The Cardinal suspended the execution of the sentence and wrote to Pope Clement, telling him that the greatest man in the world in the goldsmith's trade had fallen into his hands, and that he had just been condemned to be hanged and burned since he had made some counterfeit coins;

but that this man was simple and honest, for he claimed to have asked the opinion of his confessor who, he said, had given him permission to make them. Moreover, he said: 'If you summon this great man to Rome, Your Holiness will diminish the great arrogance of your Benvenuto, and I am absolutely certain that the works of this Tobbia will please you much more than those of Benvenuto.' As a result, the Pope immediately had him summoned to Rome. And after he had arrived, summoning both of us to him, he told us to prepare a design for mounting a unicorn's horn, the most beautiful ever seen:* it had been sold for seventeen thousand papal ducats. Since the Pope wished to present it to King Francis,* he first wanted it to be richly adorned in gold, and he commissioned both of us to execute those designs. After we had done so, each of us took his design to the Pope. Tobbia's design was in the form of a candlestick on which, like a candle, that beautiful horn would be inserted, and at the base of this candlestick he made four little unicorn heads, designed in the most rudimentary fashion, so that when I saw it I could not help laughing up my sleeve. The Pope noticed this and immediately said: 'Here, show me your design!' My design was a single unicorn's head to match the horn. I had created the most beautiful kind of head that can be imagined, because I had taken the shape partly from the head of a horse and partly from that of a stag, and embellished it with the most beautiful kind of mane and other elegant ornaments, so that the moment my design was seen everyone praised it. But because certain Milanese gentlemen of very great authority were present at this contest, they said: 'Most Blessed Father, Your Holiness intends to send this great gift to France: you must know that the French are crude people and will not recognize the excellence of this work of Benvenuto's, but they will be well pleased with this ciborium,* which will also take less time to make; Benvenuto will occupy himself with finishing your chalice, and you will have two works completed in the same amount of time; and this poor man, whom you have summoned here, will also be gainfully employed.' Anxious to have his chalice, the Pope most willingly accepted the counsel of these Milanese. So, on the following day he gave the commission for work on the unicorn horn to Tobbia, and made me understand, through his Master of the Wardrobe,* that I should complete his chalice. To these instructions I responded that I desired nothing else in the world but to complete this beautiful work of mine, and that if it were made of any other material than gold I could most easily finish it by myself, but since it was to be gold, His Holiness would have to give me some if he wished me to complete it. To my explanation this plebeian courtier replied: 'Alas, do not ask for gold from the Pope, for you will send him into such a rage that you will be in big, big trouble!' To this I answered: 'O Messer, then will Your Lordship teach me a bit about how you can make bread without flour? For without gold, that work will never be completed.' This Master of the Wardrobe, apparently thinking that I was pulling his leg, told me that he would tell everything I had said to the Pope, and so he did. The Pope, exploding into a bestial anger, said that he wanted to see if I were such a madman that I would not complete his chalice. So more than two months went by, and even though I had clearly stated that I would not do a lick of work on the chalice, I had not kept my word and had rather worked on it continuously with the greatest love. Seeing that I would not bring it, the Pope began to thwart me as much as he could, declaring that he would punish me in one way or another. His Milanese jeweller was there and heard his words. Named Pompeo, he was a close relative of a certain Messer Traiano, Pope Clement's most favoured servant.* These two, by agreement, said to the Pope: 'If Your Holiness will take the Mint away from Benvenuto, perhaps you will increase his desire to finish the chalice.' To this the Pope answered: 'On the contrary, this would lead to two evils: in the first place I would be badly served at the Mint, which is very important to me; and in the second place I would most surely never receive the chalice.' These two Milanese, seeing that the Pope was ill-disposed toward me, finally managed to have the Mint taken away from me and given to a certain young man from Perugia known by the nickname of Fagiuolo.* This Pompeo came to tell me on the Pope's behalf that His Holiness had taken away the Mint from me, and that if I did not complete his chalice he would take away some other things.* To this I replied: 'Tell His Holiness that he has taken the Mint away from himself, not from me, and that the same thing applies to the other things, and that when His Holiness wishes to return it to me I shall not take it back under any condition.' It seemed to this miserable and wretched man a thousand years before he reached the Pope and repeated all these remarks, adding a few of his own invention. Then, a week later the Pope sent this same man to tell me that he no longer wanted me to complete the chalice and that he wanted it back in exactly that state and at that point to which I had brought it so far. To this Pompeo I said: 'This chalice is not like the Mint, which he can take away from me, but it is true that there are five hundred scudi which I have that belong to the Pope, and I shall immediately return them to him; the work is mine, and I shall do with it what I wish.' Pompeo rushed off to report my remarks, along with some other biting words that I had said to him with just cause.

61. Nearly three days later, one Thursday, two of His Holiness's most favoured chamberlains came to see me; one of them is still alive today and a bishop; his name is Pier Giovanni,* the Master of the Wardrobe; the other was even more highly born than Messer Giovanni, but I do not remember his name.* When they arrived, they said: 'The Pope sends us. Benvenuto, since you have decided not to learn the easy way, he says that either you give us his chalice or we shall take you to prison.' Then, as I looked them cheerfully in the face, I said: 'My Lords, if I gave the chalice to His Holiness I would give him my work and not his, and in any case I do not intend to give him my work, for as I have brought it along very far by my own great labours, I should not wish it to fall into the hands of some ignorant beast who would ruin it with very little effort.' The goldsmith named Tobbia that I mentioned above was present when I said this, and foolishly he also asked me for the drawings for the chalice: the words that I spoke to him, worthy of such a wretched scoundrel, need not be repeated here. Since the two chamberlains were urging me to hurry up and decide what I wanted to do, I told them that I was ready and took up my cloak, and before I left my workshop I turned to an image of Christ with great reverence, my cap in my hand, and I said: 'O merciful and immortal, just and holy Lord, all the things You do are done according to Your justice, which is without equal. You know that I have just now reached the thirtieth year of my life and that never before have I been threatened with prison for any reason, but since it is now Your wish for me to go to jail, I thank You with all my heart.' Then I turned to the two chamberlains and, with one of my rather reproachful expressions on my face, I said: 'A man such as myself deserves policemen of no less merit than Your Lordships; if you will put me between the two of you, you may lead me off to prison as you wish.' These two distinguished gentlemen burst out laughing, put me between them, and continuing to chat pleasantly, they took me to the Governor of Rome, who was called Magalotto.* When I arrived the Fiscal Procurator was with him, both of whom were expecting me, and these chamberlains, still laughing, said to the governor: 'We consign this prisoner to you: take good care of him. We were very amused in carrying out the duties of your officers, because Benvenuto told us that, as this was his first arrest, he deserved officers of no lesser merit than ourselves.' They quickly left and went to the Pope, telling him everything precisely, and at first he showed signs of losing his temper but then forced himself to laugh, since there were in his presence some noblemen and cardinals who were my friends and who had greatly favoured me. Meanwhile the Governor and the Procurator were partly threatening me, partly exhorting me, partly advising me, saying it was only reasonable for a man who commissions a work from another to take it back when he likes and in any manner which pleases him. To such remarks, I replied that justice did not permit it nor could a pope do such a thing, because a pope was not the same sort of man as certain tyrannical little lords, who do the worst they can to their people, neither observing the law nor justice: a Vicar of Christ can, therefore, do none of these things. Then the Governor, employing certain of his police agent's words and expressions, said: 'Benvenuto, Benvenuto, you are trying to make me treat you as you deserve.' 'You will treat me with honour and courtesy, if you wish to treat me the way I deserve,' I replied. Once again he said: 'Send for the chalice immediately, and don't wait for me to say this again.' To this I answered: 'My lords, do me the courtesy of allowing me to say a few words about my actions.' The Procurator, who was a much more discreet policeman than the Governor, turned to him and declared: 'Monsignor, let him say a hundred words; so long as he gives up the chalice, that's enough for us.' I said: 'If he were any ordinary man and commissioned the building of a palace or a home, he could quite rightly say to the mason who walled it up: "I don't want you to work any longer on my home or on my palace;" once he had paid him justly for his labours, he could send him away. Again, if he were a nobleman who was having a jewel worth a thousand scudi set, when he saw that the jeweller did not do the work following his instructions, he could say: "Give me my jewel, for I do not want your work." But this affair has no connection to these cases, since there is neither a house nor a jewel: nobody can tell me anything except that I should return the five hundred scudi I received. So, Monsignors, do all that is in your power, but you will have nothing from me but the five hundred scudi. You will tell this to the Pope. Your threats don't scare me in the slightest, because I'm a decent man and have no fear of my sins.' Once the Governor and the Procurator rose to their feet, they told me they were going to see the Pope, and that they would return with orders that would mean trouble for me. So I remained under arrest. I was pacing up and down a hall while they remained there almost three hours, before returning from the Pope. During that interval all the most important Florentine merchants came to see me, begging me insistently not to argue with a pope, because it could spell my ruin. To their entreaties I replied that I had carefully made up my mind about what I wished to do.

62. No sooner had the Governor, along with the Procurator, returned from the palace than he had me summoned, and he spoke along these lines: 'Benvenuto, I'm certainly very sorry to have returned from the Pope with an order like the one I have received: either you come up with the chalice immediately or you had better put your affairs in order.' Then I replied that, since I had never believed up to that moment that a holy Vicar of Christ could commit an injustice, 'For this reason I want to see it first before I believe it; so, do what it is in your power to do.' Then the Governor replied, saying: 'I have two words to say to you on the Pope's behalf, and then I shall carry out the orders given to me. The Pope says that you are to bring the work here to me and that I am to see that it is put into a box and sealed; then I am to carry it to the Pope, who promises on his faith not to remove it from under his closed seal and will immediately return it to you, but he desires that this be done in order to safeguard his own honour as well.' Laughing at these words, I answered that I would most willingly give the Pope my chalice in the way he described, for I wanted to be able to determine how much the word of a pope was worth. And so I sent for my work, sealed it up in the way that had been mentioned, and gave it to the Governor. When he returned to the Pope with the chalice sealed in that fashion, the Pope took the box and, according to what the Governor told me, he turned it around a number of times; then he asked the Governor if he had seen the chalice, and he replied that he had seen it and that it had been sealed in his presence in that way; and he also added that he thought it was a most admirable work. To this the Pope said: 'You

will tell Benvenuto that popes have the power to loosen and bind greater things than this,'* and as he uttered those words, with a certain degree of disdain he opened the box, removing the cords and the seal with which it had been bound; then he looked at the chalice for a long while, and as I learned later, he showed it to the goldsmith Tobbia, who praised it very highly. At that point the Pope asked Tobbia if looking at it was sufficient for him to create a work like that one;* the Pope told him to follow my design exactly; then he turned to the Governor and said to him: 'See if Benvenuto wants to give the chalice to us, and if he gives it to us like this, pay him the price at which it is valued by worthy men; or if he truly wishes to complete it himself, select a date, and if you see that he is willing to do it, give him whatever he reasonably requests.' At that, the Governor said: 'Most Blessed Father, since I know the terrible qualities of this young man, give me the authority to give him a scolding in my fashion.' To this the Pope said that he could do what he liked with words, although he was certain that it would make matters worse; then, if he saw that he could do nothing else, he was to tell me to bring his five hundred scudi to that Pompeo, his jeweller whom I previously mentioned. After the Governor returned he had me summoned to his chamber, and with the look of a police agent on his face he said to me: 'Popes hold the authority to loose and to bind the entire world, and whatever they do is immediately confirmed in heaven as well done: here is your work unbound and seen by His Holiness.' At that point I immediately raised my voice and said: 'I give thanks to God, for I now know how to determine what the word of the popes is worth!' Then the Governor spoke to me and made many rash threats, but once he saw that this would gain him nothing, despairing in fact of the enterprise, he took on a somewhat softer manner once again and said to me: 'Benvenuto, I greatly regret that you do not wish to recognize your own interests; therefore go, take the five hundred scudi, whenever you wish, to Pompeo.' Picking up my work, I immediately took the five hundred scudi to that Pompeo. Perhaps because the Pope thought that I would not return the money so soon, because of the inconvenience or some other reason, and was anxious to reattach the thread of my servitude, when he saw Pompeo come smiling to him with the money in his hand he swore at him and complained loudly about the way the affair had turned out; then he told Pompeo: 'Go find Benvenuto in his workshop and treat him as kindly as your ignorant boorishness will allow, and tell him that if he wants to complete the chalice for me and make of it a monstrance* to carry the Host in when I walk with it in procession, I shall give him the means required to complete it, provided that he works.' When Pompeo came to me, he summoned me outside my workshop and paid me the most simpering and asinine compliments, telling me everything that the Pope had ordered him to say. To this I replied immediately that the greatest treasure I could desire in all the world was to regain the favour of such a great pope, which had been lost to me not through my own fault but rather through the fault of my lengthy illness and the wickedness of those jealous men who take delight in doing evil: 'and since the Pope has an abundance of servants, he shouldn't send you around here again if he values your health; you should mind your own business. I shall never fail either by day or by night to think about doing everything I can in the service of the Pope; and remember this well, for after you have told the Pope about my reply, don't get involved in any way in any of my affairs, for I'll make you recognize your mistakes with the punishment they deserve.' This individual reported everything I said back to the Pope in a much cruder fashion than I had employed. And so the matter remained like this for a time, and I occupied myself with my workshop and my own affairs.

63. That goldsmith named Tobbia, whom I mentioned before, was attending to the completion of the decorations and ornaments for the unicorn's horn, and in addition the Pope had told him to begin the chalice in the manner in which he had seen mine executed. But once this Tobbia began to show what he was doing, the Pope became dissatisfied and, complaining a great deal for having broken with me over it, he harshly criticized that man's work and those who had introduced him; and on a number of occasions Baccino della Croce* came to speak with me on behalf of the Pope, telling me that I should finish the monstrance. To this I replied that I had begged His Holiness to allow me to rest on account of the serious illness that I had suffered and from which I was not yet certain of being cured, but that I would show His Holiness that of those hours I was capable of working, I would spend them all in his service. I had begun to do his portrait and had secretly designed a medal for him, and I was making the steel dies for stamping this medal at home; in my workshop I kept a partner, who had been my apprentice, by the name of

Felice.* At this time, as young men are wont to do, I fell in love with a young Sicilian girl, who was very beautiful, and since she, too, showed that she liked me a great deal, her mother noticed this and suspected what might happen (that is, I had been planning for a year to elope to Florence in the greatest secrecy with this young girl without telling her mother); once aware of the plan, she left Rome one night in secret and went off toward Naples, letting it be known that she was going by Civitavecchia but then actually travelling by Ostia. I followed her to Civitavecchia and did endless crazy things to find her again. It would take far too long to describe such things in great detail: it is enough to say that I was on the verge of either going mad or dying. At the end of two months she wrote to me that she was in Sicily and very unhappy. In the meantime I had occupied myself with all the pleasures that might be imagined, and had involved myself in another love affair only to extinguish this one.

64. A number of odd things came about that caused me to strike up a friendship with a certain Sicilian priest, who had a very fine mind and a very good knowledge of Latin and Greek. Once, in the course of discussing something, we happened to speak of the art of necromancy, and I said on this subject: 'For my whole life I've had a great desire to see or hear something concerning this art.' To these words the priest answered: 'The man who sets about such an enterprise must have a strong and firm nature.' I responded that I would exhibit an overabundance of strength and resolve, provided I could find the means to undertake such a thing. Then the priest replied: 'If you have the courage for this, I shall give you your fill of all the rest.' So we agreed to begin this undertaking. This priest got everything in order one evening and told me to find a companion or, at the maximum, two. I called Vincenzio Romoli,* my very good friend, and he brought with him a man from Pistoia who understood necromancy. We went off to the Culosseum,* where the priest, dressed up like a necromancer, began to sketch out the circles on the ground with the most beautiful ceremonies imaginable in this world, and he had had precious perfumes brought there and fire and even some evil-smelling perfumes. When everything was in order he created an entrance into the circle, and taking us by the hand, one by one he placed us inside the circle; then he assigned us our tasks: he handed over the pentacle* to a necromancer friend of his; to the others he assigned the care of the fire and the perfumes; then he put his mind to his incantations. These lasted for more than an hour and a half; several legions of devils appeared, until the Culosseum was completely filled. I was attending to the precious perfumes, and when the priest saw that there were a great many devils he turned to me and said: 'Benvenuto, ask them something.' I said that they should make it possible for me to be together with my Angelica, the Sicilian girl. That night we received no reply whatsoever, but I was very satisfied with having been able to make such a request. The necromancer said that we had to go back another time and that I would receive satisfaction for everything I asked, but he wanted me to bring with us a young boy who was a virgin. I took my shop-boy, who was about twelve years of age, with me, and I once again asked Vincenzio Romoli and, as our companion, we also took a certain Agnolino Gaddi to this affair. When we arrived once again at the designated spot the necromancer made his same preparations, with the same and even more astonishing arrangements; he placed us into the circle which he had once again created with more wonderful skills and more wonderful ceremonies; he gave my Vincenzio the task of looking after the perfumes and the fire; Agnolino Gaddi joined him in this task; then he placed the pentacle in my hand, ordering me to turn it in the direction of the places he pointed out to me, and under the pentacle I held that young shop-boy of mine. The necromancer began to make those truly terrifying invocations and called up by name a great number of those demons who were leaders of their legions, ordering them by the virtue and power of Immortal God, living and eternal, with words in Hebrew and even more in Greek and Latin, so that in a brief space of time the entire Culosseum was filled up with a hundred times more demons than had materialized on the first occasion. Vincenzio Romoli was attending to the fire and a great quantity of precious perfumes, along with that Agnolino. At the necromancer's suggestion, I once again asked to be united with Angelica. Turning to me, the necromancer said: 'Did you hear what they said? That in the space of one month you'll be with her.' Once again he added that he begged me to hold fast, since there were a thousand times more legions than he had invoked and they were the most dangerous, and since they had done what I had asked of them, it was necessary to treat them kindly and to dismiss them very patiently. On the other side, the young boy under the pentacle was terrified and said there were a million fierce-looking men in that place, all of whom were threatening us: moreover, he declared that four enormous giants had appeared to him, who were armed and showed signs of wanting to enter the magic circle with us. Meanwhile the necromancer, who was trembling with fear, was trying as best he could to dismiss them in a sweet and gentle manner. Vincenzio Romoli, who was trembling like a leaf, was looking after the perfumes. While I was just as afraid as the others, I tried to show it less and emboldened them all wonderfully; but I truly considered myself a dead man when I saw the necromancer's terror. The young boy had stuck his head between his legs, saying: 'I want to die this way, we are all dead men!' Once again I said to the young boy: 'These creatures are all under our power and what you see is smoke and shadow; so lift up your eyes!' When he raised his eyes, once again he said: 'The entire Culosseum is burning, and the fire is coming toward us!' And, putting his hands to his face, he again declared that he was a dead man and that he did not want to see any more. The necromancer implored me, begging me to hold fast and to make some asafoetida fumes,* and so, turning to Vincenzio Romoli, I ordered him to light some asafoetida quickly. While I did this, Agnolino, who was looking on, was so frightened that his eyes were popping out of his head and he was half dead, so I said to him: 'Agnolo, you can't be afraid in these places, you need to get to work and help us; quickly throw some asafoetida on the fire.' This Agnolo, as soon as he turned to move, let out such a blast of farts accompanied by such an abundance of shit that it produced a far more overpowering smell than the asafoetida. The young boy, as a result of the great stink and the noise, lifted his head up a bit, and when he heard me laughing a bit of his courage returned and he said that the demons were beginning to run away in a great hurry. Thus, we stayed there until they began to ring matins.* Once again the young boy told us that only a few devils remained and were some distance away. After the necromancer had completed the rest of his ceremonies, he took off his robes and made a large pile of books which he had carried there, and all in unison with him we left the circle, staying very close to each other, especially the young boy, who had placed himself in our midst and had taken the necromancer by the robe and me by the cloak, and while we were going toward our homes in Via dei Banchi he kept on saying that two of those demons he had seen in the Culosseum were jumping along in front of us or running along on the rooftops and on the ground. The necromancer said that, as many times as he had entered the magic circle, he had never before experienced such an event, and he urged me to agree to consecrate a book* with him, from which we would make a great deal of money, because we would ask the demons to tell us the whereabouts of the treasures that fill the earth, in this way becoming extremely rich; and he added that all those questions of love were useless and crazy and never led to anything. I told him that if I knew any Latin, I would very gladly undertake such a project. He kept trying to persuade me, telling me that a knowledge of Latin would not help me a bit, and that if he wished he could have found lots of people with a good knowledge of Latin, but that he had never found a man with as stout a heart as I had; and that I ought to listen to his advice. With such arguments we reached our homes, and each of us dreamed of demons all that night.

65. Then we used to see each other every day, the necromancer pressing me to get involved in that undertaking; because of this, I asked him how much time would be spent on such a thing and where we would have to go. He replied that we would be finished with it in less than a month, and that the place best suited for it was in the mountains of Norcia,* although one of his masters had consecrated a book near there at a place called the Badia di Farfa,* but had experienced some difficulties there that would not arise in the mountains of Norcia, for the peasants of Norcia were trustworthy people who had some experience in such things and could render marvellous assistance if the need arose. The necromantic priest had most certainly convinced me to the point that I was perfectly willing to do what he asked, but I said that first I wanted to complete the medals I was making for the Pope, and that I had confided about these in him and nobody else, begging him to keep them a secret. At the same time, I kept on asking him if he believed that I would be united with my Sicilian girl Angelica at the promised time, and seeing that the time was drawing closer, it seemed a very serious thing to me that I heard nothing of her. The necromancer told me that most certainly I should find myself where she was, because the demons never fail when they make a promise in the manner that they had done to me, but that I should keep my eyes open and guard against any misfortune that might befall me in this instance. He added that I should force myself to undertake something contrary to my nature because he recognized in this situation a great danger, and that it would be

good for me to go with him to consecrate the book, since by this means such a great danger would be avoided and I would be the cause of making both him and me extremely happy. As I was beginning to grow more anxious about this than he was, I told him that a certain Giovanni da Castel Bolognese,* a man very talented in producing the same kind of medals in steel that I was making, had arrived in Rome, and that I had no greater desire in the world than to compete with this talented man and to make a name in the world with such an undertaking, through which I hoped to slay those numerous enemies of mine with my talent rather than my sword. This necromancer still went on, saying to me: 'Please, my dear Benvenuto, come with me and flee from a great danger I see hanging over you.' I was in all respects resolved first to complete my medal, and the end of the month was already drawing near, but since I was so caught up in my medal I no longer remembered either my Angelica or anything else, and was wholly intent upon my work.

66. One day, about the hour of vespers, I had occasion to go from home to my workshop outside my normal hours; I had the workshop in the Via dei Banchi and I kept a little house behind the Via dei Banchi; and I did not go to the workshop very often, for I left my partner Felice in charge of the whole business. After I had spent a bit of time in the shop, I remembered that I had to go and speak to Alessandro del Bene.* Immediately I left, and after I had reached the Via dei Banchi I ran into a very good friend of mine, named Ser Benedetto.* He was a notary and born in Florence, the son of a blind man who begged for alms by praying for the souls of his benefactors and was from Siena. This Ser Benedetto had been in Naples for many, many years; then, after he had established himself in Rome, he transacted some business affairs for certain Sienese merchants of the Chigi family. And because this partner of mine had asked him over and over again for some money that was owed for some rings Felice had entrusted to him, on this very day Felice, upon running into him in the Via dei Banchi, had demanded his money in a very rude fashion, as was his custom; this Ser Benedetto was with his patrons, so that when they saw what was going on, they severely reprimanded Ser Benedetto, telling him that they wanted to have the services of someone else so they would not have to hear any more of such vulgar yapping. This Ser Benedetto walked along with them, defending himself as best he could, and he said that he had paid that goldsmith,

and that it was not his job to restrain the frenzy of madmen. These businessmen from Siena took the word 'madmen' badly, and immediately chased Ser Benedetto away. Having taken leave of them, he went off to my workshop in a flash, perhaps to pick a quarrel with Felice. It happened that, right in the middle of the Via dei Banchi, we ran into each other: whereupon I, who knew nothing, greeted him very pleasantly in my usual manner; he replied to me with many crude insults. At this I remembered everything the necromancer had told me, so that, while restraining myself as best I could from doing what his remarks were forcing me to do, I said: 'Ser Benedetto, my brother, don't be angry with me, for I've never had a quarrel with you, and I don't know anything about these problems of yours, and whatever you have to do with Felice, pray, go settle the matter with him, for he knows very well how to respond, whereas since I know absolutely nothing, you do me wrong by attacking me in this way, especially knowing that I'm not the kind of man who puts up with affronts to my honour.' To this Ser Benedetto replied that I knew all about it, and that he was the kind of man to make me bear a greater burden than that, and that Felice and I were a couple of great scoundrels. By that time a large crowd had gathered to see this contest. Compelled by his ugly words, I quickly stooped down and took up a handful of mud, for it had been raining, and taking this I quickly went to throw it in his face with all my might. He lowered his head so that the mud struck him in the middle of his crown. Concealed in the mud was a piece of rock with many sharp edges, and as he was struck in the middle of his crown by one of those edges, he fell down like a dead man, in a faint; when the crowd saw such a quantity of blood, all the bystanders thought he was dead.

67. While Ser Benedetto was still lying on the ground and some of those people assumed the task of carrying him away, Pompeo, the jeweller mentioned earlier, passed by. The Pope had sent for him about some of his jewels. When Pompeo saw this man reduced to such a bad condition, he asked who had struck him. And he was told: 'Benvenuto struck him, because the beast asked for it.' As soon as he reached the Pope, Pompeo said to him: 'Most Holy Father, Benvenuto has just killed Tobbia—I saw it with my own eyes.'* Enraged, the Pope ordered the Governor, who was standing there with him, to take me and hang me immediately on the spot where the murder had been committed, and to make every effort to apprehend me and not

to come back again before he had hanged me. Once I had seen the poor unfortunate man lying on the ground, I immediately thought of what was in my own interest, considering the power of my enemies and what could come of such a thing. I left that place immediately and withdrew to the home of Messer Giovanni Gaddi,* a clerk of the Chamber, since I wanted to make my preparations as rapidly as possible to leave the city behind. On this matter Messer Giovanni advised me not to be in such a hurry to leave, for sometimes things are not as bad as they seem, and after he had summoned Messer Annibal Caro, who was part of his household, he told him to go and find out what the situation was. While he was giving these orders, a Roman gentleman who was part of the Cardinal de' Medici's household,* and who had been sent by him, appeared. This gentleman called Messer Giovanni and me aside and told us that the Cardinal had repeated to him the very words he had heard the Pope say, and that there was no way he could help me, that I should do everything possible to escape the Pope's first fit of rage, and that I should not trust my safety to any household inside Rome. Immediately the gentlemen departed, and Messer Giovanni looked me in the eye, showed some signs of tears, and said: 'Alas, unhappy me, for I have no way whatsoever to help you!' And I replied: 'With God's help, I shall help myself very well on my own; I only request that you loan me one of your horses.' A dark Turkish horse was already saddled, the most handsome and best horse in all of Rome. I mounted the horse and placed an arquebus with a cogwheel across the saddle-horn, ready to defend myself with that. When I had reached Ponte Sisto I found all the constable's guard there on horseback and on foot; so, making a virtue of necessity, I lightly spurred on my horse and, thanks to God who obscured their eyes, I passed through freely, and with as much haste as I could muster I went off to Palonbara,* a place belonging to Giovanbatista Savello,* and from there I sent back my horse to Messer Giovanni while letting him know where I was. After having shown me cordial hospitality for two days, Signor Gianbatista advised me that I should leave and go on to Naples until the Pope's rage passed, and giving me an escort, he set me on the road to Naples, where I encountered a sculptor friend of mine who was going to San Germano to complete the tomb of Pier de' Medici at Monte Cassino.* He went by the name of Solosmeo:* he gave me the news that Pope Clement had that very evening sent his chamberlain to find out how Tobbia was; and that the chamberlain discovered him at work, and seeing that nothing had happened to him, and that he did not even know anything about the matter, the chamberlain reported this to the Pope, who turned to Pompeo and declared: 'You are a wretched fellow, but I can guarantee you that you have stirred up a serpent that will bite you and give you what you deserve.' Then he turned to Cardinal de' Medici and ordered him to take good care of me, for on no account would he wish to lose me. And so Solosmeo and I went along singing in the direction of Monte Cassino, so that we could go on from there to Naples.

68. After Solosmeo had taken care of his business at Monte Cassino, we went on together towards Naples. When we were about half a mile from the city an innkeeper met us who invited us to stay at his inn; he told us that he had lived in Florence for many years in the service of Carlo Ginori,* and that if we went to his inn he would treat us very hospitably since we were Florentines. We told this innkeeper several times that we did not wish to go with him. This man nevertheless, riding now in front of us and now behind us, went on repeating the same thing—that he would like to have us stay at his inn. Becoming annoyed by this, I asked him if he knew anything about a certain Sicilian woman by the name of Beatrice, who had a beautiful little daughter named Angelica, both of whom were courtesans. This innkeeper, thinking that I was pulling his leg, said: 'May God send misfortune to courtesans and to all those who wish them well.' And giving the spur to his horse, he seemed determined to ride away from us. I thought I had got rid of this beast of an innkeeper in fine fashion, even though I gained no satisfaction from it, because I remembered the great love I bore for Angelica, and while I was discussing it with Solosmeo, not without a few amorous sighs, we saw the innkeeper returning to us in a great hurry, and when he reached us he said: 'Two or three days ago, next door to my inn, a woman and a young girl with those names came to stay; I don't know if they were Sicilian or from another place.' Then I said: 'That name of Angelica has so much power over me that, at any rate, I would like to come to your inn.' Agreeing together, we went with the innkeeper to the city of Naples and dismounted at his inn, and it seemed as if it took a thousand years to unpack my things, which I did very quickly; and going to the house next to the inn, there I found my Angelica, who gave me the most boundless caresses imaginable. So I stayed

with her from around ten o'clock at night until the following morning, with such pleasure that I have never had its equal. And while I
was enjoying these pleasures, I remembered that this day was the
exact end of the month that had been promised to me within the
circle of necromancy by the demons. So, any man who becomes
involved with them should consider carefully the tremendous risks
I ran.

69. By chance, I found a diamond in my purse that I happened to
show around to the goldsmiths, and even though I was still young, I
was so well known in Naples as a man of talent that I was shown
many acts of kindness. Among others, there was a certain gentleman,
a jeweller named Messer Domenico Fontana.* This worthy man
abandoned his workshop during the three days I stayed in Naples
and never left my side, showing me many of the most beautiful
antiquities in Naples and outside the city, and he even took me to pay
my respects to the Viceroy of Naples,* who had let him know that he
would like to meet me. When I met His Excellency he gave me the
most honourable welcome, and while we were talking, His Excellency's eyes fell upon this diamond; once I showed it to him he told
me that, if I had to get rid of it, I should look no further than
himself. Taking back the diamond, I offered it once again to His
Excellency and declared that both the diamond and I were at his
service. Then he said that the diamond delighted him, but that it
would delight him even more if I were to stay with him, and that he
would come to such an arrangement with me that I would sing his
praises. We both exchanged many such courteous words, but when
we came to discuss the value of the diamond His Excellency ordered
me to name a price, whatever I thought it might be, without bargain-
ing, to which request I replied that two hundred scudi was precisely
the diamond's value. His Excellency declared that he thought I was
not at all far from the mark, but that it had been set by my hand, and
recognizing me to be the best in the world, he thought that if another
man were to set it it would not appear to be of such excellent quality.
Then I said that the diamond had not been set by my hand and that
it was not well set; that the effect the diamond produced was a result
of its own brilliance; and that if I reset it, I would make it very much
more beautiful than it was. Applying my thumbnail to the edges of
the diamond's setting, I prised the diamond from its ring and
cleaned it off a bit, then offered it to the Viceroy, who, both satisfied

and astonished, wrote me out a letter of payment so that I might be paid the two hundred scudi that I had asked. After I had returned to my lodgings I discovered letters that came from Cardinal de' Medici, who told me to return to Rome with great speed and dismount directly at the home of His Most Reverend Lordship. After reading the letter to my Angelica, she begged me with the most loving tears to do her the favour either of remaining in Naples or of taking her with me. I replied that if she wished to come with me I would give her the two hundred ducats* I had received from the Viceroy for her to take care of. When her mother saw us in serious conversation, she drew near to us and said to me: 'Benvenuto, if you want to take my Angelica to Rome, leave me fifteen ducats to have my baby, and then I shall come as well.' I told the old freeloader that I would gladly give her thirty if she agreed to give me my Angelica. Once we reached this agreement, Angelica begged me to buy her a black velvet dress, since this fabric was inexpensive in Naples. I was perfectly happy to do this, and after sending for the velvet and striking the deal, the old woman, who thought I was more homesick than smart, asked me for a dress of elegant fabric for herself, as well as many other expenses for her children and much more money than I had offered. Quite pleasantly, I turned and said to her: 'Beatrice, my dear, isn't what I offered you enough?' She said that it was not. Then I said that what was not enough for her would be enough for me, and after kissing my Angelica, she in tears and myself laughing, we separated and I returned to Rome immediately.

70. I left Naples at night with my money on me in case I was ambushed or murdered, as is the custom in Naples, and when I reached Selciata* I defended myself with great skill and bravery against a number of horsemen who had come there to murder me. Then a few days later, after I had left Solosmeo to his business in Monte Cassino, I arrived one morning to eat at the inn in Adanagni:* as I approached the inn I shot at some birds with my arquebus and killed them; and an iron splinter in the lock of the gun tore my right hand. And even if this was not a wound of great severity, it seemed much greater because of the large quantity of blood that flowed from my hand. After I stabled my horse I entered the inn and walked up to a room in the attic, where I found a great many Neapolitan gentlemen about to sit down at the table; with them was a young gentlewoman, the most beautiful I have ever seen. As I arrived, close by me

my servant, a most excellent young man, was climbing up the stairs carrying a big halberd;* so that the sight of us, with the weapon and the blood, struck terror into those poor gentlemen, particularly as the area was known to be a nest of murderers; springing up from the table in great fright, they begged God to help them. Laughing, I said to them that God had helped them and that I was the man to defend them from anyone who wished to harm them, and when I asked them for a bit of help to bandage my hand, that most beautiful gentlewoman took out her own handkerchief, richly embroidered in gold, with which she wished to bandage it for me; I objected, but she quickly tore it in half, and with great gentleness she bandaged me with her own hands. After they had been reassured in this way, we dined quite happily. After our meal, we mounted our horses and went off together. They had not yet overcome their fear, for those gentlemen cleverly had me chat with the gentlewoman while they rode a short distance behind; I rode along with her on my handsome little horse, motioning to my servant that he should stay a little way behind me; and in this fashion we spoke about those things that are not for sale in a grocer's shop. And so I returned to Rome with greater pleasure than I ever had before.

When I arrived in Rome, I went off to dismount at the palace of Cardinal de' Medici, and once I found His Most Reverend Lordship, I spoke to him and thanked him for having me brought back. Then I begged His Most Reverend Lordship to protect me from prison and, if possible, from a monetary fine. This Lord saw me most willingly and said that I should not have any doubts; then he turned to one of his gentlemen, a man from Siena named Messer Pierantonio Pecci,* ordering him to tell the constable on his behalf not to dare touch me. Next the Cardinal asked Pecci how the man I had struck on the head was. This Messer Pierantonio said that he was not well and that he would become even worse, because he had learned that I was returning to Rome and declared that he wanted to die to spite me. Upon hearing this response, the Cardinal said with great laughter: 'He couldn't find a better means of ensuring that we recognize he was born a Sienese!' Then he turned to me and said: 'For the sake of both our honour and your own, be patient four or five days and don't frequent the Via dei Banchi; after that, go where you like and let madmen die as they wish.' I went to my home and set to work on finishing the medal I had already begun with the head of Pope

Clement, on the reverse of which I did a figure representing Peace.*
This figure was a small woman dressed in a girdled-up costume of
the finest fabrics with a small torch in her hand, who is setting fire to
a pile of weapons tied together in the form of a trophy; part of a
temple is also represented which contains the figure of Discord
bound with many chains, and all around there is a motto in letters
which reads: *Clauduntur belli portae.** While I finished this medal, the
man I had struck recovered and the Pope never stopped asking about
me, and I avoided going to see Cardinal de' Medici, since every time
I was in his presence, it happened that His Lordship commissioned
me to make some important work, which hindered me considerably
in the completion of my medal. It came to pass that Pier Carneschi,*
one of the Pope's great favourites, took charge of keeping track of
me, and so in a tactful way he told me how much the Pope desired
me to serve him. In reply, I said that in just a few days I would show
His Holiness that I had never left his service.

71. A few days afterwards, when I had completed my medal, I
stamped it in gold, silver, and copper.* Once I showed them to Messer
Piero he immediately took me to the Pope. It was a day in the month
of April, in the afternoon, and the weather was beautiful: the Pope
was in the Belvedere.* When I came into the presence of His Holiness
I placed in his hand the medals, along with the steel dies. He took
them from me, immediately recognized the great strength of craftsmanship they exhibited, looked Messer Piero in the face, and said:
'The ancients were never so well served with medals.' While he and
the others were examining them, first the dies and then the medals, I
began to speak very modestly and said: 'If the power of my hostile
stars had not encountered a much greater power* which prevented
them from doing what they actually threatened so violently, Your
Holiness, without any fault of Yours or mine, would have lost His
faithful and loving servant. For that reason, Most Blessed Father, it
is certainly no mistake in such matters, where one's life is at stake, to
employ the methods of poor, simple men who customarily declare
that one must mark seven times but cut only once.* Since the wicked,
lying tongue of my worst adversary* had so easily angered Your Holiness that You flew into such a rage You ordered the Governor to have
me hanged immediately, and later, after You had seen what a disadvantage this was, doing Yourself a great wrong by depriving Yourself of one of Your servants—of the kind that Your Holiness Himself

declared he was—I most certainly think that, before God and the world, Your Holiness would later have felt no little remorse. For that reason good and virtuous fathers, like good and virtuous patrons, must not precipitously allow their arm to fall upon their sons and servants; feeling regret afterwards serves no purpose. Since God hindered this evil trajectory of the stars and saved me for Your Holiness, I beg that on another occasion Your Holiness will not become enraged with me so easily.' The Pope, having stopped to examine his medals, stood there listening to me with great attention, and because there were many lords of the greatest importance in his presence, the Pope blushed a bit, looked as if he were ashamed, and knowing no other means of escaping from this embarrassing situation, he remarked that he did not remember ever having given such an order. When I saw his embarrassment I began to talk about other things, in order to move our discussion away from the cause of the shame he had shown. Once more His Holiness began to talk about the medals, and he asked me what method I had employed in stamping them so admirably, since they were so large: he had never seen ancient medals of such a size. We spoke of this for a while and the Pope, who was afraid I would deliver another little sermon to him, worse than the first, told me that the medals were most beautiful, that they pleased him a great deal, and that he would like another medal done with another reverse design following an idea of his own,* if such a medal could be stamped with two different reverse sides. I said it could be done. Then His Holiness commissioned me to create a design with the story of Moses, where he strikes the rock and water gushes forth, with a motto above the design reading: 'Ut bibat populus.'* And then he added: 'Go, Benvenuto, you shall not be finished with it before I shall have seen to all your needs.' After I had left him, the Pope bragged in the presence of all that he would give me so much that I would be able to live like a rich man without ever again having to work for other patrons. I diligently applied myself to finishing the reverse with the figure of Moses.

72. In the meantime the Pope became ill, and since his physicians judged his illness to be dangerous, that adversary of mine, being afraid of me, commissioned certain Neapolitan soldiers to do to me what he feared I would do to him.* For this reason, I was hard pressed to defend my own poor life. By working continuously, I finished the reverse side completely: taking it to the Pope, I found him in bed in

very bad condition. In spite of this he welcomed me with great affection and wanted to see the medals and dies; he had his eye-glasses and candles brought to him, but was unable to make anything out. He began to probe the medals with his fingers; then, after doing that for a while, he let out a great sigh and said that he was truly very worried about me, but that if God restored his health he would set everything right. Three days later the Pope died,* and when I discovered that I had wasted all my efforts, I screwed up my courage and told myself that, as a result of these medals, I had made myself so well known that every pope in the future would hire me with even better fortune. And so I gathered up my courage, forgetting completely and forever the great injuries that Pompeo had done me, and putting my armour all around me I went to St Peter's and kissed the feet of the deceased Pope, not without some tears; then I returned to the Via dei Banchi to ponder the great confusion that occurs on such occasions. While I was sitting in the Via dei Banchi with a good number of my friends, Pompeo happened to pass by, accompanied by ten very well-armed men, and when he was standing directly in front of me he stopped, as if he wished to pick a fight with me. The friends with me were brave young men and eager for a fight, and they motioned to me to put my hand on my sword, which I had immediately thought of doing, except that if I put my hand on my sword there might have followed some serious injury to those who had committed no fault in the world, and for this reason I judged that the best plan was to put only my own life at risk. After Pompeo had waited long enough to say two Hail Marys, with a scornful laugh in my direction he went off; his companions too laughed and shook their heads, and with other such gestures acted very threateningly. My own companions wanted to settle the challenge; I angrily told them that I was man enough to know how to end my own fights, that I needed no better soldiers than myself, and that they could all mind their own business. Angry at this, my friends left me, complaining. With them was my dearest friend, Albertaccio del Bene,* the natural brother of Alessandro and Albizo, who is today a very wealthy man in Lyons. This Albertaccio was the most wonderful young man I ever knew and the most courageous, and he loved me as much as himself, and because he realized that my patience was not a result of cowardice but of audacious courage (for he knew me very well), responding to my words, he begged me to do him the favour of calling on him to take part in whatever I intended to do. To this request, I said: 'My dear Albertaccio, dearer to me than anybody else, there may very well come a time when you'll be able to help me, but in this case, if you wish me well, stay away from me and mind your own affairs, and get away from here quickly as the others did, because there is no time to lose.' I spoke these words in a hurry.

73. Meanwhile my enemies had headed from the Via dei Banchi toward the Chiavica, as the place was named, at a slow walk and had arrived at an intersection where the streets went off in different directions, but the street where the home of my enemy Pompeo was located was the street that went directly toward the Campo de' Fiori. And having some business there, Pompeo had gone into the apothecary's shop at the corner of the Chiavica and stayed there with the apothecary for some time about his affairs, although I was told that he was boasting about the brave way in which he had confronted me. But in any case all this turned out to be his bad luck, for just as I arrived at the corner he came out of the apothecary's shop, and his hired cutthroats opened their ranks for him and then closed up around him. I grabbed a small sharp dagger, forced my way through the line formed by his escort, and grabbed him by the chest with such speed and courage that none of them could stop me. I aimed at his face, but the fear he felt made him turn it aside, causing me to stab him just under the ear; and after I struck him there only two more times, in an instant he fell down dead by my hand, which was not what I intended;* but as they say, you don't trade blows by agreement! I pulled back the dagger with my left hand, and with my right I drew my sword in self-defence, while all those cutthroats ran toward the dead body and made no move to attack me, and all alone, I retreated to the Via Giulia,* thinking about how I might save myself. When I had gone three hundred paces the goldsmith Piloto,* my very good friend, met me and said: 'My colleague, now that the damage is done, let's see about saving you.' To this I replied: 'Let's go to Albertaccio del Bene's house, since a short time ago I was telling him how very soon the time would come when I would need his help.' When we reached Albertaccio's house, his welcome was extremely warm, and soon the best young men of the Via dei Banchi of every nationality, except the Milanese,* appeared; they all offered to risk their own lives to save mine. Even Messer Luigi Rucellai* sent word to offer with amazing generosity anything of his I might need, and

many other important persons like him did the same; then they all blessed my hands in agreement, since they thought that Pompeo had offended me too greatly, and they wondered why I had put up with it for so long.

74. In the meantime, Cardinal Cornaro* found out about what happened, and he himself sent thirty soldiers, with a great many halberds, pikes, and arquebuses, to escort me to his chambers with every sign of respect; I accepted his offer and went off with them, and more than the same number of those young men accompanied me. While this was happening, that Messer Traiano, Pompeo's relative and the first chamberlain of the Pope, sent a Milanese gentleman to Cardinal de' Medici to tell him of the great crime I had committed, and that His Most Reverend Lordship was obliged to punish me. The Cardinal quickly replied, saying: 'He would have committed a grave crime by not committing this minor offence: thank Messer Traiano for me, since he has informed me of something that I did not know about.' Then he quickly turned and, in the presence of that same gentleman, he said to the Bishop of Frullí,* his attendant and friend: 'Search for Benvenuto very carefully and bring him here, for I wish to help and defend him, and anyone who acts against him acts against me.' The gentleman blushed and left, and the Bishop of Frullí came and found me with Cardinal Cornaro in his home, and he told the Cardinal how Cardinal de' Medici had sent for Benvenuto and that he wanted to be the one to protect him. This Cardinal Cornaro was as irascible as a bear, and he very angrily replied to the Bishop that he was just as capable of protecting me as Cardinal de' Medici. The Bishop asked if he might kindly speak a word to me about another matter, some other affairs of the Cardinal's. Cornaro told him that, for this day, he could consider that he had already spoken to me. Cardinal de' Medici was very indignant: but, well escorted, I went the following night to visit him without letting Cardinal Cornaro know; I then begged him to do me the favour of leaving me in Cornaro's home, and I described the great courtesies that Cornaro had employed in my regard, given that if His Most Reverend Lordship allowed me to remain with Cornaro, I would come to gain one more friend in my adversities, but that His Lordship could do with me anything he pleased. Cardinal de' Medici replied that I should do whatever I liked. After I returned to Cornaro's home, a few days later Cardinal Farnese* was elected Pope,

and after immediately settling matters of the greatest importance, the Pope next asked about me, saying that he did not want anyone else to make his coins. Hearing these words, a certain gentleman named Messer Latino Iuvinale,* who was on intimate terms with the Pope, stated that I was a fugitive from a homicide I had committed on the person of a Milanese named Pompeo, and he put all my motives in the most favourable light. At those words the Pope said: 'I didn't know about the death of Pompeo, but I knew of Benvenuto's motives perfectly well, so write him out an order of safe conduct immediately, with which he will be completely secure.' There was present a great friend of that Pompeo and close confidant of the Pope named Messer Ambruogio,* a Milanese, and he said: 'During the first days of your papacy, it would not be good to grant pardons of this sort.' Turning toward him, the Pope said: 'You don't understand the matter as well as I do. You should know that men like Benvenuto, unique in their profession, need not be subject to the law: especially not Benvenuto, since I know what good reasons he had.' And after my safe-conduct was made out, I immediately began to serve the new Pope and was treated with the greatest favour.

75. This Messer Latino Iuvinale came to see me and commissioned me to make the Pope's coins. Because of this, all my enemies bestirred themselves: they began to hinder me from doing them. When the Pope learned of it, he reprimanded them all and insisted that I make them. I began to make the stamps for the scudi, upon which I designed a half-length figure of St Paul and an inscription that read: *Vas electionis.** This coin was far more pleasing than those made by any of my rivals, so that the Pope said no one was to speak about coins to him again, because he wanted me to be the man to make them and no one else. So I freely went to work, and that Messer Latino Iuvinale led me in to see the Pope, because that Pope had given him this task. I wanted once again to obtain the *moto proprio** for the position as engraver at the Mint. In this case, the Pope allowed himself to be advised, saying that first I needed to receive the pardon for the homicide, which I could have during the Festival of the Assumption in August according to the regulations of the *caporioni* of Rome; these pardons are customarily given to these *caporioni* for twelve outlaws each year during this solemn festival; in the meantime, he would have another safe-conduct written up for me, by means of which I would be safe until the appointed time.*

When my enemies saw that they could find no way to hinder me from regaining my position in the Mint, they seized upon another expedient. When Pompeo died, he left behind three thousand ducats as a dowry for a little bastard daughter of his, and they arranged things so that a certain favourite of Signor Pier Luigi, the Pope's son,* should ask for her hand in marriage through his master's assistance: and this was done. This favourite of Pier Luigi's was a peasant who had been brought up by this lord, and by all accounts he saw very little of the money, since Pier Luigi got his hands on it and intended to use it for himself. But since the husband of this young girl had asked Pier Luigi on numerous occasions to have me arrested to please his wife, he had promised to do so when he saw that the favour I enjoyed with the Pope diminished a bit. With matters standing thus, for about two months, since this servant was trying to obtain his dowry, Pier Luigi did not respond to his enquiries about it, but let his wife know that he would avenge her father no matter what happened. Although I knew something about all of this, I presented myself on numerous occasions to Pier Luigi, who pretended to show me the greatest favour; on the other hand, he had decided to take one of two paths—either to have me murdered or to have me arrested by the constable. He commissioned a certain little devil of a Corsican soldier of his to do the job as neatly as possible, and my other enemies, especially Messer Traiano, had promised to make a present of one hundred scudi to this little Corsican, who said that he could murder me as easily as sucking a fresh egg. When I learned about this, I went about with my eyes open and a good escort, extremely well armed with a coat of mail and arm-plates, since I had the right to wear this armour. Out of avarice, this little Corsican, who was hoping to get all that money safe in his own hands, believed he could do the job by himself alone, and so one day after dinner he had me summoned by Signor Pier Luigi, whereupon I went immediately, because Pier Luigi had spoken to me about commissioning a number of large silver vases. I left the house in a hurry, although with my usual armour, and I quickly went down the Via Giulia, thinking I would not find anyone there at that hour. When I reached the end of the street to turn toward the Farnese Palace, giving a wide berth to the corners as usual, I saw that little Corsican stand up and come out into the middle of the street. I was completely unperturbed by this, but I remained on guard to defend myself, and slowing my pace somewhat, I drew near to the wall to make way for this little Corsican. As he approached the wall and we drew near to each other, I recognized clearly by his movements that he wanted to do me some harm, and seeing me alone that way, he thought that he would succeed. So I began to speak to him, and I said: 'Courageous soldier, if this were nighttime you could say that you took me for somebody else, but since it is broad daylight you know very well who I am, a person who has never had dealings with you and has never done you any harm. Yet I'd be quite capable of doing you this favour.' At these words he took a threatening stance, and did not move out of the way, telling me he did not know what I was talking about. Then I said: 'I know very well what you want and what you are saying, but that enterprise you've undertaken to accomplish is more difficult and dangerous than you imagine, and it could well go wrong. Remember that you have to reckon with a man who would defend himself against one hundred men. And this is not an honourable enterprise for courageous men such as yourself.' I started scowling, and the colour of both our faces changed. Meanwhile people had gathered and had already understood that our words meant drawn swords; and since he lacked the courage to lay hands on me, he said: 'We shall see each other another time.' To this I replied: 'I am always prepared to meet again with worthy men and with men who seem so.' I left and went to the house of Pier Luigi, who had not sent for me. After I returned to my shop, the little Corsican, through a close mutual friend, gave me to understand that I should not worry about him any longer, since he wished to be like a good brother to me, but that I should guard myself carefully from others, since I was running a very grave risk and men of great importance had sworn to have me killed. After I had sent back my thanks I protected myself as best I could. Not many days later I was told by one of my close friends that Signor Pier Luigi had given a direct order to have me arrested that evening. I heard this several hours before sunset, and because of it I spoke with several of my friends, who advised me to leave immediately. And since the order was given for an hour after sunset, I mounted a post-horse an hour before sunset and rode off to Florence, for after that little Corsican had lacked the courage to complete the undertaking as he had promised, Signor Pier Luigi on his own authority had given the order to arrest me, only to placate that daughter of Pompeo a little, who wanted to know what had happened to her dowry. Being unable to carry out her vendetta in either of the two ways that he had planned, he thought of another means which we shall describe in the proper place.

76. I reached Florence, and I went to speak with Duke Alessandro, who showed me marvellous kindness and sought to make me stay with him. In Florence there was a certain sculptor named Tribolino,* who was my close friend, since I had stood as godfather to his son, and while we were talking he told me that a certain Iacopo del Sansovino,* who had been his first master, had called and sent for him; because he had never seen Venice and because of the profit he expected from it, he was very keen to go there; then he asked me if I had ever seen Venice and I said that I had not, whereupon he begged me to go along with him, which I promised to do. For that reason, I told Duke Alessandro that I first wanted to go to Venice but that I would then return most ready to serve him; and so he wanted me to promise to do so, and he ordered me to come and speak to him before I departed. Early the next day, having put everything in order, I went to take my leave of the Duke, whom I found in the Palazzo dei Pazzi where, at the time, the wife and daughters of Signor Lorenzo Cibo were lodged.* I let His Excellency know that I wanted to go to Venice with his good wishes, and Cosimino de' Medici,* now Duke of Florence, returned with his response, telling me that I should go to find Niccolò da Monte Aguto,* and that he would give me fifty golden scudi, money that His Excellency the Duke was giving me so that I might enjoy them, out of love for him, and then return and serve him. I took the money from Niccolò and went to the home of Tribolo, who was all ready, and he asked me if I had tied the hilt of my sword to my scabbard. I told him that a man on horseback who was going on a journey did not have to tie up his sword. He said that in Florence it was customary, because there was a certain Ser Maurizio* who, for every little infraction, would have hanged even St John the Baptist, and it was therefore necessary to wear one's sword tied up until you were outside the city gates. I laughed at this, and thus we set off. We were accompanied by the courier to Venice who had the nickname 'Lamentone',* with whom we travelled in a group, and after passing Bologna, one evening we arrived in Ferrara, where we took lodgings at an inn on the piazza while this Lamentone went to find some of the *fuorusciti** to bring them letters and messages from their wives, for it was the will of the Duke that only this courier could

speak with them, while others were not allowed to do so, under penalty of the same condemnation that they had received. In the meantime, since there were still almost two hours before sunset, we went out, Tribolo and I, to see the return of the Duke of Ferrara,* who had gone to Belfiore to see the jousting. Awaiting his return we ran into a great many *fuorusciti*, who stared at us almost as if they were forcing us to speak with them. Tribolo, who was the most timid man I ever knew, never ceased telling me: 'Don't look at them or speak to them if you wish to return to Florence!' So we waited to see the Duke return; then after we went back to the inn we found Lamentone there. Now it was almost an hour after sunset and there appeared Niccolò Benintendi and Piero, his brother, and another older man, who I think was Iacopo Nardi,* along with a number of other young men, who, immediately upon arriving, asked the courier for news of their families in Florence: Tribolo and I stood off to the side to avoid speaking to them. Then, after they had talked a bit with Lamentone, this Niccolò Benintendi said: 'I know these two very well—why are they being such shits, not wanting to talk to us?' Tribolo was telling me to remain silent. Lamentone told them that the permission to speak had been given to him, not to us. Benintendi replied, saying that it was asinine, cursing us, and a thousand other such things. Then I raised my head with as much modesty as I could muster, or knew how to muster, and said: 'My dear gentlemen, you can harm us a great deal, while we cannot help you at all, and although in what you have said to us there were some words that were inappropriate, we shall not become angry with you even for this.' That old gentleman Nardi said that I had spoken like a fine young man, which I was. Then Niccolò Benintendi said: 'They and the Duke can shove it up their arses!' I replied that he was mistaken about us and that we had nothing to do with his affairs. This old man Nardi took our side, telling Benintendi that he was in the wrong; as a result, he continued to speak insults. Because of this, I told him that I would say and do some things which would displease him; so he should mind his own business and leave us alone. He once again replied that we and the duke could shove it up our arses, and that we and he were just a bunch of asses. At these words, I accused him of lying through his teeth and drew my sword; the old man, who wanted to be the first to go down the stairs, fell down after a few steps and they all fell on top of him. At this, I sprang up and scraped my sword along the wall with great force, shouting: 'I shall kill all of you!', and taking great care not to harm anyone even though I could easily have done so. At this noise, the innkeeper shouted. Lamentone was saying: 'Don't do it!' And some of the others were saying: 'Alas, our heads!'; others were yelling: 'Let me out of here!' There was unimaginable confusion: they looked like a herd of pigs. The innkeeper came in with a light, and I retreated and put my sword back into its scabbard. Lamentone told Niccolò Benintendi that he had acted badly, while the innkeeper said to him: 'It could cost you your life to draw your sword here, and if the Duke knew of your insolent actions he would have you hanged by the neck; I won't do what you deserve, but if you ever show your face in this inn again you'll be sorry.' The innkeeper came up to me, and when I wanted to make my excuses he would not allow me to say anything, telling me that he knew I had a thousand good reasons and that I should be on my guard against them during my journey.

77. After we had eaten supper a boatman showed up to take us to Venice: I asked if he would let me have the boat without other passengers, and he was happy to do so and we struck a bargain. Early in the morning we mounted our horses to go to the port, which is I do not know how many miles from Ferrara, and when we reached the port we found Niccolò Benintendi's brother there with three other companions who were waiting for me to arrive: between them they were armed with two pikes, while I had purchased a fine short lance in Ferrara. Since I was very well armed I was not at all afraid, unlike Tribolo, who cried: 'God help us, they are here to murder us!' Lamentone turned to me and said: 'The best thing you can do is to return to Ferrara, because I see danger here. Please, my dear Benvenuto, avoid the fury of these rabid beasts.' Then I said: 'Let's go forward, because God helps those in the right; and you will see how I'll help myself. Isn't this boat the one we paid the deposit for?' 'Yes,' said Lamentone. 'And we'll go aboard without them if my abilities allow it.'* Spurring on my horse, I was within fifty paces of them when I dismounted, and bravely went forward with my lance. Tribolo had stopped behind me and was crouched over his horse as if he were the very figure of cold; Lamentone the courier huffed and puffed as if he were the wind; this was his usual way of behaving, but he was doing it more than usual, as he considered how this devilish business would end. When I reached the boat, the boatman came up

to me and told me that these Florentine gentlemen wished to join us
in the boat if I were willing. I said to him: 'This boat was hired for us
and not for anyone else, and I'm very sorry but we can't have them
with us.' Hearing my reply, an arrogant young man of the Magalotti
family said: 'Benvenuto, we'll make it possible for you to do so.'
Then I said: 'If God and the right that is on my side, together with
my own strength, will it or can do it, you'll not be able to do to me
what you are saying.' As I said this I jumped into the boat. I turned
the point of my weapon toward them and said: 'With this, I'll show
you that I cannot do so.' Wanting to make a bit of a show, this
Magalotti put his hand to his sword and stepped forward, and I
leaped upon the side of the boat and struck him such a hard blow
that, if he had not fallen backward on the ground, I would have run
him through from one side to the other. His other companions,
instead of helping him, retreated backwards, and once they saw that
I could have murdered him, instead of just striking him I said: 'Get
up, brother, take your weapons and go away; you've seen very well
that I cannot do what I will not do, and that what I could have done I
did not wish to do.' Then I called for Tribolo, the boatman, and
Lamentone; and so we all went off to Venice. When we were ten
miles along the Po river these young men, who had boarded a skiff,
caught up to us, and when they pulled alongside us, this stupid Piero
Benintendi said to me: 'Go on your way now, Benvenuto, for we shall
meet again in Venice.' 'Get going then, for I am coming,' I said, 'and
by all means, just let me see you again.' And so we arrived in Venice.
I took the advice of a brother of Cardinal Cornaro, asking him to do
me the favour of allowing me to carry arms, and he told me that I
should carry them freely, since the worst that would happen to me
was to lose my sword.

78. And so, carrying our arms, we went to visit Iacopo del Sansovino the sculptor, who had sent for Tribolo; he gave me a very warm
welcome and wanted us to stay for dinner, and so we did. Speaking
with Tribolo, Sansovino told him that he did not need his services at
the moment and that he should return another time. When I heard
these words I burst out laughing, and said to Sansovino quite pleasantly: 'His house is too far away from yours if he has to come back
another time.' Timidly, poor Tribolo said: 'But I have the letter right
here that you wrote, telling me to come.' To this Sansovino replied
that men like him, honourable and talented, could do such things

and even more. Tribolo shrugged his shoulders and said 'Patience' several times. At this, without being mindful of the abundant dinner that Sansovino had offered me, I took the side of my companion Tribolo, who was in the right. Since at the dinner table Sansovino had never stopped chattering about his great enterprises, speaking badly of Michelangelo and all those who practised the art of sculpture, only praising himself to the stars, it had annoyed me so much that I had not eaten a single mouthful that was to my taste, and I only said these few words: 'O Messer Iacopo, worthy men act like worthy men, and those talented men who create those fine and beautiful works are recognized much better when they are praised by others than when they are praised with such confidence by themselves.' After saying this, he and we got up from the table, grumbling. That same day, finding myself near the Rialto Bridge in Venice, I ran into Piero Benintendi accompanied by a number of men, and realizing that they were out to do me some harm I went into the shop of a druggist until I let the storm pass by. Later I learned that the young man from the Magalotti family, to whom I had been so courteous, had yelled at them; and so the affair was settled.

79. A few days later we headed back towards Florence, and while we were staying in a certain place which is on the left going from Chioggia and approaching Ferrara, the innkeeper wanted to be paid in his own way before we went to bed, and telling him that in other places it was customary to pay in the morning, he said to us: 'I want to be paid in the evening and in my own way.' I said, in response to his words, that men who wanted to do things in their own way had better make a world in their own way, because in this world things are not done like this. The innkeeper replied that I should not bother him, since he wanted to do things that way. Tribolo trembled with fear, and he pinched me to be quiet so that they did not do any worse to us, and so we paid the innkeeper in his way, and then we went to bed. We had very fine, comfortable beds, new in every detail and really clean, but despite this I never slept a wink, thinking all that night about what I had to do to avenge myself. First I thought about setting fire to the house, then about slitting the throats of the four good horses he kept in his stable; all this I saw would be easy for me to do, but I did not see that it would be easy to save myself and my companion. As a last resort, I thought of loading my belongings and my companions in the boat, and I did so: and after I had tied the

horses to the tow-ropes which pulled the barge, I told them not to move the boat until I returned, because I had left behind a pair of slippers in the room where I had slept. So I returned to the inn and asked for the innkeeper, who sent word that he did not want to have anything to do with us and that we could go to hell. There was a young stable-boy of his standing there, half asleep, who told me: 'The innkeeper wouldn't budge for the Pope, since he is sleeping with some little wench he has been lusting after for some time.' He asked me for a tip, and I gave him some of those small Venetian coins and told him to make the man holding the tow-rope wait for a while, so that I could look for my slippers and come back. I went on upstairs and, taking a little knife for shaving, I cut into shreds all the four beds that were up there in such a way I knew I had done more than fifty scudi in damage. And after returning to the boat with some strips of that bedspread in my pocket, I hastily told the man controlling the tow-rope to shove off at once. After we had moved a short distance away from the inn, my companion Tribolo said that he had left behind some of the little straps that bound up his luggage and that he wanted to return for them no matter what. To this I replied that we were not concerned about two small straps, because I could make him straps as large and as many as he liked.* He said that I was always joking but that he wanted to go back for his little straps no matter what, and he tried to persuade the man with the tow-rope to stop, while I was saying that he should go forward, at the same time explaining to Tribolo about the great damage I had done to the innkeeper and showing him a sample of the shreds of the bedding. This made him so afraid that he could not stop telling the boatman, 'Get going, get going quickly', and he never felt safe from this danger until we were at the gates of Florence. When we arrived, Tribolo said: 'Let's bind up our swords for God's sake, and no more tricks; I've felt like I was going to get my guts ripped out the whole trip.' To this remark, I answered: 'Tribolo, my friend, you don't need to bind up your sword since you never untied it,' and I said this to him, by the way, since I had never seen him act like a man during that trip. So, looking at his sword, he said: 'By God, you are right; it has been bound in the way I fixed it before I left my house.' My friend thought I had made a very bad companion, since I had become angry and defended myself from men who had wanted to do us some harm, and I thought that he had behaved much worse toward me, in not coming to my assistance when I needed it. The unbiased observer can judge fairly for himself.

80. After I had dismounted I immediately went to find Duke Alessandro and thanked him profusely for the present of the fifty scudi, telling His Excellency that I was more than ready to do everything I could to serve His Excellency well. He immediately imposed on me the task of making the stamps for his coins, and the first that I made was a coin of forty soldi with His Excellency's head on one side and figures of St Cosmas and St Damian on the reverse.* These were silver coins, and they were so pleasing that the Duke dared to claim that they were the most beautiful coins in all Christendom. All of Florence said the same thing, as well as everyone who saw them. For this reason, I asked His Excellency to give me a fixed salary and to assign me rooms in the Mint; he told me that I should concentrate upon serving him and that he would give me much more than I had asked of him; and in the meantime he said that he had given orders to the Master of the Mint, who was a certain Carlo Acciaiuoli,* and that I should go to him for all the money I wanted. And this I found to be true, but I drew my money so prudently that I always had some left according to my accounting. Next I made the stamps for the giulio,* which had a figure of St John the Baptist in profile seated with a book in his hand, which seemed to me more beautiful than anything I had ever made; the arms of Duke Alessandro were on the other side. Shortly after this, I made the stamps for the half-giulio, in which I represented the head of a youthful St John in full-face. This was the first coin in full-face done on silver with such great subtlety that had ever been created, and such technical difficulty is not apparent except to the eyes of those who are experts in this profession.* After this I made the stamps for the golden scudi:* on one side of it was a figure of the cross with some small cherubs, and on the other was His Excellency's coat of arms. When I had completed these four kinds of coin, I begged His Excellency to confirm my salary and to assign me the previously mentioned rooms, if my service had pleased him: at these words, His Excellency kindly told me that he was very satisfied and that he would give such an order. While I was speaking to him, His Excellency was in his wardrobe and was inspecting a marvellous short carbine that had been sent to him from Germany: when he saw that I was examining it with close attention, he placed it in my hand, telling me how he knew very well what delight I took in

such things, and that as a pledge of what he had promised me I could take from his wardrobe any arquebus I liked except that one, since he knew very well that there were many more beautiful and just as good. Hearing this, I accepted his offer and thanked him; and seeing me begin to look around the room, he ordered his Master of the Wardrobe, a certain Pretino da Lucca,* to allow me to pick anything I wanted. And after he had departed with the most pleasing words, I remained and selected the most beautiful and best arquebus I had ever seen, or that I ever had, and this I carried home with me. Two days later I took His Excellency certain little designs he had requested for some works in gold, which he wanted to send as gifts to his wife, who was still in Naples.* Once again I asked him about the same business of mine and if he could expedite it for me.* His Excellency then informed me that he wanted me first to make the stamps for a handsome portrait of him like the one I had made for Pope Clement. I began the portrait in wax; for this reason, His Excellency ordered that at any time I came to work on it I should always be allowed inside. When I saw that this work of mine was going to take some time, I called a certain Pietro Pagolo* from Monte Ritondo, the one near Rome, who had been with me as a small boy in Rome; I discovered that he was with a certain goldsmith named Bernardonaccio,* who did not treat him very well, and because of this I took him away and taught him extremely well how to make dies for the striking of coins. Meanwhile I was sketching the Duke's portrait; on many occasions I found him napping after dinner all alone with this Lorenzino of his,* who later murdered him, and I was very much amazed that a Duke of this sort would be so trusting.

81. It happened that Ottaviano de' Medici,* who seemed to have control over everything, wanted to favour, against the Duke's wishes, the old Master of the Mint named Bastiano Cennini,* an old-fashioned craftsman of little skill, who, during the making of the stamps for the scudi, had meddled with my dies using some of his clumsy iron tools. Because of this I complained to the Duke who, when he saw that it was true, took it very badly and said to me: 'Go tell this to Ottaviano de' Medici, and show some of them to him.' Whereupon I went immediately, and after showing him the damage that had been done to my beautiful coins, he said to me like an ass: 'This is the way we like to do it.' To him I replied that it should not be this way, and that I did not like it. And he said: 'And if the Duke

likes it this way?' To which I answered: 'I would still not like it; such a thing is neither just nor reasonable.' He said to get out of his sight and that I would have to swallow that way of doing it, even if I were to die. After returning to the Duke, I gave him an account of everything that we had so unpleasantly discussed, Ottaviano de' Medici and I; and because of this I begged His Excellency not to allow anyone to do harm to the beautiful coins I had made for him, and to give me permission to leave. Then the Duke said: 'Ottaviano is going too far, and you shall have what you wish, for this is an injury that is being done to me.' On that very day, which was a Thursday, a comprehensive safe-conduct pass arrived from the Pope in Rome, who ordered me to go immediately to receive the pardon of the Assumption in mid August so that I could free myself of the charge of murder. When I went to see the Duke I found him in bed, for they told me he had been making merry, and having finished in little more than two hours what I needed for the wax model of his medal, I showed him the completed version, which he liked a great deal. Then I showed His Excellency the safe-conduct pass that I had received on the Pope's orders, and explained that the Pope had recalled me to do certain works for him; in this way, I would go to regain my position in that beautiful city of Rome, and at the same time I would serve him with his medal. To this the Duke said, half in anger: 'Benvenuto, do what I want and don't leave, for I shall secure your stipend and give you the rooms in the Mint along with much more than you would ever ask me for, because you only ask of me what is just and reasonable; and who would you want to make coins from those beautiful stamps that you have created for me?' Then I said: 'My Lord, I have already thought of everything, because I have here with me one of my pupils, a young Roman, whom I have taught and who will serve Your Excellency extremely well until I return with your finished medal, to remain here to serve you forever. And since I have a workshop open in Rome, with workmen and other business, as soon as I receive my pardon I shall leave all the work in Rome to one of my pupils who is there, and then, with Your Excellency's kind permission, I shall return to you.' At this conversation that Lorenzino de' Medici I mentioned before was present, and no one else. The Duke several times motioned to Lorenzino that he, too, should persuade me to stay; this Lorenzino never said anything in response but 'Benvenuto, you would do better to stay'. To this I replied that I wanted to return to Rome no matter what. Lorenzino said nothing more and stood there, constantly staring at the Duke in a treacherous way.* Since I had completed the medal the way I wanted to do it and had locked it in its little box, I said to the Duke: 'My Lord, be of good will, for I shall make you a much more beautiful medal than I made for Pope Clement: it is reasonable to assume that, since that one was the first I ever made, I shall make yours better; and Messer Lorenzo, who is a learned and extremely intelligent person, will give me some beautiful design for the reverse.' To my remarks Lorenzo immediately replied, saying: 'I have been thinking about nothing but a reverse worthy of Your Excellency.'* The Duke smiled maliciously and, looking at Lorenzino, he said: 'Lorenzo, you will give him a design for the reverse, and he will do it here and will not leave.' Then Lorenzo replied, saying: 'I shall do it as quickly as I can, and I hope that it will be something that astounds the world.' The Duke, who considered Lorenzino sometimes slightly mad and sometimes a slacker, turned in his bed and laughed at the words he had spoken to him. I departed without further leavetaking, and left them alone together. The Duke, who did not think I would leave, said nothing more to me. When he learned that I had gone he sent one of his servants after me, who caught up with me at Siena, and he gave me fifty golden ducats on the Duke's behalf, telling me that I should enjoy them for love of him and that I should return as quickly as I could. 'And on Messer Lorenzo's behalf, let me tell you that he will prepare a marvellous reverse for that medal you want to make.'* I had left all the instructions for Pietropagolo, the Roman mentioned above, as to how he was to employ the stamps, but because it was extremely difficult to do, he never used them too well. I remained a creditor at the Mint, from the making of my stamps, to the amount of more than seventy scudi.

82. I went to Rome and took with me that beautiful flintlock arquebus the Duke had given me, and with the greatest of pleasure I used it many times along the way, putting it through its paces to unbelievable effect. I reached Rome; and since I had a little house in Via Giulia, which was not ready for me, I went to dismount at the home of Messer Giovanni Gaddi, the clerk of the Chamber, to whom I had entrusted on my departure from Rome my many handsome weapons and many other items that I held most dear. I did not want to dismount at my workshop, however, and I sent for my partner

Felice and got him quickly to put everything in good order in my little house. Then, the next day,* I went to sleep there, for my clothes had been put in order as well as everything that I needed, since I wanted to go on the following morning to visit the Pope in order to thank him. I had two young boys as servants, and below my house there was a washerwoman who used to cook very nicely for me. After I had invited a number of my friends to supper, having enjoyed the meal with the greatest pleasure, I dropped off to sleep; the night was almost over and it was about an hour before sunrise when I heard a furious knocking at the door of my home, one blow after another. At this, I called this older servant of mine, whose name was Cencio: he was the boy I led through the circle of necromancy;* I told him he had to see who the madman was, knocking so ferociously at that hour. While Cencio was going to the door I lit another light, as I always keep one lit at night, and I immediately put on over my shirt a splendid coat of mail, and over that a bit of clothing picked up at random. When Cencio returned, he said: 'Alas, master, it's the constable with his entire crew, and he says that if you don't open quickly he will knock the door down; and they have torches and a thousand other things with them.' To this I replied: 'Tell them that I am putting a few clothes on my back and will come down in my shirt-sleeves.' Imagining that this was an assassination attempt, like the one already committed against me by Signor Pier Luigi, with my right hand I seized a marvellous dagger that I owned and with the left my safe-conduct pass; then I ran to the back window, which looked out over some orchards, and saw there more than thirty policemen; thus I realized that I could not run away from that side of the house. Putting the two young boys in front of me, I told them to open the door exactly when I told them to. I readied myself, the dagger in my right hand and the safe-conduct pass in my left, in a proper defensive posture, and I said to those two boys: 'Don't be afraid, open the door.' Vittorio the constable,* along with two other men, immediately leaped inside, thinking they could easily lay their hands upon me in this manner, but when they saw that I was ready for them, they retreated and declared: 'This is much more than a joking matter!' Then, throwing the safe-conduct pass to them, I said: 'Read this, and since you can't arrest me, I don't want you to touch me!' The constable then told some of his men to seize me, and that they would see later about the safe-conduct pass. To this remark, I thrust forward bravely with my weapon and cried out: 'God is on the side of the righteous: I'll either escape alive or you'll arrest a dead man!' The room was crowded; they showed signs of coming at me with force, and I showed signs of defending myself; for this reason, the constable realized that he could not arrest me in any other manner than the one I had mentioned. Calling the chancellor, while he had the safe-conduct pass read aloud he made a motion two or three times to have me seized, but I never moved from my resolve. Giving up on their undertaking, they threw my safe-conduct pass on the floor and went off without me.

83. After I returned to bed, I felt so upset I could not fall asleep again. I had made a decision that as soon as daylight came I would have myself bled, but I took the advice of Messer Giovanni Gaddi, and he sought the advice of one of his quack doctors, who asked me if I had been frightened. Just imagine what kind of medical judgement he must have had, after I had told him about such an extraordinary affair, and he asks a question like that! He was a nitwit who laughed constantly, and over the least little thing, and laughing in that way, he told me to take a good glass of Greek wine and to try to be of good cheer and not be afraid. Messer Giovanni said over and over again: 'Maestro, even a man made of bronze or marble would be afraid in a case such as this, not to mention a man of flesh and blood.' To this statement that charlatan replied: 'My Lord, we are not all made in the same way: this man is neither of bronze nor of marble but of pure iron,' and placing his hands on my pulse, with that inappropriate laugh of his, he said to Messer Giovanni: 'Just feel here: this is not a man's pulse, it's the pulse of a lion or a dragon.' In fact my pulse was beating furiously, perhaps in an unusual fashion that this idiot of a physician had never heard about in his readings of Hippocrates or Galen, and I understood very well how sick I was, but in order not to be make myself more afraid or to do myself more harm than I had already done, I made a show of being calm. Meanwhile, Messer Giovanni had supper prepared, and we all ate together: the group included, besides Messer Giovanni, a certain Lodovico da Fano, Messer Antonio Allegretti, Messer Giovanni the Greek—all very learned men—and Messer Annibale Caro, who was then a very young man, and the group* never spoke of anything during that meal but the way in which I had shown my courage. They had my servant Cencio, who was extremely clever, brave, and

handsome, recount the story for them: every time he told them about
my angry behaviour, imitating the gestures I made and repeating
very precisely the very words that I had said, it always reminded me
of some new aspect of the affair; and they often asked him if he had
been afraid, and to their question he replied that they should ask me
if I had been afraid, because he had felt the same way I felt. All this
silly, tedious talk began to annoy me, and since I was feeling quite
upset, I got up from the table, declaring that I wanted to go and get
some new clothes of blue silk for Cencio and me; that I wanted to
join the procession four days later, when the Assumption was celebrated; and that I wanted Cencio to carry a white lighted torch for
me. So, after I had left I went to have some blue cloth cut out, for a
handsome jacket made from pure blue Persian silk and a short cloak
of the same colour, and for Cencio I had made a cloak and a taffeta
jacket, also in blue. After the cloth had been cut I went to see the
Pope, who told me to speak with his Messer Ambruogio, to whom
he had given orders for me to make a large work in gold. So I went
to find Messer Ambruogio, who had been informed very thoroughly about the matter by the constable, and had been in agreement with my enemies to have me return and had yelled at the
constable for not arresting me, but the constable had the excuse
that he could do nothing in the face of a safe-conduct pass. This
Messer Ambruogio began to discuss the business that the Pope
had commissioned him to do, then he told me to draw up the
designs while he would prepare everything else. Meanwhile the
Feast of the Assumption arrived, and because it was customary for
those who received pardons to give themselves up as prisoners, I
returned to the Pope and told His Holiness that I did not want to
put myself in jail, and begged him to exempt me from going to
prison. The Pope replied that this was the custom and this was
how it must be done. To this I knelt once again and thanked him
for the safe-conduct pass that His Holiness had signed for me, for
with it I would return to serve my Duke in Florence, who was
waiting for me with great eagerness. Upon hearing these words,
the Pope turned to one of his trusted servants and said: 'Give
Benvenuto a pardon without time in prison; and see to it that his
*motu proprio** is properly written up.' When the *motu proprio* was
drawn up, the Pope signed it once again and had it registered at
the Campidoglio; then, on the appointed day, walking between two

gentlemen very honourably, I took part in the procession and obtained a complete pardon.

84. About four days later I came down with a terrible fever and unbelievable chills, and after taking to my bed, I thought I was going to die on the spot. I had the best doctors of Rome summoned, among whom was a Master Francesco da Norcia,* a very old physician with the best reputation in all of Rome. I told all these doctors what I thought had been the cause of my grave illness, and that I had wanted to have myself bled but had been advised against it; and I said that if there was still time, I begged them to bleed me. Master Francesco replied that drawing blood now was not advisable, but that it should have been done earlier when I did not suffer from any illnesses at all; now it was necessary to treat me in another way. So they set about treating me with as much care as they were able and knew how to administer, and every day I grew much worse, so that at the end of a week the illness had grown so serious that the physicians, despairing of the undertaking, had given orders that, to make me happy, I should be given anything I wanted. Master Francesco said: 'As long as he is breathing, call me at any hour, for one cannot imagine what Nature may accomplish in a young man of this type; if he faints, however, use these five medications one after the other on him and send for me, for I shall come at any hour of the night, because it would be a greater pleasure for me to save him than any cardinal in Rome.' Every day Messer Giovanni Gaddi came to visit me two or three times, and each time he would pick up my beautiful short carbines or my coats of mail, or my swords, continuously saying: 'This is beautiful, and this is even more beautiful.' And he kept saying the same about my other little models and belongings, so that I really became annoyed. With him came a certain Mattio Franzesi,* who seemed to think a thousand years would pass before I died, not that he wanted anything of mine but it seemed that he wanted Messer Giovanni to get what he wished. I had with me Felice, the partner I previously mentioned, who gave me the most help that any man ever received from another. I became weak and dispirited, and I hardly had enough strength left to breathe in and out, but the soundness of my mind was as great as it was when I was healthy. Nevertheless, even with my mind in that condition, a terrible old man came to my bed who wanted to drag me off by force into his enormous boat; because of this I called out to my partner Felice to

come to my side and to chase that old rascal away. This Felice, who was extremely fond of me, ran to me in tears and said: 'Go away, you old traitor, trying to steal all my valuables!' Then Messer Giovanni Gaddi, who was there with us, said: 'The poor man is raving and has only a few hours left!' That other fellow Mattio Franzesi said: 'He's been reading Dante,* and with this serious illness he's become delirious,' and he said with a laugh: 'Go away, you old rascal, and don't bother our Benvenuto!' Seeing that they were mocking me, I turned to Messer Giovanni Gaddi and said to him: 'My dear patron, you should know that I'm not raving and this old man really is bothering me. But you would do very well to get rid of this wretched Mattio who is laughing at my illness; later, if Your Lordship deigns me worthy of a visit, you should come with Messer Antonio Allegretti or with Messer Annibale Caro or with those other talented friends of yours, who are people of the highest discretion and intellect, unlike this animal.' Then, in fun, Messer Giovanni ordered Mattio to leave for good, but because Mattio laughed the joke became serious, for Messer Giovanni never wanted to see him again and had Messer Antonio Allegretti, Messer Lodovico, and Messer Annibale Caro summoned. When these worthy men had arrived, I took great consolation from it and spoke with them lucidly for some time, all the while urging Felice to chase the old man away. Messer Lodovico asked me what I imagined I saw and what it looked like. While I was sketching it in words, this old man seized me by the arm and dragged me away by force, because of which I screamed for them to help me, since he wanted to throw me onto the deck of his terrifying boat. While uttering that last word I fell into a deep faint, and I felt as if he had tossed me into his boat. They said that during this fainting spell I flung myself about and insulted Messer Giovanni Gaddi, saying that he was there to rob me and not out of any act of kindness whatsoever, making many other very ugly remarks which made Messer Giovanni very much ashamed. Then they said that I stopped as if I were dead, and after they waited for more than an hour they thought that I had grown cold and left me for dead. And after they returned home, this Mattio Franzesi learned about it, and he wrote to Messer Benedetto Varchi,* my dearest friend, in Florence, that at such-and-such an hour of the night they had seen me die. Because of this, Messer Benedetto, that greatly talented man and my very close friend, wrote a wonderful sonnet about my false but supposed death, which I shall cite at the proper place. More than three long hours passed before I regained consciousness, and all the remedies of the previously mentioned Master Francesco had been employed when they saw that I had not come to. My dearest friend Felice ran to the house of Master Francesco da Norcia and knocked so hard that he woke him and made him get up, and, in tears, he begged him to come home with him since he thought I had died. To this Master Francesco, who had an extremely choleric character, said: 'Son, what do you think I could do by coming there if he is dead, something that grieves me more than it does you? Do you think that by coming there with my medicine, I could blow in his arsehole and bring him back from the dead?' Seeing that the wretched young man was going away in tears, he called him back and gave him a certain oil to rub on my wrists and chest; he ordered him to squeeze my little toes and fingers very tightly, and if I regained consciousness he should send for him immediately. Felice left and he did just what Master Francesco had told him to do; it was almost daybreak and, believing that my case was hopeless, they gave orders to have me dressed in a shroud and to wash my body. In an instant I came to and called Felice, telling him right then to chase away the old man who was bothering me. Felice wanted to send for Master Francesco, and I told him not to do so but to come over by me, because that old man was moving away quickly and was afraid of him. When Felice drew near to me I touched him, and it seemed as if that old man left in a rage; I therefore begged him to stay by me. Master Francesco appeared and said that he was determined to save me no matter what, and that he had never seen greater strength in a young man in all his days; once he had written a prescription, he made me perfumes, lotions, ointments, plasters, and endless other medications. Meanwhile, I came to with more than twenty leeches fastened to my arse, which had been pricked, bound up, and pounded upon. Many of my friends had come to witness the miracle of the man raised from the dead, and a great number of very important men had appeared; in their presence I declared that the little bit of gold and money I possessed, which must have been around eight hundred scudi between the gold, silver, jewels, and cash, I wished to be given to my poor sister in Florence, whose name was Mona Liperata; all the rest of my property, all my weapons as well as everything else, I wanted my dearest partner Felice to have, as well as fifty gold ducats more, so that he could dress himself properly.* At these words Felice threw himself upon me, declaring that he wanted nothing except for me to live. Then I said: 'If you want me to live, touch me in this way and yell at that old man who is afraid of you.' Some of those present were terrified at my words, since they realized I was not delirious but that I spoke to the point with a sound mind. And so, in this way, my great illness went on changing and I became a bit better. Master Francesco, that fine man, came four or five times a day; Messer Giovanni Gaddi, who was ashamed of himself, did not come to see me again. My brother-in-law, the husband of my sister, appeared: he came from Florence for the inheritance, and because he was a very worthy man he was quite delighted to have found me alive; it gave me endless comfort to see him there; and he immediately displayed his affection for me, declaring that he had come only to treat me with his own hands, and he did so for several days. Then I sent him back to Florence, since I had almost certain hope for recovery. When he departed he left behind the sonnet by Messer Benedetto Varchi, which I cite here:

On the Supposed But Falsely Reported Death of Benvenuto Cellini

Who shall console us, Mattio? Who shall
Forbid death from weeping, since
It is indeed true, alas, that without us and
At the appointed time up to Heaven has fled
That bright and friendly soul, in whom flourished
Such talent that until his days, I believe,
No equal was ever, nor would ever, be seen
In the world, where the best depart first?
Gentle spirit, if outside our mortal veil we can love,
Look down from Heaven upon one who loved you on earth,
And see these tears that mourn your loss, not your great talent.
You have gone to contemplate in Heaven
The Creator, and you see Him living now in the same form
You once shaped with your own learned hands here below.*

85. My sickness had been so severe that it seemed impossible to put an end to it; that worthy man, Master Francesco da Norcia,

worked harder than ever, and each day he brought me new remedies, seeking to strengthen my poor, ravaged body, but despite all his endless labours it seemed impossible to put an end to its raging, so that all the doctors had almost given up in desperation and did not know what else to do. I had an unquenchable thirst, but I had abstained from drinking for many days as they had ordered me to do. Felice, who thought he had done something special in having saved me from danger, never left my side, and that old man gave me no more trouble, but he did visit me on occasion in my dreams. One day Felice had left the house, and my apprentice and a serving-girl named Beatrice had stayed behind to look after me. I asked my apprentice what had happened to Cencio and why it was that he had never attended to my needs. This apprentice told me that Cencio was even more ill than I, and that he was at the point of death. Felice had ordered them not to tell me about this. When he told me about it I was deeply upset; then I called that serving-girl, Beatrice, who was from Pistoia, and begged her to bring me some clear, fresh water in a large crystal container that would keep it cool, which stood nearby. The girl ran off immediately and brought it back to me full. I told her that if she held it to my lips and let me drink a sip from it in my own way, I would give her a new dress. This serving-girl, who had robbed me of certain items of some importance, would have greatly preferred for me to have died for fear that I might discover the theft, and she twice allowed me to drink as much of that water as I wanted, so that without exaggeration I swallowed more than a flask of it; then I covered myself and began to sweat and to fall asleep. When Felice returned later I must have been sleeping for about an hour, and he asked the boy what I was doing. The boy told him: 'I don't know. Beatrice brought him this container full of water, and he drank it all down: now I don't know if he's dead or alive.' They say that this poor young partner of mine was about to collapse on the ground for the great sorrow he felt; then he took a large stick and began beating the serving-girl in desperation, saying: 'Alas, traitor, you've killed him!' While Felice was beating her, she was screaming and I was dreaming; I thought I saw that old man holding some ropes in his hand and showing signs of wanting to tie me up, and Felice rushed up and attacked him with an axe, so that the old man fled, saying: 'Let me go, and I won't come back here for a good long while.' Meanwhile Beatrice was screaming loudly and had run into my bedchamber; this woke me up, and I said: 'Leave her alone, for perhaps by intending to harm me she has done me a great deal of good, and you have not been able, despite all your efforts, to do what she has done: get on with helping me—I'm covered with sweat—and do it quickly.' Felice regained his courage, dried me off, and comforted me, and since I felt a tremendous improvement, I hoped to regain my health. Master Francesco appeared, and when he saw my great improvement and the servant-girl in tears, the apprentice running back and forth, and Felice smiling, this commotion gave the doctor reason to believe that some extraordinary event had occurred which had been the cause of my great improvement. Meanwhile that other Master Bernardino, who at first had not wanted to bleed me, appeared. Master Francesco, that fine man, declared: 'Oh, the power of Nature! She knows her needs and physicians know nothing at all!' Immediately that bird-brain Master Bernardino responded and said: 'If he had drunk one flask more, he would have been cured immediately.' Master Francesco da Norcia, an old man of great authority, replied: 'It was the plague that God should strike you with.' Then he turned to me and asked me if I was able to drink any more water, to which I replied that I was not, because I had completely quenched my thirst. Then he turned to Master Bernardino and said: 'Do you see that Nature has taken precisely what she needed, no more and no less? In the same way, she asked for what she needed when the poor young man asked you to draw his blood: if you knew that regaining his health was a matter of drinking two flasks of water at this point, why didn't you tell us earlier? Then you would have received the credit for the cure.' At these words, the quack doctor went off sulking and never returned. Then Master Francesco ordered me to be taken away from that room, and said that they must have me carried to one of the hills of Rome. Cardinal Cornaro, hearing about my improvement, had me taken to one of his properties on Monte Cavallo;* that very evening I was carried up there with great care on a litter, well covered and without being jostled. When I arrived I began to vomit; and in the vomit that issued forth from my stomach, a hairy worm, as long as a quarter armslength, was found; it had long hair and was extremely ugly, and it was spotted with different colours, green, black, and red; and they kept it to show to the doctor, who declared he had never seen such a thing before, and then he said to Felice: 'Take good care of your friend Benvenuto, now that he's

cured, and don't allow him to commit any excesses, because if he
survived this illness another excess now could kill him. You see, his
illness was so serious that if we had brought him the holy oil* we
would have been too late; now I recognize the fact that, with a bit of
patience and time, he will once again create more beautiful works.'
Then he turned to me and said: 'My dear Benvenuto, be prudent and
don't commit any more excesses, and when you are cured, I want you
to make me an Our Lady with your own hands, as I wish to pray to
her forever out of affection for you.' I then promised him to do so;
afterwards I asked him if I could be transferred as far as Florence.
He then told me that I should wait until I was a little better, and that
we would see what Nature would do.

86. After eight days had passed the improvement was so slight
that I was almost bored with myself, for I had been suffering greatly
for over fifty days; so I made up my mind to leave, and in a pair of
litters my dear friend Felice and I were carried off to Florence, but
because I had not written ahead at all, when I arrived in Florence at
my sister's house she cried and laughed over me at the same time.
That day many of my friends came to see me: among them was Pier
Landi,* who was the greatest and dearest friend I ever had in the
world; the next day a certain Niccolò da Monte Aguto,* who was my
very close friend, arrived because he had heard the Duke say: 'Benvenuto would have done much better to die, since he has come here
to be hanged, and I shall never forgive him for what he's done.'
When Niccolò came to me, he said to me in desperation: 'Alas, my
dear Benvenuto, what have you come here for? Didn't you realize
what you did to offend the Duke? I heard him swear that you had
come to put a noose around your own neck, no matter what.' Then I
replied: 'Niccolò, remind His Excellency that Pope Clement already
tried to do the same thing to me and was greatly in error; and if I am
taken care of and allowed to get well, I'll demonstrate to His Excellency that I have been the most faithful servant he shall ever have in
his entire lifetime; some enemy of mine must have done me this bad
turn out of envy, but if he will wait for my recovery, I'll be able to
give an account of myself that will astonish him.' This bad turn had
been done by the painter from Arezzo, Giorgetto Vassellario,* perhaps in repayment for the many favours I had done him, for I had
put him up in Rome and had paid for his expenses, and he turned my
home upside down because he had a dry leprosy.* He was constantly

scratching it with his hands, and while he was sleeping with a fine young shop assistant of mine named Manno,* he thought he was scratching himself but he skinned off one of Manno's legs with those filthy little hands of his, whose nails he never clipped. Manno left my employ and wanted to kill him, no matter what: I made peace between them, and then I set up the previously mentioned Giorgio with Cardinal de' Medici* and always helped him. This was my reward—he told Duke Alessandro that I had spoken badly of His Excellency and that I had boasted of wanting to be the first to leap up onto the walls of Florence along with the exiled enemies of His Excellency. As I learned later, he had been put up to making such remarks by that fine gentleman Ottaviano de' Medici, who wished to take revenge for the irritation the Duke had shown toward him on account of the coins and my departure from Florence, but since I was innocent of the falsehood attributed to me, I had not the least fear in the world; that good Master Francesco da Montevarchi* treated me with the greatest skill; he had been brought to me by my dearest friend Luca Martini,* who stayed for the better part of the day with me.

87. Meanwhile, I had sent my faithful partner Felice back to Rome to take care of the business there. When I could raise my head up a bit from the pillow, which happened after some fifteen days, although I was unable to walk on my own two feet, I had myself carried into the Medici Palace up to where the little terrace is located: they left me resting there, waiting for the Duke to pass by. And many of my friends at the court came to speak to me, and expressed their great astonishment that I had undergone the discomfort of having myself carried up there in this fashion when I was weak from my illness; they told me that I should have waited to be cured, and then visited the Duke. A number of them were gathered together, and they all looked upon my cure as a miracle, not so much because they had heard I was dead but rather because I looked like a corpse to them. In their presence, I then related how some wicked scoundrel had told my lord the Duke that I had boasted of wanting to be the first to leap up onto His Excellency's city walls, and that subsequently I had spoken badly of him as well. For this reason, I would not have the courage to live or die had I not first cleared myself of such an infamous accusation, and discovered who this reckless scoundrel was who had made this false statement. At these

words a large group of these gentlemen had gathered, and were showing great compassion for me, some saying one thing, some saying another; I said that I wished never to leave that spot until I learned who it was who had accused me. Hearing this, Master Agostino, the Duke's tailor, came up to me from among those gentlemen and said: 'If that is all you want to know, you will learn it right now.' At that precise moment the previously mentioned Giorgio the painter was passing by, and Master Agostino then declared: 'There's the man who accused you: now you can find out for yourself if it's true or not.' Although I was unable to move, I boldly demanded of Giorgio if what had been said was true. Giorgio said no, that it was not true, and that he had never said such a thing. Master Agostino responded: 'You gallows-bird, don't you realize that I know it for certain?' Immediately Giorgio left, declaring that, no, it had not been he. A short time passed and the Duke came by: I immediately had myself raised up before His Excellency, and he stopped. Then I said that I had come there in that condition solely to vindicate myself. The Duke stared at me and marvelled that I was still alive; then he told me to work at being an honourable man and at getting well. After I returned to my home, Niccolò da Monte Aguto came to see me and told me that I had weathered one of the worst storms in the world, something he would never have believed, for he had seen my doom written down in indelible ink, and he said that I should concentrate upon getting well quickly and then be on my way, because the accusation came from a place and from a man who could do me great harm. And then he said: 'Be careful,' and he asked me: 'What offence have you given to that nasty scoundrel Ottaviano de' Medici?' I told him that I had never given him any offence, but that he had certainly given me offence more than once, and I recounted the entire case of the Mint to him, and he replied: 'Go as quickly as you can and remain in good spirits, for you shall have your revenge sooner than you think.' I did concentrate upon getting well: I gave advice to Pietropagolo concerning the stamps for the coins; and then I went off, returning to Rome, and without saying a word to the Duke or anyone else.

88. When I reached Rome* I celebrated a good deal with my friends, and began the Duke's medal. In only a few days I had completed the head in steel, the most beautiful work I had ever done in that genre, and at least once every day a certain idiot named

Francesco Soderini* came to watch, and when he saw what I was making he several times said to me: 'Alas, you bad, cruel man, you want to immortalize this mad tyrant. And since you've never before created something so beautiful, we can see by this that you are our mortal enemy as much as you are their devoted friend, even though both the Pope and the Duke have wrongly tried to have you hanged twice: like father, like son, now beware of the holy spirit!' People held it to be true that Duke Alessandro was the son of Pope Clement. Then this Messer Francesco declared and expressly swore that, if he could, he would have robbed me of the stamps for this medal. To this I replied that he had done well to tell me, and that I would take care that he would never see them again. I made it understood in Florence that Lorenzo should be told to send me the reverse of the medal. Niccolò da Monte Aguto, to whom I had written, wrote me back that he had asked that mad, melancholy philosopher* Lorenzino, who had replied that he could think of nothing else day or night, and that he would do it as soon as he possibly could; Niccolò added, however, that I should not put much hope in getting my reverse, and that I should make one for myself of my very own invention; and once it was finished, I should confidently take it to the Duke, which would be profitable for me. Since I had made the design for a reverse I thought was appropriate, with as much care as possible, I went forward with it, and because I was not completely cured of that lengthy illness, I took more delight in going hunting with my carbine along with my dear partner Felice, who knew absolutely nothing about my profession, but since we were always together, day and night, everyone imagined that he was very proficient in our craft. So, since he was a very agreeable fellow, we laughed together about the great reputation he had acquired a thousand times over, and since his name was Felice Guadagni [Happy Gains], he used to say in jest: 'I should call myself Felice Guadagni-poco [Happy Small Gains], but you have made me acquire such a high reputation that I can call myself Felice De' Guadagni-assai [Happy of the Noble Family of Huge Gains].'* And I told him that there were two ways of gaining money: the first was to gain money for yourself; the second was to gain money for others; and I praised him for the second far more than the first, since he had gained me my life. We had these discussions many times, but in particular on one day around Epiphany,* when we were near the Magliana,* and the day had almost ended:

that day I had killed a great number of ducks and geese with my carbine; and, as I had pretty well decided not to continue hunting, we were moving quickly toward Rome. I called my dog, who was named Barucco,* but not seeing him ahead of me, I turned and saw that this well-trained dog was staring at some geese that had settled down in a ditch. Because of this, I dismounted immediately. After I had prepared my carbine, I shot at them from a great distance and hit two of them with the same ball, for I never wanted to shoot with any other kind of ammunition than a single ball, with which I could shoot as far as two hundred armslengths,* and hit the mark most of the time; with those other methods you cannot do this. Thus, after I hit the two geese, one was almost dead and the other was wounded, and since it was wounded and flew very poorly, my dog chased it and brought it to me; when I saw that the other goose had taken a dive into the ditch, I sprang upon it. Relying upon my boots, which were very high, I thrust my foot forward and sank beneath the ground: even though I had caught the goose, the boot on my right leg was completely full of water. I raised my foot into the air and emptied out the water, and once I had mounted my horse we hurried to return to Rome, but because of the severe cold I felt as if I were freezing, and so I said to Felice: 'I must take care of this leg right now, for otherwise I don't think I can stand it.' That good Felice, without speaking another word, climbed off his horse, gathered up some thistles and twigs, and got ready to make a fire. In the meantime I was waiting for him, and having put my hands between the breast-feathers of the geese, I felt very warm; because of this I stopped him from building the fire, instead filling my boot with the goose-feathers, and I immediately felt so comfortable that it revived me.

89. We mounted our horses and moved steadily toward Rome. When we arrived and were on a little slope it was already night, and looking toward Florence both of us together let out a loud cry of astonishment, saying: 'O God of heaven, what is that tremendous thing we see over Florence?'* It was like a great beam of fire that sparkled and shone with a tremendous splendour. I said to Felice: 'Tomorrow we shall certainly hear about some momentous event that has occurred in Florence.' And so we reached Rome, where it was pitch-black. Upon approaching the Via dei Banchi and our house, my little horse was travelling at a gallop, and a mountain of rubbish and broken tiles had been left in the street that day which

neither my horse nor I could see, so that he charged up it at full speed, then stumbled on the descent, and took a headlong fall: he put his head between his legs, and by the power of God I suffered no harm at all. The noise and commotion brought out the neighbours with their lights, but I jumped to my feet and, without remounting, ran home laughing, for I had escaped the danger of breaking my neck. When I reached my house I found some of my friends there, and while we ate together I described to them the hardships of our hunting trip and that diabolic beam of fire we had seen, and they said: 'What the deuce could all this mean?' I said: 'Some strange event has certainly taken place in Florence.' So we completed our supper most pleasantly, and late on the following day the news of Duke Alessandro's death reached Rome.* Because of this, many of my acquaintances came to me and said: 'You were certainly right that some great event had occurred in Florence.' At this moment that Messer Francesco Soderini came bouncing along on an old mule. Laughing on his way like a madman, he said: 'This is the reverse of the medal of that wicked tyrant your Lorenzino de' Medici had promised you!' Then he added: 'You wanted to immortalize those dukes: we don't want any more dukes!'; and then he jeered at me as if I had been the leader of those sects* that elect dukes. At that point we were joined by a certain Baccio Bettini,* who was an obstinate dolt, and he also jeered at me about the Medici dukes, declaring: 'We've "unduked" them, and there will be no more dukes—and you wanted to immortalize them!', with many other such irritating remarks. As this greatly annoyed me, I said to them: 'You idiots, I'm a poor goldsmith, and I work for whoever pays me, and you're jeering at me as if I were the head of a political faction; but I don't want to reproach you on this account for the greed, madness, and the worthlessness of your predecessors.* Rather, let me say this in response to these idiotic fits of laughter you're having at my expense: before two or three days pass, at the most,* you'll have another duke, perhaps even worse than the last.' The next day Bettini came to my workshop and said to me: 'It's not necessary to spend money on couriers because you know things before they happen: what kind of spirit tells you?' And he informed me how Cosimo de' Medici, the son of Lord Giovanni, had been made Duke, but that he had been named under certain conditions that would limit him so that he could not fly about in his own way. Then it was my turn to laugh at them, and I said:

'These men in Florence have placed a young man upon a marvellous horse; then they have given him spurs and put the bridle freely in his hand, and they have set him upon a beautiful field, where there are flowers, fruits, and many delights; and then they've told him not to pass certain pre-established boundaries: now you tell me who there is who can hold him back when he has decided to cross them? You can't impose laws on a man who is master of the law.' And so they left me alone and caused me no more bother.

90. Having attended to my workshop, I was pursuing some other business dealings which were not of great importance, because I was concentrating upon the recovery of my health and still did not think I was recovered from the serious illness I had gone through. Meanwhile, the Emperor returned victorious from the expedition to Tunis, and the Pope had sent for me and was seeking my advice about what kind of honourable gift I thought should be given to the Emperor. I responded to his question, saying that I thought it would be most appropriate to give His Majesty a golden cross with a figure of Christ, an ornamental work I had almost completed and which would be entirely appropriate and would do great honour to His Holiness and to me. I had already finished three little gold figures in full relief, about a palm's-length in size: these figures were the ones I had begun for the chalice of Pope Clement; they were the representations of Faith, Hope, and Charity, to which I added the base of this cross in wax; and when I took it to the Pope with the figure of Christ in wax, along with many extremely beautiful decorations, he was enormously pleased with it, so that before I left His Holiness we had agreed on everything that was to be done and had estimated the cost of the work. This occurred one evening about four hours after sunset; the Pope had ordered Messer Latino Iuvinale* to have me given money on the following morning. This Messer Latino, who had a big crazy streak, thought he would like to offer a new idea to the Pope, one that was completely his own: he undid all that had been arranged, and in the morning, when I thought I was going to get the money, with that beastly presumption of his he declared: 'It's for us to be the designers and for you to be the workmen. Before I left the Pope yesterday evening we thought up something much better.' At his first words, without allowing him to go any further, I told him: 'Neither you nor the Pope could ever think up something better than a work in which Christ is present; now go ahead and speak as much

of that tedious courtier's nonsense as you know how.' Without another word he left me in a rage, and he sought to have the commission for this work given to another goldsmith. Still, the Pope did not want this, and he immediately sent for me and told me that I had spoken the truth, but that they wanted to make use of a Book of Offices of Our Lady,* which was marvellously illuminated and had cost Cardinal de' Medici more than two thousand scudi to have done. This book would be appropriate as a present for the Empress, while for the Emperor they would later make what I had prepared, which truly was a present worthy of him, but this was being done because time was short and the Emperor was expected in Rome within a month and a half. The Pope wanted the book to have a cover of solid gold, richly decorated and adorned with numerous jewels, which were valued at around six thousand scudi. So, when the jewels and the gold were given to me I set to work on the book, and pressing on with it, I made it look so beautiful in just a few days that the Pope was astonished and showed me the greatest favour, along with an agreement that this beast Iuvinale would not come near me. As this work was nearing completion the Emperor appeared, for whom a great number of triumphal arches had been erected; he arrived in Rome with great pomp, which other writers will describe,* since I want to treat only what concerns me, and upon his arrival he immediately gave the Pope a diamond which he had bought for twelve thousand scudi. The Pope sent for me and gave me this diamond so that I might make a ring to fit His Holiness's finger, but he first wanted me to bring him the prayer book in whatever state of completion it had reached. When I brought the book to the Pope he was very satisfied; then he asked my advice about what excuse he could give the Emperor for why the work was unfinished, and that it must be a valid one. Then I said that the most valid excuse was for me to tell him about my illness, something His Majesty would very easily believe, seeing me as emaciated and pale as I was. This suggestion pleased the Pope a great deal, but when presenting the book I was to add, on His Holiness's behalf, that I was also offering myself as a present, and he told me exactly the manner I was to assume and the words I would have to speak, which I repeated to the Pope while asking him if he liked the way in which I spoke them. He said to me: 'You will speak only too well if you are able to speak to the Emperor in the way you are speaking to me.' Then I replied that I was able to speak to the Emperor with much greater confidence, given that the Emperor went around dressed in the same way as I did, and that to me it would seem like speaking to a man who was made as I was, something which did not occur when I spoke to His Holiness, in whom I saw much greater divinity because of his ecclesiastical garb, which shone with a kind of holy aura for me, along with His Holiness's venerable old age: all these qualities caused me more fear than did those of the Emperor. Upon hearing these words, the Pope said: 'Go, my dear Benvenuto, for you are a good man: do Us honour, and it will be to your advantage.'

91. The Pope prepared two Turkish horses,* which had belonged to Pope Clement and were the most handsome ever to come into Christendom. The Pope ordered his chamberlain, Messer Durante,* to take them down to the corridors of his palace, there to present them to the Emperor, speaking a few words that the Pope had prepared for him. We went downstairs together, and when we reached the Emperor's presence those two horses entered those rooms with such majesty and strength that the Emperor and everyone else marvelled at it. At that moment Messer Durante stepped forward in such a graceless manner and, with his Brescian dialect, became so tongue-tied, that nothing worse was ever seen or heard. It moved the Emperor to laugh a bit. At that point I had already uncovered my work, and when I noticed that the Emperor had turned his eyes toward me with a gracious gesture, I immediately stepped forward and said: 'Sacred Majesty, our Most Holy Pope Paul sends this book of the Madonna as a gift for Your Majesty, which has been written by hand and illuminated by the hand of the greatest man who has ever practised that profession: this rich cover of gold and jewels is incomplete because of my illness, and for this reason His Holiness is making a present of me along with the book, so that I may come along with Your Majesty to finish the book, and in all that you might have in mind to do, for as long as I may live, I shall serve you.' To this the Emperor replied: 'The book is pleasing, and so are you, but I want you to finish it for me in Rome, and when it is finished and you are well, bring it to me and come to see me.' Then, in talking with me, he called me by name, something that astonished me, because no words had been spoken in which my name was mentioned, and he told me he had seen the morse belonging to Pope Clement, on which I had created so many marvellous figures. Thus, we prolonged our

conversation for a full half-hour, speaking of many different things, all of which were useful and pleasing, and since I felt that I had come out of this encounter with much more honour than I had anticipated, having brought our conversation to a conclusion, I made a bow and departed. The Emperor was overheard to say: 'Give Benvenuto five hundred golden scudi immediately.' But the man who carried the money upstairs asked who was the man from the Pope who had spoken to the Emperor. Messer Durante stepped forward and robbed me of my five hundred scudi. I complained about this to the Pope who told me not to worry, because he knew everything, including how well I had conducted myself in speaking to the Emperor, and that I would receive my share of that money no matter what.

92. After returning to my workshop, I set to work with great diligence to finish the diamond ring, for which four jewellers, the finest in Rome, were sent to me, because someone had told the Pope that this diamond had been set by the finest jeweller in the world, whose name was Master Miliano Targhetta,* in Venice, and since the diamond was rather thin this undertaking was too difficult to accomplish without expert advice. I welcomed the four jewellers,* among whom was a Milanese named Gaio. This man was the most presumptuous beast in the world, and a man who knew less but who thought he knew more than anyone else; the other jewellers were the most modest and talented men. This Gaio began to speak before anyone else, and said: 'Keep Miliano's tint,* and to that, Benvenuto, you should tip your cap, because tinting a diamond is the most beautiful and the most difficult part of the jeweller's craft, and Miliano is the greatest jeweller who ever existed in the world, and this is the most difficult diamond.' Then I declared that it was all the more glorious for me to compete with such a talented man in such a worthy profession; then I turned to the other jewellers and said: 'Here, I've saved Miliano's tint, and I'll see if I can improve upon it by making one myself; if not, we can keep the same colour.' This beastly Gaio declared that if I could do it that way he would gladly tip his cap to me. To this I replied: 'So if I do it better, my tint will deserve two tips of your cap.' 'Yes', he admitted, and so I began to make my own tints. With the greatest diligence, I set about making my tints, and in the proper place* I shall explain how to make them: certainly, this diamond was the most difficult that I ever came across, either before or since, and Miliano's tint was very skilfully wrought,

but this fact still did not discourage me. After sharpening the tools of my intellect,* I did it so well that I not only matched Miliano, but I surpassed him by a wide margin. Then after I realized that I had outdone him, I went ahead trying to outdo myself, and with new methods I created a tint that was better, by a long shot, than the first one I had made. Then I summoned the jewellers and I tinted the diamond with Miliano's tint, and after cleaning it off thoroughly, I retinted it with my own. When I showed it off to the jewellers, one of the most talented of them, whose name was Raffaello del Moro, took the diamond in his hand and said to Gaio: 'Benvenuto has surpassed Miliano's tint.' Gaio, who did not want to believe it, took the diamond in hand and declared: 'Benvenuto, this diamond is worth two thousand ducats more than it was with Miliano's tint.' Then I said: 'Since I've outdone Miliano, let's see if I can outdo myself.' Having begged them to wait for me a while, I went up to a small room upstairs and, out of their sight, I retinted the diamond, and when I brought it back to the jewellers Gaio immediately declared: 'This is the most wonderful thing I have ever seen in my life, for this diamond is now worth more than eighteen thousand scudi, whereas we estimated it as barely worth twelve thousand.' The other jewellers turned to Giao and declared: 'Benvenuto is the glory of our craft, and we must tip our caps to his tints and to him, because he deserves it.' Gaio then said: 'I want to go and tell the Pope, and I want him to have a thousand golden scudi for the setting of this diamond.' Running off to the Pope, he told him everything, and for that reason the Pope sent someone three times that day to see if the ring was completed. Then an hour before sunset I took the ring up, and since I was not obliged to wait in the antechamber I discreetly raised the door-curtain and saw the Pope together with the Marquis del Guasto,* who must have been pressing him to do something he did not wish to do, and I heard him say to the Marquis: 'I tell you, no, because I must be neutral and nothing else.'* As I quickly drew back, the Pope himself summoned me: so I quickly entered, and carried that beautiful diamond to him in my hand, the Pope drawing me over to one side, so that the Marquis withdrew. While he looked at the diamond, the Pope said to me: 'Benvenuto, strike up a conversation with me that seems important, and don't ever stop as long as the Marquis remains in the room.' And as he began to walk about the room I felt pleased, since the affair was in my interest, and I began to talk with the Pope about the method I had employed in tinting the diamond. The Marquis just stood there to one side, leaning against a tapestry, and performing contortions now on one leg and now on the other. The subject of our conversation was of such importance that, in order to discuss it thoroughly, it would have taken a full three hours. The Pope took such great pleasure from it that it overcame the annoyance caused him by the Marquis, who was still standing there. I had mixed into our discussion those aspects of philosophy* which belong to our profession, so that after we had been talking for almost an hour the Marquis became annoyed and left, pretty angry; then the Pope treated me with the most loving kindness imaginable, and said: 'Just wait, my dear Benvenuto, for I shall give you a reward for your talents other than the thousand scudi that Gaio knows your labour deserves.' So, when I left, the Pope praised me in the presence of his courtiers, among them this Latino Iuvenale about whom I have spoken before. Since he had become my enemy, he tried with every effort to do me a bad turn, and seeing that the Pope was speaking of me with such affection and resoluteness, he said: 'There is no doubt whatsoever that Benvenuto is a person of the most marvellous talent, but even though every man is naturally held to love people from his own native city more than others, one should still give careful consideration to the manner in which one speaks of a Pope. Benvenuto has been heard to say that Pope Clement was the most handsome prince who ever ruled and that he was just as able, but that he had bad luck, and he says that Your Holiness is completely the opposite, that your tiara weeps on your head,* that you look like a bundle of straw all dressed up, and that you have nothing but good luck.' These remarks had such force, uttered by a man who knew extremely well how to repeat them, that the Pope believed them: I had not only not said them, but to do so had never entered my mind. If the Pope had been able to do so and preserve his honour, he would have done me great harm, but since he was a person of the greatest intelligence he pretended to laugh at such remarks: nevertheless, he kept fostered in himself a boundless hatred toward me, and I began to become aware of it, because I was not allowed to enter his chambers with the same ease as before but rather only with the greatest of difficulty. Since I had been familiar with that court for many years, I imagined that somebody had done me a bad turn, and after making some skilful enquiries, I was told the entire story, but not the identity of the man who did it; I could not imagine who could have said such a thing, but if I had known I would have taken my revenge beyond all bounds.*

93. I applied myself to finishing the little book; and when I had finished it I took it to the Pope, who truly could not hold himself back from praising me lavishly. To this I said that he should send me to take it to the Emperor, as he had promised me. The Pope replied that he would do what seemed best to him, and that I had done what it was my part to do. And so he gave orders that I be well paid. For these works, in a little more than two months I earned nearly five hundred scudi: I was paid for the diamond at the rate of one hundred and fifty scudi and no more; all the rest was given to me for the work on that little book, the craftsmanship of which deserved more than a thousand scudi, since it was a work rich with many figures, foliage, enamels, and jewels. I took what I could get and decided to get out of Rome. Then the Pope sent the little book to the Emperor through a grandson of his named Lord Sforza.* When he presented the book to the Emperor, the Emperor was most grateful and immediately asked about me. The young Lord Sforza, having been instructed, said that since I was ill I had not come. All this was repeated to me. In the meantime I made preparations to go to France, and I wanted to travel alone but I was not able to do so, because of a young man who worked with me named Ascanio;* this young fellow was of a very tender age, and he was the most wonderful servant who ever existed; and when I took him on he had left one of his masters whose name was Francesco,* who was a Spaniard and a goldsmith. Since I had not wished to take on this young man, in order to avoid any disputes with this Spaniard, I said to Ascanio: 'I don't want you, because I might offend your master.' He arranged things so that his master wrote me a note telling me I was free to take him on. So he had been with me for many months, and since he came to us thin and pale, we used to call him Il Vechino;* I thought that he was a little old man, because he served me so well and because he was so knowledgeable; it did not seem reasonable that in a youngster at the age of thirteen, which he said he was, there should be so much ability. Now to return to my story, this Ascanio in those few months gained weight, and after he was rescued from privation he became the most handsome young man in Rome. Because he was as good a servant as I have indicated and learned our craft amazingly well, I

had as great a love for him as if he had been my son, and I kept him
dressed as if he were. When he saw that he had regained his health,
this young man felt he had received a stroke of good fortune to have
fallen into my hands. He often went to thank his former master who
had been the cause of his good luck, and since this master of his had
a beautiful young woman as his wife, she used to say: 'Surgetto,* what
have you done to become so handsome?' Surgetto was what they
called him when he was with them. Ascanio answered her: 'Madonna
Francesca, it was my master who made me so handsome, and much
better as well.' This spiteful little woman took what Ascanio said
very badly, and because she had the reputation of a wanton woman,
she knew how to touch this young man in a way that perhaps went
beyond the boundaries of decency. For this reason, I noticed that he
went many times more than usual to see his master's wife. It happened that one day, after he had given one of our shop-boys a bad
beating, this little boy complained to me in tears just as I arrived,
telling me that Ascanio had beaten him without any reason whatsoever. Hearing this, I said to Ascanio: 'With or without reason,
don't ever touch anyone in my house again, or you will learn that I
myself know how to give someone a beating.' He answered me back,
and so I immediately leaped upon him, and what with punches and
kicks I gave him the severest beating he ever felt. As soon as he could
escape from my clutches he fled, without cloak or cap, and for two
days I never knew where he was, nor did I look for him, but after two
days had passed a Spanish gentleman called Don Diego came to
speak to me. He was the most generous man I ever knew; I had done
and was doing some work for him, so that he had become my very
good friend. He told me that Ascanio had returned to his former
master and asked me, if I would be so good as to return the cap and
cloak that I had given him. To his request, I said that Francesco had
behaved badly and had acted like a man of ill breeding; for if he had
told me immediately that Ascanio had gone to him, since Ascanio
was in his own home, I would very gladly have given him my permission; but since Francesco had kept him there for two days and then
had not let me know anything about it, I did not want Ascanio to
remain with him, and he should make sure that under no condition
would I see him in his home. Don Diego relayed all this: Francesco,
however, made a joke of it. The following morning I saw Ascanio,
who was working on some worthless wire trinkets* at his master's

side. As I passed Ascanio bowed to me, and his master was all but
sneering at me. He sent word to me through that gentleman, Don
Diego, that if I would, I should send back to Ascanio the clothes I
had given him, but that if I would not he did not care, since Ascanio
would not lack for clothes. At these words, I turned to Don Diego
and declared: 'Signor Don Diego, in all that you do I have never seen
anyone either more generous or more honest than you, but this
Francesco is just the opposite of you, since he is a dishonourable
Marrano.* So tell him for me that before vespers sounds, if he hasn't
brought Ascanio back personally right here to my workshop, I'll kill
him no matter what, and tell Ascanio that if he doesn't get out of
there by that hour fixed upon by his master, I'll do not much less to
him.' Signor Don Diego did not make any reply to these remarks,
but he went instead and put such fear into Francesco that he did not
know what to do. Meanwhile Ascanio went to find his father, who
had come to Rome from Tagliacozzi,* which is where he was from,
and when he heard about the quarrel even he advised Francesco that
he should send Ascanio back to me. Francesco then said to Ascanio:
'Go yourself, and your father will go with you.' Don Diego said:
'Francesco, I foresee some terrible trouble: you know better than I do
what Benvenuto is like; don't be afraid to take him back to Benvenuto, and I'll come with you.' I had prepared myself, pacing about
the workshop and waiting for vespers to sound, in a mood for committing one of the most violent deeds I had ever committed in my
entire life. At that moment Don Diego, Francesco, Ascanio, and his
father, whom I did not know, arrived. When Ascanio entered I stared
at them all with eyes full of anger, and Francesco, pale as a corpse,
said: 'Here, I've brought Ascanio back. I kept him without realizing
that I was offending you.' Then Ascanio respectfully said: 'Pardon
me, master, I am here to do everything that you order me to do.'
Then I said: 'Have you come to complete the time that you promised
to put in?' Ascanio said that he had, and that he would never leave
me again. I then turned and told the shop-boy he had beaten to bring
Ascanio the bundle of his clothes, and I said to him: 'Here are all the
clothes I had given you, and with these you may have your freedom
and go wherever you wish.' Don Diego remained astonished about
this, since he was expecting something else altogether. Then
Ascanio, along with his father, begged me to forgive him and to take
him back. After I asked who it was who spoke on his behalf he told

me that it was his father, to whom, after many entreaties I then replied: 'And since you are his father, I shall take him back for your sake.'

94. As I said a short time before, I had decided to leave for France, both because I had seen that the Pope no longer held me in the same esteem as before because of the evil tongues that had cast a bad light on my exceptional service, and also for fear that these people might do even worse to me; I was therefore disposed to seek another country to see if I might better my fortune, and I was going alone. Having decided one evening to depart on the following morning, I said to my faithful partner Felice that he should enjoy all my property until my return, and if it came about that I did not return, I wanted him to have everything. And because I had an apprentice from Perugia* who had helped me finish those works for the Pope, I dismissed him, paying him for his labours. He said to me that he begged me to take him with me, and that he would come at his own expense, for if it happened that I stayed to work for the King of France, it was much better if I had with me my own Italian workmen, especially those people I knew, who would be able to help me. This boy knew so well how to persuade me that I was happy to take him with me on the condition he had offered. Ascanio, present during this conversation and half in tears, said: 'Since you took me back, I said I wanted to stay with you as long as I lived, and this is what I intend to do.' I told him that I did not want him under any condition. The poor young man prepared to follow me on foot. Once I saw that he had made such a decision I got a horse for him too, and after I placed my bag on the horse's back, I loaded myself down with much more equipment that I would otherwise have taken; and I left Rome,* going from there to Florence, and from Florence to Bologna, and from Bologna to Venice, and from Venice I went to Padua, where I was taken from the inn by that very dear friend of mine, Albertaccio del Bene.* Early the next day I went to kiss the hands of Messer Pietro Bembo,* who was not yet a cardinal. Messer Pietro treated me with the greatest kindness ever extended to anyone; then he turned to Albertaccio and said: 'I want Benvenuto to stay here with all his servants, even if he has a hundred of them; so make up your mind that if you want Benvenuto to be with you you must stay here with me, or else I shall not return him to you.' And so I stayed to enjoy the company of this brilliant nobleman. He had prepared a room for me that would have been too honourable for a cardinal, and he constantly wanted me to eat right next to His Lordship. Then he began to drop the most delicate hints, making it clear that he was anxious for me to do his portrait, and since I had no wish to do anything else in the world but that, I made some bright white stucco inside a little box and began to work; on the first day I worked for two hours in a row and sketched out this noble head of his with so much grace that His Lordship was stupefied; and although he was a very great man of letters and a superlative poet, His Lordship understood nothing at all about my profession, because he thought I had finished the work in that space of time while I had hardly begun it, so that I could not make him understand that it required more time to do it well. Ultimately, I decided to do it as best as I knew how in whatever time it required, and because he wore a short beard in the Venetian style, it cost me a tremendous effort to create a head that satisfied me. I finished it, however, and I thought it was the most beautiful work I had ever done, insofar as my craft was concerned. I saw that he was dumbfounded at all this, for he thought that, having made a model in wax in two hours, I should be able to make it in steel in ten hours. But then, when he saw that I hadn't completed the wax image after two hundred hours, and that I was asking for leave to go to France, he was very much put out, and asked me at least to make him a reverse for that medal of his, and this would show the horse Pegasus* framed by a garland of myrtle. I did this in about three hours, giving the model a good, graceful touch; and as he was very satisfied, Bembo said: 'This horse seems to me to be ten times more difficult to execute than that little head, over which you took such pains: I cannot grasp the difficulty in it.' Still, he told me and begged me to finish it in steel for him, as he said: 'Do it for me as a favour, because you could do it very quickly if you wanted.' I promised him that, although I did not want to do it there, when I settled down to work I would do it for him without fail. While we were giving more consideration to this matter I went to make a bargain for three horses to go to France, and Messer Bembo, in secret, made certain I was well treated, because he enjoyed the greatest authority in Padua, so that when I wanted to pay for the horses, which I settled on at a price of fifty ducats, their owner said: 'Since you're a man of such talent I'm making you a present of the three horses.' To this offer I replied: 'You're not the person who is giving me the gift, and I don't want to accept them from the person who is offering them, since I've not yet been able to do any of my work for him.'* The good man told me that if I did not take those horses I would not find any other horses in Padua, and would be obliged to travel on foot. At this, I went to the magnificent Messer Pietro, who pretended to know nothing about this and yet again greeted me kindly, telling me that I should stay over in Padua. Since I did not want to do this at all, and was ready to go no matter what, I was forced to accept the three horses, and with them I set off.

95. I took the route through the Swiss canton of Grisons, since the other roads were unsafe because of the wars.* We passed over the Albula and the Bernina passes: it was the eighth day of May and the snow was very deep. With very great danger to our lives, we passed over these two mountains. Once we had crossed them we stopped at a city that, if I remember correctly, was called Valdistà:* there we took lodgings. During the evening we ran into a Florentine courier whose name was Busbacca.* I had heard that this courier was a trustworthy man who was skilled in his profession, and I did not know that he had fallen on hard times through his rascally behaviour. When he saw me at the inn he called me by name, and said to me that he was going to Lyons on important business, and asked, as a favour, if I would lend him money for the journey. To this I replied that I did not have any money to lend him, but that if he wanted to come along with me I would gladly pay his expenses as far as Lyons. This scoundrel shed some tears and paid me beautiful compliments, explaining to me that, 'in matters of importance for the nation, when a poor courier lacks money a man like you is obliged to help him'; he added that he was, moreover, carrying things of the greatest importance belonging to Messer Filippo Strozzi; and since he had a goblet case covered in leather, he whispered in my ear that inside that case was a silver goblet, that inside the goblet were jewels worth many thousands of ducats, and that there was also a letter of the utmost importance which Messer Filippo Strozzi was sending. To this I replied that he should allow me to conceal the jewels on his person, which would be less dangerous than carrying them in that goblet, that he should leave the goblet, worth around ten scudi, with me, and that I would lend him twenty-five scudi. To this proposal the courier said that he would come with me, not being able to do anything else, since to leave the goblet behind would not be honourable. So we cut the

discussion short, and after departing on the following morning, we reached a lake located between Valdistate and Vessa;* this lake is fifteen miles long at the point where it reaches Vessa. After I examined the boats on the lake I became frightened, for these boats were made of fir, they were not very big nor very strong, and they were not nailed together, nor coated with pitch; and if I had not seen four German gentleman board another similar boat with their four horses I would never have set foot in this one; I would have far sooner turned back, but upon seeing their recklessness, I thought to myself that these German waters would not drown you the way those in Italy do. Nevertheless my two young companions said to me: 'Benvenuto, it's a dangerous undertaking to go aboard with four horses.' To them I replied: 'Haven't you cowards seen how those four gentlemen who went on board ahead of us are going on their way laughing? If this were wine rather than water, I'd say that they are going off happily to drown themselves, but since it's water I know very well that they're no more delighted at the thought of drowning than we are.' This lake was fifteen miles long and about three miles wide; on one side there was a very high, cavernous mountain, while on the other it was flat and grassy. When we were some four miles out a storm began to blow up on the lake, so that the oarsmen asked us if we would help them row, and we did so for a stretch. I made gestures to them and said that they should land us on the other shore; they said it was impossible, because the water was not sufficient to float the boat and that the shoals over there would immediately break up the boat and drown us all; and they went on asking us to help them. The boatmen began to shout to one another, asking for help. Once I saw that they were terrified, since I had a well-trained horse, I fastened its bridle around its neck and took one end of the halter in my left hand. The horse, which possessed, as they often do, some intelligence, seemed to sense what I wanted to do, for having turned his head toward the fresh grass, I wanted him to drag me along with him as he swam. At that moment such an enormous wave rose up from the lake that it swamped the boat. Ascanio was screaming: 'Mercy, father, help me!', and he wanted to throw himself upon me: because of this, I put my hand on my small dagger and told them to do what I had instructed them to do, since the horses would surely save their lives and that was the way I, too, hoped to escape from danger; but that if Ascanio threw himself upon me again I would kill him. So we went forward for a few miles in this mortal danger.

96. When we were halfway down the lake we spotted a bit of flat land where we could rest, and I saw that the four German gentlemen had disembarked there. When we wanted to disembark, the boatman absolutely refused. Then I said to my young companions: 'Now is the time to give a good account of ourselves: so draw your swords, and let's force them to put us ashore.' We did so with great difficulty, because they put up great resistance. Still, after we had landed we had to climb two miles up the mountainside, which was more difficult than climbing up a stepladder. I was fully armed in a coat of mail, with heavy boots and a musket in my hand, and the rain was as heavy as God knows how to make it. Those devils of German gentlemen made miraculous progress holding their horses by their bridles, but because our horses were not suitable for this purpose, we were utterly exhausted from forcing them to climb up this difficult mountain. When we were part of the way up, Ascanio's horse, which was a wonderful Hungarian animal, was a short distance ahead of Busbacca the courier, and Ascanio had given Busbacca his lance so that he could help him carry it; it happened that, because of the poor footing, the horse slipped and staggered back so forcefully that, completely helpless, it impaled itself on the tip of the lance being carried by that rascal of a courier, who had not had the good sense to move it aside; and when it pierced the horse through the throat from one side to the other, the other shop-boy of mine, anxious to help his own horse, a black one, slipped toward the lake but saved himself by holding on to a very tiny shrub. This horse was carrying a pair of saddle bags which held all my money and everything of value I owned; I told the young fellow to save his life and to let the horse go to the devil: the drop was more than a mile at a steep pitch, and it went directly into the lake. Right below this spot those boatmen of ours had stopped, so that if the horse fell he would land right on top of them. I was ahead of everyone and we stood there to watch the horse fall, since we thought it would most certainly be lost. At that moment I said to my young companions: 'Don't worry at all, let's save ourselves and thank God for everything: I feel badly only about that poor Busbacca, who tied his goblet and jewels, which are worth several thousand ducats, to the horse's saddle thinking that it would be safer: my property amounts to a few hundred scudi, and I'm not afraid of anything in the world, so long as I have God's grace.' Busbacca then said: 'I'm not bothered about my loss, but I'm very sorry about yours.' I asked him: 'Why does my small loss make you sorry while your great loss doesn't bother you?' Then Busbacca said: 'In God's name, I'll explain it to you: in such matters and in the straits we find ourselves, I have to tell the truth. I know that your losses are in scudi and are real ones, but that goblet case of mine, which I said contained so many jewels and about which I told so many lies—it's completely full of caviar.' Hearing this, I could do nothing but laugh: those young companions of mine laughed; he cried. That horse saved itself after we had given it up for lost. And so, laughing, we regained our courage and set out to climb up the mountain once again. Those four German gentlemen, who had reached the crest of this steep mountain before we had, sent some people to assist us, so that we reached those rustic lodgings where, being thoroughly soaked, exhausted, and famished, we were most pleasantly received; there we dried ourselves off, rested, and satisfied our hunger, and with some wild herbs we treated our wounded horse; they taught us that if we kept the wound constantly filled with this kind of herb, of which the hedges were full, the horse would not only be cured but would serve us as if he had no wound at all: and this is what we did. After we had thanked the gentlemen and felt greatly refreshed, we departed and went forward, giving thanks to God who had saved us from that great danger.

97. We arrived at a town beyond Vessa, where we rested for the night and heard, at every hour of the night, a guard who sang in a most pleasing manner, and since all the houses of these towns were made of pine-wood, the guard said nothing else but be careful of fire. Busbacca, who had been terrified during the day, called in his sleep at every hour when the guard sang out, yelling: 'Alas, oh my God, I'm drowning!' This was due to the fright of the day before; and in addition he had got drunk during the evening, because he wanted to compete in drinking that evening with all the Germans who were there; and sometimes he would say 'I'm burning up'; and sometimes 'I'm drowning': he thought he was being tortured in the infernal regions with that caviar hanging around his neck. This night was so cheerful that all our troubles were transformed into laughter. In the morning we arose to beautiful weather, and we went to eat at a charming town called Lacca.* There we were treated marvellously

well: we then took on guides, who were on their return trip from a town called Surich.* The guide led us along a dyke on the shore of a lake, and there was no other road; this dyke was still covered with water, so that this stupid guide slipped, and he and his horse went under the water. I was directly behind the guide, and I stopped my horse and stood to watch the idiot climb out of the water, and just as if nothing had happened he began to sing once again and motioned to me that I should go ahead. I plunged toward the right and broke through a few hedges, and in this fashion I led the way for my young companions and Busbacca. The guide yelled, telling me in German that if the people of that area saw me they would have me killed. We moved on and escaped that additional danger as well. We arrived in Surich, a marvellous city, sparkling as a jewel. We rested there for an entire day, and then in the morning we left in good time and reached another beautiful city called Solutorno;* from there we reached Usanna;* from Usanna we went to Geneva; and from Geneva to Lyons, all the while singing and laughing. In Lyons I rested for four days, and I had a very good time with some friends of mine; I was reimbursed for the expenses I had incurred for Busbacca; then at the end of four days I took the road for Paris. This was a pleasant trip except for when we reached Palissa,* where a band of highwaymen tried to murder us, and with no little valour, we saved ourselves. Then we reached Paris without any problems at all: always singing and laughing, we reached safety.

98. After I had relaxed for a while in Paris, I went to see Rosso the painter,* who was in the service of the King.* I thought this Rosso was the best friend I had in the world, because I had done him the greatest favours in Rome that one man could ever do for another, and since these favours can be described in a few words I do not wish to avoid mentioning them, to show how shameless ingratitude is. When he was in Rome he had spoken so badly with his wicked tongue about the works of Raphael of Urbino that Raphael's pupils wanted to kill him, no matter what: I saved him from that danger, protecting him day and night with great effort. Furthermore, because he spoke badly of Master Antonio da San Gallo,* a most excellent architect, Antonio had a work taken away from him that Messer Agnol da Cesi* had commissioned him to do; then Antonio began to work against Rosso so effectively that Rosso was brought to the point of dying from hunger; and as a result, I loaned him many tens of scudi to live

on. And since I had not yet been repaid, knowing that Rosso was in the service of the King, I went, as I said, to visit him: I did not really think that he would return my money to me, but I did think that he would give me some assistance and support in order to place myself in the service of that great king. When Rosso saw me he suddenly became upset, and he said to me: 'Benvenuto, you've come at too great expense on such a lengthy journey, especially in these times when people are attending to the business of war and not to our trifling works.' In answer to this, I said that I had brought enough money with me to enable me to return to Rome in the same manner in which I had come to Paris; that this was not the return I expected for the efforts I had made for him; and that I was beginning to believe what Maestro Antonio da Sangallo had said about him. He wished to treat the whole matter as a joke, since he had recognized his own mean behaviour, and I showed him a letter of exchange for five hundred scudi on the account of Ricciardo del Bene.* This rascal was then ashamed and although he wanted to keep me there practically by force, I laughed at him and went off with a painter who was there with us. People called this painter Sguazzella,* and he was also a Florentine: I went to stay at his house, with three horses and three servants at so much per week. He treated me extremely well, and I paid him even better. Then I sought to speak to the King, to whom I was introduced by a certain Messer Giuliano Buonaccorsi, his treasurer.* I waited for a good long while to do so, for I did not know that Rosso was working very diligently to make sure I did not speak to the King. When Messer Giuliano became aware of this, he immediately took me to Fontainebleau* and brought me straight before the King, with whom I was granted an audience of an entire hour. And because the King was preparing to go to Lyons,* he told Messer Giuliano that he would take me along with him, and that along the way we would discuss some beautiful works that His Majesty had in mind to commission. So I went off in the train of the court, and along the way I paid great deference to the Cardinal of Ferrara,* who had not yet received his cardinal's hat. And since I had lengthy discussions with the cardinal every evening, His Lordship told me I ought to stay in Lyons at one of his abbeys, where I could enjoy myself until the King returned from the war; the King was heading towards Grenoble, but at the abbey in Lyons I would have every convenience. When we reached Lyons I fell ill, and my young

Ascanio came down with the quartan fever, so that I became heartily sick of the French and their court, and it seemed like a thousand years before I could return to Rome. When the Cardinal saw me ready to return to Rome, he gave me enough money to make him a basin and a ewer of silver in Rome. So we returned to Rome mounted on some very good horses, going through the Sempione mountains, accompanied by some Frenchmen with whom we travelled for some distance, Ascanio with his quartan fever and I with a persistent feverishness that seemed as if it would never leave me; my stomach was so upset that I do not believe I was able to eat an entire loaf of bread during the week, and I was very eager to reach Italy, eager to die in Italy and not in France.

99. After we had passed over the Sempione mountains, we came upon a river near a place called Indevedro.* This river was very wide, extremely deep, and across it was a long and narrow little bridge, without railings. That morning there had been a very thick frost, and when I reached the bridge I found myself in front of everyone, and recognizing that the bridge was very dangerous, I ordered my young companions and servants to dismount and lead their horses by hand. So I crossed the bridge very easily, and went along talking with one of the two Frenchmen, who was a gentleman; the other was a notary, who had remained a little way behind and who made fun of this French gentleman and me, because we had preferred the discomfort of going on foot when there was nothing to fear. I turned around, and seeing him in the middle of the bridge, I begged him to tread carefully since he was in a very dangerous place. This man, who could not suppress his French character, told me in French that I was a man of little courage and that there was no danger at all there. While he was uttering those words he tried to spur on his horse a bit, as a result of which the horse immediately slid off the bridge and, with its legs turned skywards, fell beside an enormous rock. And because God is frequently merciful to the mad, this beast of a man along with the beast he was riding fell into an enormously deep pool, where they went under, both he and his horse. As soon as I saw this, with the greatest possible speed I broke into a run and, with great difficulty, I leaped upon that rock and, leaning down from it, caught hold of the edge of the gown the notary was wearing, and I pulled him up by it while he was still under the water. Because he had swallowed so much water he was just short of having been drowned,

and when I saw that he was out of danger I congratulated him on having escaped with his life. At this, he replied to me in French and told me I had done nothing at all, that the important thing was his documents, which were worth many tens of scudi; and it appeared that he was angry as he spoke to me, all drenched and sputtering. In reply, I turned to some guides who were with us and ordered them to assist this beast of a man, saying that I would pay them. One of those guides courageously, and with great effort, began to help him and fished out his documents so that he did not lose anything; the other guide never bothered to lift a finger to help him. When we later arrived at the place mentioned above, we had made up a common purse which it was my job to manage, and after we had eaten I gave a good deal of money from the purse of our company to the guide who had helped pull the notary from the water; the notary told me I should take money for that purpose out of my own pocket, since he did not intend to give him anything but what we had agreed upon for doing no more than fulfilling his duty as a guide. At this, I spoke to him very offensively. Then the second guide, the one who had not lifted a finger, confronted me and wanted me to pay him as well, and because I said: 'Only the man who has carried the cross deserves the reward,' he replied that he would very shortly show me a cross that would cause me to weep. I said to him that I would light a candle to that cross, since I hoped he would be the first to shed a tear. And since the place was on the frontier between the Venetians and the Germans,* the guide ran off to seek help and returned with a crowd of people and bearing a large spear in front of him. I was mounted on my good horse, and I lowered the muzzle of my arquebus: turning to my companions, I declared: 'First I shall kill the guide; the rest of you all do your duty, since these fellows are highway robbers and they have seized upon this flimsy excuse for the sole purpose of murdering us.' The landlord, from the inn where we had eaten, called over one of the leaders, who was an older man, and he begged him to put an end to the trouble, telling him: 'This is a very brave young man, and even if you cut him to pieces he will kill so many of you, and will perhaps still escape from your clutches after doing his worst.' The turmoil quietened down, and the older leader said to me: 'Go in peace: you wouldn't have been able to do anything even if you had a hundred men with you.' I recognized that he was speaking the truth, and had already resolved to die and considered myself a dead man, but when I no longer heard any more insults, shaking my head I said: 'I would have done everything in my power to show you the life and manliness that's in me.' Continuing our journey, that evening at the first lodging we settled our accounts, and I parted from that bestial Frenchman while remaining on good terms with the other one, who was a gentleman, and with my three horses we went on alone to Ferrara. After I had dismounted I went to the Duke's court to pay my respects to His Excellency, so that I might leave on the following morning for Santa Maria dal Loreto.* I waited until two hours after sunset, and then the Duke appeared: I kissed his hands and he gave me a very warm welcome and ordered that water for my hands be brought.* Because of this, I said jokingly: 'Most Excellent Lord, for over four months I have eaten so little that it seems a man could not survive on so small an amount. Nonetheless, realizing that I could not enjoy the regal fare of your table, I shall stay and chat while Your Excellency dines, and thus at one and the same time you and I shall take greater pleasure than if I had dined with you.' And so we struck up a conversation and passed the time until the fifth hour after sundown. Then, at the fifth hour, I took my leave, and when I went back to my inn I found the table marvellously set, because the Duke had sent me the leftovers from his own meal, with a great deal of good wine, and since it was two hours past my usual mealtime I ate with great appetite, the first time in four months I had been able to do so.

100. When I left on the following morning I went to Santa Maria dal Loreto, and there, after I had said my prayers, I travelled to Rome,* where I found my faithful Felice to whom I had left my workshop with all its tools and furnishings; I opened another much larger and more spacious workshop beside Sugherello the perfumer; and I thought that the great King Francis would no longer remember me. For this reason, I accepted commissions for many works from different gentlemen, and in the meantime I worked on that ewer and basin I had agreed to make for the Cardinal of Ferrara. I had many workmen and many large commissions in gold and in silver. I had entered into an agreement with my workman from Perugia* that he would himself write down all the money that had been spent on him—money spent on his clothing and on many other things; with the expenses from the journey, it came to around seventy scudi, which, we agreed, he would pay off at the rate of three scudi each month, since I paid him more than eight. After two months this scoundrel ran off from my workshop and left me tied up with many jobs, and he said that he did not want to pay me anymore. For this reason, I was advised to recover my money through legal means, although I had it in mind to cut off his arm; I would surely have done so, but my friends said that it would not be well to do such a thing; it might turn out that I would lose my money and perhaps lose Rome yet again, for blows are not exchanged by agreement;* and with the document written in his own hand, I could have him arrested immediately. I followed their advice, but wanted to move the matter ahead more quickly. I brought the suit, in fact, before the Auditor of the Pontifical Camera and won the case; by virtue of that verdict, which took several months, I subsequently had him thrown into prison. My workshop was charged with the most important commissions, and among them were all the golden ornaments and the jewels for the wife of Lord Gerolimo Orsino, the father of Lord Paolo, now the son-in-law of our Duke Cosimo.* The works were very nearly completed, and all the while my important commissions increased. I had eight workmen and, both for honour and for profit, I toiled together with them day and night.

101. While I pursued my undertakings so energetically, a letter came to me sent with great despatch from the Cardinal of Ferrara, who wrote in this tone: 'Benvenuto, our dear friend. In these past days the great and most Christian King* remembered you, saying that he desired to have you in his service. I replied that you had promised me that any time I sent for you on His Majesty's behalf, you would come immediately. At these words, His Majesty said: "I want him to be sent fare for the trip, according to what a man of his sort deserves." And he immediately ordered his Admiral* to pay me a thousand golden scudi from the treasurer of the Exchequer. Cardinal de' Gaddi* was present at this conversation, and he immediately stepped forward and told His Majesty that His Majesty had no need to give such an order, for he said that he had sent you enough money and that you were on your way. Now if the opposite happens to be true, as I believe is the case, after you receive my letter respond immediately, for I shall be back in touch and have you sent the money promised by this magnanimous king.'

Now let the entire world and all those who inhabit it witness how much the malignant stars and adverse fortune can do to us human beings! I had not spoken two times in all my days to this little fool of a wretched Cardinal de' Gaddi;* and this presumption of his was not meant to do me any harm at all, but rather he did it only out of stupidity and simple-mindedness, trying to show that he, too, had dealings with talented men that the King desired to have in his service, just as the Cardinal of Ferrara had. But he was so foolish that after saying what he did, he said nothing to me, for I would have certainly found some excuse to cover up his foolish presumption in order not to cast blame on a foolish puppet, out of love for my native city. When I had the letter from the Most Reverend Cardinal of Ferrara, I immediately answered that I knew nothing at all about the Cardinal de' Gaddi and that if he had made such a proposal I would not have left Italy without informing His Most Reverend Lordship, especially because I had in Rome a greater quantity of commissions than I had ever enjoyed in the past; but at a word from His Most Christian Majesty, relayed to me by such a great lord as His Most Reverend Lordship, I would depart immediately, throwing every other consideration aside. After sending my letters, that traitor of a Perugian workman of mine thought of another act of malice that immediately succeeded, because of the avarice of Pope Paul Farnese but even more because of that bastard son of his, then called the Duke of Castro.* This workman led one of the secretaries of this Signor Pier Luigi to understand that, after he had been with me as a worker for several years, he knew all my business, and as a result, he assured Signor Pier Luigi that I was a man with a patrimony worth more than eighty thousand ducats, and that the greatest part of this money I held in the form of precious stones; that these jewels belonged to the Church, and I had stolen them during the time of the Sack of Rome in Castel Sant'Angelo; and that they should seek to arrest me quickly and secretly. One morning I had worked more than three hours before daybreak on the commissions for the previously mentioned bride;* and while my workshop was opened and being swept out, I had put on my cloak to take a brief walk; after taking the path through Via Giulia, I emerged at the corner of the Chiavica, where the constable Crespino* with all of his policemen met me and said: 'You're the prisoner of the Pope.' To this I said: 'Crespino, you've arrested me by mistake.' 'No,' said Crespino, 'you're the brilliant Benvenuto and I know you very well, and I have to take you to the Castel Sant'Angelo, where gentlemen and talented men like you go.'* Because four of his corporals threw themselves upon me and violently tried to remove a dagger I wore by my side and some rings from my fingers, this Crespino said to them: 'Let none of you touch him: it's quite enough that you do your duty and stop him escaping from me.' Then he came up to me and courteously asked for my weapon. While I was giving him my weapon, I realized that I had murdered Pompeo on precisely this spot. From there they took me to Castel Sant'Angelo and locked me up as a prisoner in a room up in the keep. This was the first time I ever had a taste of prison in all my thirty-seven years.

102. When Signor Pier Luigi, the Pope's son, considered the great sum of money I was accused of stealing, he immediately asked his father the Pope to do him the favour of giving him that sum of money as a gift. The Pope, therefore, gladly granted him the money and told him, moreover, that he would help him to get it back, so that after I had been kept locked in prison for eight whole days, at the end of that time, to bring the affair to a conclusion, they sent me to be interrogated. For this purpose I was called into one of those rooms in the Castello which belong to the Pope, a very honourable place, and the interrogators included the Governor of Rome, whose name was Messer Benedetto Conversini, who came from Pistoia and later became Bishop of Jesi;* another was the Procurator Fiscal, whose name I have forgotten;* the other, the third, was the criminal judge, whose name was Messer Benedetto da Cagli. These three men began to interrogate me, first with friendly remarks, but then with the most harsh and frightening words, caused by my saying to them: 'My lords, for more than half an hour you have not ceased asking me about fantastic events and other things, so that truly one can say that you're chattering or that you're merely talking: by chattering, I mean that your words have no meaning; by mere talking, I mean that you are saying nothing; so, I beg you to tell me what you want from me, so that I might hear reasoned arguments issue forth from your mouths instead of mere talk or chatter.* At these words, the Governor, who was from Pistoia and could no longer disguise his ugly nature, said to me: 'You speak very confidently—rather too arrogantly; so much so that I shall humble your arrogance lower than a puppy in the face of the reasoned arguments you shall hear from me; this will be neither chattering nor mere talk, as you put it, but a coherent set of arguments which you will absolutely have to do your best to answer.' And he began in this fashion: 'We know for

certain you were in Rome at the time of the Sack, which was inflicted upon this unfortunate city; that during this time you were in this Castel Sant'Angelo, where you were employed as a gunner; and since your trade was that of a goldsmith and a jeweller, Pope Clement, who had known you previously, summoned you secretly because there were no other persons of your profession there, and he had you remove all the precious stones from his tiaras, mitres, and rings. Then, since he trusted you, he wanted you to sew them into his clothing, and while doing so you set aside for yourself, without the knowledge of His Holiness, a quantity of stones worth eighty thousand scudi. This was told to us by one of your workmen, in whom you confided and to whom you boasted about it. Now we say to you openly: either find the stones or the value of the stones—then we shall allow you to go free.'

103. When I heard these words I could not keep myself from bursting out laughing; and then, after I had laughed a bit, I said: 'I gratefully thank God for the fact that when, for the first time, it has pleased His Divine Majesty to have me imprisoned, I am fortunate not to have been imprisoned for some minor matter, as is usually the case with young men. If what you are saying were the truth, there would be no danger of my suffering capital punishment, since the law at that time had lost all its authority; therefore, I might excuse myself by saying that, as the Pope's minister, I had kept guard over this treasure on behalf of the Sacred and Holy Apostolic Church, waiting for the chance to return it to a good pope, or indeed to the person who asked me for it, which would now be you, if things were as you say they were.' Upon hearing these words, the enraged Governor from Pistoia did not allow me to finish my argument, for he said furiously: 'Put it any way you like, Benvenuto, all we want is to have our property back again, and be quick about it if you don't want us to use more than words.' And as they prepared to stand up and leave, I said to them: 'My Lords, I'm not yet finished with this examination, so finish examining me, and then you may go where you please.' Immediately they began to sit back down, but they were obviously very angry, looking as if they did not wish to hear another word I told them, and so—half-seated, half-standing up—they gave the impression of having discovered all they wanted to know. For this reason, I began in this tone: 'My Lords, you must know that I've lived in Rome for about twenty years, and I've never been put in prison either here or elsewhere.' At these words, that obnoxious snoop of a Governor said: 'You have certainly killed some men.' Then I said: 'You say so, not I, but if somebody came to kill you, even though you are a priest, you would defend yourself, and the holy laws would tolerate your killing the assassin; allow me, therefore, to present my arguments, if you want to refer this to the Pope and if you want to be able to judge me fairly. Once again, let me say that I've lived in this marvellous city of Rome for nearly twenty years, and in this city I've executed some very great works of art in my profession. Because I know that Rome is the Holy See of Christ, I've always been certain that, if a temporal ruler wished to do me some harm, I should have recourse to this Holy Throne and to this Vicar of Christ, who would defend my rights. Alas, where must I go now? And which ruler will defend me from such a wicked, murderous attack? Before you arrested me, shouldn't you first have discovered where I had disposed of these eighty thousand ducats? Shouldn't you also look at the record of the jewels that this Apostolic Camera has carefully kept for the last five hundred years? Then, when you had discovered something missing, shouldn't you have seized all my account books along with me? I can tell you that the account books in which all the jewels and tiaras of the Pope are inscribed are completely intact, and you won't discover anything missing that belonged to Pope Clement that is not carefully noted in them. It could only have happened that when that poor man, Pope Clement, wanted to make peace with those thievish imperial forces that had robbed Rome and brought shame upon the Church, someone called Cesere Iscatinaro, if I remember correctly, came to negotiate the settlement.* After this man had almost concluded the agreement with that defeated Pope, in order to do him a small courtesy the Pope allowed a diamond ring worth about four thousand scudi to fall from his fingers, and because this Iscatinaro bent down to pick it up, the Pope told him to keep the ring out of affection for him. I witnessed these events in person, and if that previously mentioned diamond were missing, I could tell you where it went, but I am completely confident that you'll still find it recorded. Then you might, on your part, be ashamed at having attacked a man of my sort, who has executed so many honourable projects for this Apostolic See. You should know that, had I not been the sort of man I am, the morning that the imperial troops entered the Borgo* they would have entered the Castello with no opposition whatsoever, and without being rewarded for it I threw myself vigorously upon the artillery pieces that the gunners and the soldiers of the fortress had abandoned, and I gave courage to one of my companions, by the name of Raffaello da Montelupo, the sculptor,* who had also given up and had hidden in a corner, completely terrified and doing nothing; I aroused him, and he and I alone killed so many enemy troops that the soldiers took another path. I was the one who fired the arquebus at Scatinaro, because he had spoken to Pope Clement with no respect but with a foul sneer, like the wicked Lutheran he was. For this reason Pope Clement searched the Castello for who might have done this, in order to hang him. I was the man who wounded the Prince of Orange with an arquebus-shot to his head, there below the trench of the Castello. Besides this, I have created a great many ornaments in silver, gold, and precious stones for the Holy Church, and a great many medals and coins that are both beautiful and praiseworthy. Is this, then, the proud priestly reward that you bestow upon a man who has served and loved you with so much faith and ability? Now go and repeat everything I have said to the Pope, telling him that he has all his jewels, and that I never had anything from the Church except the wounds and bruises from stones I got at the time of the Sack, and that I have never counted upon anything but a small remuneration from Pope Paul, which he had promised me. Now I'm quite clear about both His Holiness and you, his ministers.' While I spoke these words, they stood listening to me, astonished, and, looking one other in the face, they left me in amazement. They all three went of one accord to report everything I had said to the Pope. The Pope, feeling ashamed, ordered a very careful review of all the accounts regarding the jewels. Later, when they saw that nothing was missing, they left me in the Castello without saying anything else; Signor Pier Luigi, even though he felt he had been wrong, sought most diligently to bring about my death.

104. During the brief space of time in which these disturbing events took place, King Francis had already heard in detail how the Pope was keeping me in prison and what a great injustice it was. After he had sent as his ambassador to the Pope one of his gentlemen, whose name was Monsignor di Morluc,* he wrote to him that he should ask the Pope to hand me over as one of His Majesty's men. The Pope, who was a highly talented and marvellous man, but who

comported himself in this affair of mine like a worthless idiot, replied to the King's messenger that His Majesty should not trouble himself about me, since I was a man who was very dangerous when armed, and on that account he was giving His Majesty warning to leave me be, because he was keeping me in prison for murders and other wicked deeds I had committed. The King once again replied that in his kingdom high justice reigned, and just as His Majesty rewarded and granted the most marvellous favours to men of ability, so he punished those who caused trouble; he added that, since His Holiness had allowed me to leave and had not really cared about the said Benvenuto's service, when the King saw him in his kingdom, he had most gladly taken him into his service; he asked that I be released as one of His Majesty's own men. These events brought me the greatest trouble and harm, even though they also involved the most splendid favours that could possibly be desired by a man of my station. The Pope fell into such a rage, out of fear that I would go and tell about the shockingly wicked way in which I had been treated, that he thought of every means by which he could put me to death without compromising his honour. The Castellan of Castel Sant'Angelo was one of our Florentines whose name was Messer Giorgio, a knight of the Ugolini family. This worthy man showed the greatest courtesy toward me that could be imagined, allowing me to walk around the Castello freely upon my word of honour alone, and because he understood the great wrong that had been done to me, when I wanted to give him something in security for allowing me to walk freely around the Castello, he said to me that he could not accept it, since the Pope was too interested in my case, but that he would freely trust my word of honour, because everyone knew what a worthy man I was: I gave him my word of honour, and in this manner he gave me the opportunity to do a little bit of work. Meanwhile, thinking that the Pope's wrath, both because of my innocence and the King's favour, must come to an end, I still kept my shop open, and my apprentice Ascanio used to come to the Castello to bring me some things to work on. Although I was able to do very little work, seeing myself imprisoned in such a fashion for so great a wrong, I nevertheless made a virtue of a necessity: as happily as I could, I bore up under the perversity of my fortune. I became very friendly with all the guards and many soldiers in the Castello. Since the Pope used to come on occasion for supper at the Castello, during the time the Pope was there the Castello remained unguarded but completely open like an ordinary palace, and although when the Pope was there in this way they usually locked up all the prisoners with greater care, none of these things was done to me, for on all these occasions I went about freely throughout the Castello; and several times some of the soldiers advised me to escape, saying they would give me their support since they recognized the great wrong that had been done to me: I answered them that I had given my word of honour to the Castellan, who was such a worthy man and had done me so many kindnesses. One very brave and resourceful soldier told me: 'My dear Benvenuto, you should know that anyone who is in prison is not obliged, nor can he be obliged, to keep his word of honour any more than anything else; do as I tell you: get away from this rascal of a Pope and his bastard son, who will, at any cost, take your life.' Since I had resolved that I would more gladly lose my life than break my word of honour to that worthy Castellan, I endured this indescribable constraint, along with a friar from the Palavisina family* who was a very great preacher.

105. This man had been arrested as a Lutheran: he was a most excellent friend and companion, but as for being a friar, he was the greatest scoundrel in the world and indulged in all sorts of vices. I admired his fine talents and I greatly abhorred his ugly vices, and I openly criticized him for them. This friar never did anything but remind me that I was not obliged to keep my word of honour with the Castellan since I was in prison. To this I replied that even though he spoke the truth as a friar, as a man he was not speaking the truth, because a man who was not a friar was obliged to keep his word of honour in every kind of situation in which he found himself: for this reason, since I was a man and not a friar, I would never have failed to keep my simple and good word of honour. After this friar had realized that he was incapable of corrupting me through the keen and clever arguments he set out in such a marvellous fashion, he made up his mind to tempt me in another way, and after allowing many days to go by, while he read me the sermons of Fra Girolamo Savonarola,* he provided such an admirable commentary that it was finer than the sermons themselves. As a result I remained spellbound, and there was not anything in the world I would not have done for him, except to break my word of honour, as I have already said. When this friar saw I was amazed by his abilities, he thought of another way: he very

skilfully began to ask me what means I would have employed, had I felt the wish when they had shut me up, to open the prison in order to escape. Since I also wanted to display some measure of the subtlety of my wit, I said to this clever friar that I could certainly open even the most difficult lock, and especially those in this prison, which would have been no harder than eating a bit of fresh cheese. This friar, in order to force me to reveal my secret, tried to humiliate me, declaring that there are many things people say when they have gained some reputation for being resourceful, and that if they were obliged to put the plans they boasted of into effect they would lose a great deal of credit and it would go badly for them; and that he had heard me speak of things so far from the truth that, if I were put to the test, he thought I would come out of it with little honour. At this, feeling provoked by this devil of a friar, I said I was accustomed to promising in words much less than I knew how to do in fact, and that what I had promised concerning the keys was the most simple thing to do. In a few words, I completely persuaded him that things were as I had said, and, as I spoke, I thoughtlessly demonstrated for him with great ease everything I had told him. The friar, pretending not to pay any attention, immediately learned everything in the cleverest fashion. And as I explained above, that worthy Castellan allowed me to go freely throughout the Castello, and he never even locked me in during the night as he did with all the other prisoners; he still allowed me to work on everything I wished, whether in gold and silver or in wax; and even though I had worked for several weeks upon a certain basin that I was making for the Cardinal of Ferrara, I discovered that I was disheartened by prison life, and that working upon such projects grew tedious. In order to ease my tedium, I only worked upon some small wax figures; this friar stole a piece of the wax from me, and with it he used the method for making keys which I had foolishly taught him. He had taken as a companion and assist-ant a clerk who worked with the Castellan. This clerk, named Luigi, was from Padua. They wanted to make a set of keys but were betrayed by the locksmith, and since the Castellan came to see me in my room on several occasions and had seen me working on some wax figures, he immediately recognized the wax and said: 'Although this poor Benvenuto has suffered one of the greatest wrongs ever inflicted on anyone, he should not have done such a thing to me, because I did him favours that I should not have done for him. Now I shall keep him tightly locked up, and never will I do him any more favours.' So he had me locked up, the whole affair being very unpleasant, especially because of the remarks of some of his most devoted servants, who were also extremely fond of me, and who constantly mentioned all the good things their lord the Castellan had done for me, to such an extent that in this unfortunate situation they called me an ingrate, false and untrustworthy. And because one of his servants insulted me a bit more boldly than he should have, I responded fearlessly, since I felt I was innocent, saying that I had never broken my word of honour and that I would be bound to uphold it with all my energy, and that if he or anyone else made such unfair statements I would say that whoever said such a thing would be lying in his throat. Unable to tolerate this insult, he ran to the chamber of the Castellan and brought me the wax that contained the imprint of the keys. As soon as I saw the wax I informed him that we both were right, but that he should allow me to speak to the Lord Castellan, since I would tell him plainly how matters stood, a question of much greater consequence than they thought. The Castellan immediately had me summoned, and I explained the entire affair to him; as a result, he put the friar into solitary confinement, and the friar betrayed the clerk, who was nearly hanged for it. The Castellan hushed the matter up, but it had already reached the ears of the Pope; he saved his clerk from the gallows, and allowed me to go about in the same way as I had previously.

106. When I saw how rigorously this matter had been pursued, I began to think about my own affairs, saying to myself: 'If, on another occasion, one of these storms arises and this man loses confidence in me, I'd no longer be obliged to him, and I'd like to use some of my own ingenuity, which I am certain would bring me more success than that rascally friar;' and I began to have new and coarser sheets brought to me without sending the dirty ones back. When my servants asked for them I told them to be quiet, because I had given them to some impoverished soldiers, and if this became known these poor men would run the risk of being sent to the galleys. As a result, my young servants, especially Felice, most faithfully kept this matter of the sheets completely secret. I set about emptying a straw mattress and I burned the straw, since in my prison cell there was a fireplace in which one might build a fire. I began to make strips from these sheets about a third of an armslength wide: when I had made as

many of them as I thought I would need to descend the great height from the keep of the Castel Sant'Angelo, I told my servants that I had given away the ones I wished to give away, that they could bring me some finer sheets, and that I would always give them back the dirty ones. The matter was forgotten. Cardinal Santiquattro and Cardinal Cornaro* had my workers and servants close up my workshop, telling me plainly that the Pope would hear nothing about letting me go, and that the great favour shown me by the King of France had done me more harm than good, because the last words Monsignor di Morluc had said on the King's behalf were these: Monsignor di Morluc told the Pope that he should hand me over to the ordinary judges of the court, and that if I had committed some error he could punish me, but if I had not, reason demanded that he allow me to go free. His words annoyed the Pope to such an extent that he had no mind at all to free me. The Castellan most certainly helped me as much as he could. During this time, when my enemies saw that my workshop had been locked up, every day they disdainfully made some insulting remarks to my servants and friends who came to visit me in prison. One day it happened that Ascanio, who came to see me twice a day, asked me if I might have a certain garment made for him out of my blue satin robe, which I never wore: I had only worn it that one time when I had gone with it in a procession; I told him, however, that these were not the times, nor was I in a place, for the wearing of such garments. The young man took it so badly that I did not give him this wretched garment that he told me he wanted to leave and go to his home in Tagliacozze. Infuriated, I told him that he would do me a favour if he would get himself out of my sight, and he swore with the greatest of passion that he would never come near me again. While we were saying this, we were passing by the keep of the Castello. It happened that the Castellan was also taking a walk; just when we ran into His Lordship, Ascanio said: 'I'm leaving, so goodbye—forever.' To this I said: 'I hope it will be forever, and let it be so: I'll order the guards never to allow you to come inside again,' and turning to the Castellan, with all my heart I begged him to give instructions to the guards never to allow Ascanio to come inside again, saying to His Lordship: 'This little peasant comes to me to add insult to injury; so My Lord, I beg you never to give him entrance again.' The Castellan was very sorry about this, for he recognized Ascanio as a young man of marvellous gifts; besides this, he was so handsome a fellow that, on seeing him only once, everyone immediately became fond of him. This young man left in tears, and he was carrying a small scimitar that he sometimes wore secretly under his clothing. Leaving the Castello, his face bathed in tears, he ran into two of my greatest enemies, one of whom was that Girolamo from Perugia* mentioned previously; and the other a certain Michele,* both of whom were goldsmiths. Since he was a friend of that Perugian scoundrel and an enemy of Ascanio, this Michele said: 'What does Ascanio's weeping mean? Perhaps his father is dead? I mean his father in the Castello.' To this Ascanio replied: 'He is alive, but you are going to die right now,' and raising his hand, with his scimitar, he gave him two blows, both upon the head, and with the first blow he knocked him onto the ground, while with the second he cut off three fingers of his right hand, striking him in the head as well. He lay there as if dead. The attack was immediately reported to the Pope; and the Pope, in a great rage, spoke these words: 'Since the King wishes that he be judged, go to him and give him three days to prepare his defence.' The magistrates immediately came to me and executed the order the Pope had given them. That worthy Castellan immediately went to the Pope and made it very clear that I was not aware of this event, and that I had chased Ascanio away. He defended me so marvellously that he saved my life from the Pope's great rage. Ascanio fled to his home in Tagliacozze, and from there he wrote to me, begging me for forgiveness a thousand times, since he recognized that he was wrong in adding this annoyance to my more serious problems, but he declared that if God were to grant me the grace to leave that prison he would never again abandon me. I let him know that he had to pay more attention to learning his trade, and that if God granted me my freedom I would send for him, no matter what.

107. Every year this Castellan suffered from an illness that made him go out of his mind, and when it began to come on he talked a great deal, in a chattering manner; these humours* of his were different every year, for on one occasion he thought he was a jar of oil; another time he thought he was a frog, and hopped about like a frog; yet another time he thought he had died and it was necessary to bury him: every year a different humour arose in him. This time he began to imagine he was a bat, and while he was out walking he sometimes squeaked as quietly as bats do; he also made a motion with his hands

and body as if he wanted to fly. His doctors, when they saw this, as well as his old servants, offered him all the pleasant diversions they were able to devise, and since they thought he took great pleasure in hearing me speak, every so often they came for me and took me to him. Because of this, the poor man sometimes kept me for four or five entire hours without ever allowing me to stop speaking with him. He used to keep me at his table to sit opposite him and eat, and he never stopped talking or making me talk, but in the midst of these discussions I managed to eat very well. The poor man neither ate nor slept, with the result that he wore me out, so that I could not go on any longer; and sometimes when I looked at him in the face I saw that the pupils of his eyes looked terrified, for one went in one direction and one in another. He began to ask me if I had ever had a wish to fly: to his question, I replied that I had most eagerly tried to do and had done all those things that were the most difficult for a man to accomplish, and as for flying, since the God of Nature had given me a body which was very suitable and fit for running and jumping much higher than the average, with that small amount of ingenuity that I could utilize in working with my hands, I felt I certainly had the courage to fly. This man began to ask me what means I would consider using: to this I answered that, judging from the animals that fly, and wishing to imitate with art what they possessed from Nature, there was no animal that one could imitate except the bat. When the poor man heard the word 'bat', which was the humour he was suffering that year, he raised his voice, saying: 'He speaks the truth, he speaks the truth; that's the proper way to fly, that's it!' And then he turned to me and said: 'Benvenuto, if somebody gave you the means, would it give you the courage to fly?' To this I responded that, if he were willing to give me my freedom afterwards, I would be capable of flying all the way to Prati,* making myself a pair of wings from waxed Rheims linen. Then he said: 'And I, too, would have enough courage, but the Pope has ordered me to keep watch over you as if with his own eyes; I realize that you're a resourceful devil and that you'd escape. So I'll lock you up with a hundred keys so that you don't get away from me.' I began begging him, reminding him of the fact that I could have escaped but, for the sake of my word of honour, which I had given him, I would never betray him; I begged him, therefore, for the love of God and for the many kindnesses he had shown me, not to add a greater ill to the

Icarus

enormous ill I was already suffering. And while I said these words to him, he gave express orders that I be bound and taken to a tightly locked prison cell. When I saw that there was no other remedy, I said to him in the presence of all his guards: 'Lock me and guard me well, for I'll escape no matter what.' And so they led me off and locked me up with the greatest care.

108. I then began to think about the method I had to use to escape. As soon as I saw myself shut up, I went about examining what the prison cell where I was confined was like, and when I thought I had surely discovered the method of escaping from it, I began to think about the method I should use to descend from the great height of that keep, which was what they called this high tower. After I had taken my new sheets, which, as I already explained, I had made into strips and had sewn together very tightly, I set about investigating how many of them would enable me to make the descent. Once I had calculated how many would be appropriate and had put them all in order, I found a pair of pincers I had taken from a man from Savoy,* who was a member of the guard at the Castello. He was in charge of the casks and the cisterns and took great delight in woodworking, and since he had several pairs of pincers, among which was a very heavy and large pair, thinking that they might serve my purposes, I took them from him and hid them inside my straw mattress. When the time then came for me to use them, I began by testing the nails that held the iron bars on the cell door, and since the door was a double door, it was not possible to see the riveting of the nails, so that I had a good deal of trouble in trying to pull one of them out, but then in the end I succeeded. Once I had pulled out this first nail I set about inventing a way to prevent my jailers from noticing it. Hastily, I mixed some scrapings of rusty iron with a little wax, which was the same colour as the heads of the nails I had extracted; with this wax I very carefully began to simulate the heads of the nails in the iron bands; and one after another, as many nails as I pulled out, I counterfeited them in wax. I left the iron bars attached at both the top and the bottom by replacing some of the nails I had pulled out, but they were cut short and then replaced lightly, just enough to hold the bars. The difficulty I had in doing this was enormous, because the Castellan dreamed every night that I had escaped and he therefore had my cell inspected from hour to hour, and the man who came to do this had both the name and the manner of a jailer. His name was Bozza, and he always brought another man with him, whose name was Giovanni but who had the nickname Pedignione: Pedignione was a soldier, while Bozza was a servant.* This Giovanni never came a single time to my cell without saying something insulting to me. He was from the area around Prato, where he had worked in a druggist's shop: every evening he carefully inspected those iron bands and the entire cell, and I used to say to him: 'Watch me well, for I want to escape, no matter what.' My words caused the greatest enmity to arise between him and me; so that I was extremely careful to replace all my iron tools—that is to say, the pincers, a largish dagger, and other items appropriate to my task—inside my straw mattress; I did the same with those strips I had made, which I continued to store inside the mattress. When daylight came I would immediately sweep the room myself, and although by nature I take pleasure in neatness, I was at that time unusually tidy. After I had swept up, I remade my bed with great care, placing upon it some flowers that almost every morning I had brought to me by a certain fellow from Savoy.* This Savoyard took care of the cisterns and the casks, and he also enjoyed woodworking; it was from him that I stole the pincers with which I removed the nails from the iron bands.

109. To get back to my bed, when Bozza and Pedignione came into the cell I never said anything to them except that they should stay away from my bed, so that they would not soil it or dirty it or mess it up for me. When I would say this to them, sometimes, merely to taunt me, they would touch my bed very lightly, so that I would then say: 'Ah, you filthy idlers! I'll set my hand to one of your swords and do you such mischief that I'll make you wonder. Do you think you're worthy of touching the bed of a man like me? If this happens again I won't worry about my own life, because I'll be certain of taking yours away from you. So leave me alone with my trials and tribulations, and don't cause me any more trouble than I already have; if not, I'll show you what a desperate man can do.' They repeated these words to the Castellan, who gave them express orders never to go near my bed, and that when they came to my cell they should come without their swords, but for the rest, they were to watch me very carefully. After I had made my bed secure I thought I had accomplished everything, because that was the crux of the entire business. One feast-day evening the Castellan felt very ill-disposed

and his humours had increased, for he never said anything else except that he was a bat, and that if they should hear that Benvenuto had flown away they should let him go and he would catch up with me, because he could certainly fly better than I at night. He declared: 'Benvenuto is a counterfeit bat, and I'm a real bat, and since he has been given to me to guard, leave this to me, for I shall surely catch him.' After passing a number of nights in this humour he had worn out all his servants, and through various means I had heard about everything, mainly from that Savoyard who was fond of me. On that feast-day evening I had resolved to escape at no matter what cost, but first I most devoutly prayed to God, begging His Divine Majesty to defend me and to assist me in such a dangerous enterprise; then I took out all the items I wanted to use and worked for the entire night. Two hours before daybreak I removed the iron bars with a great deal of trouble, because the wooden door-frame, as well as the bolt, offered such resistance that I could not open it: I had to chip off the wood, yet I opened it in the end, and shouldering those strips which I had wound up like reels of thick thread on two small pieces of wood, I left the cell and went toward the latrines in the castle's keep; and after I had exposed two roof-tiles from inside, I quickly and easily climbed up on them. I was wearing a white great-coat, a pair of white stockings, and, as well, a pair of high boots, inside which I had placed that dagger of mine. Then I took one end of my strips and secured it to a piece of old tile mortared into the keep: by chance, this piece of tile jutted out almost four fingers. The strip was prepared like a stirrup. After I had attached it to that piece of tile, I turned to God and declared: 'Lord God, help my cause, for I'm in the right as You know, and because I've helped myself.' Letting myself go, little by little, holding myself up with the strength of my arms, I reached the ground. There was no moonlight, but the sky was bright with the first light of dawn. When I reached the ground I looked at the great height from which I had descended so courageously, and happily I moved away, thinking that I was free. But it was not so, because the Castellan had had built two very high walls on that side, and he used them for a stable and a chicken coop: the place was closed up with enormous bolts from outside. Seeing I could not get out from there made me tremendously upset. While I paced back and forth, thinking about my problem, I tripped over a large pole that was covered with straw. I raised it up with great difficulty to the wall; then, with the strength of my arms, I climbed up the pole to the top of the wall. And because the wall had a jagged edge, I could not muster the strength to pull the pole up; therefore, I decided to tear off a piece of the strips on the other reel, since I had left one of the two reels attached to the castle's keep. So I took a piece of this other reel, as I said, and once I tied it to that beam I climbed down the wall, which required an enormous effort that left me thoroughly exhausted, and meanwhile I had also skinned the palms of my hands, which were bleeding. For this reason I took a rest, and I bathed my hands in my own urine. Standing there, when I thought my strength had returned, I climbed up the last of the outer circle of walls facing toward Prati: then I set out my reel of strips, which I wanted to tie around one of the battlements and use the same method to descend from this lesser height that I had used with the greater one; having positioned my reel, as I said, I noticed one of those sentinels who were keeping guard almost on top of me. Once I saw my plan threatened and my life endangered, I decided to confront the guard. When he saw my determined spirit and realized I was going for him with a weapon in my hand, he quickened his step, showing that he was trying to avoid me. Since I had moved away somewhat from my strips, I very quickly turned around, and although I saw another guard he, perhaps, did not see me. Reaching my strips, I tied them to the battlement and let myself down, but either because I thought I was actually near the ground and had opened my hands to jump down, or else because my hands were weak and could no longer stand the strain, I fell, and in my fall I struck the back of my head* and remained unconscious for more than an hour and a half, as far as I can determine. Then, as day began to break, that slight coolness that comes before the sun rises revived me, but I was still not completely conscious, since I thought that my head had been cut off and that I was in Purgatory. Standing there, little by little my faculties returned to normal, and I noticed that I was outside the Castello and immediately remembered everything I had done. And because I felt the blow to the back of my head before I realized that my leg was broken, putting my hands to my head, I drew them away covered with blood. Then, exploring my body thoroughly, I surmised and concluded that I had not suffered any serious harm, but when I wanted to stand up I found my right leg broken three fingers above the heel. Not even this discovery dismayed me: I took out my large dagger along with its scabbard, which had a metal tip with a very heavy ball at the end; this had caused me to break my leg, because the bone could not bend when it was struck with that heavy ball, which broke it in that exact place. So I threw away the scabbard of the dagger, and with the dagger I cut off a piece of those strips that were hanging down, and as best I could I bound up the leg with it, and then, crawling with my dagger in my hand, I went toward the gate. But when I reached the gate I found it closed; and seeing there was a stone right under the gate which I judged not to be very firmly fixed, I tried to remove it; I put my hands upon it and when I felt it shift, it easily yielded to me and I pulled it out; and I entered through the hole.

110. It was more than five hundred standard paces from the spot where I fell to the gate through which I had entered. When I came into Rome some mastiffs threw themselves on me and bit me badly; they returned several times to attack me, and I drew out my dagger and stabbed one of them so deeply that he was howling loudly, and the other dogs, as is their nature, ran to that dog; and I hurried to leave, crawling toward the Church of the Trespontina.* When I reached the beginning of the street that turns toward Sant'Angelo, I took the path from there to go towards St Peter's, since it was growing light all around me and I felt that I was running into danger; I then met a water-carrier who had his donkey loaded up with jugs of water. I called him over and begged him to lift me up and carry me to the top of the steps of St Peter's, saying to him: 'I'm a poor young man who, for the sake of a love affair, tried to climb down from a window, when I fell down and broke a leg. And since the house I left is one of great importance, I run the risk of being cut to pieces, so I beg you to carry me off quickly and I'll give you a gold scudo.' And I reached for my purse, inside of which I had a good number. The man immediately picked me up and readily carried me off on his back to the top of the stairs of St Peter's, where I made him leave me and told him to run back to his donkey. I immediately went on my way, still on all fours, going to the home of the Duchess, the wife of Duke Ottavio and a natural, not legitimate, daughter of the Emperor, who had been the wife of Alessandro, Duke of Florence;* I did so because I knew most certainly that there were many of my friends with this great princess, who had come with her from Florence. I did so as well because she had done me a service through the Castellan, who, wishing to help me, informed the Pope, at the time the Duchess

made her entry into Rome,* that I had been the cause of saving the city from more than a thousand scudi's worth of damage as a result of a very heavy rain. The Castellan said that he had been in despair on account of the rain, but that I had revived his spirits, and he described how I had aimed several heavy artillery pieces towards where the clouds were thickest, and where an extremely heavy rain had already begun to fall; how, after I began to fire the artillery pieces, the rain stopped; and how, after the fourth salvo, the sun came out. He said that I had been the sole reason why that celebration had turned out so well, and because of this, when the Duchess heard him, she had said: 'That Benvenuto is one of those brilliant men who stood in high favour with my husband, Duke Alessandro, and I shall always remember such men whenever the occasion to do them a good turn presents itself;' and she had also spoken about me to her husband Duke Ottavio. Because of this I went straight to Her Excellency's home, which was located in Borgo Vecchio* in an extremely beautiful palace; and there I would have been very sure that the Pope would not touch me, but since the deed I had accomplished up to that point was too marvellous for a mere human body and God was unwilling for me to become too arrogant, for my own good he wanted me to undergo an even harsher test than the one I had just passed through: and it turned out like this, that while I was crawling up those stairs a servant in the service of Cardinal Cornaro* recognized me—the Cardinal was staying in the palace. This servant ran to the Cardinal's bedchamber and awakened him, saying: 'My Most Reverend Lord, your Benvenuto is there down below, he has escaped from the Castello and is crawling along covered in blood: it looks like he has broken a leg, and we don't know where he is heading.' The Cardinal said straightaway: 'Run and carry him here to me in my bedchamber!' When I was brought to him he told me I should not be afraid, and he immediately sent for the best doctors in Rome, by whom I was treated; one of them was a certain Master Iacopo da Perugia,* a very fine surgeon. He set my bone admirably well, then bandaged me up, and he bled me with his own hand, but because my veins were much more swollen than was normal, and also because he wished to make a rather wide incision, the flow of blood was so strong that it spurted on his face, which was covered with so much blood that he was unable to treat me. Since he took this as a very bad omen, he treated me with great reluctance; and many times he wanted to

abandon me, once he realized that he ran the risk of no small punishment for having treated me or completing the treatment. The
Cardinal placed me in a secret chamber, and he immediately went off
to the Vatican Palace with the intention of asking the Pope for my
freedom.

111. At this moment an enormous disturbance arose in Rome,
since the strips attached to the great tower of the castle's keep had
already been noticed, and everyone in Rome ran to see this extraordinary occurrence. Meanwhile the Castellan had fallen into one of
his greatest attacks of madness, and he wanted, despite the resistance
of all his servants, to fly off from the keep himself, declaring that no
one could recapture me except himself, by flying after me. While this
was happening, Messer Roberto Pucci, the father of Messer Pandolfo, having heard about this great event, went in person to see it for
himself; then he came to the Vatican, where he encountered Cardinal
Cornaro, who had described everything that had taken place and
how I was in one of his bedchambers and had already been treated.
These two worthy men went together and fell to their knees before
the Pope, who declared to them, before he allowed them to speak: 'I
know everything that you wish from me.' Messer Roberto Pucci
replied: 'Most Blessed Father, we ask you to pardon this poor man
who, because of his talents, deserves to receive some consideration,
and who, in addition to those talents, has demonstrated such bravery
along with such ingenuity that it hardly seems human. We do not
know for which sins Your Holiness has held him for so long in
prison. Still, even if these sins exceeded all bounds, Your Holiness is
holy and wise and your will may be done in everything and through
everything, but if they are matters that are in your power to grant,
we beg you to do us this favour.' The Pope, feeling ashamed at this
request, declared that he had kept me in prison at the request of
some of the members of his household, 'for being a bit too arrogant,
but recognizing his talents and wishing to retain him in Our service,
We have ordered that he be treated so well that he will not have any
reason to return to France. I am very grieved* over his serious injury;
tell him that he should concentrate upon getting well, and after he is
well we shall compensate him for his suffering.' These two great men
came to me and gave me the good news on behalf of the Pope. In the
meantime all of the Roman nobility came to visit me, both young
and old of every rank. The Castellan, who was beside himself, had

himself carried to the Pope, and when he came before His Holiness he began to scream, declaring that if the Pope did not return me to him in prison he would be doing him a great injustice. He said: 'He fled from me after giving me his word of honour: alas, he has flown away from me and he promised me not to fly away!' Laughing, the Pope said: 'Go away, go away, for I shall return him to you no matter what.' The Castellan, speaking to the Pope, added: 'Send the Governor to him. He will discover who helped him to escape, because if it were one of my men I want to hang him by the neck from the same battlement by which Benvenuto escaped.' After the Castellan had left, the Pope, smiling, called the Governor and said: 'Benvenuto is a brave man, and this is a marvellous feat, although when I was young I also descended from that very spot.' In this instance, the Pope was telling the truth, because he had been imprisoned in the Castello for having forged a brief, when he was abbreviator for the *Parco Maioris*:* Pope Alexander* had kept him in prison for a long time; then, since the affair was such an ugly one, he decided to have him decapitated; but since he wanted to wait until after the feast of Corpus Domini, Farnese learned of everything. He had Pietro Chiavelluzzi* come with several horses, and he bribed some of the guards at the Castello with money, so that on the day of Corpus Domini, while the Pope was in see 198 the procession, Farnese was placed in a basket and was lowered to the ground with a rope. The outer circle of walls had not yet been constructed at the Castello and there was only the great tower, so that the Pope did not encounter the same enormous difficulties in his escape that I had; moreover, his arrest was justified, while mine was wrong. All he wanted was to brag to the Governor about how he, too, had been bold and courageous in his youth, and he did not realize that he was revealing his own dirty tricks. He said: 'Go and tell Benvenuto that he is free to say who helped him; no matter who it might be, it's enough that he be pardoned, and you may promise that to him freely.'

112. This Governor, who two days earlier had been named Bishop of Jesi, came to me, and when he arrived he said to me: 'My dear Benvenuto, although my office is one that terrifies men, I come to you to reassure you; and thus, I have the authority to make a promise to you, on the express orders of His Holiness, who has told me that he also escaped from the Castello, but that he had a great deal of assistance and many accomplices, since otherwise he would

not have been able to do so. I swear to you by the Sacraments which I
am carrying on me—for I was named Bishop only two days ago—
that the Pope has freed and pardoned you, and that your serious
injury causes him a good deal of regret, but you must think about
getting well and take everything as being for the best, for this
imprisonment, which you have surely endured in complete innocence, will always be your salvation, for you will trample down poverty and will never need to return to France or to trouble yourself
travelling from one place to the next. So, tell me openly exactly how
you did it and who offered you assistance; then you may take comfort, rest, and get well.' I started at the beginning and recounted the
entire affair exactly as it had occurred, and I gave him the most
convincing details, down to the water-carrier who had carried me on
his back. Once the Governor had heard everything, he said: 'These
feats are truly too great for one man alone: no other man but you
would be capable of them.' And so, after having me hold out my
hand, he said: 'Be of good cheer and take comfort, for by this hand
with which I am touching you, you are free and, while you live, you
shall be happy.' He left me, having inconvenienced many important
gentlemen and lords who had come to visit me, saying to one
another: 'Let's go and see this man who works miracles;' these
people remained with me; and some of them offered me assistance
and others gifts. Meanwhile, the Governor reached the Pope and
began to relate the story that I had told him; it so happened that his
son, Lord Pier Luigi, was present; and everyone expressed very
great astonishment. The Pope said: 'This is surely too great a feat.'
Lord Pier Luigi then remarked: 'Most Holy Father, if you set him
free he will accomplish even greater exploits, because this man has a
nature that is far too audacious. I want to tell you another story about
him that you don't know. Before he was imprisoned, this Benvenuto
of yours, after he had words with a gentleman in the service of
Cardinal Santa Fiore,* caused by some trifling little remark that this
gentleman had made to Benvenuto, replied so defiantly and with
such daring that he gave signs of wanting to start a quarrel; the
gentleman related all this to Cardinal Santa Fiore, who said that if he
could lay his hands upon Benvenuto, he would relieve this madman
of his head. When Benvenuto heard about it he kept his guns
ready, with which he continuously practised by firing at a coin, and
one day, when the Cardinal showed himself at the window, since this

Benvenuto's workshop was located under the Cardinal's palace,* he took up his gun and prepared to fire at the Cardinal. And since the Cardinal was warned of this, he quickly got out of the way. To disguise what he was doing, Benvenuto fired at a pigeon nesting in a hole high up on the palace, and he struck the pigeon on the head—an unbelievable feat. Now Your Holiness may do whatever you wish with him; I did not want to fail to tell you about this. And he might even wish, since he feels he has been wrongly imprisoned, to fire a round at Your Holiness. His is a nature that is too ferocious and too self-assured. When he killed Pompeo he stabbed him twice in the throat in the midst of ten men who were guarding him, and then he escaped, to their no little disgrace, since they were nevertheless worthy men and of some account.'

113. That nobleman in the service of Santa Fiore with whom I had exchanged words was present when these words were spoken, and he confirmed to the Pope everything his son had said. The Pope was enraged and said nothing. I do not wish to fail to provide, justly and forthrightly, my own explanation for this affair. This nobleman of Santa Fiore one day came to me and handed me a little golden ring which was all discoloured by quicksilver, and he said: 'Clean off this dirty ring for me and do it quickly.' I had many commissions in gold and precious stones before me, and hearing myself being given haughty orders by someone I had never spoken to nor even seen, I told him that I had no tool for cleaning off quicksilver* at the moment and that he should go to someone else. This man, without any reason in the world, told me that I was an ass. To this remark I replied that he was not speaking the truth, and that I was a man in every respect of greater worth than he, but that if he stirred me up I would kick him harder than an ass. The man related all this to the Cardinal and painted it like a scene from Hell.* Two days later I was behind the palace shooting at a wild pigeon that was nesting high up in a hole; on many occasions I had witnessed a goldsmith by the name of Giovan Francesco della Tacca,* who was from Milan, firing at it without ever hitting it. On that particular day when I was shooting the pigeon was showing only his head, being suspicious on account of the other times that he had been fired upon, and because this Giovan Francesco and I were rivals in hunting with a musket, while some gentlemen and friends of mine were in my shop they pointed out the pigeon to me and said: 'Look up there at Giovan Francesco

della Tacca's pigeon—the one he has fired at so many times. Look at how suspicious the poor animal is—he will hardly show his head.' Looking up, I said: 'That little bit of his head would be enough for me to kill him, if he'll only wait until I can take aim.' Those gentlemen declared that even the inventor of the musket could not hit him. To this I said: 'Let's wager a carafe of Greek wine from Palombo, my good innkeeper, that if he just waits until I can aim my amazing "Broccardo"—the name I had given my musket—I shall hit him on that little part of his head that he's showing me.' Taking aim immediately, and holding the musket with my arms without any other support, I did what I had promised, neither thinking of the Cardinal nor anyone else; on the contrary, I considered the Cardinal very much my benefactor. Let all the world witness how many different means Fortune employs when she wishes to destroy a man. The Pope, enraged and sulking, went on thinking about what his son had told him.

114. Two days later Cardinal Cornaro went to the Pope to request a bishopric for one of his gentlemen, whose name was Messer Andrea Centano.* The Pope, it is true, had promised him a bishopric, and since it became vacant, when the Cardinal reminded the Pope that he had made him such a promise the Pope agreed that this was true and said that he was willing to give it to him, but that he desired a favour from His Most Reverend Lordship: he wanted him to put Benvenuto back into his hands. Then the Cardinal said: 'Oh, if Your Holiness has pardoned him and given me his liberty, what will everyone then say of both Your Holiness and of me?' The Pope replied: 'I want Benvenuto, and let them say what they like if you want the bishopric.' The good Cardinal said that His Holiness should give him the bishopric and that he should think over the rest by himself, and then do whatever His Holiness wished and would allow to be done. The Pope, although somewhat ashamed at the wickedness of going back on his word of honour, said: 'I shall send for Benvenuto, and as a small satisfaction to myself I shall place him down in those rooms of my secret garden, where he can concentrate upon getting well; I shall not prohibit any of his friends from going to see him, and I shall even provide for his expenses* until this little whim of mine has passed.' The Cardinal returned home and sent for me immediately by the man who was waiting for the bishopric, who told me how the Pope wanted me back in his hands but that he would keep me in a lower room in his secret garden, where I could be visited by anyone, just as

if I were in his home. Then I begged this Messer Andrea to be so kind as to tell the Cardinal not to give me up to the Pope and to allow me to look after myself, because I would have myself rolled up in a mattress and carried outside Rome to a safe spot, since if he gave me back to the Pope he would most certainly send me to my death. The Cardinal, when he heard this, would, it seems, have been glad to do what I asked, but that Messer Andrea, who was waiting to have this bishopric, revealed the plan. And in the meantime, the Pope sent for me immediately and had me put, just as he said, in a lower room in his own secret garden. The Cardinal sent word to me not to eat any of the food the Pope sent me, and that he would send me food himself; he said that what he had done he could not have avoided doing, and that I should be of good cheer, for he would give me so much help that I would have my freedom. Under these conditions I received visits every day, and many important gentlemen offered me many fine presents. From the Pope came the food I did not touch; instead, I ate what came from Cardinal Cornaro, and so I remained there. I had, among my other friends, a young Greek who was twenty-five years old; he was enormously strong and handled a sword better than any other man in Rome; he was faint-hearted, but was an extremely trustworthy man and very credulous. He had heard that the Pope had said that he wanted to compensate me for my pains and hardships. And it was true that, at the beginning, the Pope had said such things, but he ended up saying something quite different. For this reason, I took this young Greek into my confidence and said to him: 'My dearest brother, these people want to assassinate me, so now is the time to help me: they think that, with all the extraordinary favours they are doing me, I won't realize that they are being done to betray me.' This worthy young man replied: 'My dear Benvenuto, all over Rome it's reported that the Pope has given you an appointment worth five hundred scudi in revenue, so I humbly beg you not to allow your suspicions to deprive you of such a great benefit.' And I continued to implore him, with my arms crossed over my breast, to carry me away from there, for I knew very well that while a pope like this one could do me a great deal of good, I knew for certain that he was trying to do me great harm in secret, in defence of his honour; I urged him therefore to act quickly and to try to save me from that pope: if he would get me away from there and in the way I had told him, I would always acknowledge that I owed my life to him, and whenever the need arose I would gladly give my life for him. Weeping, this poor young man said to me: 'O my dearest brother, you really want to ruin yourself, but I can't fail to do what you ask of me; tell me the way and I'll do everything that you say, even though it's against my will.' Thus, we resolved the matter, and I gave him the entire plan, which would very easily have succeeded. When I thought that he had come to set the plan into operation, he came to tell me that, for my own safety, he wanted to disobey me and that what he had heard came from men who were close to the Pope and who knew the entire truth about my case. Since I could not help myself in any way, I remained there unhappy and desperate. This was the day of Corpus Domini* in the year 1539.

115. After this dispute the whole day passed, until nightfall came and an abundance of food arrived from the Pope's kitchen, while from the kitchen of Cardinal Cornaro arrived the most excellent provisions. As several of my friends happened by I had them stay for supper with me; in bed, with my leg in splints, I dined heartily with them; and so they stayed with me. When one hour of night had passed they left; two of my servants got me ready to sleep, and then they retired to the antechamber. I owned a dog that was as black as a mulberry, one of those hairy dogs, and he served me admirably well when I went hunting with my musket, never staying more than a step away from me. That night, while he was lying under my bed, I summoned my servant three times to come and take him from under the bed, because he was howling in a frightful manner. When my servants arrived this dog threw himself upon them to bite them. They were terrified and were afraid that the dog was rabid, since he was howling continuously. And this went on until the fourth hour of the night. At the stroke of the fourth hour the Chief Constable entered my bedchamber with a large escort: then the dog jumped forward and threw himself upon them with such fury, ripping apart their capes and stockings and frightening them to such an extent that they thought he was rabid. Because of this the Chief Constable, who was an experienced man, said: 'This is the nature of all good dogs, who always divine and foretell the harm about to befall their masters: get a couple of sticks and defend yourselves from the dog, while the rest of you tie Benvenuto into this chair and take him where you've been told.' As I said, this was the day after Corpus Domini,* and the time was around the fourth hour of the night. They carried me

gagged and covered, and four of them walked ahead, pushing aside those few men who were still to be found on the streets. Thus they carried me to Torre di Nona,* as the place was called, and they placed me in the cell of the condemned, setting me down on a small piece of mattress and leaving one of the guards with me, who commiserated with me all night over my bad luck, telling me: 'Alas, poor Benvenuto, what have you done to them?' So I was very well aware of what was going to happen to me, given the kind of place it was and what the guard had said. I remained for part of the night in thought, racking my brains over why it pleased God to inflict such punishment upon me, and since I could not uncover the reason I was enormously troubled. The guard then began, as best he could, to comfort me, so I implored him for the love of God to say nothing to me and to avoid speaking to me, since I would more quickly arrive at some resolution if I did it on my own. And so he promised to do this. Then I turned with all my heart to God; I devoutly prayed that He would be willing to accept me into His kingdom; I said that although I was lamenting my fate, since it seemed to me I did not deserve to die according to the rules the law prescribed, and although I had committed some murders, His Own Vicar had summoned me from my native city and had pardoned me under His own authority as well as that of the law; and what I had done had been done entirely in the defence of that body which His Divine Majesty had lent to me. So I did not recognize how, according to the rules under which one lived in the world, I deserved that kind of death, but it seemed that what was happening to me was what happened to those unfortunate people who, walking down the street, are struck on the head by a stone from a great height and killed, which happens clearly under the influence of the stars, not so much because the stars have conspired against us to do us either good or evil, but rather, because such things happen during the conjunction of the stars to which we are subject; although I realize that I have free will, and that if I demonstrated my faith in the manner of a saint I am entirely certain that the angels from Heaven would carry me out of this prison and would surely rescue me from all of my afflictions, since God does not seem to have made me worthy of such a thing it is, therefore, necessarily true that these celestial influences have brought down all malignancy upon me. So I debated for a little while, then resigned myself and quickly fell asleep.

116. After dawn had broken, my guard awakened me and said: 'Oh unfortunate but worthy man, now there is no more time for sleep, because someone has arrived to give you some bad news.' At this I said: 'The sooner I escape from this earthly prison the more grateful I shall be, particularly since I'm certain that my soul is saved and that I'm dying unjustly. Christ the Glorious and Divine makes me the companion of his disciples and friends who—both He and they—were put to death unjustly; and so I'm unjustly being put to death, and I devoutly thank God for this. Why doesn't the man who is to pronounce sentence upon me step forward?' Then the guard said: 'He's far too upset about it and is crying.' Then I called him by name, which was Messer Benedetto da Cagli.* I said: 'Come forward, my dear Messer Benedetto, now that I'm very much better prepared and more resolute; dying unjustly brings me much more glory than if I deserved to die. Come forward, I beg you, and give me a priest so that I can exchange a few words with him; there is no real need to do so, since I've made my holy confession with My Lord God, but I would do so only to observe what our Holy Mother Church commands; for although she is doing me this cruel injustice, I pardon her.* So come forward, my dear Messer Benedetto, and send me off before other feelings begin to master me.' After I had spoken this worthy man told the guard to lock the door, for without him it would be impossible to carry out the execution. He then went to the home of the wife of Signor Pier Luigi, who was together with the Duchess I mentioned before,* and coming before them this man said: 'My most illustrious patron, I pray you for the love of God to be so kind as to send word to the Pope that he should send someone else to pronounce that sentence upon Benvenuto and to execute my official duties, because I renounce them and will never be willing to perform them.' And sighing, with the deepest sorrow he left them. The Duchess, who was present, said with a frown: 'This is the fine justice upheld in Rome by the Vicar of God! The Duke, my former husband,* was extremely fond of this man because of his excellence and his talents, and he did not wish him to return to Rome, keeping him by his side with great affection.' And she went away, muttering many angry words. The wife of Signor Pier Luigi, who was called Signora Girolama, went to the Pope, and throwing herself upon her knees—she was in the presence of a number of cardinals—this lady spoke with so much energy that she made the Pope blush, and he said: 'For your sake we shall leave him alone, although we've never had any bad intentions toward him.' The Pope said this because he was in the presence of those cardinals, who had overheard the remarks made by this marvellous and courageous lady. I waited with very great uneasiness, my heart pounding furiously. All those men who were appointed to carry out that evil task also remained uneasy until it was late—the hour for supper; at that time they all went about their other business, so that I was brought something to eat. Amazed by this, I said: 'Here truth has prevailed over the malignity of the celestial influences; I therefore pray God, if it is His will, to rescue me from this tempest.' I began to eat, and just as I had earlier resigned myself to my evil fate, so now I began to hope for my great good fortune. I ate my supper with a hearty appetite. So I remained there, without seeing or hearing from anyone until an hour after sundown. At that time the Chief Constable arrived with a good part of his escort, and placed me back in that chair on which he had carried me off there the evening before, and then, telling me in a very kind tone not to be afraid, he ordered his policemen to be careful not to jostle the leg I had broken and to treat me as carefully as their own eyes. They did so, and carried me to the Castel Sant'Angelo from which I had escaped; and when we were high up inside the keep, where a small courtyard is located, they locked me up for a while.

117. Meanwhile, the previously mentioned Castellan had himself carried up to the place where I was waiting, and as sick and tormented as he was, he said: 'See how I captured you again?' 'Yes,' I replied, 'but do you see how I escaped as I said I would? And if I had not been sold under a papal guarantee for the price of a bishopric by a Venetian cardinal and a Roman of the Farnese family, both one and the other of whom have disfigured the face of God's sacred, holy laws, you would never have retaken me. But seeing that they've acted now in such an evil way, you also can do your worst, since I no longer have a care in this world.' This wretched man began to scream very loudly, saying: 'Alas! Alas! He doesn't care whether he lives or dies, and he is even bolder now than when he was well: put him down there under the garden, and never again speak to me of him, since he will be the death of me!' I was carried under a garden into a very dark room where there was a great deal of water, full of tarantulas and many poisonous worms. They threw me a miserable mattress made of flax on the floor, and that evening I was not given

supper and I was locked up behind four doors: I remained in this situation until the nineteenth hour of the following day. Then they brought me something to eat: I asked them to give me some of my books to read. None of these men spoke to me, but they reported to that poor Castellan, who had asked what I had said. Later the next morning I was brought my Bible in the vernacular and another book containing Giovanni Villani's *Chronicles*.* When I asked for some of my other books I was told that I would not get any more and that I had too many as it was. And so, unhappily, I lived on that mattress, which was soaking wet since after three days everything was covered with water; I remained there without ever being able to move, because of my broken leg; and when I wanted to leave my bed for the necessity of relieving myself, I crawled with the greatest difficulty in order not to dirty the place where I slept. For an hour and a half each day I had a bit of indirect light, which entered my wretched cell through an extremely small hole; only during that small bit of time did I read, while for the rest of the day and night I remained patiently in the constant darkness, never far from thoughts of God and our human frailty; and it seemed to me certain that in a few days I would end my miserable life in that fashion and in that place. Yet, as best I could, I consoled myself, considering how much more distressing it would have been to have ended my life feeling the unbelievable agony of the executioner's axe,* whereas, in this condition, I was passing away as if drugged by a sleeping potion, which had become more agreeable to me than that other way of dying; and little by little I felt myself fading away to the point that my sound constitution became accustomed to that purgatory. Then, when I felt that I had become adapted and accustomed to it, I made up my mind to endure that unbelievable discomfort for as long as my strength could stand it.

118. I began the Bible from the beginning, and I read and contemplated it most devoutly; and I was so enthralled by it that if I could have done so, I would have done nothing but read; but, as I lacked light, all my discomforts immediately assaulted me and tormented me so greatly that on many occasions I resolved to find the means of killing myself, but because they did not permit me to have a knife, I lacked a way of doing it. Nonetheless, on one occasion I had arranged a large log that was there and had propped it up like a weighted trap, and I wanted to spring it right above my head, which

would have crushed it at once. But after I had arranged this entire apparatus and was moving resolutely to spring the device, when I tried to push it with my hand I was seized by some invisible force and thrown four armslengths away from that spot; I was so terrified that I remained unconscious, and I lay there like that from dawn until the nineteenth hour, when they brought me my supper. They must have come in several times, but I had not heard them, because when I did hear them, Captain Sandrino Monaldi* entered and I heard him say: 'Oh, unhappy man, see what an end has befallen such a rare talent!' Hearing those words I opened my eyes, and I saw priests wearing vestments who were saying: 'Oh, you told us he was dead!' Bozza replied: 'I found him dead, and for that reason I told you so.' They immediately lifted me up from where I was lying, and after removing the mattress, which had become so completely soaked it was like macaroni, they threw it out of the room. Once they reported these matters to the Castellan he gave me another mattress. And so, recalling to myself what that force might have been that had deterred me from such an act, I thought that it must have been something divine, and my protector.

119. The following night a marvellous creature in the form of an extremely handsome young man appeared to me in a dream, and as if to rebuke me he said: 'Do you know Who it is who loaned you that body you wanted to destroy before its time?' I seemed to respond that I knew it was the God of nature. 'Therefore,' he said to me, 'you think so little of His works that you wish to destroy them? Let Him guide you and do not lose hope in His power,' and he added so many other wonderful words that I do not recall the thousandth part of them. I began to consider that this angelic figure had told me the truth; and after I glanced around my prison cell, I saw a bit of crumbling brick. So I rubbed some of the fragments together, and in this way I produced a bit of a runny mixture; then I crawled over to one corner of the door and gnawed on it with my teeth until I bit off a small splinter; and after I had done that I waited for the hour when the light would come into my prison, which was from the twentieth hour to an hour-and-a-half later. Then I began to write as best I could on some blank pages that were left in my Bible; and I reproached the spirits of my intellect for loathing life in the world; they replied to my body, excusing themselves on account of their

misfortunes, and my body gave them hope of better things. And so I wrote this out in dialogue form:*

> —'Afflicted spirits of my soul,
> Alas, how cruel you are to hate this life!'
> —'If you against Heaven now stand,
> Who will be on our side? Who will give us protection?
> Let us, let us go to a better life.'
> —'Ah, do not depart as yet,
> for Heaven promises us happier and more pleasant joys
> than you have ever known.'
> —'We shall remain for a little while
> since the great God has granted you
> such grace that you will suffer no greater woes.'

Having once again regained my vigour after I had consoled myself by my own efforts, I continued to read my Bible, and I had in a way accustomed my eyes to that dimness, so that while earlier I was in the habit of reading for an hour and a half, I now read for three entire hours. As I marvelled greatly over the effects of God's power on those men of enormous simplicity who, with such fervour, believed that God granted them all that they dreamed of, I too promised myself that God would help me, both because of His divinity and mercy and because of my own innocence; and sometimes through prayer and sometimes through rational arguments directed toward God, I remained totally absorbed in lofty thoughts of Him, which brought me such great delight that I no longer remembered any discomfort ever experienced in the past; rather, all day long I sang psalms and many of my own compositions, wholly dedicated to God. Only my nails, which continued to grow, gave me great distress, because I was unable to touch myself without their wounding me, nor could I dress, because they turned inwards or outwards, causing me great pain. My teeth also died in my mouth, and I became aware of this because once those dead teeth were pushed out by those that were alive, little by little my gums became perforated and the ends of the roots began to break through the bottoms of their canals. When I became aware of this I pulled them out as if I were drawing a sword from its scabbard, without feeling any pain or drawing any blood: in this way, I lost a good many. Somehow I also grew accustomed to these new discomforts, sometimes singing, sometimes praying, and sometimes writing with that brick paste I mentioned before, and I began to compose a *capitolo** in praise of prison in which I recounted all those events that had befallen me. I shall write it down later in the appropriate place.*

120. The good Castellan often secretly sent for news about what I was doing, and because on the last day of July I was rejoicing greatly by myself, remembering the grand celebration that was usually held in Rome on the first day of August,* I said to myself: 'All those past years I have celebrated this pleasant holiday with the vanities of this world, but this year I shall observe it in the holiness of God.' And I said to myself: 'Oh, how much happier I am with the latter rather than the former.' Those who overheard me speaking these words recounted everything to the Castellan, who with the greatest displeasure said: 'Oh, God! He triumphs and survives in such misfortune, while I live in such comfort and I am dying solely on his account. Go quickly and place him in the cell farthest underground, where the preacher Foiano was starved to death:* perhaps when he finds himself in such harsh conditions that will break his will.' Immediately Captain Sandrino Monaldi came to my prison cell with about twenty of the Castellan's men; they found me on my knees, and I did not turn toward them, for I was adoring a figure of God the Father surrounded by Angels and another figure of Christ Rising Again Victorious which I had drawn on the walls with a bit of charcoal that I had found covered up by the dirt. It was now four months since I had been stretched out on the bed with my leg broken, and I had dreamed so many times that angels came to heal me that after four months I had become as strong as if my leg had never been broken. For that reason they came to me armed to the teeth, as terrified as if I were a poisonous dragon. This captain declared to me: 'You're well aware that there are a lot of us and that we've come to you with a great deal of noise, and you don't even turn around.' To these words and imagining very well the worst that might happen to me, but having grown familiar with misfortune and able to resist it, I told them: 'To this God who bears me up, the One who rules the heavens, I've turned my soul, my contemplation, and all my vital spirits; and to you I've turned exactly what belongs to you, because you're not worthy to look upon what good there is within me, nor can you touch it, so to what belongs to you, you may do whatever you're able to do.' This captain, who was frightened and unsure of what I intended to do, told four of his strongest men: 'Put your weapons aside.' Once they had done so, he said: 'Hurry! Hurry! Jump on him and take him. Even if he were the devil, should we be afraid of him, since there are so many of us? Hold him tightly, now, so that he can't escape!' Taken by force and roughly handled by them, expecting much worse than what eventually happened to me, I raised my eyes to Christ and said: 'Oh Just God! You have paid for all our sins on Your High Cross; why, then, must my innocence pay for the sins of someone I do not know? Oh! Still may Your will be done.' Meanwhile they were carrying me away by the light of a large torch; I thought that they wanted to toss me into the pit called Sammalò,* the name given to a frightful place which had swallowed alive so many men, for they fall down into a well in the foundations of the Castello. This did not happen to me, and on this account I thought I had got a good bargain, because they placed me in that horrible cavern mentioned earlier, where Foiano died of starvation, and they left me there without doing me any further harm. When they had left I began to sing a *De profundis clamavit*, a *Miserere*, and an *In te Domine speravi*.* All that day of the first of August I celebrated with God, and my heart constantly rejoiced with hope and faith. On the second day they took me out of that hole and brought me back to the place where my first drawings of the images of God were located. When I reached that spot, in the presence of those sketches I wept profusely from delight and joy. Afterwards the Castellan wanted to know every day what I was doing and saying. The Pope, who had heard about everything that had occurred, and to whom the doctors had already given up the previously mentioned Castellan for dead, said: 'Before my Castellan dies I want him to put to death, in his own way, that Benvenuto, who is the cause of his death, so that he will not die without having his revenge.' When the Castellan heard these words from the mouth of Duke Pier Luigi, he said to him: 'So the Pope gives Benvenuto to me and wants me to take my revenge? Don't give it another thought, and leave everything to me.' Though the heart of the Pope was cruelly disposed towards me, that of the Castellan showed itself at first to be worse and more malicious; and at that point the invisible being who had deterred me from killing myself came to me, still invisibly but with clear words, shook me, raised me up, and said: 'Alas! my dear Benvenuto, quickly, very quickly turn to God again with your usual prayers, and cry out loudly, very loudly.' Terrified, I immediately fell to my knees and I said many of my prayers in a loud voice; after all of them I said a *Qui habitat in aiutorium*;* after this I talked with God for a while; and after a moment the same voice said to me, plainly and clearly: 'Go and rest now, and have no more fear.' And this was because the Castellan, after issuing the ugliest orders for my death, immediately took them back and said: 'Isn't this the Benvenuto, the man I've defended so firmly, who I know for certain is innocent, and who has suffered all these evils unjustly? Oh, how will God ever have mercy upon me and upon my sins if I do not pardon those who have done me the greatest injuries? Oh, why am I harming a worthy man, an innocent man, who has served and honoured me? Go, and instead of putting him to death I shall grant him life and liberty; and I shall leave in my will the instruction that no one should ever ask him for any part of the enormous expenses he should pay here.' When the Pope learned of this he took it very badly.

121. Meanwhile, I was saying my usual prayers and writing my *capitolo*, and every night I began to have the happiest and most pleasant dreams anyone could imagine; it seemed to me that I was always visibly in the company of that Invisible Being that I had heard and continued to hear quite often, to whom I asked no other favour except that I begged him, and most insistently, that he take me to a place where I might see the sun, saying to him that this was as much of a desire as I had, and that if I could only see it a single time I could then die happy. All the things in this prison that were painful had become like friends and companions to me, and nothing bothered me. Although those devoted servants of the Castellan, who were waiting for him to hang me from the same battlement from which I had descended (as he had declared he would), had then seen him make another decision completely contrary to that one, they could not bear it and constantly tried to frighten me in some way or other, to scare the life out of me. As I said, I had become so familiar with all these things and no longer had any fear of them, and nothing disturbed me except for this desire, that dream of seeing the sphere of the sun. So I carried on with my fervent prayers, all of which were directed with affection toward Christ, saying constantly: 'Oh, true Son of God, I beg You by Your birth, by Your death on the cross, and by Your glorious resurrection, make me worthy of seeing the sun, if not otherwise then at least in a dream; but if You make me

worthy of seeing it with these mortal eyes of mine, I promise to come pay a visit to Your Holy Sepulchre.' I made this resolution and these fervent prayers of mine to God on the second day of October in the year one thousand five hundred and thirty-nine. On the following morning, which was the third of October of the same month, I got up at the crack of dawn, about an hour before sunrise; once I had risen from that wretched bed of mine, I dressed myself with that bit of ragged clothing I had, since it had begun to be chilly; and standing there uplifted in spirit, I said my prayers more devoutly than I had ever said them in the past. In those prayers I made special entreaties to Christ, asking Him to grant me enough grace to know by divine inspiration for which of my sins I was paying such great penance, and asking that if His Divine Majesty did not see fit to make me worthy of the sight of the sun at least in a dream, that by all His power and might He should at least make me worthy of knowing the cause of my punishment.

122. Once I had said these words, I was seized by that Invisible Being and carried away as if by a wind,* and I was led into a chamber where my Invisible Being now showed himself to me in visible human form in the shape of a very young man, with a most marvellous face, handsome but austere and not lascivious; he directed me into that chamber, telling me: 'All those men that you see are all of those who up to this time have been born and later have died.' For this reason, I asked him why he had brought me here, and he answered me: 'Come along with me and you will soon see why.' I found myself with a dagger in my hand and wearing a coat of mail, and he led me dressed in that manner through that enormous room, pointing out to me the infinite number of people who were walking in one direction or another. Leading me on, he went out before me through a very small door into a place that resembled a narrow street, and when he drew me after him into that same street, upon leaving that room I found myself disarmed, and I was dressed in a white shirt, with nothing on my head, and I was standing at the right side of my companion. When I saw myself in that condition I was amazed; I did not recognize the street; and after lifting up my eyes I saw that the brightness of the sun was striking an inside wall, as if upon the façade of a house, above my head. Then I said: 'Oh, my friend, what must I do to be able to rise up high enough to see the sphere of the sun itself?' He pointed out a flight of stairs on my right

and said to me: 'Go up there by yourself.' Having moved away from him a bit, I climbed backwards up several of the steps and began, little by little, to realize I was near the sun. I hastened to ascend, and I went on up in that way until I saw revealed the entire sphere of the sun. And because the force of its rays made me close my eyes, as is customary, when I realized my error I opened them, and looking straight into the sun I said: 'Oh, my very own sun, the sun I have desired so much! I never want to see anything else again, even if your rays blind me.' Thus I remained with my eyes fixed on it, and after I stood there for a while suddenly I saw the entire force of those enormous rays cast itself to the left side of the sun; when the sun was left clear, without its rays, I gazed upon it with the greatest delight; and it seemed a marvel that those rays had been removed in that way. I remained there, considering the divine grace that I had that morning from God, and I was crying out loudly: 'O, how wonderful is Thy strength! O, how glorious is Thy power! How much greater grace You are bestowing upon me than what I'd expected!' This sun without its rays appeared to me neither more nor less than a bath of the purest molten gold.* While I was contemplating this momentous thing, I saw that the centre of this sun began to swell up and to expand, and in a moment it was transformed into the figure of a Christ on the cross, made from the very material that made up the sun; it was of such elegant beauty and so gracious in appearance that the human intellect could not imagine even a thousandth part; and while I was contemplating such a vision I said out loud: 'Miracles, miracles! O God, O Thy mercy! O Thy Infinite power! What marvels You have made me worthy of seeing this morning!' And while I was contemplating this vision and speaking these words, this figure of Christ moved towards the part of the sun from which its rays had disappeared. Once again the middle of the sun swelled up, as it had done before, and after the swelling had grown larger it suddenly changed into the form of an extremely beautiful Madonna, displayed as if She were seated on high with Her son, Her arms in the most delightful pose, almost as if She were smiling; She was placed between two of the most beautiful angels the imagination could conceive. I also saw at the right of this sun a figure dressed like a priest:* this figure turned his back on me and kept his face turned toward that Madonna and that Christ. All these things I saw truly, clearly, and vividly, and I continuously gave thanks to the glory of God in a very loud voice. When this wonderful vision had been before my eyes for little more than an eighth of an hour it left me, and I was brought back to that hovel of mine. I immediately began to cry out in a loud voice: 'God's power has made me worthy of witnessing all His glory, something perhaps never before seen by another mortal eye, by reason of which I recognize myself as being free and happy and in the grace of God; and you scoundrels—you will remain scoundrels, wretched and without God's grace. You should know I'm completely convinced that on All Saints' Day, the same day that I came into the world in the year one thousand five hundred—on the first of November four hours after the end of day—on the day which is approaching,* you will be compelled to remove me from this gloomy prison, and you'll not be able to do otherwise, because I've seen this with my own eyes and on the very throne of God Himself. St Peter was the priest who was turned toward God and who stood with his back to me, pleading on my behalf, since he was ashamed that such ugly injustices were inflicted upon Christians in his own home. So, tell this to anyone you wish, since no one has the power to do me further harm, and tell that lord who's holding me here that if he'll provide me with either wax or paper, the means by which I may express the Glory of God that has been revealed to me, I'll most assuredly make clear that about which he may perhaps be doubtful.'

123. Although all his doctors had no hope whatsoever of his recovery, the Castellan remained of sound mind, and those humours of madness that used to bother him every year had left him. Once he devoted himself completely to the state of his soul his conscience pricked him, since he believed I had suffered and continued to suffer an enormous injustice, and when he informed the Pope about the momentous events I described, the Pope—like a man who believed in nothing, neither in God nor in anything else—sent word telling him that I was mad, and that he should attend to his own health as much as possible. When the Castellan heard these replies he sent word to comfort me and sent me writing materials, wax, and certain small tools for working wax, along with many courteous words, that were reported to me by one of his servants who liked me a great deal. This particular fellow was completely unlike that bunch of those other scoundrels who would have liked to see me dead. I took up the paper and the wax and I began to work; and while I was working I wrote this sonnet addressed to the Castellan:

My Lord, if I could show you the truth
of the eternal light in this base world
that God has shown me, you would value
my faith more than the most powerful emperor's.
And if the Great Pastor of the clergy might believe
that God has shown Himself in His infinite glory,
something no living soul has ever seen, before His Glory
departed from this base, cruel, and harsh kingdom,
You would see the gates of holy and saintly Justice
unbarred, and wretched, impious Fury would fall in chains,
and she would send her cries to Heaven.
If only I possessed the light, alas, at least
my great talent might sculpt the lower portions of Heaven,
and my misfortune might not be such a heavy burden to bear.

124. On the following day, when that servant of the Castellan—
the one who was very fond of me—came to bring me my meal, I gave
him this sonnet I had written, and secretly, without telling those
other malicious servants who detested me, he gave it to the Castellan,
who would have gladly allowed me to leave because he felt that the
injustice inflicted upon me was the chief cause of his dying. After he
took the sonnet and read it more than once, he said: 'These are
neither the words nor the ideas of a madman but, rather, those of a
good and worthy man,' and he immediately ordered one of his secretaries to take it to the Pope and to put it into the Pope's own hands,
begging him to release me. While this secretary carried the sonnet to
the Pope, the Castellan sent me light for both day and night, with all
the comforts that one could desire in such a place; because of this I
began to recover from my lack of vital energy, which had become
quite serious. The Pope read my sonnet many times; then he sent
word to the Castellan that he would shortly do something that would
please him. And certainly the Pope would have then willingly
allowed me to go, but Lord Pier Luigi, his son, whom I have mentioned, almost against the Pope's wishes, kept me there by force. As
the Castellan's death grew ever closer, I had meanwhile sketched that
wonderful miracle and made a model in wax. On the morning of All
Saints the Castellan sent his nephew, Piero Ugolini, to show me
certain jewels, and when I saw them I immediately said: 'This is the
sign forewarning my liberation.' Then this young man, who was a

person of very little intelligence, replied: 'Don't ever think about that, Benvenuto.' Then I answered: 'Take away your precious stones, for I'm reduced to such a state that I can see no light except in this dark cavern, where it's impossible to discern the quality of jewels, but as for getting out of this prison, this day will not end before you come to take me away from here; and this must come to pass, and you can do no less.' The young man left and had me locked up again, and he went off and stayed for more than two hours by the clock; then he came for me without armed guards, and, accompanied by two young boys who helped hold me upright, he led me in that fashion back to those large quarters I had occupied previously (this was in 1538*), supplying me with all the comforts I requested.

125. A few days later the Castellan, who thought I was outside the prison and free, was overcome by his severe illness and passed from this life, and in his place remained Messer Antonio Ugolini, his brother,* who had given the deceased Castellan to understand that he had let me go. This Messer Antonio, as far as I could tell, had orders from the Pope to allow me to remain in that spacious prison cell until he could tell him what to do with me. That Messer Durante from Brescia, whom I mentioned previously,* came to an agreement with that soldier—the one who had been a druggist in Prato—to mix some sort of liquid into my food that would be deadly, but not immediately; it would take effect at the end of four or five months. They went about imagining how to put some crushed diamond in my food, which is not in any way poisonous in itself, but it retains its sharp edges and does not act like other stones because of its incredible hardness. Other stones, when crushed, lose their sharpest edges and become almost rounded, while the diamond alone retains its sharpness. So when diamond dust enters the stomach along with other food, turning around in the process of digestion that foods undergo, the diamond sticks to the cartilage of the stomach and intestines, and as the new food constantly pushes it forward, the diamond stuck to them perforates them before very long; and as a result the person dies; but no other sort of stone or glass mixed with food has the power to stick, and as a result it passes through with the food. To this end, that Messer Durante whom I mentioned gave a diamond of very little value to one of these guards. It was said that the task of pounding the stone had been given to a certain Lione,* a goldsmith from Arezzo who was a great enemy of mine. This Lione

had the diamond in order to crush it; but since he was extremely poor and the diamond could have been worth several tens of scudi, he gave the guard to understand that the powder which he gave him was from that diamond that the guard had been ordered to feed me; and that morning when I ate it, which was a Friday, they mixed it up in all my food: I had it in my salad, in my sauces, and in my soup. I was anxiously awaiting my meal, because I had fasted in the evening. That day was a feast day. And it is very true that I heard my food crackling between my teeth, but I never imagined such rascally behaviour. After I had finished eating, a bit of salad remained on my plate, and my eyes fell directly upon some extremely fine chips that stood out. Immediately I took them up and, drawing closer to the light from the window, which was very bright, while I examined them I remembered the unusual crunching of my food that morning, and after thinking the matter over thoroughly, as far as my eyes could judge, I was absolutely convinced that this substance was crushed diamond. I was absolutely certain that I was a dead man, and in great sorrow I raced to pray with great devotion; utterly convinced, I thought for certain that I had been sold out and murdered; and for a solid hour I prayed most fervently to God, thanking Him for such a pleasant death. Since my stars had settled my destiny in this way, I thought I had struck a good bargain in leaving this life by such an easy path; I was content and had blessed the world and the time I had passed in it. Now I was turning toward a better kingdom with the grace of God, which I most certainly thought I had acquired, and while I was immersed in such thoughts I held in my hand some of the finest particles of what I believed to be a diamond and what I had been convinced was one. But since hope never dies, I allowed myself to be moved by a bit of vain hope: this led me to take a small knife and some of those particles, and I placed them on an iron bar in the prison; then I gently placed the point of the knife on them, pressed down hard, and felt them disintegrate; and when I examined them carefully with my eyes, I saw the truth. Suddenly I was clothed once again with new hope, and I said: 'This isn't a diamond from my enemy, Messer Durante, but it's a poor, soft stone that couldn't do me any harm at all.' And although I had resolved to remain quiet and to die peacefully in that way, I conceived a new plan, but first I thanked God and blessed poverty, which on many occasions has been the cause of human death, but in this instance was the very cause of my survival, because after my enemy Messer Durante (or whoever it might have been) had given a diamond worth more than one hundred scudi to Lione to be crushed and fed to me, he had taken the diamond for himself because of his poverty, and had ground up for me a greenish beryl worth only two carlini, thinking perhaps that since it too was a stone, it would produce the same effect as the diamond.

126. At that time the Bishop of Pavia, the brother of the Count of San Secondo—called Monsignor de' Rossi of Parma*—was a prisoner in the Castello because of some disturbances that had taken place earlier in Pavia, and since he was a good friend of mine I pressed myself to the opening of my prison cell and called out to him at the top of my lungs, telling him that in order to kill me those thieves had given me a powdered diamond to eat. I had one of his servants show him some of the powdered grains that remained, but I did not tell him I had realized the particles were not from a diamond; I did tell him, however, that they had most certainly poisoned me after the death of that worthy Castellan, and that during the short time left to me I begged him to give me one of his loaves of bread each day, because I never again wished to eat anything they brought; and so he promised to send me some of his provisions. That Messer Antonio, who most assuredly knew nothing about the entire affair, raised a great ruckus and wanted to examine the powdered stone, since he still thought that it was a diamond, but supposing that this plan originated with the Pope, he passed it off lightly once he had thought the matter over. I took care to eat the food that the Bishop sent me, and I continued to write that *capitolo* of mine about my prison, recording daily all those incidents that had recently befallen me. Messer Antonio still sent me food through the previously mentioned Giovanni, the druggist from Prato who was a soldier in the Castello. I told this man, who was my mortal enemy, and who had been the one to bring me the powdered diamond, that I would eat nothing of the food he brought me unless he tasted it first, while he said that such tasting is done only for the popes. To this I answered that just as gentlemen were obliged to taste food for the popes, so he too—soldier, druggist, and knave from Prato—was obliged to taste the food of a Florentine of my rank. He spoke angrily to me and I did likewise to him. This Messer Antonio, growing somewhat ashamed of himself but still determined to make me pay those expenses the poor, dead Castellan had granted me, found another of his servants who was my friend, and he sent him with my food, which he happily tasted without any further argument. This servant told me that the Pope was pestered every single day by that Monsignor di Morluc,* who continually asked about me on behalf of the French King, that the Pope had very little inclination to give me up, and that Cardinal Farnese,* formerly my great patron and friend, had been forced to say that I should not plan to get out of that prison for a long time: to all this I said that I would get out in spite of them all. This worthy young man begged me to remain silent and to avoid being overheard saying such a thing, for it would do me very great harm; and that with the faith that I placed in God I ought to await His grace, remaining silent myself. I told him that the powers of God have no need to fear the wickedness of injustice.

127. After a few days had passed the Cardinal of Ferrara* arrived in Rome, and when he went to pay his respects to the Pope, the Pope entertained him for such a long time that the supper hour arrived. Since the Pope was a very clever man, he wanted to have the leisure to speak with the Cardinal about French court gossip.* When men eat together they often say things that they would never say except at such times; and since that great King Francis was extremely generous in all his affairs, and the Cardinal, who understood the King's wishes quite well, also conceded far more to the Pope than even he imagined possible, the Pope became quite merry because of it, and also because he had the habit of engaging in an energetic debauch once a week, so that he vomited afterwards. When the Cardinal saw the Pope's good mood, one in which he was likely to grant favours, he asked for me very earnestly in the name of the King, insisting that the King was very anxious for such a favour. Then the Pope, feeling the time for his vomiting drawing near and the overly abundant quantity of wine doing its work, said to the Cardinal with a loud laugh: 'I want you to take him home with you right now.' After he gave these express orders he rose from the table, and the Cardinal sent for me immediately before Signor Pier Luigi knew anything about it, because he would have never have allowed me to leave the prison under any circumstances. The Pope's messenger arrived along with two noble gentlemen who served the Cardinal of Ferrara, and when the fourth hour of the night had passed they took me away from that prison and led me to the Cardinal, who greeted me very

warmly; there, in comfortable lodgings, I stayed on to enjoy myself. Messer Antonio, brother of the Castellan and his successor, wanted me to pay for all my expenses, as well as those extras that constables and other such people are used to charging, and he did not want to observe any of the instructions that the deceased Castellan had left behind concerning how I was to be treated. This affair cost me many tens of scudi; and moreover, the Cardinal told me afterwards that I should keep a sharp guard if I truly valued my life, and that if he had not removed me from that prison on that particular evening I would never have left it: for he had already heard that the Pope greatly regretted releasing me.

128. I must now take a step backwards, because all these events that I am describing are repeated in my *capitolo*. When I stayed those several days in the Cardinal's chamber and then in the Pope's private garden, among my other dear friends, one of Messer Bindo Altoviti's* cashiers, by the name of Bernardo Galluzzi,* to whom I had entrusted the sum of several hundreds of scudi, came to see me. This young man came to visit me in the Pope's private garden and wanted to return the entire amount to me, whereupon I told him that I did not know a dearer friend to whom I could entrust my property or a place in which I might think it could be more secure; my friend, as it seemed, twisted and turned to make me understand that he did not want the money, and I made him keep it almost by force. When I finally left the Castello I discovered that this poor young man, Bernardo Galluzzi, had been ruined, and as a result I lost my property. Also, during my time in prison, I had a terrible dream in which words of the greatest importance were written upon my forehead with a pen, and the person who did this to me repeated to me three times over to remain silent and not to relate this to anyone else. When I awoke I felt that my forehead had been marked. So, in the *capitolo* about my imprisonment many such events take place. I also foretold, without knowing what I was saying, everything that subsequently happened to Signor Pier Luigi,* so clearly and so exactly that I myself thought it was an angel from heaven who told me about it. Also, I do not wish to omit one more thing, the greatest that has ever happened to any man, and I say this to demonstrate the divinity of God and His secrets of which He deigned to make me worthy: that is, from the time I experienced my vision there has remained over my head a brilliant splendour (a marvellous thing!); this is visible to every sort of man to whom I have been willing to show it, though they have been very few. This brilliant splendour may be seen above my shadow in the morning from sunrise until two hours after sunrise, and it can be seen much better when the grass is bathed in the soft dew; it can also be seen in the evening at sunset. I became aware of this in France, in Paris, for the air in that part of the world is so much freer from fogs that it can be seen there much more clearly than in Italy, because in Italy the fogs are so much more frequent; but, at any rate, there is no occasion when I cannot see it, and I can show it to others, but not so well as in that location.* I want to transcribe the *capitolo* I composed in prison and in praise of my imprisonment; then I shall continue with an account of what has happened to me from time to time, both good and bad, as well as what will happen to me during my life to come.

I Address This Capitolo *To Luca Martini, Calling Upon Him in It, As Will Be Evident Here**

He who would know God's power,
   And in what way a man may resemble Him,
   Should, in my opinion, spend time in prison;
He should be burdened with cares and family problems,
   And with some concern for his own safety,
   Dragged a thousand miles away from home.
Now, if you wish to achieve some worthy goal,
   Be unjustly arrested, remain in prison for some time,
   And remain without assistance from anyone.
Let them rob you of the little you possess,
   And run the risk of death as you are mistreated,
   Without hope of ever reaching salvation.
And be driven into desperation
   To break out of prison and to leap over the Castello wall:
   Then be locked up once again in an even more terrible spot.
Listen, Luca, now here comes the good part:
   Have a broken leg and be deceived,
   And lie soaking wet in prison without a cloak.
And permit not a soul speak to you,
   While the man who brings you food to eat and bad news
   Is a soldier, druggist, and scoundrel from Prato.

Now hear how Glory puts you to the test:
 There is no place to sit except the toilet;
 And yet you remain ready to undertake something new;
Express orders are to the servant given
 That he is not to heed you or to speak to you;
 And the door is only opened wide enough to let him in.
Now this is a fine pastime for the brain:
 No paper, no pen, no ink, no tool nor fire,
 And full of beautiful thoughts from the cradle on.
The great sense of anguish, which is saying very little,
 That makes every worry increase a hundredfold,
 And for each worry I have reserved a section and a place.
Now, to return to our first intention,
 That is, to praise the prison and present its merits:
 For this, a celestial spirit would not suffice.
No honest people are ever sent there
 Unless it be through evil ministers, bad government,
 Envy, malice, or some other quarrel.
But to tell the truth as I see it,
 Here one knows God, constantly crying out to Him,
 Feeling at every moment the tortures of Hell.
However evil a man's reputation may be in the world,
 After he remains in prison for two harsh years,
 He leaves it holy and wiser and beloved by all.
Here inside, soul, body, and garments are all refined;
 And every ignorant lout becomes sharper,
 And sees into Heaven up to the thrones of the Blessed.
I want to relate a miracle to you:
 When a capricious thought to write came to me,
 In need, a man seizes upon anything.
I pace the room, with my brow and head bent,
 Then I spot an opening of the door,
 And with my teeth I bite off a piece of wood;
And taking a piece of brick I happen to find on the floor,
 I break it up a bit into powder;
 Then make a paste of it with stagnant water.*
Then and only then does the flame of poetry
 Enter my body, and, I believe, through
 The place where bread goes out; for there is no other spot.

To return to my first fantasy:
    Before a man wishes to know what the Good may be,
    He must first know the Bad that God gives him.
Prison knows how to create and maintain every craft:
    If you want to learn the pharmacist's trade,
    It will sweat the blood from your veins.
And then prison has within it a certain natural force,
    For it renders you eloquent, fierce, and audacious,
    And laden with beautiful thoughts of good and evil.
Lucky is the man who lies in a dark prison
    For a long time and then, finally leaves it behind:
    For he can speak of war, truce, and peace.
Inevitably he succeeds in all things;
    For prison fills a man with such ability
    That his brain no longer dances the *moresca*.*
You may well tell me: 'But he has so many fewer years!'
    But that's not the case, for prison teaches you a way
    Of filling your heart and your brain.
As for me and insofar as I know, I praise prison;
    But I would prefer that at least one law be adopted there:
    That whoever deserves prison should not escape.
Every man who is given a poor flock to govern,
    Should take his scholarly degree in prison,
    For then he would know very well how to govern.
He would then rule wisely,
    And never swerve from the true path,
    Nor ever be caught up in great confusion.
During the time I spent there,
    I saw friars, priests, and soldiers as well,
    But far fewer people who deserved such punishment more.
If you only knew the great grief I felt there
    When one of that kind was let out before me!
    A man would almost repent for having been born.
I don't wish to say more: I have become like gold,
    The kind of gold that is not spent so easily,
    Nor is useful to create an excellent piece of work.
Another thought has come to mind, Luca,
    Something I haven't told you: where I wrote my *capitolo*
    Was in a book about one of our kinsmen,*

There in the margins I wrote it out at length,
    Describing the enormous suffering that has twisted my
      body,
    So that even my ink would not run, as I told you;
For in order to form the letter 'O', three times
    I had to dip my stick; what other punishment
    Greater than this one is suffered by the spirits in Hell?
Now, since I am not the first to be unjustly condemned,
    I shall hold my peace and return to the theme of my
      imprisonment,
    Where I rack both my brain and my heart with suffering.
I praise my imprisonment more than others;
    And wishing to enlighten those without such understanding,
    For without such enlightenment, nothing good can be
      accomplished.
Oh, as I read some time ago, if only one might come to me
    And say, like the one who spoke at the Pool of Bethesda:
    'Take your clothing, Benvenuto, and go!'*
I would sing the *Credo*, the *Salve regina*,
    And the *Paternoster*,* and then I would give alms
    To the blind, poor, and lame every morning.
Oh, how many times have those lilies* made my cheeks
    Grow pale and lifeless, to such an extent that I
    No longer desire either Florence or France ever again!
And if it happens that I must go to the hospital
    And I see the Annunciation painted there,
    I shall flee away,* looking like a wild beast!
I don't say this on Her account, She who is worthy and sacred,
    Nor on account of Her glorious and holy lilies
    That have illuminated heaven and earth.
But I do so because in every angle of the street I see
    Those lilies whose petals are hook-shaped in form,
    And I am afraid that there are so many lilies of the Farnese.
Oh, how many others, like me, lead a wretched life,
    Born slaves and servants of this family crest,
    Yet who are celebrated, noble, lofty and divine souls!
I have seen* that deadly crest plummet down
    From the swiftest heaven* among the vain people,
    Then on the stone a new lamp is lit;

First the bell of the Castello must be broken*
    Before I go free; and He told me this,*
    He who, both in Heaven and on earth, reveals the truth;
Beside the stone I then saw a dark bier,
    Decorated with broken lilies,* crosses and sad lamentations,
    And many afflicted men suffering on their beds.
I then saw Her who afflicts and tortures souls,*
    Now terrifying first this one, now another; and then this
        figure declared:
    'I shall carry off whoever seeks to harm you!'
This worthy angel* then wrote words upon my brow
    With St Peter's quill, and when this was done,
    He ordered me three times to keep silent my tongue.
I then saw Him who makes the sun rise and set,*
    Dressed by the sun's light in the midst of His court,
    A sight no mortal eye is ever accustomed to behold.
A solitary sparrow sung loudly
    Upon the castle keep; at this, I said:
    'This bird surely predicts life for me and for you death.'
And I sang and wrote about my dire troubles,
    Only begging God for pardon and assistance,
    While I felt my eyes grow dim in death.
There was never a wolf, a lion, a tiger, or a bear
    More thirsty of human blood than he,
    Nor viper with a more venomous bite.
This man was a cruel captain and thief,*
    And the worst rascal with others as wicked,
    But so everyone will know, I shall speak clearly.
If you have ever seen famished policemen
    Enter a poor man's home to despoil him,
    They hurl to the ground images of Our Lady and of Christ,
And on a day in August they came scornfully
    To carry me off to an even more wretched tomb:
    'November: when it comes, you'll be lost and cursed.'*
I heard in my ears the sound of such a trumpet
    That told me all, and I told all to them,*
    Without thinking of anything but diminishing my sorrow.
And when they had lost all hope,*
    To murder me, they gave me a diamond

Ground up to eat, one not set in gold.
I asked that rascally villain who brought my meals
　To taste them first; and I said to him:
　'This can't have been done but by my enemy Durante.'
But first of all, I turned my thoughts to God,
　Begging Him to forgive my sins,
　And in tears, I said the *Miserere*.*
And when my great grief had been somewhat softened,
　I gave my soul willingly up to God,
　Content to be going toward a better kingdom and another
　　condition,
And then I saw an angel with a glorious palm
　Descend from Heaven; and He then with a joyous face
　Promised to my life a longer stay on earth,
Telling me: 'God shall remove your every adversary
　With bitter war, and then you shall remain
　Happy, content, and freed, and in grace
With Him who is the Ruler in Heaven and on earth.'

BOOK TWO*

1. I was living in the palace of the Cardinal of Ferrara* I mentioned before. Everyone without exception thought very highly of me and I received many more visits than previously, since everyone was amazed by my having escaped and lived through so much. While I was catching my breath and doing my best to remember my skills, I took the greatest pleasure in rewriting this *capitolo*. Then, in order to regain my strength more quickly, I made up my mind to take a trip to the country for several days, with the permission and horses of my good Cardinal, and accompanied by two young Romans: one of them was a worker in my own craft, and his companion was not from the profession but came along to keep me company. After leaving Rome I went toward Tagliacozzo, thinking I would find my pupil Ascanio there, and when I arrived I found him along with his father, brothers, sisters, and stepmother. I was so well treated by them for two days that it would be impossible to describe; I then left for Rome and took Ascanio with me. On the road we began to discuss our craft,* so that I was consumed by the desire to return to Rome in order to recommence my work. After we had reached Rome I immediately prepared myself to work, and recovered a silver basin that I had begun for the Cardinal before I had been incarcerated; along with the basin I had begun an extremely beautiful ewer (this was stolen from me, together with a great quantity of other things of significant value*). I had Pagolo, whom I mentioned previously, work on the basin. I too began work once again on the ewer, which was composed of small figures in full and low relief; the basin, also composed of figures in full relief and fish in low relief, was so rich and so well arranged that everyone who saw it was amazed, both by the strength of its design as well as by its inventiveness and the clean finish those two young men gave to these works. The Cardinal came at least twice every day to spend time with me, accompanied by Messer Luigi Alamanni and Messer Gabbriel Cesano,* and several hours would go by pleasantly. Although I had a great deal to do, the Cardinal still overloaded me with new works, and he commissioned me to make his pontifical seal, which was as large as the hand of a twelve-year-old boy. On the mould for casting this seal I engraved two small scenes, one of which

was St John preaching in the desert, while the other was St Ambrose on horseback with a whip in his hand driving out the Arians.* It was executed with such daring and good design and was so cleanly finished that everyone said I had surpassed even the great Lautizio,* who executed only works of this kind; the Cardinal compared it, out of personal pride, to the other seals of the cardinals of Rome which were almost all from the hand of this Lautizio.

2. Once more the Cardinal asked me to make, along with the two works mentioned above, a model for a salt-cellar,* but he insisted that it be different from the usual kind of thing made by those who had designed salt-cellars. Messer Luigi made many admirable observations concerning such a salt-cellar; Messer Gabbriello Cesano also made many fine remarks on this subject. The Cardinal, who was a most gracious listener and who had been pleased beyond all measure by the designs which these two brilliant men had sketched out in words, then turned to me and said: 'My dear Benvenuto, the designs of Messer Luigi and Messer Gabbriello please me so much that I would not know which one of the two to choose; I therefore refer the question to you, since you must execute the design.' So I said: 'You know, my lords, just how important the sons of kings and emperors are and what marvellous splendour and divinity are visible in them. Nevertheless, if you ask a poor and humble shepherd for whom he has more love and affection—for these sons or for his own—he will most certainly declare that he loves his own sons more. For the same reason, I too harbour great love for the sons I give birth to through this profession of mine: so, the first design that I shall show to you, my reverend monsignor and my patron, will be my own work and my own invention, because many things are beautiful when described in words, but when executed they do not match their design.' And turning to those two talented men, I said: 'You have spoken, and I shall create.' Then Messer Luigi Alamanni, while laughing, very charmingly added many worthy remarks in my favour, remarks which suited him, because he was handsome and well-proportioned and spoke in a pleasant voice, while Messer Gabbriello Cesano was completely the reverse, quite ugly and unpleasant, and he spoke in accordance with his physical appearance. Messer Luigi had sketched out in words how I might execute the figure of a Venus with a Cupid, along with many appropriate decorations; Messer Gabbriello had sketched out in words how I might

execute the figure of Amphritite, the wife of Neptune, along with Neptune's Tritons and many other things that were extremely beautiful to describe but not to execute. I made an oval shape the size of more than half an armslength—in fact, almost two thirds of an armslength—and on it, as if to show the Sea embracing the Land, I placed two nicely executed figures larger than a palm in size, seated with their legs intertwined in the same fashion as certain long-branched arms of the sea can be seen running into the land; and in the hand of the male figure of the Sea I placed a lavishly wrought ship, within which a great deal of salt could easily and well be accommodated; underneath this figure I placed four seahorses, and in the hand of this figure of the Sea I placed his trident. The Land I had represented as a woman whose beautiful figure was as full of as much loveliness and grace as I was able and knew how to produce, in whose hand I had placed a rich and lavishly decorated temple which rested upon the ground, and she was leaning on it with her hand; I had created the temple in order to hold the pepper. In her other hand I had placed a Horn of Plenty adorned with all the beautiful things I knew to exist in the world. Under this goddess and in the part that portrayed the earth, I had arranged all the most beautiful animals that the earth produces. Under the part devoted to the sea god I represented all the beautiful kinds of fishes and small snails that tiny space could contain; in the widest part of the oval space I created many extremely rich decorations. Then, after waiting for the Cardinal, who came accompanied by these two brilliant men, I brought out this wax model of mine, about which Messer Gabbriel Cesano, loudly blustering, was the first to speak, and he said: 'This is a work that couldn't be executed in the lives of ten men; and you, my most Reverend Monsignor, who would like to have it, will not have it in your lifetime; so Benvenuto has wished to show you his children but not to give them to you, as we did, when we spoke of those things that might be done; and he has shown you those things which can't be done.' On hearing this, Messer Luigi Alamanni took my side. The Cardinal said that he did not wish to enter into such a great undertaking. Then I turned to them and said: 'My most Reverend Monsignor and you men of talent, let me tell you that I hope to execute this work for anyone who is to have it, and each one of you will see it finished one hundred times more richly than the model, and I hope that there is yet enough time left for us to execute even greater works than this one.' The Cardinal replied angrily: 'Unless you make it for the King, to whom I am taking you, I don't believe you can make it for anyone else,' and when he showed me the letters where the King of France, in one passage, wrote that the Cardinal should return soon, bringing Benvenuto with him, I raised my hands toward the heavens and said: 'Oh, when will that moment ever arrive?' The Cardinal said that I should put in order and settle all my affairs in Rome within ten days.

3. When the time for my departure arrived, the Cardinal gave me a good and handsome horse; he had named it Tornon, because the Cardinal Tornon had given it to him.* My pupils Pagolo and Ascanio were also provided with mounts to ride. The Cardinal divided his court, which was extremely large: the noblest part he took with him, and with it he took the road to Romagna in order to visit the Madonna of Loreto and then subsequently to go to Ferrara, which was his home; the other part he ordered to go in the direction of Florence. This was the largest part, and it included a large number of people, including the majority of his knights. To me he said that, if I wished to travel in safety, I should go with them: if I did not do so my life was at risk. I expressed my intention to His Most Reverend Lordship of travelling with him, but since that which is ordered by Heaven necessarily occurs, it pleased God for me to remember my poor sister,* who had suffered such great distress at my great misfortunes. I also remembered my first cousins, who were nuns in Viterbo, one an abbess and the other a chamberlain, so that they were the administrators of this rich convent; and since they had experienced such grievous sorrow for me and had said so many prayers for me, I was quite certain that the prayers of those poor virgins had obtained God's grace for my safety. And so, as I recalled all these matters, I wanted to go toward Florence; and whereas I might have travelled free of any expense either with the Cardinal or with his retinue, I preferred to go on my own; and I was accompanied by a most excellent master clockmaker whose name was Master Cherubino,* a great friend of mine. Meeting by chance, we made that very pleasant journey together. Having left Rome on Monday of Holy Week,* we three* proceeded alone, and at Monteruosi* we came upon the company I mentioned before; and since I had already expressed my intentions of travelling with the Cardinal, I did not think otherwise that any of my enemies would keep watch for me. I

certainly came off badly at Monteruosi, because a band of well-armed men had been sent ahead of us to cause me trouble; and as God would have it, while we were eating dinner, since they had been informed that I was coming without the Cardinal's retinue, they had prepared to do me harm. At that moment the Cardinal's retinue arrived, and with it I happily travelled in safety as far as Viterbo, since from there on I anticipated no further danger, and I went on a few miles ahead with much greater security, while the best of the men in the Cardinal's retinue kept a close eye on me. Thanks be to God, I arrived safe and sound in Viterbo, and there I received the warmest greetings from my cousins and all the rest of the convent.

4. After I had left Viterbo with the people mentioned above, we went on our way on horseback, sometimes ahead and sometimes behind the Cardinal's retinue, so that by the twenty-second hour on Holy Thursday we found ourselves one post station from Siena;* and seeing that there were several mares for exchange and that the people at the post station were waiting to give them to travellers who, for a small fee, would take them back to the post station inside Siena, I dismounted from my horse Tornon, placed my saddle-pad and stirrups upon one of those mares, and gave one of the stable-boys a giulio.* After I left my horse with those young men, who were to bring it back to me, I immediately went ahead to reach Siena a half-hour earlier, in order to visit a certain friend of mine and to conduct some other business: yet, although I went hurriedly, I did not race the mare in question. After I reached Siena I took rooms at an inn suitable for the needs of five people, and I sent the mare back with the inn-keeper's young servant to the post station, which was located outside the Porta Camollìa; but I had left my stirrups and my saddle-pad on that horse. We passed the evening of Holy Thursday very pleasantly. The next morning, which was Good Friday,* I remembered my stirrups and my saddle-pad. When I sent for them, the postmaster declared that he refused to return them because I had raced his mare. We sent messages back and forth, and this post-master kept on saying that he was not going to return them to me, along with many intolerable insults; the innkeeper where I was lodging said to me: 'You should consider yourself lucky if he does nothing but refuse to return your saddle-pad and stirrups,' and he added: 'You should know that this fellow is the most brutal man we've ever had in this city; he has two sons here, both extremely brave soldiers,

even more brutal than he is; so just buy again what you need and move along without saying anything.' I bought another pair of stirrups, yet all the while thinking about getting back my excellent saddle-pad by means of kindly words; and because I was very well mounted and well armed, with both a coat of mail and gauntlets, as well as an admirable arquebus at my saddle-horn, I was not at all frightened by the tremendous brutality the innkeeper said that mad beast embodied. I had also trained those young men of mine to wear coats of mail and gauntlets, and I put a great deal of faith in that young Roman,* since it seemed to me that while we were in Rome he never took his armour off. Even Ascanio, who was still a young boy—even he wore it, and since this was Good Friday I thought to myself that even the madness of the mad might take a holiday. We reached Porta Camollìa, where I saw and recognized the postmaster from the distinctive marks that had been described to me, for he was blind in the left eye. Having gone forward to meet him, I left behind me those young men and my companions, and I said very pleasantly: 'Postmaster, if I assure you that I did not race your mare, why won't you please return my saddle-pad and my stirrups?' To this question he replied precisely in the brutal, mad way I had been told about. So I said to him: 'How's that? Aren't you a Christian? Or do you want both of us to cause a scandal on Good Friday?' He answered that it did not worry him whether it was Good Friday or Fiendish Friday, and that if I did not get out of his way he would knock me to the ground, along with the arquebus I held in my hand, with a pike he had picked up. At such threatening words an old Sienese nobleman dressed in civilian clothes approached; he was returning from the performance of the devotions customary on such a holiday, and after having heard all my explanations from afar, he boldly drew near to admonish the postmaster, taking my side in the argument, and he reproached his two sons as well, because they had not done their duty to the strangers who were passing by, and in so doing had acted against God and brought down blame upon the city of Siena. These two young men, the postmaster's sons, shook their heads without saying a word and went away back inside their home. Their angry father, enraged by the remarks of that honourable gentleman, immediately lowered his pike with shameful curses, swearing that he wanted to murder me with it no matter what. When I had seen his brutish resolution, in order to keep him at some distance I made signs of showing him the muzzle of my arquebus. This madman threw himself upon me even more violently, and the arquebus— which I held in my hand for self-defence and which I still had not lowered to aim at him, but kept with the muzzle pointed upwards— went off by itself. The ball struck the arch of the gate, and after it ricocheted backwards it struck the man's windpipe, and he fell down dead on the ground. His two sons ran up quickly, and while one of them seized his weapons from a rack, the other picked up his father's pike; when they attacked my young men, the son with the pike first wounded Pagolo the Roman on the left breast; the other son rushed at a man from Milan who was in our company, who looked like a fool; and it did not do him any good to ask for mercy, saying he had nothing to do with me, nor to defend himself from the point of a heavy pike with a little cane he was holding in his hand: with this he was unable to save himself from getting a slight wound in the mouth. Messer Cherubino was dressed as a priest, for although he was a most excellent clockmaker, as I said, he had benefices from the Pope that produced good revenues. Ascanio, seeing that he was very well armed, made no sign of fleeing as the man from Milan had done, so that he and the clockmaker remained untouched. I had spurred my horse, and while it was galloping I had hurriedly prepared myself and loaded my arquebus; turning back furiously, it seemed to me that I had taken the matter as a joke but now I had to treat it seriously, and thinking that those young men of mine had been killed, I too resolutely went off to die. The horse had not gone back many paces when I met them coming towards me, and I asked them if they were hurt. Ascanio answered that Pagolo had been mortally wounded by a pike. Then I declared: 'Oh, Pagolo, my son! So the pike pierced your coat of mail?' 'No,' Pagolo replied, 'I had put the coat of mail into the saddle-bag this morning.' 'So coats of mail are supposed to be worn in Rome to make yourself look handsome to the ladies, and in dangerous places, where they are necessary, you keep them in your saddle-bags? You deserve all the misfortunes that you have suffered, and it's your fault that I'm now riding to my death as well,' and while I was uttering these words I continued to turn back boldly. Ascanio and Pagolo begged me to be satisfied with saving myself and them as well, because most certainly I was riding to my death. At that moment I ran into Messer Cherubino, along with the man from Milan who had been wounded: the Milanese immediately

shouted out that nobody was injured and that the blow that struck
Pagolo had gone so far up to the right that it had not penetrated
deeply, and he said that the old postmaster remained dead on the
ground, while his sons, along with a great number of other people,
were making preparations to attack us, and that they would certainly
cut us all to pieces: 'So, Benvenuto, since Fortune has saved us from
the first onslaught, let's not tempt her further, since she may not save
us again.' Then I said: 'Since you are satisfied, I'm satisfied too,' and
turning to Pagolo and Ascanio, I said to them: 'Spur your horses and
let's gallop on to Staggia* without stopping, and we'll be safe there.'
The wounded man from Milan declared: 'Blast our sins! This wound
I received was only for the sin of eating a bit of meat soup yesterday,*
since I had nothing else to eat.' For all our trials and tribulations, we
had to laugh a bit at this numbskull and at the silly words he had
uttered. We spurred our horses and left behind Messer Cherubino
and the man from Milan, who came along at their leisure.

5. Meanwhile the dead man's sons ran to the Duke of Melfi* for
light horses, in order to catch up with us and take us. When this
Duke learned that we were in the service of the Cardinal of Ferrara,
he refused to give them either horses or permission to leave. In the
meantime we reached Staggia, where we were safe. When we arrived
there we looked for a doctor, the best to be found in that place, and
we had Pagolo examined; the wound was only superficial, and I
realized that it would cause no harm. Then we arranged to have
dinner. In the meantime Messer Cherubino arrived with that fool
from Milan, who was continuously cursing violent quarrels, and said
that he had been excommunicated because he had been unable to
recite a single Paternoster that entire holy morning. This man had an
ugly face and nature had given him a large mouth; the wound he had
received enlarged his mouth by more than three fingers, and with
that silly Milanese accent of his and his foolish tongue, the words he
spoke gave us so many occasions for laughter that, rather than complaining about our misfortunes, we could not do anything but laugh
at every word the man uttered. The doctor wanted to stitch the
wound in his mouth, and he had already put in three stitches when
the wounded man told him to stop a moment, since he did not want
him to stitch him up completely out of some hostility toward him; he
picked up a spoon and he said that he wanted him to leave enough
room for that spoon to enter his mouth, so that he could return alive

to his family and friends. These words, which he spoke while tossing his head about in a particular way, gave us such a wonderful excuse to laugh that, instead of complaining over our bad luck, we never stopped laughing; and so, laughing all the way, we went on to Florence. We dismounted at the home of my poor sister, where we were treated with marvellous kindness by her and by my brother-in-law. This Messer Cherubino and the man from Milan went off to attend to their own affairs. We stayed in Florence for four days, during which Pagolo recovered: but it was quite something that, whenever we talked about that fool of a Milanese, it made us laugh just as hard as our other mishaps moved us to tears, so that we were continually laughing and crying at the same time. Pagolo healed quickly; then we went on toward Ferrara, and we discovered that even before our Cardinal had arrived in Ferrara he had heard all about our misfortunes, and consoling us, he said: 'I pray to God that He will grant me the grace to bring you safe and sound to that king to whom I have promised you.' The Cardinal assigned me to one of his own palaces in Ferrara, an extremely beautiful place called Belfiore which adjoins the city walls; here he arranged things so that I could work. Afterwards he made arrangements to set out for France without me, and when he saw that I was very unhappy about this, he said: 'Benvenuto, everything I am doing is to your advantage, because before I take you out of Italy I want you to know beforehand exactly what you are going to do in France: in the meantime work as hard as you can on my basin and ewer, and I shall leave orders for my steward to give you everything that you need.' And after he left I remained extremely discontented, and more than once I felt like going away, but what held me back was the fact that he had liberated me from Pope Paul, and for the rest, I remained there in discontent and to my great personal loss. Yet, having dressed myself in the gratitude that such a favour deserved, I resolved to be patient and see what conclusion these affairs might reach; and having set myself to work with my two young men, I made marvellous progress with this basin and the ewer. The air where we were lodged was unhealthy, and as summer was approaching we all became rather ill. During our indisposition we went about exploring the place where we were staying, which was enormous, and which left wild almost a mile of open terrain, inside of which were numerous domesticated peacocks that nested there like wild birds. When I noticed this I loaded my musket with some noiseless powder; I then lay in wait for these young peacocks, and every two days I killed one of them, which nourished us so completely, but with such potency that all our ailments disappeared; and we applied ourselves to our work there quite happily as we moved ahead on the ewer and the basin, a task that required a great deal of time.

6. At this time the Duke of Ferrara reached an agreement with the Roman Pope Paul, resolving a number of their old differences of opinion regarding Modena and certain other cities. As the Church had a right to them, the Duke concluded this peace agreement with the Pope through the power of money—it was a very large sum: I believe that the total surpassed three hundred thousand ducats of the Camera.* At this time the Duke had an aged treasurer, who had been raised by his father Duke Alfonso, by the name of Messer Girolamo Giliolo. This old man could not endure the outrage of so great a sum going to the Pope, and he went yelling through the streets, saying: 'His father, Duke Alfonso, would rather have captured Rome with this money than as much as shown it to the Pope,' and no orders could induce him to pay it out. At last, when the Duke had forced him to make the payment, the old man suffered such an attack of dysentery that he almost died. Meanwhile, as the old man lay ill, the Duke summoned me and wanted me to do his portrait, which I did upon a round piece of black stone which was as large as a small plate for the table. These labours of mine pleased the Duke, along with my numerous pleasant conversations; those two things often caused him to remain still for four or five hours to let me do his portrait, and sometimes he had me eat at his table. In the space of eight days I finished this portrait of his head; then he ordered me to execute the reverse, where I depicted Peace as a woman with a torch in her hand, who was setting fire to a pile of weapons, the trophies of war; I executed this woman in a joyful pose, with extremely delicate drapery, and extraordinary grace; and underneath her feet I represented the vexed and sorrowful figure of Fury,* in despair and bound by many chains. I executed this work with great care, and it brought me great honour. The Duke could not get his fill of saying how pleased he was, and he gave me the inscriptions for the head of His Excellency and for the reverse. The inscription for the reverse read: *Pretiosa in conspectu Domini.** It showed that this peace had been bought at a high price.

7. During the time that I set about executing this work, the Cardinal had written telling me that I should prepare myself, because the King had asked for me, and that his next letters would contain all the arrangements that he had promised to make for me. I carefully packed my basin and my ewer in a case; I had already shown them to the Duke. A gentleman from Ferrara, whose name was Messer Alberto Bendedio,* took care of the Cardinal's affairs. This man had been confined to his home for twelve years without ever going outside because of some illness. One day he sent for me with the greatest haste, telling me that I was to take the post immediately to go and join the King, who was asking for me with great insistence, as he thought I was in France. The Cardinal had excused himself by saying that I was rather ill and had remained in one of his abbeys in Lyons, but that he would arrange for me to come promptly to His Majesty; and so he entreated me to travel by post.* This Messer Alberto was a very worthy man, but he was arrogant, and insufferably so as a result of his illness; and as I said, he told me to get ready immediately to travel by post. To his order I replied that my profession did not travel by post; that if I had to go I wanted to do so at comfortable intervals, and that I would take my two workers whom I had brought from Rome, Ascanio and Pagolo, with me; and that, moreover, I needed a servant with us on horseback to assist me and enough money to get me there. This sick old man answered me, with the most arrogant words, that the Duke's sons travelled in the way I had described, and other than them no one did. I immediately answered that the sons of my profession travelled in the manner I had described; that since I had never been the son of a duke I did not know how such people travelled; and that if he spoke such unfitting words in my ears I would not go on any account, for since the Cardinal had broken his word of honour with me and such rude words had been spoken to me, I would certainly decide not to trouble myself with people of Ferrara any longer; and turning my back on him, I grumbling and he threatening, I left. I went to find the Duke, with his completed medal; he showed me the most honourable kindness ever shown to any man, and he entrusted to his Messer Girolamo Giliolo the task of finding a ring with a diamond worth two hundred scudi and of giving it to his chamberlain Fiaschino, who would give it to me. And so it was done. This Fiaschino, on the evening of the day that I had delivered the medal, at the first hour of

the night offered me a ring set with a diamond that had a fine appearance, and he said these words on behalf of his Duke—that such a uniquely talented hand, which had worked so well, should, in remembrance of His Excellency, be adorned by that diamond. When daylight came I examined the ring, which contained a very thin, wretched diamond worth about ten scudi. Yet I did not want to think that all those marvellous words the Duke had directed him to address to me should be accompanied by such small reward, believing the Duke had been very satisfied with me; and since I imagined that this was the doing of that rascally treasurer of his, I gave the ring to a friend of mine who was to return it to the chamberlain Fiaschino in any way he could. This friend was Bernardo Saliti,* who carried out this task admirably. This Fiaschino immediately came to see me, making the greatest outcry, telling me if the Duke learned that I had sent him back a present in that way, one that he had so kindly given to me, he would take it very badly and I would perhaps repent of my action. To this I responded that the ring His Excellency had given me was worth about ten scudi, while the work I had executed for His Excellency was worth more than two hundred; but in order to show His Excellency that I valued his act of kindness, he had only to send me a ring that worked against the cramps,* of the kind that came from England and cost about a carlino. This I would cherish in memory of His Excellency as long as I lived, along with the honourable words His Excellency had him offer me; because I recognized that the splendour of His Excellency had more than paid me for my labours, while this jewel of little value brought them reproach. These words so upset the Duke that he called his treasurer and berated him far worse than he had ever done in the past; to me he gave orders that, under pain of his displeasure, I should not leave Ferrara without his giving me permission; and he commanded his treasurer to give me a diamond worth up to three hundred scudi. The miserly treasurer found one worth barely more than sixty scudi, and he gave it to be understood that this diamond was worth well over two hundred.

8. In the meantime Messer Alberto, whom I mentioned above, had returned to the right path and had provided me with all that I had requested. At all events I was ready to leave Ferrara that very day, but that zealous chamberlain of the Duke had arranged things with this Messer Alberto so that I would have no horses that day. I had loaded a mule with much of my baggage, and on this mule I had

packed up the basin and the ewer I had executed for the Cardinal. At this point I was joined by a gentleman from Ferrara, who was called Messer Alfonso de' Trotti.* This gentleman was very old, and an extremely cultivated person who took great delight in the arts, but he was one of those people who are extremely difficult to please, and if by chance they ever happen to see anything that they like, they picture it in their minds as being of such excellence that they think they will never again see anything else that will please them. This Messer Alfonso came up to me, causing Messer Alberto to say to him: 'I am sorry you came so late, because we have already packed the basin and the ewer that we are sending to the Cardinal in France.' This Messer Alfonso said that he did not mind about that, and he made a sign to one of his servants and sent him to his home; this servant brought back a white ceramic ewer, the kind that came from Faenza, which was very delicately decorated. While the servant was going and returning, this Messer Alfonso said to Messer Alberto: 'I want to tell you why I don't care to see any more vases: the reason is that I once saw a silver one, an antique that was so beautiful and so marvellous that the human imagination would never even arrive at the thought of such excellence, and so I don't mind not seeing anything else, so that such a sight will not spoil my marvellous memory of that one. The owner of the vase was a great and talented gentleman who was travelling to Rome on some business of his, and he was secretly shown this antique vase; by means of an enormous quantity of scudi, he corrupted the man who owned it and brought it back with him to our neighbourhood, but he keeps it secretly hidden so that the Duke doesn't know anything about it, since he is frightened of losing it in some way.' This Messer Alfonso paid no attention to me while he told these tall tales of his, although I was present, since he did not know me. Meanwhile this blessed ceramic model appeared, and was displayed with so much ostentation, pretence, and pomposity that, when I had seen it, I turned to Messer Alberto and said: 'How lucky of me to have seen it!' Angered, Messer Alfonso replied offensively: 'So who are you, who doesn't know what he is talking about?' To this I said: 'Now listen to me, and then you will see which of us knows better what he is talking about.' I turned to Messer Alberto, a very serious and intelligent person, and I said: 'This is a little silver goblet of such and such a weight that I made at such and such a time for that charlatan Maestro Jacopo, the surgeon from Carpi, who came to Rome and stayed there for six months; he smeared with one of his ointments many dozens of lords and poor noblemen, from whom he extracted many thousands of ducats. At that time I made this vase for him and another different from it; he paid me very badly for both the one and the other, and now all those unfortunate people he anointed are crippled and reduced to a very bad state. I consider it a very great honour for me that my works should be held in such high esteem by you other wealthy lords, but let me tell you quite plainly that during all those many years since that time I've applied myself to learn as much as possible, so that I believe the vase I'm carrying to France is much more worthy of the Cardinal and the King than was the vase belonging to that quack doctor of yours.' After I had spoken my piece this Messer Alfonso actually seemed to be consumed by the desire to see the basin and the ewer, the sight of which I continued to deny him. After we had gone on in this way for a time, he said that he would go to the Duke and that he would see them through His Excellency's intervention. Then Messer Alberto Bendedio, who was, as I said earlier, extremely arrogant, said: 'Messer Alfonso, before you leave here you shall see them without using the Duke's influence!' At these words I left, and allowed Ascanio and Pagolo to show them the works, and Pagolo said later that the two gentlemen had given me high praise. Then Messer Alfonso wanted to become more friendly with me, and as a result I thought a thousand years would pass before I could leave Ferrara and get away from them. All the good I derived from this experience had been an acquaintance with Cardinal Salviati and the Cardinal of Ravenna,* as well as with some of those talented musicians* and no one else, because the people of Ferrara are extremely avaricious and the property of others pleases them in whatever way they can get it: they are all like that. At the twenty-second hour Fiaschino, whom I mentioned above, turned up and handed me that diamond worth around sixty scudi; he told me, with the most melancholy expression and in few words, that I should wear it out of love for His Excellency. To this I answered: 'And I shall do so.' Placing my feet in my stirrups in his presence, I began my journey to get away from there. He noted my action and my words and reported them back to the Duke, who, enraged, was extremely eager to make me return.

9. That evening, trotting all the way, I went more than ten miles, and the next day when I was outside the territory of Ferrara I was

extremely pleased about it, because except for those young peacocks I had eaten there, which were the cause of my good health, I knew of no other benefit from that place. We travelled by the Mont Cenis road, avoiding the city of Milan on account of my previously mentioned fear,* so that we reached Lyons safe and sound. Counting Pagolo, Ascanio, and a servant, there were four of us with four very good mounts. After we reached Lyons we stopped for several days to wait for the muleteer who was carrying the basin and the silver ewer, along with our other baggage: we were lodged in an abbey that belonged to the Cardinal.* After the muleteer arrived we placed all our belongings in a cart and started out toward Paris. So we went toward Paris, and we experienced some trouble along the road, but nothing very notable. We found the court of the King at Fontainebleau:* we presented ourselves to the Cardinal, who immediately had us assigned lodgings, and we were very comfortable that evening. The next day the cart arrived, and once we had taken our belongings, the Cardinal heard about its arrival and told the King, who immediately wanted to see me. I went to His Majesty with the basin and the ewer, and when I was in his presence I kissed his knee, and he received me most kindly. Meanwhile, I thanked His Majesty for having liberated me from prison, telling him that every ruler in the world who was good and unique, in the way he was himself, was obligated to free men who were talented in some fashion—especially those who were innocent as I was—and that such good deeds were first to be written down in the books of God, rather than any others that could be done in the world. This good King waited to listen until I had spoken, with very great courtesy and with a few words worthy of him alone. After I had finished he took the ewer and the basin, and then he said: 'Truly, I do not believe that such a beautiful method of working was ever seen by the ancients: I well remember having seen all the best works executed by the best masters in all of Italy, but I never saw anything that moved me as profoundly as this.' The King spoke these words in French to the Cardinal of Ferrara, along with many other remarks even more laudatory than these. Then he turned to me and spoke to me in Italian, saying: 'Benvenuto, pass your time pleasantly for several days, take heart, and see that you enjoy some good dinners; and meanwhile we shall think about how to give you a good opportunity to create some beautiful works of art for us.'

10. The Cardinal of Ferrara, whom I mentioned above, saw how

very pleased the King had been by my arrival, and he also saw that on the basis of these few works the King hoped to be able to fulfil his wish to carry out certain great works that he had in mind. At this time we were following behind the court—it could be said that we were struggling along, because some twelve thousand horses always trail along behind the king's retinue. And this is the smallest number, for when the court is fully attended in peacetime there are some eighteen thousand horses, so that there are always more than twelve thousand. The result was that we were following the court into places where there were sometimes not even two houses available; and as the gypsies do, they made tents of linen, and many times we suffered great discomfort. I therefore continuously begged the Cardinal to urge the King to set me to work; the Cardinal told me that it was best in this case to wait until the King remembered to do so himself, and that I should allow myself to be seen by His Majesty on occasion while he was eating. While I was doing so, one morning as the King was dining, he called me over: he began to speak with me in Italian, and said that he had intended to carry out many great works and that soon he would make arrangements about where I was to work and would provide me with everything that I needed, making many other pleasant and diverse remarks. The Cardinal of Ferrara was present, since he almost always ate in the morning at the King's own table, and after he had heard all these remarks, as the King got up from the table the Cardinal of Ferrara spoke in my favour, as it was later reported to me: 'Sacred Majesty, this Benvenuto has a very strong desire to work; it could almost be said to be a sin to make such a skilled artisan waste his time.' The King replied that he had spoken well, and added that he should arrange with me all that I wished for my allowance. On the following evening, after the Cardinal had received this commission, he sent for me after supper and told me, on behalf of His Majesty, how His Majesty had determined that I should set to work, but first he wanted me to know what my allowance was to be. The Cardinal said: 'It seems to me that if His Majesty gives you an allowance of three hundred scudi per year you can make out very well indeed; subsequently, let me say that you should leave the arrangements to me, since every day the occasion arises to do well in this great kingdom, and I shall always give you my utmost help.' Then I answered: 'Without my seeking out Your Most Reverend Lordship, when you left me in Ferrara you promised never to make me leave Italy if I did not know beforehand the conditions under which I was to remain with His Majesty; Your Most Reverend Lordship, instead of sending me a message to tell me the conditions under which I was to work, sent me an express order to come by post, as if such art could be executed by post; and if you had sent me a message speaking of three hundred scudi, as you are saying now, I would not have bestirred myself for even six hundred. But I still thank God and Your Most Reverend Lordship for everything, because God has employed you as His instrument for such a great good, that is, my liberation from prison. On that account, let me say to Your Lordship that all the great ills I am now experiencing at your hands can't equal even a thousandth part of the great good that I have received from you, and I thank you for it with all my heart; and I take my leave of you, and wherever I might be, and as long as I may live, I shall always pray to God for you.' Enraged, the Cardinal replied angrily: 'Go wherever you like, since it's impossible to help someone by force.' Some of his good-for-nothing courtiers said: 'This man thinks he's something very special, since he's refusing an income of three hundred scudi.' Others, the ones with more understanding, said: 'The King will never find this man's equal: and this Cardinal of ours wants to trade him as if he were a load of firewood.' It was Messer Luigi Alamanni who said this, as I was later informed. This took place in Dauphiné and in a castle whose name I cannot remember, and it was the last day of October.

11. After I left the Cardinal I went to my lodgings three miles away, accompanied by a secretary of the Cardinal who was also heading toward the same accommodations. During the entire distance this secretary never stopped asking me what I wanted done for me and what would have been my expectations for an allowance. I never answered him except with one phrase, saying: 'I knew everything.' Then, after reaching our lodgings, I found Pagolo and Ascanio who were there, and when they saw how upset I was they forced me to tell them what was wrong. When I saw how dismayed these poor young men were, I told them: 'Tomorrow morning I'll give you enough money so that you can comfortably return to your homes, and I shall go on without you to take care of a very important bit of my own business, which I have had in mind to do for some time now.' Our room shared walls with the room of the secretary, and it is quite possible that he wrote to the Cardinal about everything I had in mind

to do, although I never knew anything about it. I spent a sleepless night: it seemed like a thousand years before dawn broke, so that I might carry out the decision I had taken. When dawn came I gave the orders for my horses, and I quickly organized myself and gave everything that I had taken with me to those two young men, as well as an additional fifty gold ducats; I set aside an equal amount for myself, plus the diamond that the Duke had given me; I carried only two shirts and some riding clothes that I was wearing, which were none too good. I could not get away from the two young men, who wanted to come with me no matter what, and for that reason I really humiliated them, telling them: 'One of you has his first beard, while the other is just beginning to grow one, and you've learned from me as much of this poor craft as I've been able to teach you, since you are today the foremost young men in this trade in Italy—and aren't you ashamed that you don't have the courage to abandon the stroller that always carried you?* This is really disgraceful! Oh, what would you say if I let you leave without any money? Now get out of my sight, and may God bless you a thousand times over—goodbye!' I turned my horse and left them in tears. I took a most beautiful road through the woods in order to get at least forty miles away that day, to a place as unknown as could be imagined. I had already gone around two miles; and in that brief journey I had decided never to practise my craft again in any place where I was known, nor did I ever want to execute any work again except a figure of Christ some three armslengths in height, approaching as near as I could to that boundless beauty that He Himself had shown to me.* Once I had come to this decision I set off in the direction of the Holy Sepulchre. Just when I thought I had gone far enough away that nobody could ever find me, I heard the sound of horses behind me; this aroused my suspicions, because in those parts there are certain bands of men called 'adventurers' who quite happily murder people on the highway; and even though many of them are hanged every day, it almost seems as if they do not worry about it. When these riders came closer I recognized that among them was a messenger from the King, along with that young man of mine, Ascanio, and after the messenger caught up with me he said: 'On behalf of the King, I'm telling you to come to him immediately.' To this man, I said: 'You come on behalf of the Cardinal: and for that reason, I don't wish to come.' The man said that since I did not want to return voluntarily, he had the authority to command the locals to bind me like a prisoner. Ascanio, too, as best he could, begged with me, reminding me that when the King imprisoned somebody it took at least five years before he decided to release him. This mention of the word prison, reminding me of that prison in Rome, terrified me so greatly that I turned my horse in the direction the King ordered. The messenger, continuously babbling in French, never once stopped during the whole journey until he had brought me back to the court: sometimes he threatened me, then he would say one thing and then another, until I was almost ready to renounce the world.

12. When we reached the King's quarters we passed before those of the Cardinal of Ferrara. Standing in the door, the Cardinal called me over to him and said: 'Our Most Christian King, on his own authority, has provided you with the same allowance that His Majesty gave to the painter Leonardo da Vinci, of seven hundred scudi a year; and what's more, he will pay you for all the works that you execute for him; for your journey here he will give you five hundred golden scudi, which are to be paid to you before you leave.' When the Cardinal had finished speaking, I replied that these were, indeed, gifts worthy of such a King. The King's messenger, not knowing who I was, begged my pardon many times when he saw those great offerings from the King. Pagolo and Ascanio remarked: 'God has helped us return to such an honoured stroller!' Then, on the following day I went to thank the King, who ordered me to make the models for twelve silver statues which he wanted to serve as twelve candlesticks around his table; he wanted them to represent six gods and six goddesses, of exactly the same size as His Majesty himself, which was a little less than a height of four armslengths. After he had given me this commission, he turned to his treasurer* and asked if he had paid me the five hundred scudi. The treasurer said that no one had told him anything about that. The King took this very badly, for he had entrusted the Cardinal with the task of telling the treasurer to do so. The King also told me to go to Paris and to look for accommodations that would be suitable for producing such works, because he would give them to me. I took the five hundred golden scudi and went to Paris, to an apartment belonging to the Cardinal of Ferrara, and there, in the name of God, I began to work, and I made four small models in wax, each about two thirds of an armslength in size: Jupiter, Juno, Apollo, and Vulcan. Meanwhile the King came to

Paris, and for this reason I went to see him immediately, and I took these models with me, along with my two young men, that is, Ascanio and Pagolo. After I saw that the King was satisfied with the models, he ordered me to execute the figure of Jupiter in silver, at the stated height, as the first of these works. I presented to His Majesty the two young men whom I had brought from Italy to serve His Majesty; and since I had trained them myself, I would receive much greater assistance from them in the first phases of my work than from the young men of the city of Paris. To this the King replied that I must provide the two young men with a salary that seemed fair to me and which was appropriate for their maintenance. I said that one hundred golden scudi would be fine for each of them, and that I would make certain they earned their wages. Thus, we reached an agreement. I also told the King that I had found a place which seemed very suitable for the execution of these works; this place was the property of His Majesty and was called the Le Petit Nesle,* and it was, at that time, held by the Provost of Paris, to whom His Majesty had given it; but since this Provost did not use it, His Majesty could give it to me, and I would use it in his service. The King immediately said: 'This place belongs to me, and I know very well that the man to whom I gave it does not live there and does not use it; you can, therefore, use it for our business,' and he immediately ordered his lieutenant to install me in Le Petit Nesle. The man offered some resistance to this, telling the King that he was unable to do so. To this, the King angrily replied that he wanted to give his property to whomever he pleased and to a man who was serving him, since the Provost was not doing anything for him: he should, therefore, say no more to him about the matter. Still, the lieutenant added that it would be necessary to use a little force. To this the King said: 'Go right now, and if a little force is not sufficient, use a great deal of it.' The man immediately took me to the place, and he had to use force to put me in possession of it; then he told me that I should take great care not to be murdered there. I went inside and immediately took on servants and purchased a good many large pikes, and for several days I stayed there with great unease, because this Provost was a great Parisian gentleman, and the other gentlemen were hostile to me to such an extent that they directed more insults at me than I was able to bear. I do not want to omit the fact that this period during which I arranged to work for His Majesty was in the year of 1540, which was exactly the fortieth year of my life.

13. On account of these intense attacks I returned to the King, begging His Majesty to accommodate me somewhere else, to which the King replied: 'Who are you and what is your name?' I remained very confused and did not know what the King meant to say, and while I was standing there in silence, the King asked me the same question, almost angrily. Then I answered that my name was Benvenuto. The King said: 'Well, if you are the Benvenuto I have heard about, act as you customarily do, for I give you full leave to do so.' I told His Majesty that it was enough for me to remain in his favour— as for the rest, I knew nothing could harm me. With a slight smile, the King said: 'Go, then, and my favour will never fail you.' He immediately ordered his first secretary, whose name was Monsignor di Villurois,* to give instructions to provide for me and to arrange for all my needs. This Villurois was a very close friend of the gentleman called the Provost who had possession of Le Petit Nesle. This place was in the shape of a triangle and adjoined the city walls; it was an old castle, but did not hold a garrison: it was of a considerable size. This Monsignor di Villurois advised me to look for another place and to abandon this one at all costs, because the individual who owned it was a man of the greatest power, who would most certainly have me murdered. To this I responded that I had left Italy for France only to serve that marvellous King, and that as for dying, I knew very well that I had to die eventually but that a bit earlier or later did not worry me at all. This Villurois was a man of extraordinary spirit, admirable in everything he did, and extremely wealthy: there was nothing in the world he would not have done to cause me trouble, but he showed nothing of this; he was a serious person, handsome in appearance, and he spoke slowly. He entrusted my case to another gentleman, who was called Monsignor di Marmagna* and was the treasurer of Languedoc. The first thing this individual did was to search for the best rooms in the place and have them prepared for his own use: I said to him that the King had given me the place so that I could serve him, and that I did not want anyone else to live there except me and my servants. This man was arrogant, bold, and spirited; he told me that he would do whatever suited him, that I was knocking my head against a wall if I wanted to oppose him, and that for everything that he was doing, he had received a commission from

Villurois permitting him to do it. Then I told him that I had received a commission from the King, and that neither he nor Villurois could do such things. When I said this, this haughty man spoke to me in his French, using many ugly words, to which I answered in my own language that he was lying. Moved by anger, he made a motion as if he were about to draw one of his small daggers; at this, I set my hand on one of the large daggers I always wore at my side for self-defence, and I said to him: 'If you dare to unsheathe your weapon, I'll kill you on the spot.' He had two servants with him, and with me I had my two young men; and while this Marmagna was standing there a little uncertainly, not knowing what to do but more inclined to do some harm, he said, muttering: 'I shall never put up with such a thing!' I saw things taking a bad turn, and I quickly made up my mind and said to Pagolo and Ascanio: 'When you see me unsheathe my dagger, throw yourselves upon his two servants and kill them if you can, for I shall kill him with the first blow, and then we shall immediately leave together.' When Marmagna heard my decision he thought it would be enough to leave that place alive. I wrote about all these events to the Cardinal of Ferrara, toning things down a little, who immediately told them to the King. The King, angered, put me in the care of another of his guards, whose name was Monsignor lo Iscontro d'Orbech.* With as much pleasantness as one could imagine, this man provided for all my needs.

14. After I had made all the most appropriate arrangements for the house and workshop, so that I could work and serve the King and make the most honourable use of the house, I immediately set to work making three models, of the exact size that they had to be in silver: these figures were of Jupiter, Vulcan, and Mars.* I made them of clay, very well reinforced by an iron framework; and then I went to the King, who had me given, if I remember correctly, three hundred pounds of silver so that I could begin work. While I was giving instructions about these things, the little ewer and the oval basin which had involved several months' work were brought to completion. After I had completed them, I had them very well gilded. They seemed to be the most beautiful works that had ever been seen in France. I immediately took them to the Cardinal of Ferrara, who thanked me profusely; then, without me, he took them to the King and made him a present of them.* The King held them very dear, and he praised me beyond the limits that any man of my condition had

ever been praised, and in response to this present he gave the
Cardinal of Ferrara an abbey producing seven thousand scudi of
revenue, but he also wanted to give me a gift. At that point the Cardinal stopped him, saying to His Majesty that he was doing this too
quickly, since I had not yet delivered any works to him. The King,
who was most generous, replied: 'Then I wish to give him encouragement to deliver some to me.' Ashamed at this remark, the Cardinal
said: 'Sire, I beg you to let me attend to this, for I shall give him a
pension of at least three hundred scudi as soon as I have taken possession of the abbey.' I never received the pension, and it would take too
much time to tell of the diabolical deceptions of this Cardinal; but I
want to save my narrative for things of greater importance.

15. I returned to Paris. With so much favour shown to me by the
King, I was admired by everyone. I procured the silver and began the
statue of Jupiter I mentioned previously. I hired a great many workmen, and with the greatest care I never stopped working both day
and night, so that after I had completed the clay figures of Jupiter,
Vulcan, and Mars and had already began to move ahead rather well
on the Jupiter in silver, my workshop already looked very prosper-
ous. At this time the King appeared in Paris: I went to visit him, and
as soon as His Highness saw me he cheerfully summoned me and
asked if there was anything beautiful in my house to show him, for
then he would come there. In response, I told him everything that I
had done. He was immediately seized by the desire to come; and
after his dinner he made arrangements with Madame d'Étampes,* the
Cardinal of Lorraine,* and with certain other noblemen, including
the King of Navarre, the brother-in-law of King Francis,* and the
Queen, the sister of King Francis;* the Dauphin and the Dauphiness*
also came, so that all the nobility of the court arrived on that day. I
had gone on home and I had begun to work. When the King
appeared at the door of my castle, on hearing the blows of several
hammers he ordered everyone with him to be quiet: in my house
everyone was at work, so that when the King turned up I did not
expect him. He entered my hall, and the first thing he saw was me,
working on a large plate of silver that I was using for the body of the
Jupiter: someone else was working on the head, another the legs, so
that it was extremely noisy. While I was working, I had a little French
boy of mine helping me, and since he had annoyed me in some small
way or another I had given him a kick, and as luck would have it I

caught him with my foot in his crotch and had thrust him more than four armslengths, so that when the King entered this small lad knocked against the King: it caused the King to burst out laughing, and I was very embarrassed. The King began to ask me what I was doing and wanted me to work; then he told me that he would be much happier if I did not exhaust myself, but rather took on as many men as I liked and had them do the work: because he wanted me to keep healthy so that I could serve him for longer. I replied to His Majesty that I would immediately fall ill if I did not work, 'nor would the works be of the kind I want to create for His Majesty'. Since the King thought that what I said was for the purpose of bragging and was not, in fact, the truth, he had the Cardinal of Lorraine say the same thing to me, to whom I revealed my reasons so fully and clearly that he was fully convinced: he advised the King, therefore, to let me work a little or a good deal, just as I wished.

16. Pleased with my works, the King returned to his palace,* and he left me with such an abundance of favours that it would take too long to describe them. The next day, during his dinner, he had me summoned. In his presence was the Cardinal of Ferrara, who was dining with him. When I joined them, the King was still on the second course: as I approached His Majesty he immediately began talking with me, saying that since he now owned such a beautiful basin and such a beautiful ewer from my hand, he required a beautiful salt-cellar to keep such things company; and he wanted me to make a design for one, but he wanted to see it very soon. I then replied, saying: 'Your Majesty will see such a design even sooner than you request, because while I was working on the basin I thought that a salt-cellar ought to be made to keep it company', and I added that such a design had already been made, and that if he liked I could show it to him immediately. The King became very animated and, turning toward such noblemen as were with him, the King of Navarre, the Cardinal of Lorraine, and the Cardinal of Ferrara, he said: 'This truly is a man who knows how to gain the love and admiration of everyone who knows him.' Then he told me that he would gladly look at the design I had executed for such an object. I set off, and was quick to go and return, for I had only to cross over the river, that is, the Seine: I carried with me a wax model, which I had already made in Rome at the request of the Cardinal of Ferrara. When I returned to the King I uncovered the model, and amazed,

the King said: 'This is something a hundred times more divine than anything I might have imagined. This is a magnificent piece of work by this man! He should never stop working!' Then he turned to me with an expression full of delight, and told me that this was a work that pleased him enormously and that he wanted me to execute it in gold. The Cardinal of Ferrara, who was there in person, looked me in the eye and made a sign to show me that he recognized this as the model I had made for him in Rome. At this, I told him that I had already said I would make this work for whoever was to have it.* The Cardinal, recalling those same words, and almost indignant, for it seemed to him that I meant to take my revenge, said to the King: 'Sire, this is a very great work, and my only doubt about the thing is that I don't believe we shall ever see it completed: because the talented men who have such grand conceptions in this craft are very keen to begin them, without really considering when they will complete them. Consequently, in commissioning such great works, I'd like to know when I would be able to have them.' To this the King replied, saying that whoever looked so closely into the completion of a work would never even begin one; and he said this most particularly, to show that such works were not a matter for men with little courage. Then I said: 'All princes who encourage their servants in the way in which His Majesty acts and speaks succeed in facilitating all great enterprises; and since God has given me such a marvellous patron, I hope to finish and present him with many great and marvellous works.' 'And I believe him,' continued the King, and he rose from the table. He called me into his chamber and asked me how much gold would be necessary for the salt-cellar: 'a thousand scudi's worth,' I answered. The King immediately called one of his treasurers, whose name was Monsignor lo risconte d'Orbeche,* and he ordered him then and there to provide me with one thousand old scudi* of good weight. Leaving His Majesty, I had the two notaries summoned who had provided me with the silver for the Jupiter and many other things, and after crossing the Seine I picked up a very small basket that my cousin the nun had given to me when I passed through Florence, and it was my good fortune to have taken that basket and not a bag. Thinking that I would carry out this task in daylight, since it was still early and I did not wish to distract my workmen, I did not even take the precaution of bringing a servant with me. I arrived at the home of the treasurer, who had already set

the coins out before him and was selecting them just as the King had
ordered. As far as I could see, that thieving treasurer deliberately
delayed counting out this money for me until the third hour of the
night. Not lacking in caution, I summoned some of my workmen to
come and keep me company, because this was a matter of grave
importance. When I saw that they did not arrive, I asked the messenger if he had delivered my message. A certain thieving servant said
that he had, and that they had said they were unable to come, but
that he would gladly carry this money for me: I said to him that I
wished to carry my money by myself. Meanwhile the contract was
completed, the money was counted out, and everything done. After
placing the money in the basket, I then thrust my arm through its
two handles; and because my arm passed through them with a good
deal of force, the handles were tightly closed; and I carried it more
conveniently than if it had been a bag. I was well armed with my
coat of mail and gauntlets, along with my sword and dagger, and I
speedily set out on my way by foot.

17. At that moment I saw certain servants who, whispering, also
left the house quickly, appearing to go down a different street from
the one I was taking. I walked along briskly, and after passing the
Pont au Change I came up along a riverside wall which led me to my
home at Le Petit Nesle. Then I reached the monastery of the Augus-
tinians, a most dangerous spot, although only five hundred paces
from my home; the residential part of the castle was another five
hundred paces inside, so that nobody would have heard my voice if I
had called out; but I decided, as soon as I clearly saw four men armed
with swords behind me, to cover that basket quickly with my cape,
and putting my hand on my sword, since I saw that they were carefully surrounding me, I said: 'You can gain nothing from soldiers but
a cape and a sword, and before I give this one to you, I hope that you
will earn it with very little profit to yourselves.' And attacking them
boldly, I several times opened my cape so that, if they had been
informed by those servants who had seen me take the money, they
would have reason to believe that I did not have such a sum of money
on my person. The scuffle only lasted a short while, because little by
little they withdrew; and they said to themselves in their native
language: 'This is an Italian *bravo*, and he is certainly not the man we
are looking for; or, if he really is, he has nothing on him.' I spoke in
Italian, and with constant blows, thrusting and slashing, I sometimes

came close to taking their lives, and because I had handled my weapons very well they thought I was more of a soldier than anything else; after closing ranks, they moved away from me little by little, continuously muttering under their breath in their own language; and I continued to say, still modestly, that anybody who wanted my weapons and my cape would not take them without a good deal of trouble. I began to quicken my steps, while they continued to follow right behind me at a slow pace; for this reason, I grew more fearful, thinking of how to avoid falling into an ambush with several other such men who might have me surrounded, so that when I was about a hundred paces from home I began running at top speed, and I cried out loudly: 'To arms! To arms! Outside! Outside! I am being murdered!' Immediately, four young men with four lances ran out, and even though they wanted to follow those men, who could still be seen, I stopped them, saying very loudly: 'Those four cowards were against one single man but they could not rob me of a booty worth a thousand scudi of pure gold, even though the gold has been breaking my arm; so let's go first and put the money away, and then I'll keep you company with my two-handed sword wherever you like.' We went to deposit the money, and my young men, terribly upset over the great danger I had incurred, said to reproach me: 'You put too much trust in yourself, and one day you are going to give us all something to weep about.' I said many things, and they answered me in turn; my adversaries had fled; and all of us ate supper together, merry and glad, laughing at the great strokes of Fortune, as often for the good as for the bad; and when she misses, it is as if nothing has happened. It is certainly true what they say: 'You'll learn for another time.' This rule is worthless, however, because Fortune always strikes in different and unimagined ways.

18. On the following morning, I immediately began the great salt-cellar, and with great diligence I made progress on it as well as on the other works. I had already hired many workers, some from the craft of sculpture and others from the craft of goldsmithing. These workers were Italians, Frenchmen, Germans, and I sometimes employed a good number of them, depending on whether I could find good ones, because I changed them from day to day, taking on those who knew the most. These I prodded so much that, trying to follow my example of working tirelessly, they could not bear up under this hard labour, since they lacked my constitution, and they

thought they could restore themselves by much drinking and eating; some of the Germans who knew more than the others wanted to imitate me, but since their natures could not endure such strain, it shattered them. While I was making progress with the silver Jupiter, and realizing that a good deal of the silver was left over, without the King's knowledge I began working on a large vase with two handles, of a height of approximately one-and-a-half armslengths. I was still anxious to cast the large model I had made for the silver Jupiter in bronze; and setting to work on this new undertaking, something I had never done before, after consulting with certain of the older Parisian masters I told them all about the methods that we use in Italy to carry out such an enterprise. They told me that they had never proceeded in that way, but that if I let it be done according to their own methods they would make it and cast it for me just as cleanly and beautifully as the clay model. I wanted to strike a bargain, entrusting this work to them: and over and above the sum they requested, I promised them several scudi more. They began work on the project, and when I saw that they were not going about it in the best fashion I quickly began work on a head of Julius Caesar, with his bust in armour and much larger than life-size, which I had copied from a small model I had brought with me from Rome, imitated from a truly marvellous ancient bust. I also began work on another head of the same size that I had drawn of a very beautiful young girl, whom I kept with me for my physical pleasure. I gave it the name of Fontainebleau after the place the King had selected for his own pleasure. After I built a fine little furnace to melt the bronze and had prepared and baked our moulds—the Parisian masters prepared the Jupiter and I prepared the two heads—I said to them: 'I do not believe that your Jupiter will come out right, because you haven't left enough air-holes at the bottom for the air to circulate: so you're wasting your time.' They said to me that if their work did not come out successfully they would return all the money I had given them on account and would refund all my lost expenses, but that I should be careful, because those fine heads of mine that I wanted to cast by my Italian method would never come out right. Present during this dispute were those treasurers and other noblemen who had come to see me on the King's orders, and they reported everything that was said or done to the King. The two old masters who wanted to cast the Jupiter held off in giving the order for the casting, because they said they would have liked to prepare the two moulds for my heads, since the method I was using could not possibly succeed, and it would be a great pity to lose such beautiful works. When they informed the King, His Majesty replied that they should apply themselves to learning rather than seeking to teach the master. With loud laughter they placed their work in the furnace, and I, steadfast, without any sign of laughter or of anger (which I felt), placed my two moulds on either side of the Jupiter: when our metal was nicely melted, with great satisfaction we made a passage for the metal, and it filled the mould of the Jupiter beautifully; at the same time it filled the moulds of my two heads, so that they were glad and I was content, because I truly wanted to have been mistaken about their working methods, and they seemed truly to want to have been mistaken about mine. They then asked, with great rejoicing and in the French fashion, for something to drink: I very willingly provided them with a magnificent breakfast. Then they asked me for the money they were to receive and that additional sum I had promised them. To this, I said: 'You were laughing over something I'm very much afraid may cause you to weep, because I thought that much more metal ran into your mould than should have done; so I don't want to give you any more money than you have already had until tomorrow morning.' These poor men began to think over what I had told them, and without saying another word they went home. When the next morning arrived they very, very carefully began to dig out the furnace, but they could not uncover their large mould until they had first dug out my two heads, which they took out—properly formed—and placed upright so that they could be seen very well. Then they began to uncover the Jupiter, and they had not gone down more than two armslengths when these masters and their four workmen uttered a cry so loud that I heard it. Thinking that these were cries of joy, I set out running, since I was in my bedchamber about five hundred paces away. When I reached them, I found them in a pose that is usually employed to depict those people looking at the Sepulchre of Christ, sorrowful and frightened. When I glanced at my two heads and saw that they were fine, I combined my pleasure with displeasure, while they made excuses by saying: 'It's just our bad luck!' To this I said: 'Your luck is just fine, but your lack of knowledge has been very bad indeed. If I had seen you put the soul* into the mould, with a single word I could have taught you how to make the figure come out perfectly; such a result would have brought me great honour and a handsome profit for you: I shall be able to find excuses for my honour, but you will come out of this with neither honour nor profit. Another time you should, therefore, learn how to work and not to make fun of others.' Nevertheless they begged me, saying that I was right, but that if I did not help them they would have to cover their huge expenses, and that this loss would force them to go begging, together with their families. To this I said that when the treasurer of the King wanted to make them pay what they owed, I promised them to pay it myself, because I had seen quite clearly that they had done in good faith everything that they knew how to do. These acts earned me so much goodwill on the part of these treasurers and the ministers of the King that it was incredible. Everything was recounted to the King, who was an extremely generous man, and he ordered that everything should be done as I said.

19. At this time the most wonderful, valiant soldier Piero Strozzi* arrived, and when he reminded the King of his letters of naturalization, the King immediately ordered that they be drawn up. 'And along with these', the King added, 'write up some for Benvenuto, *mon ami*,* and take them immediately on my behalf to his home and give them to him without any expense.' The naturalization papers of the great Piero Strozzi cost him many hundreds of ducats; mine were brought to me by one of the first of the King's secretaries, who was named Messer Antonio Massone.* This gentleman handed me the papers with marvellous ceremony on His Majesty's behalf, as he remarked: 'The King makes you a present of these papers so that you may serve him with even greater confidence. They are letters of naturalization.' And he told me how the King, after the passage of so much time and as a special favour, had given such papers to Piero Strozzi at the latter's own request, while those for me had been sent to me as a gift, and that such a favour had never before been granted in that kingdom. To his words, I replied thanking the King with great ceremony; then I begged the secretary to kindly tell me what such 'letters of naturalization' meant. The secretary was extremely able and kind, and he spoke Italian fluently: at first he burst out laughing, then regained his solemnity and he told me in my language (that is, in Italian) the meaning of 'letters of naturalization', which were one of the greatest honours that could be bestowed upon

a foreigner; and he said: 'This is a far greater honour than to be made a Venetian nobleman.' After he left me he returned to the King and related everything to His Majesty, who laughed a bit, and then he said: 'Now, I want him to know why I sent him these letters of naturalization. Go and make him lord of the castle of Petit Nesle in which he lives, which is part of my patrimony. He'll know what this implies much more easily than he understood what the letters of naturalization were.' A messenger came to me with this gift, for which I wanted to treat him generously; he did not want to accept anything, declaring that such was His Majesty's command. When I went back to Italy I carried with me these letters of naturalization, along with those concerning the gift of the castle, and wherever I go, and wherever I may end my life, I shall always do my best to keep them with me.*

20. I shall now return to the story of my life. Having to make progress with the above-mentioned projects—that is, the silver Jupiter already begun, the salt-cellar, the large silver vase, and the two bronze heads—I worked upon them assiduously. I also gave orders to cast the base of the Jupiter, which I executed in bronze, covered in the richest decorations, among which in low relief I sculpted the rape of Ganymede* and, on the other side, Leda and the swan:* I cast this base in bronze, and it came out extremely well. Then I executed another similar one to hold the statue of Juno, waiting to begin this as well until the King gave me the silver to be able to carry out such an undertaking. By working diligently I had already put together the silver Jupiter; I had also put together the golden salt-cellar; the vase was far advanced; and the two bronze heads were already finished. I had already completed several little works for the Cardinal of Ferrara; I had also made a small, richly decorated silver vase to give to Madame d'Étampes; and I had executed many works for many Italian noblemen—that is, Signor Piero Strozzi, the Count of Anguillara, the Count of Pitigliano, the Count della Mirandola,* and many others. Returning to my great King, as I have said, after I had made good progress on these works of his he came back to Paris, and on the third day after his return he came to my house with a large number of the finest nobility from his court, and he was greatly amazed by how many works I had on hand or had brought to completion; and because his Madame d'Étampes was with him, they began to discuss Fontainebleau. Madame d'Étampes told His

Majesty that he should commission me to execute something beautiful to adorn his Fontainebleau. The King immediately said: 'What you have said is a good idea, and here and now, I resolve that something splendid be made for that place.' Turning to me, he began to ask what I thought I could make for that beautiful fountain.* To his query, I put forward some of my own creative ideas: His Majesty then expressed his own opinion. Then he told me later that he wanted to spend fifteen to twenty days at San Germano dell'Aia,* which was twelve leagues from Paris. Meanwhile I was to make a model for his beautiful fountain with the richest inventions that I knew how to make, because this spot was the best place for relaxation that he had in his kingdom; he ordered and beseeched me, however, to exert myself to create something beautiful; and I promised him that I would do so. Once he had seen so many beautiful works all around him, the King said to Madame d'Étampes: 'I have never had a man in this profession who pleases me more, nor who deserves to be rewarded more than this one; we must think, therefore, about how to keep him here. Because he spends openly, is a good sort, and works very hard, we must therefore keep him in mind: the reason for this is, if you think about it Madame, that he has come to me many times and I have come here many times, but he has never asked me for anything: his heart is clearly intent upon his work, and we must do something good for him very soon in order not to lose him.' Madame d'Étampes said: 'I shall remind you to do so.' They went away, and with great diligence I set about working on the things I had already begun, and also began making the model of the fountain, which I brought forward with great care.

21. At the end of a month and a half the King returned to Paris, and as I had been working day and night, I went to see him and brought with me my model so beautifully sketched out that it could be clearly understood. By that time the devilish war between the Emperor and the King had broken out again,* so that I found him very disconcerted; I spoke to the Cardinal of Ferrara, and told him that I had with me certain models that His Majesty had ordered; I also begged him to say a few words if he saw an opportunity so that I could show these models, and I said 'I think that the King would take great pleasure in this.' The Cardinal did so: he mentioned the models to the King, and the King immediately came to where I had put them. First of all I had fashioned a model for the portal of the palace

of Fontainebleau,* trying to alter as little as possible the design of the doorway that had been built for this palace, which was both wide and squat in that bad French style of theirs;* the opening was little more than a square, above which there was a half-circle flattened like the handle of a basket; and in this half-circle the King wanted to have a figure representing Fontainebleau.* I gave this opening the most beautiful proportions: above this space I then placed a correct half-circle; and on the sides I made some delightful reliefs, with socles at the bottom to harmonize with what was above; I did likewise on the part above; and instead of two columns that were clearly required according to the moulding done below and above, I fashioned a satyr in place of each column.* One of them was in more than half-relief and seemed to support with one of his arms the part of the doorway that rests upon the columns; in his other hand he held a huge club, and with his bold and fierce head he struck fear in the onlooker. The other figure had a similar stance, but it was distinct and varied in its head and in some other respects: it held in its hand a whip with three balls attached to some chains. Although I say 'satyrs', these figures had nothing of the satyr in them except for their little horns and their goatish heads: all the rest of the figure was of human form. In the half-circle I fashioned a woman reclining in a beautiful pose: she had her left arm resting upon the neck of a stag, which was one of the King's emblems; on one side I fashioned in half-relief some little fawns, some wild boars, and other wild game in lower relief; on the other side there were hunting dogs and greyhounds of various types, for such animals are found in this beautiful wood where the fountain rises. I then enclosed this entire work within an oblong shape, and in each of the upper angles, I drew a figure of Victory* in low relief with those small torches in her hand, like those the ancients used to depict. Above this oblong I fashioned a salamander,* the personal emblem of the King, along with many other charming decorations in keeping with the work, which was in the Ionic style.

22. When the King saw my model it immediately cheered him up, and it took his mind off the trying discussions which had occupied him for more than two hours. When I saw that he was happy, as I wished, I showed him the other model, which he did not expect at all, since he thought he had seen a good deal of work in the first one. This model was larger than two armslengths in height, and in it I had created a fountain in the form of a perfect square, with the most

beautiful flights of stairs around it which intersected with one another, something that had never before been seen in those parts and which was extremely rare in Italy. In the middle of the fountain I had drawn a base, which rose a bit higher than the basin of the fountain; on this base I had placed a nude figure of a corresponding size, full of beauty and grace. The figure held a broken lance high in his upraised right hand, while his left hand rested upon the hilt of a most beautifully shaped curved sword: the figure rested on its left foot, and its right foot rested upon a helmet that was as richly worked as can be imagined; and at the four corners of the fountain I placed in each one a seated figure, raised up with its own pleasing emblems. The King began to ask me to explain to him this beautiful vision I had created, saying that everything I had done for the portal he had understood without needing to ask about anything, but that he understood nothing about this conception of the fountain, even though it seemed extremely beautiful to him; and he knew very well that I had not done it like those other fools, who produce things with a bit of grace but without any kind of meaning whatsoever. At this I prepared myself to reply, for since he had been pleased with what I had done, I wanted him to be equally pleased with what I had to say: 'You know, Sacred Majesty, that this entire little work is very carefully measured on a reduced scale, so that in its execution the same grace you see here will still be present. The figure in the middle is fifty-four feet high' (upon hearing this the King gave signs of great astonishment), 'and it is meant to represent the god Mars. These other four figures are made to represent the virtues in which Your Majesty takes so much delight and to which he gives so much support. The one on the right symbolizes the knowledge of Letters: you see that it has its own distinguishing attributes, which portray Philosophy with all her accompanying virtues. The other figure portrays the entire art of Design: that is to say, Sculpture, Painting, and Architecture. The third figure symbolizes Music, which appropriately accompanies all these branches of knowledge. The final figure, which looks so pleasant and kind, symbolizes Liberality, since without her none of the marvellous virtues that God displays to us could be demonstrated. The huge statue in the middle, which is a figure of the god Mars, symbolizes Your Majesty himself, for you are the only brave man in the world, and you employ this bravery in a just and holy fashion in the defence of your own glory.' The King had scarcely enough patience to allow me to finish what I had to say before, crying aloud, he said: 'Truly, I have found a man after my own heart.' And so he summoned the treasurers charged with paying me and ordered them to provide me with everything I might need, whatever the expense required: then he patted me upon the shoulder, as he said: '*Mon ami* (which means 'my friend'), I don't know which is the greater pleasure, that of a prince who has discovered a man after his own heart, or that of a talented artist who has discovered a prince who gives him so much help that he can express his most brilliant conceptions.' I answered that if I were that man of whom His Majesty spoke, mine would be much the greater fortune. He replied with a laugh: 'Let's say that it's equal.' He left me in a very cheerful mood, and I returned to my works.

23. As my bad luck would have it, I was not prudent enough to act in the same manner with Madame d'Étampes, for when she had heard that very evening from the King's own mouth everything that had happened, these remarks generated such a poisonous rage in her breast that she said with contempt: 'If Benvenuto had shown me his beautiful works, he would have given me reason to remember him at the proper time.' The King tried to make excuses for me, but nothing worked. I heard all about this, and some fifteen days later—after they had travelled through Normandy to Rouen and to Dieppe, and then had returned to San Germano dell'Aia—I took the beautiful little vase I had made at Madame d'Étampes's request, thinking that if I gave it to her I would regain her favour. So I carried it with me; and trying to let her know through one of her nurses, I showed this nurse the beautiful little vase that I had executed for her lady and explained how I wanted to give it to her; the nurse showed me unbounded kindness and told me that she would have a word with Madame, who was not yet dressed, and that as soon as she told her about it she would immediately receive me. The nurse told everything to Madame, who replied disdainfully: 'Tell him to wait!' When I heard this, I clothed myself in patience, which was a most difficult thing for me. I managed, however, to wait patiently until after she had dined: but as the hour had become late, hunger made me so furious that I could no longer stop myself and, having devoutly sent her to the devil in my heart, I left; and I went to find the Cardinal of Lorraine and gave him the little vase, imploring him only to keep me in the King's good graces. He said there was no need, and that

whenever it became necessary he would gladly do so: then he summoned one of his treasurers and whispered in his ear. This treasurer, having waited for me to leave the Cardinal's presence, said to me: 'Benvenuto, come with me, and I'll give you a glass of very good wine.' To this I replied, not knowing what he meant to say: 'Thank you, Monsignor Treasurer, have them give me just a glass of wine and a good mouthful of bread, because I am truly about to faint, for I have fasted from early this morning until now, as you see me, at the door of Madame d'Étampes in order to give her that beautiful little gilded silver vase, and I let her know all about it, but in order to keep me in torment she sent word that I was to wait. Now hunger has overcome me and I feel faint; and as God has willed it, I've given the thing and my labour to someone who really deserves it, and I ask you for nothing but a little to drink, for since I'm somewhat over-choleric by nature, fasting depresses me so greatly that I could fall down unconscious.' While I was struggling to say these words some admirable wine and other delicacies were brought for me to lunch on, so that I felt much refreshed, and once my vital spirits were restored my anger left me. The good treasurer handed me one hundred golden scudi, to which I offered some resistance, since I did not wish to accept them under any circumstances. He went to report this to the Cardinal, who spoke to him outrageously, ordering him to force me to accept the money and not to come to him again otherwise. Very distressed, the treasurer returned to me, saying that he had never been shouted at by the Cardinal like that in the past; and when he tried to give me the money and I made a bit of resistance, he said in great distress that he would force me to accept it. I took the money. I wanted to go and thank the Cardinal, but he gave me to understand through one of his secretaries that he would always do whatever he could to please me, and would do so gladly: I returned to Paris the same evening. The King found out everything. They made fun of Madame d'Étampes, which caused her to become even more venomous in her desire to do me harm, so that I was in danger for my very life, as will be related in the proper place.

24. I should have recorded long before this how I earned the friendship of the most brilliant, most lovable, and most courteous gentleman that I have ever known: this man was Messer Guido Guidi,* an excellent physician and doctor and a noble Florentine citizen. Because of the countless problems caused by my perverse

fortune, I have neglected him somewhat. I did not think, however, that this was of great importance, since it was enough to keep him continually in my heart, but when I realized that the story of my life would not be right without him, I have introduced him in the midst of my greatest trials so that, since he gave me comfort and assistance in my life, I may here record that blessing. This Messer Guido happened to come to Paris, and after I had got to know him, I took him to my castle and there I gave him a free apartment for his use; and in this fashion we enjoyed several years together. Then the Bishop of Pavia also arrived—that is, Monsignor de' Rossi, brother of the Count of San Sicondo.* I took this lord from the inn and brought him to my castle, also providing him with a free apartment where he was very well accommodated with his servants and his mounts for many months. Yet another time I put up Messer Luigi Alamanni* and his children for several months: God granted even to me the grace to be able to offer some favours to men both great and talented. Messer Guido and I enjoyed a friendship for as long as I lived in France, feeling great pride in the fact that we were both learning some skill, each of us in his own profession, with the support of such a great and marvellous prince. I can truly say that what I am, and whatever I have created that has been good and beautiful, is all because of that marvellous King: I must therefore pick up the thread of my story and discuss the great works that I executed for him.

25. I had in my castle a tennis court, from which I derived much profit while I made use of it. The place contained some small rooms where all sorts of men were living, including among them a very skilful book printer: this man had almost his entire workshop in my castle, and he was the one who printed that first handsome book on medicine* for Messer Guido. Wishing to use those rooms I sent him away, but with more than a little difficulty. A maker of gunpowder was also living there, and when I decided to use his small rooms for some of my good German workers, this master craftsman did not want to move; I had told him pleasantly on more than one occasion that he should vacate my rooms, since I wanted to use them as living quarters for my workmen in the service of the King. The more humbly I spoke, the more arrogantly this beast answered me: in the end I gave him a deadline of three days. He laughed at me, and told me that in the space of three years he would begin to think about it. I

did not know that he was a domestic servant of Madame d'Étampes, and if it had not been for the fact that my encounter with Madame d'Étampes had made me think a bit more about these matters than I had done before, I would have quickly sent him packing; but I wanted to be patient for those three days. When they had passed, without saying anything else I took my Germans, Italians, and Frenchmen with weapons in hand, and many workmen that I employed, and in a short time I tore apart the entire place and threw his property outside my castle. I committed this rather drastic act because he had told me that he knew of no Italian strong or courageous enough to make him move one stitch from its place. After this deed was done, however, he arrived; I said to him: 'I'm the least of all the Italians in Italy, and I've done nothing to you compared to what I'd have the courage to do to you , and what I'll certainly do, if you say just one word!' And I said this along with other insulting remarks. This man, dumbfounded and frightened, arranged his property as best he could; then he ran to Madame d'Étampes and painted a picture of hell for her; this great enemy of mine, who was so much more eloquent and powerful than her servant, painted an even worse picture for the King; and I was later told that the King had twice become angry with me and wanted to take harsh measures against me, but that Henry, the Dauphin—his son, who is now King of France—had suffered some annoyance from that far too audacious woman, and he, along with the Queen of Navarre, the sister of King Francis, took my side so cleverly that the King laughed off the entire incident: for this reason, with very real assistance from God, I passed through a great storm.

26. I had to do the same thing to another individual like this one, but I did not wreck his place, even though I tossed all his property outside. Because of this, Madame d'Étampes was bold enough to say to the King: 'I think this devil will eventually sack Paris!' To this the King angrily replied to Madame d'Étampes that I was doing quite well in defending myself from the rabble who wanted to keep me from serving him. The anger of this cruel woman grew greater every hour: she summoned a painter who lived at Fontainebleau, where the King stayed almost continually. This painter was an Italian and a Bolognese, and he was known as 'Il Bologna': his own name was Francesco Primaticcio.* Madame d'Étampes told him that he should ask the King for the commission concerning the fountain that His

Majesty had entrusted to me, and that she would help him with all her power: and so they were in agreement. This Bologna felt as cheerful as he had ever felt, and reckoned that it promised to be a sure thing, even though this was not his kind of work; but because he was quite skilled in the art of design he had come to an agreement with some workmen who were trained by Il Rosso, one of our Florentine painters, and a truly marvellous and worthy man: and whatever this Bologna did that was good he had taken from the wonderful style of this Rosso, who was already dead. These clever arguments, along with the great assistance of Madame d'Étampes, and the constant hammering away night and day—now Madame, now Bologna—had their effect in the ears of that great King. The strongest reason that made the King give in was when she and Bologna said together: 'How is it possible, Sacred Majesty, that while you want Benvenuto to make you twelve silver statues, he hasn't yet finished a single one? If you employ him in such a great undertaking you'll necessarily deprive yourself of these other works, which you so strongly desire, for one hundred of the most talented men could never complete as many great works as this talented man has organized. It is obvious that he has a great desire to work: that very thing will be the cause of Your Majesty's losing both him and his works in one stroke.' These arguments, along with many other similar ones, presented to the King when he was in a compliant frame of mind, persuaded him to yield to all their requests: and he had not as yet seen either the designs or the models from the hand of this Bologna.

27. At this same time, in Paris, the second tenant that I had chased from my castle moved; he brought a suit against me, declaring that I had stolen a great deal of his property when I had evicted him. This lawsuit was very troublesome to me and took a great deal of my time, and many times, in desperation, I wanted to leave immediately. In France they have the custom of making a great deal of money out of a lawsuit that they begin against a foreigner, or any other person who they see is somewhat unaccustomed to litigation; straightaway, as soon as they start to see some advantage in this lawsuit, they try to sell it; and some have even given lawsuits as dowries to the kind of men who make their entire profession out of buying them. They have another ugly custom, which is that the men of Normandy, or most of them, make a profession of giving false testimony, so that the men who buy lawsuits immediately instruct

four such witnesses, or six, according to their needs, and through this means anyone who is not forewarned to produce as many witnesses to the contrary—a man who is not familiar with the customs—has sentence immediately pronounced against him. I too met with such incidents; the affair seeming to me extremely dishonest, I appeared to defend my rights at the Great Hall of Justice in Paris, where I saw a judge, the lieutenant of the King for civil cases, seated up on a high tribunal. This man was tall, heavy, and fat, with the most austere appearance: he was surrounded on both sides by many prosecutors and lawyers, all lined up on the right and left; others came up, one at a time, and they put forward a case to this judge. I sometimes saw those lawyers on the sides speaking all at once, so that I stood in amazement at the sight of this admirable man, the veritable image of Pluto, who lent his ear with evident attention now to one lawyer and now to another and most skilfully replied to all. Because seeing and tasting every sort of skill has always delighted me, this seemed so marvellous to me that I would not have missed seeing it for anything. Since the hall was extremely large and was filled with a great number of people, it happened that they took care not to allow anyone to enter unless he had a reason to be there, and they kept the door locked and a guard at the door; this guard, in opposing someone he did not want to let in, would occasionally drown out that wonderful judge with the great racket he was making, angering the judge, who would then hurl insults at the guard. I found myself before him several times, and I pondered the incidents; these very words that I heard were spoken by this same judge, who noticed two noblemen who had come to watch the proceedings; and as this porter offered them the greatest resistance, the judge said, crying at the top of his voice: 'Be quiet! Be quiet Satan, get out of here and be quiet.' In the French tongue these words sound like this: '*Phe phe, Satan, phe phe, Satan, alè, phe.*'* When I heard this expression, since I had learned the French tongue very well, I realized what Dante meant to say when he went with Virgil, his master, inside the gates of Hell. In the time of Giotto, the painter, Dante was with him in France, mainly in Paris, and for these reasons one can say that the spot where litigation takes place is an inferno. Dante, therefore, understanding the French language very well, employed this very expression, and it seems strange that it has never been understood in this way: so that I say and believe that these commentators make Dante say things he never thought of.*

28. Returning to my own affairs, when I saw the court hand down certain judgments to me through these lawyers, not seeing any other method of helping myself, I had recourse for such self-defence to a large dagger that I owned, for I have always enjoyed keeping fine weapons; the first one I attacked was the man most responsible for filing this unjust lawsuit against me; and one evening I gave him so many wounds in the legs and arms, taking care not to kill him, that I deprived him of the use of both his legs. Then I encountered the other man who had purchased my lawsuit, and I handled him as well in such a way that the lawsuit ended. Always thanking God for this and all other blessings, and thinking that for the time being I would remain without being bothered, I told the young men in my household, especially the Italians, that for the love of God they should all look after their own business and help me out for a time until I could bring the works that I had begun to completion, for I would finish them shortly; then I wanted to return to Italy, since I could not adapt to the roguish behaviour of the French; and if that good King should ever become angry with me, he could make things turn out badly for me on account of the many such things I had done in my self-defence. The Italians were, first and the dearest, Ascanio, from Tagliacozzo in the kingdom of Naples; the other was Pagolo, a Roman and a man born under humble conditions who did not know his father: these two were the young men I had taken with me from Rome and who had been living with me there. Another Roman, who had also come from Rome for the purpose of finding me, was also named Pagolo, and he was the son of a poor Roman gentleman of the Macaroni family:* this young man knew little about my profession, but he was extremely brave with weapons. I had another young man from Ferrara, by the name of Bartolomeo Chioccia.* I had still another one: he was a Florentine by the name of Pagolo Micceri.* He had a brother who bore the nickname of Gatta and who was skilled in keeping account books, but had spent too much when managing the property of Tommaso Guadagni,* a very wealthy merchant: this Gatta set some of my books in order, in which I kept the accounts of the great and Most Christian King as well as of others; this Pagolo Micceri, after learning from his brother the method of keeping my books, continued to keep them for me, and I gave him a very good

salary. And because I thought him to be a very fine young man, since I saw that he was devout, hearing him constantly muttering psalms with his rosary in hand, I trusted his feigned goodness. Calling him aside on his own, I said to him: 'Pagolo, my dearest brother: you see how well off you are with me, and you know that you have no other means and, besides this, you are a Florentine; for these reasons I trust you, and even more since I can see how devout you are in your religious duties, which is something that pleases me very much. I beg you to help me, because I don't trust any of the others too much; I beg you, therefore, to take care of two very important matters that give me a great deal of bother: the first is that you must take very good care of my property so that it's not stolen from me, and you should, therefore, not touch it yourself; you also see that poor little girl Caterina, whom I keep primarily to assist me in my profession and whom I could not do without. Also, because I am a man, I use her for my own carnal pleasures, and it's possible that she will give me a child. I do not want to support other people's children, nor would I tolerate anybody inflicting such an injury upon me. If anyone in this house were so daring as to do such a thing, and I found out about it, I believe I would certainly kill the both of them. I therefore beg you, dear brother, to help me, and if you see anything tell me about it immediately, for I shall send to the gallows both her and her mother and anyone who would be a party to such a thing: but first of all, be sure to keep an eye on yourself.' This rogue made a sign of the cross that travelled from head to toe, and said: 'Oh blessed Jesus! God keep me from ever even thinking of such a thing! First, because I am not given to such wicked deeds; and then, don't you think that I know the great benefits I've received from you?' At these words, seeing they were said in a simple manner and with affection towards me, I believed that everything was exactly as he said.

29. Two days afterwards, when the feast day arrived, Messer Mattia del Nazaro,* also an Italian and a servant of the King, a most worthy man in my own profession, invited me along with those young men of mine to enjoy a garden party. And so I got myself ready and told Pagolo, too, that he should come along to enjoy some merrymaking, since I thought that the tiresome lawsuit had died down a bit. This young man answered me, saying: 'Truly, it would be a mistake to leave the house so empty: you see how much gold, silver, and jewels you have here. Since this is a city of thieves, you must be

on your guard both day and night: I'll attend to my prayers, while I guard the house; go on and set your mind at rest, amusing yourself and having a good time; another time, somebody else can do this job.' Thinking I could leave with my mind at rest, Pagolo, Ascanio, and Chioccia and I went off to enjoy ourselves, and we passed most of the day very happily. After midday, as evening began to draw on, I grew uneasy, and I began to think about the words that miserable villain had said to me with such feigned simplicity; I mounted my horse and with my two servants returned to my castle, where I discovered Pagolo and that slut of a Caterina almost in the very act, because when I arrived her pandering French mother yelled: 'Pagolo, Caterina, your master is here.' Seeing them coming, both of them frightened and all dishevelled, not knowing what they were saying nor, as if stupefied, where they were going, it was clear they had been committing a sin. As a result, my reason overcome by anger, I put my hand to my sword, having decided to murder them both. Pagolo ran away, the girl threw herself to the ground on her knees and screamed to high heaven for mercy. I had wanted to go after the man first but, unable to reach him with the first blow, when I subsequently caught up with him I had in the meantime come to the conclusion that it would be better to throw them both out, because with so many other incidents having taken place so close to this one, it would have been difficult to escape with my life. I therefore told Pagolo: 'If my eyes had witnessed what you—you scoundrel—make me believe has happened, I would have run your belly ten times through with this sword: now get out of my sight, and if you ever say an Our Father again, make sure it's San Giuliano's.'* Then I drove out the mother and daughter with shoves, kicks, and punches. They thought they would take revenge for this injury, and conferred with a lawyer from Normandy who instructed them that Caterina should say that I had relations with her in the Italian fashion—that is to say, against nature, like a sodomite—saying: 'At least when this Italian hears of it and knows how great the danger is, he will immediately give you several hundred ducats so that you will say no more about it, considering the severe punishment they inflict in France for this kind of sin.' And so they came to an agreement: they lodged the accusation against me, and I received a summons.

30. The more I sought repose, the more my tribulations increased. Harmed every day by Fortune in different ways, I began

to think about which of two things I should do: either leave and let France go to the devil, or honestly fight this attack and see what end God had in store for me. I had worried over this matter for a long time; then, finally, I took the decision to leave, not wishing to tempt my perverse Fortune any further, since it might yet break my neck. When I had arranged everything, quickly taking steps to dispose of the property I could not carry with me, and had packed the light luggage as best I could, accommodating it on my own person or on my servants, then, with the greatest unhappiness, I determined to make my departure. I remained alone in one of my studios, for I had informed my young assistants who had advised me I should leave that I needed some time by myself to think things over, even though I realized that what they were telling me was in large measure correct, because later, as long as I was not in prison and had given this storm time to pass, I could much better make my excuses with the King, telling him in private letters how this murderous attack upon me was made solely out of envy. As I said, I had resolved to do just that; and as I started off, I was seized by my shoulder and spun around, and a voice said boldly: 'Benvenuto, do as you always do, and do not be afraid!' I instantly took the opposite decision to the one I had chosen, and said to those young men of mine: 'Take your best weapons and come with me, and do what I tell you and don't think about anything else, because I want to appear in court. If I leave here you will all go up in smoke the next day, so do as I say and come with me.' In unison, the young men replied: 'Since we are here and owe our livelihood to him, we must go with him and help him do whatever he proposes as long as there is life in us: because he has spoken more truly than we thought. As soon as he left this place his enemies would drive us all out. Let us consider the great works that have been initiated here, and of what immense importance they are: we lack the vision to complete them without him, and his enemies will say that he has left because he lacks the vision to complete such undertakings.' They said, besides, many other things of importance. That young Roman of the Macaroni family was the first to give them courage: he also summoned some of the Germans and Frenchmen who were fond of me. We were ten in all: I took the path I had decided upon, resolving never to allow myself to be put in prison alive. We arrived before these criminal judges, where I found Caterina and her mother. When I came upon them they were laughing with one of their lawyers: I entered the hall and boldly asked for the judge, who was puffed up, massive, and fat, sitting up high above the others on a tribunal. When this man spotted me, shaking his head menacingly, he said in a deep voice: 'Although you bear the name Welcome, on this occasion you are certainly Unwelcome.'* I heard him, and I called out in turn, saying: 'Take up my case immediately and tell me what I'm here for!' Then the judge turned to Caterina and said to her: 'Caterina, tell us everything that happened in your dealings with Benvenuto.' Caterina said that I had used her in the Italian fashion. The judge turned to me and said: 'You hear what Caterina says, Benvenuto.' Then I answered: 'If I had used her in the Italian fashion, I would have done so only out of the desire to have a son, just as you Frenchmen do.' Then the judge replied, saying: 'She means that you used her outside the place where you produce children.' To this I answered that such was not the Italian method; rather, it must be the French method, since she knew it and I did not; and that I wanted her to describe in detail this method that I had used with her. This sluttish whore wickedly described, openly and clearly, the method that she meant. I forced her to confirm the description three times in a row, and when she had finished I said loudly: 'My Lord Judge, Lieutenant of His Most Christian Majesty, I ask you for justice, for I know that the laws of the Most Christian King for such a sin prescribe burning at the stake for both the agent and the recipient; she confesses her sin, however, while I have not known her in any way whatsoever.* Her pandering mother is here, and for both one crime and the other they deserve to be burned at the stake;* I demand justice.' I repeated these words frequently and loudly, continuously demanding the stake for Caterina and her mother, and telling the judge that if he did not put her in prison in my presence, I would run to the King and would inform him of the injustice committed against me by one of his criminal lieutenants. At this loud uproar of mine they all began to lower their voices, and then I raised mine even more: the little whore began to cry, along with her mother, and I shouted at the judge: 'To the stake, to the stake!' When that great coward saw that matters were not going the way he had planned, he began to excuse the weaker sex with many soothing words. At this, I thought it seemed I had won a great battle and, muttering and threatening, I most gladly went away; but I would have certainly paid five hundred scudi not to have shown

up at all. After I had escaped from that sea of troubles I thanked God
with all my heart, and most happily I returned with my young men
to my castle.

31. When perverse Fortune, or our contrary star, if we wish to
speak truthfully, begins to persecute a man, it never lacks new
methods of taking the field against him. It seemed that I had escaped
from an immeasurable sea of troubles, and I even thought that this
perverse star of mine ought to leave me alone for a little time, but I
had not yet caught my breath from that inestimably great danger
when she had placed two of them before me all at once. In the space
of three days two things happened to me: in each of the two my life
rested on the balance of the scales. It so happened that I went to
Fontainebleau to speak with the King, who had written me a letter in
which he wanted me to execute the dies for the coinage of his entire
realm, and in this letter he had sent me some little designs to show
me something of what he wanted, but he gave me the freedom to do
whatever I pleased: I had made new designs following my own ideas
and the standards of beauty in my profession. So, when I arrived at
Fontainebleau one of those treasurers who had the commission from
the King to provide for my needs—this man's name was Monsignor
della Fa*—immediately said to me: 'Benvenuto, Bologna the painter
has received the commission from the King to execute your great
colossus,* and all the commissions that our King had told to us to give
you he has taken away from you, and told us to give them to him.
This has displeased us greatly, and it has seemed to us that this
Italian of yours has behaved most arrogantly towards you, because
you had already earned the commissions by virtue of your models
and your labours; this man has taken them away from you solely
through the favour of Madame d'Étampes: many months have
already passed since he received this commission and he has not
given any sign yet of beginning anything.' Amazed, I said: 'How is it
possible that I knew nothing about all this?' Then he told me that
Bologna had kept it completely secret, and that he had received the
commission only with the greatest difficulty, since the King did not
want to give it to him, but that the diligence of Madame d'Étampes
alone had caused him to obtain it. Having heard that I had been
harmed and greatly wronged in this fashion, and seeing myself
deprived of a work I had earned with my enormous efforts, I was
disposed to commit some serious act with my weapon, and I went

swiftly to find Bologna. I found him in his chambers and immersed in his studies: he had me called inside, and with some of his Lombard expressions of welcome he asked me what fine business had brought me there. Then I said: 'An extremely fine and important business.' The man directed his servants to bring us something to drink, and he said: 'Before we discuss anything I want us to share a drink together: that is the custom in France.' Then I said: 'Messer Francesco, you know that the discussion we need to have doesn't require drinking beforehand: perhaps afterwards we may drink.' I began to reason with him, saying: 'All men who claim to be honourable execute their works in such a way that they are known through them to be honourable men; if they do the contrary, they no longer enjoy the reputation of being honest men. I know that you knew the King had given me the commission to execute this great colossus, which was the subject of discussion for eighteen months, and neither you nor others had ever come forward to say anything about it; for this reason, I had made myself known through my great efforts to this great King, who, since he liked my models, had commissioned me to execute this great work, and for many months I have heard nothing else to the contrary. Only this morning I learned that you had received the commission and had taken it away from me; I earned my work with my marvellous deeds, and you have taken it away from me only with your empty words!'

32. To this Bologna replied, and said: 'Oh, Benvenuto, everyone seeks to serve his interests in every way possible: if the King wants it this way, how can you object? You'd be wasting your time, for I have received the commission and it's mine. Now say whatever you like, and I shall listen to you.' I spoke as follows: 'You know, Messer Francesco, that I'd have to say a great deal to you, and that with admirable and true reasoning I would make you confess that such methods as those you have described and employed are not used among rational animals; I shall, however, come quickly to the point and conclude in a few words; but open your ears and hear me well, because it is important.' He wanted to rise from his seat, because he saw that my face was flushed and my expression had changed greatly: I said that it was not yet time to get up—that he was to remain seated and listen to me. Then I began, speaking in this manner: 'Messer Francesco, you know that the work was mine first, and that by any rational standard the time has passed for anyone to speak

about it further: now let me tell you that I'll be satisfied if you execute a model, and in addition to the one I have already executed, I will do another one; then we shall very quietly carry them to our great King; and whoever earns in this way the distinction of having done the better work, that man shall be truly worthy of making the colossus; and if the commission comes to you, I'll forget all this great wrong you have done me, and I'll bless your hands as worthier than mine to achieve such glory. And so let's leave it at this, and we'll be friends; otherwise we'll become enemies; and since God always helps those in the right, and I'm making my way straight to the right, I'll show you how very mistaken you have been.' Then Messer Francesco said: 'The work is mine, and since it was given to me I don't want to compromise what is mine.' To him I responded: 'Messer Francesco, since you don't want to take the proper path, which is just and reasonable, I shall show you the other; it will be like your path, which is ugly and distasteful. Let me tell you, then, that if I ever hear in any way that you have spoken of this work of mine, I'll immediately kill you like a dog; and since we are neither in Rome nor Bologna nor Florence—here people live in a different way—if I ever find out that you have spoken about this to the King or to others, I'll kill you no matter what. Think about which path you wish to choose: either that first good one, which I described, or this last evil path, which I am describing now.' This man did not know what to say or to do, and I was prepared to carry out my threat right then and there rather than to waste further time. Bologna said only this: 'When I do the things that a worthy man should do, I'll have nothing in the world to fear.' To this I said: 'You've spoken well; but in doing the contrary you should be afraid, because it is a serious matter.' And I immediately left him and went to the King; and with His Majesty I discussed the making of his coinage for some time, about which we were in full agreement, but because his Council was present there, they persuaded him that the coins should be minted in the French style, as they had been minted up to that time. To this I replied that His Majesty had brought me from Italy to execute works that were good, and if His Majesty ordered me to do the contrary, I would never in good conscience agree to it. This matter was postponed to be discussed at another time: I immediately returned to Paris.

33. I had no sooner dismounted when one of those fine people who take delight in uncovering evil came to tell me that Pagolo

Micceri had taken a house for that little whore of a Caterina and her mother, that he went there continually, and that in speaking about me he always said, with scorn: 'Benvenuto set the geese to guard the lettuce, and he thought I wouldn't eat it; it's enough that he now goes around acting brave and believing that I'm afraid of him: I have strapped on this sword and this dagger by my side to give him to understand that my sword cuts too, and that I'm a Florentine just like him, from the Micceri family, a much better family than his Cellinis.' The scoundrel who brought me this story told it so effectively that I immediately felt a fever coming on—and I mean a real fever, not a figure of speech. And since I might have died from such a bestial passion, I found a remedy by giving it the outlet such an opportunity had afforded me, just as I wished. I told my worker from Ferrara, who was called Chioccia, to come with me, and I had my horse brought behind me by the servant, and when I reached the house where this spiteful man was living, I found the door half-closed and went inside. I saw that he had his sword and dagger by his side, and that he was sitting on a chest with his arm around Caterina's neck: I had hardly arrived when I heard him joking with her mother about my affairs. I pushed in the door, and at the same time I put my hand to my sword and placed its point at his throat, not giving him time even to think about the fact that he had a sword too, and all at once I said: 'Vile coward, commend yourself to God, for you are a dead man!' Paralysed, he cried out three times: 'Oh, Mother, help me!' I wanted to murder him no matter what, but when I had heard his silly cries half of my anger left me. Meanwhile, I had told my workman Chioccia not to allow either Caterina or her mother to leave, for once I had attended to him I wanted to do equal harm to these two whores. Keeping the point of my sword constantly at his throat, after a little time I pricked him a bit, uttering terrifying words. When I saw that he was making no effort at all to defend himself I did not know what else to do, and I thought that my threats had no point whatsoever. I came up with the clever idea of choosing the lesser evil and making them marry, with the design of taking my revenge on them later. So, once I made up my mind, I said: 'Take off that ring you're wearing on your finger, you coward, and marry her, so that I can take the revenge that you deserve later on.' He immediately replied: 'As long as you don't murder me, I'll do anything!' 'Then,' I said, 'put the ring on her finger.' I moved the sword slightly from his throat, and he put the ring on her. Then I said: 'This is not enough—I want to have two notaries found so that this matter can be put into a legal contract.' After telling Chioccia to go for the notaries, I quickly turned to Caterina and her mother. Speaking in French, I said: 'The notaries and other witnesses are coming here: the first one of you I hear saying anything about this I'll kill immediately, and I'll kill all three of you; so keep that in mind.' And to Pagolo I said, in Italian: 'If you make any objection to anything I propose, even the slightest thing you might say, I'll stab you so many times with this dagger that I'll make everything in your guts spill out.' To this he answered: 'It's enough for me that you don't kill me, and I'll do whatever you wish.' The notaries and witnesses arrived, they drew up an authentic, admirable contract, and both my anger and my fever passed. I paid the notaries and went off. The following day Bologna came on purpose to Paris and had Mattio del Nazaro summon me: I went and found Bologna, who greeted me with a pleasant expression, begging me to consider him a good brother and telling me that he would never again speak of this work, because he knew very well that I was right.

34. If I did not say that I admit to having done some harm in some of the events that have occurred to me, I would not be considered truthful when I say, on the other hand, that I know I have sometimes done what is right; I know, however, that I made an error in wanting to take such a strange revenge upon Pagolo Micceri. Although had I thought him to be such a weak man, it would have never entered my mind to take such a humiliating revenge on him as I did: because it was not enough for me to have forced him to take as his wife such a wicked little whore, but to put the finishing touches on my vendetta I also had her summoned and drew her portrait. Every day I gave her thirty soldi; and since I made her pose nude, the first thing she wanted was for me to pay her the money in advance; the second thing she wanted was a good meal; the third thing was that I had sex with her out of revenge, reproaching her and her husband with all the various horns I was giving him; the fourth thing was that I made her stand there in great discomfort for hours and hours, and the more annoyed she became, standing in that uncomfortable position, the more I took pleasure from it, because she had a very beautiful figure and brought me great honour; and since she thought I did not treat her with the same consideration as I

once had, before she was married, this annoyed her greatly and she began to complain. In that French fashion of hers, she threatened me with words, bringing up her husband who had gone to stay with the prior of Capua, the brother of Piero Strozzi.* As I said, she kept bringing up this husband of hers, and when I had heard her speak about him I became exceedingly angry. Still, I unwillingly put up with it as best I could, reckoning that for the purposes of my profession, I could not find anywhere a more suitable model than she was, and I said to myself: 'I am getting two kinds of revenge out of this: the first is that she is married; these horns are not empty ones like hers, when she betrayed me like a whore; and so, if I am taking this great revenge upon him, while I am treating her maliciously by making her stand here in so much discomfort—which, besides pleasing me, will bring me so much honour and profit—what more can I desire?' While I was adding up my account books in this fashion, this wretch of a woman redoubled her insults, still talking about her husband; she did and said so much that she drove me beyond the bounds of reason; and giving in to my rage, I pulled her by the hair and dragged her around the room, giving her so many kicks and blows that I was worn out. And no one was able to enter here to help her. After I had thoroughly pummelled her she swore she would never return to my house; because of this, for the first time I thought I had acted wrongly, since I thought I was losing a marvellous opportunity to do myself honour. Besides, when I saw her all torn up, bruised, and swollen, I thought that even if she were to return it would be necessary to give her medical treatment for a fortnight before I could get any use out of her.

35. Returning to the girl, I sent one of my servants to help her get dressed, an old woman by the name of Ruberta who was extremely kind, and when she came to that little scoundrel she again brought her something to drink and eat; she then rubbed some beef dripping on the bad bruises I had given her, and together they ate the dripping that was left over. Once she had dressed she took her leave, blaspheming and cursing all the Italians and the King who kept them there. And so she went away, crying and muttering until she reached home. For the first time I certainly thought that I had done something wrong, and my Ruberta reproached me, constantly saying to me: 'You were very cruel to treat such a beautiful little girl so harshly.' Trying to make excuses for myself to my Ruberta, I told her

all the wicked things Caterina and her mother had done when they lived with me, and at this Ruberta scolded me, saying that this was nothing at all, because it was the custom in France, and she knew for a fact that there was not a husband in France who did not have his pair of horns. Her words moved me to laughter, and I then said to Ruberta that she should go and see how Caterina was, since I would be very pleased to be able to finish that work of mine, using her as a model. My Ruberta admonished me, telling me that I did not know how to live: 'for as soon as day breaks she'll come here by herself, whereas if you should send for her or visit her, she will put on airs and won't want to come here at all.' When the next day arrived this same Caterina came to my door and began knocking on it furiously, so that, since I was downstairs, I ran to see if it was a maniac or someone inside my household. Opening the door, this wild animal flung herself round my neck laughing, and once she had embraced and kissed me she asked me if I was still angry with her. I said I was not. She replied: 'Then give me a good breakfast.' I gave her a good breakfast, and I ate with her as a sign of peace. Then I set to drawing her portrait: in this way the usual carnal pleasures followed; then, at the same hour as on the day before, she provoked me so much that I had to give her the same beating; and in this fashion we went on for several days, every day doing the very same things after the same pattern, with only the slightest variation. Meanwhile, I had brought myself great honour and finished my figure, and I made preparations to cast it in bronze; in the process I encountered some difficulties, which it would be very valuable to describe in recounting the details of my profession, but since they would take me too much time I shall pass them over. It is enough to say that my figure came out extremely well, and it was as beautifully cast as anything ever has been.*

36. While I was moving forward with this work, I set aside certain hours of the day and worked sometimes on the salt-cellar and sometimes on the statue of Jupiter. Since the salt-cellar was worked upon by many more people than I had to assist me on working on the Jupiter, I had already completely finished it by this time. The King had returned to Paris and I went to find him, taking him the completed salt-cellar; it was, as I have said before,* oval in shape, about two-thirds of an armslength in size, all in gold, and decorated using a chisel. And as I said when I discussed the model, I had represented the Sea and the Land both seated, and they intertwined their legs,

just as certain branches of the sea run into the land and the land juts out into the sea: I had, therefore, very appropriately given them this kind of grace. In the right hand of the Sea I had placed a trident, and in the left I had placed a boat that was very delicately adorned, to hold the salt. Underneath this figure were his four seahorses, whose breast and front hooves were like horses; all the rest, from the middle backwards, was like a fish: these fishes' tails were intertwined together in a very delightful manner; and above that group the Sea was sitting in a very proud pose: he had all around him all kinds of fish and other sea-creatures. The water was represented with its waves, and then most beautifully enamelled in its own proper colour. For the Land I depicted an extremely beautiful woman, with her horn of plenty in her hand and completely naked like her male counterpart, and in her left hand I had fashioned a small temple in the Ionic order, most delicately decorated, in which the pepper was placed. Under this female figure I created the most beautiful animals the land produces, and I had partly enamelled and partly left in gold the rocks of the earth. I had then positioned this work and set it upon a base of black ebony: it was of a certain suitable thickness, and had a small moulding in which I had distributed four figures in gold, executed in more than half-relief, which represented Night, Day, Twilight, and Dawn.* Also, there were four other figures of the same size to represent the four major winds, enamelled in part and as carefully finished as one could imagine. When I placed this work before the King's eyes he exclaimed in astonishment, and could not get his fill of looking at it: then he told me to take it back to my house, and that he would tell me what I was to do with it. Having taken it back home, I immediately invited my closest friends, and with them I dined in great happiness, placing the salt-cellar in the middle of the table; we were the first people to use it. Later, I set out to finish the silver Jupiter and a large vase, previously mentioned, which I completely adorned with many extremely delightful decorations and numerous figures.

37. During this period the painter Bologna, whom I mentioned previously, gave the King to understand that it would be to His Majesty's advantage to allow him to go to Rome, and to write him letters of introduction, so that he might take casts of those fine and foremost ancient statues, that is to say, the Laocoön, the Cleopatra, the Venus, the Commodus, the Zingara, and the Apollo.* These are

truly the most beautiful things in Rome. And he told the King that, after His Majesty had seen these amazing works, he would then know how to discuss the art of design, because everything he had seen done by us modern artisans was very far removed from the good craftsmanship of the ancients. The King was agreeable, and gave him all the letters of introduction he requested. And so this beast went off on his own damned way. Not having the vision to compete with me by working with his own hand, he had chosen that typical Lombard expedient of seeking to devalue my works by becoming an imitator of those by the ancients. And although he executed his casts extremely well, he succeeded in producing quite the opposite result to what he had imagined, something that I shall describe in the proper place.* I had chased that wretched Caterina away altogether, and the poor, unfortunate young man who was her husband had left Paris; and since I wanted to put the finishing touches to my Fontainebleau, which was already cast in bronze, and also to execute carefully the two Victories, which were to go in the angles beside the half-circle of the doorway, I took on a poor little girl of about fifteen years of age. She had an extremely beautiful body and was somewhat dark; and since she was rather wild and a girl of very few words, swift in her movements, with eyes that glared, all these traits caused me to give her the name Scorzone:* her real name was Gianna. With this young girl, I finished very nicely the bronze of Fontainebleau, as well as the two figures of Victory for the doorway. This young girl was pure and a virgin, and I made her pregnant; she gave me a daughter on the seventh of June, at the thirteenth hour of the day in 1544, which was in the course of my forty-fourth year. I gave the name of Costanza to this little girl, and she was held at her baptism by Messer Guido Guidi, the King's physician and my very dear friend, as I have written previously. He was the only godfather, because in France they follow the custom of having only one godfather and two godmothers, one of whom was Signora Maddalena, the wife of Messer Luigi Alamanni, a Florentine gentleman and a wonderful poet; the other was the wife of Messer Ricciardo del Bene, one of our fellow Florentine citizens and a great merchant; she was a great French noblewoman.* This was the first child I ever had, as far as I remember. I consigned to this young girl a sufficient sum of money for a dowry to satisfy her aunt, into whose care I entrusted her, and I never ever had anything to do with her again.*

38. I pressed on with my works, and had clearly moved ahead with them: the Jupiter was almost completed, as was the vase; the doorway began to display its beauties. During this time the King turned up in Paris, and even though I mentioned 1544 as the birth-day of my daughter, the year of 1543 had still not yet ended, but since it came to me to speak of this daughter of mine just now, in order to avoid being prevented from turning to other matters of more importance I shall say nothing further about her until the proper time. The King came to Paris, as I said, and he immediately came on to my house, and found all those many works before him, which could very well delight his eyes; as indeed they did: this marvellous King was as pleased with them as anyone might desire who had endured the hardships I had undergone; he immediately recalled, of his own accord, that the Cardinal of Ferrara, whom I mentioned before, had given me nothing—neither a pension nor anything else—of what he had promised me; and muttering to his Admiral,* he said that the Cardinal of Ferrara had behaved very badly in giving me nothing, but that he wanted to find a remedy for this improper situation, because he saw that I was a man of few words, and that in a blink of the eyes I might leave him, without saying a thing to him. He went home, and after dining His Majesty told the Cardinal to give orders on his behalf to the royal treasurer to pay me seven thousand golden scudi as soon as he could, in three or four instalments, whichever was convenient to him, provided that he did not fail to do this; and moreover, he said repeatedly: 'I gave Benve-nuto into your custody, and you have forgotten him.' The Cardinal said he would gladly do everything His Majesty had ordered. This Cardinal, because of his wicked nature, allowed the King's wish to be neglected. Meanwhile, the wars grew worse, and this was in the period when the Emperor, with his powerful army, marched toward Paris.* When the Cardinal saw that France was very short of money, one day he went to speak about me with the King, and said: 'Sacred Majesty, acting in your best interests, I did not have the money given to Benvenuto: one reason is because now we need it too much; the other is because a large disbursement of money would have caused you to lose Benvenuto more quickly, for if he thought himself rich he would have purchased property in Italy, and the first time he was taken by the whim he would happily have left you; I thought, there-fore, that the best policy would be for Your Majesty to give him something inside your kingdom, if you want him to remain here a long time in your service.' The King considered his arguments to be good ones, since he was short of money; nevertheless, as a most noble spirit, truly worthy of the king that he was, he thought that the Cardinal had done such a thing more out of a wish to ingratiate himself than due to any necessity he had imagined, so far in advance, concerning the needs of such a great kingdom.

39. And as I have said, although the King showed that he had accepted the Cardinal's arguments as good ones, privately he did not think like this: for, as I said above, he returned to Paris, and on the following day, without my urging him to do so, he came of his own accord to my home, where I myself met him and led him through a number of rooms in which there were various kinds of works, and beginning with the most humble items, I showed him a great quantity of works in bronze, more than he had seen for a good long while. Then I took him to see the silver Jupiter and showed it to him completed, with all of its exquisitely beautiful decorations: he thought that this was a much more admirable work than it would have seemed to any other man, as the result of a certain terrible event that had befallen him a few years earlier: for after the capture of Tunis, when the Emperor passed through Paris* in agreement with his brother-in-law King Francis, the said King, wishing to give him a gift worthy of such a great emperor, had a statue of Hercules executed for him in silver, of the exact size that I had made this Jupiter; the King confessed that this Hercules was the ugliest work he had ever seen; and so, after he had condemned it as such to the most talented men in Paris, who pretended to be the most talented men in the world in that profession, they gave the King to understand that this figure represented the best that could be achieved in silver and, nevertheless, wanted two thousand ducats for their filthy work. For this reason, after the King had seen this work of mine he perceived in it such an elegant finish that he would never have believed it. So, he made a fair judgement, and wanted my work on Jupiter to be appraised likewise at two thousand ducats, saying: 'I provided these men with no salary: to Benvenuto I give about a thousand scudi as a salary, and he certainly can make this for me for the price of two thousand gold scudi, since he has the advantage of his salary.' Then I took him to see other works in silver and gold, and many other models for the creation of new works. Then, at the last moment

before his departure, in the meadow of my castle I uncovered that enormous giant,* which amazed the King yet more than anything ever had, and turning to the Admiral, whose name was Messer Aniballe,* he said: 'Since the Cardinal has provided nothing for this man, and he is inevitably also slow to ask, I want him to be provided for without saying another word about it: for men such as these, who are not used to asking for anything, are certain that their works ought to ask a great deal on their behalf; take care, therefore, to provide him with the first abbey that becomes vacant with revenues worth up to two thousand scudi; and if no single vacancy of that kind occurs, let him have it made up in two or three, because it will be all the same for him.' Standing in the King's presence I heard everything, and I quickly thanked him as if I had already received it, telling His Majesty that, once this gift had come to me, I wanted to work for His Majesty without any other reward, either in salary or in other compensation for my work, until such time as I was constrained by old age and no longer able to work, when I could in peace find rest for my weary life, living honourably on this income, and remembering how I had served such a great king as His Majesty was. At my words the King with great openness, turned toward me cheerfully and said: 'And let it be so!' And His Majesty, quite content, left me, and I remained there.

40. When Madame d'Étampes learned of my affairs, she became even more greatly embittered against me, saying to herself: 'Today I rule the world, and a little man like this gives me no respect!' She put all her efforts into working tirelessly against me. When a certain man, who was an expert distiller, fell into her clutches, and gave her some wonderful fragrant waters which smoothed her skin, something never before used in France, she presented him to the King: this individual offered some of these distillations, which greatly pleased the King, and in the midst of these delights she had him ask His Majesty for a tennis court I had in my castle, along with some little apartments which he said I did not need. This good King, who recognized the origin of the request, gave no reply whatsoever. Madame d'Étampes set about entreating him by those methods that women employ with men, so that her plan easily succeeded, for finding the King in an amorous mood, to which he was very susceptible, he granted to Madame as much as she desired. This distiller, whom I mentioned before, came together with the treasurer Grolier,*

an extremely important nobleman in France, and since this treasurer spoke Italian very well, he visited my castle and came before me, speaking to me jokingly in Italian. When he saw the time was ripe, he said: 'On behalf of the King, I place this man here in possession of the tennis court, along with those little apartments that belong with the court.' To this I said: 'All things come from our sacred King; you could, therefore, have entered here more openly; for acting in this manner, by means of notaries and the court, seems more a kind of deception than a genuine order from so great a King; I protest therefore that, before I go to complain to the King, I shall defend myself in the way that His Majesty ordered me to do the other day; and unless I see another express order written in the King's own hand, I shall throw this man, whom you have placed here, out of the window.' At these words of mine, the treasurer went off, threatening and muttering, and I remained, doing the same thing, nor did I wish at that time to make any other move: then I went off to find those notaries who had placed this man in possession. They were all very well known to me, and they told me that this was a formal procedure done on the order of the King, but that it did not matter very much; that if I had offered a bit of resistance he could not have taken possession, as he had; and that these were the acts and customs of the court, which did not in the least touch on obedience to the King: so that, when I succeeded in stripping him of possession in the same manner in which he had come into it, it would be well done and nothing would come of it. It was enough for me to have received the suggestion, and on the following day I began to put my hand to my weapons; and even if I did in fact encounter some difficulties, I considered it part of the fun. Every day I would make a sudden assault with rocks, pikes, and arquebuses, shooting without bullets, but I frightened them to such an extent that no one wanted to come to his assistance any longer. For this reason, one day, finding his resistance weak, I entered the house by force and drove him out, throwing after him every little thing that he brought there. Then I went to the King and told him that I had done absolutely everything His Majesty had commanded me to do, defending myself from all those who wished to prevent me from serving him. The King laughed about this and sent me new letters of ownership,* through which I would have no more disturbance.

41. Meanwhile, with great diligence I completed the beautiful

silver Jupiter, along with its gilded base which I had placed upon a wooden plinth which was scarcely visible; in this wooden plinth I had inserted four balls of hard wood which were more than half-hidden in their sockets, like the button on crossbows.* These objects were so delicately arranged that a small boy could easily, and without the slightest effort, push the statue of Jupiter back and forth and turn it around in every direction. When I had set everything in order in my own way, I went off with it to Fontainebleau where the King was. At this time Bologna, whom I mentioned before, had brought back from Rome the previously mentioned statues,* and with a great deal of care he had cast them in bronze. I did not know anything about this, both because he had done this work very secretly, and because Fontainebleau is more than forty miles from Paris; I could not, therefore, have known anything about it. When I was trying to find out from the King where he wished me to place the Jupiter, Madame d'Étampes, being present, told the King that there was no spot more appropriate in which to place it than in his beautiful gallery. This was, as we would say in Tuscany, a loggia, or actually a wide corridor; it could more properly be called a corridor, since we call a room open on one side a loggia. This room was more than one hundred paces in length, and it was elegant and full of paintings from the hand of our marvellous Florentine Rosso, and among the paintings very many pieces of sculpture were arranged, some in the round and others in low relief: the corridor was about twelve paces wide. This Bologna had brought into this gallery all the above-mentioned ancient works, cast in bronze and carefully finished, and he had placed them in a very beautiful arrangement, elevated upon their bases; and as I mentioned above, these statues were the most beautiful objects copied from the antique statues of Rome. Into this same corridor, I brought my Jupiter;* and when I saw that grand arrangement, all done with skill, I said to myself: 'This is like running the gauntlet.* Now may God help me!' After putting the figure in its place and arranging it as best I could, I waited for the great King to arrive. The Jupiter held his thunderbolt in his right hand, as if he were about to hurl it, while in his left hand I had placed a globe. Among the flames I had very skilfully fitted a piece of a white taper. Madame d'Étampes had kept the King occupied until nightfall to do me one of two evil turns: either he would not come at all, or my work would certainly show itself to be less beautiful because of the night;

Margot + Henri of Navarre

but as God grants to those creatures who have faith in Him, exactly the contrary happened. Once I saw that night had fallen, I lit the taper in the hand of Jupiter, and because it was somewhat elevated above the head of Jupiter, the illumination fell from above and produced a far more beautiful sight than it might have done in daytime. The King appeared together with his Madame d'Étampes, his son the Dauphin (now king),* the Dauphiness, the King of Navarre, his brother-in-law, Madame Margherita, his daughter,* and many other great lords, who were all expressly instructed by Madame d'Étampes to speak badly of me. When I saw the King enter I had the statue pushed forward by that young man of mine, Ascanio, who gently moved the handsome Jupiter toward the King. Since I had executed the work with some skill, the slight motion given to the figure, which was well executed, made it seem alive, and since the antique figures had been left by me somewhat in the background, I first provided great delight to the onlookers' eyes with my own work. The King immediately declared: 'This is much more beautiful than anything anyone has ever seen, and even though I take pleasure in such things and understand them, I would have never imagined the hundredth part of it.' Those lords, who were supposed to have spoken against me, seemed to be unable to give my work sufficient praise. Then Madame d'Étampes impertinently exclaimed: 'It seems quite clear you have no eyes. Don't you see all those handsome ancient bronze figures placed behind this one, in which the true genius of this craft exists, rather than in these modern trifles?' Then the King moved and the others with him, and after he had glanced at these other figures which, lighted from below, were not well displayed, he declared: 'Whoever wished to remove this man from my favour actually did him an enormous favour, because through a comparison with these admirable figures we can see and recognize that his statue is by far more beautiful and more wonderful than those. Therefore, we must hold Benvenuto in high esteem, for not only do his works withstand the comparison with the ancient ones, but they actually surpass them.' To this Madame d'Étampes claimed that, if one saw such a work by day, it would not appear a thousandth part as beautiful as it did by night; it was also to be noted that I had placed a veil over the figure in order to cover up its embarrassing defects. This was a very thin veil, which I had draped very gracefully around Jupiter in order to increase its majestic appearance: I heard her remark, I took the veil, and lifting it up from below, revealed its fine genital organs, and with a touch of obvious annoyance I ripped it off completely. She thought I had uncovered that part of the statue to mock her.* When the King noticed her indignation and saw me overcome with passion and wishing to speak, the wise monarch immediately said these exact words in his own language: 'Benvenuto, I am cutting off your reply; so be quiet, and you shall receive a thousand times more treasure than you desire.' Unable to speak, I twisted and turned in great distress: this caused her to grumble even more indignantly, and the King left much sooner than he might have done otherwise, declaring in a loud voice, to give me courage, that he had brought out of Italy the greatest man ever born, the perfection of his profession.

42. I left the Jupiter there, and since I wished to leave in the morning, I was given a thousand gold scudi: part was my salary and part was on account for the personal expenses I had incurred. After I took the money I returned to Paris happy and content, and having arrived and immediately celebrated in my own home, I then, after dining, had all my clothes brought in, which consisted of a vast quantity of silk, the finest furs, and some similarly fine and most delicate cloth. I made a present of these to all my workers, giving to them according to the merits of their service, down to the serving girls and the stable-boys, which gave them all the inclination to assist me with a willing heart. Once I had recovered my strength, with the greatest study and diligence I set about finishing that great statue of Mars,* which I had constructed in timber, extremely well fitted together to form a frame; over this frame its flesh was a crust, an eighth of an armslength thick, made from plaster and very carefully finished; then I had prepared to cast the figure in many pieces and later to dovetail it as best as our profession might allow, something which was very easy for me to do. I do not want to fail to mention something about this huge work, which is truly worthy of laughter: I had given orders to all those on my payroll not to bring prostitutes into my home or my castle, and I was very careful to see that such a thing did not happen. Ascanio, that young man of mine, was in love with an extremely beautiful girl, and she with him. For this reason, she had run away from her mother, coming one night to find Ascanio and then not wishing to leave; not knowing where to hide her, but being an ingenious person, as a last resort he placed her inside this

statue, and he prepared a place for her to sleep right in its head; and she stayed there for some time, while during the night he sometimes quietly brought her out. I had left that head very close to completion, and I had left it uncovered, somewhat out of my own pride, so that it could be seen by most of the city of Paris: those living nearby had begun to climb up on the rooftops, and many people used to come just to see it. In Paris there was a rumour circulating that a spirit had been dwelling from ancient times in this castle of mine, even though I never saw any indication to make me believe this was true—the common people of Paris all called this spirit by the name of Lemmonio Boreò,*—and because this young girl who was living in the statue's head could not prevent some of her movements being seen through the statue's eyes, some of these foolish people were saying that this spirit had entered into the body of this great statue, and was making the eyes in that head and its mouth move as if it wanted to speak. Terror-stricken, many of them fled, while others, who were more astute and who came to see it, could not deny the flashing of the eyes in the statue, and they too affirmed that there was a spirit inside, not knowing that there was indeed a spirit, but also some good flesh as well.

43. Meanwhile, I turned my attention to putting together my beautiful doorway with all the previously mentioned details. Since I do not wish to write in this story of my life about matters that concern those who write chronicles, I have therefore omitted the arrival of the Emperor with his great army, and the King with all his forces mustered.* And during this time the King sought my advice in order to fortify Paris quickly: he came to my home for that purpose and led me around the entire city; when he heard how I would fortify Paris for him quickly and in an efficient way, he gave express orders for me to do immediately what I had described; and he ordered his Admiral to command the citizens to obey me under pain of incurring his displeasure. The Admiral, who had been named to this rank through the favour of Madame d'Étampes and not because of his good works, was a man of little talent, and his name—Monsieur d'Anguebò, which in our language means Monsignor d'Aniballe— has such a sound in their language that the people usually called him Monsignor Ass-Ox.* This beast had related everything to Madame d'Étampes, and she had ordered him to summon Girolimo Bellarmato* as quickly as possible. This man was a Sienese engineer and

was at Dieppe, little more than a day away from Paris. He came immediately, and having put into operation the most tedious method of building fortifications, I retired from the entire undertaking; and if the Emperor had pressed forward he would have taken Paris with great ease. It was, indeed, maintained that in the subsequent treaty Madame d'Étampes—who was involved in the matter more than anyone else—had betrayed the King.* I do not need to speak further of this, since it is not part of my subject. I set myself with great diligence to assemble my bronze doorway and bring to completion that large vase and the two other medium-sized ones made of silver. After these tribulations the good King came to rest for a while in Paris. That damned woman* must have been brought into the world only for its ruination, and it seemed to me that since she considered me her sworn enemy, I was a person of some importance. She happened to begin talking with this good King about my affairs, and she spoke so badly of me that this good man swore, to please her, that he would never again take any more notice of me, just as if he had never known me. A page of the Cardinal of Ferrara, who was called Villa, immediately came to tell me this, and he informed me himself that he had heard these words from the King's own mouth. This drove me into such a fit of anger that I threw all my tools and all my works as well up in the air, prepared to take my leave immediately, and went at once to find the King. After his dinner, I entered the chamber where His Majesty was with only a few people; and when he saw me enter, after I paid him that dutiful reverence that is owed to a King, he immediately bowed his head toward me with a cheerful expression. I took hope from this and drew nearer little by little to His Majesty, and since they were showing off a number of items from my own profession, after discussing these things for a time, His Majesty asked me if I had anything beautiful to show him at my house; and then he said that whenever I liked he would come to see them. Then I said that I was prepared to show him something right away, if he wanted to see it. He immediately said that I should head for home, and that he would come straightaway.

44. I went off to wait for this good King, who then went to take his leave of Madame d'Étampes. She wanted to know where he was going since she said she wanted to keep him company, and when the King told her where he was going, she informed His Majesty that she did not want to accompany him, and begged him that he do her

the favour of not going himself that day. She had to repeat her request more than twice in her desire to dissuade the King from his intention: but that day he did not come to my home. The following day I returned to the King at around the same hour: he immediately spotted me and swore that he wanted to come to my house right away. As usual, he went to take his leave of Madame d'Étampes, and when she saw that, with all her power, she was unable to change his purpose, she began, with that biting tongue of hers, to speak as badly of me as could be spoken of a man who was the mortal enemy of that worthy throne. At this, the good King said he wanted to go to my house for the sole purpose of bawling me out in order to terrify me, and he gave his word to Madame d'Étampes that he would do this. He came to my house right away, where I guided him through some of the large downstairs rooms in which I had assembled the whole of that great door of mine, and when the King saw this he remained so speechless that he could not find a way to give me the bawling-out that he had promised to Madame d'Étampes. Nevertheless, he did not want to miss the opportunity of insulting me as he had promised, and he began by saying: 'There is indeed something important that you artisans, even though you may be talented, must understand— that you cannot demonstrate such talent without the assistance of others; and you demonstrate your greatness only when you receive the opportunity from us. Now you should be a bit more obedient and not so proud and capricious. I remember having given you express orders to make me twelve silver statues, and that was all I wanted. You wanted to make me a salt-cellar, vases, heads, doorways, and so many other things that I am disconcerted, seeing the way you have abandoned all the desires of my heart and concentrated on satisfying all your own desires: if you think you can act in this man- ner, I shall show you subsequently how I am accustomed to act when I want people to do things my way. And so, I say to you: make sure you do what you are told, for by sticking obstinately to these fan- tasies of yours, you will run headlong against a wall.' And while he was saying this, all the noblemen stood attentively, watching as the King shook his head, glowered with his eyes, and gesticulated with one hand or the other; everyone who was present there trembled out of fear for me, but I was resolved not to have a fear in the world.

45. As soon as the King had completed the display of bravado he had promised his Madame d'Étampes, I kneeled upon the ground,

kissed the robe upon his knee, and said: 'Sacred Majesty, I admit that everything you say is true; only let me say that my heart has been continuously, both day and night and with all my vital spirits, intent only upon obeying you and upon serving you; and as for anything which might seem to go contrary to what I am saying, Your Majesty should know that this was not Benvenuto but was, instead, my evil fate or my adverse fortune, which has wanted to make me unworthy to serve the most marvellous ruler the earth ever had: therefore, I beg you to pardon me. Only it seemed that Your Majesty gave me enough silver for only one statue: and not having any silver myself, I was unable to execute more than that one; and of the little bit of silver that was left over from the figure of Jupiter, I fashioned that vase to show Your Majesty that beautiful style of the ancients, some-thing you had perhaps never seen before. And as for the salt-cellar, if I remember correctly, it seems to me that Your Majesty ordered it of your own accord one day, after you had been discussing another salt-cellar that was brought to you; because of this I showed you a model, which I had already executed in Italy, and then, only at your request, you had me immediately given a thousand golden scudi to make it, telling me that you were grateful to me for the inspiration: and I thought that you thanked me even more when I gave you the com-pleted work. As for the doorway, it seems to me that, speaking of this by chance, Your Majesty gave the commission to Monsignor di Villurois, your first secretary, who gave orders to Monsignor di Marmagna and Monsignor de la Fa to keep me working on the project and to supply me with provisions for it; for without these commissions I would never have been able to bring forward such a great undertaking alone. And as for the bronze heads, the base of my Jupiter, and other things, to tell the truth, I executed the heads for myself in order to experiment with the clays of France, about which, as a foreigner, I knew nothing; for without experimenting with these clays, I would never have set about casting those greater works. As for the bases, I executed them believing that these items were quite appropriate to accompany such figures; everything I have done, how-ever, I thought I did for the best, and never wanted to stray from Your Majesty's wishes. It is certainly true that I have made all of that great colossus, up to the point it has reached, with the expenses of my own purse; I did so thinking only that, since you are such a great King and I am such an insignificant artisan, I ought to execute a

statue for your glory as well as my own, a work the ancients have
never fashioned. Now that I see God is unwilling to make me worthy
of the honour of being in your service, I beg you that, instead of that
honourable reward Your Majesty had intended for my works, you
give me only a bit of your good grace, and with it your kind permission to take my leave; for at this point, if you make me worthy of
such favours, I shall leave and return to Italy, always thanking God
and Your Majesty for the happy hours that I have spent in your
service.'

46. The King took hold of me with his own hands and, with great
courtesy, raised me up from my knees; then he told me that I must be
content to serve him, and that everything I had made was good and
was pleasing to him. Turning to the noblemen, he said these exact
words: 'I surely believe that if Paradise had to have doors, it could
never have more beautiful ones than these.'* When I saw that the
vehemence of his words, which were all in my favour, had made him
pause, I once again thanked him with the greatest of reverence,
nevertheless repeating that I should like permission to leave, because
my annoyance had not yet passed away. When this great King perceived that I had not valued these extraordinary and enormous kindnesses of his in the way they deserved, with a loud and frightening
voice he ordered me not to speak another word, or I would be very
sorry; and then he added that he would drown me in gold and would
give me licence to work as I wished, for in addition to the works
commissioned by His Majesty, he was extremely satisfied with everything that I had done between one work and another on my own
account; that I would never more have differences with him, since he
now understood me; and that I should try to understand His Majesty, as my duty required. I said that I thanked God and His Majesty
for everything, then I begged him to come and see the great figure,
and how I had made progress on it: and so he came along with me. I
had it uncovered: it astonished him so much that it was unbelievable;
and he instantly ordered one of his secretaries immediately to repay
all my own money that I had spent, whatever sum I wished, it being
sufficient for me to give a written account in my own hand. And then
he departed, and he said to me: 'Goodbye, *mon ami*'—an intimate
expression rarely used by a King.

47. Returning to his palace, he began to repeat the lofty words, so
amazingly humble and so haughtily proud, that I had used towards

His Majesty, words that had made him very angry; and he recounted
some details of my expressions in the presence of Madame
d'Étampes, who was accompanied by Monsignor di San Polo, a great
baron of France.* This individual had, in the past, made a very
public profession of being my friend, and certainly on this occasion
he showed his friendship very skilfully in the French fashion.* After
a great deal of discussion, the King complained about the Cardinal
of Ferrara, into whose custody he had given me and who had never
given much thought to my affairs, saying that it was no thanks to him
that I had not already left his kingdom, and that he was seriously
thinking of putting me into the care of someone who understood me
better than the Cardinal of Ferrara did, because he did not want to
give me another opportunity to leave. Hearing these remarks, Monsignor di San Polo offered himself, telling the King that he should
give me into his care, and that he would really make very sure that I
would never have further reason to leave his kingdom. To this
request the King replied that he was very delighted to do so, if San
Polo was prepared to explain to him the method by which he
intended to prevent me from leaving. Madame d'Étampes, who was
present was pouting a great deal, but San Polo stood on his dignity,
not wishing to tell the King what method he wanted to employ.
The King asked him once again, and in order to please Madame
d'Étampes, he said: 'I would hang him by the neck, this Benvenuto
of yours, and in this way you would not lose him from your kingdom!' Madame d'Étampes immediately burst out laughing, saying
that I certainly deserved this. In reply, the King laughed to keep
them company, and said that he would be delighted if San Polo
hanged me, if first he could find another man who was my equal; for
even though I had never deserved it, he gave him his full permission.
In this fashion the day came to an end, and I remained safe and
sound: for which God be praised and thanked.

48. During this period the King had settled the war with the
Emperor but not with the English, and these devils kept us in great
tribulation.* Having something on his mind other than pleasure, the
King had commissioned Piero Strozzi to take a number of galleys
into those English waters, which was a very great and difficult thing
to undertake, even for that astonishing soldier, who was unique in
those times in his profession and equally unique in his misfortune.
Several months had passed and I had not received either money or

commissions, and so I had dismissed all my workmen except for the two Italians, whom I set to work on the two large vases to be made with my own silver, since they did not know how to work in bronze. When these two vases had been completed, I went with them to a city which belonged to the Queen of Navarre, by the name of Argentana,* which is many days away from Paris. After I reached the town I found the King, who was indisposed; the Cardinal of Ferrara told His Majesty that I had arrived there. To this news the King said nothing, which was the reason why I was forced to remain there in great discomfort for many days. In truth, I never experienced greater discomfort: and so, after several days I presented myself one evening and placed these two beautiful vases before the King's own eyes, and they pleased him beyond all measure. When I saw the King was well disposed, I begged His Majesty to do me the favour to grant me permission to take a trip clear down to Italy, and said that I would leave behind seven months of salary that I was owed and which His Majesty could deign to pay me afterwards if I had need of it on my return trip. I begged His Majesty to grant me this favour, especially since then was a time for making war and not for casting statues; besides, since His Majesty had granted the same request to his painter Bologna, I most devoutly begged him to be pleased to treat me in the same worthy fashion. While I said these words the King was looking with the closest attention at the two vases, and from time to time he would wound me with a ferocious glance; nevertheless, I begged him to grant me this favour as best I could and knew how. All of a sudden I saw he was furious, and he rose from his seat and said to me in Italian: 'Benvenuto, you are a great idiot; bring these vases to Paris, for I want them gilded.' And without giving me any other answer, he left. I approached the Cardinal of Ferrara, who was present, and I begged him, since he had done so much for me when he brought me out of the prison in Rome, along with so many other benefits, to obtain this favour for me as well, so that I could return to Italy. The Cardinal told me he would very gladly do everything he could to obtain this favour for me; that I should freely leave him in charge of this; and that if I wished I was free to go, for he would keep me on the best of terms with the King. I told the Cardinal that, since I knew His Majesty had given me into His Most Reverend Lordship's custody, if he gave me permission I would most willingly depart, to return upon receiving the slightest sign from His Most

Reverend Lordship. Then the Cardinal told me to go to Paris and to remain there for eight days, and that during this time he would obtain permission from the King for me to leave; that in case the King would not permit me to leave, he would send word to me without fail; and that if he did not write to me to the contrary, that would be a sign that I could leave freely.*

49. Going to Paris, as the Cardinal had told me, I made some admirable carrying cases for those three silver vases. After twenty days passed I prepared myself, placing the three vases in the pack of a mule that had been loaned to me as far as Lyons by the Bishop of Pavia,* whom I had lodged once again in my chateau. I left with my bad luck, along with Signor Ippolito Gonzaga, a nobleman in the King's pay and in the service of Count Galeotto della Mirandola, and with certain other noblemen of the Count. Lionardo Tedaldi, our Florentine fellow-citizen, also accompanied us.* I left Ascanio and Pagolo in charge of my chateau and all my property, among which were some vases which I had begun and left behind so that these two young men would not lack work. There was also a great deal of valuable furniture, for I lived there very honourably: the value of all this property of mine was more than one thousand five hundred scudi. I told Ascanio not to forget the great benefits he had received from me, and that up to that moment he had been a lad of little intelligence: now it was time for him to acquire the intelligence of a man, for I wished to leave him in charge of all my property, along with all my honour; and that if he should hear anything out of these French brutes he should immediately notify me, for I would ride post-haste and fly back there from wherever I might be, both from the great obligation I had towards this good King as well as for my own honour. This Ascanio, with feigned and thievish tears, said to me: 'I've never known any better father than you, and in whatever way a good son ought to act towards a good father, I shall always act towards you.' And so, after settling our affairs, I left with my servant and with a little French boy. When it was past noon, some of those treasurers who were not my friends came to my chateau. This rascally rabble immediately said I had gone off with the King's silver, and told Messer Guido and the Bishop of Pavia to send for the King's vases quickly, for if they did not they should send after me in a way I would not like very much. The Bishop and Messer Guido were more afraid than they should have been, and they immediately

sent that traitor Ascanio after me by post-horse, who turned up around midnight. I was not asleep, and was worrying, saying to myself: 'To whom have I left my property, my chateau? Oh, what kind of destiny is this, that forces me to take such a journey? Let's hope that the Cardinal is not in league with Madame d'Étampes, who desires nothing else in the world except for me to lose the favour of this good King!'

50. While I was having this debate with myself I heard Ascanio call me; and I instantly arose from the bed and asked him if he brought me good or bad news. Then the thief replied: 'I bring good news; only you have to send back the three vases, because these scoundrel treasurers are screaming "stop thief!",* and so the Bishop and Messer Guido say that you should send them back no matter what: otherwise there's nothing to worry about, and carry on enjoying this felicitous journey.'

I immediately returned the vases, although two of them were mine, along with the silver and everything else. I was carrying them to the abbey of the Cardinal of Ferrara in Lyons, for although they had accused me of wanting to carry them to Italy, everyone knows very well that you cannot export either money or gold or silver without special permission. So one can just imagine that I wanted to carry away these three large vases, which, with their carrying cases, took up an entire mule. It is, of course, true that these objects were very beautiful and valuable, and that I was afraid of the King's dying, since I had certainly left him in poor health; and I said to myself: 'If such an event were to occur, having entrusted them to the care of the Cardinal, at least I would not lose them.' Now, to conclude, I sent back this mule with the vases and other items of value, and with the companions I mentioned I set off next morning on my journey, never once during the entire trip being able to keep myself from sighing and weeping. Sometimes, however, I took comfort from God by praying to him, as I said: 'Lord God, You know the truth, You realize that this journey of mine is made solely to carry alms to those six poor wretched virgin sisters and to their mother, my own sister; and while they do have a father, he's so old and his profession earns him so little, so that these girls could easily choose an evil path; but by doing this pious deed I hope to receive assistance and counsel from Your Majesty.' This was the only recreation I took as I travelled forward. One day, when we were a day's journey from Lyons, at about the twenty-second hour, the sky began emitting some sharp claps of thunder and the sky was covered in white clouds: I was about a crossbow's shot ahead of my companions; and after the claps of thunder the sky made a noise that was so loud and so terrifying that I thought to myself it was Judgement Day; and as I stopped momentarily, a hailstorm began, without a drop of water. The hail was larger than the bullets in a musket, and when it struck me it hurt me a great deal: little by little the hail began to increase in size until it grew to about the size of a crossbow bullet. Seeing that my horse was sorely frightened, I turned back at a tremendous gallop until I met up with my companions again, who had stopped inside a pine grove because of the same fear. The hailstones increased to the size of large lemons: I sang a *Miserere*; and while I prayed so devoutly to God, a hailstone fell that was so large it broke a very thick branch of the pine tree under which I thought I was safe. Another lot of hailstones fell on my horse's head, who showed signs of falling to the ground; one struck me, but not with full force, or I would have been killed. Likewise, another struck that poor old man Lionardo Tedaldi, so that while he was, like me, upon his knees, it made him go on all fours on the ground. Then, when I saw that the branch could no longer protect me, and that along with my *Miserere* I had to take some action, I began to wrap my clothing around my head: and I told Lionardo, who was crying out 'Jesus! Jesus!' for help, that Jesus would help him if he helped himself. I spent more energy on saving that old man than on myself. The hailstorm lasted for a while, then ceased, and, all pounded as we were, we set out again on horseback as best we could; and while we were riding towards our lodgings, showing each other our scratches and bruises, we discovered a mile further on destruction so much greater than our own that it is impossible to describe. All the trees were stripped of leaves and broken, with as many livestock killed as happened to have been under them; many shepherds were also killed: we saw a lot of these hailstones which were so large that you could not get your two hands around them. It seemed to us that we had escaped with little damage, and we recognized then that our prayers to God and our *Misereres* had done us more good than we might have been able to do on our own. And so, giving thanks to God, we went on to Lyons next day, and we remained there for eight days.* After the eight days had passed and we were much refreshed, we continued our journey and most happily passed over the mountains. There I bought a little pony, since some of our small luggage had rather tired my horses.

51. After we had been in Italy for a day Count Galeotto della Mirandola joined us, passing through by post-horse, and while he stopped with us he told me I had make a mistake in leaving and that I ought to go no further, since by returning immediately my affairs would go better than ever; but that if I went ahead I would leave the field to my enemies, and give them the opportunity of doing me evil, for if I returned instantly I would block the way to what they had planned against me; and that those in whom I placed most faith were those who were deceiving me. He did not want to say anything else, even though he knew this very certainly: that the Cardinal of Ferrara had come to an agreement with those two scoundrels of mine whom I had left in charge of all my belongings. The Count repeated to me many times that I ought to return at all costs. After taking the post-horse, he went on his way, and I, along with my companions, was still resolved to go ahead. My heart struggled to make a choice, either to get to Florence as soon as possible or to return to France. I was so confused and so undecided that I finally determined to take the post to arrive quickly in Florence. I had made no arrangement to travel by the first post; and through this I became fixed in my absolute decision to go to my sufferings in Florence. Having left the company of Signor Ippolito Gonzaga, who had taken the road to go to Mirandola while I had taken the road for Parma and Piacenza, after reaching Piacenza I encountered Duke Pier Luigi* in one of the streets, who stared at me and recognized me. As I knew that all the evil I had suffered in the Castel Sant'Angelo in Rome had been entirely his fault, it made me very angry to see him; but not knowing any other means of escaping his clutches, I decided to go and visit him; and I arrived just as they had removed his food, and with him were those members of the house of Landi who later were the ones who murdered him. When I reached His Excellency's presence the man gave me the kindest welcome imaginable: and among his kind gestures, he began speaking of this subject of his own accord, saying to all those in his presence that I was the first man in the world in my profession, and that I had spent a long time in prison in Rome. Turning to me, he said: 'My dear Benvenuto, the evil you've suffered grieves me very much; I knew you were innocent but could not help you in any way, because my father was determined to satisfy certain

enemies of yours who had given him to understand that you had spoken badly of him: something I know very, very well was never true; and I grieved a great deal for you.' And to these remarks he added so many similar ones that it almost seemed as if he were begging my pardon. Then he asked me about all the works I had executed for the Most Christian King; and while I was explaining them to him, he remained most attentive, granting me the most pleasing audience possible. Then he asked if I wanted to work for him: to this I answered that, upon my honour, I could not do so; for if I had left all the many grand works I had begun for this great King in a completed state, I would abandon every great lord only to serve His Excellency. Now here we can recognize how the great power of God never leaves unpunished any sort of man who commits wrongs and inflicts injustice upon the innocent. This man as much as begged my pardon in the presence of those who, shortly afterwards, brought about my revenge, along with the revenge of many others who had been murdered by the Duke: and therefore let no lord, no matter how important he might be, scoff at God's justice, as do some of those whom I know and who have brutally attacked me, as I shall relate in the proper place. I do not write of these affairs of mine out of worldly arrogance, but solely to thank God, who has brought me through so many trials. And in the trials by which I am daily afflicted, I appeal to Him, I call upon Him as my own protector, and I commend myself to Him. And always, although I help myself as much as possible, when I begin to weaken and my feeble strength is insufficient, that great power of God is immediately made manifest to me, which descends unexpectedly upon those who do wrong to others and upon those who pay but little attention to the important and honourable duties God has given to them.

52. I returned to my inn and found that the previously mentioned Duke had sent me very abundant gifts of food and drink, most honourably: I ate with a hearty appetite; then, mounting my horse, I rode toward Florence; and after I reached Florence I found my sister with her six daughters, including one who was of marriageable age and another who was still with the wet-nurse. I found her husband, who as a result of various incidents in the city no longer worked at his profession. More than a year before I had forwarded jewels and golden jewellery made in France, to the value of more than two thousand ducats, and I had brought with me more, to a value of

around a thousand scudi. I discovered that even though I carried on giving them four golden scudi each month, they still carried on receiving large sums from those works in gold of mine that they sold from day to day. This brother-in-law of mine was such an honest man that, for fear I might be angry with him, since the money I sent for their provision out of charity was insufficient, he had pawned almost everything that he owned in the world, letting himself be eaten up by the interest, only to avoid touching the money that was not intended for him.* From this, I realized that he was a very honest man, and my desire to help him financially grew: and before I left Florence I wanted to provide for all his daughters.*

53. At this time (we were in the month of August of 1545), our Duke of Florence was at Poggio a Caiano,* a place some ten miles from Florence, and I went to find him, simply to pay my respects, since I was a Florentine citizen and my ancestors had been very close friends of the Medici family, and because more than anyone else I loved this Duke Cosimo.* And as I said, I went to this Poggio only to pay my respects and never with the slightest intention of staying with him, which it pleased God, Who does all things well, to have me do: on seeing me, the Duke then showed me the most unlimited kindness, and he and his Duchess* asked me about the works I had executed for the King; and I described them quite willingly and all in full detail. Having heard me, he said that he had understood as much, that such was the case; and then, in a tone of compassion, he said: 'Oh, how small a reward for such beautiful and imposing labours! My dear Benvenuto, if you're willing to make something for me, I shall pay you very differently than this King of yours did, whom you praise so highly out of your good nature.' At these remarks, I mentioned in addition the great obligations I was under with His Majesty, since he had removed me from such an unjust imprisonment and then had given me the opportunity to create the most astonishing works that were ever executed by any artisan of my kind ever born. And while I spoke in this fashion my Duke twisted about and seemed unable to wait until I stopped speaking. Then, when I had finished, he said to me: 'If you want to do something for me, I shall treat you so kindly that you'll perhaps be astonished, providing that your works please me, something that I do not doubt for a moment.' Poor, unlucky creature that I was, wanting to demonstrate to this wonderful School* that, although I had been away from

it, I was skilled in other crafts besides that branch which this School did not esteem very highly, I answered my Duke that I would most willingly execute for him, either in marble or in bronze, a large statue for that fine piazza of his.* To this the duke replied that, as a first work, all he wanted from me was a Perseus.* This is what he had wanted for some time, and he begged me to make him a little model of it. I gladly set about making this model, and in a few weeks I had completed it, with a height of about an armslength: this was in yellow wax and very well finished; it was very well made, with the greatest study and skill. The Duke came to Florence, and before I could show him this model a number of days passed: so that it seemed just as if he had never seen or acknowledged me, with the result that I felt I had misjudged my relations with His Excellency. Later, one day after dinner, when I had brought the model to his wardrobe chamber,* he came to see it, along with the Duchess and a few other noblemen. As soon as he saw it, it pleased him, and he praised it beyond all measure: as a result, I had a little hope that he understood it to some extent. And after he had examined it a great deal, his pleasure increasing greatly, he spoke these words: 'My dear Benvenuto, if you execute this small little model as a large work, it will be the most beautiful work in the piazza.'* Then I said: 'My Most Excellent Lord, in the piazza stand the works of the great Donatello and the wonderful Michelangelo, who were the two greatest men* from ancient times to the present. For all that Your Most Illustrious Excellency is very enthusiastic about my model,* nevertheless I have vision enough to make the work more than three times better than the model.' There arose no small debate about this, for the Duke insisted that he understood the matter very well and knew exactly what could be accomplished. In answer to this, I said that my works would decide this question and would remove any of his doubts, and that I would most certainly fulfil for His Excellency much more than I promised, but that he must give me the means to complete such an undertaking, for without such conveniences I could not fulfil the great undertaking I was promising him. To this, His Excellency told me that I should make a petition for the amount I was requesting, and in it I should enumerate all my needs, for he would give orders that they be provided in full. Certainly, if I had been astute enough to bind with a contract everything that I needed for these works of mine, I would not have suffered the great tribulations that later came upon me through my own fault: for the Duke seemed extremely willing, both in wanting to execute these works and also in giving proper orders in their regard. However, not realizing that this lord acted more like a merchant than a duke, I proceeded with His Excellency as a duke [and not as a merchant].* His Excellency responded most generously to my requests. Where-upon I said: 'My most extraordinary patron, the true petitions and the true agreements between us do not consist in these words or these papers, but rather they depend entirely upon how I succeed with my works as I have promised; and if I succeed, then I am certain that Your Illustrious Excellency will remember how much he has promised me.' Charmed by these remarks, as well as by my manner and my speech, His Excellency and the Duchess showed me the most unlimited favours imaginable in the world.

54. As I had an enormous desire to begin working, I told His Excellency that I needed a house, which should be of the kind where I could set myself up with my furnaces, and work there in both clay and bronze, and then, separately, in gold and silver; for I realized that he knew how well I was qualified to serve him in this profession; and I had need of comfortable rooms in order to do such things. And so that His Excellency might see how strong my desire to serve him was, I had already located the house,* which was to my liking, and it was in a place that pleased me a great deal. And because I did not want to importune the Duke about money or anything until he had seen my works, I had brought two jewels with me from France with which I begged His Excellency that I might buy myself this house, and that he should keep them until I had paid for them with my works and my labours. The jewels were very beautifully set by my workmen, following my designs. And after he had looked at them, he spoke these encouraging words, which clothed me with false hope:* 'Take your jewels back, Benvenuto, for I want you and not them; and you may have the house free.' After this he made me out a deed * following my request, which I have always kept with me.* The deed read as follows: 'Let the house be examined and who it is that sells it and the price he asks for it; for we wish to please Benvenuto.' I thought that, with this deed, I was sure of my house; for I promised myself that my works would certainly be much more pleasing than I had promised; after this, His Excellency had given an express order to a certain majordomo of his named Ser Pier Francesco Riccio.* He

was from Prato, and he had been the Duke's pedantic pedagogue.* I
spoke to this brute, and described to him all the things I needed, for
there was an orchard by the house where I wanted to set up my shop.
This man immediately gave the order to a certain dried-up, skinny
paymaster called Lattanzio Gorini.* It was an evil hour when this
little wimp of a man, with his spidery little hands, a tiny little voice
like that of a mosquito, and the rapidity of a snail, had delivered for
me at my home stones, sand, and lime, that would have sufficed only
with great difficulty for erecting a pigeon-coop. When I saw matters
going ahead with such excessive sluggishness, I began to feel dismayed, but I said to myself: 'Small beginnings sometimes have great
endings.' And I also gave myself a little hope when I saw how many
thousands of ducats the Duke had thrown away on some ugly and
monstrous works of sculpture executed by the hand of that beastly
Blockhead Bandinello.* Recovering my spirits by myself, I would
give that Lattanzio Gorini a kick in the arse to move him along; yell
at some lame donkeys and a blind boy who was leading them; and by
such efforts, and then by using my own money, I had the site of the
workshop marked out and the trees and vines uprooted: nevertheless, in my usual manner, I went about my business boldly, with a
touch of frenzy. On the other hand, I was dependent on Tasso the
carpenter, my very dear friend, and it was to him that I assigned the
task of making the wooden frameworks to begin the large Perseus.
This Tasso was a most excellent and talented man, and I believe he
was the best that ever exercised his profession: on the other hand, he
was easygoing and cheerful, and every time I went to see him he met
me laughing, singing a little song in falsetto. And I was already more
than half desperate, for I was beginning to hear about affairs in
France that were going badly, while I expected little from matters
here because of their sluggishness; and I therefore always forced
myself to listen to at least half of these songs of his: finally, I would
nevertheless cheer up a bit, forcing myself to forget, as best I could,
some of those desperate thoughts of mine.

   55. Having organized all the above-mentioned matters and begun
to move ahead in preparing myself more quickly for the undertaking
discussed above—part of the lime was already used up—I was suddenly summoned by this majordomo, and going to see him, I found
him after His Excellency's dinner in the room called the Clock Hall.*
When I went up to him with the utmost courtesy, he, with the

greatest coldness, asked who it was had installed me in that house, and with what authority I had begun building on it; and he said he was most astonished at me for my bold presumption. To this I answered that His Excellency had installed me in the house; that His Lordship* in His Excellency's name had given the commission to Lattanzio Gorini; and that this Lattanzio had delivered stones, sand, lime, and arranged for all the things I had requested: 'And for all this, he said that he had received the orders from Your Lordship,' I added. After I had spoken these words, that beast turned to me with greater harshness than before, and said that neither I nor anyone else to whom I had referred was speaking the truth. Then I became angry, and I said to him: 'Oh, Majordomo! As long as Your Lordship speaks in keeping with your most noble rank, I shall respect you and speak to you as submissively as I do to the Duke; but if you do otherwise, I shall address you as merely Ser Pier Francesco Riccio.'* The man flew into such a rage that I thought he would go mad on the spot, and in advance of the time* the celestial powers had determined for him; and along with some insulting remarks, he said that he was most astonished that he had considered me worthy to speak to him as an equal. At these remarks, I was moved to say: 'Now, listen to me, Ser Pier Francesco Riccio, while I tell you who my equals are and who yours are—yours are schoolmasters who teach reading to children.' When I said these words, this man, with his face contorted, raised his voice and repeated what he had said before, even more rashly. In reply, still looking daggers at him, I clothed myself in a bit of presumption on his account and said that my equals were worthy to address popes, emperors, and a great king; and that my equals numbered perhaps one in all the world, while ten of his equals could be found on every doorstep. When he heard these words he jumped upon a little window-seat which is in that hall, then told me to repeat one more time what I had said to him; I repeated it even more boldly than I had done before, and I told him furthermore that I no longer cared to serve the Duke and that I would go back to France, where I could return at will. This beast remained stupefied, his face the colour of clay, while I, burning with anger, went off with the intention of leaving: and I wish to God I had done so! His Excellency the Duke must not have known about this devilish occurrence immediately, because I remained for several days, having put aside all my thoughts of Florence, except those concerning my sister and my nieces, for whom I was making arrangements; with that small amount of money I had brought I wanted to leave them taken care of as best I could, and then I wanted to return to France as quickly as possible, never caring to see Italy again. After I had resolved to hurry away as quickly as possible and to leave without the permission of the Duke or anyone else, one morning this majordomo, of his own accord, summoned me very humbly, and embarked on a certain kind of pedantic oration typical of him, in which I heard neither style, grace, skill, beginning, nor end: I only understood that he said he professed to be a good Christian and did not wish to harbour hatred against anyone, and he asked me on the Duke's behalf what salary I wanted for my upkeep. At this I stood for a while hesitating and did not answer, with the clear intention of not staying. Seeing me stand there without answering, he had sufficient wit to say: 'Oh, Benvenuto, you must respond to dukes; and what I'm saying to you, I'm saying on behalf of His Excellency.' Then I said that, since he was speaking to me on behalf of His Excellency, I would most gladly respond; and I told him to tell His Excellency that I did not wish to be second to anyone in my profession whom he kept in his employment. The majordomo said: 'Bandinelli is given two hundred scudi for his upkeep, and if you are satisfied with that, your salary is set.' I replied that I was satisfied, and that if I deserved more it would be given to me after my works were seen, and that I left everything to the good judgement of His Most Illustrious Excellency: so, against my will, I picked up the thread again and set to work, while the Duke continued to show me the most boundless favours imaginable.

56. I had received frequent letters from France from my most faithful friend, Messer Guido Guidi: these letters up to that time told me nothing but good news; that Ascanio of mine also sent me advice, telling me that I should concentrate on enjoying myself, and that if anything happened he would let me know. It was reported to the King that I had begun to work for the Duke of Florence; and since he was the best man in the world, he often said: 'Why doesn't Benvenuto return?' And when he asked those young men of mine separately, they both told him that I had written to them that I was doing very well, and that they thought I no longer wanted to return and serve His Majesty. Enraged at this, and after hearing these arrogant words which never came from me, he said: 'Since he has left us without any reason, I shall never ask for him again: so let him stay

where he is!' These thieving assassins had brought the matter to the point they desired, because once I had returned to France they would have gone back to being labourers serving under me as they were at first; whereas, so long as I did not return, they would remain free and in my place, and for this reason they used all their efforts to ensure that I would not return.

57. While I was having the workshop built in which to begin the Perseus, I worked in a room on the ground floor, where I fashioned the Perseus in plaster in what was to be its actual size, with the idea of casting it from that plaster model. When I saw that executing it in this way would take me a little longer, I chose another expedient, because there was already set up, brick by brick, some small part of a broken-down workshop, constructed so poorly that it pains me to remember it. I began the figure of the Medusa, and constructed an iron framework; then I began to prepare the clay; and once I had made the model in clay, I baked it. I was working only with two young boys, one of whom was very handsome: he was the son of a prostitute called Gambetta.* I used this young boy as a model for drawing, since we have no other books to teach us our profession besides Nature. I tried to find workmen to advance this work of mine, but I could not find any, and I could not do everything by myself. There were some workers in Florence who would gladly have come, but Bandinelli immediately prevented them from coming to me, and while he was causing me difficulties over a good long period of time, he told the Duke that I was going around trying to hire his workmen, since I could never possibly know how to assemble so large a figure on my own. I complained to the Duke that this beast was annoying me greatly, and I begged him to let me have some of the workers from the Opera.* My requests caused the Duke to believe what Bandinelli was telling him. When I realized this, I decided to do as much as I could by myself. And while I set about it with the most enormous efforts imaginable, labouring day and night, my sister's husband fell ill, and died within a few days. He left behind my sister, still young, with six daughters ranging from very young to grown-up. This was the first great distress that I suffered in Florence: to be left father and guardian of such an unfortunate woman.

58. I was, however, anxious that nothing should go wrong, and when my garden was filled up with a good deal of rubbish, I sent for two day-labourers, who were brought to me from the Ponte Vecchio:

one of them was an old man of sixty, while the other was a young man of eighteen. After I had kept them for three days, the young man told me that the old man did not want to work and that I would do better to send him away, because not only did he not want to work but he also kept the young man from working; and he told me that the little there was to do he could do by himself, without throwing money away on other people: this young man's name was Bernardino Manelli from the Mugello.* Seeing that he was so willing to work hard, I asked him if he would like to arrange with me to be my servant: we came to an agreement at once. This young man looked after a horse for me, worked the garden, and then tried his best to help me in the workshop, so that little by little, he began to learn this profession, with such ease that I never ever had a better assistant than he. Resolving to work with him on every project, I began to show to the Duke that Bandinelli was telling lies, and that I could do perfectly well without Bandinelli's workmen. Around this time I began to suffer some pain in the small of my back; and since I was unable to work, I gladly remained in the Duke's wardrobe, with certain other young goldsmiths by the names of Gianpagolo and Domenico Paggini,* whom I had make a little golden vessel, all decorated in low relief with figures and other beautiful decorations: this was for the Duchess, which she had made as a vessel for drinking water from. I was also asked to make a golden girdle, and this work, too, was most richly adorned with jewels and many pleasing inventions, including ornamental heads and other details: this was made for her. Every now and then the Duke came to this wardrobe, and he took great pleasure in watching me work and in talking with me. My back began to improve a bit, and I had clay brought to me, and while the Duke stayed there to pass the time, I did a bust portrait of him that was larger than life-size.* His Excellency took great delight in this work, and treated me so kindly that he told me it would give him enormous pleasure if I arranged to work in the palace, and that he would look for some spacious rooms in the palace that I might fit out with the furnaces and everything I needed, because he took great pleasure in such things. At this, I told His Excellency that it was not possible, because I would not have finished my works in a hundred years.*

59. The Duchess did me endless favours, and she would have liked me to concentrate upon working for her and not to worry about

either the Perseus or any other commissions. When I saw these empty favours, I knew for certain that my perverse and biting fortune could not restrain itself from causing me some new calamity; for all the while I had in mind, above all, the great evil I had done when I sought to do a great good: I am speaking of my affairs in France. The King could not swallow that great displeasure he felt over my departure, and yet he would have liked me to return, as long as he could save face: I thought I was completely in the right and did not want to ask his pardon, because I thought that if I had been inclined to write humbly, those men, acting in the French manner, would have declared that I had been in the wrong, and that certain vices falsely attributed to me were true. For this reason, I stood on my honour and wrote with conviction as a man who is in the right, which gave the greatest possible pleasure to those two treacherous pupils of mine. In writing to them, I bragged about the great kindness shown to me in my native land by a lord and a lady, absolute rulers of the city of Florence, where I was born. When they received one of these letters they would go to the King and press His Majesty to give them my castle, in the same way he had given it to me. The King, who was a good and admirable person, never wanted to agree to the bold demands of these great young thieves, because he had begun to recognize their evil aspirations; and in order to give them a bit of hope and me a reason to return immediately, he had a rather angry letter written to me by one of his treasurers, whose name was Messer Giuliano Buonaccorsi, a Florentine citizen.* The letter contained this message: that if I wished to maintain the reputation of an honest man that I had earned in France, since I had departed without any reason I was truly obliged to render an accounting of everything that I had managed and done for His Majesty. When I received this letter it gave me such pleasure that I myself would not have asked for either more or less. Setting myself down to write, I filled nine sheets of ordinary paper, where I recounted in minute detail all the works that I had executed, all the unexpected problems I had experienced in making them, and all the money that was spent on these same works, which had all been given to me under the signature of two notaries and one of his treasurers, and underwritten by the very men who had received these funds, some of whom had provided materials and others their labour. As for this money, I had not put a single penny in my pocket, nor had I received anything at all for my completed works; all I had brought with me to Italy were some favours and royal promises, truly worthy of His Majesty. Although I could not boast of having derived anything from these works other than certain wages that His Majesty had ordered for my recompense—and I was still owed more than seven hundred gold scudi in wages—I had left this money behind, because it was to have been sent to me for my safe return: 'I know that some malicious individuals, out of their own envy, have made some evil allegations, but the truth will always prevail: I glory in His Most Christian Majesty, and I am not moved by avarice. Although I know that I have done much more for His Majesty than I had offered to do, and although I never obtained the compensation promised me, I have no other care in the world but to remain in His Majesty's opinion a worthy and honest man, such as I have always been. If Your Majesty harboured any doubt on this matter, at the slightest sign I would come flying to render an account of myself, even at the risk of my own life; but seeing that I am held in such slight account, I have not returned to offer myself, knowing that I shall always have enough bread wherever I go: when I am summoned, however, I shall always respond.' In this letter were many other details worthy of that marvellous King and of saving my honour. Before I sent this letter I carried it to my Duke, who was pleased to see it; I then immediately sent it to France, addressed to the Cardinal of Ferrara.

60. Around this time Bernardone Baldini, His Excellency's agent in precious stones, had brought from Venice a huge diamond of more than thirty-five carats in weight; Antonio di Vittorio Landi* was also interested in having the Duke purchase it. This diamond had already been cut to a point, but since the cutting did not result in the brilliant clarity desired from such a jewel, the owners of the diamond had cropped it off,* and indeed it was not much good for cutting either flat or to a point.* Our Duke, who took great pleasure in precious stones but understood little about them, gave some hope to this rascal of a Bernardaccio* that he would buy this diamond, and since Bernardo wanted to have all the honour of this fraud he wanted to inflict upon the Duke of Florence, he never conferred at all with his partner, the previously mentioned Antonio Landi. This Antonio had been my very dear friend from childhood, and since he saw that I was on such intimate terms with my Duke, he called me aside one day— it was close to noon in a corner of the New Market*—and said to me:

'Benvenuto, I am sure that the Duke will show you a diamond, which he has shown signs of wanting to buy: you will see that it is a large diamond. Help us with the sale; and let me tell you that I can let it go for seventeen thousand scudi. I am certain that the Duke will want your advice, and if you see him truly inclined to buy it, make sure that he takes it.' This Antonio showed that he was quite certain he could conclude this business with the jewel. I promised him that if it were shown to me, and if my opinion was subsequently requested, I would say everything I thought without damage to the stone. As I said above, the Duke came every day to the goldsmith's workshop* for several hours, and one day after dinner more than eight days after Antonio Landi had spoken to me, the Duke showed me this very diamond, which I recognized by the distinctive marks Antonio Landi had described to me and by its shape and weight. Since this diamond was of a rather murky brilliance, as I said previously, which caused them to crop off the point, when I saw that the stone was of this type I would certainly not have advised him to make such a purchase; but when he showed it to me I asked His Excellency what he wanted me to say about it, for there was a difference between a jeweller's evaluating a stone after a lord had purchased it and his setting a price on it before it was purchased. Then His Excellency told me that he had bought it, and that I should only give my opinion. I did not want to neglect giving him a modest indication of how little I thought of this stone. He told me to consider the beauty of those large edges* that it possessed. Then I said that this beauty was not as great as His Excellency imagined, and that its point was cropped off. At these remarks, my lord, who realized I was speaking the truth, pulled a long, disagreeable face and told me that I should apply myself to appraising the stone and to judging what it seemed to me to be worth. Since Antonio Landi had offered the stone to me for seventeen thousand scudi, I thought it possible that the Duke might have had it for fifteen thousand scudi at the most. For this reason, when I saw that he took it badly after I had told him the truth, I thought I would sustain him in his false opinion, and handing the diamond to him, I said: 'Eighteen thousand scudi is what you spent on it.' At these words the Duke cried out, making an 'O' larger than the mouth of a well, and said: 'Now I believe you understand nothing about these things!' And I replied to him: 'My Lord, how wrong you are: you attend to upholding the reputation of your jewel, and I shall attend to understanding such matters. At least tell me what you paid for it, so that I can learn to understand such matters following Your Excellency's methods.' The Duke stood up with a slightly scornful smile, and said, 'Benvenuto, it cost me twenty-five thousand scudi and more'; and he left. These words were spoken in the presence of Gianpagolo and Domenico Poggini the goldsmiths; and Bachiacca the embroiderer,* who was also working in a room near ours, ran in when he heard the commotion, and as a result I said: 'I would not have advised him to buy it, but had he still wanted it, nonetheless, Antonio Landi offered it to me eight days ago for seventeen thousand scudi; I believe I could have bought it for fifteen or even less. But the Duke wants to uphold the reputation of his stone, and since Antonio Landi offered it to me for such a price, how the devil can Bernardone have worked such a shameless swindle on the Duke?' Refusing to believe that this was possible—as it was—we passed off the Duke's naivety with a laugh.

61. Having already started the figure of the large Medusa, as I said, I had constructed its iron framework; then I covered it in clay, following the anatomical structure, only half-a-finger thick, and baked it thoroughly; then I put wax over it and finished it as I wanted it to be. The Duke, who had come to watch this on numerous occasions, was so fearful that I would not succeed with it in bronze that he would have liked me to call in some other master to cast it for me. Since His Excellency was continually, and with very great approval, talking about my technical skills, his majordomo was continually seeking out some little snare to make me break my neck, and this majordomo had the authority to command the chief constables and all the officials of this poor, unfortunate city of Florence*—a native of Prato, our enemy, the son of a cooper, an ignoramus, had achieved such great authority simply by having been the rotten tutor of Cosimo de' Medici before he became Duke! As I said, constantly seeking to do me a bad turn, seeing that he could find no way of putting me in fetters, he thought of another way that something could be done. Having gone to find the mother of my shop-boy, whose his name was Cencio, while hers was Gambetta, they worked out a plan—this roguish tutor and that rascally whore—to give me a scare in order to drive me away. Gambetta, employing the wiles of her profession, went out on the orders of that crazy, knavish pedant of a majordomo; and since he had also instructed the sheriff—who

was a certain individual from Bologna, later banished by the Duke for doing just this kind of thing—on Saturday evening, three hours after sundown, this Gambetta came to see me with her son, and she told me she had kept him locked up for several days inside the house for my safety. To this I replied that she need not keep him locked up on my account; and, laughing at her whorish wiles, I turned to her son in her presence and said to him: 'You know, Cencio, if I've sinned with you,' and crying, he said that I had not. Then the mother, shaking her head, said to her son: 'Ah, you little rascal, maybe you think I don't know what's going on?' Then she turned to me, saying that she kept him hidden in the house because the sheriff was looking for him, and would arrest him at any cost if he were outside, but they would not touch him in my house. To this I said that in my house, I already had my widowed sister with six saintly little daughters, and that I did not want anyone else in my house. Then she said that the majordomo had given the order to the sheriff, and that, in any case, I would be arrested; but since I did not want to take her son into my house, if I gave her one hundred scudi I would have nothing more to fear, for since the majordomo was such a great friend of hers I could rest assured that she would make him do anything she liked, provided I gave her the hundred scudi. I was so enraged that I told her: 'Get out of my sight, you shameless whore, for if it were not for my reputation in the world and the innocence of that unhappy son you have there, I would already have slit your throat with this dagger that I've put my hand on two or three times.' And with these remarks, along with a good many pushes and shoves, I drove her and her son out of my house.

62. After I had given careful thought to the dirty tricks and the power of that evil pedant, I judged that it would be best to allow a bit of time for this devilishness to blow over, and early the next morning, after consigning to my sister my precious stones and possessions worth close to two thousand scudi, I mounted my horse and headed towards Venice,* taking with me that Bernardino of mine from the Mugello. When I reached Ferrara I wrote to His Excellency the Duke, saying that although I had left without being sent away, I would return without being summoned. Then, when I reached Venice, I gave some thought to the many different methods my cruel fortune used to torture me, but finding myself nonetheless healthy and hearty, I decided to fight her off in my usual fashion. And while I

was going about, thinking of my affairs in this way and passing my time in this beautiful and extremely wealthy city, I went to pay my respects to that wonderful painter Titian* and our Florentine citizen, the brilliant sculptor and architect Iacopo del Sansovino, who was very well treated by the Signoria of Venice, and whom I had known from the time of our youth in Rome and Florence as one of our fellow-citizens, and these two talented men showed me many signs of affection. The following day I ran into Messer Lorenzo de' Medici,* who immediately took me by the hand with the warmest possible welcome, for we had become acquainted with each other in Florence when I was minting the coins for Duke Alessandro, and later in Paris when I was in the service of the King. He was staying in the home of Messer Giuliano Buonaccorsi,* and since he had nowhere else to go to pass his time without running grave risks, he stayed in my house* most of the time, watching me make these great works. And as I said, because of this past friendship he took me by the hand and led me to his house, where the Lord Prior degli Strozzi,* brother of Signor Piero, was staying; and, glad to see me, they asked how long I was going to remain in Venice, believing that I intended to return to France. To these lords I said that I had left Florence on account of the circumstances described above, and that after two or three days I wanted to return to Florence to serve my great Duke. When I said this the Lord Prior and Messer Lorenzo turned toward me with such severity that I was very much afraid, and they said to me: 'You'd do much better to return to France, where you are rich and well known, than to return to Florence, where you'll lose everything you had earned in France, and gain nothing but trouble!'* I did not reply to their words, and left the following day as secretly as I could and went in the direction of Florence; and in the meantime these devilish plots came to a head, for I had written to my great Duke about all the circumstances that had taken me to Venice. Given his usual prudence and severity, I paid him a visit without any ceremony; for a while he showed that same severity, then he turned to me pleasantly and asked where I had been. To which I replied that my heart had never moved more than a finger-length's distance away from His Most Illustrious Excellency, although for some legitimate reasons it had been necessary to take my body for a bit of a stroll. Then, becoming more agreeable, he began to ask me about Venice, and so we talked for a while; then he finally told me to concentrate upon working, and to finish his Perseus for him. So I returned home, joyful and happy, and I cheered up my family, that is to say, my sister with her six little daughters; and taking up my works again, I made progress, taking as much care as possible.

63. And the first work I cast in bronze was that large head, the portrait bust of His Excellency, that I had fashioned of clay in the goldsmith's workshop when I had that pain in my back. This was a very pleasing work, and I made it for no other reason than to experiment with the clays for casting in bronze. Although I saw that the wonderful Donatello had executed his works in bronze, which he had cast with Florentine clay, it seemed to me that he had produced them with great difficulty; and thinking that this might have arisen from some defect in the clay, before I set out to cast my Perseus I wanted to do these initial experiments; through them I discovered that the clay was good, even though it had not been completely understood by that wonderful Donatello, because I saw he had produced his works with great difficulty.* So, as I said above, I mixed the clay with professional skill, and it worked very well for me; and, as I said, I cast the head with this clay, but because I had not yet built the furnace, I used the furnace of Master Zanobi di Pagno, the bellfounder.* When I saw that the head had come out very cleanly, I immediately set to work on the construction of a small furnace in the workshop that the Duke had built for me on my own orders and design, and in my own house that he had given me; and immediately after I built the furnace, with as much care as possible I prepared myself to cast the statue of the Medusa, which is that contorted female figure under the feet of the Perseus. Since this casting was a very difficult undertaking I did not want to overlook any of those technical details I had learned, so that I would make no errors. The first casting that I made in this small furnace came out splendidly well, and it was so clean that my friends did not think there was any need for me to retouch it further; this way of doing things had been discovered by certain Germans and Frenchmen, who talk and boast about fine secret methods of casting bronze statues without retouching them; this is truly the claim of madmen, because once bronze has been cast it must be reworked with hammers and chisels, just as the most marvellous ancients did and as modern artists still do—I am speaking about those moderns who have known how to work in

bronze. This casting greatly pleased His Illustrious Excellency, who came many times to see it at my house, giving me the greatest encouragement to work well. But the rabid envy of Bandinelli was so potent that, by persistently whispering into His Most Illustrious Excellency's ear, he made the Duke believe that although I had cast some parts of this statue well, I would never put them together, because this was a new profession for me, and that His Excellency should be very careful not to throw his money away. These remarks had such influence in those glorious ears that part of the allowance for my workers was reduced, to the point that I was forced to take the liberty of showing my resentment to His Excellency: one morning, waiting for him in the Via dei Servi, I declared to him: 'My Lord, I suspect that Your Excellency lacks confidence in me, so let me say once again that I possess enough vision to bring off this work three times better than the model, just as I promised you.'

64. Having spoken these words to His Excellency, and understanding that they were bearing no fruit whatsoever, since I received no reply, suddenly anger welled up in me, together with unbearable passion, and once again I began to speak to the Duke, saying to him: 'My Lord, this city has truly always been the school of the most brilliant talents; but once a man, having learned something, has made his reputation here, if he wishes to add to the glory of his native city and his glorious prince he will do well to go and work somewhere else. And to show that this is the truth, My Lord, I know that you understand who Donatello was, who the great Leonardo da Vinci was, and now who the miraculous Michelangelo Buonarroti is. These men bring glory to Your Excellency through their talents; I also hope, for this reason, to do my part; and so, My Lord, allow me to do so. But let Your Excellency be well advised not to let Bandinelli leave, on the contrary, always give him everything that he asks of you: for if he goes outside the city his ignorance is so presumptuous that he is capable of bringing shame upon this most noble School. Now give me your permission to leave, Lord; nor do I ask any other reward for my labours up to now than Your Most Illustrious Excellency's favour.' When His Excellency saw my resolve, with some indignation he turned to me and said: 'Benvenuto, if you want to finish the work you shall lack for nothing.' Then I thanked him, and said that I had no other desire than to demonstrate to those envious individuals that I had the vision to complete the work I had

promised. So, after I hurried away from His Excellency, I was given some little degree of assistance; I was forced, as a result, to reach into my own pocket if I wanted my work to move forward a bit more quickly than at a walk. And nevertheless I always went in the evening to work a little in His Excellency's wardrobe, where Domenico Poggini and his brother Gianpagolo were working on a golden vessel for the duchess, which I mentioned previously, and on a golden girdle; His Excellency also had me make a little model for a pendant in which the large diamond that Bernardone and Antonio Landi had made him purchase was to be set. Although I did everything I could to avoid doing such a thing, through his great affability the Duke made me work there every evening until nearly ten o'clock. He also tried, with the most charming methods, to oblige me to work there during the day as well, but I would never agree to this, and as a result I believe for certain that His Excellency was angry with me. One evening, having arrived a bit later than was my custom, the Duke said to me: 'You are *malvenuto*.'* To this remark, I said: 'My Lord, this is not my name, for my name is Benvenuto; and since I think Your Excellency is joking with me, I shall say no more about it.' To this the Duke said that he was speaking in deadly earnest and was not joking, and that I had better watch what I was doing, because it had come to his ears that, presuming upon his favour, I was deceiving now one person and now another. At these words, I begged His Illustrious Excellency to do me the honour of telling me about just one man I had ever deceived. He immediately turned to me in anger and said: 'Go and give back what you have that belongs to Bernardone: there's one for you!' To this I said: 'My Lord, I thank you, and I beg you to do me the honour of listening to a few words from me: it's true that he loaned me a pair of old scales, two anvils, and three little hammers; fifteen days ago today I told his workman Giorgio da Cortona to send for these tools; and this Giorgio came for them himself. If Your Most Illustrious Excellency ever finds that, from the day I was born until now, I have ever kept anything from anyone in this fashion, including anyone in Rome or in France, gather the information from those who have reported these things or from others, and if such accusations are found to be true let me be punished in full measure.'* When the Duke saw my great anger, like a most discreet and kindly lord he turned to me and said: 'Such a reproof is not meant for those who are not guilty; if things are as you say, I shall always receive you most willingly, as I have done in the past.' To this I said: 'Your Excellency should know that the rascally deeds of Bernardone compel me to demand and beg Your Lordship to tell me the price of that large diamond with the cropped point, because I hope to show you why this evil wretch is seeking to put me in disgrace.' Then His Excellency said to me: 'The diamond cost me twenty-five thousand ducats: why are you asking me about it?' 'Because, My Lord, on such and such a day at such and such an hour, on the corner of the New Market, Antonio di Vettorio Landi told me I should try to strike a bargain with Your Most Illustrious Excellency, and on the first request he asked sixteen thousand ducats for it; now Your Excellency knows what You have bought it for. And that this is the truth, you may ask Ser Domenico Poggini and his brother Gianpagolo, who are right here. I told them immediately and since then have said no more about it, because Your Excellency said that I did not understand such matters, at which point I thought that you wanted to uphold the reputation of this precious stone. Know now, My Lord, that I do understand such matters; and as for the rest, I profess that I am as honest as any other man who has ever been born in the world, whoever he might be. I shall not seek to rob you of eight or ten thousand ducats at a time, rather I shall work to earn them by my labours; and I shall stay to serve Your Excellency as sculptor, goldsmith, and master of coin-making; but to report to you on the affairs of others—never! And what I am saying now I say in my own defence, and I don't want a fourth as a reward:* I say this in the presence of the many honest men standing here, so that Your Most Illustrious Excellency won't believe what Bernardone says.' The Duke immediately flew into a rage and sent for Bernardone, who was forced to flee clear away to Venice, both he and Antonio Landi; Antonio told me that he had not meant to refer to that particular diamond. They went to Venice and came back, and I sought out the Duke and said: 'My Lord, what I've said to you is the truth, and what Bernardone told you about the tools was not the truth; and you would do well to put this to the test, and I will head for the chief constable.' At these words the Duke turned to me, saying: 'Benvenuto, concentrate upon being an honest man, as you have done in the past, and never have any more doubts about anything else.' The affair went up in smoke, and I never heard any more talk about it. I applied myself to finishing his jewel; and one day, when it was completed, I brought it to the Duchess, who told me herself that she valued my setting as much as the diamond that Bernardaccio had made her buy. She wanted me to put it on her bosom with my own hand; and she placed a large pin in my hand, with which I attached it, and I left very much in her good graces. Afterwards* I heard that they had had the jewel reset by a German or some other foreigner, if I am not mistaken, because Bernardone told them that the diamond would be shown off better by a less elaborate setting.

65. Following my designs, Domenico and Gianpagolo Poggini, goldsmiths and brothers, as I believe I have already said, worked in His Most Illustrious Excellency's wardrobe on certain small gold vases engraved with narrative scenes with little figures in low relief, and other items of great importance. And I often said to the Duke: 'My Lord, if Your Illustrious Excellency would pay for several workmen, I would make the coinage for your Mint and medals bearing Your Most Illustrious Excellency's head. I would make them in competition with the ancients and would have hope of surpassing them: because since I made Pope Clement's medals I have learned a great deal, and I would therefore make them much better than his; and so I would make better coins than I made for Duke Alessandro, which are still considered beautiful. I would also make you large vases in gold and silver, like the many I executed for that wonderful King Francis of France, only because of the great assistance he provided for me—and I never lost any time on the execution of his great colossal statues or on any of the others.' At these words of mine, the Duke said to me: 'Do this, and I shall see.' He never gave me any such assistance, nor did he provide me with any help at all. One day His Most Illustrious Excellency had me given several pounds of silver, and told me: 'This is the silver from my mines*—make me a handsome vase.' And since I did not want to abandon my Perseus, but still had a strong desire to serve him, I handed over the vase, along with my designs and little wax models, to a certain scoundrel named Piero di Martino,* a goldsmith; he made a bad beginning then did not even work on it, so that I lost more time than if I had done everything myself. And so, after he had been tormenting me for several months, I saw that this Piero was not working on the vase, much less putting anyone to work on it; I made him give it back to me; and it took a good deal of trouble to retrieve, along with the body of the vase so poorly begun, as I said, the rest of the silver I had given

him. The Duke, who heard something about this dispute, sent for the vase and the models, but he never again spoke to me about it, either about why or how; enough to say that, using some of my designs, he had it made by different people both in Venice and elsewhere, and he was very poorly served. The Duchess often used to tell me that I should work on jewellery for her: to which I often said that everyone—and all of Italy—knew very well that I was a good goldsmith; but Italy had not yet seen works of sculpture from my hand: 'and in the profession certain angry sculptors laugh at me, calling me the novice sculptor; I hope to demonstrate to them that I am a veteran sculptor, if only God will grant me the grace to exhibit my completed Perseus in that honoured piazza of His Most Illustrious Excellency.' Returning home, I set myself to work day and night, and I did not show myself in the palace. Thinking, however, of a way to keep myself in the good graces of the Duchess, I had made for her some little vases, as large as a little twopenny saucepan, in silver, with beautiful little masks of an extremely rare type, in the ancient manner; and when I brought these little vases to her she gave me the most gracious welcome imaginable, and she paid for the silver and gold that I had put into them. Still, I commended myself to Her Most Gracious Excellency, begging her to tell the Duke that I had very little help for such a great work, and that Her Most Gracious Excellency should tell the Duke not to give so much credence to Bandinelli's evil tongue, with which he was hindering my efforts to finish my Perseus. At these tearful words of mine, the Duchess shrugged her shoulders and then said to me: 'The Duke certainly ought to recognize that this Bandinelli of his is worthless.'

66. I remained at home, rarely presenting myself at the palace, and I laboured with great diligence to complete my work; I was obliged to pay the workers with my own money, because after the Duke had Lattanzio Gorini pay some of my workers for about eighteen months and it began to irritate him, he took away the order of payment from me. For this reason, I asked this Lattanzio why he was not paying me. He answered, waving his spidery hands at me, in a tiny little mosquito-like voice: 'Why don't you complete this work of yours? Some people think you'll never finish it.' I immediately replied in anger and said: 'Blast you and all those who don't believe I'll finish it.' And so, in desperation, I returned home to my unfortunate Perseus, and not without tears, because I recalled the

fine position I had left behind in Paris in the service of that marvellous King Francis, who provided me with everything—and here I lacked for everything.* Several times I was tempted to give myself up to despair; and one such time I mounted my handsome little horse, put a hundred scudi in my purse, and went to Fiesole to see a natural son of mine, whom I put out to wet-nurse with a friend of mine, the wife of one of my workmen. When I reached my little boy I found him in good health and, as unhappy as I was, I kissed him; when I wanted to leave he would not let me, for he held me tightly with his little hands and with a storm of tears and cries, which in a child of the age of about two was more than astonishing. And since I had decided that if I ran into Bandinelli, who was accustomed to go every evening to that farm of his above San Domenico, I wanted, like a desperate man, to kill him, I detached myself from my baby boy, leaving him to his wild weeping. Travelling toward Florence, when I arrived at the square of San Domenico, Bandinelli himself entered from the other side of the piazza. I decided at once to commit that bloody act and went up to him, but when I raised my eyes I saw him unarmed and mounted on a little mule that looked like a donkey, and he had with him a young boy of about the age of ten; as soon as he spotted me he turned the colour of death and trembled from head to toe. Realizing what a vile act it would be, I said: 'Don't be afraid, you filthy coward, for I don't consider you worthy of my blows.' He looked at me weakly and said nothing. Then I regained my senses and thanked God, who through His true power had not wanted me to commit such an intemperate act. So, set free from this devilish fury, my courage mounted and I said to myself: 'If God grants me sufficient grace to finish my Perseus, I hope with this work to overcome all my rascally enemies: I shall, in this way, take much greater and more glorious revenge than if I had taken it out on one man alone.' With this firm resolution I returned home. At the end of three days I learned that my friend had smothered my only little son,* which caused me much greater pain than I have ever experienced. I knelt upon the ground, however, and not without tears I thanked my God, as was my usual custom, saying: 'My Lord, you gave him to me and now you have taken him away from me, but I thank you for everything with all my heart.' Although this great pain had almost stripped me of my reason, still, in my usual way, I made a virtue of necessity and, as best I could, resigned myself to it.

67. At this time a young man named Francesco, son of Matteo the blacksmith, left Bandinelli's employment. This young man asked me if I would give him work and, happy to do so, I set him to cleaning the figure of the Medusa, which had already been cast. After fifteen days this young man told me that he had spoken with his master—that is to say, Bandinelli—and he told me on Bandinelli's behalf that if I wanted to do a statue in marble, he was sending me the offer to give me a beautiful piece of marble. I quickly replied: 'Tell him I accept it; and it could end up as his tombstone, because he goes about provoking me, and he doesn't remember the great risk he ran with me in the piazza of San Domenico. Now tell him that I want the marble in any case. I never speak about him, but that beast is always bothering me; and I believe you were sent by him to work with me, for the sole purpose of spying on my affairs. Now go and tell him that I'll have the marble in spite of him; and come back here with it.'*

68. Many days having passed since I had allowed myself to be seen at the palace, I went there one morning when the fancy struck me, and the Duke had almost finished dining. From what I understood, His Excellency had been talking, and had spoken most favourably about me that morning, and among other things, he had very highly praised my skill in setting precious stones. For this reason, when the Duchess saw me she had me summoned to her by Messer Sforza,* and when I approached Her Most Illustrious Excellency, she begged me to set a small, pointed diamond into a ring, telling me that she would wear it on her finger always; she gave me the measurements and the diamond, which was worth about one hundred scudi; and she begged me to make it quickly. The Duke immediately began to discuss the matter with the Duchess, and told her: 'Benvenuto certainly was without equal in this art, but now that he has given it up I believe that making a little ring, as you wish, would be too much trouble for him: so I beg you not to weary him with this trifling matter, which would be a large problem for him, since he is out of practice.' Upon hearing these words I thanked the Duke, and then I begged him to allow me to do this small service for Her Ladyship the Duchess: I set my hand to it immediately, and in a few days I had it completed. The ring was for the little finger: so I fashioned four cherubs in full relief with four little masks, which formed the ring, and I also adorned it with some fruit and small links in enamel, so that the jewel and the ring were shown off very well together. I immediately took it to the Duchess, who in gracious words informed me that I had done a truly fine job and that she would remember me. She sent this ring as a gift to King Philip,* and after that, she was always ordering something from me, but in such a kindly way that I always forced myself to serve her, even though I saw very little money: and God knows that I needed a great deal of it, because I longed to complete my Perseus, and I had found some young men to assist me whom I paid out of my own pocket; and once again I began to allow myself to be seen more often than I had done in the past.

69. On one particular feast day, I went to the palace after dinner, and when I had reached the Clock Room I saw the door of the wardrobe open, and when I drew a bit nearer the Duke called to me and, with a pleasant greeting, said: 'You are welcome: look at this chest which has been sent to me as a gift from Signor Stefano di Pilestina;* open it and let's see what it is.' As soon as I opened it I said to the Duke: 'My Lord, this is a statue in Greek marble, and it's a marvellous thing. Let me say that, as a statue of a young boy, I don't remember having seen such a beautiful work among the ancient works, nor one executed in such a beautiful style; so let me offer to restore it for Your Most Illustrious Excellency—the head, arms, and feet. And I will add an eagle, so that we can christen it a Ganymede. And although it's not really advantageous for me to restore statues, since that is the profession of certain bunglers, who do it rather badly, still, the excellence of this great master summons me to serve him.' The Duke was delighted that the statue was so beautiful, and he asked me a great number of questions, saying to me: 'Tell me clearly, Benvenuto, what is it about the great talent of this master that amazes you so greatly?' Then I tried in the best way I knew to make His Most Illustrious Excellency understand such beauty, such intelligent skill, and such rare style; I spoke of these matters at length and did so most gladly, knowing that His Excellency took the greatest pleasure in it.*

70. While I was thus pleasantly entertaining the Duke, it happened that a page went out of the wardrobe, and as he left Bandinelli entered. When the Duke saw him, half-perturbed and with a harsh expression, he said: 'What are you doing here?' Bandinelli, without any other reply, immediately cast his eyes on the chest which contained the uncovered statue, and with one of his derisive laughs, shaking his head, he said, turning toward the Duke: 'My Lord, here

you have one of the things I have so frequently told Your Most Illustrious Excellency about. You should know that these ancients understood nothing about anatomy, and for this reason their works are full of errors.' I remained silent, paying no attention to what he said; rather, I had turned my back on him. As soon as this beast had finished his unpleasant chattering, the Duke said: 'Oh, Benvenuto! This is exactly the opposite of what you have just now demonstrated to me with so many fine arguments: so defend your position a little.' To these noble words, directed at me with such charm, I quickly responded and said: 'My Lord, Your Most Illustrious Excellency has to bear in mind that Baccio Bandinelli is composed entirely of badness, and he has therefore always been that way: so that whatever he looks upon, the moment he sets his disagreeable eyes on it, even though it is of superlative quality, is immediately converted into something as bad as possible. But I, who am drawn only toward the good, perceive the truth more purely: so that what I said about this most beautiful statue to Your Most Illustrious Excellency is the absolute truth, and what Bandinelli said about it only reflects that badness of which he is composed.' The Duke stood listening to me with great pleasure, and while I was making these remarks Bandinelli was twisting and turning and making the ugliest expressions with his face—which was, in fact, extremely ugly—that could be imagined. The Duke suddenly moved away, heading toward some of the apartments on the ground floor, and Bandinelli followed him. The chamberlains took me by the cape and led me after them, and in this manner we followed the Duke, so that when His Illustrious Excellency entered one of the apartments he sat down, while both Bandinelli and I stood, one on the right and one on the left of His Most Illustrious Excellency. I remained quiet, and those who were gathered around, several servants of His Excellency, all stared at Bandinelli, snickering a little among themselves at the remarks I had made to him in the apartment upstairs. And so this Bandinelli began to prattle on, and said: 'My Lord, when I uncovered my Hercules and Cacus,* I'm certain that more than a hundred vile sonnets were addressed to me which said the worst that might be imagined from this rabble.' I then responded and said: 'My Lord, when our Michelangelo Buonarroti unveiled his Sacristy,* where so many beautiful statues can be seen, this admirable and talented Florentine School, the friend of truth and goodness, addressed more than a hundred sonnets to him, competing with each other to see who could praise him best: and just as the statue by Bandinelli deserved all the nasty things he says were said about it, so Buonarroti's work deserved all the good things said about it.' At these words of mine Bandinelli flew into such a rage that he was about to explode, and he turned to me and said: 'And what criticism would you be capable of offering?' 'I'll tell you if you've enough patience to know how to listen to me.' Then he said: 'Speak up, then.' The Duke and the others who were there were all waiting attentively. I began, and first said: 'You know it grieves me to have to tell you about defects in this work of yours; but I'll avoid saying such things, instead, I'll tell you everything this brilliant School says about it.' And because this wretched little man was now making some unpleasant remark, now gesturing with his hands and feet, he made me so angry that I began in a much more disagreeable fashion than I would otherwise have done: 'This talented School says that if Hercules' hair were sheared off, there wouldn't be enough of his potato head to contain his brain; that it's impossible to tell whether his face is that of a man or a lion-ox;* that he is not paying attention to what he is doing; that it is badly attached to its neck, with so little skill and so much less grace that nothing worse has ever been seen; that his ugly shoulders look like two pommels on an ass's pack-saddle; and that his two breasts and the rest of his muscles are not copied from a man, but are instead copied from an old sack full of melons propped up against a wall. Likewise, his back seems to be copied from a sack full of zucchini squash; it's impossible to tell how his legs are attached to that ugly torso, because it's impossible to know which leg he is standing on, or which leg he is putting pressure on; still less does he seem to be standing upon both legs, as is done sometimes by those masters who understand something about the matter; it can easily be seen that he is unbalanced, tilting forward by more than a third of an armslength: this alone is the greatest and most intolerable mistake that such maestros of the vulgar herd can commit! As for his arms, they say that both hang downwards with no grace, nor is there any skill in them, as if you had never seen any live naked figures; they said that the right leg of Hercules and that of Cacus come together in the middle of their calves in such a way that, if one of the two figures were separated from the other, not just one but both of them would remain without calves at the point where they touch; and they say that one of Hercules' feet is buried and that the other looks as if someone had lit a fire under it.'

71. The man could not bear to wait patiently while I went on to describe the great defects of the Cacus: first because I was telling the truth, and secondly because I was clearly making the Duke and the others in our presence recognize it, for they were making obvious signs of astonishment and then of recognition that I was telling the truth. All at once this wretched man said: 'Ah! You wicked slanderer, what do you make of my design?' I said that whoever was good at design could never execute the design badly: 'I therefore believe that your sense of design is just like your works.' Now when he saw from the faces of the Duke and the others that they were tearing him to shreds with their glances and their gestures, he allowed himself to be overcome by his insolence and, turning toward me with that hideous, ugly face of his, he suddenly said to me: 'Oh, keep quiet, you dirty sodomite!' At his remark the Duke frowned at him angrily, and the others pursed their lips and glared at him. I felt grossly insulted, and impelled by anger, I instantly came up with the remedy and said: 'Oh, you madman, you've taken leave of your senses; but I wish to God that I knew how to exercise such a noble art, for we read that Jove practised it with Ganymede in paradise, while here on earth it is practised by the greatest emperors and the greatest kings in the world. I am but a lowly and humble little man, who neither could nor would ever know how to meddle in such a marvellous matter.' No one knew how to restrain himself at this remark, for the Duke and the others caused a great uproar with the loudest laughter imaginable. And in spite of the fact that I made a show of being amused, you should know, kind readers, that inside my heart was bursting when I considered how someone, the dirtiest, most wicked scoundrel ever born on earth, could have had the audacity, in the presence of such a great ruler, to make an enormously insulting remark of that sort to me. But you should know that he insulted the Duke and not me; if I had been outside such an august presence, I would have struck him dead. When this dirty, clumsy scoundrel saw that these lords would not stop their laughing, in order to divert them from making so much fun of him, he began to change the subject by saying: 'This Benvenuto is going around bragging that I have promised him a block of marble.' At these words I immediately said: 'What? Didn't you send me Francesco, the son of Matteo the

blacksmith and your own shop-boy, to ask me if I wanted to work in marble, and to say you wanted to give me a block of it? And I accepted it and I want it.' Then he said: 'Well, you can count on never getting it.' Since I was full of rage over the unjust insults aimed at me earlier, having set reason aside and forgotten the Duke's presence, in a great frenzy I said: 'I tell you most explicitly that if you do not send that block of marble to me at my house, you'd better search for another world, for in this one I'll rip the wind out of you, one way or another!' Suddenly aware again that I was in the presence of such a great Duke, I humbly turned to His Excellency and said: 'My Lord, one madman produces a hundred; this man's madness has made me neglect Your Illustrious Excellency's dignity as well as my own; please forgive me.' Then the Duke said to Bandinelli: 'And it's true that you've promised him the block of marble?' Bandinelli admitted that it was true. The Duke said to me: 'Go to the Opera* and select a block to your liking.' I said that he had promised to deliver the block to my house. There was a terrible argument, but I would not have the block in any other way. On the following morning the block of marble was brought to my house, and I asked who sent it to me: the workmen said that Bandinelli had sent it to me and that this was the block of marble he had promised me.

72. I had it carried at once into the workshop and began to work on it with a chisel; and while I was working I made the model: I had such a strong desire to set to work in marble that I had not the patience to settle myself to make a model with that judgement required by such a profession. And because I heard the marble ring false, I was sorry more than once ever to have begun the work: I still got from it what I could—the Apollo and Hyacinth that may still be seen incomplete in my workshop.* And while I was working on it, the Duke came to my house and often said to me: 'Set aside the bronze for a while and work for a bit on the marble, so that I can watch you.' I straightaway took out my tools for carving marble and worked away with confidence. The Duke asked me about that model I had fashioned for this marble, and I said: 'My Lord, this marble is all cracked, but despite that, I'll get something out of it; I have not, however, been able to make a decision about the model, but I'll go ahead in this fashion, doing the best I can.' With great haste, the Duke had me brought a block of Greek marble from Rome so that I might restore his antique Ganymede, which had been the cause of

my dispute with Bandinelli. Once this Greek marble was brought to me, I thought it was a shame to cut it into pieces to fashion a head, arms, and other things for the Ganymede; I provided myself with some other marble, and for that block of Greek marble I made a very small model in wax, which I called Narcissus.* Since this block of marble had two holes going into it more than a quarter of an armslength and a good two fingers wide, I fashioned it in the attitude that can be seen in order to avoid them, in such a way that I entirely eliminated them from my figure. But the block had been rained on for so many decades that those holes always remained full of water, which had penetrated the block to such an extent that the marble was weakened; how rotten it was in the part above the hole was later proven when those great flood waters of the Arno came down,* which rose in my workshop up to the level of more than an armslength and a half. Because the Narcissus was standing on a wooden frame the water overturned it, and it broke above the breast, where I had to rejoin it; and to conceal the crack where I repaired it, I fashioned that garland of flowers that can be seen on its breast;* I went on completing it, working a few hours before dawn or even on feast-days, solely to avoid losing any time from my work on the Perseus. One morning I was preparing some small chisels for my work on it, and an extremely fine splinter of steel flew into my right eye, and it was so far embedded into my pupil that I could not find a way to remove it. I thought for certain that I would lose the sight of that eye. After several days I summoned Master Raffaello de' Pilli, a surgeon,* who took two live pigeons, and making me lie on my back on a table, he took the pigeons, and with a little knife, pierced a large vein they have in their wings so that the blood ran into my eye; I immediately felt relief as a result, and in the space of two days the steel splinter came out and I remained free of pain and my vision improved. As the feast of St Lucy* fell three days later, I fashioned an eye in gold from a French scudo and had it offered to the saint by one of my six little nieces, the daughter of my sister Liperata, who was about ten years of age, and with this I gave thanks to God and to St Lucy. For a long while I did not want to work on the Narcissus, but I pressed ahead with the Perseus, with the previously mentioned difficulties, and I was hoping to complete it and get away, in God's name.

73. Having cast the Medusa—and it had come out well—with

great hopes I brought my Perseus toward completion; I had done it in wax, and I promised myself that it would turn out as well in bronze as the Medusa. Since the Duke saw it so well finished in wax, and it looked so fine when he saw it in that state that he thought it very beautiful, it may be that someone had made him believe that it could not come out so well in bronze, or it may be that the Duke imagined such a thing on his own, but, coming more often than usual to my house, on one occasion he said to me: 'Benvenuto, this figure cannot come out in bronze, since the rules of this craft do not permit it.' His Excellency's words greatly offended me, and I replied: 'My Lord, I know that Your Most Illustrious Excellency has little faith in me; and this, I believe, comes about either because Your Most Illustrious Excellency far too easily believes those people who speak so much evil of me , or because you truly do not understand the matter.' He hardly allowed me to complete my sentence before he said: 'I make it my business to understand it and do understand it extremely well.' I immediately replied and said: 'Yes, you do, but as a nobleman and not as a craftsman: because if Your Most Illustrious Excellency understood this in the manner in which you think you understand it, you would believe me by reason of the beautiful head in bronze that I have made, that large portrait of Your Most Illustrious Excellency that you sent to Elba; by reason of my having restored the beautiful marble statue of Ganymede with such enormous difficulty, calling for much greater effort than if I had made it entirely new from the start; and also by reason of my having cast the Medusa, which is here now in Your Excellency's presence: this casting was so difficult that in it I accomplished what no other man had ever done before me in this diabolical profession. See, My Lord! I have rebuilt the furnace in a way that makes it different from the others,* for besides many other variations and skilful technical devices that can be seen in it, I created two outlets for the bronze, because this difficult and contorted figure could never come out well in any other way: only because of these intelligent refinements of mine has it come out so well, something no other practitioners of this craft could believe. You should know for certain, My Lord, that all the great and very difficult works I completed in France under that most marvellous King Francis all came out extremely well for me solely because of the great encouragement this good King gave me, along with those generous provisions and the satisfaction of my demands for as many workmen as I requested; it sometimes happened that I was employing more than forty workers, all of my own choosing; and for these reasons I created such a large number of works in such a brief space of time. Now, My Lord, believe in me and help me with the assistance I need, for I hope to bring to conclusion a work that will please you; but if Your Most Illustrious Excellency discourages me and fails to provide me with the assistance I need, it is impossible for me or any other man in the world to produce something good.'

74. Only with great difficulty did the Duke contain himself as he stood listening to my argument, now turning one way and now another; and poor desperate me, as I remembered the fine position I had enjoyed in France, so I suffered. Suddenly the Duke said: 'Now tell me, Benvenuto, how is it possible for that beautiful head of the Medusa which is high up there in Perseus's hand to ever come out well?' I said straightaway: 'Now you see, My Lord, that if Your Most Illustrious Excellency possessed the understanding of this craft you say you possess, you wouldn't worry that this beautiful head you describe would not turn out well, but you'd worry instead about this right foot, which is hidden down here.' At my remarks, the Duke, half-angry, turned suddenly to some noblemen who were with His Most Illustrious Excellency, and said: 'I think this Benvenuto acts like this out of presumptuousness, just for the sake of contradicting everything.' He immediately turned toward me in an almost scornful way, which all those in his presence imitated, and began to say: 'I'm prepared to have sufficient patience with you to listen to the arguments you'll dream up, so that I'll believe you.' Then I said: 'I'll provide you with an argument so credible that Your Excellency will be completely persuaded,' and I began: 'You must know, My Lord, that the nature of fire is to go upwards, and for this reason I can promise you that this head of the Medusa will turn out very well; but because the nature of fire is not to go downwards, and we must force it down some six armslengths by means of our craft; for this fundamental reason I say to Your Most Illustrious Excellency that it's impossible for this foot to come out well. But it will be easy for me to redo it.' The Duke asked: 'So why didn't you think to make it so that the foot would come out in the same way the head came out?' I said: 'I would have been forced to build a much larger furnace, in which I would have been able to construct a pipe as wide as my leg, and with the weight of the hot metal I could have forced it to go down;

whereas my conduit, which as I said goes a distance of six arms-lengths down to the feet, is no thicker than two fingers. It wasn't, however, worth the expense, for I can easily repair it. But when my mould has filled up more than halfway, as I hope it will, from that point on the fire will rise according to its nature, and this head of the Perseus and that of the Medusa will come out extremely well: of that you can be quite certain.' After I had stated those fine arguments of mine, along with countless others that I shall not write down here for fear of going on too long, the Duke, shaking his head, went away.

75. Having taken courage, I drove away all those thoughts that now and again presented themselves before me, which often made me weep bitterly with regret for having left France and come to Florence, my sweet native city, for the sole purpose of being charitable to my six little nieces. I saw that having done so marked the beginning of so much evil, but all the same I promised myself, with assurance, that once I had completed the work on the Perseus I had already begun, all my tribulations would be transformed into the highest satisfaction and glorious prosperity. In this way, having regained my vigour, with all my powers—both of my body and my purse, though little money remained to me—I began to search for several loads of pine-wood, which I procured from the Seristori pine forest near Monte Lupo;* and while I waited for the wood I clad my Perseus in those clays that I had prepared several months before, so that they might be properly seasoned. After I had made this clay tunic—they call it a tunic in our craft—and had properly strengthened and enclosed it very carefully with iron supports, with a slow fire I began to draw out the wax, which came out through the many air-vents that I had made: for the more one makes, the better the moulds will fill. Once I had finished removing the wax, I constructed a funnel-like furnace* around my Perseus—that is, around the previously mentioned mould—made of bricks, laying one on top of the other, and I left numerous spaces through which the fire might breathe better; then I began to place the wood inside, very, very slowly, and I kept the fire going continuously for two days and two nights, until, after all the wax was extracted and the mould had been well baked, I immediately began to excavate the trench in which to bury my mould, with all those skilful methods my fine craft demands. When I had finished excavating the ditch, I then took my mould and, by means of winches and strong hemp ropes, I very

carefully raised it up: and I suspended it an armslength above the height of my furnace, having set it properly upright so that it hung down exactly over the middle of the trench; then very, very slowly I lowered it beneath the furnace and set it down with all the care it is possible to imagine. Once I had completed this difficult operation I began to cover it with the same earth I had excavated, and little by little, as I piled the earth up, I placed the air-vents in it, which were little tubes of terracotta of the kind employed for water pipes and such things. I saw that it was suitably fixed in place and that the method of covering it up and inserting those tubes in their places was properly followed; I saw that my workmen had very clearly understood my method, which was very different from all the other masters in my profession; and assuring myself that I could put my confidence in them, I turned to my furnace, which I had made them fill with many blocks of copper and other pieces of bronze. After I had piled them one on top of the other, employing the method that our craft has taught us—that is, one separated from the other to make a path for the flames of the fire, so that the metal heats up much faster and thus melts and becomes liquefied—I then confidently told them to light the furnace. By putting in that pine-wood, which exudes an oily resin that the pine tree produces, and having built my little furnace so well, it worked so perfectly that I was obliged to check it, now on one side and now on the other, with so much exertion that it was unbearable; and yet I forced myself to do it. And to add to my problems the workshop caught fire, and we were afraid that the roof would collapse upon us; on the other side of the workshop, toward the orchard, the heavens were driving so much rain and wind against me that it cooled off the furnace. And so, fighting against these perverse occurrences for several hours, I made an effort even greater than my robust constitution could withstand, so that I was seized by a sudden attack of fever, the worst that could ever be imagined, and for this reason I was forced to go and throw myself on the bed. So, much against my will, I had no choice but to go to bed, and I turned to all those who were assisting me, who numbered around ten or even more, including masters of casting bronze, labourers, peasants, and my own shop-workers (among whom was Bernardino Mannellini from the Mugello,* whom I had trained for several years); and to the said Bernardino, after I had given my instructions to all the others, I said: 'Now see, my dear

Bernardino, follow the instructions I've given you, and do what you can quickly, because the metal will be ready shortly; you can't make any mistakes, and these other worthy men will quickly make ready the conduits, and you will surely be able to drive in the two pegs with these iron hooks;* I'm certain my mould will fill up very well indeed. I feel sicker than I've ever felt since I came into the world, and I believe for certain that in a few hours this great illness will have killed me.' And so, extremely unhappy, I left them and went to bed.

76. After I put myself to bed, I ordered my servants to bring everyone in the workshop something to eat and to drink; and I said to them: 'I shall not be alive tomorrow morning.' They gave me courage, however, telling me that my great illness would pass and that it was the result of too much exertion. And so I lay there for two hours, fighting hard against my fever, but I constantly felt it rising, and I kept on saying: 'I feel like I'm dying.' My servant, who took care of the entire house, was called Mona* Fiore di Castel del Rio: she was the most worthy woman ever born and just as kindly, and she constantly yelled at me, saying that I was frightening myself, while on the other hand she showed me the greatest kindness in her service that anyone could have shown. Nevertheless, seeing me so ill and so terrified, despite her brave heart she could not hold back a few tears that fell from her eyes; but even so, she tried as best she could to take care that I did not see them. As I was suffering these boundless tribulations, I saw a certain man entering my room; his body seemed to be as twisted as a capital S; and he began to speak in a particular tone of sorrow or affliction, like the men who give comfort to those who are condemned to death,* and he said: 'Oh, Benvenuto, your work is ruined, and there's no way out of it at all!' As soon as I heard the words of this wretched man I let out a cry so loud that it could have been heard from the sphere of flame;* and, getting out of bed, I grabbed my clothes and began to dress; and to the servants, my shop-boy, and everyone who drew near to help me I gave either kicks or punches, and I complained, saying: 'Ah! You jealous traitors! This is a deliberate betrayal; but I swear by God that I'll get to the bottom of it, and before I die I'll give such a proof of my worth to the world that I'll leave more than one person astonished.' Having finished dressing, I went in a foul mood toward my workshop, where I saw all those people whom I had left with such self-assurance: they were all astonished and dismayed. I began by saying: 'Now get up and listen

to me, and since you've neither known how nor wanted to comply with the method I've taught you, obey me now that I'm with you in the presence of my work; and no one had better contradict me, because this matter calls for help, and not for advice.' At my words a certain Master Alessandro Lastricati* answered me, saying: 'Look here, Benvenuto! You're setting yourself to accomplish an undertaking that our craft does not allow; nor can it be done in any way whatsoever!' At these words I turned about with such fury, resolved to do my worst, that he and all the others, all with a single voice, said: 'Come now, give your orders, for all of us will help you as long as you can give us orders, as long as we can hold out with our lives.' And I thought to myself that they said these kind words thinking I would very shortly drop dead. Immediately I went to examine the furnace, and I saw the metal all congealed, something that people call 'having been caked'.* I told two workmen to go across the street to the house of Capretta, the butcher, for a load of wood from young oak trees which had been drying out for more than a year, wood that Madonna Ginevra, Capretta's wife, had offered me; and when I saw the first armfuls arrive I began to load the pit under the grate.* And because oak of that kind produces a more vigorous fire than all the other kinds of wood—so that alder and pine-woods are used to cast artillery pieces, since their fire is more gentle—oh! when the cake began to feel that terrible flame it began to glow and sparkle. At the same time, I was hurrying to make ready the conduits, and had sent others up to the roof to protect it from the fire which, on account of the greater force of the fire in the furnace, had spread more quickly; and on the side toward the orchard I had them erect some boards, carpets, and some other cloths to protect me from the water.

77. As soon as I had found the remedy for all these great disasters, with the loudest cries I was shouting now to one person and now to another: 'Bring it here! Take it there!', so that, when they saw that the cake was beginning to liquefy, the entire troop obeyed me with such good will that each man did the work of three. Then I had a half-bar of pewter brought, which weighed about sixty pounds, and I threw it onto the cake inside the furnace, which, along with the help caused both by the wood and by stirring it, now with iron pokers and now with iron bars, in a short space of time became liquid. Now when I saw that we had brought a corpse back to life, contrary to the opinion of all those ignorant workmen, I regained so much energy

that I no longer realized whether I still had any fever or any fear of death. All at once we heard a noise accompanied by an enormous flash of fire, as if a thunderbolt had been produced there in our very presence; the extraordinary and terrifying fear this brought about dismayed everyone, and I more than the others. When this enormous noise and brightness had passed, we began to look one another in the face again; and when we saw that the cover of the furnace had exploded and had been lifted in such a way that the bronze had overflowed, I immediately had the mouths of my mould opened, and at the same time drove in the two plugs. Once I saw that the metal did not run with the speed that it usually had, I realized that the cause was perhaps that the alloy* had been consumed through the heat of that terrible fire, and I had all my pewter plates, bowls, and platters brought, which weighed around two hundred pounds.* One by one I placed them in front of my conduits, and some of them I threw directly into the furnace, so that once everyone saw that my bronze was turning nicely to a liquid and that my mould was filling up, enthusiastically and happily they all assisted and obeyed me; and, now here, now there, I kept giving orders, helping out, and saying: 'Oh God, who with Your immense power has raised Yourself from the dead and ascended gloriously into heaven!' So, in an instant, my mould filled up, and on that account I knelt down and thanked God with all my heart; I turned to a plate of salad lying on an old bench, and with the greatest appetite I ate and drank along with the entire company; then I went back to my bed healthy and happy, for it was two hours before dawn, and I slept as peacefully as if I had never had a care in the world. That good servant of mine, without my saying anything to her, had procured for me a fat young capon, so that when I arose from bed, which was at around the dinner hour, she brought it to me joyfully, saying: 'Oh! Is this the man who felt like he was dying? I think those kicks and punches you gave us yesterday even-ing, when you were in such a tearing hurry, with that diabolical temper you showed, perhaps struck so much terror into that high fever that it took flight for fear of such a beating.' And so all my poor household servants, freed from such fright and such extravagant labours, went out at once to purchase enough earthenware dishes and pots in place of those pewter plates and bowls, and we all dined so happily that I never remember in my whole life eating with greater joy or better appetite.

After dinner all those who had assisted came to see me, and they celebrated merrily, thanking God for all that had happened, and they kept saying that they had learned and seen how to do things that other masters held to be impossible. I too, rather self-confidently, thinking myself to be quite knowledgeable, exulted in it a little; and then I put my hand in my purse and paid them all to their satisfaction.

That evil man, my mortal enemy Messer Pier Francesco Riccio, the Duke's majordomo, sought with great diligence to learn how things had gone: so that those two workmen whom I always suspected had caused the metal to cake told him that I was not a mere man but was, instead, an authentic powerful devil, because I had done what my craft was incapable of doing, along with so many other great things that they would have been too much even for a devil. Even though they made much more of it than had actually occurred, perhaps to excuse themselves, this majordomo quickly wrote to the Duke, who was at Pisa, even more sensationally, filling his account with even greater marvels than those which they had told him.

78. After I let the work I had cast cool down for two days I began to uncover it little by little; and the first thing I found was the head of the Medusa, which had come out extremely well by virtue of the air vents, just as I had told the Duke that the nature of fire was to rise up; then I continued to uncover the rest, and I discovered the other head, that of the Perseus, had likewise come out extremely well; and this astonished me a great deal, for as can be seen, it is much lower than that of the Medusa. And because the outlets of the work had been placed above the head of the Perseus and by his shoulders, I discovered that the last of the bronze that was in my furnace had been completely used up in filling the head of the Perseus. It was a marvellous thing that in the conduits made for the castings not a bit of the metal remained, nor was anything missing; this amazed me greatly, for it seemed to be a miraculous thing, truly guided and carefully managed by God Himself. I went happily on to finish the uncovering of the statue, and I found that every detail had consistently come out extremely well, until I arrived at the foot of the right leg, upon which the statue rests, where I discovered that the heel had come out well; moving on, I saw that it was all complete, so that on one hand I was glad, but on the other I was almost displeased, only because I had told the Duke that it could not come out well. And so

when I finished uncovering it, and found that the toes of this same
foot had not come out, and not only the toes, but a small part over
the toes was missing, so that about half was missing, even though it
would give me a little more work, I was very pleased, if only to
demonstrate to the Duke that I understood what I was doing.
Although much more of the foot had come out than I thought possible, the cause of this had been that, through these various incidents
I mentioned, the metal was hotter than the rules of our craft allow
for; and also that I had had to help it along with the alloy in the way I
described with those pewter plates, something that has never been
done by anyone else. Now, when I saw how well the work had come
out I immediately went off to Pisa to find my Duke; he greeted me as
cordially as anyone could imagine, and his Duchess did the same.
Although that majordomo of theirs had informed them about everything, it seemed to Their Excellencies something even more stupen-
dous and more marvellous to hear me tell about it in my own words;
and when I came to the foot of the Perseus and how it had not come
out, just as I had initially predicted to His Most Illustrious Excellency, I saw he was filled with astonishment, and he told the Duchess
just how I had said so beforehand. Now when I saw these noble
patrons of mine were so gracious toward me, I then begged the Duke
to allow me to go down to Rome. So he kindly gave me permission,
and told me to return soon to complete his Perseus, and he gave
me letters of introduction to his ambassador, who was Averardo
Serristori:* this was during the first years of Pope Julius de' Monti.*

79. Before I left I gave instructions to my workers to continue
following the method I had shown them. The reason why I left was
that I had done a life-size bronze bust of Bindo di Antonio Altoviti,*
and had sent it to him in Rome; he had placed this portrait bust in a
study of his, which was very richly decorated with antiquities and
other beautiful objects. But this study was not designed for displaying sculptures, no less than paintings, because the windows were
below these beautiful works, so that the sculptures and paintings had
the light opposite them and were not shown off very well, as they
would have been if they had received proper illumination. One day it
happened that, while Bindo was standing in his doorway, the sculptor Michelangelo Buonarroti passed by, and Bindo begged him to do
him the honour of coming into his home to see his study; and so he
led him inside. As soon as he entered and had seen it, he exclaimed:

'Who was the master who has done such a fine portrait of you and in such a beautiful style? You should know that this bust pleases me as much, and even a little more, than the antique ones, although some excellent ones can be seen among them. If these windows were above them instead of below, they would show them off so much better that your bust would hold a place of distinction among so many fine works.' As soon as Michelangelo left Bindo's home he wrote me the most delightful letter, in which he said this: 'My dear Benvenuto, I have known you for many years as the greatest goldsmith we have ever heard of, and now I shall recognize you to be a sculptor of equal talent. You should know that Messer Bindo Altoviti took me to see a bust depicting him in bronze and he told me it was by your hand; I liked it very much, but I was very sorry that it was placed in such bad light, for if it received proper illumination it would show itself as the beautiful work that it is.' This letter was filled with the most kind and favourable words towards me, so that before I left for Rome I had shown it to the Duke, who read it with kind interest and said to me: 'Benvenuto, if you were to write to him and make him want to return to Florence, I would make him one of the Forty-Eight.'* So I wrote him a most affectionate letter,* and in it I said on the Duke's behalf a hundred times more than I had instructions to do. In order not to make any mistakes I showed it to the Duke before I sealed it, and I said to His Most Illustrious Majesty: 'My Lord, perhaps I have promised him too much?' The Duke replied and said: 'He deserves even more than you have promised, and I shall make sure that the promises are generously kept.' Michelangelo never replied to this letter of mine, and as a result the Duke made clear to me that he was very annoyed with him.

80. Now, when I was in Rome I went to take lodgings in the home of this previously mentioned Bindo Altoviti: he immediately told me that he had shown his bronze portrait bust to Michelangelo and that he had praised it very highly; and so we discussed this at length. But since this Bindo had twelve hundred gold scudi belonging to me, which he had held for me along with five thousand scudi he had loaned to the Duke—that is, four thousand belonged to Altoviti and my money was in his name—Altoviti gave me the interest on my share that was due me;* this was the reason why I began his bust. When Bindo saw the wax model he sent me a gift of fifty golden scudi through one of his notaries, Ser Giuliano Paccalli,* who lived

with him, but I did not want to take the money and sent it back to him by the same man; and I later said to Bindo: 'It's enough for me that you keep this money of mine alive,* and that you make it earn something for me.' I noticed that he had bad intentions, because rather than welcoming me warmly, as he usually did, he seemed very stiff with me; and although he put me up in his home, he never acted frankly but was rather sulky. Nevertheless, with a few words we resolved the matter: I lost my pay for the labour on his bronze bust as well as the cost of the metal, and we agreed that he should keep this money of mine at fifteen per cent interest* for the rest of my natural life.

81. First I went to kiss the Pope's feet, and while I was speaking with the Pope Messer Averardo Serristori, our Duke's ambassador, arrived: I had made certain proposals to the Pope on which, I believe, I could have easily reached agreement with him, and I would have gladly returned to Rome because of the great difficulties I was experiencing in Florence, but I became aware that this ambassador had worked against me. I went to find Michelangelo Buonarroti and repeated what I had written to him in the letter sent from Florence on the Duke's behalf. He replied that he was employed on the building of St Peter's,* and that he could not leave for that reason. Then I told him that as soon as he had made a definite decision about the model for this building, he could leave his Urbino in charge,* who would strictly obey the orders he had given to him; and I added many other promises, speaking on the Duke's behalf. Suddenly he stared at me, and said with a sarcastic smile: 'What about you, how happy are you with him?' Although I said that I was very happy, and that I had been well treated, he showed that he knew about most of my problems, and so he answered me that it would be very difficult for him to leave. Then I added that he would be better off to return to his native city, which was ruled by an extremely just lord and the greatest lover of talent of any lord who had ever been born. As I said above, he had with him one of his young men, who was from Urbino; he had been with him for many years and had worked for him more as an errand boy and domestic servant than anything else; and this was evident because this fellow had learned nothing about the profession. Since I had pressed Michelangelo with so many good arguments that he did not know how to answer me quickly enough, he turned to his Urbino for the purpose of asking him what he thought

of the matter. Instantly this Urbino of his, in his coarse way and in a very loud voice, said: 'I never want to leave my Messer Michelangelo until I skin him or he skins me.' At these foolish words I was forced to laugh; and without saying goodbye, with a dejected shrug of my shoulders, I turned and left.

82. Since I had conducted my business so badly with Bindo Altoviti, losing my bronze bust and giving him my money for the rest of my life, I was very clear about just what the word of merchants was worth, and so, most unhappily, I returned to Florence. I immediately went to the palace to visit the Duke; His Most Illustrious Excellency was at Castello, just above Ponte a Rifredi.* I found the majordomo, Messer Pier Francesco Riccio, in the palace, and when I tried to approach him to greet him in the usual manner, suddenly, with unbounded astonishment, he said: 'Oh, you've come back!' And with the same astonishment, clapping his hands, he said: 'The Duke is at Castello,' and turning his back on me, he left. I could neither understand nor imagine why this beast had acted in this way. I immediately went to Castello and entered the garden where the Duke was; I saw him at a distance, and when the Duke saw me he made a gesture of astonishment and gave me to understand that I should go away. And I, who was expecting His Excellency to treat me the same way or even better than before I went away, now, seeing such strange conduct, very unhappily returned to Florence. After taking up my business again, eager to conclude my work, I could not imagine what could be the source of this change; until, noticing the manner in which Messer Sforza and others who were close to the Duke looked at me, I was seized by the desire to ask Messer Sforza what all this meant; he said to me with a smile: 'Benvenuto, concentrate on being an honest man and don't worry about anything else.' A few days later I had the opportunity to speak to the Duke, and he greeted me in a lukewarm fashion and asked me what was going on in Rome. I opened the conversation as best as I knew how, and told him about the bust that I had made in bronze for Bindo Altoviti, with everything that ensued. I noticed that he was listening to me most attentively; I likewise told him everything about Michelangelo Buonarroti. At this he showed some annoyance; and at the remarks of Michelangelo's Urbino about the skinning, he roared with laughter; then he said, 'So much the worse for him', and I left. It is certain that this majordomo, Ser Pier Francesco, must had done me some

bad turn with the Duke which did not succeed: because God, the lover of the truth, defended me, just as up to this point in my life He has always saved me from so many endless dangers, and I hope that He will continue to save me until the end of my life, troubled though it may be. Nonetheless, I go boldly forward, solely through His power, nor does any frenzy of Fortune or the perverse stars frighten me: if only God sustains me in His grace.

83. Now, gracious reader, listen to a terrible mishap. With as much care as I knew how to muster, I concentrated on completing my work, and in the evenings I would go to work in the Duke's wardrobe, assisting those goldsmiths who were working there for His Most Illustrious Excellency: the greater part of the works they executed were done following my designs. Since I saw that the Duke took great pleasure in this, as much from seeing us work as from chatting with me, I also thought it was a good idea to go there several times during the day. One day when I was in the wardrobe, the Duke came as usual and rather more willingly, since His Most Illustrious Excellency knew I was there; and as soon as he arrived he began to talk with me about many different and most delightful things. I replied to him in turn; and I had so amused him that he treated me more graciously than he had in the past. All of a sudden one of his secretaries appeared and said something in His Excellency's ear, which must have been very important, for the Duke immediately arose and went into another room with this secretary. And meanwhile the Duchess had sent a page to see what His Most Illustrious Excellency was doing, and this page told the Duchess: 'The Duke is speaking and laughing with Benvenuto, and he is in a good humour.' Once she heard this the Duchess quickly came into the wardrobe and, not finding the Duke there, she sat down beside us, and after she had watched us work for a while, with great kindness she turned to me and showed me a necklace of enormous pearls* which were truly extremely rare, and when she asked me what I thought of them, I replied that the necklace was a very beautiful thing. Then Her Most Illustrious Excellency said to me: 'I want the Duke to buy it for me; so, my dear Benvenuto, praise it to the Duke as highly as you are capable of doing.' At her words, with as much respect as I knew how, I replied frankly to the Duchess, saying: 'My Lady, I thought that this pearl necklace belonged to Your Most Illustrious Excellency, and there was no reason to compel me to say anything at all about those

things, but now, knowing that they do not belong to Your Illustrious Excellency, I must speak, indeed I am bound to tell you this: Your Most Illustrious Excellency should know that, since this is my particular profession, I recognize a great many defects in these pearls, and on this account I would never advise Your Excellency to purchase them.' In reply to my remarks, she said: 'The merchant is offering them to me for six thousand scudi: for if the necklace did not have some of these little defects it would be worth more than twelve thousand.' Then I said that even if the necklace had been absolutely perfect I would never advise anyone to pay more than five thousand scudi for it; because pearls are not precious stones; pearls are fish-bones,* and in the course of time they deteriorate, but diamonds and rubies and emeralds do not grow old, and neither do sapphires. These four are precious stones, and it is best to buy these.' At my words, in a rather haughty way, the Duchess said to me: 'I want these pearls now, and so I am asking you to take them to the Duke and to praise them as highly as you are capable of doing; and if this seems like telling a few lies, do it to serve me, and it will be well worth your while.' I have always been totally devoted to the truth and the enemy of lies, but compelled by necessity, since I did not wish to lose the favour of such a great princess, I took those damned pearls, unhappy as I was, and went with them to the other apartment where the Duke had retired. As soon as he saw me he said: 'Oh, Benvenuto! What are you up to?' Uncovering these pearls, I replied: 'My Lord, I come to you to show you a very beautiful pearl necklace, one that is extremely rare and truly worthy of Your Most Illustrious Excellency; and for eighty pearls, I don't think that so many of them could ever be strung together so well to make a better display in a necklace; so you should buy them, My Lord, for they are wonderful.' The Duke immediately said: 'I don't want to buy them, because they are not pearls of the quality you describe, for I have seen them and I don't like them.' Then I said: 'Forgive me, My Lord, but these pearls surpass in infinite beauty all the pearls that were ever strung on a necklace.' The Duchess had got up and was standing behind the door, and she was listening to everything I was saying; and when I had said more than a thousand things more than I shall write here, the Duke turned to me with a kindly expression and said to me: 'My dear Benvenuto, I know that you understand such matters very well, and if these pearls possessed these rare qualities that you attribute to them, it would not bother me to purchase them, either to please the Duchess or to have them; for I need these kinds of things not only for the Duchess but for my other affairs concerning my sons and daughters.'* Hearing his words, having begun to tell lies I continued to tell them, with even more audacity, tingeing them with the colour of truth so that the Duke would believe me, and trusting in the Duchess to reward me at the proper time. And since I might expect to receive more than two hundred scudi if I could bring about such a sale, and the Duchess had hinted as much to me, I had resolved and was determined not to take a penny of this money, in order to avoid compromising myself, so that the Duke would never think that I had done it out of greed. Once again, the Duke, with the kindliest of words, began saying to me: 'I know that you understand these matters very well; nonetheless, if you are the honest man I've always thought you to be, tell me the truth now.' Then, my eyes red and somewhat wet with tears, I said: 'My Lord, if I tell the truth to Your Most Illustrious Excellency, the Duchess will become my mortal enemy, which will force me to leave and my enemies will immediately assail the reputation of my Perseus, which I have promised to this noble School of Your Most Illustrious Excellency; so I commend myself to Your Most Illustrious Excellency.'

84. After he realized that I had been constrained to say everything I had said, the Duke answered: 'If you have faith in me, you've nothing in the world to fear.' Once again, I said: 'Alas, My Lord, how can it possibly be that the Duchess won't find out?' At this the Duke raised his hand, as if taking an oath, and said: 'You can consider these words buried in a casket of diamonds.'* Hearing these noble words, I quickly told him the truth about the pearls as I understood, it and that they were not worth much more than two thousand scudi. The Duchess saw us calm down, since we were speaking as softly as we could, and she came forward and said: 'My Lord, will Your Excellency kindly buy me this string of pearls, since I am very keen to have them, and your Benvenuto had said that he has never seen a necklace more beautiful.' Then the Duke answered: 'I don't wish to buy it.' 'My Lord, why does Your Excellency not wish to please me by buying this pearl necklace?' 'Because I don't want to throw money away.' Once again the Duchess said: 'Oh! How are you throwing money away, when your Benvenuto, in whom you quite deservedly place so much trust, told me that it would be a great

bargain at more than three thousand scudi? ' Then the Duke said:
'My Lady, my Benvenuto told me that if I buy it I shall be throwing
my money away, because these pearls are neither round nor equal in
size, and many of them are old; and to see that this is so you should
look at this one or at that one, and look here and there: so, they're
just not for me.' At these remarks the Duchess stared at me with
great animosity, and threatening me with a nod of her head she left,
and I was tempted to leave, disappearing from Italy; but because my
Perseus was almost completed I did not want to lose the chance of
displaying it. Still, everyone should consider the serious trouble I
found myself in. The Duke had, in my presence, ordered his porters
always to allow me to enter his chambers or wherever His Excellency
was; and the Duchess had ordered them to chase me away every time
I arrived at the palace: so that, whenever they saw me, they immediately came outside the doors and chased me away. But they were
careful that the Duke did not see them, for if the Duke saw me
before those wretches did he either summoned me or made a sign for
me to come over. The Duchess summoned that Bernardone, her
broker, about whose laziness and despicable worthlessness she had
often complained to me, and she asked for his assistance, just as she
had done with me; he replied: 'My Lady, leave everything to me.'
This great scoundrel went before the Duke with the necklace in his
hand. As soon as the Duke saw him he ordered him to get out of his
sight. Then this great scoundrel, with his ugly little voice braying
through his ugly ass's nose, said: 'Ah! My Lord, buy this necklace for
your poor lady; she's dying to have it and can't live without it.'
Adding many other of his stupid remarks, he became very annoying
to the Duke, who said to him: 'Either get out of my sight, or puff
yourself up at once.'* This dirty scoundrel, who knew very well what
he was doing—because if either by puffing up his cheeks or by
singing 'La bella Franceschina'* he could convince the Duke to make
the purchase, he would earn the Duchess's favour and his broker's
fee as well, which amounted to several hundred scudi—and so
he puffed himself up. The Duke gave him several heavy slaps on
those ugly cheeks of his, and to get him out of his sight the Duke
gave him even harder slaps than he normally did. These blows were
so violent that not only did his cheeks redden but tears streamed
down his face. For all that, he began to say: 'Ah! My Lord, see how
one of your faithful servants is trying to do his best and is happy to

bear any kind of discomfort, provided that this poor lady of yours is happy.' Since the Duke had begun to get really sick of this wretched man, both because of the slaps on the cheeks and out of love for the Duchess, whom His Most Illustrious Excellency always wished to please, the Duke suddenly said: 'Get the hell out of here and go strike a bargain, for I'm happy to do anything the Lady Duchess wishes.' Now here one can recognize the way in which evil Fortune rages against a poor man, and how shameless Fortune favours a wicked man: I lost the favour of the Duchess completely, which was reason enough to lose that of the Duke as well; while he earned that large commission and their favour: it is, therefore, not enough to be an honest and talented man.

85. During this time, war broke out with Siena,* and wishing to fortify Florence, the Duke assigned the gates to his sculptors and architects; I was assigned the Prato gate and the small side postern leading to the Arno, which is near the meadow going toward the mills; Cavaliere Bandinelli was assigned the San Frediano gate; Pasqualino d'Ancona the San Pietro Gattolino gate; Giuliano di Baggio d'Agnolo, the cabinet-maker, the San Giorgio gate; Antonio Particini, the cabinet-maker, the gate at Santo Niccolò; Francesco da San Gallo, the sculptor known as Margolla, the Santa Croce gate; and Giovanbattista, called Tasso, the Pinti gate; and in this way certain other bastions and gates were distributed among various engineers, but I neither remember their names nor does it matter much to my argument.* The Duke, who was certainly always a very capable man, went around his city himself, and when His Most Illustrious Excellency had examined everything closely and had made up his mind, he summoned Lattanzio Gorini, who was one of his paymasters. Since this Lattanzio also liked this kind of work, His Most Illustrious Excellency had him sketch out all the ways in which he wanted to fortify these gates, and to each one of us he sent the appropriate design for his gate. So, when I saw the gate that was assigned to me I thought the method was not as it should have been and was, indeed, entirely incorrect, and with this design in hand I immediately went to find my Duke. Wishing to show His Excellency the defects of the design given to me, no sooner had I begun to speak when the Duke, infuriated, turned to me and said: 'Benvenuto, in creating the most excellent statues I shall yield to you, but in this profession I want you to yield to me; so, follow the design I've given you.' To these

blustering words I replied as gently as I knew how, and said: 'My Lord, even in the fine method of making statues I've learned something from Your Most Illustrious Excellency; we have, nonetheless, always discussed this together to some extent, and so, in this matter of fortifying your city, a question of much greater importance than that of creating statues, I beg Your Most Illustrious Excellency to do me the honour of hearing me out, and thus, in reasoning with Your Excellency, it will be easier for me to demonstrate the manner in which I'm to serve you.' And so, when he heard these extremely charming words of mine, he kindly began to discuss the matter with me, and after I had demonstrated to His Most Illustrious Excellency with vivid and clear arguments that the method which he had designed for me would not be satisfactory, His Excellency said to me: 'Now go and draw up a plan yourself, and I shall see if I like it.' So I drew up two plans, following the logic of the true method of fortifying the two gates, and brought them to him, and after he recognized which design was correct and which incorrect, His Excellency declared very affably: 'Now go and do it your way, and I shall be happy with that.' And so I began to do so with great diligence.

86. There was a captain from Lombardy on guard at the Prato gate: he was a terribly stocky man, and extremely coarse in his speech; and he was presumptuous and extremely ignorant. This man immediately began to ask what I wanted to do; in response, I graciously showed him my designs and took great pains to make him understand the method I wanted to follow. But this villainous beast would now shake his head and then turn this way and that, shifting his weight from one leg to the other again and again, twisting the ends of his moustache, which he wore very long, and again and again he would pull down the peak of his cap over his eyes, muttering over and over: 'Come now! Blast you! I don't understand this plan of yours!'* Because of this, when this beast had begun to annoy me I said: 'Now, just leave everything to me, since I understand it.' Then, as I turned my back on him to return to my work, this man began giving me threatening looks; and with his left hand on the pommel of his sword, he raised the point of it a little and said: 'Look, Master, are you trying to start a fight with me?' I turned around in great anger, for he had really irritated me, and I said: 'I think it will be less trouble for me to fight with you than to fortify this gate.' In an instant we both put our hands to our swords, but before we could

draw them, a number of honest men, both Florentines and other courtiers, rushed up; and most of them cried out to him, telling him that he was in the wrong, that I was a man who would give a good account of himself, and that if the Duke knew about this he would be in trouble. And so he went about his business, and I began work on my bastion. When I had given the directions for this bastion I went to the other little gate on the Arno, where I found a captain from Cesena, the most courteous and gallant man I have ever known in such a profession: he had the manners of a charming young girl, and when necessary he was one of the boldest and most bloodthirsty men imaginable.* This courteous man watched me so closely that he often made me embarrassed: he wanted to understand, and I was delighted to explain everything to him, and we tried to outdo each other in paying each other the greatest courtesies, so that I built that bastion a good deal better than the other one. When I had nearly completed my bastions some of Piero Strozzi's men conducted a raid, and frightened the countryside around Prato so badly that all the inhabitants left their homes, and because of this all the carts from that district arrived loaded, each person carrying his belongings inside the city. Since the endless number of carts jostled one another, I saw such confusion that I warned the guards at the gates to take care that the same kind of rioting that occurred at the gates of Turin* did not happen here: for if it were necessary to use the portcullis it would not perform its function, because it would be held up on the top of one of the wagons. When that great beast of a captain heard my remarks, he turned to me with insulting words and I replied to him in kind, so that we were at the point of having a much worse fight than the first time: we were separated, however, and after completing my bastions I received several scudi unexpectedly, which delighted me, and I gladly returned to complete my Perseus.

87. In those days* some antiquities were discovered in the countryside around Arezzo, including among them the Chimera,* which is the bronze lion that can be seen in the chambers near the great hall of the palace; and along with this Chimera was discovered a number of very small statues, also of bronze, covered with clay and rust, and each of them lacking either a head or the hands or the feet; the Duke enjoyed cleaning them himself with some small goldsmiths' chisels. It happened that I chanced to speak with His Most Illustrious Excellency; and while I was talking with him he handed me a small

hammer, with which I would strike the small chisels the Duke was holding in his hand. In this way the little statues were cleaned of the dirt and rust. So, after passing several evenings in this fashion the Duke put me to work on beginning to redo the missing limbs for the little statues. And since the Duke took so much delight in the small matter of these little things, he had me work during the day as well, and if I was late in arriving His Most Illustrious Excellency sent for me. I frequently made His Excellency understand that, if I strayed from working on my Perseus in the daytime, several disadvantages would arise from this: the first, which frightened me most, was that the great length of time I saw that my work was taking would cause His Most Illustrious Excellency to be annoyed, as later happened to me; the second was that I had several workers, and when I was not there with them, they caused two particular kinds of trouble. The first was that they ruined my work, and the second was that they did as little work as possible: so the Duke contented himself with my going there only after sundown. And because I had so mollified His Most Illustrious Excellency, during the evening when I arrived in his chambers he welcomed me ever more warmly. In those days the new apartments toward Via dei Leoni were being built, so that when His Excellency wanted to retire to more private quarters he had a certain little chamber arranged in these recently built apartments, and he ordered me to go through his wardrobe, where I was to pass secretly above the ceiling of the great hall and then go through certain cubby-holes to this most secret chamber. Then, in the space of a few days, the Duchess deprived me of this privilege, having all those passageways locked up, so that every evening when I arrived at the palace I had to wait for a long time while she was in those antechambers through which I had to pass, engaged in her private affairs; and because she was unwell,* I never once arrived without inconveniencing her. Now, for this or another reason she had become so hostile to me that she could not bear to see me; and in spite of all this great discomfort and infinite annoyance, I patiently continued to go to the palace; the Duke had issued express orders in this regard, so that when I knocked on the gates they were immediately opened to me, and without saying anything to me they allowed me to enter anywhere, so that it sometimes happened that, upon entering quietly and unexpectedly through those secret chambers, I would come upon the Duchess engaged in her private affairs; she would immediately get angry, flying into such a rabid fury against me that I was terrified, and she always said to me: 'When will you ever be finished with fixing those little statues? Because by now I've had more than enough of your comings and goings.' To this I graciously replied: 'My lady and my only patroness, I desire nothing else than to serve you with faith and the utmost obedience; and because these works, which the Duke has ordered me to complete, will take me many months, tell me, Your Most Illustrious Excellency, if you do not wish for me to come here any longer; I'll not come here under any circumstances, no matter who summons me; and even if the Duke summons me, I'll say I feel ill, and under no circumstances will I ever come here again.' To these words of mine, she said: 'I'm not saying that you are not to come, and I'm not saying you shouldn't obey the Duke; but it certainly seems that these works of yours will never come to an end.' Whether the Duke got wind of this, or whether it was for some other reason, His Excellency began it all again: as soon as sunset drew near he would have me summoned; and the man who came to summon me was always saying to me: 'Take care not to fail to come, for the Duke is waiting for you.' And so I continued with these same difficulties for several evenings. Then one evening, while I was entering as usual, the Duke, who had to speak with the Duchess about some matters that were perhaps secret, turned upon me with the greatest possible fury; and since, somewhat alarmed, I wanted to leave immediately, he suddenly said: 'Come in, my dear Benvenuto, and go in there to your work, and I shall come to join you in a little while.' While I was passing through, Signor Don Grazìa,* a little boy still very young, took me by the cloak and gave me the most charming signs of affection that such a young child could offer; wondering at this, the Duke said: 'Oh! How delightfully friendly my children are with you!'

88. While I was working on those things of little importance, the Prince, Don Giovanni, Don Fernando,* and Don Grazìa would stay near me every evening, and unseen by the Duke, they used to pinch me: so I begged them kindly to keep still. They answered me, saying: 'We can't.' And I said to them: 'What is impossible should not be desired: so go ahead, do as you like.' The Duke and Duchess instantly burst out laughing. Another evening, after I finished those four small bronze statues that are set in the base, the Jupiter, the Mercury, the Minerva, and the Danaë, the mother of Perseus, with

her infant Perseus sitting at her feet,* I had them brought into the chamber where I used to work in the evenings and arranged them in a row a bit higher than our level of vision, so that they made a truly beautiful sight. When the Duke learned of this he came somewhat earlier than normal; and because the person who informed His Most Illustrious Excellency must have told him they were much better than they were, employing such phrases as 'better than the ancients' and other such remarks, my Duke appeared with the Duchess, happily discussing my work; and I immediately arose and went forward to greet them. The Duke, greeting me in his fine, aristocratic way, raised his right hand, in which he was holding a very large and beautiful branch from a pear tree, and said: 'Take this, my dear Benvenuto, and plant this pear in the garden of your house.' To his remark I replied with good-humour, saying: 'Oh, My Lord, does Your Most Illustrious Excellency really mean that I should plant it in the garden of *my* house?' Once again, the Duke said: 'In the garden of the house, which is yours. Have you understood me?'* Then I thanked His Excellency and did the same with the Duchess, as ceremonially as I knew how. Then they both sat down opposite the small statues, and for more than two hours they spoke of nothing except these beautiful little figures: so that the Duchess was seized with so enormous a desire for them that she said to me: 'I don't want these beautiful little statues to be lost on that base down in the square, where they will run the risk of being ruined; rather, I want you to arrange them for me in one of my apartments, where they will be treated with the reverence that their extremely rare qualities deserve.' I opposed this request with countless arguments; but seeing that she was determined I should not set them into the base where they are now, I waited until the following day and went to the palace two hours before dusk; and finding that both the Duke and the Duchess were out riding, having already prepared my base, I had the little statues brought down and immediately soldered them in as they were intended to stand. Oh! When the Duchess learned about this she became so angry that, if it had not been for the Duke, who vigorously helped me, I would have ended up in very serious trouble: on account of her anger over the pearl necklace and over this, she fixed things so that the Duke was deprived of that little bit of pleasure he enjoyed; this was the reason why I could no longer go there, and I immediately ended up with the same problems as before when entering the palace.

89. I returned to the Loggia, where I had already brought the Perseus, and I went on finishing it with the difficulties previously mentioned, that is, with no money and with so many other misfortunes, the half of which would terrify a man in adamantine armour. Nonetheless, I went on in my usual fashion, and one morning, after hearing Mass in San Pier Scheraggio,* I crossed paths with Bernardone, the broker and worthless goldsmith, who, through the Duke's kindness, had become purveyor to the Mint; and he was scarcely outside the door of the church when this filthy pig let loose four farts that could be heard all the way to San Miniato.* At this I said: 'So, you pig, lazy coward, ass—this is the sound of your filthy talents?' And I ran to find a stick. He quickly went back into the Mint, and I stood at the crack in my door while I kept a little boy of mine outside who would give me a signal when that pig left the Mint.* Now, when I saw that I had been waiting for a long time and was getting sick of it, my irritation had subsided a bit, and when I considered that you do not trade blows by agreement and that some trouble might arise from this, I decided to take my revenge in a different way. Since this incident occurred at around the time of the Feast of our San Giovanni,* within a day or two I wrote these four verses and tacked them up in the corner of the church where people go to piss and shit, and it read as follows:

> Here lies Bernardone, that ass and dirty pig,
>   Spy, thief, broker, in whom
> Pandora placed her worst evils, and from whom
>   That blockhead Master Buaccio inherited them.*

The story of the incident and the verses went around the palace, and the Duke and Duchess laughed about them; and before he himself had realized it, a large number of people had stopped there and had a huge laugh over it. Because they were looking toward the Mint and staring at Bernardone, once his son Master Baccio became aware of it he immediately tore the verse down in a great rage, and Bernardone bit his thumb in anger, making threats in that ugly little voice of his which came out of his nose: he made a great scene.

90. When the Duke learned that my whole work of the Perseus could be exhibited as if complete, he came to see it one day and gave

many clear signs that he was hugely satisfied with it; and, turning to some noblemen who were with His Most Illustrious Excellency, he said: 'Although the work seems very beautiful to us, it still has to please the people; so, my dear Benvenuto, before you give it your final touches I want you, out of affection for me, to open up a small part of the scaffolding facing my piazza for half a day to see what the people say about it. For there's no doubt that seeing it displayed out in the open will show it in a very different way from seeing it in such a confined space.' At these words, I humbly said to His Most Illustrious Excellency: 'Rest assured, My Lord, that it will look twice as good. Or how is it that Your Most Illustrious Excellency doesn't remember seeing it in the garden of my house, where it was displayed so well out in the open that Bandinelli came to see it from the garden of the Innocenti,* and for all his spiteful and wicked nature, the work compelled him and he spoke well about it, a man who never in his life said anything good about anyone? I realize that Your Most Illustrious Excellency puts too much faith in him.' At my words, smiling a little contemptuously, yet with many kindly words, the Duke said: 'Do it, my Benvenuto, only to give me a little satisfaction.' Once he went away I began to give orders to uncover it; and since there was a little gold, certain varnishes, and some other little things missing that are part of the finishing of a work, I grumbled indignantly and complained, cursing the damned day that brought me to Florence. I already saw the great and certain loss that I had incurred upon my departure from France, and I still neither saw nor knew any way to hope for anything good from this lord of mine in Florence: for from beginning to middle and end, everything I had done was always accomplished to my enormous disadvantage; and so, discontented, the following day I unveiled the statue. Now, as it pleased God, as soon as it was seen it evoked an endless outpouring of praise that brought me some consolation. And the people never stopped affixing verses around the door, which was covered with a bit of fabric, while I gave the statue its finishing touches. Let me say that on the very day it was kept uncovered for several hours, more than twenty sonnets were affixed there, all in boundless praise of my work; after I covered it up again a number of sonnets were put up every day, along with verses in Latin and Greek, because it was vacation time at the University of Pisa and all those most excellent learned men and scholars were vying with one another. But what gave me the greatest satisfaction, along with the hope of enjoying greater respect from my Duke, was that even those in the profession—that is, sculptors and painters—competed with each other about who could say the best about it. Among others, the one I esteemed most was the talented painter Iacopo da Puntorno,* and more than him his excellent pupil, the painter Bronzino,* for whom it was not enough to tack up several sonnets to the door but he sent his Sandrino* to my house with some of them, which spoke so well of the statue in that beautiful style of his, which is most rare, that it gave me a little consolation. And so I covered it up again and worked diligently to finish it.

91. Although His Excellency had heard the approval that had been shown to me after this brief exposition by this most excellent School, he said: 'I'm truly delighted that Benvenuto has received this little bit of satisfaction, which will cause him to finish the work as it deserves, more quickly and with greater diligence; but he must not think that afterwards, when it's completely unveiled and can be seen from every angle, the people will speak of it in this way; on the contrary, all its defects will be discovered, and others which it does not even possess will be added to them; so he should arm himself with patience.' Now these were words spoken by Bandinelli to the Duke, citing the works of Andrea del Verrocchio, who executed that handsome group of Christ and St Thomas in bronze* that can be seen on the façade of Orsanmichele; he cited many other works, down to the wonderful David of the divine Michelangelo Buonarroti, saying that that figure looked fine only when viewed from the front; and then he spoke of his Hercules and Cacus and the countless and insulting sonnets that were attached to it, and he spoke badly of the people of Florence. Bandinelli had induced my Duke, who believed him all too well, to make these remarks, and the Duke thought for sure that for the most part things would happen in the same way, because that envious Bandinelli never stopped speaking evil. On one particular occasion, when that scoundrel of a broker Bernardone happened to be present, to substantiate Bandinelli's words Bernardone said to the Duke: 'You must know, My Lord, that making large statues is a different kettle of fish from making smaller ones: I don't mean to say that the small statues he has executed have not come out well, but you'll see that he will not succeed with the large one.' And he mixed these nasty remarks with a great many more, engaging

in his craft of being a slanderous spy, into which he mixed a mountain of lies.

92. Now, as it pleased my glorious Lord and immortal God, I completely finished it, and on a Thursday morning* I completely unveiled it. Immediately, although it was not yet daylight, such a large number of people gathered there that it would be impossible to describe it, and they were all competing with one voice* to say the best things about the statue. The Duke was standing at a lower window in the palace, which was above the gate, and so, half-hidden inside the window, he heard everything that was being said about the work, and after he had listened for several hours he stood up with so much confidence and satisfaction that he turned to his Messer Sforza and said this to him: 'Sforza, go and find Benvenuto, and tell him on my behalf that I'm much more satisfied than I expected, and tell him that I shall satisfy him in such a way that I shall astonish him: so tell him to be of good cheer.' So Messer Sforza brought me this glorious message, which comforted me that day, both because of this good news and because the people kept pointing out to me now this detail and now that one as something both marvellous and new. Among the others were two gentlemen who had been sent by the Viceroy of Sicily* to our Duke on business. These two agreeable men encountered me in the piazza, for I was pointed out to them as I was passing: so that they ran furiously to catch up with me, and immediately, with their caps in their hands, delivered to me a speech so ceremonious that it would have been too much even for a pope. As much as I was able, however, I responded modestly;* but they overwhelmed me to such an extent that I began to beg them, as a favour, to leave the piazza, because people were stopping to stare at me more closely than at my Perseus. And in the middle of these ceremonious speeches they were so bold as to ask me to come to Sicily, and they would make such arrangements with me that I would be satisfied: they told me how Fra Giovanagnolo de' Servi* had made them a whole fountain adorned with many figures, but that they were not of the excellent quality they saw in the Perseus, although they had made him rich. I did not allow them to finish saying all that they would have liked to say, and I told them: 'I'm truly astonished by you, because you are asking me to abandon such a lord, who is more a lover of the arts than any other ruler ever born, and also because I'm in my native city, the School of all the greatest talents. Oh, if I had

an appetite for great profit I could have remained in France in the service of that great King Francis, who gave me a thousand golden scudi for my upkeep, and what's more, paid the costs of all my works, so that every year I had more than four thousand golden scudi left over; and I left in Paris my labours from four years of work.' With these and other remarks I cut short their protestations and thanked them for the high praise they had given me, which was the greatest reward that could be offered to any man who worked with great skill; and I said that they had so increased my desire to do well that I hoped within a few years to be able to exhibit another work, which I hoped would please the wondrous Florentine School much more than this one. The two gentlemen would have liked to pick up the thread of their ceremonious speeches once again, but with a tip of my cap, and a deep bow, I said goodbye.

93. After I had let two days pass and had seen that the high praise was continuously increasing, I decided then to go and present myself to My Lord Duke, who with great kindness said to me: 'My dear Benvenuto, you have satisfied me and made me happy; but I promise that I shall make you happy in a way that will astonish you; and furthermore, let me tell you that I don't intend to wait until beyond tomorrow.' At these wonderful promises I immediately turned all my highest powers of soul and body towards God, thanking Him sincerely, and in the same instant I approached my Duke and, half-weeping for joy, I kissed his robe. Then I added this remark: 'Oh, My Glorious Lord, true and most generous lover of the arts and of those men who work in them, I beg Your Most Illustrious Excellency to do me the favour of allowing me, first of all, to go away for eight days in order to give thanks to God: because I know very well the tremendous extent of my toil, and I recognize that my honest faith has moved God to come to my assistance. For this and for every other miraculous assistance, I want to go on a pilgrimage of eight days, constantly giving thanks to my Immortal God who always helps those who truly call upon Him.' Then the Duke asked me where I wanted to go. I said to him: 'Tomorrow morning I shall depart and go to Vallombrosa, then to Camaldoli and the Eremo, and I shall go as far as the Bagni di Santa Maria and perhaps even as far as Sestile, for I understand that there some beautiful antiquities there; then I shall return by San Francesco Della Vernia, and always giving thanks to God, I shall return content to serve you.'* The Duke

at once said to me, cheerfully: 'Go, and then return, for you truly please me; but leave me a couple of lines as a reminder, and leave everything to me.' I immediately wrote four lines in which I thanked His Most Illustrious Excellency and gave them to Messer Sforza, who placed them, on my behalf, in the Duke's hand. He took them; then he entrusted them to Messer Sforza and told him: 'Make sure to show them to me every day, because if Benvenuto returns and discovers that we have not expedited the matter, I believe he will kill me.' And so, laughing all the while, His Excellency said that he must be reminded of it. These exact words were repeated to me in the evening by Messer Sforza, who, laughing, was also astonished by the great favour the Duke was showing me; and, most pleasantly, he said to me: 'Go, Benvenuto, and come back again, for I envy you.'

94. In God's name I left Florence, continuously singing psalms and prayers to the honour and glory of God throughout the entire journey; I took the greatest pleasure in this, because the season was extremely beautiful; it was summertime, and the journey and the countryside, where I had never been before, seemed so beautiful to me that it made me astonished and happy. Since a young workman of mine from Bagni, named Cesare,* had come as my guide, I was warmly welcomed by his father and by the entire household; among whom was an old man of more than seventy, who was most charming: he was Cesare's uncle, and he pursued the profession of a surgeon and dabbled a bit in alchemy. This good man showed me that Bagni had a gold and silver mine, and he pointed out many splendid things in the countryside, so that I enjoyed myself as much as I ever had. When, in his own way, he had grown familiar with me, he said to me one day: 'I don't want to fail to mention one of my concerns which, if His Excellency should lend an ear, I believe would be something very useful: and this is, that around Camaldoli there is a pass that is so undefended that Piero Strozzi could not only pass through safely but could also plunder Poppi without any opposition whatsoever.'* And in addition, not only did he explain it in words but he also took out a sheet of paper from his pocket on which this good old man had sketched out all of the countryside, so that it could be seen very easily and the danger clearly recognized. I took the sketch and immediately left Bagni, and as fast as I could, returning by Prato Magno and San Francesco della Vernia, I went back to Florence, where, without stopping except to take off my riding

boots, I went to the palace. And when I was near the Badia I ran into my Duke, who was coming along by the Palace of the Podestà;* he greeted me warmly, with a touch of astonishment, as soon as he spotted me, saying to me: 'But why have you come back so soon? I wasn't expecting you for eight days.' And I said: 'I have returned in the service of Your Most Illustrious Excellency, for I would have gladly spent several days wandering through that beautiful country-side.' 'And what good affair brings you back?' said the Duke. I said: 'My Lord, I must speak to you and show you things of great import-ance.' And so I went with him to the palace. When we reached the palace he led me secretly into a room, where we were alone. Then I told him everything and showed him that little sketch; he seemed very glad to have it. And explaining to His Excellency that it was necessary to provide for this situation immediately, the Duke stood there a moment lost in thought, and then he said to me: 'Know that we have an agreement with the Duke of Urbino,* who has to take care of this pass; but keep this to yourself.' After this, with many signs of his good favour, I returned home.

95. The next day I presented myself, and after a little conversa-tion the Duke said to me, happily: 'Tomorrow without fail I wish to expedite your business; so be of good cheer.' I considered the matter entirely settled, and with great anticipation I awaited the following day. When the day came I went to the palace, and as always, it seems that bad news travels faster than good, for Messer Iacopo Guidi,* the secretary to His Most Illustrious Excellency, summoned me, with his twisted mouth and haughty voice, and drawing himself up as stiff as a rod,* he began to speak in this manner: 'The Duke says that he wants to know from you what you are asking for your Perseus.' This bewildered and astonished me, and I immediately replied that I was not in the habit of asking prices for my labours, and that this was not what His Excellency had promised me two days earlier. Instantly this man, in an even louder voice, told me that, on behalf of the Duke, he was ordering me expressly to state what I wanted for it, under pain of His Most Illustrious Excellency's utter displeasure. The great courtesies shown to me by His Most Illustrious Excellency had not so much led me to hope that I would earn something, but rather, and more importantly, to hope that I had won the Duke's favour completely, because I never asked for anything greater than being in his good graces: now this way of proceeding, completely unexpected

by me, caused me to fly into a great rage; and all the more so because
the request was made in this manner by this poisonous toad. I said
that if the Duke were to give me ten thousand scudi he would not
pay for it, and that if I had ever imagined descending to these discussions of money I would have never remained here. This contemptible man straightaway made a number of insulting remarks to me;
and I did the same to him. The next day, when I was paying
my respects to the Duke, His Excellency made a sign to me; I
approached, and he said to me angrily: 'Cities and palaces are built
with tens of thousands of ducats.' To this I replied straightaway
that His Excellency could find countless men who would know
how to construct cities and palaces, but as for making statues like
the Perseus, he would perhaps not find a single man who would
know how to accomplish such a feat. And I immediately left without saying or doing anything else. A few days later the Duchess sent
for me, and told me to entrust her with the unpleasantness I was
having with the Duke, for she boasted that she could arrange matters
so that I would be happy. To her kind words I replied that I had
never requested any greater reward for my labours than the good
grace of the Duke, and that His Most Illustrious Majesty had promised me this; and that there was no need for me to entrust into Their
Most Illustrious Excellencies' hands what, from the first days I had
begun to serve them, I had already entrusted to them in complete
freedom: I added, moreover, that if His Most Illustrious Excellency
would give me only a crazia,* which is worth five quattrini,* for
my labours, I would call myself content and satisfied, provided
His Excellency did not deprive me of his favour. To my words the
Duchess said, smiling a little: 'Benvenuto, you would do better to
do what I tell you;' and, turning her back on me, she left. I thought
that the best thing I could do was to employ such humble words,
but it turned out that they produced the worst effect for me, for
although she had been somewhat angry with me before, there was
in her, nonetheless, a certain way of doing things that worked to
good effect.

96. At this period I was on friendly terms with Girolimo degli
Albizi,* who was commissioner of His Excellency's troops; and one
day he said to me: ' Oh, Benvenuto, it would be a good thing to find
some way out of this trouble you're having with the Duke; let me
tell you that if you place your trust in me, I'm confident that I can

arrange it, for I know what I'm talking about. As the Duke goes on
getting really angry, you will come out of the matter very badly: let
this suffice; I can't tell you everything.' Someone had told me—
perhaps someone malicious—that after the Duchess had spoken to
me he had heard that the Duke, on I do not know what occasion, had
said: 'For less than two quattrini, I would throw away this Perseus,
and so end all these disagreements.' Now, on account of this fear, I
told Girolamo degli Albizi that I would entrust the entire matter to
him, and that I would be completely satisfied by whatever he did,
provided that I remained in the Duke's good graces. This gallant
man, who understood the military profession very well, especially
how to lead the militias, who are all peasants, had no appreciation of
the craft of sculpting and, moreover, understood absolutely nothing
about it, so that when he spoke to the Duke, he said: 'My Lord,
Benvenuto has placed himself in my hands and has begged me to
commend him to Your Most Illustrious Excellency.' Then the Duke
said: 'And I likewise place myself in your hands, and I shall be happy
for you to decide everything.' As a result, this Girolamo wrote a very
clever letter and one very much in my favour, and he decided that the
Duke should give me three thousand five hundred golden scudi,
which was intended not as an adequate price for such a beautiful
work, but only to provide a small sum for my maintenance: it was
enough that I should say that I was satisfied; it contained many other
words, which essentially confirmed the price.* The Duke agreed most
willingly to the letter, for all that I was very unhappy with it. When
the Duchess heard about it she said: 'It would have been much better
for that poor man if he had entrusted the matter to me, for I would
have had him given five thousand golden scudi;' and one day when I
went to the palace the Duchess said these very same words to me, in
the presence of Messer Alamanno Salviati,* and she made fun of me,
saying that I deserved all the bad luck I was having. The Duke
ordered that I should be paid one hundred gold scudi each month up
to the said amount, and thus several months passed by. Then Messer
Antonio de' Nobili,* who had received the Duke's orders, began
giving me fifty scudi, and then sometimes he gave me twenty-five,
and sometimes nothing at all: so that, seeing the payment being
prolonged, I spoke to this Messer Antonio in a very friendly way,
begging him to tell me the reason why he did not complete the
payments. He also answered me most graciously: in his reply I

thought he wandered off the point rather too much—let whoever
understands it be the judge: first, he told me the reason he did not
continue my payments was the severe shortage of money the palace
was suffering, but he promised me that as soon as he had the money
he would pay me; and then he added: 'Alas! If I didn't pay you I
would be a great scoundrel!' I was surprised to hear him say such a
thing, and assured myself, for that reason, that he would pay me
when he could. In this affair things happened in exactly the opposite
way, so that when I saw myself being badly treated I became angry
with him and said many angry and resentful things to him, reminding him of everything he had said would happen. He died, however,
and I am still waiting to receive five hundred golden scudi, and it is
now near the end of the year 1566.* I was still owed the rest of my
salary, which I thought they no longer had any intention of paying
me, because almost three years had passed; but the Duke was struck
by a perilous illness, remaining forty-eight hours without being able
to urinate, and when he realized that the doctors' remedies were not
helping him, perhaps he turned to God and wanted everyone to be
paid what he was owed, and I too was paid, although I was still not
paid the balance from the Perseus.

97. I had all but half-decided not to say anything more about my
unfortunate Perseus; but the occurrence that forces me to do so was
so notable that I shall once again take up the thread of my narrative,
going backwards a little. I thought I was doing the best for myself
when I told the Duchess I could not discuss something that was no
longer in my control, because I had told the Duke that I would be
happy with whatever His Most Illustrious Excellency would give me.
I said this, thinking I would ingratiate myself to some degree; and
with that little display of humility I sought every available means of
placating the Duke somewhat, because a few days before he had
come to an agreement with Albizi, the Duke had given many signs of
being angry with me. The reason was that I complained to His
Excellency of the dirty, arrogant acts that Messer Alfonso Quistello,
Messer Iacopo Polverino the fiscal minister, and, more than all of
them, Ser Giovanbatista Brandini of Volterra were committing
against me;* and as I was making my arguments with some show of
passion, I saw the Duke become so angry it was unbelievable. After
His Most Illustrious Excellency had flown into this great fit of rage,
he said to me: 'This case is just the same as the one about your

Perseus, for which you have asked ten thousand scudi: you let yourself be overcome by your self-interest; I want it to be valued, therefore, and I shall give you everything it's judged to be worth.' At those
words I immediately answered a little too boldly and half-angrily—a
tone that is inappropriate to use with great lords—and I said: 'Oh!
How is it possible to set a price for my work when there is not a
single man in Florence today who even knew how to create it?' Then
the Duke became even more furious, and he spoke many angry
words, among which he said: 'In Florence there is one man today
who would know how to make such a statue and, moreover, he will
know very well how to judge it.' He meant Bandinelli, knight of
Saint Jacopo. Then I replied: 'My Lord, Your Most Illustrious
Excellency has given me the ability to execute in the greatest School
of the world a great and most difficult work, which has been more
praised than any work ever unveiled in this most divine School; what
makes me even more confident is that among these excellent men,
who know this profession and are members of it, the painter
Bronzino has laboured and written me four sonnets, using the most
well-chosen and glorious words possible; and because of this astonishing man, perhaps the entire city has been moved to such great
excitement. I must say, moreover, that if Bronzino had devoted himself to sculpture as he has to painting, yes, he would perhaps have
understood how to do it. And I must tell Your Most Illustrious
Excellency as well that, although my master, Michelangelo Buonarroti, might have executed such a statue when he was younger, he
would not have exerted any less effort than I have; but now that he is
a very old man* he certainly would not do so: so that I do not believe
that today there is any man we know of who would understand how
to accomplish this feat. My work has already received the greatest
reward that I could possibly desire, especially since Your Most Illustrious Excellency has not only described yourself as content with my
work but you have also praised it to me more than any other man.
Oh, what greater or more honourable reward can anyone desire? Let
me say absolutely for certain that Your Excellency could not pay me
in more glorious coin; nor could any treasure whatsoever be equal to
this: I have been paid too much, and for this I thank Your Most
Illustrious Excellency with all my heart.' To these words the Duke
replied, saying: 'On the contrary, you think that I don't have enough
money to pay you; but let me tell you that I shall pay you much more

than the statue is worth.' Then I said: 'I did not expect to have any other reward from Your Excellency, but I count myself well paid by the recognition the School has given me, and with this I wish to leave right away, without ever again returning to the house Your Most Illustrious Excellency gave me, nor do I ever care to see Florence again.' We were near Santa Felicità,* and His Excellency was return-ing to the palace. At my angry words the Duke suddenly turned in great fury and said: 'You are not to leave, and take care that you do not leave!' Half-frightened, I accompanied him to the palace. When His Excellency reached the palace he called Bishop de' Bartolini,* who was the Archbishop of Pisa, and summoned Messer Pandolfo della Stufa,* and he told them to tell Baccio Bandinelli on his behalf to study carefully this Perseus of mine and to value it, because the Duke wanted to pay me a just price for it. These two honest men immediately found that Bandinelli and, carrying out their mission, Bandinelli informed them that he had carefully studied this work and that he knew all too well what it was worth; but since he was in dispute with me over other past matters, he did not want to get involved in my affairs in any way whatsoever. Then these two noblemen added: 'The Duke has told us that, under pain of his displeasure, he commands you to state a price; and if you want two or three days of time to study it well, you may take them. Afterwards, tell us what you think this work is worth.' Bandinelli answered that he had studied it very carefully, that he could not neglect the Duke's orders, and that this work had turned out very rich and beautiful, so that he thought it was worth sixteen thousand golden scudi and even more. These excellent noblemen immediately reported this to the Duke, who became extremely angry; and similarly they repeated it to me. In response, I said that I had no wish to accept the praises of Bandinelli, since that evil man spoke ill of everyone. These remarks of mine were reported to the Duke, and it was for this reason that the Duchess wanted me to entrust everything to her. All this is the plain truth: it is sufficient to say that I would have done best to allow myself to be judged by the Duchess, because I would have been paid very quickly and I would have had a greater reward.

98. The Duke gave me to understand through Messer Lelio Torello,* his auditor, that he wanted me to depict certain stories in low relief and in bronze around the choir of Santa Maria del Fiore; but since this choir was an undertaking of Bandinelli, I did not want

to embellish his ugly works with my own labours. And although the
design for the choir was not his, because he understood nothing at all
about architecture (the design was by Giuliano, the son of Baccio
d'Agnolo, the woodcarver, who ruined the cupola*)—suffice it to say
that there was no skill in it whatsoever; and for one reason or another
I did not want to do such a work under any circumstances, but I kept
telling the Duke humbly that I would do everything His Most Illustrious Excellency ordered me to do, so that His Excellency ordered
the administrators at the Opera di Santa Maria del Fiore to come to
an agreement with me: His Excellency would give me only my allowance of two hundred scudi per year, and he wanted the administrators to provide for anything else from their own funds. As a result,
I appeared before these administrators, who outlined the orders they
had received from the Duke, and since I thought I could explain my
arguments to them much more safely, I began to point out to them
that so many narratives in bronze would be a very large expense, all
of which would be thrown away, and I stated all my reasons, which
convinced them completely. The first reason was that the arrangement of the choir was all wrong and had been done without any
judgement, nor could any craftsmanship, convenience, grace, or
design be seen in it; the other reason was that these narratives were
to be placed down too low, so that they would be much lower than
the line of sight and would become a urinal for dogs, constantly
covered with every sort of filth; and for these reasons, I had no wish
to execute them. Only to avoid throwing away the rest of my best
years and to avoid failing to serve His Most Illustrious Excellency,
whom I so greatly desired to please and to serve, I said therefore that
if His Excellency wanted to make use of my labours he should allow
me to make the central door of Santa Maria del Fiore, which would
be a work that would be seen and would bring His Most Illustrious
Excellency much more glory; and that I would bind myself by a
contract stating that if I did not execute this better than the door
which is the most beautiful of the doors of San Giovanni,* I wanted
nothing for my labours. But if I completed the door according to my
promise, I would be happy if he had it valued and afterwards gave me
a thousand scudi less than the amount for which the men of my
profession had appraised it. The administrators liked what I had
proposed to them very much, and they went to speak to the Duke
about it, including one among them named Piero Salviati,* who

thought he was saying something that would be very pleasing to the Duke; but it turned out completely the opposite; the Duke said that I always wanted to do exactly the opposite of what he wanted me to do; and without any other decision being taken, this Piero left the Duke. When I learned about this, I immediately went to find the Duke, who seemed rather angry with me; I begged him to do me the honour of listening to me, and he promised to do so. So I began from the beginning, and with many fine arguments I gave him to understand the truth of the matter, showing him it would be a good deal of money thrown away. So that I greatly placated him, saying that if His Most Illustrious Excellency did not wish for me to execute the door, two pulpits had to be executed for the choir, and these would be two great works and would bring glory to His Most Illustrious Excellency. I added that I would fashion a large number of narratives in bronze in low relief for them, with many decorations. Thus, I calmed him down, and he ordered me to make the models. I made several models and it took great effort. Among the others, I made one model with eight panels, and took much greater pains than I had with the others, and I thought it was much more suitable for the purpose it was to serve. And because I had brought the models to the palace several times, His Excellency gave me to understand by Messer Cesare,* the keeper of his wardrobe, that I was to leave them there. After the Duke had seen them I saw that His Excellency had chosen the least beautiful among them. One day His Excellency summoned me, and in discussing these models I told him and showed him with many arguments that the one with eight panels would be much more suitable for this purpose, and much more beautiful to see. The Duke replied that he wanted it to be made square, since he liked it much more that way; and so, very agreeably, he discussed it with me for quite some time. I did not hesitate to say everything that occurred to me in defence of my craft. Oh! If only the Duke might have seen that I was speaking the truth, but he still wanted it to be made his way, and a great deal of time passed before anything else was said to me about it.

99. It was during this period* that the great marble block for the Neptune was transported on the Arno river and then brought by way of the Grieve* along the road by Poggio a Caiano, in order to convey it to Florence more easily along that flat road, where I went to see it. And although I knew for certain that the Duchess, through her own

personal favour, had arranged for the Cavaliere Bandinelli to have it,
I went not out of any jealousy I bore for Bandinelli but rather
because I was moved by pity for this poor, unfortunate block of
marble (it should be noted that, whatever the thing may be, when it
is subjected to an evil destiny, if one tries to rescue it from some
obvious evil it will happen that it falls into one that is much worse, as
did this block of marble at the hands of Bartolomeo Ammannati,*
about whom I shall speak in the appropriate place). When I saw that
extremely beautiful marble, I immediately measured its height and
its width from all points and returned to Florence, where I executed
a number of models suitable for it. Later I went to Poggio a Caiano,
where the Duke, Duchess, and their son the Prince* were staying; and
finding them all at the dinner-table, since the Duke was eating alone
with the Duchess, I began to talk with the Prince. After I had entertained him for quite a long while, the Duke, who was in a room
nearby, heard me, and with great kindness he had me summoned;
and once I arrived in Their Excellencies' presence, with many
charming remarks the Duchess began to talk with me. In that conversation I began to discuss, little by little, that extremely beautiful
block of marble I had seen. I began to describe how their most noble
ancestors had made their most noble School so very brilliant only by
making all the most talented men in their professions compete; and it
was in this way of testing skill that the wonderful cupola,* the most
beautiful doors of San Giovanni, and so many other beautiful
churches and statues had been created, which formed a crown of so
many excellences for their city that its equal had never been seen
since the time of the ancients. The Duchess immediately told me,
with irritation, that she knew very well what I was trying to say; and
she said that I should never speak further of that block of marble in
her presence, for I would make her annoyed. I said: 'Do I, therefore,
cause you annoyance by wishing to act as Your Excellencies' repre-
sentative, doing everything so that you may be better served? Consider this, My Lady: if Your Most Illustrious Excellencies would
agree to have everyone make a model of a Neptune, although you are
resolved that Bandinelli will have the block, this will cause Bandinelli, for his own honour, to take greater pains to produce a beautiful
model, which he would not do if he knew he had no competitors. In
this way you, My Lords, would be much better served, and you
would not dishearten this brilliant School, and you would see who

would do the best: I mean, in the beautiful style of this wonderful art; and Your Lordships would show that you take pleasure in it and understand it.' In great anger, the Duchess told me that I had wearied her and that she wanted this marble block to be Bandinelli's, saying: 'Ask the Duke about it, since His Excellency also wants Bandinelli to have it.' After the Duchess had spoken, the Duke, who had remained silent, said: 'Twenty years have passed since I had that fine block of marble quarried specially for Bandinelli, and so I want Bandinelli to have it, and it will be his.' I immediately turned to the Duke and said: 'My Lord, I beg Your Most Illustrious Excellency to do me the favour of allowing me to speak four words in your service.' The Duke told me to say everything I wished and that he would listen to me. Then I said: 'You should know, My Lord, that the block of marble from which Bandinelli carved Hercules and Cacus was quarried for that wonderful Michelangelo Buonarroti, who had made a model of a Samson with four other figures which would have been the most beautiful work in the world; and your Bandinelli carved only two figures out of it, which were badly executed and all cobbled together: as a result, this brilliant School is still crying out about the great wrong that was done to that beautiful marble. I believe that more than a thousand sonnets were tacked up in reproach of that ugly work, and I know that Your Most Illustrious Excellency remembers this very well. And so, My Noble Lord, if those men who had such responsibility were so ignorant that they took away that beautiful piece of marble from Michelangelo, which was quarried for him, and gave it to Bandinelli, who ruined it, as can be seen—Oh! Can you ever tolerate that this even more beautiful piece of marble, even though it belongs to Bandinelli who will spoil it, should not be given to another worthy man who can use it properly? Arrange it, My Lord, so that everyone who wishes to do so can make a model and then they will all be unveiled to the School, and Your Most Illustrious Excellency will hear what the School says; and with your good judgement, Your Excellency will know how to select the best, and in this fashion you will not throw your money away, nor will you diminish the brilliant spirit of such a wonderful School, which is unique in the world today: all of which is to Your Most Illustrious Excellency's glory.' After the Duke had kindly listened to me, he immediately arose from the table and turned to me, saying: 'Go, my dear Benvenuto, and make a model, and earn yourself that beautiful block of marble, because you are telling me the truth and I recognize it.' Nodding threateningly at me, the Duchess was indignant and spoke, muttering I know not what; and I made them a bow and returned to Florence, where it seemed like a thousand years before I set my hand to making the model.

100. When the Duke came to Florence, without notifying me he came to my house, where I showed him two little models,* one different from the other; and although he praised them both, he told me that one of them pleased him more than the other and that I should finish the one that he liked carefully, for it would be to my advantage: and although His Excellency had seen what Bandinelli and also some of the others had done, His Excellency praised my model far more and at much greater length, or so it was reported to me by many of his courtiers who had overheard him. Among other remarkable and memorable things to take special note of, it happened that the Cardinal of Santa Fiore* came to Florence, and while the Duke was taking him to Poggio a Caiano he saw, in passing, the previously mentioned block of marble and praised it highly, and then asked to whom His Excellency had offered it to work on. The Duke immediately replied: 'To my Benvenuto, who has produced a very beautiful model for it.' This was recounted to me by men worthy of trust: and because of this I went to find the Duchess and brought her some delightful little trifles of my craft, which Her Most Illustrious Excellency obviously loved dearly; then she asked what I was working on, to which I said: 'My Lady, I have undertaken, for my pleasure, to make one of the most difficult works that has ever been made: this is a representation of the crucified Christ in very white marble on a cross of the blackest marble, and it will be the size of a tall living man.' She asked at once what I wanted to do with it. I answered her: 'Know, My Lady, that I would not give it to anyone even for two thousand golden ducats, because no man has ever expended such great effort to realize such a work; still less would I have obliged myself to execute it for any lord, for fear of humiliating myself. I bought the blocks of marble with my own money, and I've kept a young boy for around two years who has assisted me; what with the marble blocks, the iron scaffolding upon which it stands, and wages, it has cost me more than three hundred scudi, so that I would not part with it for two thousand golden scudi. But if Your Most Illustrious Excellency wishes to do me a most innocent kindness, I shall

gladly make you a free gift of it: I only beg Your Most Illustrious Excellency not to show me disfavour nor any favour in the matter of the models of Neptune that His Most Illustrious Excellency has commissioned to be made for the large block of marble.' She replied with great indignation: 'So, you think nothing of my assistance or my opposition?' 'On the contrary, My Lady, I value it; or why would I offer to give you something that I value at two thousand ducats? But I have so much faith in my own painstaking and systematic studies that I count on earning the prize myself, even if the contest were against that great Michelangelo Buonarroti, from whom—and never from others—I've learned everything I know; it would be even more pleasing to me if he were to make a model himself: he who knows so much, while these others know so little: because by competing with that great master of mine I could gain a great deal, whereas by competing with those others it's impossible to gain a thing.' When I had spoken she rose, half-angry, and I returned to my work, expending as much care on my model as I could. After I had completed it the Duke came to see it and with him were two ambassadors, one from the Duke of Ferrara and the other from the government of Lucca;* they liked it very much, and the Duke said to them: 'Benvenuto truly deserves the commission.' Then, by their words, these two men greatly encouraged me, especially the ambassador from Lucca, who was a learned person and a scholar. I had withdrawn a little so that they could say everything they thought, but hearing myself being praised I quickly approached them and, turning to the Duke, I said: 'My Lord, Your Most Illustrious Excellency should impose another excellent test: order anyone who wishes to do so to produce a model in clay of exactly the same size as the figure will emerge from this block of marble, and in this way Your Most Illustrious Excellency will see much better who deserves the commission; and let me tell you that if Your Excellency gives it to someone who does not deserve it, you will not wrong the person who deserves it, but rather you'll do a huge wrong to yourself, because you'll suffer both loss and shame; whereas if you do the contrary, by giving it to the person who deserves it, first you'll acquire great glory and you'll spend your money wisely, and the skilled people will continue to believe that you delight in such matters and understand them.' As soon as I had said these words the Duke shrugged his shoulders; and as he set out to leave, the ambassador of Lucca said to him: 'My Lord, this Benvenuto of yours is a formidable man!' The Duke replied: 'He's more formidable than you realize, and it would be better for him if weren't so formidable, because he would have had now things that he hasn't had.' The ambassador himself recounted these exact words to me, practically admonishing me not to act in this way. I said to him that I wished My Lord well, as his loving and faithful servant, but that I did not know how to play the flatterer. Several weeks later Bandinelli died;* it was believed that, besides his ailments, his annoyance over seeing himself lose the block of marble was the main cause of it.

101. This same Bandinelli had learned that I had executed the Crucifix I mentioned above: he immediately set his hand to a piece of marble and created that Pietà* that can be seen in the Church of the Annunziata. And although I had already offered my Crucifix to Santa Maria Novella and had already attached the hooks for mounting it there, I asked only for permission to dig under the feet of my Crucifix, in the ground, a small tomb to receive me after I was dead. The friars told me that they could not concede such a thing without asking the administrators of their works department, and I said to them: 'Oh, brothers, why didn't you first ask the administrators about providing a place for my beautiful Crucifix, since you let me put up the hooks and other things?' For this reason, I no longer wanted to give the Church of Santa Maria Novella the fruits of my greatest labours, even though the administrators of the church later came to see me and begged me for the work. I immediately turned to the Church of the Annunziata, and when I proposed to give the Crucifix, on the same terms as those I had wanted from Santa Maria Novella, these holy friars of the Annunziata all agreed and told me that if I placed it in their church I could construct my tomb in any way that I found proper and pleasing. Having heard about this agreement, Bandinelli set to work with great diligence to complete his Pietà, and he asked the Duchess to procure for him the chapel that belonged to the Pazzi family; it was procured with some difficulty; and as soon as he had it he very hastily set up his work, which was not completely finished, and he died. The Duchess said that, just as she had helped him in life, she would help him in death as well, and that although he was dead I should never expect to have that block of marble. After Bernardone the broker told me one day, when he ran into me in the villa, that the Duchess had assigned the

block of marble, I said to him: 'Oh, unfortunate marble! Certainly it would have suffered at the hands of Bandinelli, but at the hands of Ammannati it will suffer a hundred times worse!' I had received orders from the Duke to construct the clay model in the size that it would turn out in marble, and he had provided me with wood and clay, had a small partition set up for me in the loggia where my Perseus stood, and paid for a workman for me. I set to work with all possible diligence and made the wooden skeleton following my usual good standard, and I was happily approaching its completion without worrying about doing the statue in marble, for I knew that the Duchess was determined not to let me have it, and because of this I was not concerned about it. Only, I was pleased to undergo that labour, promising myself that once I had completed it, the Duchess, who was, for all this, a person of intelligence, if she chanced to see it later would be sorry to have done both the block of marble and herself such an immeasurable wrong.* Giovanni the Fleming* made a model in the cloisters of Santa Croce, and Vincenzio Danti* of Perugia made one in Messer Ottaviano de' Medici's home; the son of Moschino* began another one in Pisa, and yet another one was being executed by Bartolomeo Ammannati in the Loggia, which we had divided between ourselves. When I had it all well sketched out and wanted to begin to finish the head, to which I had already given the first touches, the Duke came down from the palace and Little George the painter* took him to Ammannati's workshop to show him his Neptune, upon which this same Little George had worked with his own hands for many days together with Ammannati and all his workmen. While the Duke looked it over he was very little satisfied by it, so I was told, and even though Little George wanted to fill him up with that chattering of his, the Duke shook his head and, turning to Messer Gianstefano,* he said: 'Go and ask Benvenuto if his giant is far enough advanced that he would be willing to give me a look at it.' Messer Gianstefano very properly and graciously brought me the message on the Duke's behalf, and he told me, moreover, that if I thought my work was not ready to be shown I should say so quite freely, since the Duke knew very well that I had had little help in this great undertaking. I said that I would be delighted for him to come, and although my work was not too far advanced, His Most Illustrious Excellency's intellect was such that he could easily judge how it would turn out when completed. And so this gentleman took my message to the Duke, who came eagerly. As soon as His Excellency entered the workroom he glanced at my work and showed that he took great satisfaction in it; then he walked around it, stopping at all the four points of view just as a man would have done who was an expert in the art; then, by many clear signs and gestures, he showed his great pleasure, and said only: 'Benvenuto, you only have to give it a final touch.'* Then he turned to those who were with His Excellency, and he spoke very well about my work, saying: 'The little model that I saw in his home pleased me a great deal, but this work of his has surpassed the quality of the model.'

102. As it pleased God, who always works for our best interests (I am speaking of those who acknowledge and believe in Him, for God always defends them), at around that time I ran into a certain scoundrel from Vicchio named Piermaria d'Anterigoli, nicknamed Sbietta:* he was a sheep-farmer by profession, and since he was a close relative of Messer Guido Guidi,* a physician and today the Provost of Pescia, I gave him a hearing. This fellow offered to sell me one of his farms for the term of my natural life, which I did not want to see, because I was eager to complete my model for the gigantic Neptune statue; and also because there was no need for me to see it, since he was selling me only its revenue: this he had calculated for me in so many bushels of wheat, so much wine, oil, corn, chestnuts, and other profits, which by my own accounting at the period we were in was worth much more than one hundred golden scudi, and I gave him six hundred and fifty scudi, including the taxes.* So, since he had left me a written guarantee in his hand stating that he would always provide me, for as long as I lived, with the said income, I did not worry about going to see this farm, but I informed myself as best I could about whether this Sbietta and Ser Filippo, his brother, were sufficiently well enough off for me to be safe. And so, many different people who knew them told me that I was extremely safe. By common agreement we summoned Ser Pierfrancesco Bertoldi, notary for the Mercatanzia;* and first of all I gave him the document containing everything this Sbietta wanted to provide for me, thinking that this written agreement would have to be mentioned in the contract. In any case, this notary, who drew up the contract, was attending to the twenty-two boundaries that Sbietta described to him, and in my opinion he did not remember to include in this contract what the seller had offered me. While the notary wrote I continued to work, and since he

took several hours to write it out I completed a good part of the Neptune's head. And so, after the contract was completed, Sbietta began to show me the greatest possible kindness, and I did the same with him. He presented me with kids, cheeses, capons, ricotta, and many kinds of fruit, so that I began to feel almost embarrassed; in return for these kindly gestures, every time he came to Florence I took him from the inn to my home; and on many occasions he was accompanied by some of his relatives, who came along as well. In a pleasant manner, he began to tell me that it was a shame I, having bought a farm, had let so many weeks go past already without resolving to leave my business to my workmen for the short space of three days to go and see it. He flattered me so well that, to my misfortune, I went to see it, and this Sbietta received me in his home with such kindness and so much honour that one could not do more for a Duke, while his wife gave me an even warmer welcome. And so we went on like this for a while, until all that they had plotted to do, he and his brother Ser Filippo, came to pass.

103. I did not neglect to work diligently on the Neptune, and I had already completely sketched it out, as I said above, using the best method, which no one had ever used or even knew about before me. So, although I was certain I would not receive the marble, for the reasons I previously stated, I thought I would complete the model and immediately allow it to be seen in the square, solely for my own satisfaction. The season was hot and pleasant, and after being so well treated by those two scoundrels I started out one Wednesday, which was a double feast day,* toward my villa in Trespiano.* I had eaten a good lunch, so that it was more than three hours before dusk when I arrived in Vicchio; I immediately found Ser Filippo at the gate of Vicchio, who seemed to know I was coming; he gave me an extremely warm welcome and took me to Sbietta's house, where his shameless wife also treated me with extreme kindness; and I gave her a very fine straw hat, about which she said she had never seen one more beautiful. Sbietta was not there at the time. As evening drew near we all ate together very pleasantly; then I was given a splendid bedroom, where I slept in an extremely clean bed; and two of my servants were given similar quarters according to their rank. In the morning, when I arose, I was paid the same courtesies. I went to see my farm, which pleased me; I was given a great deal of wheat and other kinds of corn; and then, as we returned to Vicchio, this priest, Ser Filippo,

said to me: 'Benvenuto, don't be worried; for although you haven't found everything exactly as you were promised, you can be very sure that the farm will be maintained for your profit, because you are dealing with honest people; and you should know that we have fired this labourer, because he was a bad sort.' The labourer, whose name was Mariano Rosegli, told me many times: 'Keep an eye on your affairs, for in the end you will discover which of us is the worst sort.' When this peasant said this to me he snickered in a particularly nasty way, shaking his head as if to say: 'Go there and you'll see for yourself.' I had a bad feeling about the matter, but I never imagined anything like what happened to me. Having returned from the farm, which was two miles outside Vicchio toward the mountains, I found this priest waiting for me, with his usual warm welcome, and so we all went to have lunch together: this was not a full dinner, but it was an excellent meal. Then I went for a stroll around Vicchio, where the market had already opened: I saw that I was stared at by everybody in town as if something about me was strange to see, but more than all the others by an honest man who has lived many years in Vicchio and whose wife bakes bread to sell. He holds some good properties about a mile away, but he is, however, happy to remain as he is. This worthy man lives in a house belonging to me, which is located in Vicchio and which was consigned to me along with the farm, which is called the Farm of the Fountain; and he said to me: 'I am in your house, and at the proper time I'll give you your rent; or, if you want it beforehand, I'll do what you wish in every respect: it's enough for me that we're always in agreement.' And while we were talking I saw that this man was staring fixedly at me, so that, constrained by such a thing, I asked him: 'Ah, tell me, my dear Giovanni, why do you keep staring at me so intently?' This honest man said: 'I'll gladly tell you if you, as the fine man you are, promise not to tell that I've told you.' So I promised him. Then he said to me: 'You should know that that filthy priest, Ser Filippo, not too many days ago went around bragging about the shrewdness of his brother Sbietta, saying that he had sold his farm to an old man for the course of his natural life, who wouldn't last out the whole year. You are mixed up with some real rascals, so do your best to live as long as you can, and keep your eyes open, for you will need them: I don't want to say any more.'

104. Strolling through the market, I met Giovanbatista Santini, and he and I were taken to supper by the priest; as I said before, it

was around four hours before sunset, and it was on my account that we were eating at such an early hour, for I had said I wanted to return to Trespiano in the evening. Because of this they hastily arranged everything, with Sbietta's wife working very hard, and among the others present was a certain Cechino Buti, their accomplice. After the salads were made and we began to sit down at the table, this evil priest, with a certain wicked little laugh of his, said: 'You must forgive me, for I cannot have supper with you because a matter of great importance to my brother Sbietta has come up. As he's not here I have to take his place.' We all begged him but could not change his mind: off he went, and we began to eat. After we had eaten the salads out of certain common platters, they began to give us boiled meat, and a bowl arrived for each person. Santino,* who was sitting opposite me at the table, said: 'They're giving you all different crockery from what they're giving to the rest of us: now have you ever seen anything more beautiful?' I told him I had not noticed. He also told me I should call Sbietta's wife to the table, for she and that Cecchino Buti were running back and forth, both bustling about in an extraordinary fashion. Finally I begged the woman so persistently that she came; she complained, saying to me: 'You didn't like my cooking, for you've eaten very little!' After I had praised the supper many times, telling her that I had never eaten with greater appetite, or a better dinner, I finally said that I had eaten precisely what I required. I would never have imagined why that woman was putting so much pressure on me to eat. After we had finished supper it was already less than three hours to sunset, and I was anxious to return that evening to Trespiano in order to go to my work in the Loggia on the following day. So I said goodbye to all, thanked the woman, and left. I had not gone three miles when I it seemed to me my stomach was in flames, and I was in such torment that I felt it would take a thousand years to reach my farm in Trespiano. As God willed it I arrived during the night, but only with great difficulty, and I immediately prepared to go to bed. I never got to sleep during the night, and in addition my bowels kept moving, which forced me to go to the toilet several times, until, when daybreak came, I felt my anus burning and turned around to see what it was: I found that the cloth was all covered with blood. I at once imagined I had eaten something poisonous, and over and over again I asked myself what it might have been: I remembered how Sbietta's wife had given me those plates, bowls, and saucers which were different from the others, and how that evil priest, Sbietta's brother, had worked so hard to do me such honour and then had not wanted to have supper with us; and then I recalled how the priest had said that his brother Sbietta had struck such a great bargain when he sold a farm to an old man for the rest of his natural life, a man who would never live out the year: for his words had been repeated to me by that honest man Giovanni Sardella. So I concluded that they had given me a pinch of sublimate* in a bowl of sauce (which had been very well made and was very pleasing to eat), because sublimate causes all those symptoms that I saw I had; but although I am in the habit of eating few sauces or spicy condiments with meat, other than salt, I did happen to eat two little mouthfuls of that sauce, since it was so good and tasty. I went on to remember how many times Sbietta's wife kept on urging me in one way or another, telling me to eat that sauce: so that I knew for absolutely certain that they had given me a small dose of sublimate with that sauce.

105. Even though I found myself very ill, I still went to work at the Loggia on my giant: I was so sick that a few days later this violent illness overcame me, so that I was confined to my bed. As soon as the Duchess heard I was sick she had the work to be done on that unfortunate piece of marble freely given to Bartolomeo Ammannati, who sent Messer —— to tell me that I could do what I liked with the model I had begun, for he had won the marble. [This Messer —— was one of the lovers of the wife of Bartolomeo Ammannati; and because he was both kind and discreet, he was the most favoured, and this Ammannati gave him every opportunity]—and on this topic there would be a great deal to say.* Nevertheless, I do not want to be like Bandinelli, his master, who in his arguing raised issues irrelevant to our profession;* suffice it to say that I said I had always foreseen this, and that I told Bartolomeo that he should work hard so that he could prove himself grateful to the fortune that had so undeservedly bestowed so much favour upon him. And so I unhappily stayed in bed, and I put myself in the care of that most excellent man, Master Francesco da Monte Varchi, the physician, and along with him I was being treated by the surgeon, Master Raffaello de' Pilli,* because that sublimate had burned out the guts of my bowels so that I could not keep my bowels from running. Once Master Francesco recognized that the poison had done its worst, since it had not been enough to

overcome the strength of the sound constitution he found I had, he said to me one day: 'Benvenuto, thank God, for you've won; and have no doubts, for I want to cure you just to spite the scoundrels who wanted to do you harm.' Then Master Raffaellino said: 'This will be one of the finest and most difficult treatments ever known: you should know, Benvenuto, that you've eaten a mouthful of sublimate.' When he heard these words Master Francesco interrupted him, and said: 'Perhaps it was some poisonous caterpillar.' I said I knew for absolutely certain what poison it was and who had given it to me: and then we all fell silent. They attended to my treatment for more than six whole months; and it was more than a year before I felt on top of things.

106. At this time the Duke went to make his entry into Siena,* and Ammannati had gone several months before to construct the triumphal arches. A bastard son of Ammannati remained in the Loggia, and he had pulled up some of the curtains that were hanging over my model of the Neptune, for since it was not completed I had kept it covered. I immediately went to complain to My Lord Don Francesco, the Duke's son, who seemed to like me, and I described to him how my statue had been unveiled while it was still incomplete, and told him that I would not have minded if it had been finished. To this the Prince replied, nodding rather menacingly, and said: 'Benvenuto, don't worry about it being unveiled, for that just does them even more injury; but if you would be happier for me to have it covered up again, I shall have it done immediately.' And along with these words, His Most Illustrious Excellency added many other remarks that were very favourable to me, in the presence of many noblemen. Then I said that I begged His Excellency to give me the means to complete it, for I wanted to make a present of it, along with the little model, to His Excellency. He answered that he would gladly accept both the one and the other, and that he would provide me with all the assistance I asked for. And so I fed upon this small show of favour, which had the effect of saving my life: because I saw my strength declining, from so many immeasurable evils and misfortunes that befell me all at once. This small degree of favour comforted me with some hope of going on.

107. A year had already passed since I had taken the Farm of the Fountain from Sbietta, and besides all the unpleasant things done to me, both the poison and their other robberies, when I saw that this

farm did not produce for me half of what they had promised, and that besides the contracts I possessed a written document in the hand of Sbietta, who had bound himself before witnesses to maintain the previously mentioned income for me, I went to the Lords of the Council; for at that time Messer Alfonso Quistello* was alive and was the Fiscal Chancellor; he met with the Lords of the Council, and the councillors were Averardo Serristori* and Federigo de' Ricci:* I don't remember all their names, but there was also someone from the Alessandri family; it is enough to say that they were a group of very influential men. Now, after having set forth my arguments to the magistrates they all, with one voice, wanted this Sbietta to return my money, except for Federigo de' Ricci, in whose service the said Sbietta was at the time: so that they all made their apologies to me that Federigo de' Ricci wished to keep them from expediting the case; among them was Averardo Serristori along with the others, although he made a great fuss about it, and so did the man from the Alessandri family. But when this Federigo had so delayed the case that the magistrates' mandate had expired, Serristori found me one morning after they came out into the Piazza of the Annunziata, and without a care for anyone he said, in a loud voice: 'Federigo de' Ricci has so much more power than all the rest of us that you've been destroyed against our will.' I do not want to add anything to this point, because it would be too offensive to the person who holds supreme power in the government; suffice it to say that I was destroyed by the will of a rich citizen, solely because that sheep-farmer was in his employ.

108. The Duke was in Livorno, and I went to find him simply to ask for my dismissal. Feeling my strength return, and seeing that I was not being employed in any way, it grieved me to do so much harm to my studies; so that, making my mind up, I went off to Livorno and there I found the Duke, who gave me a most agreeable welcome. And since I stayed there several days, I went riding with His Excellency every day and had all the time I needed to say everything I wanted to say, for the Duke would leave Livorno and ride four miles along by the seashore, where he was building some fortifications. To avoid being bothered by too many people he liked me to chat with him, so that one day, when I saw he was showing me special favour, I began talking about Sbietta, that is, Piermaria d'Anterigoli, and I said: 'My Lord, I want to recount to Your Most

Illustrious Excellency an amazing affair, through which Your Excellency will learn why I was prevented from completing my clay Neptune which I was working on in the Loggia. I must tell Your Most Illustrious Excellency how I had purchased a farm for the course of my natural life from Sbietta.' It was enough for me to outline all the details, never staining the truth with falsehoods. When I reached the part about the poison, I said that, if I had ever been a good servant in His Most Illustrious Excellency's opinion, rather than punishing Sbietta or those who gave me the poison he should give them some reward: because the poison was not strong enough to kill me, but it was, nevertheless, powerful enough to purge me of a deadly catarrh, an inflammation in my stomach and my intestines. 'Which has had such an effect that, while I remained as I was, I might have lived three or four years, and this type of medicine has worked so that I think I have gained at least twenty more years of life; for which, with greater devotion than ever, I thank God still more. And so, what I've sometimes heard some people say is true, when they say: "God sends us evil to do us good."' The Duke listened to me for more than two miles of the journey, always paying close attention; all he said was: 'Oh, what evil people!' I concluded by saying that I was obliged to them, and took up other, more pleasant topics. I waited for an appropriate time, and when I found the Duke in an agreeable mood, I begged His Most Illustrious Excellency to grant me leave to depart, so that I would not throw away several years while I was still capable of working on something, and I said that as for what was still owed me for my Perseus, His Most Illustrious Excellency could give me what he pleased. And along with these reasons, I overflowed with much elaborate politeness and expressions of thanks to His Most Illustrious Excellency, who did not respond to me in any way at all but, on the contrary, seemed to show signs that he had taken this very badly. On the following day Messer Bartolo Concino,* a secretary of the Duke's, and among the most important of them, ran into me and said, in a half-threatening way: 'The Duke says that if you want his permission to leave he will give it to you; but if you want to work he will put you to work: and may you be able to do as much as His Excellency gives you to do!' I answered him that I did not desire anything but to work, and especially for His Most Illustrious Excellency, more than for all the rest of the men in the world, whether they were popes, emperors, or kings: I would more willingly serve His Most Illustrious Excellency for a penny than all the others for a ducat. Then he said to me: 'If you are of this opinion, you and the Duke are in agreement without saying anything further; so return to Florence and be of good cheer, for the Duke wishes you well.' And so I returned to Florence.*

109. As soon as I was in Florence, a certain man named Raffaellone Scheggia, a weaver of golden cloth, came to see me, and he said to me: 'My dear Benvenuto, I want to settle your dispute with Piermaria Sbietta.' To this I answered that no one except the Lords of the Council could settle the dispute, and that in this session of the Council Sbietta would not have a Federigo de' Ricci who, for a gift of two fat kids and without caring either for God or his own honour, was willing to hold back such a wicked suit and do so ugly a wrong to holy reason. After I had made these remarks, along with many others, this Raffaello told me, still in a very kindly way, that it was much better to eat a thrush in peace than to win the fattest capon in such a long war, even if one was certain of getting it. And he told me that the course of lawsuits was such that they sometimes went on forever, and that I would do much better by spending this time on creating some beautiful work, for which I would acquire much greater honour and much greater profit. Recognizing that he was telling the truth, I began to lend an ear to his words, so that he soon settled the dispute in this fashion: Sbietta would lease the farm from me for seventy gold scudi a year for the entire duration of my natural life. When we were about to sign the contract, which was drawn up by Ser Giovanni, the son of Matteo da Falgano, Sbietta said that the way we had calculated it would involve paying the most tax, but that he would not back out—'and so, it would be good for us to make this lease for five years at a time'—and that he would keep his promise without ever again reopening any more lawsuits. And so that scoundrel of a priest, his brother, promised me the same thing, and after that was settled we made a contract for five years.

110. Although I want to discuss some other matters, and abandon for a moment the recounting of this endless roguery, I am first bound to describe what happened with this five-year lease; for once it expired these two scoundrels did not want to keep any of the promises they had made, but rather they wanted to return their farm to me and no longer wished to lease it. Because of this I began to complain, and they waved the contract under my nose, so that as a

result of their bad faith I could do nothing to help myself. Once I saw this, I told them that the Duke and the Prince of Florence would not allow men in their cities to be ruined in such a wicked fashion. Now, the terror of this was so effective that they sent the same Raffaello Scheggia who drew up the first contract back to me; and they said that they did not want to give me the seventy gold scudi as they had done for the past five years: to this I responded that I would accept nothing less. This Raffaello came to see me, and he said: 'My dear Benvenuto, you know that I'm on your side: now they have entrusted the whole matter to me.' And he showed me some document in their handwriting. Since I did not know he was a close relative of theirs, this seemed to be perfectly acceptable to me, and so I placed myself completely and entirely in his hands. This fine fellow came to see me one evening half-an-hour after sundown in the month of August, and, with a great deal of talk, he compelled me to draw up the contract, solely because he knew that if he put it off until morning, the trick he wanted to play on me would not have succeeded. So the contract was drawn up, and they were to give me sixty-five scudi in coin* for the lease, in two instalments per year, for the rest of my natural life. And despite the fact that I struggled against this and did not want to accept it on any account, this Raffaello showed the writing in my own hand, with which he convinced everyone to say I was in the wrong; and he was saying that he had done everything for my own good, and that he was on my side; and since neither the notary nor any of the others knew he was their relative, they all said I was in the wrong: for this reason I soon gave in, but I shall try to live as long as possible. Shortly after this I made another mistake, in the following year during the month of December 1566. I bought half the farm of Poggio from them—that is, from Sbietta—for two hundred scudi in coin; it adjoins on that first one, my Farm of the Fountain, and it was to revert to them in three years, while I gave it back to them on a lease. I did this with the best intentions. I would have to make too long a digression in my writing if I wanted to describe the great cruelties they inflicted upon me; I want to place it entirely and completely in the hands of God, Who has always defended me from those who have wished to do me harm.

111. I had completely finished my marble Crucifix, and it appeared to me that, by raising it upright and setting it up some armslengths above the ground, it would look much better than if I

kept it on the ground. And although it did look fine, when I set it up it looked so much better that I was very pleased with it; and so I began showing it to anyone who wished to see it. As God willed, it was mentioned to the Duke and the Duchess, so that when they had returned from Pisa the two of Their Most Illustrious Excellencies, with all the nobility of their court, came to my house unexpectedly one day, for the sole purpose of seeing the Crucifix: it pleased them so much that the Duke and Duchess never stopped praising me, and consequently all those lords and gentlemen who were in their presence did the same. Now when I saw that they were extremely satisfied, I began to thank them most graciously, telling them that having been stopped from working on the marble for the Neptune had been the real cause of my having executed such a work, one that no one before me had ever attempted. And although it had taken a greater effort than I had ever before endured, it seemed to me to have been well expended, and especially since Their Most Illustrious Excellencies had praised me so highly for it; and since I could never believe it would be possible to find anyone who would be more deserving of the Crucifix than Their Most Illustrious Excellencies, I would gladly make them a present of it.* I only begged them that, before they left, they should do me the honour of visiting the ground floor of my home. Upon hearing my courteous words they immediately rose and left my workshop, and when they entered my house they saw my little model of the Neptune and of the fountain, which the Duchess had never seen before that moment. When the Duchess saw them they had such a powerful effect upon her that she immediately uttered a cry of indescribable astonishment, and turning to the Duke, she said: 'I swear on my life, I have never imagined the tenth part of such beauty.' In response to her words the Duke kept saying: 'Oh! didn't I tell you?' And so they discussed it between themselves for a good long while, to my great credit; then the Duchess called me over and, after offering me many words of praise by way of excusing herself—since in the course of her remarks she showed that she was almost begging my pardon—she then said she wanted me to have a block of marble excavated suitable for my needs, so that I could set to work on it. To these kindly words I said that, if Their Most Illustrious Excellencies gave me the means, I would most gladly set myself to work on such a difficult undertaking out of love for them. To this the Duke quickly replied, and said: 'Benvenuto, you shall be given all the assistance you can ask for, and besides this, what I shall give you on my own account will be of much, much greater value.' And with these pleasing words they went away, and left me feeling very happy.

112. After many weeks had passed and nothing more was said about me, when I saw no orders being given for me to do something, I was half desperate. At that time, the Queen of France sent Messer Baccio del Bene* to our Duke to request a loan; and the Duke most kindly assisted her, or so it was said. Since Messer Baccio del Bene and I were very close friends, when we recognized one another in Florence we most eagerly got together. So he told me all the great favours that His Most Illustrious Excellency had done for him, and while we were talking he asked me whether I had any great works in hand. Because of this I told him, as it had happened, the entire affair of the great Neptune and the fountain and the great wrong that the Duchess had done me. At these words, he told me, on behalf of the Queen, that Her Majesty had the greatest desire to complete the tomb of King Henry, her husband; he said that Daniello da Volterra* had undertaken to execute a large bronze horse and had already gone past the time when he had promised it to her, and that this tomb was to have the most splendid decorations. So, if I wanted to return to France to my castle, she would provide me with all the assistance I could ask for, provided that I was willing to serve her. I said to Messer Baccio that I would ask permission from my Duke, and that if My Most Illustrious Excellency was satisfied, I would gladly return to France. Messer Baccio cheerfully said: 'We'll return together;' and he considered it settled. And so on the following day, when he was speaking with the Duke, my name came up in the conversation: so that he told the Duke that the Queen would engage my services if he was willing. To this request the Duke replied at once and said: 'Benvenuto is the magnificent man the entire world knows, but he no longer wants to work;' and they took up other issues. The next day I went to see Messer Baccio, who repeated everything to me. At this I could no longer stop myself, and said: 'Oh if, after His Most Illustrious Excellency gave me nothing to do, I created on my own account one of the most difficult works that has ever been made by anyone in the world, and it cost me more than two hundred scudi, which was paid for out of my poverty; oh! what would I not have done if His Most Illustrious Excellency had put me to work! I tell you truly that he has done me a great wrong.' The kind

gentleman repeated to the Duke everything I had said in reply. The Duke told him that he had been joking, and that he wanted me for himself: and as a result I insisted on leaving, on numerous occasions. The Queen did not wish to discuss it any longer to avoid upsetting the Duke; and so I remained, very discontented.

113. At this time the Duke left with his entire court and all his children, except for the Prince, who was in Spain.* They went through the marshes of Siena, and by that route they went to Pisa. That bad air poisoned the Cardinal before the others:* so that after a few days he was attacked by a pestilential fever that quickly killed him. He was the apple of the Duke's eye: a handsome and good man, and his death was a tremendous loss. I let a few days pass until I thought their tears had dried; and then I set off for Pisa.*

EXPLANATORY NOTES

3 *I write*: the original manuscript of *My Life* (Manuscript Mediceo-Palatino 2342 in the Biblioteca Mediceo-Laurenziana in Florence, Italy) contains this autograph sonnet on its first page, although some translations of the work omit it. After the sonnet and the opening declaration in Cellini's hand, manuscript pages 1–460b are written in the hand of his scribe; pages 464b to 520a, the last page, are again in Cellini's hand. Some pages contain additions and corrections in Cellini's hand, as well as suggested emendations added by others. An alternative title of the work, crossed out by Cellini on the manuscript, was: 'In the Name of the Living and Immortal God, The Life of Benvenuto Cellini: Goldsmith and Sculptor, Written by His Own Hand.'

In the flower of this worthy Tuscan land: that is, in Florence. Cellini's reputation as a writer clearly rests upon his prose, not his poetry. Generations of scholars have even claimed that the second quatrain of the poem makes little or no grammatical sense in the original Italian, even though Cellini had submitted his manuscript with its important opening sonnet to the literary critic Benedetto Varchi (1503–65) without receiving such a negative judgement of either his Tuscan grammar or his meaning. The editor of the critical edition we follow in this translation, however, suggests at least two interpretations of the poem, the second of which we have accepted as the only one that makes logical or grammatical sense. See Lorenzo Bellotto (ed.), *Benvenuto Cellini, La vita* (Parma: Fondazione Pietro Bembo, 1996), pp. xliv–xlviii.

Michele Goro from Pieve a Groppine: in a document dated 29 July 1557, Cellini entrusts his writings to this man. Pieve a Groppine is in the Arezzo area near Terranuova Bracciolini.

I dictated: recent scholarship casts doubts on Cellini's description of how his autobiography was nonchalantly dictated while he was working in his studio; for this argument, see Paolo L. Rossi, '*Sprezzatura*, Patronage, and Fate: Benvenuto Cellini and the World of Words', in Philip Jacks (ed.), *Vasari's Florence: Artists and Literati at the Medicean Court* (Cambridge: Cambridge University Press, 1998), 55–69, 263–5.

5 *those things of special merit*: Cellini uses the term *le virtù* to refer to the special qualities that might be associated with a heroic deed, a useful action, or even an artistic creation, which exhibited exceptional skill, ingenuity, or ability and brought outstanding results. The term in Machiavelli's political thought refers to the special skill and ability exhibited by a leader, who succeeds in establishing order, stability, or new successful institutions in a civil society.

such a fine undertaking: in this passage, Cellini links the presumably heroic composition of his autobiography not only to the impressive deeds that mark his life (mentioned in the opening sonnet) but also to the magnificent artistic works he has created. In fact, his *Trattato dell'oreficeria* or the *Treatise on Goldsmithing* speaks of 'such a fine undertaking,' (*una cotale bella impresa*) in referring to this specific art in its introduction. See Benvenuto Cellini, *I trattati dell'oreficeria e della scultura*, ed. Carlo Milanesi (Florence: Felice Le Monnier, 1857; repr. 1994), 6; for an English translation, see Benvenuto Cellini, *The Treatises of Benvenuto Cellini on Goldsmithing and Sculpture*, trans. C. R. Ashbee (New York: Dover, 1967).

5 *continue to grow older*: while some scholars consider this an unfinished sentence in the Italian original, Bellotto notes in his critical edition (p. 8) that Cellini's contemporaries would not have felt so, since they followed grammatical rules that did not yet conform to the reforms instituted by Pietro Bembo in the same century. We have made the syntax conform to modern English practice.

Giovanni Villani writes: Villani (*c.*1275–1348) was a Florentine businessman, political figure, and historian associated with several of the most powerful of the medieval city's banking firms. His *Cronaca* (*Chronicle*, first published in 1537–54) covers the history of Florence from its legendary past to the year 1346, and is a major source for information about the city from Dante's time to the Black Plague of 1348. It appears to have been one of Cellini's favourite books (he reads it in prison), probably because Villani's historiography presents a vast historical drama of divine justice in which human sin is inevitably punished by retribution.

can still be seen: Villani refers to the remains of some of the Roman buildings which were still visible in early Florence (a coliseum and the baths). The Capitol and temple (now the baptistery of San Giovanni) were located in what is now the city centre.

the Rotunda: a name that came to be given to the Pantheon in Rome. Cellini found the story about the temple of Mars, which was transformed into the baptistery, in Villani.

6 *two miles from Montefiascone*: Cellini found this reference to a commander by the name of Fiorino in Villani (I, 34); the *Istorie fiorentine* (*Florentine Histories*, II, 2) by Niccolò Machiavelli (1469–1527) also mentions him. Cellini invents the notion that this man came from the town of Celleno (about 14 km. from Montefiascone in the area around Viterbo), and that he was the founder of his own family.

'Let us go to Fiorenze': Florence is *Firenze* in modern Italian. This explanation for the foundation and naming of Florence is, of course, completely invented by Cellini. He embellishes his life-story with such archetypal details from the lives of literary heroes in a completely self-conscious fashion.

on the flowing Arno: here, Cellini argues that the Italian word for 'Florence' (*Firenze*) does not derive from the word for 'flowing' (*fluente*). Such a plausible etymology for the name of Florence had already been advanced by both Vespasiano da Bisticci (1421–98) in his work *Le vite d'uomini illustri del secolo XV* (*Renaissance Princes, Popes and Prelates*, published only in 1839) and by Machiavelli (*Florentine Histories*, II, 2).

and in this state: the Grand Duchy of Tuscany, successor to the republican city-state of Florence.

in the ring: in tournaments, contests of single combat were normally held in an area enclosed by a fence of some kind. Vicorati is near Florence.

of exceptional ability: given Cellini's notorious penchant for brawling and physical violence, it is not surprising that he claims to have fighting men, rather than artists, in his family tree.

7 *which is not yet a subject of great importance*: this passage has bothered some critics, since Cellini seems to be stating that his artistic contributions are of little value. Hence, we translate the line to reflect what we assume to be Cellini's view that his artistic triumphs have simply not occurred at this point in time. We agree that it would be remarkable for the most boastful artist of the Italian Renaissance to imply that his work was of little value, since in fact the entire autobiography is a paean to Cellini's artistic genius.

Val d'Ambra: in the western part of the territory near Arezzo.

in Via Chiara: Cellini was born at no. 6, near what is today an open market for leather goods near San Lorenzo Cathedral.

through this craft: Andrea was a bricklayer or mason, but during the Italian Renaissance many artisans practised the skills of architecture without receiving any special training in that science. Indeed, few distinctions were made between artists, architects, and other craftsmen, especially in the early years of the Renaissance.

experience in music and good design: like many artists of his day, Cellini was familiar with the *De architectura* or *Ten Books of Architecture* by Vitruvius, whose Latin treatise was rediscovered in 1414 and circulated after 1487 in various printed editions; Leon Battista Alberti (1401–72) was primarily responsible for popularizing Vitruvius' work in his *De re aedificatoria* (*Ten Books of Architecture*, begun 1449, printed 1485). The passage in Vitruvius is probably I. i. 8: 'qui se architectum profiteatur . . . litteratus sit, peritus graphidos, musicam scierit.'

8 *a bit irascible*: Cellini must have inherited his grandfather's temperament.

my father's mother: Cosa, the diminutive form for Niccolosa, was born in 1499 and, like many women of the time, died very young in 1528.

in the year 1500: actually the birth happened not on 2 November but on Tuesday, the 3rd. An unusual birth and concern with the naming of a child are typical topoi in the literature celebrating the birth of great heroes and artistic geniuses. See e.g. the description of the birth of Michelangelo or other major figures in the history of Italian Renaissance art in *The Lives of the Artists* (1st edn., 1549–50; definitive edn., 1568) by Giorgio Vasari (1511–74).

9 *let him be welcome [benvenuto]*: in Italian, this is a play on words, as Cellini's father says 'e sia il Benvenuto', or 'let him be welcome', to explain how he came to be called Benvenuto.

Realizing it was a scorpion: Cellini calls the animal both a 'nice crab' and a 'scorpion'. Both animals, as Rossi notes, are related to Cellini's astrological signs: the crab (Cancer) is his ascendant sign, and the scorpion (Scorpio) is his dominant sign. Throughout the autobiography, Cellini claims that the negative influence of the stars was the cause of many of his misfortunes. See Rossi, '*Sprezzatura*, Patronage, and Fate', 67.

10 *is a salamander*: the ancients considered the salamander capable of living within a fire without being destroyed by it, and medieval bestiaries transmitted this folklore to the Renaissance (Petrarch, Michelangelo, and other poets employ the salamander as a popular poetic image); it is significant that Cellini's future patron, the French monarch Francis I (1494–1547), employed the salamander and an Italian motto ('Nutrisco al buono, stringo el reo'—'I nourish the good and destroy the bad') as his *impresa* or symbol.

the flautists of the Signoria: the republican government of the city-state of Florence, the Signoria, was composed of fewer than ten elected officials. These officials were housed in the Palazzo della Signoria or what came to be called the Palazzo Vecchio (the 'Old Palace'), after the Medici family, who had seized control of what had become the Grand Duchy of Tuscany, moved their residence to the Palazzo Pitti in the sixteenth century. Apparently, the city government paid musicians to perform at various official functions.

Lorenzo de' Medici and his son Piero: Cellini refers to Lorenzo 'Il Magnifico' (1448–92) and his son Piero dei Medici (1471–1503), the latter of whom was forced to flee Florence in 1494 when republican rule was restored to the city after an anti-Medicean revolution.

the seven virtues: that is, the three theological virtues (Faith, Hope, Charity) of Christianity and the four cardinal virtues (Justice, Prudence, Fortitude, Temperance) of classical antiquity. These virtues were often represented by personifications in artistic works.

11 *quoquo me verto stat virtus*: Cellini feels obliged to provide an Italian paraphrase (though not a literal translation) of his father's Latin motto because his imaginary audience was probably unfamiliar with literary Latin.

the major guilds of the silk and wool trade: in republican Florence before the Grand Duchy of Tuscany was established, the *Arti maggiori* or major guilds (at first twelve, then seven in number) and the *Arti minori* or minor guilds (at first nine, then fourteen of them) not only offered a means to acquire wealth, but membership in them was obligatory before political participation was allowed in the city's republican form of government, since the republican city-state was based upon an economic oligarchy. Guilds should not be confused with modern unions, since guilds were controlled by the owners of wool or silk manufacturing or trading businesses, not the humble workers they employed. Workers were not allowed guild membership, and therefore lacked access to governmental participation as well. The guilds devoted to wool and silk were among the most ancient and venerable of them all, since the trade in such textiles was in large measure the foundation of Florentine economic prosperity. Florentine banks were initially developed in order to foster the manufacturing and trading of such textiles. The Italian word *arte* meant 'guild' (thus the Arte della Lana was the Wool Guild), not 'art', and only came to be associated with 'art' as the social status of the Renaissance craftsman was exalted in the sixteenth century. In good part, works like Cellini's autobiography, or the even more influential *Lives of the Artists* by Vasari, helped to raise the Renaissance painter or sculptor from the humble status of artisan or craftsman to the more exalted position of artist or, in the case of a Promethean figure such as Michelangelo, artistic genius.

when Piero was sent into exile: Piero de' Medici was driven out of Florence on 9 November 1494, after he had ceded Pisa and Livorno to King Charles VIII of France.

the magnificent Piero Soderini: Piero di Tommaso Soderini (1452–1522) became Gonfaloniere or Standard-bearer of the Florentine Republic, and served from 1502 until he was driven out in 1512 by pro-Medici factions within the city who had allied themselves with foreign troops. Niccolò Machiavelli's service in politics was in Soderini's government, and he too was exiled from power when Soderini fell from grace.

some of the old priors: the *Signori* or Priors were guild members elected by the districts into which the city was divided; they made up the political body that formed the council or priorate that, together with the *Gonfaloniere*, ruled Florence.

until the Medici returned: on 4 November 1512.

who later became Pope Leo: when Giovanni de' Medici (1475–1521), the son of Lorenzo Il Magnifico, was elected to the papacy in 14 March 1513 to succeed Pope Julius II, he took the name Leo X.

12 *decorated it very beautifully*: as Christopher Hibbert notes in his *The House of Medici: Its Rise and Fall* (New York: Morrow, 1975), there are a number of explanations for the Medici coat of arms: the balls may have represented the cupping glasses of doctors or apothecaries (as their name suggests) or, possibly, coins to symbolize the trade of the pawnbroker.

Iacopo Salviati: the husband of Lucrezia de' Medici, Lorenzo il Magnifico's elder daughter, Jacopo was elected Standard-bearer in 1514.

away from him: his father's problems with the Medici family foreshadow the many difficulties Cellini would later have with his Medici patrons in Florence.

12 *From Pinzi di Monte*: Michelangelo Brandini actually came from Gaiole in Chianti, part of Sienese territory, rather than from the Pizzidimonte, a small town near Prato. He was the son of a blacksmith, not a charcoal vendor. As the reader will soon discover, Cellini's arch-enemy at the Medici court was Baccio Bandinelli (1488–1560), whose true name was Brandini, which he changed in 1530 when Charles V bestowed upon him the knighthood of San Jacopo. At the time Baccio claimed falsely that he was a relative of the noble patrician family from Siena, the Bandinelli, in order to receive the knighthood. This award provoked a number of satirical barbs directed at Cellini's adversary.

13 *Marcone the goldsmith*: Antonio di Sandro di Paolo Giamberti.

I had a brother: Giovanfrancesco or Giovanni Francesco, called Cecchino Cechino del Piffero (1504–29).

the father of Duke Cosimo: Giovanni de' Medici (1498–1526), the military leader known as Giovanni delle Bande Nere; his son Cosimo (1519–74) became duke and later Grand Duke of Tuscany when Pope Pius V gave him the title in 1569.

14 *the Eight*: the *Otto di guardia*, composed of eight judges, was an important tribunal in the city that administered criminal and civil law, with its seat in the Bargello Palace.

Master Francesco Castoro: a goldsmith from Lucca who worked at the Duomo of Siena.

who later became Pope Clement: Giulio de' Medici, the natural son of Giuliano de' Medici (killed in the Pazzi conspiracy of 1478), was elected to the papacy as Clement VII (1523–34).

15 *on the street of Our Lady of Baraccan*: Cavalletti worked in the Cathedral of San Petronio, Bologna's famous central cathedral, from 1519 to 1523; the street is the present Via del Baraccano.

17 *marvellous Signor Giovannino de' Medici*: Giovanni delle Bande Nere, the father of Duke Cosimo I.

who he thought was lost: in this passage of *My Life* dealing with his brother Cecchino and himself, Cellini injects the biblical story of the Prodigal Son to embellish the story of his life, much as he had made his own father something of a biblical prophet in his dealings with Piero.

18 *Master Ulivieri della Chiostra*: Ulivieri di Filippo della Chiostra, a Pisan goldsmith who worked at the Duomo of Pisa from 1513 to 1515.

the Campo Santo: the Campo Santo near the Pisan Duomo (or main cathedral) and the leaning tower date from 1278. This graveyard is famous for the remains of frescos painted there in the fourteenth and fifteenth centuries.

19 *gold and silver sweepings*: like the frugal Tuscans they all were, Cellini and his colleagues were careful to gather up all the filings, shavings, and fragments of metal, coral, ivory, and other precious materials used in

their trade in order to recover some of the costs of the original materials.

20 *Piero Torrigiani*: Torrigiani (1472–1528), a Florentine who worked for King Henry VIII in England and executed the tomb of Henry II in Westminster Abbey (1518) before moving to Spain, where, pursued by the Inquisition, he reportedly died by suicide in prison. Torrigiani was originally exiled from Florence after a fight with Michelangelo Buonarroti, whose nose he broke.

Michelangelo Buonarroti: Florence's most famous artist and Cellini's idol (1475–1564). Cellini hoped his own works in metal would be compared favourably with Michelangelo's marble sculpture.

a cartoon of the most divine Michelangelo: the cartoon is one made in 1504 for the fresco of the *Battle of Cascina*, and it does not refer to the eventual capture of Pisa in 1406. (The so-called Battle of Cascina was actually a minor skirmish which took place in 1364 between the Pisans and the besieging Florentines.) Michelangelo made the cartoon in preparation for the frescos in the Palazzo della Signoria commissioned by the Standard-bearer Piero Soderini. It became so famous that, along with a similar preparatory drawing done by Leonardo da Vinci for the same palace at the same time, it was copied by numerous artists. Both the original drawing and the copy by Cellini have been lost. The subject-matter of the preparatory drawings was less important to the Florentine artistic community than were the brilliant solutions of various technical problems involved in large paintings.

the first beautiful work: actually this was Michelangelo's first *painting* commissioned by a public patron (in this case, the republican government of Florence); he had already completed a number of major sculptures for public sites, including the *Pietà* for St Peter's in Rome (1497–99) and the *David* (1501–4) for the Piazza della Signoria, now in the Accademia Museum in Florence.

as one could possibly imagine: Leonardo (1452–1519) did not actually select the theme of the fresco; it was given to him and Michelangelo by the Florentine government. Leonardo's painting represented an episode in the Battle of Anghiari (1440) between the Florentines and the Milanese. The work has not survived but drawings of it remain.

the rooms of the Pope: Michelangelo's cartoon was in what is now known as the Palazzo Medici-Riccardi, while Leonardo's was placed in the Pope's quarters inside the Church of Santa Maria Novella.

the great chapel for Pope Julius later on: the Sistine Chapel, the frescos on the vault of which were commissioned by Julius II and painted in 1508–12; later, in the same chapel, Michelangelo painted the *Last Judgement* (1534–41) for Paul III.

21 *from Masaccio's chapel*: the Brancacci Chapel in Santa Maria del Carmine, frescoed by Masaccio between 1424 and 1428, was studied by many

great Italian artists of the Renaissance. Some drawings by Michelangelo from this chapel have survived.

21 *as long as he lives*: in his *Lives of the Artists*, Vasari also reports this anecdote in his biography of Torrigiani, but he attributes Torrigiani's action to his jealousy of Michelangelo's talents, not to his anger over being mocked while at work sketching in the chapel.

Michelangelo's beautiful style: like Vasari, the word Cellini employs for 'style' is *maniera*, from which is derived the period term 'Mannerism', itself largely inspired by Michelangelo's works. Cellini can best be described as a Mannerist in his own artistic production.

a most excellent painter: Giovanfrancesco Lippi (1501–?), son of Filippino Lippi (*c*.1457–1504)—the painter who had completed some of the unfinished frescos left by Masaccio in the Brancacci Chapel, and had painted the Carafa Chapel in Santa Maria sopra Minerva in Rome. He was also grandson of the famous Fra Filippo Lippi (*c*.1406–69).

a certain Giambattista: Giambattista Tasso (1500–55), one of the most skilled wood-carvers of his day, who executed the ceiling designed by Michelangelo for the Laurentian Library in Florence; he also designed the Loggia of the New Market (1547–51) in Florence.

22 *at the San Piero Gattolini Gate*: this is the present Porta Romana—the gate one must take when leaving Florence to go towards Rome. Its earlier name derives from a church, now demolished, that stood near the gate.

horse that is making a return journey: post-horses being returned to their original stables were often rented out at very low prices in order to have them returned without much expense.

the same age as the century: in 1519.

from Firenzuola in Lombardy: Giovanni de' Giorgis, who came from Fiorenzuola d'Arda in the Piacentino territory (not the better-known town of Firenzuola near Florence), was an officer in the goldsmiths' guild in Rome.

23 *Giannotto Giannotti*: Giannotto was the brother of the historian Donato Giannotti (1492–1573), who was a great friend of Michelangelo and one of the important historians of the sixteenth century in Italy. In some respects, Donato Giannotti and Benvenuto Cellini share certain features as writers: both came from humble artisan origins and both produced important works of historical and literary value written in the Florentine vernacular.

of the door of the Rotunda: the Pantheon in Rome (now actually a church called Santa Maria della Rotonda). The word Cellini employs here to describe the object (*cassonetto*) is not found in any other text of the sixteenth century: some scholars have translated it as 'cup', others as 'casket' or 'oblong box'. It would have been shaped something like a Roman urn.

Master Pagolo Arsago: Paolo d'Arzago was a member of the goldsmiths' guild who had his shop near the church of Sant'Eligio (the patron saint of goldsmiths) in Rome; documents attest to his activity around 1521–2 and to his death by 1563.

24 *Master Antonio da San Marino*: Antonio di Paolo Fabbri, called Antonio di San Marino, a goldsmith who worked in Rome and eventually became one of the heirs of Raphael.

25 *called Salvadore and Michele Guasconti*: Salvatore and Michele were two cousins from a family of important goldsmiths in Florence who owned three workshops in the city. Cellini actually praises Salvatore's skill in his treatise on goldsmithing, declaring: 'Salvatore Guasconti was an all round man, more especially good in small things. His work in niello and enamel is well worthy of praise' (*The Treatises of Benvenuto Cellini on Goldsmithing and Sculpture*, 4).

26 *in the mantle and hood of well-bred people*: while Cellini's adversaries had on the normal clothing worn by craftsmen in their workshops, Cellini sported a Spanish-style cloak; in his day, anyone wearing such a garment who was not a soldier was considered to be a dissolute troublemaker.

Prinzivalle della Stufa: Pandolfo Prinzivalle della Stuffa (1489–1566), a follower of the Medici family who was part of an unsuccessful plot to overthrow Piero Soderini in 1510.

Fra Girolamo's faction: Girolamo Savonarola (1452–98), the Dominican reformer and political leader whose political treatise, *On the Constitution and Government of the City of Florence* (1498), attacked a narrowly olig-archic form of republican government in Florence (that practised by the Medici family). He was excommunicated by Pope Alexander VI in 1497 and burned at the stake in the Piazza della Signoria in the following year. Savonarola's political followers were called the *Piagnoni* or 'weepers', and were apparently still wearing the special garments with the oddly shaped hoods associated with his political movement some twenty-five years after the friar's execution. They constituted an important force in the 1527 revolt against Medici power after the Sack of Rome that restored the republic for a few short years, until Medici control was reaffirmed in 1530. Although Cellini had numerous problems with his Medici patrons, he was no supporter of Medici opponents even though their populist ideas might well have appealed to artisans such as he. The fact that a Medici supporter managed to save Cellini from harsher punishment by the Eight underlines how the struggles between supporters of the Medici and their adversaries permeated every aspect of daily life in Cellini's Florence, even the sentencing of a citizen for a minor scuffle.

as harshly as possible: Cellini actually says *a misura di carboni* or 'meas-ured out like charcoal'; this means literally in abundance or a great deal, and refers to a time when wood charcoal was relatively cheap and, there-fore, would be doled out without too much attention paid to the precise measure.

four bushels of flour: the records of the Eight reveal that the punishment was higher: Cellini was fined twelve bushels of flour, not four. For an indispensable study of the archives regarding the many scrapes Cellini had with the law during his lifetime, see Paolo L. Rossi, 'The Writer and the Man: Real Crimes and Mitigating Circumstances: *Il caso Cellini*', in Trevor Dean and K. J. P. Lowe (eds.), *Crime, Society and the Law in Renaissance Italy* (Cambridge: Cambridge University Press, 1994), 157–83.

26 *Convent of the Murate*: today a prison, the Convent of SS Annunziata delle Murate was in Cellini's day a nunnery associated with the Franciscan rule.

27 *the father of Messer Librodoro Librodori*: in a document written on 18 December 1570, Cellini names Librodoro Librodori as the executor and heir to his will.

28 *any harm whatsoever*: actually, according to period documents, Cellini wounded both Gherardo and Bartolomeo Salvatori, who had rushed to Gherardo's aid. The incident occurred on 13 November 1523.

for my circumstances or for my actions: Cellini was actually condemned to death on 13 November 1523, but on 20 February 1527 peace was made between Michele and Gherardo Guasconti, on the one hand, and Cellini and his father on the other. Cellini was certainly no stranger to brushes with the law: on 14 January 1523 (the same year that witnessed this fight with the Guasconti family), he was forced to pay another twelve bushels of flour for 'libidinous acts' with Giovanni Rigogli committed against a certain Domenico di Giuliano da Ripa. See the previously cited article by Russo, 'The Writer and the Man'.

to the country with the lancers: that is, he would be sent with the troops outside of town to be hanged. As Russo (ibid. 163) notes, executions in Florence were normally carried out at least 1000 braccia (armslengths or yards) outside the city walls.

Piero di Giovanni Landi: the son of an important Florentine banker and one of Cellini's most faithful friends.

29 *Messer Benedetto da Monte Varchi*: Benedetto Varchi—critic, historian, and academician—whose *Florentine History*, begun in 1527 at the request of Duke Cosimo, treated the period 1527–38, precisely the years when Medici hegemony over Florence was re-established. Varchi was a good friend of Cellini's, and it is not surprising that in one of his books on language, *The Dialogue of Ercolano* (1570), he defends the supremacy of the Italian vernacular over Latin. Varchi echoes the opinion of Giambattista Gelli (1498–1563), one of Cellini's contemporaries, who was a popularizer and an educator and who, like Cellini, wrote numerous literary works in the Italian vernacular. Gelli was trained as a shoemaker, but like Cellini he became a talented master of Italian prose style.

the Paglia river: one of the streams running into the Tiber near Orvieto.

Pope Clement: Cardinal Giulio de' Medici was elected to the papacy in November 1523 as successor to Adrian VI, taking the name Clement VII (d. 1534).

Master Santi, a goldsmith: this figure has been identified with Santo di Cola, a Roman goldsmith who also served as mace-bearer to the Pope.

called Luca Agnolo: Luca Agnolo was apparently one of Master Santi's assistants. According to the custom of the times, a goldsmith's workshop could be inherited by someone not skilled in the profession so long as the shop was managed by an artisan who met the guild's criteria for membership.

the Spanish Bishop of Salamanca: Don Francisco de Cabresa y Bodadilla (d. 1529); the bishop came to Rome in 1517 for the Lateran Council and remained until the Sack of Rome in 1527, when he fled with Pope Clement VII to refuge inside the Castel Sant'Angelo. None of the works Cellini made for this prelate has survived. In fact, nothing made by Cellini before 1528 has survived.

and nicknamed 'Il Fattore': Giovan Francesco Penni (1488–c.1528), called 'Il Fattore' or 'The Artisan', was an assistant of Raphael and subsequently of Giulio Romano (c.1499–1546); Penni's talents, while less than those of Romano, were nevertheless sufficient to cause Raphael to bequeath his workshop to Penni and Romano together. Penni was best known for his grotesque figures and designs (a very popular style at the time, following the discovery of similar figures in the classical ruins of the Emperor Nero's Domus Aurea). See also note to p. 53.

30 *in Michelangelo's chapel*: the Sistine Chapel.

Agostino Chigi from Siena: Agostino Chigi (1465/6–1520), who made his fortune as the church's banker, was not only extremely wealthy but was also a grand patron of the arts in Rome. His palazzo on what is today Via della Lungara was built by Baldassarre Peruzzi between 1508 and 1511. The building contains famous frescos by Peruzzi, Sodoma, Sebastiano del Piombo, and Raphael. In 1580 the palace passed to Cardinal Alessandro Farnese, and from that time on has been called 'La Farnesina'.

Messer Gismondo Chigi: Sigismondo Chigi, the younger brother of Agostino, married Sulpicia Petrucci in 1507; she was the daughter of Pandolfo Petrucci, the lord of Siena during the period before the city-state was absorbed into the Grand Duchy of Tuscany.

that I sketched far too well to be a goldsmith: during Cellini's entire career he wished to be considered an artist of the highest aspirations, such as his idol Michelangelo or Raphael, but his originally chosen profession (goldsmithing) was usually considered a more menial craft or trade. While it is certainly true that the sixteenth century witnesses the birth of the figure of the artist and the rise of the artist above the artisan in terms of social standing, wealth, and status, some aspects of artistic life were still less valued than others. Much of the drama of Cellini's life stems from the fact that, while he considered himself equal to all other artists, it was not uncommon for other artists or patrons to denigrate his talents because of his artistic origins as a goldsmith.

30 *Madonna Porzia*: Porzia was the younger sister of Sulpicia Petrucci. Here, Cellini's narrative seems to make a fundamental error: the wife of Chigi is definitely Sulpicia, to whom Cellini is speaking; when the Roman noble lady descends the stairs, the woman to whom Cellini has been speaking, and who is commissioning the resetting of the golden lily, suddenly becomes Porzia. It is difficult to understand why either Cellini or Benedetto Varchi did not catch this error.

31 *better by one half than the model*: here Cellini means to say that he has promised to make the reset jewel *twice* as beautiful as the original setting.

33 *twenty-five scudi di giuli*: this was a silver coin minted in Rome in honour of Pope Julius II (1503–13); ten giuli ('giulios') corresponded to one ducat, and the 'scudi di giuli' were worth roughly nine to ten giuli.

at least half again as much as his: once again, Cellini employs this expression to mean that his wages were double his opponent's.

34 *Raphael from Urbino*: the painter, Giovan Francesco Penni.

Master Giovanpiero della Tacca: a goldsmith of whom little is known, except that he may have belonged to either the Crivelli or the Carpani family.

35 *gods in the heavens*: In the original, Cellini shifts gears in mid-sentence and his syntax is faulty. The first dependent clause is left dangling. We have modified the sentence somewhat, to make it syntactically correct in English.

he might have pushed them further off the deep end: while Cellini is careful to call what the Greeks wrote about beautiful young boys 'foolish remarks', he nevertheless implies that his Paulino would surpass figures such as Ganymede in their beauty.

than the Faustina about whom the ancient books are always rattling on: Faustina, the wife of the Roman Emperor Marcus Aurelius, was famous for her beauty and infamous for her lustfulness.

that a certain Gianiacomo: Giangiacomo Berardini, an artisan who did inlaid work (*intarsia*) and who was the leader of the Pope's fife players.

our Duke: Cosimo I de' Medici.

for the Pope's celebration of Ferragosto: Ferragosto in Italy is the feast of the Assumption, which was celebrated in Cellini's day on 1 August rather than the 15th, as it is today.

the Belvedere: actually the gardens and courtyard built for Pope Julius II that connected the Belvedere Palace with the Pope's residence in St Peter's.

36 *scudi di Camera*: that is, scudi from the papal treasury.

38 *You Marrani*: this was a particularly offensive insult to the Spanish, who employed the word to refer to Jews and Muslims who pretended that they had converted to Christianity. We have left the word here to under-line the fact that Cellini knew Spaniards well enough to appreciate how to

offend them. A good English equivalent for 'Marrani' might be 'swine', since these animals were considered unclean by both Jews and Muslims.

the jennet: a small but agile horse of Spanish origin.

the painter: Giovan Francesco Penni.

39 *a third like Cancer*: that is, they looked like animals (a lion, a scorpion, and a crab, the species that symbolize these signs of the Zodiac).

Cardinal Cibo: Innocenzo Cibo Malaspina (d. 1550), Archbishop of Genoa and the son of Maddalena de' Medici, the sister of Pope Leo X.

Cardinal Cornaro . . . Cardinals Ridolfi and Salviati: Marco Cornaro (d. 1524), Venetian nobleman and the son of Giorgio Cornaro, the brother of the last Queen of Cyprus, Caterina Cornaro; Niccolò Ridolfi (d. 1550), a Florentine who was one of Michelangelo's patrons; and Giovanni Salviati (1490–1553), another Florentine and the son of Jacopo Salviati (see note to p. 12). None of Cellini's work for these patrons is extant.

40 *Gabbriello Ceserino*: Gabriello Cesarini, the *Gonfaloniere* or Standard-bearer of Rome, a high government official.

Leda and the swan: in Greek mythology, Leda (the wife of Tyndareus, King of Sparta) was loved by Zeus, who came to her by the river in the form of a swan.

the Feast of St John: St John the Baptist is the patron saint of Florence. His feast-day is celebrated on 24 June.

Rosso the painter: Giovanni Battista di Jacopo, called Il Rosso Fiorentino (1495–1540); like Cellini, Rosso eventually went to France, where he died. He was one of the most important artists at the court of Francis I.

a pupil of Raphael of Urbino: the same Giovan Francesco Penni referred to earlier.

one of Rienzo da Ceri's soldiers: Lorenzo Orsini, the lord of Ceri (d. 1528), was one of the *condottieri* employed after 1515 in the Pope's service and head of the papal militia.

41 *and delivered from my opponent*: the original Italian phrase ('restando dal mio avversario') has been interpreted in two entirely different ways, either as indicating that the duel ended with the opponent's withdrawal (our choice), or that Cellini actually fled from his opponent, an intriguing possibility but one that seems to contradict both his normal arrogance and bravado and the rest of the sentence. It is difficult to believe that Cellini would state that he came out of the affair with much honour if he had been the one to run away.

man from Perugia by the name of Lautizio: Lautizio Rotelli (d. 1527), who worked for the Mint of Perugia until about 1518 and is mentioned in Cellini's *Treatise on Goldsmithing* (XIII). There, Cellini says: 'In my time in Rome, that was about 1525, there was a certain master from Perugia, called Lautizio, who practised nothing else but the making of seals for the bulls of cardinals. These seals are about the size of a ten-year-old child's hand, and they are made in the shape of an almond. The cardinal's title is engraved on them, usually in the form of a rebus, or allegorically. Lautizio used to get at least 100 scudi for each seal he made' (*The Treatises of Benvenuto Cellini on Goldsmithing and Sculpture*, 61).

41   *his coat of arms*: rather than the normal coat of arms belonging to a family or clan, the designs on a cardinal's seals were usually episodes or symbols linked to the specific Roman church to which their cardinal's office was attached.

42   *Messer Caradosso*: Cristoforo Foppo, called Il Caradosso (*c.*1452–*c.*1527) was from Pavia and worked as a goldsmith and a minter of coins. In Rome, Il Caradosso worked for a number of popes (Julius II, Leo X, Clement VII), and executed, among other works, the bronze doors of San Giovanni in Laterano, as well as a famous tiara for Julius II that was subsequently destroyed.

   executed some 'Pace' tabernacles: these were silver objects in the shape of a tabernacle that were kissed by the faithful before the Eucharist in substitution for the kiss of peace; they were often decorated with religious imagery connected with the Passion of Christ.

   Amerigo: Amerigo Righi (1420–91), of whom Cellini declares in the *Treatise on Goldsmithing* that he 'was far and away the first craftsman in it either before or after his time. He too, great as he was, made use of the designs of Antonio del Pollaiuolo' (*The Treatises of Benvenuto Cellini on Goldsmithing and Sculpture*, 2).

43   *by nature melancholy*: it was a common belief during the Renaissance, thanks in large measure to remarks by Vasari in his biographies of artists, that a melancholic disposition derived from one of the body's four humours was a natural state for the visual artist.

44   *large beans used in political ballots*: very often in communal elections in Florence and other city-states, votes were cast originally by beans and later by small balls or *palline*.

   tying up the three-faced Cerberus: one of the Twelve Labours of Hercules was the capture of Cerberus, the guard-dog posted at the gate of Hades.

   Master Iacomo da Carpi: Giacomo Berengario da Carpi (1470–1530), a doctor from Bologna and professor of surgery at the university there from 1502 on; he was one of the first to fight syphilis with medicines containing mercury. An important prelate paid this doctor with a major painting for his services, as Vasari relates: 'Raphael painted a Saint John on canvas for Cardinal Colonna, who bore a great love for the painting because of its beauty, and when he was struck down by an illness, the doctor who cured him, Messer Jacopo da Carpi, asked for the painting as a gift, and since Messer Jacopo wanted it, the cardinal, who felt he was under an endless obligation to him, gave it up, and it is now in Florence in the possession of Francesco Benintendi' (Vasari, *The Lives of the Artists*, trans. Julia Conaway Bondanella and Peter Bondanella (Oxford: Oxford World's Classics Paperback, 1998), 329).

the French disease: around the end of the fifteenth century, the 'great pox' or venereal disease was a scourge widespread in Europe. According to some accounts—for example, the widely circulated *History of Italy* (1561–4) by Francesco Guicciardini (1483–1540)—the disease had been carried back from the Americas by the crew of Christopher Columbus. The most virulent kind of pox eventually became known as syphilis. The origin of the word 'syphilis' is a Latin poem by Girolamo Fracastoro (1478–1553) entitled *Syphilis or the French Disease* (1530), in which a shepherd named Syphilis offends Apollo and is the first human being to be stricken by the disease. For a treatment of the subject, see Claude Quétel, *History of Syphilis* (Cambridge: Polity Press, 1990). In general, each nation blamed one of its traditional enemies for importing the disease (thus, for the Italians and the English syphilis was the 'French' disease; in France, it was sometimes called the 'Italian' disease; others blamed it on the Spanish or the English).

45 *Duke of Ferrara*: Alfonso I d'Este (1476–1534), the patron of the poet Ludovico Ariosto, author of the *Orlando Furioso*, and noted for his generosity.

those vases: Cellini's syntax is defective here, reflecting the rush with which he narrates the doctor's deception. Instead of 'he wanted those vases' the clause should read, 'he must give him those vases'.

Messer Alberto Bendedio: a nobleman from Ferrara at Alfonso I's court, who is discussed later (II, 6).

46 *journeyed many miles*: an erotic metaphor frequently employed by such writers as Giovanni Boccaccio.

the fat cow, and the little one: that is, Faustina and her serving girl.

Cardinal Iacoacci: Domenico di Cristofano Jacobacci (d. *c*.1528), a member of a Roman noble family, appointed cardinal in 1517 by Leo X.

how can I go back to the Cardinal again?: the doctor was naturally afraid of exposing the prelate to the plague.

47 *Giovanni Rigogli*: in 1523 Rigogli and Cellini were fined by the Eight of Florence for 'obscene acts'.

by the Count dell'Anguillara called Cervetera: either Flaminio dell'Anguillara or his son Averso; the place is Cerveteri.

so many months ago: see I, 26.

48 *was a sculptor named Michelangelo*: Michelangelo di Bernardino di Michele (*c*.1470–1540), who worked on the tomb of Pope Adrian VI (1524) at the Church of Santa Maria dell'Anima in Rome, following designs by Baldassarre Peruzzi (1481–1536).

the painter Giulio Romano and Gian Francesco: Giulio Pippi, called

Romano (*c.*1499–1546), the best of Raphael's students; Gian Francesco is the same Gianfrancesco Penni mentioned previously (pp. 34, 38, 40).

48 *bring along his 'crow'*: Cellini actually employs the word *cornachia* or crow; he means a paramour or mistress.

Il Bachiacca: Francesco di Ubertino Verdi (1494–1557), a pupil of Perugino, well known for the tapestry designs he created for the Medici family.

49 *Antinous*: the extremely handsome young lover of the Emperor Hadrian; after his death in AD 130 Hadrian erected altars, temples, and statues all around the empire in his memory.

50 *'also women'*: Cellini actually employs both a masculine (*Angeli*) and feminine form (*Angiole*) of the word 'angel' in Italian.

51 *a certain Aurelio Ascolano*: perhaps Eurialo d'Ascoli, an improviser of verse in Greek and Latin who had such important literary friends as Pietro Aretino (1492–1556) and Annibale Caro (1507–66).

52 *the dead Pope Adrian*: Adrian VI, a Flemish pope who was in office from January of 1522 until September of 1523. He was the last non-Italian pope elected until Pope John Paul XXIII from Poland ascended the throne of St Peter in the twentieth century.

the Marquis of Mantua: Giulio left Rome in October 1524 to work for Federico II Gonzaga in Mantua.

'grotesques': as Cellini explains, the discovery of Roman interiors underground in the fifteenth and sixteenth century, especially Nero's Domus Aurea and the baths of Diocletian and Titus, revealed rooms called 'grottos' after the walls decorated by paintings or frescos—i.e. grotesques—of fanciful plant and animal figures.

54 *this troubled life of mine*: see the first line of the sonnet that opens Cellini's autobiography.

when a young man named Luigi Pulci: not Luigi (1432–84), the famous poet and author of *Il Morgante*, but his grandson; the poet's son and this man's father, Jacopo Pulci, was executed for incest in Florence on 15 November 1532.

the French pox: syphilis.

Piloto: Giovanni di Baldassarre, called 'Il Piloto' (1460–1536), a Florentine goldsmith and sculptor, who is a protagonist in several tales from Anton Francesco Grazzini's collection of novelle entitled *Le cene* (*The Suppers*, 1549).

55 *called Bishop Gurgensis*: Girolamo Balbi (1470–1555), a Venetian humanist and church diplomat who was sent on many diplomatic missions by the Roman Curia. At the Diet of Worms in 1521 he was named Bishop of Gurck or Gorizia (in Latin, Gurgensis). Bishops and cardinals were frequently known by the name of the town or church to which their office was attached.

57 *the Prati district*: the zone around the Castel Sant'Angelo (still known by this name today) was in Cellini's time a green area full of fields, as the name implies.

named Canida: probably a diminutive form of Candida (but used by Cellini, according to all his editors, because of its similarity in pronunciation to the word *cagna* or bitch).

behind the Banchi: this was the Via dei Banchi (now Via Banco Santo Spirito), so named because of the many benches the merchants employed in their banking. When Cellini established his own workshop, he eventually located it in this zone of the city, which was also associated with the Florentines living in Rome. In fact, the Florentine Church in Rome, San Giovanni dei Fiorentini, is across the street Cellini mentions and on the Tiber's banks.

'pal': the exact word Cellini employs is *compare*, which can mean anything from godfather or sponsor at a baptism to friend, crony, accomplice, or confederate. Especially in the south of Italy (and frequently in *The Decameron* of Giovanni Boccaccio), it is used as a form of friendly address.

a certain Messer Benvegnato: Benvegnato Narducci.

58 *By God's arsehole*: while the manuscript is almost illegible at this point, scholars claim that 'per lo cul di Dio' is a typical example of Perugian blasphemy and is the phrase cited by Cellini here. Some earlier translations (Cust, for example) omit the word 'arsehole'.

59 *already at war*: in 1521 war broke out between Francis I of France and the Emperor Charles V. The wars between these two rivals would last until 1559.

Giovanni de' Medici: Giovanni delle Bande Nere (1498–1526), the cousin of Pope Clement VII and the leader of a group of mercenary soldiers in the papacy's employ. Giovanni's soldiers were brought to the city to protect the pope from his bitter enemies in the Colonna family, who had been exiled from Rome by the Pope. Because of the mercenary troops' behaviour, the Pope sent most of them away, and this contributed to his inability to protect himself during the Sack of Rome in 1527.

60 *already died in Lombardy*: Giovanni delle Bande Nere was killed on 25 November 1526 at Governolo near Mantua, in a battle with German troops under the command of Charles V. Cellini wrote a sonnet on the occasion of his death.

Borbone: Charles de Bourbon (1490–1527), cousin of Francis I who, after quarrelling with the French king, passed into the service of Charles V; he died during the Sack of Rome while commanding the imperial forces. For a detailed account of the Sack of Rome and its historical protagonists, see André Chastel, *The Sack of Rome, 1527* (Princeton: Princeton University Press, 1983).

Alessandro: Alessandro del Bene, the son of Piero del Bene; Piero was a rich merchant, one of the pope's bankers, and one of Cellini's patrons.

60 *the Colonna came back to Rome*: on 19 September 1526 members of the exiled Colonna family, led by Cardinal Pompeo Colonna, attacked the Vatican and the area around it known as the Borgo, and forced the Pope to sign an accord with Charles V.

appeared outside the walls of Rome: on 5 May 1527 Charles de Bourbon and Georg von Frundsberg brought some 40,000 troops to the city gates. The next day they began their attack. As Chastel points out, the imperial army consisted of some three groups: around 10,000 lansquenets led by von Frundsberg (all Lutherans and violent opponents of the papacy); some 6,000 *tercieros*, Spanish troops whose cruelty had become legendary after they sacked Prato in 1513; and a third group of Italian soldiers led by *condottieri* or mercenary soldiers of fortune, such as Fabrizio Maramaldo, Marc'Antonio Colonna, and Ferrante Gonzaga. This third group lived entirely on pillage and extortion, since they received no wages, while the first two groups were held in check during the invasion of Italy only by the promise of sacking Rome as their eventual reward.

the Campo Santo: the German cemetery near the Vatican.

61 *one of our shots had killed Borbone*: Francesco Guicciardini's account of the Sack of Rome claims that Charles de Bourbon was killed early in the conflict (actually on the morning of 6 May) by a shot from an arquebus (*History of Italy*, XVIII). The fog that morning, described by other historians, makes it difficult to determine who killed him but lends credence to Cellini's account.

Signor Orazio Baglioni: for Lorenzo Orsini, see note to p. 40; Orazio Baglioni (1493–1528) was the son of Giovan Paolo Baglioni and a member of the most important family of Perugia; Baglioni assumed command of the Bande Nere after the death of Giovanni de' Medici, and the pope entrusted to him the defence of the city when the imperial army reached the city gates.

Captain Pallone de' Medici: perhaps a reference to a certain Marcello Pallone, a Roman soldier who years later was in the Medici's service.

the retinue of the Castello: because Cellini was inscribed in the group of Clement VII's fife players, he had the right to take refuge within the Castel Sant'Angelo.

the corridors: the elevated passageways between the Vatican and the Castel Sant'Angelo (originally Hadrian's tomb) still exist.

62 *Messer Antonio Santa Croce*: this individual is mentioned by a number of documents and sixteenth- and seventeenth-century historians (Guicciardini, Scipione Ammirato) as being an artillery captain during the Sack of Rome.

called the Angel: this site took its name from the marble statue of an angel placed at the highest point of the Castel Sant'Angelo. Executed by a friend of Cellini's, Raffaello da Montelupo (1505–57), it was replaced by a bronze statue in 1740.

For an entire month: from 6 May to 5 June 1527; although Clement VII officially surrendered on 5 June 1527, he remained a prisoner inside the Castel Sant'Angelo until December, when he escaped in disguise.

63 *the Duke of Urbino*: Francesco Maria della Rovere (1491–1538), a relative of Pope Julius II and at the time Captain-General of the Venetian militia.

help from the Duke never came: the Duke of Urbino and his Venetian army did attempt to stop the imperial troops, but without success.

in this diabolical business of mine: Cellini means that artillery is literally an affair of the devil; several Renaissance thinkers (Ariosto, in particular) speak of gunpowder and firearms in this fashion as something fundamentally different from other and supposedly more 'humane' sorts of weapon.

Cardinal Ravenna and Cardinal de' Gaddi: Benedetto Accolti (1497–1549) from Arezzo, Archbishop of Ravenna after 1524, was named cardinal in 1527 and appointed Papal Legate to the Marches in 1532. Later, under Pope Paul III, he fell into disfavour and was sentenced to death for treason but later pardoned. Niccolò Gaddi (named cardinal in 1527; died in 1552) was a member of one of the oldest and noblest of Florentine families, Bishop of Fermo, and Papal Legate to France. Following the Sack of Rome, Gaddi tried to re-establish republican rule in Florence after the assassination of Alessandro de' Medici, but without success.

the Torre de' Bini: actually the tower of the palace owned by the same Bene family to which Alessandro Del Bene belonged.

64 *Cardinal Farnese*: Alessandro Farnese (1468–1559), originally elevated to the rank of cardinal by Alexander VI in 1493 and subsequently elected pope in 1534, taking the name Paul III. He and his family eventually became Cellini's nemesis in Rome, and this incident foreshadows future difficulties.

for causing the Sack of Rome: Farnese believed Salviati was at fault because he had advised the Pope to dismiss the mercenary soldiers guarding the city.

65 *the cause of even worse*: 'one of them' refers to Salviati; Farnese is the individual who will be even more disastrous to the papacy, not to mention the fact that he and his family (especially his son Pier Luigi) will later become Cellini's implacable enemies and plot to imprison him.

[. . . better if I had killed him]: in the original manuscript the entire passage enclosed in brackets from 'Would to God' to 'better if I had killed him' has been cancelled. Perhaps Cellini thought better of putting into print his opinion of one of Rome's most powerful families.

66 *in that cruel, hellish place*: note Cellini's earlier characterization of firing artillery as a 'diabolical business' (see note to p. 63).

the Santo Spirito gate: a large gate near a church by the same name.

67 *whose name was Gian di Urbino*: Giovanni d'Urbino (d. 1529), a captain in the Spanish army known for his bravery and cruelty.

Cavalierino: probably Niccolò Vespucci, a member of the famous Florentine family that produced Amerigo (the origin of the name America), one of the favourites of Pope Clement. He is portrayed in Giulio Romano's Vatican fresco, *The Baptism of Constantine*. Cellini's statement that Vespucci was a Frenchmen is obviously an error, although many Florentines lived and worked in France, as Cellini would do later.

Filippo Strozzi: Giovanni Battista Strozzi (*c.*1489–1538), known as Filippo, a member of one of Florence's noblest families and one of the richest men of his time, having served as the administrator of papal finances under Leo X and Clement VII. He later participated in the uprising against Medici rule in Florence made possible by the Sack of Rome in 1527. Held captive by Cosimo I, he eventually died in prison, perhaps by suicide.

68 *the Prince of Orange*: Philippe de Châlons, Prince of Orange (*c.*1500–30); after leaving the service of Francis I this soldier passed into the army of his enemy, Charles V; he became the commander of the imperial militia after the death of Charles de Bourbon and earned the title of Viceroy of Italy. He was actually eventually killed near Pistoia in a skirmish with Francesco Ferrucci, the *condottiere* commanding Florentine republican forces, during the siege of Florence in 1530.

69 *Cardinal Orsino*: Francesco or Franciotto Orsini, named cardinal in 1518 (d. 1534). At the time of Cellini's cannon shot he was heading the negotiations between the forces of Charles V and the papacy.

the peace accord was signed: under the terms of the agreement signed on 5 June 1527, Cardinal Orsini and four other cardinals were taken as hostages, while Pope Clement VII remained a prisoner inside the Castel Sant'Angelo, until he escaped in disguise on 8 December 1527.

that had been placed on me in Florence: Cellini needed to pay a sum of money to lift the ban imposed upon him in 1523 during his scuffle with the Guasconti family (see I, 17–18), which resulted in his exile in Rome and other places.

70 *Cosa*: her full name was Niccolosa (d. 1528).

my other, younger sister: her name was Reparata.

Bartolomeo: he was more likely a stone-cutter or mason; like Cosa, he died in the plague of 1528.

71 *the Duke of Mantua*: Federigo II Gonzaga (1500–49), the son of the celebrated Isabella d'Este, was actually a marquis at the time but received the title of Duke of Mantua in 1530. Nominally allied with the papacy, he had in fact allowed the imperial troops to pass the Po river on his way to the Sack of Rome, and was later rewarded by being appointed captain of the imperial troops in Italy (1529). Subsequently, he received the title of Duke from Charles V, who made two important visits to Mantua in 1530

and 1532. Giulio Romano, who had worked for the Pope, came to Mantua in 1524, and, filling it with mythological and historical frescos, made the Duke's Palazzo del Tè into one of the most beautiful palaces in Italy.

at a place called Tè: the decoration of the palace, of which Romano was also the architect, was begun in 1524 and finally completed in 1542.

by Longinus: according to legend, Longinus was the Roman soldier who thrust a lance into Christ's side to certify that he was dead on the cross; he supposedly was later converted to Christianity and was believed to have carried to Mantua a vial filled with earth from Golgotha that had been soaked with the blood of the crucified Christ. As a result of this legend, Longinus became the patron saint of Mantua (along with St Andrew).

to the Cardinal, his brother: Ercole Gonzaga (1505–63), Bishop of Mantua and cardinal after 1527. He would preside over the concluding sessions of the Council of Trent.

pontifical seal: this seal, for which he received 200 ducats, depicts the Ascension of the Virgin with the Twelve Apostles; it is mentioned in Cellini's treatise on goldsmithing (ch. XIII).

by the quartan fever: that is, malaria, then sometimes called the 'quartan fever' because its symptoms were intermittent fevers followed by a spasm or convulsion every four days.

72 *Governo ... Lord Giovanni was killed*: actually Governolo, where Giovanni delle Bande Nere met his death in battle (see I, 34).

no more than two hours!: that is, I hope you die within two hours.

named Mona Andrea de' Bellacci: 'Mona' was the polite term of address for a married woman (from Madonna) at this time, the feminine equivalent of 'Messer'.

Giovanni Rigogli: the same man condemned along with Cellini for 'obscene acts' according to a sentence of the Eight in 14 January 1523.

Bertino Aldobrandi: the favourite pupil of Francesco Cellini, Benvenuto's brother, who was killed in a duel in 1530.

73 *during that delightful wedding meal*: Cellini apparently means to imply that this meal not only celebrated his return but also his sister Liperata's second marriage (just before she had shed tears for the members of the family lost to the plague, including her first husband and their child).

Piero di Giovanni Landi: see I, 18.

the Medici had been chased out of Florence (that is, Signor Ippolito and Signor Alessandro . . .): on 17 May 1527 anti-Medici forces proclaimed a second republic that lasted until August 1530, when the Medici returned. The Sack of Rome had loosened the Medici hold over Florence, since Clement VII was of the Medici family and was using papal power to bolster Medici rule in his native city. Ippolito dei Medici (1511–55) was the illegitimate son of Giuliano, Duke of Nemours; he became cardinal at the age of 18. Alessandro de' Medici (1512–37) was the natural son either of Lorenzo, Duke of Urbino, or of Giulio de' Medici (who became Pope Clement VII). He was declared Duke of Florence in 1532, and was subsequently assassinated by his cousin Lorenzino.

73 *Girolamo Marretti*: Marretti is also mentioned in Cellini's *Treatise on Goldsmithing* (ch. XII).

the lion's mouth: the Twelve Labours of Hercules became a popular theme for Renaissance medals, as well as fresco painting. Cellini's theme on the medal for Marretti represented the first of the Twelve Labours: a lion that terrorized the citizens of Nemea was invulnerable to normal weapons, forcing Hercules to kill it by ripping its jaws apart.

this praise was invaluable: in ch. XII of *The Treatise on Goldsmithing* Cellini is more specific about Michelangelo's praise, quoting his reaction as follows: 'If this work were made in great, whether of marble or of bronze, and fashioned with as exquisite design as this, it would astonish the world; and even in its present size it seems to me so beautiful that I do not think ever a goldsmith of the ancient world fashioned aught to come up to it!' (*The Treatises of Benvenuto Cellini on Goldsmithing and Sculpture*, 48). This medal is no longer extant.

Federigo Ginori: this individual is praised in ch. XII of Cellini's *Treatise on Goldsmithing* for his aesthetic judgement and patronage of the arts.

74 *Giuliano Bugiardini*: a Florentine artist (1475–1554) who studied with both Ghirlandaio and Piero di Cosimo; he was one of Michelangelo's assistants in the painting of the Sistine Chapel ceiling, and is remembered chiefly for his *Martyrdom of Saint Catherine* in the Rucellai Chapel in Santa Maria Novella (Florence).

Summa tulisse juvat: translations suggested for this motto range from the literal—'I like carrying the heaviest weights'—to the more abstract—'I like supporting the highest things' or 'It is pleasant to support sublime things'. In his *Treatise on Goldsmithing* (ch. XII) Cellini gives an even more detailed account of the work, noting that the motto was suggested by Ginori because he was of lowly rank and in love with a woman of higher social status. The difference in social class between the lover and his lady might suggest the less literal translation.

Messer Luigi Alamanni: Luigi Alamanni, poet and humanist (1495–1556), best known for a didactic poem in blank verse in imitation of Virgil's *Georgics* called *La coltivazione* (*Agriculture*, 1546). One of those many fascinating literary figures that Florence was to produce during Cellini's lifetime, he was a great friend of Machiavelli, who made him one of the interlocutors in *The Art of War* and dedicated his *Life of Castruccio Castracani* to him. Alamanni also attended the meetings of the young republican intellectuals of Florence at the Orti Oricellari, and was deeply involved in an unsuccessful conspiracy against the Medici in 1522. After Medici power was restored in Florence in 1530 he was forced into exile to France, where he enjoyed the patronage of Francis I, Henry II, and

Catherine de' Medici. After Ginori's death, the Atlas medal fell into Alamanni's possession; it was taken with him to France and was given to Francis I, who asked to meet Cellini as a result. Cellini and Alamanni will meet again at the French court.

Pope Clement . . . Florence: as part of the peace treaty Clement VII signed with Charles V on 29 June 1529, the Emperor sent his troops to restore Medici power in Florence, and the siege of Florence began in October of 1529, lasting until 12 August 1530, when the Medici were finally restored.

Master Iacopino della Barca: a weaver and master craftsman who created designs of flowers, foliage and ornaments engraved on tablets to be transferred and woven into fabrics.

75 *I would have ended up very badly*: as an artist, Cellini needed his patrons in the aristocracy and in the church, but as a citizen of a republican city-state, his patriotic duties sometimes clashed with his economic interests. Cellini's situation was not unusual, for both he and Michelangelo found themselves at this moment in a republican Florence controlled by anti-Medici forces, while they had both enjoyed or would later enjoy Medici patronage. Michelangelo even organized the city's fortifications, and was forced to hide after the city fell to the Medici troops until he received a pardon from the Pope.

76 *Raffaello del Moro*: a well-known Roman goldsmith who worked on numerous occasions for the Pope; he receives praise in several places in Cellini's *Treatise on Goldsmithing*.

(this was Maundy Thursday): Holy Thursday—'Maundy' Thursday, as it is traditionally known in England—is the day before Good Friday. The term 'Maundy' derives from a Latin phrase linked to the ceremony of footwashing (*Mandatum novum*, 'a new command', in John 13: 34). As Cellini is about to confess to the Pope that he has stolen some of the gold he earlier melted down during the Sack of Rome, it is fitting for him to meet the Pope on a day that recalls Christ washing the feet of the disciples, since the Pope traditionally imitated Christ's act and was expected to be in a humble, generous mood in imitation of Christ.

the Archbishop of Capua: Nikolaus von Schomberg (1472–1537), a Dominican from Saxony who was once a disciple of Savonarola, and later became one of Clement VII's most trusted counsellors. Pope Paul III made him a cardinal in 1535.

77 *the two holidays*: Good Friday and Easter Sunday.

78 *I went off like a shot*: the button or clasp (also known as a morse) for the Pope's cope was, by every account of it, an extraordinary work of art. Sir John Pope-Hennessy's discussion of the work in *Cellini* (London: Macmillan, 1985), 47–9, is invaluable in understanding why Cellini's technique on this piece was so strikingly original. As Pope-Hennessy notes, the technique of Caradosso (Cellini's predecessor; see note to p. 42)

began with a wax model like Cellini's, but Caradosso first cast the piece in bronze and then applied the gold to the bronze relief; sections in high relief were worked up, and two kinds of solder were used to attach them and to repair defects in the gold's surface. This was a very slow and painstaking process. Cellini dispensed with the bronze model and began work directly on the gold, employing the wax model as a guide. Chapters VII and XII of Cellini's *Treatise on Goldsmithing* actually provide a much more detailed description of the work than is offered in the autobiography. The diamond itself was reputed to be the second largest in the world. Cellini's morse was tragically destroyed in 1797 when, under the terms of the Treaty of Tolentino, it was melted down to cover the cost of the indemnity that Pope Pius VI was forced to pay Napoleon. Pope-Hennessy points out that the morse is the first major work by Cellini for which documents exist: before the piece was melted down, an Italian draughtsman, Francesco Santi Bartoli, did three beautiful coloured drawings of its back, front, and profile in 1729. The drawings are preserved in the British Museum in London.

78 *Micheletto*: Michele di Francesco Naldini or Nardini, a goldsmith who is recorded in the papal registry between 1513 and 1531.

79 *Pompeo*: Pompeo de' Capitaneis, goldsmith and *pesatore di zecca* (i.e. the person responsible for insuring the value of the metal in the papal coins). Cellini kills him in 1534.

Messer Traiano: Traiano Alicorni, a notary and cleric from Milan.

80 *the difference between my model and their drawings*: as Cellini himself notes in ch. VII of *The Treatise on Goldsmithing*, and as Pope-Hennessy explains in great detail (*Cellini*, 47), the original feature of Cellini's design was to employ the enormous diamond as a seat for the figure of God the Father, rather than placing the diamond in the breast of God the Father as the drawings did and as the Pope had originally requested.

five hundred papal golden ducats: he actually requests 500 'ducati d'oro di Camera', which would be the kind of coin minted by the papal treasury.

81 *Messer Tommaso from Prato*: Giovanni Tommaso de' Cortesi (1480–1543), a well-known jurist who was named by Clement VII to be the papal datary (the head of a branch of the papal chancery, the 'dateria', which was charged with the concession of dispensations, benefices, patents, petitions, etc.). He eventually became Bishop of Cosenza and Avignon and finally cardinal.

a gold doubloon: 'un doppione largo d'oro', or the double (from the Spanish *dobla*), of the value of two golden scudi.

the inscription 'Ecce Homo': 'Behold the man!' (John 19: 4–6), the words of Pontius Pilate to the Jews gathered after the flagellation and the crowning with thorns of Christ.

Unus spiritus et una fides erat in eis: 'one spirit and one faith were in them both'. This citation, from Ephesians 4: 5, refers to the recent accord between Clement VII and Charles V. As Pope-Hennessy notes (*Cellini*, 50), Cellini's account of the coins he produced for the Pope is confused in the autobiography, while it is more accurate in *The Treatise on Goldsmithing* (ch. XIV), where it is clear that Cellini made three coins for Clement VII: one gold coin with the 'Ecce Homo'; a second gold coin with the figure of the Pope and the Emperor as described here; and a third silver coin called a *doppio carlino*, which featured the head of the Pope on one side and St Peter on the other. Pope-Hennessy's *Cellini* reproduces the second and third of these coins in extremely clear plates (see plates 25–8). For other illustrations, see Charles Avery, *L'opera completa di Cellini* (Milan: Rizzoli, 1981).

the sculptor Bandinello: Baccio Bandinelli (1488–1560), sculptor and painter, who becomes Cellini's nemesis later on in the autobiography, was apparently known for his efforts to denigrate the work of other artists. His statue of *Hercules and Cacus* stands in the Piazza della Signoria of Florence, near the location where Cellini's *Perseus* would eventually rest. In addition to numerous Mannerist works of sculpture, Bandinelli also did the tombs for the Medici popes Leo X and Clement VII in Santa Maria Sopra Minerva in Rome. Bandinelli's artistic style becomes the target for ferocious attacks by Cellini in *My Life*.

his craft: in Bandinelli's case, sculpture. With his remarks to his future rival, Cellini underlines his aspiration to move from goldsmithing to sculpture early on in his career.

82 *a 'motto proprio'*: Cellini confuses his own petition for the position with the decree the Pope eventually pronounced. A decree spontaneously and directly announced by a ruler personally, or in his own words, was technically referred to as a *motu proprio* in Latin.

Master of the Dies of the Mint: this position was also called the *incisore*, and it included the responsibility for making the designs and dies for papal coins. Cellini obtained this position in 16 April 1529 and held it until January 1534.

83 *a certain Master Iacomo from Perugia*: Giacomo Rastelli (1491–1566), a surgeon at the papal court who treated Pope Pius III and Paul III, was on friendly terms with many of the city's artists and writers.

with a certain Messer Giovanni Gaddi: Giovanni di Taddeo Gaddi (1493–1542), dean of the Apostolic Chamber and member of a very prominent Florentine family; he had close relations with many artists and writers.

a very distinguished scholar: Giovanni has never been conclusively identified, although several suggestions have been made: Giovanni Battista Vergerio (d. 1548), who was actually not Greek but Istrian; Giovanni Andrea Vergerio, a sixteenth-century humanist known through several letters; or the diplomat and scholar from Constantinople named Giovanni Lascaris or Laskaris (1445–1534), who established himself in Rome after 1513.

83 *a Messer Lodovico da Fano*: an erudite poet who died in 1541.

Messer Antonio Allegretti: Florentine writer and friend of Luigi Alamanni and Annibale Caro.

Messer Annibal Caro: the secretary to the Giovanni di Taddeo Gaddi mentioned above, Annibale Caro (1507–66) later became secretary to Pier Luigi Farnese and Alessandro Farnese. He is remembered today for his classic blank-verse translation of Virgil's *Aeneid*, first published in 1581.

Messer Bastiano the Venetian: Sebastiano Luciani (1485–1547), the painter better known as Sebastiano del Piombo, who left Venice in 1511 to work for Agostino Chigi in the decoration of the Farnesina Palace. In 1531 he was given the office of the Piombo or the Papal Seal over Cellini, and he was known thereafter as Sebastiano del Piombo. In the same year, however, Cellini applied for and received the position of *mazziere* or papal mace-bearer (men who proceeded the Pope in ceremonial processions), which yielded some 200 scudi per year, a position he held until 1533, when his rival Pompeo de' Capitaneis caused him to lose this coveted benefice.

blackberries are from January: blackberries generally mature in the summer, not in the dead of winter.

84 *completing my work*: the button or morse for the Pope's cope.

Quare dubitasti?: 'Why have you doubted me?' (Matthew 15: 31).

Sanga: Giovanbattista Sanga (1496–1532), Roman humanist and Latin poet who served Clement VII. His life was apparently ended by an accidental poisoning.

had procured the duchy of Penna: actually, Alessandro de' Medici (1510–37) received the duchy of Civita di Penne in the Abruzzi in 1522 when he married Margherita d'Austria, the daughter of Charles V. Before he became pope, Clement VII may have had a role in the matter.

that great Lord Giovanni de' Medici: Giovanni delle Bande Nere.

Baccino della Croce: a goldsmith working in Rome for the pope *c.*1530–5.

Captain Cattivanza degli Strozzi: Bernardo Strozzi, an officer of the mercenary soldiers led by Giovanni delle Bande Nere, who eventually became a commander in the army of the short-lived Florentine republic in 1530.

86 *Maffio*: Maffeo di Giovanni, constable or sheriff (*bargello*) of Rome from 1529 to 1530

87 *the Torre di Nona*: at the time a prison for common criminals was located here, near the church of San Salvatore in Lauro behind the Piazza Navona.

in the Florentine church: the Florentine church in Rome was and still remains San Giovanni dei Fiorentini, located on the Tiber riverbank a stone's throw away from the Banchi, where Cellini set up his workshop.

88 *Obiit die XXVII Maii MDXXIX*: 'To Francesco Cellini, a Florentine,

who after achieving numerous victories at yet a tender age under the command of Giovanni de' Medici and being his standard-bearer, gave clear proof of how much strength and intelligence he would have been capable of, had he not been struck down through a cruel fate by an arquebus and had not died in his twenty-fifth year. Erected by his brother Benvenuto. He died on 27 May 1529.'

twenty-five years old: actually 27.

Cecchino del Piffero: Cecchino the Fifer's son.

the true coat of arms of the Cellini family: in the National Library of Florence (in the Cassetta Palatina, along with the Cellini archival documents) there is a drawing of the Cellini coat of arms in Cellini's own hand.

89 *there was only the paw*: that is to say, there was a paw without the body of the lion.

Torre Sanguigna: near Piazza Navona, this place took the name of the Sanguigni family.

large dagger of the type made in Pistoia: a dagger with a double-edged blade.

90 *lived between Piazza Navona and the Rotonda*: Alessandro de' Medici lived in what is today known as the Palazzo Madama (named for his wife, Margherita d'Asburgo, also known as Margherita d'Austria, the daughter of Charles V, who, after the Duke's death, married Ottavio Farnese). Today the Palazzo Madama houses the Italian Senate. The Rotonda is the nearby Pantheon.

Giovan Bandini: Giovanni Bandini, a Florentine gentleman serving Duke Alessandro, who became famous for a duel fought against Ludovico Martelli during the siege of Florence in 1529–30.

Now that you are cured: that is, now that you have avenged your brother's death. Note that almost no one in Cellini's society thought his act was reprehensible, including the Pope.

across from Raffaello's: Raffaello del Moro, not the better-known painter Raphael from Urbino (Raffaello Sanzio).

92 *Francesco del Nero*: Niccolò Machiavelli's brother-in-law (d. 1563), who served as the papal treasurer.

the Bishop of Vasona: Girolamo da Schio (1481–1533) was named Bishop of Vison near Avignon in 1523; he also served as Clement's personal confessor.

93 *welcome*: the Pope continues the play on words that Cellini's father began by naming him Benvenuto (*benvenuto* in Italian means 'welcome').

Iacopo Balducci: superintendent of the pontifical Mint, 1529–41; he was eventually imprisoned and tortured after being accused of making counterfeit money himself.

94 *arrested one of the coin finishers*: Ceseri Macheroni was a goldsmith who

was arrested, tried, tortured twice, and finally hanged in 1532 as a counterfeiter; the coin-finisher or *ovolatore di zecca*, as Cellini calls him, was named Raffaello di Domenico, and the work of this particular craftsman was to make the teethmarks or chiselled edges on the coins.

94 *Donnino*: Donnino di Lorenzo Rippa.

95 *engulfed all of Rome in water*: this occurred between 7 and 9 October 1530.

Monte Cavallo: the Quirinale, the hill upon which the Quirinale Palace stands, the papal residence in Rome until the establishment of the Italian Republic in the nineteenth century. It now serves as the residence of the President of Italy.

and Bastiano Veniziano, the painter: see previous notes to Giovanni Gaddi and Sebastiano del Piombo in I, 46.

a vacant position as mace-bearer: the post of *mazziere* was essentially a sinecure, since the person holding the position usually persuaded others to perform the chore for a pittance. Cellini held the position, which paid 200 scudi per year, from 1531 to 1533.

96 *a magnificent chalice*: this chalice or ostensory, apparently commissioned in 1531, was to be employed in a procession when the Host was carried along with the Pope. Cellini left the work unfinished and Cosimo I later commissioned another goldsmith (Niccolò Santini) to complete the job; it was given by Cosimo to Pope Pius V in 1569 when Cosimo became Grand Duke of Tuscany, and was subsequently lost.

Faith, Hope, and Charity: the three 'theological virtues' (1 Corinthians 13: 13), as opposed to the four 'cardinal virtues' from classical antiquity (Justice, Prudence, Fortitude, Temperance).

a vacant position for a friar in the Piombo: the post of 'sealer' in the Papal Chancery (*piombatore* or *sigillatore*) was originally reserved for members of the Cistercian monastic order. By Cellini's day it had customarily been awarded to laymen, who would adopt a clerical habit when performing the duties associated with placing the seals on papal bulls.

Bramante, that most excellent architect: Donato Bramante (1444–1514), the architect from Urbino whose work in Rome for papal patrons, especially Julius II (1503–13), included the Tempietto at S Pietro in Montorio, the creation of major new streets in the city (Via Giulia, Via de' Banchi, Via della Lungara), and the foundation for the new St Peter's Cathedral.

97 *Messer Bartolomeo Valori*: Bacio Valori, a Florentine and one of the pope's confidants; subsequently Valori fought against Duke Cosimo and the Medici family along with Filippo Strozzi. Captured at the disastrous Battle of Montemurlo, he was eventually beheaded on 20 August 1537.

Messer Ruberto Pucci: Roberto d'Antonio Pucci (1464–1547), an ardent supporter of the Medici family; after he was widowed he took holy orders and pursued a career in the church, becoming Bishop of Pistoia, then

Ravello, and eventually received the cardinal's hat from Pope Paul III in 1542.

98 *After the Pope went off to Bologna*: Clement VII left Rome for his historic meeting with Charles V in Bologna on 18 November 1532: their topic of discussion was essentially who would have hegemony within the Italian peninsula, but it also included the plan to marry Catherine de' Medici to Henry, son of Francis I of France. Clement had previously met Charles in Bologna, where he crowned him emperor in 1530.

Cardinal Salviati: Giovanni Salviati (1490–1553), son of Jacopo Salviati and a nephew of Pope Leo X, who was eventually named Archbishop of Ferrara.

The Pope returned from Bologna: in March 1533.

100 *'Benvenuto'... occasion*: yet another pun on *benvenuto*, 'welcome'.

that French pox: probably syphilis or some other venereal illness.

101 *I decided to take 'lignum vitae'*: the resin of a tropical American tree with evergreen leaves (*Guaiacum officinale*) was used in this period to treat syphilis. Its Latin name means 'wood of life'.

by the name of Tobbia: Tobbia or Tobia da Camerino was, as his name implied, actually from Camerino in the Marches, not Milan; he is documented as working for the Vatican between 1537 and 1546.

102 *the most beautiful ever seen*: since the unicorn does not exist, the object in question may have been an ivory tusk or a precious stone cut in the form of such a horn.

King Francis: Francis I of France (1494–1547) was to receive this gift for the marriage of his second son Henry, Duke of Valois (the future King Henry II) to Catherine de' Medici, the niece of Clement VII, a ceremony celebrated in Marseilles in 1533.

this ciborium: a covered metal cup holding hosts for Communion, the inside of which must be gold-plated; apparently Tobia's design resembled one of these.

Master of the Wardrobe: the *guardarobiere* was a court dignitary, and the position at the time was held by a certain Pier Giovanni Aliotti, later public accountant of the papal buildings, and eventually the Bishop of Forlì.

103 *Pope Clement's most favoured servant*: for Pompeo and Messer Traiano, see notes to p. 79.

Fagiuolo: Tommaso d'Antonio di Perugia, who took over Cellini's position at the Mint in January of 1534; his nickname means 'Bean'.

some other things: in fact, Cellini also lost his post of mace-bearer, thus losing two different sources of income.

104 *his name is Pier Giovanni*: this is the same Pier Giovanni Aliotti mentioned just above.

104 *but I do not remember his name*: one of the few times Cellini's remarkable memory for names fails him.

105 *Magalotto*: Gregorio Magalotti (d. 1537), a well-known man of letters and Roman judge who was made Bishop of Lipari in 1532 and of Chiusi in 1534 by Clement VII, to whom he was close.

107 *loosen and bind greater things than this*: Clement refers to the passage in Matthew 16: 19, where his predecessor, St Peter, is given the power by Christ to bind and loosen anything in heaven or on earth, the biblical text upon which the papacy's power has always been based.

a work like that one: at this point in the manuscript (fo. 158ʳ) there is a lacuna. Earlier editors added a phrase here to indicate that Tobbia had replied affirmatively to the Pope's question.

108 *a monstrance*: also called an ostensory; this is a vessel used to expose the eucharistic bread to view on the altar or sometimes in a procession.

Baccino della Croce: see note to p. 84.

109 *by the name of Felice*: little else is known of this partner named Felice Guadagni.

Vincenzio Romoli: a Florentine and an agent at the Mint where Cellini had worked.

Culosseum: in employing this spelling for the famous ancient Roman monument (*Culiseo*), as well as a number of *–culo* endings for other words in this passage (*circulo* for 'circle', *pentàculo* for 'pentacle'), Cellini is probably punning on the word for 'arse' (*culo*), in light of the scatological direction the account of this necromancy eventually takes.

the pentacle: a five-pointed star traced upon pieces of parchment, rock, or metal.

111 *some asafoetida fumes*: a foul-smelling gum resin from various Asiatic plants of the carrot family, once employed by doctors as an anti-spasmodic.

until they began to ring matins: around the break of dawn, when the first religious services would take place.

112 *consecrate a book*: to create a book about spirits and demons possessing magic powers.

the mountains of Norcia: this Umbrian city was associated with necro-mancy and magic by popular tradition.

the Badia di Farfa: the Benedictine abbey of Farfa, some 20 km. from Rome, was, according to legend, founded by San Lorenzo Siro in the fifth century on the spot where he had killed a fire-spouting dragon that terrorized the region with its breath.

113 *a certain Giovanni da Castel Bolognese*: Giovanni Bernardi (1495–1555), an artist who specialized in coins, cameos, and gem-cutting. Bernardi came to Rome and entered the service of Clement VII at the request of Paolo Giovio (1483–1552), the humanist scholar and historian from Como who was always associated with Medici patrons in both Rome and

Florence, and who left the papal court in disgust in 1549 after Pope Paul III (a Farnese) denied him the position of cardinal at Como. It was Giovio who apparently encouraged Vasari to complete his celebrated collection of lives of the great Italian artists. Like Cellini, Bernardi was a mace-bearer of the pope.

to Alessandro del Bene: see note to p. 60.

Ser Benedetto: a Florentine notary who worked in both Rome and Naples.

114 *I saw it with my own eyes*: Pope-Hennessy (*Cellini*, 52) suggests that Pompeo mistook Ser Benedetto for Tobbia, Cellini's rival, because of the darkness at that hour.

115 *Messer Giovanni Gaddi*: see note to p. 83.

the Cardinal de' Medici's household: Ippolito (1511–35), the natural son of Giuliano, Duke of Nemours, to whom Machiavelli initially dedicated *The Prince*; Clement VII named him as a cardinal in 1529 at the age of 18. In spite of this, he generally supported the anti-Medici forces (the so-called *fuorusciti*), and was part of a plot against Duke Alessandro, who perhaps had him poisoned. He was a popular patron of the arts and letters in Rome.

Palonbara: Palombara Sabina, about 37 km. from Rome.

Giovanbatista Savello: Giovambattista or Gianbattista Savelli, a Roman nobleman and soldier of fortune who served Pope Clement VII, fought with the Medici forces at the siege of Florence, and was later employed by Duke Cosimo I of Tuscany until his death in 1553.

. . . Monte Cassino: the Benedictine abbey at Monte Cassino was known as San Germano until 1871; the son of Lorenzo de' Medici, Piero de' Medici, died in 1503 after being exiled from Florence and was buried at this abbey, where Clement VII wanted to erect his tomb, a monument finally completed in 1559.

Solosmeo: Antonio Solosmeo or Antonio di Giovanni da Settignano, a disciple of Andrea del Sarto and Sansovino who was both painter and sculptor; he completed the tomb in 1559 following the design of Antonio da Sangallo.

116 *Carlo Ginori*: Carlo di Leonardo Ginori, *Gonfaloniere* or Standard-bearer of the Florentine Republic during the first few months of 1527, and friend of Vasari and other artists.

117 *Messer Domenico Fontana*: little is known of this goldsmith except for what Cellini tells of him here.

the Viceroy of Naples: Pedro Alvarez di Toledo, named Viceroy in 1532 (d. 1553), the father of Eleonora, the wife of Cosimo I de' Medici.

118 *the two hundred ducats*: a moment ago the price was two hundred scudi.

Selciata: Selice near Santa Maria Capua Vetere.

in Adanagni: Anagni.

119 *a big halberd*: a pike armed with a steel point and a crosspiece of steel resembling an axe with one or two cutting blades.

Messer Pierantonio Pecci: after serving Cardinal Ippolito, Pecci passed to the service of Catherine de' Medici in France; in 1551 he was declared a rebel by the Florentine government because he had tried to deliver his native city, Siena, to the French.

120 *a figure representing Peace*: for a colour photograph of both the original die and one of the medals with the Allegory of Peace, see Pope-Hennessy, *Cellini* (plates 31–2).

Clauduntur belli portae: actually, the surviving examples of this medal completed in 1534 reveal an allegorical figure of Peace clad in a long robe and holding a cornucopia in her left hand and a rather large torch in her right hand. The quotation comes from Virgil's *Aeneid* (I, 294): 'Claudentur belli portae' or 'The gates of war shall be closed'. The quotation refers to the doors of the temple of Janus, which were locked in ancient Rome during peacetime.

Pier Carneschi: Pietro Carnesecchi (1508–67), a humanist of great culture who rose from being secretary to Clement VII to the position of Protonotary Apostolic, an official of the Roman Curia who notarizes certain important documents concerning the acts of the church, the lives of the martyrs, and so forth. Because of his adherence to heretical doctrines associated with such church figures as Juan de Valdés, Erasmus, Melanchthon, and Cardinal Pole, he was accused of heresy, absolved by the Inquisition in 1546, then condemned again in 1558 to decapitation and burning at the stake. This sentence was finally carried out on 3 October 1567, after Cosimo I had consigned him into the hands of Pope Pius V.

I stamped it in gold, silver, and copper: according to Pope-Hennessy (*Cellini*, 53), Cellini produced his medals by a technique described as 'striking with the screw' (*stampare con la vite*) rather than normal stamping (*coniare*); this process was slower and more expensive, but did not wear out the dies and produced much finer impressions.

the Belvedere: the courtyard of the Vatican palaces.

a much greater power: that is, God; Cellini wants his reader and the Pope to believe that God alone saved him from the hostile influence of the stars and the Pope.

one must mark seven times but cut only once: that is, one must reflect before acting hastily. The image is taken from what was probably a popular saying among tailors, who needed to check and recheck their measurements before actually cutting the fabric they were sewing.

of my worst adversary: Pompeo de' Capitaneis.

121 *following an idea of his own*: this remark underlines the interesting fact that Cellini's first medal was designed without any instructions from

the Pope, an unusual situation for any Renaissance artist with such a demanding and erudite patron as Clement VII.

Ut bibat populus: for illustrations of the die and the alternative reverse of the first medal, see Pope-Hennessy, *Cellini* (plates 33–4). The motto comes from Exodus 17: 6: 'so that the people may drink.' The story is also repeated in Numbers 20: 1–11. According to most commentators, the motif was intended to commemorate the drilling of an important civic well in Orvieto, the Pozzo di San Patrizio. The older town well had proved inadequate during the period (December 1527 to June 1528) when the papal court was temporarily located in Orvieto following the Sack of Rome. The new well was finally completed in 1532, a few years after Clement's death.

what he feared I would do to him: it was common practice for a general amnesty to be declared after the death of one pope and the election of another. Consequently, it was not uncommon for violent crimes to be committed while a pope was dying in the hopes of benefiting from such an amnesty. Cellini is referring to a thwarted assassination plot engineered by his arch-enemy Pompeo de' Capitaneis which justifies, to some extent, Cellini's subsequent homicide.

122 *the Pope died*: on 25 September 1534.

Albertaccio del Bene: another of the three sons—Alberto or Albertaccio, Alessandro, and Albizzo—of the rich Roman merchant Piero del Bene, whose family palace Cellini guarded during the Sack of Rome; Pietro Bembo mentions Albertaccio in a letter dated 1547 as both a highly literate man and a skilled connoisseur of art. He was killed in 1554 at the Battle of Marciano.

123 *not what I intended*: since the successor to a dead Pope almost always proclaimed an amnesty, it is difficult to believe that Cellini's killing of Pompeo was not premeditated; the murder occurred on 27 November 1534.

Via Giulia: so called because Pope Julius II created the street, now one of Rome's most elegant addresses; during Cellini's day it was much frequented by artists, such as Raphael.

the goldsmith Piloto: Giovanni di Baldassare Piloto (1460–1536), Florentine goldsmith and sculptor who worked in Florence, Venice, and Rome. One of his works was the sphere, designed by Michelangelo, that was placed atop the New Sacristy of San Lorenzo in Florence.

except the Milanese: since Pompeo was from Milan, his fellow citizens were reluctant to assist his murderer from Florence. Note that Cellini calls the various cities 'nations', since in fact the major cities of Italy represented separate political entities, or city-states.

Messer Luigi Rucellai: (1495–1549), a rich Florentine patrician hostile to the Medici who had retired to Rome after the fall of the Florentine Republic in 1530. It is interesting to note how the Florentine origins of Cellini's friends move them to assist him even though some of the

Florentines living in Rome were staunch anti-Medici foes, while Cellini and his family were deeply indebted to Medici patronage. Civic loyalty, even in the cosmopolitan microcosm of papal Rome, was extremely strong during the Renaissance.

124   *Cardinal Cornaro*: Francesco Cornaro (1478–1543), nephew of the Queen of Cyprus and a Venetian soldier, named cardinal in 1528. Subsequently, he became Bishop of Brescia.

the Bishop of Frullì: Bernardo di Michelozzo Michelozzi (dates uncertain) had been in the service of Leo X and later served both Paul III and Cosimo I. At this time he was Bishop of Forlí, but later resigned this position to take up the bishopric of Cassano.

a few days later Cardinal Farnese: on 13 October 1534 Alessandro Farnese (1468–1549) was elected pope, taking the name Paul III.

125   *Messer Latino Iuvinale*: Latino Giovenale Manetti (1486–1553), humanist and friend of many Italian writers of the period, including Baldassare Castiglione, author of *The Book of the Courtier*. A member of the Papal Curia, he was responsible for the preservation of Rome's ancient monuments and served as the guide for Charles V's historic visit to the city in 1530.

Messer Ambruogio: Ambrogio Recalcati, canon of San Ambrogio in Milan, the Protonotary and powerful secretary of Paul III who was later imprisoned for a time in the Castel Sant'Angelo by the Pope for abuse of his office.

Vas electionis: 'the chosen vessel' or 'the chosen instrument'; in Acts 9: 15, as well as in Dante's *Inferno* (II, 28), this epithet is used to refer to St Paul, who is chosen by God Himself to spread the faith. This Pauline reference underlines the fact that Paul III was elected by acclamation and not by written or verbal ballots, something that had not occurred in a papal election for many years. In the surviving copies of the coins, the figure of Paul is full-length. Some scholars deny that the surviving coins are by Cellini's hand. For black-and-white photographs of two of these golden *scudi*, see Barbaglia, *L'opera completa di Cellini* (plates 167r, 167v, 168r, 168v).

once again . . . the 'moto proprio': see note to p. 82.

safe until the appointed time: for the Feast of the Assumption on 15 August, it was the custom to allow the *caporioni*, or the heads of the various city districts, as well as the leaders of the guilds, to pardon twelve men accused of a crime. In fact, Cellini was eventually pardoned with the patronage of the guild of the *beccai* or butchers.

126   *Pier Luigi, the Pope's son*: Pier Luigi Farnese (1503–47), natural son of Paul III, who married Girolama Orsini, was named *Gonfaloniere* of the Church, as well as Duke of Parma and Piacenza, by his father, and Duke of Castro by Charles V. A very violent man noted for his sodomitic proclivities (he was reported to have once raped the Bishop of Fano), he

was finally murdered by his own courtiers at the wishes of Ferrante I Gonzaga. Cellini considered him to be his most implacable enemy.

128 *Tribolino*: Niccolò di Raffaello de' Pericoli, called Il Tribolo (1500–50), a Florentine sculptor and architect who was the pupil of Sansovino. He collaborated with Michelangelo on the New Sacristy of San Lorenzo Cathedral in Florence, and spent perhaps too much time and energy arranging decorations and constructions for the lavish festivals given by the Medici family. His best-known work is the fountain he designed for the Medici villa at Castello.

a certain Iacopo del Sansovino: Jacopo Tatti (1486–1570), called Sansovino, left Rome after the Sack (1527) and went to Venice, where he became the city's most important architect; Cellini surely knew him in Rome, and calls him 'one Iacopo del Sansovino' not because he was unknown at the time (which he most certainly was not) but because he later came to dislike him after visiting him (1535, 1546) in Venice.

Signor Lorenzo Cibo were lodged: the Pazzi Palace on Florence's Via del Proconsolo had been designed by Giuliano da Maiano for Jacopo de' Pazzi, hanged after the unsuccessful Pazzi Conspiracy against the Medici in 1478. At the time in question, Ricciarda Malaspina, the wife of Lorenzo Cibo (1500–49) occupied the palace; the couple were separated, and it seems that Ricciarda had an amorous relationship with Duke Alessandro. In 1530 Pope Clement VII named Lorenzo Cibo commander of the papal army.

Cosimino de' Medici: then still a young boy (thus Cellini employs the diminutive for his name), he would later become Cosimo I, Grand Duke of Tuscany.

Niccolò da Monte Aguto: one of Duke Alessandro's favourite courtiers.

a certain Ser Maurizio: this individual from Milan served as the Chancellor of the Eight in Florence around 1535, and was infamous for being a stickler about the regulations, so strict—as Cellini says—that he would have hanged or tortured the town's patron saint for a minor offence.

the nickname 'Lamentone': 'Complainer'; a man by this name is listed in the register of men paid by Cosimo I in 1545.

fuorusciti: 'outcasts', i.e. some of the exiled opponents of the Medici family.

129 *the Duke of Ferrara*: Ercole II d'Este (1508–59), who in 1534 had succeeded his father Alfonso I as Duke of Ferrara and Modena; Belfiore was one of the Este villas near Ferrara.

Iacopo Nardi: a member of a staunchly anti-Medici family and follower of Savonarola, Nardi (1476–1563) was exiled to Venice and deprived of his property; he translated Livy into the vernacular and was the author of a major historical work (*History of the City of Florence*, 1582) that analysed Florentine affairs between 1494 and 1538 from the viewpoint of the defeated Savonarolian republicans. Benintendi was one of the Eight and captain of the republican militia in 1529; he was exiled by the Medici in 1530 along with his brother Piero.

130 *if my abilities allow it*: here Cellini employs the Italian word *virtù*, the same term employed by Machiavelli in *The Prince* to mean ability, strength, and courage in accomplishing a worthy enterprise.

133 *as large and as many as he liked*: Cellini is playing on the double meaning of the word *coregge*, which can mean both 'straps' and 'farts'.

134 *St Damian on the reverse*: Saints Cosmas and Damian were the patron saints of the Medici family because they were reputed to have been physicians (*medici*, in Italian). These famous coins, one example of which is preserved in the Bargello Museum in Florence, were called *ricci* ('curly heads') because Duke Alessandro's portrait on one side of the silver coin sported very curly hair. For a very detailed photograph of this coin, see Pope-Hennessy, *Cellini* (plates 35, 38). Pope-Hennessy believes that Michelangelo's sculpture provided Cellini with the inspiration for the figures on both sides of the coin: the prophets and ancestors of Christ in the Sistine Chapel resemble the style of the Duke's portrait; and Michelangelo's models for statues of the two Medici saints flanking the Virgin and Child in the Medici Chapel seem to have been the inspiration for the figures of Cosmas and Damian.

Carlo Acciaiuoli: Carlo di Roberto Acciaiuoli was in charge of the Mint after 1530 for several years.

the stamps for the giulio: this was a silver coin depicting the patron saint of Florence; see Pope-Hennessy, *Cellini* (plate 39), for a photograph of the figure of St John.

experts in this profession: Pope-Hennessy (*Cellini*, 74) is in complete agreement with Cellini's high estimation of his originality. For reproductions of both sides of this coin, see *Cellini* (plates 40, 41). The half-giulio was a silver coin of the same size (24 mm. in diameter) as the giulio.

golden scudi: in addition to the Greek cross with cherubs on one side, there is a Latin inscription: 'Virtus est nobis Dei.' See Pope-Hennessy (*Cellini*, plates 42, 43) for colour photographs of this coin.

135 *a certain Pretino da Lucca*: a Francesco da Lucca, called Pretino, is listed as the Master of the Wardrobe in the registry of the Medici court some years later (1543–45).

his wife, who was still in Naples: Margherita d'Asburgo, of the Habsburg family—also known as Margaret of Austria (1522–86) and natural daughter of Charles V—was then in Naples but was to come to Florence for the wedding in the following year, 1536. After Alessandro's assassination in 1537 she became the wife of Ottavio Farnese (the future Duke of Parma) in 1538; in 1559 she became governess of the Low Countries.

expedite it for me: that is, his fixed salary and the rooms at the Mint.

Pietro Pagolo: Pietropaolo Galeotto (1520–84), goldsmith and pupil of Cellini from Monterotondo, who later accompanied him to France and assisted him during the casting of the statue of *Perseus* in December 1552.

Bernardonaccio: Bernardo Baldini, a goldsmith always treated with contempt by Cellini in his autobiography, was named Superintendent of the Florentine Mint by Duke Cosimo I.

this Lorenzino of his: Lorenzo de' Medici (1513–48), son of Pierfrancesco de' Medici and Maria Soderini; called 'Lorenzaccio' because of his dissolute and violent disposition. In spite of his character, he was a great friend of writers and scholars and wrote plays and verse himself. After assassinating his cousin Alessandro between 5 and 6 January 1537, he fled to Venice, where a hired assassin sent by Duke Cosimo I eventually killed him. In some circles Lorenzaccio's act was seen as the last gasp of Florentine republicanism, and he was sometimes depicted as a classical tyrannicide in the tradition of the Roman Brutus, who assassinated Julius Caesar. For a treatment of the mythology and artistic iconography of Renaissance republicanism, with particular reference to Italy, see Peter Bondanella, *The Eternal City: Roman Images in the Modern World* (Chapel Hill, NC: University of North Carolina Press, 1987).

Ottaviano de' Medici: although not belonging to the noble branch of the Medici family, Ottaviano (d. 1546) exercised a great deal of power under Alessandro and later under Cosimo I, and was praised by Vasari as a friend of artisans.

Bastiano Cennini: in spite of his supposedly old fashioned artistic techniques in the making of coins, Cellini praises Cennini (1485–1535) in the introduction to his *Treatise on Goldsmithing*.

137 *in a treacherous way*: Cellini seems to imply that even Lorenzino's physical manner foreshadowed his subsequent assassination of Duke Alessandro.

a reverse worthy of Your Excellency: Lorenzino thus obliquely refers to the Duke's future assassination.

that medal you want to make: Cellini's medal for Alessandro was never finished.

138 *Then the next day*: the first few days of June in 1535.

the circle of necromancy: see I, 64 for the earlier reference to Vincenzo Mantovano, who later became a famous goldsmith.

Vittorio the constable: according to records of the period, a Vittorio Politi was the constable only after May 1539; between 1534 and 1535, the constables were Nardo Castaldo and Pier Francesco dei nobili di Baro (called Il Riccio or 'Curly').

139 *the group*: for earlier notes on Annibale Caro and Giovanni Vergerio (the full name of Giovanni the Greek), see notes to p. 83. Ludovico da Fano was a noted scholar and poet with an extravagant character who died in 1541; Antonio Allegretti was a Florentine poet.

140 *his 'motu proprio'*: for an explanation of this term, see note to p. 82.

141 *Master Francesco da Norcia*: Francesco Fusconi (d. after 1550), court doctor to popes Adrian VI, Clement VII, and Paul III, who specialized in curing malaria, a very common disease in the Rome of Cellini's day. He was also a collector of classical sculpture.

a certain Mattio Franzesi: Matteo Franzesi, a Florentine burlesque poet active in Rome during Cellini's lifetime, who eventually became secretary to Cardinal Niccolò Ardinghelli.

142 *been reading Dante*: the image of the old man in the boat probably refers to Charon, the boatman of Hell, in Dante's *Inferno* (III, 82–111). Dante's picture of the afterlife was a popular source of inspiration for many Renaissance artists, whose frescos of scenes from Hell almost always drew inspiration from the poet's descriptions.

Benedetto Varchi: see note to p. 29.

144 *dress himself properly*: in an outfit appropriate to mourning the passing of his best friend.

here below: an allusion to the image of God the Father that Cellini had fashioned for the morse of Pope Clement VII.

146 *on Monte Cavallo*: the Quirinale (see note to p. 95).

147 *the holy oil*: the oil administered by the priest during the last rites of extreme unction.

Pier Landi: see note to p. 28.

a certain Niccolò da Monte Aguto: see note to p. 128.

the painter from Arezzo, Giorgetto Vassellario: this sarcastic reference to Giorgio Vasari (1511–74) cannot be verified. Vasari actually spoke well of Cellini in the brief reference to him in *The Lives of the Artists*, although he does not devote a chapter to him in this important collection of artists' lives. The diminutive name employed by Cellini might be translated as 'little Georgie the Potter'.

a dry leprosy: Cellini calls it 'una lebbrolina secca', which must have been either a mild form of leprosy or, more likely, some undetermined skin disease such as scabies.

148 *named Manno*: Manno di Bastiano Sbarri (1536–76), a Florentine goldsmith and Cellini's pupil, who worked in Pisa and Rome. In 1529 Vasari and Manno apparently took refuge in Pisa during the siege of Florence. His most famous work is considered to be the silver frame of the Cassetta Farnese (*Cofanetto farnese*) in the Capodimonte Museum in Naples. Accusing Vasari of sodomy was a serious charge, as it could be punished by the death sentence.

with Cardinal de' Medici: with Ippolito de' Medici (see note to p. 115).

good Master Francesco da Montevarchi: Francesco Catani da Montevarchi, a famous physician and, according to both Vasari and Benedetto Varchi, a connoisseur of the fine arts.

Luca Martini: a burlesque poet and student of Dante, whose portrait was done by Bronzino and who is mentioned by Pontormo in his diary; besides Caro, Varchi, and Cellini, Martini was on familiar terms with most of the writers and artists of his time in Florence. In 1555 Duke Cosimo I appointed him to the position of *provveditore* (Superintendent) in Pisa; Cellini would later dedicate the long poem he composed during his imprisonment in the Castel Sant'Angelo to Martini. He also corresponded with him in 1536 concerning a medal for Pietro Bembo and wrote a sonnet at his death. For the letter and the sonnet, see Milanesi (ed.), *I trattati*, 270, 390.

149 *When I reached Rome*: Cellini arrived in Rome in 1536.

150 *idiot named Francesco Soderini*: not to be confused with the cardinal from the same family, this Francesco Soderini (d. 1551) had been exiled to Spello with other opponents of the Medici, returning in 1530. The proof that Cellini was an honest man may be found in the fact that both sides of the political spectrum found his straight talk irritating.

that mad, melancholy philosopher: it was not uncommon to consider brooding, studious, or taciturn personalities both melancholy (i.e. associated with a particular humour of the body) and philosophical. Lorenzino was characterized in this way by several contemporary historians (Varchi, Paolo Giovio) who discussed his life and his assassination of Duke Alessandro.

[. . . of Huge Gains]: one of the cleverest of the many puns in Cellini's autobiography, these remarks are based upon simple translations of the name of the character Felice Guadagni; the punch line (De' Guadagni-assai) is amusing because this sort of family name was normally associated with the Florentine upper classes.

one day around Epiphany: the Christian feast on 6 January celebrating the visit of the Three Magi to see the infant Jesus.

near the Magliana: a castle on the Tiber about 10 km. from Rome, where the papal game reserve was located.

151 *named Barucco*: according to Bellotto (318, n. 18), the origin of the name of Cellini's dog comes from the Hebrew *barukh* (meaning *benvenuto* or 'welcome'—that is to say, his own name). He could have known of this, Bellotto argues, because Roman Jews used the two words *barukh abbà* as a common greeting, meaning 'welcome is he who comes'.

two hundred armslengths: a bit more than 100 m.

that tremendous thing we see over Florence?: portents, such as unusual movements or lights in the heavens, were traditionally seen as signs of momentous change during the Renaissance. It is doubtful that Cellini could see the skies over Florence from the outskirts of Rome.

152 *reached Rome*: Duke Alessandro de' Medici was assassinated by Lorenzino de' Medici between the night and morning of 5 and 6 January 1537.

the leader of those sects: like Machiavelli and other writers of the period,

Cellini sometimes employs a word with a religious connotation (*sette* or sects) when he means factions or political groups.

152 *by a certain Baccio Bettini*: another Florentine exile Vasari mentions in his life of Michelangelo. Michelangelo provided him with a cartoon for a painting of Cupid kissing Venus.

worthlessness of your predecessors: the republican opponents of the Medici.

before two or three days pass, at the most: Cosimo de' Medici took the title of Duke at the age of 17 on 9 January 1537. Both the opponents and the allies of the Medici regime soon discovered that Cosimo was a far cleverer political leader than they had imagined. It is also interesting to note that Cellini begins his discussion of the Medici dukes with the medal proposed in 1535, and continues that narrative until the death of Alessandro in 1537; he then turns back several years and continues the actual historical chronology to discuss the visit of Charles V to Naples on 30 November 1535 after his victory against the corsairs of Tunis. In such instances, it is clear that Cellini's art, and not the history of the times, provides the structure for the narrative.

153 *Messer Latino Iuvinale*: see note to p. 125.

154 *a Book of Offices of Our Lady*: an illuminated book of prayers to the Virgin that has not survived. In his *Treatise on Goldsmithing* (VIII), Cellini says that Ippolito de' Medici originally ordered this book for Giulia Gonzaga. The Florentine miniaturist Iacopo del Giallo, according to recent scholarship, illuminated the work. Chapter VIII of Cellini's *Treatise* should be compared to the passages in Cellini's autobiography describing the proposed crucifix, the illuminated book of prayers, and the diamond ring that will be discussed shortly, since it provides more details (sometimes different ones) about these works.

which other writers will describe: Charles V reached Rome on 5 April 1536 and left on the 18th of the month. His arrival was by all accounts spectacular, for he was attended by a retinue of some 6,000 people, which passed through the various ancient Roman arches still standing, then moved on to the Capitoline and concluded at the Vatican. The *Diario* of Biagio Baronio Martinelli of Cesena, Master of Ceremonies to Popes Leo X, Adrian VI, Clement VII, and Paul III, provides a description of the event. A letter from Pietro Aretino to Vasari, dated 7 June 1536, contains a briefer description.

155 *two Turkish horses*: we would say Arabian today, but Cellini's use of Turkish as a synonym for Arab or Arabian reminds us that, in his day, it was the Ottoman Empire of Turkey that dominated Arabic culture and competed with the Christian kingdoms and empires of Europe for hegemony in the Mediterranean.

Messer Durante: Durante Duranti (1486–1557), a learned prelate from Brescia who was Prefect of the Apostolic Chamber to Paul III, who made him a cardinal in 1544 and subsequently the Bishop of Brescia.

156 *Master Miliano Targhetta*: a goldsmith who worked in both Rome and Venice; in ch. VIII of the *Treatise on Goldsmithing* Cellini declares that 'never did any one better know how to fix foils and tint stones'. By this time, 1537, Targhetta was an elderly man.

the four jewellers: in his discussion of this episode in his *Treatise on Goldsmithing* Cellini says that there were three jewellers: the Florentine Raffaello del Moro (see note to p. 76); Gasparo Gallò, known as Guasparre Romanesco, a papal jeweller who was active from 1519 to 1549; and Giovanni Pietro Marliano (Cellini calls him Gaio), who was working in the Roman Curia from 1523 to 1548, the year of his death.

tint: the tint of a diamond is a coloured stucco inserted within the setting; Cellini discusses tints in ch. IX of his *Treatise on Goldsmithing*, with specific reference to the Emperor's diamond.

in the proper place: in his *Treatise on Goldsmithing*, Cellini devotes separate chapters to making foils for jewels (VII), cutting diamonds (VIII), tinting diamonds (IX), and giving diamonds a reflector (X).

157 *the tools of my intellect*: Cellini says 'i mia ferruzi dello ingegno', as if his mind had the same kind of tools employed in his profession as a jeweller.

Marquis del Guasto: Alfonso d'Avalos (1502–46), a Spanish *condottiere* serving Charles V, who was named, for his services, Marquis of Vasto in the Abruzzi in 1535 and subsequently governor of Milan in 1538. He was the Emperor's lieutenant at the siege of Tunis.

neutral and nothing else: the hard lesson from the Sack of Rome was that the papacy could not really compete in the political arena with such larger nation states as France or the empire of Charles V. Paul III was elected as a neutral force standing between the French monarch and the Emperor, and he wisely did not wish to change this policy. Nonetheless, he must have been reluctant to oppose the Emperor's policies in Italy. In fact, it was with the Emperor's support that Pope Paul III managed to establish his family as the ruling dynasty of Parma and Piacenza in 1545. The Farnese family remained in control of the small but important duchy in northern Italy until 1751.

158 *those aspects of philosophy*: Cellini means the theoretical principles of goldsmithing, not the formal philosophy of the humanist tradition.

that your tiara weeps on your head: that is, the tiara does not fit because of Paul III's lack of looks and talent.

159 *my revenge beyond all bounds*: here Cellini employs an idiomatic expression, *a misura di carboni*, which means without limit or measure, or in abundance (see note to p. 26 for another occurrence of the same expression).

Lord Sforza: Sforza Sforza (1521–73), the son of Costanza Farnese (the legitimate daughter of Pope Paul III) and the Count of Santa Fiora; he was named Captain General of the cavalry in the army of Charles V.

159 *Ascanio*: Ascanio di Giovanni de' Mari (1524–?), a goldsmith who worked
     for Cellini in Rome and accompanied him to France, where he remained
     for the rest of his life, working for King Henry II. French documents
     attest to his activity up to 1566 but not to the date of his death. Alexandre
     Dumas *père* used him as the model for the protagonist of a swashbuckling
     novel entitled *Ascanio*.

     Francesco: perhaps a goldsmith named Francisco de Valencia who is
     recorded as working for the papal court around 1535.

     Il Vechino: 'the Little Old Man'.

160 *Surgetto*: Bellotto (336, n. 18) suggests that this nickname for Ascanio is
     derived from the Latin *surcellus*, the diminutive of *surus* ('branch'). It
     obviously refers to Ascanio when he was very thin, and might be
     translated as 'Twig' or 'Little Branch'.

     some worthless wire trinkets: the original Italian (*certi pappolate di filo*) is
     even stronger, since *la pappolata di porci* is pig swill.

161 *a dishonourable 'Marrano'*: calling Francesco a traitor, Cellini once again
     (see note to p. 38) demonstrates that he knows the worst kind of an
     insult to be used in speaking with a Spaniard.

     to Rome from Tagliacozzi: Tagliacozzo in the Abruzzi region.

162 *an apprentice from Perugia*: Girolamo Pascucci, whose accusation that
     Cellini had stolen some of Clement VII's jewels during the Sack of Rome
     was later the cause of his imprisonment in the Castel Sant'Angelo (see I,
     101). Pascucci accompanied Cellini and Ascanio to France in 1537. After
     Cellini's escape from the Castel Sant'Angelo, a historical document dated
     April 1538 attests to a pledge Cellini gave to Pascucci, guaranteed by
     Felice Guadagni and others, not to harm him, and this pledge was
     renewed in 1539. Subsequently Cellini and Pascucci had another falling
     out, resulting in legal battles in Florence between 1558 and 1560.

     I left Rome: apparently on 3 April 1537.

     Albertaccio del Bene: see note to p. 122.

     Messer Pietro Bembo: (1470–1547), Venetian poet, courtier, humanist,
     and cardinal after 1539, whose relationship with Cellini is documented in
     some of his correspondence (*Lettere*, III). Bembo was a central literary
     figure during the sixteenth century: his *Prose della volgar lingua* (*Writings
     in the Vernacular*, first published 1525) constitutes the first history of
     Italian literature; it argues that the Tuscan linguistic models, as refined
     by Petrarch and Boccaccio, should be adopted by Italian writers as an
     ideal literary language. His *Rime* (*Rhymes*, published in 1530 with sub-
     sequent editions in 1535 and 1548) marks the high-water mark of Italian
     Petrarchism. Finally, *Gli Asolani* (1505), dedicated to Lucrezia Borgia,
     presents three dialogues held at the villa of Caterina Cornaro in Asolo:
     the third dialogue is an exaltation of Platonic love, and had a strong
     influence upon poets and philosophers of the Renaissance. Bembo's other
     works, including a history of Venice and a voluminous correspondence to

contemporaries, provide invaluable information about the cultural and intellectual life of sixteenth-century Italy.

163 *the horse Pegasus*: in the Greek myth, when Perseus decapitated the Medusa, the winged horse Pegasus sprang from her blood and became the mount Perseus rode when he rescued Andromeda. Bembo's medal is one of the first references to the myth of Perseus in Cellini's life and work. Pegasus became a symbol of fame, since both the horse and the symbolic female figure representing the concept of Fame were represented with wings. The myrtle of the garland, a plant sacred to Venus, represents love, and the winged horse, poetry.

164 *any of my work for him*: as Pope-Hennessy notes in his discussion of Cellini and Bembo (*Cellini*, 80), the possibility of Cellini making a medal for Bembo had been under discussion for several years, since 1535, and was documented in numerous extant letters written to discuss the work. Several medals of Bembo by other artists created in the early 1530s exist, including one by Valerio Belli and another by Leone Leoni. There is a third medal, the best copy of which is in silver and preserved at the Museo Bargello in Florence, which has often been attributed to Cellini. Its reverse shows Pegasus creating the spring of Hippocrene (in Greek, 'the horse's spring'), which arose when his hoof struck Mount Helicon, home of the Muses: the whole design serves as an emblem of poetic inspiration. There is no myrtle wreath, and Bembo has a long, not a short, beard. Pope-Hennessy believes that since this medal of very high quality was struck (not cast) in much the same manner as a medal of Francis I Cellini made while he was in France, it must have been the modification of Cellini's original wax model of 1537, and that it is indeed by his hand. For enlarged photographs of both sides of this medal, see Pope-Hennessy, *Cellini* (plates 44 and 45).

because of the wars: one of the numerous struggles between the French monarch and the Emperor, this one marked by a successful French invasion of Piedmont in late summer of 1537.

called Valdistà: Walenstadt in the canton of San Gallo (Cellini elsewhere calls the town Valdistate).

whose name was Busbacca: Cellini's various editors suggest that this nickname derives from the word *busbo*, meaning trickster, swindler, or cheat (an appropriate choice, given his character).

165 *located between Valdistate and Vessa*: that is, between Wallenstadt and Weesen, on the western side of Lake Walen.

167 *charming town called Lacca*: Lachen.

168 *a town called Surich*: Zurich.

beautiful city called Solutorno: Solothurn.

Usanna: Lausanne.

Palissa: La Palice.

168 *Rosso the painter*: Rosso Fiorentino (see note to p. 40).

the King: Francis I.

Master Antonio da San Gallo: Antonio di Bartolomeo Cordini, called Antonio da Sangallo the Younger (1484–1546) to distinguish him from his uncles, the architects Giuliano da Sangallo (1445–1516) and Antonio da Sangallo the Elder (1455–1534). Sangallo assisted Bramante as architect of the Vatican Basilica, and in 1516, along with Raphael, he began working on St Peter's Cathedral, eventually receiving the title of architect for the entire project in 1536. He was associated with some of the most impressive architectural projects of the period, including the Palazzo Farnese, the Church of Santa Maria in Loreto, the Pozzo di San Patrizio in Orvieto, and the Fortezza da Basso in Florence.

Messer Agnol da Cesi: a member of a noble Roman family and a close friend of Agostino Chigi; around 1524 Antonio da Sangallo worked on the Cesi Chapel in the Roman church of Santa Maria della Pace, a church in which Raphael also painted some frescos for the Chigi Chapel.

169 *Ricciardo del Bene*: another member of the family of Alessandro del Bene that was so important to Cellini in Rome, Ricciardo was most likely a banker in Paris.

Sguazzella: Andrea Chiazzella or Sguazzella, a pupil of Andrea del Sarto, with whom Sguazzella travelled to Paris in 1518, remaining there for some time working for the French king.

Messer Giuliano Buonaccorsi, his treasurer: (d. 1563), treasurer of the French King; he may also have been one of the Florentine merchants in Lyons in 1530 who attempted to recover the debts contracted by the French monarch during the siege of Florence.

Fontainebleau: a medieval castle transformed into a magnificent Renaissance chateau from 1529 onwards by Francis I with the assistance of both Rosso Fiorentino and Francesco Primaticcio (1500–70, also known as Il Bologna), as well as a host of other Italian artists and artisans.

preparing to go to Lyons: the group arrived on 6 October 1537.

the Cardinal of Ferrara: Ippolito d'Este (1509–72), brother of Duke Ercole II of Ferrara (1508–59), was created cardinal in 1539 by Pope Paul III, perhaps at the behest of the French king whom he had served. He built the splendid Villa d'Este outside Rome at Tivoli, and was a renowned patron of writers and artists.

170 *a place called Indevedro*: Cellini must be referring to the River Divèria in the Val di Vedro or Divedro in Piedmont.

171 *the frontier between the Venetians and the Germans*: if Cellini descended into Italy through the Sempione mountains, then he must have actually been in Milanese territory at this point. It was common, however, for Italians of Cellini's day to call the nearby Swiss 'Germans'.

172 *Santa Maria dal Loreto*: Santa Maria di Loreto, located in the Italian Marches, is a sanctuary including a wooden building incorporated into a basilica that is purported to be the house of the Blessed Virgin Mary, transported by angels from Nazareth to Loreto in 1294. Established in the city of Loreto in the thirteenth century, it became a site for pilgrimages where the faithful sought indulgences, and was as famous in its time as Lourdes and Fatima are today. A number of important artists worked at the site, including Giuliano da Maiano, Giuliano da Sangallo, Bramante, Antonio da Sangallo the Younger, and Andrea Sansovino.

water for my hands be brought: in other words, the Duke invited Cellini to dine with him.

I travelled to Rome: Cellini reached Rome on 16 December 1537.

with my workman from Perugia: Girolamo Pascucci (see note to p. 162).

173 *for blows are not exchanged by agreement*: for another use of this expression, see I, 73.

our Duke Cosimo: Girolamo Orsini, a famous *condottiere* and Lord of Bracciano, married Francesca Sforza; his son Paolo di Giordano Orsini was named Duke of Bracciano in 1560 and married Isabella, daughter of Cosimo de' Medici, in 1553, later murdering her in 1576 because of jealousy.

the great and most Christian King: Francis I.

his Admiral: while famous sailors such as Andrea Doria had once held the title of Admiral of France, by the time Cellini visited the French court it had become primarily an honorific title for a courtier and confidant of the king rather than a rank held by a real sailor.

Cardinal de' Gaddi: see note to p. 63.

174 *this little fool of a wretched Cardinal de' Gaddi*: never one to mince words when angry, Cellini describes him as 'questo pazzerellino di questo cardinaluccio de' Gaddi'.

the Duke of Castro: Pier Luigi Farnese was named Duke of Castro in 1530.

previously mentioned bride: Isabella de' Medici, future bride of Paolo di Giordano Orsini and daughter of Cosimo I.

the constable Crespino: on 16 October 1538 the *bargello* Crispino de' Boni arrested Cellini.

men like you go: in fact, this fortress was employed to house only important prisoners.

175 *later became Bishop of Jesi*: Conversini (d. 1553) was nominated Bishop of Forlimpopoli in 1538 and subsequently of Jesi in 1540; he was governor of Rome during the years 1537–8.

whose name I have forgotten: Benedetto Valenti (see I, 61 and 116).

instead of mere talk or chatter: Cellini makes the same distinction between chattering (*cicalare*) and mere talking (*favellare*) in his *Treatise on Goldsmithing* (IX). There he discusses four different human methods of communication: two which are praiseworthy—reasoning (*ragionare*) and speaking (*parolare*); and two which are foolish, mere talking (*favellare*) and chattering (*cicalare*). The crucial distinction between speaking and mere talking seems to be that speaking implies employing words of substance and beauty which may be related to a process of reasoning; mere talking, on the other hand, involves words of little substance, which may be pleasant on occasion or injurious on others. For the original Italian, see Milanesi (ed.), *I trattati dell'oreficeria e della scultura*, 52.

177 *negotiate the settlement*: Giovan Bartolomeo da Gattinara (and not Cesere, as Cellini remembers incorrectly), a nephew of Mercurio di Gattinaro, Grand Chancellor to Charles V and Regent of the Kingdom of Naples. He was the man who finally concluded the terms of Pope Clement's capitulation on 6 June 1527. While he was apparently wounded after he left Clement, it is unclear whether it resulted from Cellini's actions.

the Borgo: this is the term employed to indicate the area around the Vatican which was eventually torn down during Mussolini's era to open up such wide avenues as the Via della Conciliazione; in Rome, 'Borgo' became a shorthand term for the area of the Vatican outside the Vatican Palace itself.

178 *Raffaello da Montelupo, the sculptor*: Raffaello de' Sinibaldi (1505–67), a sculptor and architect who worked with Antonio da Sangallo and Michelangelo, and who was the architect of the Castel Sant'Angelo. In an autobiographical fragment that Vasari published in his *Lives of the Artists*, Raffaello notes that someone fired upon the negotiator as he left the Castel Sant'Angelo. He does not say that Cellini was the man. A number of the statements Cellini makes in his description of the siege of the Castello are, however, confirmed in Raffaello's account.

Monsignor di Morluc: Jean de Montluc (d. 1579), the brother of the Marshal Blaise de Montluc who was named Bishop of Valence in 1553. His presence is documented in Rome at this time. He had entered the service of Francis I because of the support of Queen Marguerite of Navarre.

180 *a friar from the Palavisina family*: a priest from the noble Pallavicini family (not Palavisina) was arrested and held in the Castello for his supposed Lutheran leanings, according to documents of the period.

Girolamo Savonarola: see n. to p. 26.

183 *Cardinal Santiquattro and Cardinal Cornaro*: Antonio Pucci (1484–1544), given the cardinal's hat associated with the Church of the Quattro Santi Coronati (the Church of the Four Crowned Saints) in Rome in 1531, was from one of Florence's most aristocratic families. For Cardinal Cornaro, see the note to p. 124. It was standard practice in the Renaissance to refer to a cardinal by the name of the church to which his title was connected.

184 *that Girolamo from Perugia*: see the note to p. 162.

a certain Michele: possibly the Michele Nardini mentioned in I, 44.

these humours: in the Renaissance it was common to associate different personality types and temperaments with various 'humours' (the choleric, the melancholic, the sanguine, and the phlegmatic).

185 *all the way to Prati*: see note to p. 57.

186 *a man from Savoy*: this may refer to a certain Enrico de Oziaco, known as 'Il Savoia' ('the Savoyard'), since he came from that region of Italy. At this time he was a guard and gunner at Castel Sant'Angelo, and even appears in frescos executed at the fortress in 1545.

187 *Pedignione was a soldier, while Bozza was a servant*: Pedignione means 'chilblains', while 'Bozza' may be translated as 'swelling' or 'protuberance'. Needless to say, these names reflect something of Cellini's contempt for the two individuals.

by a certain fellow from Savoy: this is the same Enrico de Oziaco Cellini mentions in the note to p. 186.

189 *I struck the back of my head*: Cellini actually says he struck 'la memoria', meaning the spot on the back part of the head where the faculty of memory was believed to reside.

190 *toward the Church of the Trespontina*: Santa Maria della Trespontina, known by that name because it was on the 'other side of the bridge' from the Castello and St Peter's Cathedral.

the wife of Alessandro, Duke of Florence: see note to p. 35.

191 *made her entry into Rome*: this occurred on 3 November 1538, some time after Cellini had been imprisoned.

Borgo Vecchio: the Borgo or the medieval quarter near St Peter's Cathedral.

Cardinal Cornaro: see note to p. 124.

Master Iacopo da Perugia: Giacomo Rastelli (see note to p. 83).

192 *I am very grieved*: although the Pope usually refers to himself in the first-person plural, in this instance he seems to drop into the more familiar form ('I am very grieved', not 'We are very grieved') in order to convince his interlocutors that he is truly personally concerned over Cellini's well-being.

193 *for the Parco Maioris*: the College of the Abbreviators of the Parco Maggiore e Minore, founded by Pope Pius II, was composed of some seventy-two of the most learned prelates in Rome, who were charged with the composition of papal bulls and briefs.

Pope Alexander: it was not Alexander VI but actually Innocent VIII (1484–92) who imprisoned the future Pope Paul III, then known merely as Alessandro Farnese.

193 *Pietro Chiavelluzzi*: a relative of Alessandro Farnese whose real name was Marganio, and who helped him escape from the Castel Sant'Angelo.

194 *Cardinal Santa Fiore*: Guido Ascanio Sforza (1518–64), the son of Bosio (Count of Santa Fiore) and Costanza Farnese, the Pope's natural daughter; Sforza was made a cardinal at the age of 16 in 1534 by Paul III.

195 *located under the Cardinal's palace*: this is the Palazzo Sforza-Cesarini, constructed by Cardinal Rodrigo Borgia (later Pope Alexander VI) and substantially rebuilt in the nineteenth century; the palace overlooks Via dei Banchi Vecchi, where Cellini's workshop was originally located.

tool for cleaning off quicksilver: here Cellini uses the technical term *svivatoio*; in ch. XXVI of his treatise on goldsmithing Cellini calls the tool an *avvivatoio*.

a scene from Hell: Cellini says literally that he depicted 'a Hell'.

Giovan Francesco della Tacca: this may well be a relative or brother of the Giovampiero della Tacca mentioned earlier in I, 22.

196 *Andrea Centano*: Venetian patrician and Bishop of Limassol (Cyprus) 1539–60, removed on a charge of heresy.

provide for his expenses: under normal circumstances, a prisoner in the Castel Sant'Angelo was required to pay for his own meals and incidentals: by agreeing to provide for Cellini's upkeep, the Pope is attempting to make his return to prison seem more like a visit to the Pope as his guest, or a stay at a convalescent hospital.

198 *Corpus Domini*: the feast of Corpus Christi.

the day after Corpus Domini: 10 June 1539.

199 *Torre di Nona*: the papal prison was located near the church of San Salvatore in Lauro near the Piazza Navona. Unlike the Castel Sant'Angelo, which was reserved for important prisoners, this prison was for common criminals, and the fact that the Pope was sending Cellini there underscored his evil intentions.

200 *Messer Benedetto da Cagli*: see note to p. 175.

doing me this great injustice ... pardon her: Cellini's desire to surpass everyone extends even to this deathbed situation: not only does he claim he needs no priestly intermediary for his confession, having made his confession privately and directly to God, something that would have been considered heretical and far too close to Protestant thinking, but he himself pardons the Church and the Pope for this injustice, an action that would be considered at the very least highly presumptuous.

with the Duchess I mentioned before: Margaret of Austria. Pier Luigi's wife was Girolama Orsini, daughter of Lodovico Orsini, Count of Pitigliano; she had the reputation of being a very honest and pious woman.

my former husband: Alessandro de' Medici.

202 *Giovanni Villani's 'Chronicles'*: this history of early Florence by Villani (see note to p. 5) was eventually published between 1537 and 1554.

Thus, if Cellini had a printed copy of Villani's history rather than a manuscript, it would have been a partial edition, perhaps that of the first ten books which appeared in the 1537 Venetian edition.

unbelievable agony of the executioner's axe: Cellini's actual words are the 'passione del coltello', or literally the 'martyrdom of the axe'. Employing the word *passione*, used to refer to Christ's death or to the martyrdom of a saint, is one more means of describing his plight in religious terms.

203 *Captain Sandrino Monaldi*: Alessandro Monaldi was a captain in the Florentine militia during the siege of 1529–30, when the city held out against an invading army sent to restore the Medici to power; in 1530, after the Medici victory, he was imprisoned in Piombino.

204 *in dialogue form*: this dialogue between Cellini's body and his soul has reminded some scholars of Dante's *Vita Nuova* (particularly ch. XII): Cellini's lyric powers, as he proves here and elsewhere in his attempts to write verse, were not equal to those enjoyed by Dante.

205 *to compose a 'capitolo'*: a capitolo is a verse form whose name derives from the term Petrarch employed to describe the six parts or 'chapters' of his *Triumphs*, the form of which originated in Dante's *terza rima* verse. While originally used in allegorical or moral poetry, during the Renaissance, the *capitolo* developed into the classic verse form for satirical poetry, and was used by such poets as Ludovico Ariosto, Francesco Berni, and Lorenzo de' Medici. There is no essential metrical difference between Dante's *terza rima* and the *capitolo*, although some critics consider the *capitolo* a corruption of Dante's more lofty poetic purposes. The classic form of *terza rima* consists of tercets of hendecasyllabic verse in rhyme (*rima incatenata*: *aba, bcb, cdc, ded . . . xyx, yzy, z*), in which the first line rhymes with the third, the second with the first of the following tercet, and so forth.

in the appropriate place: see I, 128.

the first day of August: the holiday known today in Italy as Ferragosto, which now coincides with the Feast of the Assumption on 15 August.

the preacher Foiano was starved to death: Benedetto Tiezzi (from the town of Foiano in the Valdichiana) was a Dominican friar from the Santa Maria Novella Monastery in Florence who, as a follower of Savonarola, opposed the Medici during the siege of Florence; in 1530 Clement VII condemned him to die of starvation in the Castel Sant'Angelo.

206 *the pit called Sammalò*: this was a subterranean cell into which prisoners were lowered by a rope and left to die. The name given to the place by Cellini presents some difficulties. One theory is that the name derives from an image of a saint named Marocco (deformed into Sammaraco) which was to be found there. One difficulty of this is that there seems to be no such saint. Others have suggested that the name derives from a corruption of another foreign name, and the name Moroc, a Scottish bishop from the ninth century whose feast day falls on 8 November, has

been suggested. Bellotto (431, n. 22) suggests that the name may derive from the corrupted name of Saint Maclou or Malò, who died in 640 and for whom the French city in Normandy is named. Bellotto also suggests that Cellini employs this name because it may recall Guillaume Briçon-net (d. 1514), the Bishop of St Malò, who lived in Rome at the beginning of the century and who was infamous for his many evil deeds, especially against Florentines.

206 *De profundis . . . speravi*: *De profundis clamavit* are the opening lines of Psalm 130 of the Latin Bible, which should actually be *clamavi* rather than *clamavit* (*De profundis clamavi a te, Domine*—'Out of the depths I have cried to thee, O Lord!'); *Miserere*: the opening of Psalm 51 of the Latin Bible (*Miserere mei, Deus, magnam misericordiam tuam*—'Have mercy on me, O God, according to thy steadfast love'); *In te Domine speravi*: the opening of Psalm 31 of the Latin Bible 'In you, Lord, I have trusted'.

207 *a 'Qui habitat in aiutorium'*: the first line of Psalm 90 in the Latin Bible actually reads *Qui habitat in adiutorio Altissimi*—'He who dwells in the shelter of the Most High.'

208 *as if by a wind*: some commentators have noted that Cellini may have found his inspiration for this dream vision from Ezekiel 1: 4, where a strong wind precedes a series of visions. Cellini could have derived the notion of a prophetic dream from the long tradition of classical, medi-eval, and Renaissance dream visions, including those in Petrarch; see Julia Conaway Bondanella, *Petrarch's Visions and Their Renaissance Analogues* (Madrid: José Porrúa Turanzas, 1973).

209 *a bath of the purest molten gold*: the aesthetic vision Cellini describes here is exactly what one might expect from a goldsmith—a glorious vision of liquid gold, the tool of his trade now sublimated into a religious appar-ition in a mystical experience of the divine. Cellini's description of the sun may also have connections to alchemy.

a figure dressed like a priest: commentators identify this figure with that of St Peter in his pontifical robes.

210 *on the day which is approaching*: i.e. 2 November.

212 *this was in 1538*: Cellini was in these large quarters originally in 1538; when he is returned to them it is 1539.

Messer Antonio Ugolini, his brother: Antonio replaced his brother on 1 December 1539.

whom I mentioned previously: see I, 108.

a certain Lione: Leone Leoni (1509–90), medal-maker, sculptor, and goldsmith whose chequered life included many scrapes with the law, not unlike those of Cellini. Vasari wrote his life, and he worked for a number of important patrons (including Charles V, Ferrante Gonzaga, and

Andrea Doria). In November 1538 he became the engraver at the Roman Mint, a position Cellini considered his due. Leone retained the position until 1540, after an attack upon another papal jeweller, reminiscent of Cellini's own violent actions.

214 *called Monsignor de' Rossi of Parma*: Giovanni Girolamo dei Rossi di San Secondo (d. 1564), brother to Pier Maria de' Rossi, the Count of San Secondo, was appointed Bishop of Pavia by Clement VII in 1530. He was deposed and imprisoned in the Castel Sant'Angelo on suspicion of complicity in the murder of Count Alessandro Langosco in 1538; released in 1544 but stripped of his position, he went into exile in Milan and France, where he met Cellini again. In 1550 Pope Julius III restored him to his bishopric and named him Governor of Rome. His various writings include a sonnet praising Cellini's *Perseus*.

215 *Monsignor di Morluc*: see note to p. 178.

Cardinal Farnese: Alessandro Farnese (1521–89), the son of Pier Luigi, named Archbishop of Parma and Cardinal by Paul III at the age of 14 in 1534; he was an ambitious church politician, who aspired to the papacy but never achieved his goal, although he served on diplomatic missions to the most important rulers of Europe (Francis I, Charles V). He commissioned the Palazzo Farnese at Caprarola and was a great patron of the arts.

the Cardinal of Ferrara: see note to p. 169.

about French court gossip: Cellini employs the word *francioserie*, a derogatory term that refers to the politics of the French court. Even though Cellini seems contemptuous of such matters, he was very anxious to work in France.

216 *Messer Bindo Altoviti's*: Bindo Altoviti (1491–1557), a rich Florentine banker who opposed Medici power and provided substantial patronage for Roman artists. His palace on the Tiber river was frescoed in part by Vasari. In 1898 Bernardo Berenson purchased this bronze bust of Altoviti Cellini had made and sent it to Isabella Stewart Gardner in Boston, where it now remains in the Isabella Stewart Gardner Museum in that city. See II, 79–80 for more information on the bust.

Bernardo Galluzzi: a Florentine of a noble family.

everything that subsequently happened to Signor Pier Luigi: Pier Luigi was killed in 1547, some eight years after Cellini was supposedly forewarned of his demise.

217 *as in that location*: Cellini's halo was not a figment of his imagination but a phenomenon called *Heiligenschein* (German for 'halo'), created by something called 'back scattering', which happens whenever sunlight enters a dewdrop and bounces backwards out to the front. The halo is the glare from this backward-bouncing sunlight. Because of the path of the beam, one can normally only see the halo around one's own shadow. (Eric Sonstroem, 'Your Sainted Shadow', from the radio programme *A Moment of Science*, Indiana University, 1996).)

217 *Evident Here*: Cellini's fame certainly does not rest upon his lyric talents. In spite of the pride he obviously feels toward the composition of this *capitolo*, it never measures up to the standard set by Francesco Berni or other Florentine poets who made such satirical poems famous. We have not rendered it in verse, in an attempt to express its literal content.

218 *with stagnant water*: some commentaries to the autobiography interpret this *acqua morta* as urine.

219 *the moresca*: the *moresca* was a frenetic dance associated with the Moors.

    in a book about one of our kinsmen: a book about God (man's common parent), in other words, the Bible.

220 *Take your clothing, Benvenuto, and go!*: Cellini refers here to the healing of the paralytic at the Pool of Bethesda in Jerusalem, which had miraculous restorative powers, as recounted in John 5: 1–15. It was reputed that an angel (such as the archangel Raphael) would come and stir the waters from time to time, and that the first individual to enter the pool subsequently would be healed. The paralytic, however, never succeeded in arriving first in line and had to wait until he encountered Christ there, who ordered him to take up his bed and walk: he then discovered that he was cured.

    and the 'Paternoster': Cellini refers here to: (1) the Credo or Nicene Creed (Lat. *credo*, for 'I believe'), the statement of Christian belief formulated by the Council of Nicea in 325; (2) the *Salve, Regina* (Lat., 'Hail, Holy Queen'), the opening words of an antiphon in honour of the Virgin Mary, probably composed in the eleventh century and usually sung at the conclusion of evening prayer in the Liturgy of the Hours; and (3) the *Paternoster* or Lord's Prayer (see Luke 11: 2–4 and Matthew 6: 9–13), which became an important part of the Mass.

    those lilies: the Farnese coat of arms contained six lilies; Cellini has been tortured by the Farnese to such an extent that he no longer wishes to have anything to do with other places using lilies in their coats of arms— Florence (one lily) or France (three lilies).

    I shall flee away: continuing the not altogether successful conceit, Cellini says he would avoid even the painted representations of the Annunciation, which usually contained the archangel Gabriel holding a lily, if it reminded him of the Farnese lilies.

    I have seen: the next few verses represent more or less obscure allusions to visions (some prophetic) that Cellini experiences.

    the swiftest heaven: the *Primum Mobile*, the fastest part of Heaven and origin of all motion in the Ptolemaic universe.

221 *First the bell of the Castello must be broken*: apparently a reference to the death of the Castellan.

    He told me this: God.

a dark bier, Decorated with broken lilies: this appears to be a prophecy of the death of Pier Luigi Farnese.

saw Her who afflicts and tortures souls: probably Death.

This worthy angel: i.e. the angel of the vision.

Him who makes the sun rise and set: God.

a cruel captain and thief: probably the Monaldi mentioned in I, 120.

November: when it comes, you'll be lost and cursed: Cellini had learned in his vision that he would be freed and his jailers undone on 2 November, although he was actually finally freed on 24 December 1539.

to them: i.e. to the other prisoners and jailers.

lost all hope: i.e. all hope of killing Cellini.

222 *I said the 'Miserere'*: see note to p. 206.

223 *BOOK TWO*: the reader should bear in mind that the division of Cellini's manuscript into two books (as well as into numbered chapters) is the work of subsequent editors, not Cellini himself. The original manuscript contains no divisions by chapter, book, or subject-matter.

the Cardinal of Ferrara: see note to p. 169. Ippolito d'Este actually resided in the palace of Cardinal Gonzaga while Cellini stayed with him in Rome in 1540. Ippolito's treasurer, Tommaso Mosti, kept a register of the cardinal's accounts, which reveals a number of expenses recovered by the cardinal for matting to cover the floor of Cellini's workplace, the cost of erecting a goldsmith's furnace, and other disbursements for items Cellini made for the cardinal, including: four silver candlesticks, a chalice, a bronze bust of the Emperor Vitellius, gold wire for a rosary, not to mention the salaries for two of Cellini's assistants, Pagolo (Paolo) Romano and Ascanio di Tagliacozzo.

our craft: as was the fashion during most of the Italian Renaissance, Cellini refers to his profession by the word *arte*, but the term did not yet embody the meaning of 'art' as we know it today, but rather 'craft', 'trade', or 'profession'. It is, however, the noble example of such geniuses as Michelangelo, as well as the writings of Cellini and Vasari, that eventually elevate painting, sculpture, and architecture from the realm of workmanship (that is, craft) to the realm of art, defined more as we employ the term today.

other things of significant value: in fact, an inventory of 23 October 1538 made after Cellini's imprisonment mentions several pieces that could fit the works he describes here.

Messer Luigi Alamanni and Messer Gabbriel Cesano: for Luigi Alamanni, see the note to p. 74. Gabriello Maria da Cesano (1490–1568) was a lawyer and humanist who was a friend to most of the important intellectuals of the time. Claudio Tolomei dedicated a dialogue to him in 1556 that presents Cesano as a defender of Tuscan as the model for a literary language in Italy. He was named Bishop of Saluzzo by Pope Paul IV in 1556. A manuscript of a work by Cesano on Aristotle's *Ethics* is conserved in the Vatican Library.

224 *driving out the Arians*: the two illustrations refer to the Cardinal's titles, the primary sources of his great wealth—the first to the archdiocese of Lyons; and the second to the archbishopric of Milan. St Ambrose is the patron saint of Milan, and it was popularly believed that he came to the assistance of the Milanese when they defeated the troops of the Emperor Ludwig of Bavaria on 21 February 1339. This popular belief was apparently grafted onto another tradition concerning the supposed role of Ambrose in driving the Arians out of Italy. In his *Treatise on Goldsmithing* (XIII), Cellini describes this seal in detail and says that he was paid 300 ducats for it. The original has been lost but a copy is preserved in the Musée des Beaux-Arts in Lyons.

surpassed even the great Lautizio: see note to p. 41.

a model for a salt-cellar: this will eventually become the famous salt-cellar finally executed for Francis I. As Pope-Hennessy notes (*Cellini*, 85), the question of which design to follow provided Cellini with the occasion for making an important pronouncement on the relationship between art and iconography. As the cardinal was a very wise patron, he left the ultimate choice to Cellini.

226 *because the Cardinal Tornon had given it to him*: François de Tournon (1489–1562), a counsellor of Francis I; after the king's defeat at the Battle of Pavia, Tournon negotiated his liberation and was made a cardinal in 1530. While he was a great patron of the arts and letters, his religious policies, hostile to both the Valdensians and the Huguenots, were instrumental in bringing about the Wars of Religion in France.

my poor sister: Liperata (see I, 40).

Master Cherubino: Cherubino Sforzani (nicknamed Il Parolaro or 'Chatterbox') was from Modena, and worked for the Este family as well as the Pope.

on Monday of Holy Week: on 22 March 1540.

we three: Cellini set out on this trip with only Pagolo and Ascanio as company.

at Monteruosi: a small town between Rome and Viterbo.

227 *ourselves one post station from Siena*: this was a place where travellers changed tired horses for fresh ones, usually an inn. The place in question was outside the gate of Siena known as the Porta Camollìa, to the north-east of the city.

a giulio: see n. to p. 33.

Good Friday: 26 March 1540.

228 *in that young Roman*: this would be Pagolo, mentioned earlier.

230 *Staggia*: the next post-station on the road toward Florence, a fortified hamlet about 15 km. between Siena and Poggibonsi.

a bit of meat soup yesterday: meat was prohibited on Good Friday.

the Duke of Melfi: Alfonso Piccolomini, the Duke of Amalfi, governed Siena for Charles V as Captain-General from 1529 until 1541.

232 *three hundred thousand ducats of the Camera*: in 1539 Duke Ercole II of Ferrara paid Pope Paul III a large sum (historians cite a somewhat lower figure than Cellini provides, between 100,000 and 180,000 golden ducats) to confirm the investiture of the towns and provinces, including Modena and Reggio, that the Este family had previously received from Pope Alexander VI. It should not be forgotten that the Renaissance papacy was also a secular power, with lands extending far beyond present-day Vatican City.

figure of Fury: many commentators have noted that the description of this reverse alludes to a medal made for Clement VII (see I, 70). Pope-Hennessy (*Cellini*, 87–8) notes that three portrait commissions date from Cellini's time in Ferrara: two gesso moulds of a head of Ippolito d'Este; a portrait of Benedetto Accolti; and this portrait of the duke, which has not survived except in a possible plaster cast from a wax model that is in the Goethe Museum at Weimar.

Pretiosa in conspectu Domini: literally, 'Precious in the sight of the Lord', referring to the cost of the agreement the Duke had made.

233 *Messer Alberto Bendedio*: see I, 28.

to travel by post: travelling by post would allow Cellini to change horses and to arrive more quickly than if he was forced to allow a single animal to rest periodically.

234 *Bernardo Saliti*: little is known of this individual except for his assistance to Cellini on this occasion.

a ring that worked against the cramps: Cellini uses the expression *un anello del granchio*, which were usually rings of copper or lead that supposedly functioned to counteract illnesses and had little monetary value.

235 *Messer Alfonso de' Trotti*: a minister of both Duke Alfonso I and Ercole II in Ferrara, who was involved in a dispute with Ludovico Ariosto, the author of *Orlando furioso*. Some years later (1568–70) Cellini rented Trotti a house near the Piazza Santa Maria Novella in Florence.

236 *with Cardinal Salviati and the Cardinal of Ravenna*: see respectively I, 25 and I, 36 (the Cardinal of Ravenna was Benedetto Accolti).

those talented musicians: although Cellini does not specify their names, Ferrara was famous for its musicians and composers during the Renaissance.

237 *my previously mentioned fear*: actually, Cellini never mentions fearing anything, but he is probably referring to the possible threat of being pursued by the Duke's men after his departure from Ferrara. He could have been afraid of some other danger in Milan, such as an outbreak of the plague or a report of some enemy in the area.

237 *an abbey that belonged to the Cardinal*: the Abbey of Esnay (see I, 98).

at Fontainebleau: Cellini spells the name *Fontana Beleò*, or *Biliò*, and believed that its name derived from the phrase 'fountain of beautiful water' rather than from Fontem Bilhaud, which is a more likely origin. Cellini arrived there in mid-September, 1540.

240 *to abandon the stroller that always carried you?*: Cellini actually calls it the 'father's stroller' (*il carruccio del babbo*). Today the 'carruccio' is called a *girello*—a four-wheeled cart used by small children when they are first learning to walk by themselves.

to that boundless beauty that He Himself had shown to me: a reference to Cellini's visions in the Castel Sant'Angelo during his imprisonment.

241 *his treasurer*: in 1540 the treasurer was a certain Guillaume Proudhomme, Signeur de Fontenay-en Brie.

242 *Le Petit Nesle*: this building, which Cellini calls the *Picol Nello*, was part of the castle of Nesle situated on the left bank of the Seine. It was acquired by Philippe VI in 1308 from the Lord of Nesle in Picardy, the origin of its name. In 1522 Francis I had given Le Petit Nesle to a judge, and the property was eventually passed to the Provost of Paris, who was, at the time Cellini arrived in Paris, Jean d'Estouteville, the Lord of Villebon and a counsellor to the King. Cellini's desire to have this particular spot would, of course, set him on a collision course with one of the city's most powerful men.

243 *Monsignor di Villurois*: Nicolas de Neuville (d. 1598), Lord of Villeroy, who served the King as a counsellor and secretary of state in charge of the royal finances.

Monsignor di Marmagna: Jean Lallemant, Lord of Marmaignes, who became the King's secretary in 1561. Cellini mentions him in his *Treatise on Goldsmithing* (XII), where he is called 'a shrewd old fellow and terribly fierce' (p. 60) who tries to embarrass Cellini by presenting the French King with an ancient bronze statuette at the same time that Cellini was presenting his famous salt-cellar: the King responded by saying that he was fortunate to live in an age when modern artists could surpass the ancients!

244 *Monsignor lo Iscontro d'Orbech*: Iscontro is a corrupted form of the title Visconte. Orbech is a town in the Calvados region of Normandy.

these figures were of Jupiter, Vulcan, and Mars: Cellini worked on the silver figures for the entire five years he lived in France, and when he left in 1545 only the Jupiter was complete.

made him a present of them: Cellini received 74 scudi for this project on 12 December 1540; the King received the gifts on 16 March 1541.

245 *Madame d'Étampes*: Anne de Pisseleu (1508–c.1580), the wife of Giovanni de Brosse whom the King had named Count d'Étampes. She was

the mistress of Francis I until his death in 1547, and a very powerful figure at the court.

the Cardinal of Lorraine: Jean de Lorraine, son of the Duke of Lorraine, was named a cardinal by Pope Leo X in 1518; a generous patron of the arts, he was a good friend of the French King, and died in 1550.

the King of Navarre, the brother-in-law of King Francis: Henry II (1503–55), Duke of Albret, who married the sister of Francis I in 1527 and went with the King on his ill-fated Italian invasion that ended with his capture after the disastrous defeat at Pavia in 1525. Henry managed to escape capture, but lived most of his life at the French court.

and the Queen, the sister of King Francis: Marguerite d'Angoulème or de Navarre (1492–1549), widowed after the death of her first husband, married Henry II in 1527. An important writer of religious texts, her best-known work is a collection of *novelle* entitled the *Heptameron* that follows the literary tradition established by Boccaccio's *Decameron*. She spent much of her life at her brother's court.

the Dauphin and the Dauphiness: Henry, second son of Francis I, who reigned as King of France as Henry II from 1546 until 1559. In 1533 he married Catherine de' Medici (1519—89), daughter of Lorenzo de' Medici, Duke of Urbino (the man to whom Niccolò Machiavelli dedicated *The Prince*). Catherine de' Medici acted as Regent of France, and during the minority of her two sons, Francis II (1559–60) and Charles IX (1560–63), she became a powerful force in French politics. She is best known for her role in the Massacre of St Bartholomew in 1572.

246 *his palace*: the Louvre.

247 *for whoever was to have it*: see II, 2.

Monsignor lo risconte d'Orbeche: in II, 13 Cellini had already referred to this individual as Monsignor lo Iscontro d'Orbech, and the fact that he spells his name and title quite differently points to the fact that he never seriously edited his manuscript for such minor inconsistencies. According to Cellini's Italian editor (Bellotto, 507, n. 16), Cellini may not merely have miswritten the Italian term for the French title (*iscontro* or *riscontro* for Visconte), but he may also have thought that the term *riscontro* was similar to the term employed in Florence in the sixteenth century (as in *notaio di riscontro*) for a notary charged with registering the notarized acts and various taxes.

one thousand old gold scudi: the King specifies the old form of coinage as opposed to the new coins minted in silver.

251 *the soul*: Cellini employs the technical word *anima* or 'soul' to refer to the internal block or core placed inside a statue before casting that keeps the interior hollow by not allowing the molten metal to fill up the space and become solidified. He discusses bronze casting not only in his autobiography but in several important sections of his *Treatise on Sculpture* (chs. I–III).

252 *the most wonderful, valiant soldier Piero Strozzi*: a member of the Florentine family that provided the focal point for opposition to Medici domination of their native city, Piero (1510–58) was a soldier of ability who
passed into the service of the French monarch after anti-Medici forces
lost the disastrous Battle of Montemurlo (1537) to Medici troops backed
by Spanish allies. He was named Marshal of France in 1557 and fought
for Henry II in numerous battles, finally losing his life in the French
King's service at the siege of Thionville.

Benvenuto, mon ami: Cellini reports the term of endearment ('my friend')
used by the King in his native tongue to call attention to his personal
relationship with the French ruler.

Messer Antonio Massone: Antoine Le Maçon, secretary to Queen Marguerite of Navarre; upon her suggestion, he completed the first French
translation of Giovanni Boccaccio's *Decameron*, which appeared in print
in 1545.

253 *keep them with me*: these documents were retained by Cellini until the end
of his life, when they passed to his heirs. The materials apparently passed
into the archives of the Confraternity of the Buonomini of San Martino
in 1662 after Cellini's line died out. Then they passed into the National
Archive in Florence, where they are stored today. They bear the date of
July 1542.

the rape of Ganymede: according to Ovid (*Metamorphoses*, X. 152–61),
Ganymede's beauty caused Jupiter to fall in love with him; after transforming himself into an eagle, Jupiter carried the young boy to Olympus,
where he was made his cup-bearer.

Leda and the swan: see n. to p. 40. As a result of their union (according to
different variants), the heavenly twins Castor and Pollux, Helen of Troy,
and Clytemnestra were born. The various transformations of Jupiter
became important artistic themes in Italian Renaissance art.

Count of Anguillara . . . Pitigliano . . . Mirandola: scholars have so far not
provided absolutely certain identifications of these three individuals.
Anguillara and Pitigliano were places associated with the Orsini family:
the first count may well have been Flaminio Anguillara da Stabbia (d.
1565), who was a soldier in Francis I's army under the command of Piero
Strozzi, or it may have been his son Averso. The Count of Pitigliano was
probably either Giovan Francesco Orsini or his son Nicola. The Count of
Mirandola, Galeotto Pico (d. 1550), one of Francis I's generals, murdered his uncle Giovanni Francesco II in 1533 and fled to France in 1536
to escape the wrath of Charles V.

254 *for that beautiful fountain*: Cellini thinks the name of the King's villa refers
to an actual fountain.

at San Germano dell'Aia: Saint Germain-en-Laye, a small town on the
banks of the Seine with a royal castle.

had broken out again: even though the Treaty of Nice (signed in 1537) was to prevent war between the two leaders for twelve years, hostilities between Francis I and Charles V broke out again in May 1542 and continued until 1544, after a French victory led to a new truce signed at Crèpy-en-Laonnois.

255 *the portal of the palace of Fontainebleau*: the so-called Porte Dorée on the south side of the castle.

that bad French style of theirs: in accordance with the terminology of his era, Cellini uses the word *maniera* (literally 'manner'—the origin of the term Mannerism to refer to the period style of Cellini's day) for 'style'.

a figure representing Fontainebleau: this became one of Cellini's most famous works, the *Nymph of Fontainebleau* (now in the Louvre in Paris), which was cast before 2 March 1543 and which was never placed over the Porte Dorée. It was eventually given by Henry II to his mistress Diane de Poitiers, who placed it above the entrance to her castle in Anet. The casting of this relief is described in Cellini's *Treatise on Sculpture* (I). Excellent reproductions of the complete work in colour and details in black and white may be consulted in Pope-Hennessy, *Cellini* (plates 69; 75–82).

a satyr in place of each column: these figures were never cast but were left by Cellini in Paris in a form ready for casting. A preparatory drawing exists in the Woodner Collection in New York. The J. Paul Getty Museum in Malibu, California, also contains a bronze model for one of the two figures. See Pope-Hennessy, *Cellini* (plates 70—4) for an excellent colour illustration of this drawing in pen and brown ink and wash and for several views of the bronze model in colour.

a figure of Victory: two plaster casts remain of these figures in the Louvre in Paris. The bronze originals were moved to Anet with the Nymph at the castle of Diane de Poitiers, but were eventually destroyed in the nineteenth century. Pope-Hennessy, *Cellini* (plates 83–4) reproduces the plaster casts.

a salamander: according to medieval legend, the salamander was not only impervious to fire but had the power to extinguish flames. The emblem of Francis I was a salamander amidst the flames (it appears, for example, on the famous salt-cellar that Cellini fashioned), and it is not beyond the realm of possibility that Cellini invented the early incident about the salamander during his childhood (see I, 4) in order to make a connection to his future patron.

258 *Messer Guido Guidi*: (*c*.1500–69), the grandson of the painter Domenico Ghirlandaio, Guidi practised medicine at the court of France from 1542 until 1548, when he was recalled to Florence to the court of Duke Cosimo I. He also served as professor of medicine and philosophy at the University of Pisa until his death.

259 *Monsignor de' Rossi, brother of the Count of San Sicondo*: this churchman is the same man who was imprisoned with Cellini in the Castel Sant'Angelo

(see I, 126). His brother, Pier Maria, was a general in the French army. He dedicated a number of poems to members of the French court while in Paris.

259 *for Messer Luigi Alamanni*: see I, 41, 44 and II, 10, 24, and 37. Alamanni, like so many other Florentine exiles, had opposed Medici control of his native city, and arrived in France in 1530.

first handsome book on medicine: Guidi had the printer Pierre Gauthier publish an important Latin translation of works on surgery by Hippocrates, with commentary by Galen and Oribasius, which was of some historical importance.

260 *Francesco Primaticcio*: (1505–70), native of Bologna and an important painter, sculptor, and architect, who worked with Giuliano Romano on the Palazzo del Té in Mantua. The Duke of Mantua sent him to the French court in 1532, where he completed a number of important works at Fontainebleau and worked with Rosso Fiorentino. Together, the two Italian exiles established an important branch of Mannerism in France known as the School of Fontainebleau.

262 *Phe phe, Satan, phe phe, Satan, alè, phe.*: in French, probably 'paix paix, Satan, paix paix, Satan, allez, paix' ('Peace, peace, Satan, depart, peace').

263 *these commentators make Dante say things he never thought of*: at the very beginning of Canto VII of Dante's *Inferno*, Pluto addresses Dante and his guide Virgil with the gibberish phrase 'Pape Satàn, pape Satàn, aleppe!' Cellini provides an utterly fantastic explanation of this phrase, claiming that judges of the sixteenth century were still using the phrase Dante learned during the time he supposedly spent in Paris, a visit that early commentators on Dante's life (Boccaccio, Giovanni Villani) claimed to have taken place. In the biography of Giotto contained in the *Lives of the Artists*, Vasari makes the probably false claim that Giotto too visited Paris.

the Macaroni family: little is known of this goldsmith who accompanied Cellini to France.

by the name of Bartolomeo Chioccia: little is known about this goldsmith from Ferrara, whose name was probably Bartolomeo Perini.

Pagolo Micceri: a Florentine goldsmith, who was driven out of Cellini's house in 1543 because of a sexual liaison he had with Cellini's model Caterina.

Tommaso Guadagni: a Florentine living in Lyons, Guadagni commissioned a painting of the Incredulity of St Thomas from Francesco Salviati that he brought with him to Lyons and to the Florentines in Lyons around 1547 (it is now in the Louvre).

264 *Mattia del Nazaro*: a native of Verona (called Mattia del Nassaro by Vasari in the 'Life of Valerio Vicentino'), who came to France around 1517 to practise his various trades as goldsmith, die-caster, and musician. He died *c*.1547.

265 *make sure it's San Giuliano's*: in Boccaccio's *Decameron* (II, 2), the

character Rinaldo d'Asti attributes his success in love to his practice of addressing an Our Father to San Giuliano every day upon leaving his lodgings.

267 *you are certainly Unwelcome*: another of the frequent puns on Cellini's first name in the Italian (*benvenuto*/welcome; *malvenuto*/unwelcome).

not known her in any way whatsoever: here, of course, Cellini uses 'knowing' in the biblical sense of sexual relations.

they deserve to be burned at the stake: Caterina for the crime of sodomy she has explicitly confessed to and the mother for giving false testimony at the trial.

268 *Monsignor della Fa*: Jacques de la Fa was treasurer of Francis I from 1541 until the year of his death in 1545; extant documents attest to the fact that he was in charge of works executed at Le Petit Nesle by Cellini and others.

your great colossus: the statue of Francis I as Mars.

273 *the brother of Piero Strozzi*: Leone Strozzi (1515–54), the son of Filippo Strozzi, became the prior of Capua at an early age under the protection of Clement VII. After Clement died, he became a soldier for France and distinguished himself in the Mediterranean. He was killed during a war that the Strozzi fought in a fruitless attempt to free Siena from Medici control.

274 *as anything ever has been*: this figure must refer to the lunette which was part of the *Nymph of Fontainebleau* described in II, 21.

as I have said before: Cellini describes this work twice in his auto-biography and once in his *Treatise on Goldsmithing* (XII). The descriptions in his autobiography and his treatise differ in certain respects, no doubt due to the amount of time that had passed between the composition of the two works, as well as to Cellini's lapses of memory. The single best discussion of its composition, iconography, and casting may be found in Pope-Hennessy, *Cellini* (ch. 5), which also contains extremely beautiful colour or black-and-white plates of the work from a variety of angles (plates 51; 55–68). The work was completed in 1543 and remained the property of the French monarchs until it was presented as a gift by Charles IX in 1570 to Archduke Ferdinand of the Tyrol. Today it is preserved in the Kunsthistorisches Museum in Vienna, and is the only one of Cellini's major jewellery projects that has survived.

275 *Night, Day, Twilight, and Dawn*: as Pope-Hennessy notes (*Cellini*, 109), Cellini's figures refer to the Medici Chapel in Florence's San Lorenzo by Michelangelo, where reclining figures represent Morning, Evening, Night, and Day, and which Cellini must have seen during the time he was in Florence, when the figures were already carved and lying on the floor of the chapel, only to be installed over the Medici tombs after Cellini's return to Florence in 1546.

Laocoön . . . Apollo: the Laocoön is the renowned marble group that was discovered in Rome in 1506 and is now in the Vatican Museum; the Cleopatra is, in fact, a statue of a sleeping Ariadne or a Bacchante now in the Vatican; the Venus alluded to here is not the more famous Capitoline or Medicean Venuses but the one in the Museo Pio Clementino in the Vatican; the Commodus is a statue of Hercules in the Vatican Museum; the Zingara is probably a statue of Diana in the Galleria Borghese Collection in Rome; and the Apollo is the renowned Belvedere Apollo unearthed at Anzio in 1495 and now in the Vatican Museum. The works mentioned by Bologna number among the most famous statues recovered from classical antiquity during the Renaissance.

276 *in the proper place*: see II, 41.

the name Scorzone: while some commentators note that this is the name of a small, poisonous serpent, Cellini most likely refers to the thick-skinned toughness of rustics. *Scorza* in Italian means bark or rind, and *scorzone* means a tough, thick-skinned, or boorish individual.

a great French noblewoman: parochial records for the church of Saint-André-des-Arts (which no longer exists) attest to the identity of the godparents: Alamanni's wife was Maddalena Bonaiuti; Ricciardo del Bene's wife was Jehanne Louan. Cellini's daughter Costanza must have died quite young, even before he left Paris.

I never ever had anything to do with her again: although Cellini's remarks seem callous, in fact according to customs of his day he actually did the honourable thing by his young model, providing her with a dowry that would ultimately make her fortune.

277 *to his Admiral*: Claude d'Annebaut, made Marshall of France in 1538 and Admiral from 1543 until his death in 1552.

marched toward Paris: in June 1544 Charles V occupied Luxembourg and some of the cities in Flanders, invaded the Champagne district, and seemed to be on the verge of marching against Paris.

278 *when the Emperor passed through Paris*: Tunis was taken by the Emperor in 1535; in January 1540 Charles came to Paris, and Rosso Fiorentino and Primaticcio executed the various triumphal arches and decorations for this occasion.

279 *that enormous giant*: a reference to the statue of Mars for the fountain in Fontainebleau.

whose name was Messer Aniballe: see note to p. 277, on Claude d'Annebaut.

the treasurer Grolier: Jean Grolier (1479–1565), Superintendent of Finances from Lyons, a great patron of the arts and a collector of books and medals.

280 *new letters of ownership*: they still exist and are dated 15 July 1544.

281 *the button on crossbows*: the button is the part of the crossbow to which the string is attached to load the weapon.

previously mentioned statues: not the actual statues, of course, but the plaster casts of the works listed in II, 37.

I brought my Jupiter: Cellini provides a long description of the *Jupiter* in his *Treatise on Goldsmithing* (XXV). It was the only statue of the twelve ordered by Francis I to be completed, but no other information about it can be found, including drawings or models.

is like running the gauntlet: Cellini literally says like 'running between the pikes', since one form of punishment inflicted upon prisoners was to be forced to pass through two rows of soldiers armed with pikes, who killed them. This is one of the most striking metaphors to be found in Renaissance literature for the continuous comparison between the ancients and the moderns. In Cellini's mind, there is no question that his works (or, for that matter, the works of other masters such as Michelangelo) not only match but even surpass those of classical antiquity.

282 *his son the Dauphin (now king)*: since Henry II, the son of Francis I, died on 14 July 1559, it can be presumed that Cellini wrote this part of his autobiography before that date.

Madame Margherita his daughter: Marguerite de Valois (1523–74), daughter of Francis I, married the Duke of Savoy, Emanuele Filiberto, in 1559.

283 *to mock her*: a letter from the ambassador of Ferrara to his master the Duke, dated 29 January 1545, attests to the veracity of Cellini's description.

that great statue of Mars: Cellini's *Treatise on Sculpture* (VII) contains another lengthy description of his statue of Mars, about which nothing is heard after 1546.

284 *by the name of Lemmonio Boreò*: it has been suggested that this strange name is a distortion of two French phrases: either *le moine bourreau* (literally 'the monk executioner') or *le moine bourru* ('the ghost of a monk clad in drugget', which is a coarse wool cloth called *bure* in French). Le Petit Nesle had a poor reputation because of some murders committed there in the fourteenth century by Jeanne, the wife of Philip V.

with all his forces mustered: at the end of August 1544 an imperial army sacked towns within a few miles of Paris.

Monsignor Ass-Ox: while it is possible that Cellini felt the French pronunciation of the name of Claude d'Annebau (see II, 38–9) sounded like the French words *âne* ('ass') and *boeuf* ('ox'), it is more likely that he is using this name to show his contempt for the individual in question.

Girolimo Bellarmato: Gerolamo Bellarmato or Bellarmati (1493–1555) was a military architect and cosmographer from Siena who had been banished from his native city and had moved to France, where Francis I appointed him his chief engineer. One of his many projects was the design of the harbour at Le Havre.

285 *betrayed the King*: some historians have claimed that out of enmity against Diane de Poitiers, the mistress of the Dauphin, Madame

d'Étampes arranged for the bridge at Épernay to be cut too late to stop imperial forces from threatening Paris, thus forcing Francis I to accept the harsh conditions of the Treaty of Crépy (18 September 1544).

285   *That damned woman*: Madame d'Étampes.

288   *more beautiful ones than these*: Cellini seems to be repeating the words supposedly pronounced by Michelangelo when he examined the Baptistery doors in Florence executed by Lorenzo Ghiberti. Michelangelo's assessment is reported in Vasari's 'Life of Ghiberti' in *The Lives of the Artists* (trans. Julia and Peter Bondanella, p. 100).

289   *a great baron of France*: François de Bourbon (1491–1545), Count of Saint Paul and Duke of Estouteville, one of the King's best friends and a general who shared his imprisonment after the disastrous defeat at the Battle of Pavia in 1525.

      in the French fashion: given Cellini's generally negative opinion of the French, it is obvious that this remark should be taken ironically.

      these devils kept us in great tribulation: the Peace of Crépy (18 December 1544) ended hostilities between Francis I and Charles V, but the Emperor's ally, Henry VIII of England, continued to battle against the French after taking Boulogne, and war continued until the Treaty of Campe (7 June 1546).

290   *name of Argentana*: Argentan in Normandy (since Marguerite de Navarre had first been married to the Duke d'Alençon she retained his fiefs, one of which included this town).

291   *a sign that I could leave freely*: another version of Cellini's last words with the King and his ultimate departure from France is found in his *Treatise on Sculpture* (VIII).

      by the Bishop of Pavia: Giovangirolamo de' Rossi.

      also accompanied us: Ippolito Gonzaga was a relative of Galeotto della Mirandola (see II, 20). Nothing concrete is known of Tedaldi, but he may have been the son of one Bartolo di Leonardo Tedaldi who was an opponent of Medici tyranny. Many of the anti-Medici exiles lived in France after the government of Florence had become part of a pro-imperial Italian alliance.

292   *screaming 'stop thief!'* : the actual cry is *accorr'uomo*, an exclamation made from the two Italian words *accorrere* (to run to help) and *uomo* (man), normally translated 'help!'.

293   *we remained there for eight days*: Cellini's presence in Lyons is confirmed by a letter dated 7 July 1545 and written by the son of Luigi Alamanni (Battista) to Benedetto Varchi in Florence. Cellini apparently stayed in the home of the Panciatichi, a wealthy merchant family from Florence.

294   *Duke Pier Luigi*: Pier Luigi Farnese (Pope Paul III's son) was not formally named ruler of Parma and Piacenza until September 1545, and Cellini's use of the title 'Duke' at this point refers to his rank as Duke of

Castro. He was assassinated on 10 September 1547 by a conspiracy involving Count Giovanfrancesco Angosciuola and Count Agostino Landi, which had been instigated by Ferrante Gonzaga, governor of Milan.

296 *the money that was not intended for him*: Cellini seems to be saying that his brother-in-law sold the jewellery entrusted to him but did not spend the profits, keeping it safe for Cellini's arrival, and in the process lacked enough money for his ordinary expenses and was forced to turn to moneylenders and pawnbrokers.

wanted to provide for all his daughters: providing for six girls in Cellini's day would mean supplying them all with dowries for their eventual marriage, no small task even for Cellini. Two of these nieces apparently joined the Convent of Sant'Orsola in 1555 and 1569. Raffaello Tassi (the husband in question here, the second husband of his sister Liperata) died in 1545. Liperata apparently remarried a third time, to a goldsmith named Paolo Paolini who worked with Cellini on the *Perseus*.

at Poggio a Caiano: the Duke in question is Cosimo I de' Medici, who became Duke in 1537 and Grand Duke in 1569. Poggio a Caiano is the important villa built for Lorenzo de' Medici 'Il Magnifico' by Giuliano da San Gallo, and which contains important frescos and works of art by Andrea del Sarto, Franciabigio, Pontormo, and Alessandro Allori.

I loved this Duke Cosimo: the claim that Cellini's ancestors were close friends of the Medici dynasty can only be more of the same kind of posturing that opens his autobiography and links his ancestors to those of the ancient Romans. Whether or not Cellini really admired Duke Cosimo, he certainly needed his patronage, since he had burned his bridges in France with Francis I. However, given the fact that Cosimo's alliances were with the enemies of France and that many anti-Medici exiles populated the French court, the Duke was naturally a little suspicious of Cellini's motives (in fact, Cellini notes further on in his meeting that 'my Duke twisted about and seemed unable to wait until I stopped speaking').

his Duchess: Eleonora di Toledo (1522–62), daughter of the Viceroy of Naples, married Cosimo in 1539, giving him many daughters and firmly establishing dynastic ties with Spain and the Emperor. She is immortalized in a fine portrait of her by Bronzino in the Uffizi Collection in Florence.

this wonderful School: some scholars assume that Cellini's remark here about a school (he writes *Iscuola* with a capital letter) could refer to the Accademia delle arte del disegno, but this was founded by Cosimo I in 1563, years after Cellini's return to Florence. Cellini certainly desired to be considered a true artist and not merely a goldsmith (a trade that was not included in the more illustrious artistic endeavours by architects, painters, or sculptors that the Accademia honoured). By his sculpture Cellini would eventually qualify for membership in this distinguished body, and in fact, upon his death, the Accademia celebrated his funeral with a great deal of pomp, and he was buried in the Chapel of SS Annunziata in Florence dedicated to the guild of artists. It is also possible that Cellini means by 'School' another academy, the Accademia fiorentina, which was founded in 1541 and included as its members such artists as Bronzino and Michelangelo. However, this body was primarily concerned with the protection of the purity of the Tuscan language. It is most probable that Cellini merely means by 'School' the artistic environment of Florence during his day—one of the most influential 'schools' for painting, sculpture, and architecture that the world has ever known.

297   *a large statue for that fine piazza of his*: Piazza della Signoria, 'his' because Cosimo lived in the Palazzo Vecchio in front of the square.

all he wanted from me was a Perseus: in Greek mythology, Perseus was born of the union of Jupiter and Danaë, when the god came to Danaë in the form of a shower of golden rain. One of antiquity's most dashing heroes, he is pictured with a curved sword, given to him by Mercury, and a polished shield, provided by his protectress Minerva; he also wears winged sandals and his helmet may also have wings. His heroic deeds include the beheading of the Medusa (one of the Gorgons with snake-like hair whose gaze would turn an ordinary human into stone); the rescue of the beautiful damsel in distress, Andromeda, from a sea monster; and many minor events. His exploits are recounted most famously in Ovid's *Metamorphoses*, and in addition to Cellini's famous statue, Perseus became a popular figure in Renaissance art and literature.

his wardrobe chamber: this was a large space where Cosimo kept a number of works of art and in which he had also set up a goldsmith's shop.

the most beautiful work in the piazza: both Cellini and Cosimo I knew very well that some of Florence's most important and most symbolic sculptures were standing in the square outside the Duke's palace. Donatello's *Judith and Holofernes* was at the time in the Loggia dei Lanzi to the left of the façade of the Palazzo Vecchio, while Michelangelo's *David* was placed upon the steps of the palace facing the square. However, from the perspective of Renaissance symbolism or iconography, both Judith's slaying of Holofernes and David's triumph over Goliath represented an essentially republican message—the triumph of the weak over the strong, the people over the powerful. What Cosimo I intended to show with *Perseus* was a quite different vision of power: the triumph of order and stability associated with his household over the chaos of republican disorder linked to the very exiles that Cellini had associated with in France or Rome. Of course, Cellini revelled in the situation of being challenged to place a statue in competition with the two acknowledged geniuses in this form—Donatello and Michelangelo. If his *Perseus* was a success, it would set aside forever any doubts that he was a mere goldsmith (a tradesman) and would place him in the pantheon of the geniuses of which Florence was so rightly proud.

the two greatest men: note that Cellini calls them neither artisans nor artists but the greatest *men* since classical antiquity.

my model: this may well be the wax model now in the Museo Nazionale del Bargello in Florence. Cellini certainly made a number of models, both in wax and in bronze; the Museo del Bargello holds one in wax and one in bronze (for colour plates of the models, see Pope-Hennessy, *Cellini*, plates 87–90). A bronze model for the head of Medusa is preserved in London's Victoria and Albert Museum (see Pope-Hennessy, *Cellini*, plates 93–4).

298 *as a duke [and not as a merchant]*: in the original manuscript, the words 'acted more like a merchant than a duke', were erased and replaced, perhaps by a second copyist, with the words 'had a great desire to execute the most important undertakings'. The second part of the phrase '[and not as a merchant]' was also heavily erased in the manuscript. Apparently a second copyist was also a Medici supporter, or it could have been one of Cellini's relatives who had inherited the manuscript and did not wish to circulate a work containing such disparaging remarks about the ruling dynasty of Florence.

already located the house: now on Via della Colonna, formerly Via del Rosaio, which was entered from Via della Pergola, 59.

with false hope: in the original manuscript this word 'false' in the phrase 'false hope' is erased and the adjective 'good' is written in the right margin, once again underlining how the copyist tried to soften the criticism of the Duke.

a deed: Cellini calls the document a *rescritto* or 'rescript', which is closer to an official decree or order having the force of law than a traditional deed. As a citizen of one of the most legalistic societies in Renaissance Europe, Cellini should have known that any act of this sort should have been certified by a notary and made permanent and not susceptible to the whims of a monarch. He should have learned this lesson in France with Francis I and his chateau. On the rescript Cellini wrote a note in his own hand, declaring that since the Duke had given him this rescript in his own handwriting, he decided not to return to France, for he was much happier living in a house in his own native land under such a virtuous man as the Duke than living in a chateau in France.

I have always kept with me: both the Duke's deed or rescript and Cellini's petition are conserved in Florence's Biblioteca Nazionale.

Ser Pier Francesco Riccio: Riccio or Ricci (*c.*1490–1564) was secretary, provost of the cathedral, and majordomo of the duke. *Ser* is a shortened form of the title *Messer* that Cellini most frequently employs. It was most frequently used with a person who worked as a notary, and subsequently became a common form of address like Mr in English.

299 *the Duke's pedantic pedagogue*: in this chapter, introducing some of the

Duke's collaborators, Cellini employs a number of negative diminutives or distortions of spellings to underline his dislike for these individuals. In Riccio's case, he is described as the *pedantuzo* of the Duke.

299 *Lattanzio Gorini*: Purveyor to the Otto di Pratica (a Florentine government office) from 1543 to 1545.

that beastly Blockhead Bandinello: Cellini's great rival in Florence is Baccio (Bartolommeo) Bandinelli (see note to p. 8), but here he distorts his first name Baccio to Buaccio, or 'blockhead', 'great ox'.

the Clock Hall: The Sala del Oriolo in the Palazzo Vecchio was called the Clock Hall because it contained the cosmographic clock erected there around 1484 by Lorenzo della Volpaia for Lorenzo de' Medici, Il Magnifico. It was considered to be a technological marvel in its day.

300 *His Lordship*: this form of polite address (*Sua Signoria*) refers to Riccio, not the Duke.

as merely Ser Pier Francesco Riccio: as was previously noted, *Ser* is the title employed with non-noble individuals, generally priests or notaries. *Messer* or *Messere* is a title above *Ser* and would be employed with the lesser nobility. *Signore*, finally, is the title reserved for people of importance and noble rank. Shifting from 'Your Lordship' to *Ser* is the equivalent of downgrading Riccio's rank or status and would be taken, in this context, as an insult.

in advance of the time: Cellini is referring to the fact that later in 1553 Riccio was apparently struck by a mental illness.

302 *the son of a prostitute called Gambetta*: the boy's name was Cencio (a diminutive of Vincenzo), and his mother's name was Margherita di Maria di Iacopo da Bologna.

workers from the Opera: the Opera del Duomo was the Office of the Works of Santa Maria del Fiore, the Florentine Cathedral or Duomo. It was a public office set up to administer, repair, and protect the vast public edifice, and employed a large number of people.

303 *Bernardino Manelli from the Mugello*: Cellini used Manellini as an assistant and as a model for the Mercury at the base of the *Perseus*.

Gianpagolo and Domenico Paggini: Domenico (1520–90) was a sculptor, engraver, and master of the mint for Pope Sixtus V in Rome; Gianpagolo (1518–82) was a lapidary and coin maker who eventually entered the service of Philip of Spain and died in that country.

did a bust portrait of him that was larger than life-size: this would eventually become the bronze bust of Cosimo I that Cellini completed before 20 May 1548, and which is now in the Museo Nazionale del Bargello in Florence. The bust, a handsome and ornate neoclassical work portraying Cosimo in armour, was set up over the fortress in Portoferraio (Elba) in 1557 and remained there until 1781. For detailed photographs, see Pope-Hennessy, *Cellini* (plates 117–20). Another, marble, bust on which Cellini may have assisted, and which is modelled after the bronze original, is in the Fine Arts Museum of San Francisco (Pope-Hennessy, *Cellini*, plate 121).

in a hundred years: because he would enjoy speaking with the Duke so much that he would never get any work done.

304 *Messer Giuliano Buonaccorsi, a Florentine citizen*: see I, 98.

305 *Antonio di Vittorio Landi*: a Florentine merchant and writer who lectured to the Florentine Academy. His prose comedy *Commodus* was presented in 1539 on the occasion of Cosimo's marriage to Eleonora of Toledo, and published in 1566. Landi had a legal dispute with Cellini between 1559 and 1560 and apparently also bought a jewel from him in 1555.

cropped it off: the word Cellini employs is *schericato*, which was usually employed to describe priests who had been defrocked or removed from office.

either flat or to a point: as Cellini explains in his *Treatise on Goldsmithing* (VIII), there were three methods of cutting diamonds and other precious stones: a *tavola* (a table cut, a flat surface); a *faccette* (faceted); or *per punta* (cut to a point).

this rascal of a Bernardaccio: once again, Cellini employs a diminutive of a name to underline his contempt for the individual.

the New Market: near the Palazzo Vecchio on Via Calimala.

306 *to the goldsmith's workshop*: in II, 53 Cellini noted that the Duke wanted Cellini and the Poggini brothers to work inside the palace, and this must be the workshop in question.

those large edges: the word Cellini employs is *filetti*, which actually refers to the angles or sharp lines of the cut stones that divide one facet from another.

307 *Bachiacca the embroiderer*: Antonio Ubertino (1499–1572) was the brother of Francesco Ubertini (see I, 30), and like him was called Il Bachiacca.

of this poor, unfortunate city of Florence: this original statement implicitly criticizing the effects of Medici rule in Florence was erased by the same hand that erased other negative remarks about the Duke in previous chapters, and it was replaced by the simple word 'city'.

308 *headed toward Venice*: at this point in the original codex the part written by the son of Michele di Goro Vestri ends, and it is not known who wrote the next three and a half pages before Cellini himself began to write in his own hand. The soiled state of the back of the folio leads some scholars to believe that the writing of the autobiography was interrupted here for some time. Since this second copyist's hand is evident in a number of other letters and memos that Cellini wrote, he may have been a close associate or a relative, but he has never been identified.

309 *that wonderful painter Titian*: Tiziano Vecellio (1477–1576), the greatest painter of his day, was living at this time in regal splendour in Venice. This is the only reference to Titian in Cellini's autobiography.

309 *Messer Lorenzo de' Medici*: see I, 99. Lorenzino de' Medici, the assassin of Duke Alessandro de' Medici, upon whose head Cosimo I had placed a bounty, was eventually murdered in Venice by an assassin in Cosimo's pay in 1548.

Messer Giuliano Buonaccorsi: see I, 98.

he stayed in my house: it seems incredible that Cellini would first work for Cosimo I, then pass the time with a man Cosimo had dispatched assassins to kill in Venice, without being overly concerned about how Cosimo would take such easy familiarity with one of his bitterest enemies. But during his sojourn in France Cellini was equally unconcerned about spending much of his time with Florentine exiles, also Cosimo's enemies.

the Lord Prior degli Strozzi: Leone Strozzi (1515–54), prior of Capua who, like his brother, served Francis I and Henry II (see II, 34).

nothing but trouble!: while it is surprising that Cellini maintained friendly relations with Florentine anti-Medici exiles and did not think it would bother his patron, the ruler of Florence, it is equally puzzling that Cellini thought the bitter opponents of Cosimo I would not react in a negative manner when he spoke of him as a great lord.

310 *works with great difficulty*: the repetition of the same phrase in the same paragraph underscores how little pruning or editing Cellini did with his manuscript.

Master Zanobi di Pagno, the bell-founder: a member of the Portigiani family of Fiesole, most of whom were founders. This artisan also assisted Gianbologna (1529–1608) in the casting of the monumental Neptune Fountain in Bologna (1563–6).

312 *You are malvenuto*: yet another play on Cellini's first name, Benvenuto ('Welcome') and its opposite, *malvenuto* ('Unwelcome'), which he frequently employs.

in full measure: again Cellini employs the idiom *a misura di carboni* (see notes to pp. 26 and 129).

313 *a fourth as a reward*: in Cellini's day, an informer was given one-fourth of the fine levied upon the criminal who was spied upon. In other words, Cellini says he wants no reward for telling the truth.

314 *Afterwards*: at this point in the manuscript the pages written in Cellini's own hand begin. The rest of the manuscript up to the end of his narrative is in his own hand.

from my mines: Cosimo apparently operated mines in Campiglia and Pietrasanta (in the Maremma district of Tuscany) as a kind of hobby, since they never turned a profit and were finally abandoned in the seventeenth century.

Piero di Martino: Piero Spigliati, a goldsmith in Florence active around 1545; in the following year Cellini had him condemned for failure to repay a loan.

316 *and here I lacked for everything*: by Cellini's own account of his time in France, his life was not quite so idyllic as he suggests. In fact, given his personality, his problems with all his rivals and patrons repeat themselves wherever he goes. Still, the support Cellini received from King Francis, when compared to that he grudgingly received from Duke Cosimo, appears to have been more generous and dependable.

smothered my only little son: infants were often smothered carelessly by wet-nurses and other adults, because the babies often slept in the same bed as adults.

317 *come back here with it*: on 23 June 1546 Cellini wrote a letter laden with irony to request the marble, in which he sarcastically states he has no other master in sculpture than Bandinelli and that he hopes to surpass his master's achievement!

Messer Sforza: Sforza Almeni from Perugia was Duke Cosimo's chamberlain; the Duke murdered him with his own hands on 22 May 1566 in a fit of rage after Almeni had revealed the details of his affair with Eleonora degli Albizzi.

318 *King Philip*: Philip II of Spain (1527–98), son of Charles V, who became ruler of Spain in 1556.

Signor Stefano di Pilestina: Stefano Colonna, a member of the Palestrina family, served in France and later after 1542 was Cosimo's lieutenant-general. He died in 1548.

the greatest pleasure in it: the *Ganymede* is now in the Museo Nazionale del Bargello in Florence (for photographs, see Pope-Hennessy, *Cellini*, plates 129–30). In Greek mythology, Jupiter fell in love with Ganymede and abducted him, making him his cup-bearer. Like the myth of Apollo and Hyacinth (see note to p. 322), this story was often used as an argument for homosexual love.

319 *my Hercules and Cacus*: Bandinelli's marble work was presented in the Piazza della Signoria on April 1534. It was the custom in Florence and Rome to write poems or comments on newly inaugurated statues, and those composed about Bandinelli's work (including one by Cellini himself) were not uniformly complimentary. The marble was originally meant for Michelangelo, who was supposed to use it for a figure of Hercules that would stand with his *David*, but in 1525 Clement VII gave the material to Bandinelli, who eventually completed the statue between 1530 and 1534. The mythological inspiration behind the statue is mentioned in a number of classical sources, including Livy, Virgil, and Ovid: Cacus, a fire-breathing giant and son of Vulcan, steals some cattle from Hercules, who eventually kills the monster in an epic battle and regains his livestock.

his Sacristy: the Sacrestia Nuova (New Sacristy) at the Church of San Lorenzo, where Michelangelo erected the Chapel of the Medici Tombs between 1520 and 1534, but left them unfinished; they were assembled by his assistants and shown to the public in 1545. The works there include statues of two Medici princes (Giuliano and Lorenzo, the two people to whom Niccolò Machiavelli dedicated *The Prince*), as well as the famous statues of *Day*, *Night*, *Dawn*, and *Twilight* that were so important an influence upon Cellini's salt-cellar and the rest of his sculpture.

320 *a lion-ox*: Cellini invents an animal to underline the monstrous nature of Bandinelli's statue.

322 *the Opera*: see note to p. 302.

incomplete in my workshop: the *Apollo and Hyacinth* is now in the Museo Nazionale del Bargello in Florence (see Pope-Hennessy, *Cellini*, plate 131, for an excellent photograph). As with Jupiter's passion for Ganymede, Apollo's love for Hyacinthus, a Spartan prince, is a story of homosexual love. According to the version told by Ovid in his *Metamorphoses* (X, 162–219), while Apollo was teaching Hyacinthus to throw the discus the jealous west wind caught the discus and threw it against the young boy's skull, killing him. The hyacinth flower sprang up where his blood fell.

323 *which I called Narcissus*: now in the Museo Nazionale del Bargello in Florence (see Pope-Hennessy, *Cellini*, plate 132, for a colour photograph). According to Ovid's account (*Metamorphoses*, III, 339–510), as punishment for rejecting the love of the nymph Echo, Narcissus was made to fall in love with his own reflection in a pool of water; when he died he was changed into the narcissus flower.

those great flood waters of the Arno came down: probably in the disastrous flood of August 1557.

on its breast: the garland no longer exists and was probably in bronze; the crack above the figure's breast is clearly visible, however.

Master Raffaello de' Pilli, a surgeon: a Florentine surgeon active 1550–60.

St Lucy: St Lucy is the patron saint of the eyes, who died in AD 304 during Diocletian's persecution of the Christians. She is a popular figure in Italian art, often represented as carrying a dish with two eyes on it.

324 *that makes it different from the others*: in chs. I–IV of his *Treatise on Sculpture* Cellini describes in great detail the construction of furnaces employed in the casting of bronze.

326 *near Monte Lupo*: about 25 km. from Florence, in what is today Montelupo Fiorentino.

a funnel-like furnace: Cellini calls it a *manica* ('sleeve' in Italian). The furnace was sleeve-shaped or funnel-like—wide at the mouth and narrow at the base, much like the relationship between the wider part of a shirt-sleeve and its narrower cuff.

327 *Bernardino Mannellini from the Mugello*: see II, 58.

328 *the two pegs with these iron hooks*: as Cellini himself explains in various

chapters of his *Treatise on Sculpture*, the *mandriano* or *mandriale* (iron hook) is a piece of bent iron with a long handle used by workmen to drive the peg (*spina*) into the furnace to allow the molten metal to escape. The *forma* (mould) is composed of two parts: the exterior *tonaca* (tunic), which is composed of clay and is hollow; and the other interior part (usually filled with wax), which was called the *anima* (literally, the soul). The hot metal reaches the mould and enters the space filled with wax between the *tonaca* and the *anima*: the heat drives out the wax, which is replaced with metal. This is why this ancient method of casting bronze is usually referred to as the 'lost wax' method.

Mona: the abbreviated title for Madonna, the polite term of address to a woman without important titles or family position; see note to p. 72. Subsequently, this woman, praised by Cellini now, was driven away as a thief, according to a memorandum he wrote in 1561.

just like the men . . . to death: besides priests, there were also confraternities of men who actually spent the night with condemned criminals until the morning of their execution.

sphere of flame: according to the Ptolemaic system, the sphere of flame was that which existed between the sphere of air and that of the first sphere of the moon.

329 *a certain Master Alessandro Lastricati*: a sculptor of the period who helped Cellini cast the body of the Medusa and the figure of Perseus. Alessandro's brother Zanobi (1508–90) also helped in the casting of the *Perseus*. Both were often in the employ of Cosimo I. In 1564 Alessandro played an important role in the funeral procession of Michelangelo, executing a figure of Fame for the event.

having been caked: the actual expression Cellini uses here is quite colourful (*l'essersi fatto un migliaccio*), for it refers not just to any cake but to a *castagnaccio*, a cake made from chestnut flour that retains a fairly firm, sticky consistency within its form after baking. It is still produced in many parts of Italy in different ways, especially in the winter and early spring.

the pit: the Italian term is *braciaiuola*, which is a pit below the grating of the furnace which receives the burning ashes and cinders (*brace*), as Cellini points out in ch. IV of his *Treatise on Sculpture*.

330 *the alloy*: Cellini uses the technical term *la lega* for the alloy or the base metal that is employed to bind together (*legare*, in Italian) the most important metals in the statue's composition.

two hundred pounds: literally, 'which were about two hundred'; it is most likely that Cellini means to refer to the weight of the pewter, not the number of individual items involved; in the *Treatise of Sculpture* (III) he refers to 200 *pounds* of pewter.

332 *Averardo Serristori*: in 1537 ambassador of Duke Cosimo to the court of Charles V and, from 1550 to 1564, to the papal court in Rome.

332 *Pope Julius de' Monti*: Giovanni Maria Ciocchi del Monte Sansovino (1487–1555), elected to the papacy with the name of Julius III in 1550. He was an ally of Cosimo, and an important patron of the arts, commissioning the Villa Giulia in Rome from a succession of architects (Vasari, Ammannati, Vignola, and finally Michelangelo).

Bindo di Antonio Altoviti: see n. to p. 216. For excellent photographs of the bust, see Pope-Hennessy, *Cellini*, plates 123–6. This work would be Cellini's second bronze bust in the antique style after the one he did of Duke Cosimo I. When Cellini found time to pose his subject remains problematic. We have no record of his presence in Rome between 1539 and 1550, nor can we trace Altoviti's time in Florence during Cellini's return to their native city with any certainty.

333 *one of the Forty-Eight*: after the institutions of the Florentine Republic were abolished upon the return of the Medici, Pope Clement VII established three councils for the government of Florence in 1532: the Forty-Eight or *Quarantotto*, a type of Senate; the Two Hundred or *Dugento*, a larger deliberative body similar to a chamber of deputies; and a smaller group of four people chosen from the senate called the Magnates or *Gli Ottimati*, who held office for three months and had executive functions.

a most affectionate letter: the letter is dated 14 March 1559 and still exists. In spite of the fact that Michelangelo's original letter to Cellini praising his bust is no longer extant, there is no reason to believe that it was not written, or that Cellini was inventing such high praise from the man he considered to be the greatest artist of all time.

interest on my share that was due me: the description is somewhat confusing, but Cellini means that Altoviti gave him the interest on his original 1,000 scudi, for a total of 1,200 scudi. It would be interesting to know what Duke Cosimo might have thought of his artist who was, in effect, engaged in loaning his patron money through the bank of one of the most powerful anti-Medici enemies.

Ser Giuliano Paccalli: nothing seems to be known of this notary.

334 *keep this money of mine alive*: as always, the master of the idiomatic expression, by this remark Cellini indicates that he wants his banker-patron to invest his money, and to receive the interest from it himself.

fifteen per cent interest: the contract exists and is dated 9 April 1552. The interest rate is only apparently high (Altoviti loaned Henry II, king of France, a much larger sum at 16 per cent; usurious rates were considered during this period to range between 25 and 30 per cent). Cellini's animosity toward his patron may seem surprising, but it probably has a financial basis. After Altoviti's support for anti-Medici conspirators came to nothing at the Battle of Marciano, Altoviti's property was confiscated in Tuscany by Cosimo I. As a result, Altoviti ceased payments to Cellini in 1554. Cellini petitioned the Florentine government for redress. It is only one more example of how easily financial transactions between artist and patron could go sour, especially when two hard-headed characters like Cellini and Altoviti were involved.

employed on the building of St Peter's: Michelangelo took charge of the project in 1546.

his Urbino in charge: Francesco di Bernardino d'Amadore, known as Urbino. After his death in 1555, Michelangelo composed a sonnet to mourn his passing.

335 *Castello, just above Ponte a Rifredi*: a Medici villa some 6 km. from Florence.

336 *a necklace of enormous pearls*: according to Pope-Hennessy (*Cellini*, 224), the pearls could be those shown in Bronzino's famous portrait of Eleonora of Toledo, now in the Uffizi.

337 *pearls are fish-bones*: this was the common belief in Cellini's day.

338 *my other affairs concerning my sons and daughters*: Cosimo would need such impressive pieces of jewellery for engagements, marriages, or gifts of state.

buried in a casket of diamonds: that is, you can consider these words concealed in the most secret place imaginable, safe from the Duchess.

339 *puff yourself up at once*: court buffoons would puff up their cheeks so that their patrons could enjoy the pleasure of slapping them. In other words, the Duke is saying: 'if you don't leave at once, I shall slap your face.'

singing 'La bella Franceschina': a popular song, the lyrics of which are still extant; here Cellini means that Bernardone could have done something else amusing, if not allow his cheeks to be slapped.

340 *war broke out with Siena*: in 1552, supported by French troops under the leadership of Piero Strozzi and the assistance of the French monarch Henry II, as well as anti-Medici Florentine exiles, the city of Siena rose up against imperial troops allied with Cosimo. After the French and Sienese were defeated at the Battle of Marciano, Cosimo laid siege to Siena, which capitulated on 12 April 1555. Siena was subsequently annexed to Cosimo's Tuscan duchy, and its demise signalled the true end of Renaissance republicanism in the peninsula, except for the Venetian Republic.

my argument: by the end of the Renaissance almost all the major Italian cities were surrounded by fortified walls which have, in this century, generally been torn down. The gates that remain today in Florence are those toward Prato, San Frediano, San Giorgo, and Santa Croce. Several of the individuals mentioned by Cellini are worthy of mention. Pasqualino d'Ancona, known as Il Boni, was a sculptor active in Florence around the middle of the century. Giuliano Baglione (1491–1555) was the son of Baccio Baglioni, called Baccio d'Agnolo (1462–1543, the architect of the Palazzo Bartolini in Florence's Piazza Santa Trinita); Giuliano eventually replaced his father as the architect of the Opera del Duomo. Antonio Particini is remembered by Vasari, among others, as a rare master of woodcarving; he worked on the settings for the entry of Charles V into Florence in 1536, and for other important court weddings and ceremonies, which required massive sets and façades. Francesco da San Gallo (1494–1576), the son of Giuliano da San Gallo, became renowned for his military fortifications and succeeded Baccio d'Agnolo as the head of the Opera del Duomo in 1543. Archival records in Florence dated 23 August 1554 contain instructions to pay Cellini and others ten scudi per month for their work in building these fortifications.

341 *'Come now! Blast you! I don't understand this plan of yours!'*: Cellini transcribes the Lombard idiom in this sentence as best he can.

342 *bloodthirsty men imaginable*: the identity of this bloodthirsty soldier with the manners of a young girl is unclear. It may have been Giovanni Masini (d. *c.*1587), a soldier who fought with Cosimo's troops in the war against Siena, and who eventually became Governor of the Order of San Stefano after Cosimo nominated him to the order in 1565.

at the gates of Turin: during the occupation of Turin by French soldiers, in February 1543, a Spanish captain attempted to enter the city by hiding in wagons loaded with hay.

In those days: probably during the first months of 1544.

the Chimera: an Etruscan bronze of the fifth century BC, now in the Museo Archeologico in Florence. The Chimera was a mythological animal with a lion's head, a goat's body, and a dragon's tail, and like a dragon it breathed fire. According to Greek mythology, Bellerophon killed the Chimera with his arrows from the back of Pegasus, the winged horse that sprang from the blood of Medusa when Perseus beheaded her.

343 *she was unwell*: in fact Eleonora di Toledo died a number of years later, on 18 September 1562.

344 *Signor Don Grazìa*: Garzia (1547–62), the fourth child of Cosimo and Eleonora, who died prematurely. At the time Cellini encountered the child he was either 6 or 7 years old.

the Prince . . . Fernando: the Prince is the first-born, Francesco Maria de' Medici (1541–87), who succeeded Cosimo as Grand Duke of Tuscany in 1574, and whose daughter Maria would marry Henry IV of France, establishing a historic link between the French monarchy and Florence; Giovanni de' Medici (1543–62) was made a cardinal in 1560 and became Archbishop of Pisa the following year; Fernando (Hernando) I de' Medici (1549–1609) succeeded his brother Francesco I as Grand Duke of Tuscany in 1587. The children are called by the honorific title 'Don' because of Eleonora's Spanish background.

345 *sitting at her feet*: the small bronzes (from 84 to 96 cm. in height) were placed around the base of the statue of Perseus, along with a relief of Perseus freeing Andromeda. Copies replaced them, and the originals were taken to the Museo Nazionale del Bargello in Florence. For photographs, see Pope-Hennessy, *Cellini*, plates 86, 108–16.

have you understood me?': in other words, the Duke was making Cellini a permanent gift of a house in which he might live and work.

346 *San Pier Scheraggio*: a very ancient and once important church by the Palazzo Vecchio that was eventually demolished by Vasari in the construction of the Uffizi complex in 1561 (*scheraggio* was the old Tuscan term for a conduit, ditch, or sewer for rainwater).

San Miniato: San Miniato al Monte, the great Romanesque church, is situated on a hill overlooking Florence on the south side of the Arno.

when that pig left the Mint: since the Mint (Zecca) was behind the Loggia de' Lanzi, Cellini's screen of scaffolding surrounding the work on the *Perseus* was very close by (this explains why he refers to *his* door).

Feast of our San Giovanni: since Florentines celebrate the day devoted to their patron saint (John the Baptist) on 24 June, the date was 22 or 23 June.

Master Buaccio inherited them: Cellini had already used the name Buaccio to refer to Baccio Bandinelli; here he uses it again to refer to Bernardone's son, Baccio Baldini (d. 1585), who was a physician to Duke Cosimo and the first librarian of the Laurentian Library in Florence. Pandora was the mythological figure whose box, unfortunately opened because of her female curiosity, contained all the evils and misfortunes that would subsequently plague humankind.

347 *the Innocenti*: a famous foundling hospital that still exists.

348 *Iacopo da Puntorno*: Jacopo Carucci, called Pontormo (1494–1556), one of the founders of Florentine Mannerism.

the painter Bronzino: Agnolo di Cosimo di Mariano Allori, called Bronzino (1503–72), a pupil of Pontormo, who became the great court painter for the Medici family; also a poet, he wrote two poems in celebration of the *Perseus* which still exist.

sent his Sandrino: the nephew and pupil of Bronzino, Alessandro Allori (1535–1607), who also became one of the great Medici court painters.

Christ and St Thomas in bronze: Verrocchio (1435–88), Leonardo's teacher, cast the *Incredulity of St Thomas* for an external niche on the façade of the church of Orsanmichele in Florence, working on this statue between 1466 and 1483.

349 *on a Thursday morning*: it was actually a Friday morning, on 27 April 1554.

with one voice: here Cellini exaggerates a little; at least one poem remains by Alfonso de' Pazzi that attacks the statue, claiming that it has the body of an old man but the legs of a young girl! Yet Cellini's masterpiece has stood the test of time, and as Pope-Hennessy puts it (*Cellini*, 186), the *Perseus*, 'in the pantheon of Renaissance sculpture, still stands, in terms of popular appeal, second only to the *David* of Michelangelo'.

Viceroy of Sicily: Don Juan de Vega, Spanish viceroy from 1547 to 1557.

349 *I responded modestly*: this could also read 'I humbled myself', and is one of the few times in *My Life* when Cellini does so!

Fra Giovanagnolo de' Servi: Giovanni Angelo da Montorsoli (1507–63), whose Orion and Neptune fountains in Messina were completed between 1547 and 57.

350 *return content to serve you*: Vallombrosa, Camaldoli, the Eremo di Camaldoli, and Bagni di Santa Maria are all places with monasteries or hermitages that were popular places for pilgrimages. Sestile probably refers to Sestino. San Francesco della Vernia is Verna, a monastery founded by St Francis in 1215, and where he received the stigmata in 1224. All the sites are in various parts of the Tuscan territory.

351 *Cesare*: Cesare di Niccolò di Mariano dei Federighi (d. 1560), a sculptor who worked with Cellini on the pedestal of the *Perseus* and then was active in Milan from 1560 until his death.

without any opposition whatsoever: in the margin of the manuscript and in Cellini's own hand, there is a note that reads: 'this was during the time that Piero passed through and came with his army to Siena.' On 14 July 1554 Piero Strozzi was in the Valdichiana, pillaging Medici territory around Florence and Arezzo.

352 *by the Palace of the Podestà*: today this building houses the Museo Nazionale del Bargello, but in Cellini's day it was called the Palace of the Podestà. The meeting would have taken place on what is today called the Via del Proconsolo. The Badia (still called that today, traditionally considered to be Dante's church) is the Benedictine Church of Santa Maria Assunta and Santo Stefano near the Bargello Museum.

with the Duke of Urbino: Guidobaldo II della Rovere (1514–74).

Messer Iacopo Guidi: a theologian from Volterra who became Cosimo's secretary, and Bishop of Penna in 1561; he took part in the Council of Trent (sent by Pope Pius IV), and died in 1582. Judging from letters exchanged with Baccio Bandinelli, he was not a friend of Cellini's.

as stiff as a rod: the Italian word *incamatita* means as rigid as the rod (*il camato*) used for beating wool.

353 *crazia*: a Tuscan coin of very little value coined by Cosimo I and similar to a penny.

quattrini: another coin of very little value.

Girolimo degli Albizi: Girolamo degli Albizzi (d. 1555) was a cousin to Cosimo's mother, Maria Salviati, and one of the most fervent Medici supporters, even though he belonged to the family that had traditionally opposed the rise of Medici power. He was actually banned from Florence in 1529 for his political views, but returned with the re-establishment of Medici rule in 1530. He occupied a number of important positions, including that of Commissioner-General of the Ordinanza Fiorentina, a militia that Machiavelli had originally suggested for defending the city. It was rumoured that he had poisoned his best friend and the period's greatest historian, Francesco Guicciardini.

354 *confirmed the price*: in *I trattati dell'oreficeria e della scultura di Benvenuto Cellini*, ed. Carlo Milanesi (Florence: Le Monnier, 1857; repr. 1994), 259–60, Milanesi publishes a copy of the letter written on 2 September 1554 by Albizzi to the Duke, which set the price Cellini reports, as well as a rescript written by the Duke on the same day which accepts the proposal. Cellini was nonetheless clearly not satisfied by this decision, since he assumed that there would be a substantial payment for the statue itself in addition to the cost of his maintenance. In another memorandum which he wrote on 25 September 1557, Cellini complains of Albizzi's decision, calling him a man 'who lived the low life.' For the translation of these documents, see *The Life of Benvenuto Cellini*, trans. Robert Cust (London: G. Bell, 1910), ii. 383, n. 1.

Messer Alamanno Salviati: brother of the mother of Cosimo I (Maria Salviati) and of Cardinal Giovanni Salviati.

Messer Antonio de' Nobili: one of the Duke's treasurers from 1553 until 1562.

355 *the end of the year 1566*: the Florentines maintained their peculiar calendar, which began the New Year on 25 March—the traditional date assigned to the Incarnation—from the tenth century until 1749, when it was changed to conform to most European calendars, that begin the New Year on 1 January. Thus, the date in question, crucially important for dating the composition of the autobiography, is probably February 1567.

committing against me: Quistello, from Mirandola, was auditor of the treasurer; Iacopo Polverini of Prato was one of the Duke's ministers, who became famous because of a law he sponsored in 1548 that confiscated the property of the families of anti-Medici rebels; we only know that Brandini was one of Cosimo's many functionaries. It is unclear why these men would be hounding Cellini, but one can only suppose that it had something to do with the house that Cellini assumed the Duke had given him. If this were the case, it would not be the only promise made to Cellini by the often capricious, unfair, and ungenerous Duke that he did not keep.

356 *now that he is a very old man*: Michelangelo was 80 in 1555, but he was still working on a number of major projects.

357 *near Santa Felicità*: the church off Via Guicciardini between the Palazzo Vecchio and the Palazzo Pitti, and just before reaching the Ponte Vecchio.

Bishop de' Bartolini: Pope Leo X named Onofrio Bartolini of Florence Archbishop of Pisa in 1518; he died in 1556. During the Sack of Rome in 1527 he was trapped inside the Castel Sant'Angelo with Clement VII.

Messer Pandolfo della Stufa: for many years he was the cup-bearer for Caterina de' Medici, wife of the Dauphin of France; he was imprisoned for several years in France after being suspected of passing information about French foreign and military policy to Duke Cosimo I. Upon his release he returned to Florence, where he was very warmly received and made a senator in 1561. He died in 1568.

357 *Messer Lelio Torello*: (1489–1576), a native of Fano; jurist and literary figure, he was appointed by Cosimo as Chief Auditor in 1539; in 1546 he served as Cosimo's First Secretary. He died at the age of 87 after being named a senator by Grand Duke Francesco I. Unlike many of Cosimo's functionaries, Torello had a very high reputation for honesty and integrity.

358 *who ruined the cupola*: it was the architect and woodcarver Baccio Baglioni (1462–1543), called Baccio d'Agnolo, and not his son Giuliano, who built the gallery around the inside top drum of the cathedral dome, a project that Michelangelo was reported to have called 'a cricket cage'.

the doors of San Giovanni: Cellini intends to compete with perhaps the greatest artist in the execution of bronze doors in history, Lorenzo Ghiberti (1378–1455), who began working on the various doors of the Baptistery of San Giovanni in front of the Florentine Duomo (Santa Maria del Fiore) in 1401 after winning a famous contest for the best design. Ghiberti's doors were considered so beautiful that most people agreed with Michelangelo when he was quoted as saying that they deserved to be the gates of Paradise.

Piero Salviati: Piero di Alamanno Salviati (1504–64), first a republican opponent of the Medici; later he became the staunch supporter of Cosimo I and was named senator by the Duke in 1553.

359 *Messer Cesare*: little is known of this functionary.

during this period: the events Cellini describes in this section of the autobiography actually take place in 1559, four years after the events in the preceding chapter, which took place in 1555. During this interval before the arrival of the marble block, Cellini had served time in prison on at least two occasions. Imprisoned in August 1556 for assaulting the goldsmith Giovanni di Lorenzo, he had apparently beaten him so badly with a cudgel that his bones were exposed! After being imprisoned for a time and forced to pay a sum of money as a guarantee that he would behave, he was again arrested in early 1557 on a charge of sodomy over a period of five years with one of his apprentices, Ferrante da Montepulciano. Initially he received a prison sentence of four years in the notorious Stinche, the public prison of Florence. By petitioning the Duke he had his sentence commuted to strict house arrest for four years. The charge of sodomy had been made against Cellini on several previous occasions, and it is not surprising that he omits this rather dismal period in his life.

by way of the Grieve: actually it is the Ombrone, and not the Grieve, that runs near Poggio a Caiano.

360 *Bartolomeo Ammannati*: Bartolomeo di Antonio Ammannati (1511–92), a native of Settignano and student of Michelangelo. He built the courtyard

of the Palazzo Pitti, designed the Boboli Gardens, and rebuilt Ponte a Santa Trinità, a bridge Michelangelo designed, after the flood of 1557. The gigantic statue of Neptune was placed in a fountain in the Piazza della Signoria in front of the Palazzo Vecchio in October 1556 for the wedding celebration of Francesco de' Medici.

their son the prince: Francesco, their first-born and heir to the throne of the Grand Duchy.

the wonderful cupola: the dome of the Duomo (Santa Maria del Fiore), constructed by Filippo Brunelleschi after winning a contest in 1418; Ghiberti had bested Brunelleschi in the earlier contest of 1402 to decide who would execute the second door of the Baptistery of San Giovanni.

362 *two little models*: two models of Neptune were, in fact, mentioned in the inventory taken of Cellini's possessions after his death, but they have since disappeared.

the Cardinal of Santa Fiore: Guido Ascanio Sforza (see I, 112) was charged in 1560 by Pope Pius IV with bringing the cardinal's scarlet cap to Giovanni, Duke Cosimo's second-born son, who was between 15 and 16 years old at the time.

363 *the government of Lucca*: respectively the Cavaliere Conegrano of Ferrara and Girolamo Lucchesini of Lucca.

364 *Bandinelli died*: on 7 February 1560.

that Pietà: Bandinelli's *Dead Christ Supported by Nicodemus* (1554–60) is located in SS Annunziata in Florence in a chapel that originally belonged to the Pazzi family, a clan hostile to the Medici domination of Florence. In 1559 the chapel was assigned to Bandinelli for his tomb. Both Bandinelli and Cellini are buried in the same church, an amusing coincidence, since their lives were characterized by so much personal animosity. Cellini and other artists, however, are buried in the Chapel of the Confraternity of St Luke, which was the confraternity to which Florentine artists belonged.

365 *such an immeasurable wrong*: in one of his letters written in 1570 Cellini claims that the Duchess later repented of her action after seeing Cellini's beautiful marble Crucifix, and decided to procure for him another block of marble to do the work, but died before this was accomplished.

Giovanni the Fleming: Giovanni Bologna or Gianbologna (Jean de Boulogne, 1529–1608), one of the most important sculptors of the late sixteenth century. Among his major commissions are: the Neptune fountain in Bologna (1563–66), probably based upon his design for the Florentine contest; the equestrian statue of Cosimo I in the Piazza della Signoria; the *Rape of the Sabines* in the Loggia de' Lanzi in Florence; and the *Mercury* in the Museo Nazionale del Bargello in Florence.

Vincenzio Danti: a sculptor and goldsmith from Perugia (1530–76), who also wrote a book on proportion in 1567.

365 *the son of Moschino*: not the son Simone but the father, Francesco di Simone Mosca delle Pecore, called Il Moschino, an obscure artist.

Little George the painter: Cellini employs the derogatory diminutive (*Giorgetto*; a few sentences later, *Giorgino*) when referring to Giorgio Vasari (1511–74), the architect, painter, and biographer of artists' lives, because Vasari took an active role in assisting his protégé Ammannati to obtain this commission, for which Cellini never forgave him. Vasari's corresponding antipathy for Cellini is apparent from the fact that he does not devote a biography to him in his monumental *Lives of the Artists*, an oversight that cannot be explained merely by a lack of information, since he knew Cellini and his works quite well and must have realized that his statue of *Perseus* was one of the great masterpieces of the period.

Messer Gianstefano: Gianstefano Alli, a Roman and one of Cosimo's most trusted chamberlains, who was often sent to Rome to procure antiquities for the Duke.

366 *a final touch*: one last coat of plaster.

nicknamed Sbietta: Piermaria di Vespasiano Ricci di Anterigoli from Vicchio, a small town in the Mugello about 30 km. from Florence. His nickname apparently refers to his slippery quality (*sbiettare* means to slip away in haste; Cellini actually spells his name Sbetta).

Messer Guido Guidi: see II, 24.

including the taxes: the contract for this transaction, dated 26 June 1560, is still extant. This kind of a contract was written to provide cash to the farmer while avoiding the laws against usury: Cellini would receive revenue as well as payments in kind.

the Mercatanzia: this was the tribunal that decided cases related to commercial law.

367 *a double feast day*: that is, both Wednesday and the following day were feast days.

my villa in Trespiano: about 8 km. from Florence toward Bologna, acquired by Cellini on 26 October 1548; he subsequently bought more land there in 1556.

369 *Santino*: Giovanbatista Santini, the friend introduced at the beginning of the chapter.

370 *a pinch of sublimate*: Cellini writes *silimato* for *sublimato corrosivo*, or bichloride of mercury. A lethal dose of this substance would be about one gram. It may cause burning of the mouth, abdominal pain, vomiting, ulceration, and bloody diarrhoea. It may affect the central nervous system, causing weak pulse, shallow breathing, or exhaustion, and may also cause renal failure.

a great deal to say: In the original manuscript the name of the wife's supposed lover has been erased to the point of illegibility. The portion of the manuscript that we have translated within brackets was also erased but can still be made out. It is difficult to tell whether Cellini himself erased the passages, perhaps feeling remorse for the aspersions cast against the reputation of Laura Battiferri, Ammannati's wife. She was regarded as a woman beyond reproach, and Cellini even exchanged Petrarchan sonnets with her.

irrelevant to our profession: the reader should recall how Bandinelli (II, 71) called Cellini a sodomite in the midst of a discussion about his sculpture. Cellini announces that he is taking the high road, but his first impulse was to cast doubts upon his rival's wife's virtue.

Master Raffaello de' Pilli: see notes to pp. 148 and 323 for information on Cellini's doctors.

371 *his entry into Siena*: Cosimo's triumphant entry into Siena took place on 28 October 1560.

372 *Messer Alfonso Quistello*: see II, 97.

Averardo Serristori: see II, 78.

Federigo de' Ricci: elected senator in 1532, Ricci (d. 1572) became immensely rich and was one of Cosimo's confidants.

373 *Messer Bartolo Concino*: the son of a peasant, Concino succeeded in amassing great wealth by serving as a notary for the criminal tribunals of Tuscany. He became one of Cosimo's confidants, eventually being raised to the rank of count.

374 *I returned to Florence*: in a request dated 13 April 1561, in which Cellini had requested his leave, the Duke appended to Cellini's petition a rescript stating that the sculptor could leave if he wished, since the Duke kept no one by force in his service.

375 *in coin*: previously Cellini was supposed to be paid in gold; now he is being paid in coin or money of account, usually reckoned in the silver equivalent of gold—a much less advantageous bargain.

376 *gladly make them a present of it*: the marble Crucifix was completed in 1562 and was not accepted as a gift; rather, it was acquired in 1565 by Cosimo, who paid fifteen hundred golden scudi for it. Kept in the Palazzo Pitti until 1576, Grand Duke Francesco I sent it to King Philip II of Spain, where it is now preserved in the Escorial.

377 *Queen of France sent Messer Baccio del Bene*: the Queen (regent at the time) was Catherine de' Medici (1519–89), after 1559 the widow of Henry II and the mother of his successor, Charles IX.

Daniello da Volterra: Daniello dei Ricciardelli di Volterra (*c.*1509–1566), painter and sculptor who studied with Sodoma and was one of the followers of Michelangelo; the figure of a horse he cast was placed upon the tomb of Henry II which Catherine had commissioned as a mausoleum for her family after a design by Primaticcio. Daniello da Volterra is best known, however, for his nickname Il Braghettone ('The Breeches Maker'), for he was ordered by the Pope to cover some of the nudes in Michelangelo's *Last Judgement* in the Sistine Chapel with garments to hide their nakedness.

378 *who was in Spain*: Francesco Maria de' Medici left for Spain in May of
1562 for a formal state visit, and returned only in June 1563.

before the others: Cardinal Giovanni de' Medici died at Rosignano on
21 November 1562. His brothers Don Garzia and Ferdinando also fell ill,
and Garzia died at Pisa on 6 December 1562. On 18 December 1562
Eleonora di Toledo died as well. Needless to say, these sudden deaths
within a single family aroused suspicions of poison, but letters written by
Duke Cosimo to his son Francesco at the Spanish court speak of an
epidemic of influenza, and this is a much more likely explanation. Marsh-
lands in Italy were extremely unhealthy, of course, and malaria has been
prevalent in them down to the twentieth century.

then I set off for Pisa: Cellini ends his account abruptly in 1562, but since
he lived until 13 February 1571, his autobiography omits a treatment of
the last nine years of his life. They were not particularly happy ones,
since he had managed to lose the favour of Cosimo, was often ill, and
worked on very few major works. The fact that no great works were
produced seems to have silenced his narrative. During the last years of
his life he completed his treatises on sculpture and goldsmithing, which
were published in 1568, and wrote a number of poems. The abrupt
ending of Cellini's autobiography, referring as it does to a destination for
one of his many journeys, reminds the reader that the work has many
affinities with the picaresque genre.

INDEX

Note: Cellini may refer to a character as simply the 'Cardinal of Ravenna'. We index the character exactly as he is mentioned in the text and provide additional information, or cross-references if necessary. Thus the 'Cardinal of Ravenna' is indexed under 'Ravenna, Cardinal of (Benedetto Accolti)'. We employ the spellings of names and places Cellini uses and correct them, if necessary, in the footnotes that annotate the text.

The Oxford World's Classics Website

www.oup.com/uk/worldsclassics

- Information about new titles
- Explore the full range of Oxford World's Classics
- Links to other literary sites and the main OUP webpage
- Imaginative competitions, with bookish prizes
- Articles by editors
- Extracts from Introductions
- Special information for teachers and lecturers

www.oup.com/uk/worldsclassics

American Literature

Authors in Context

British and Irish Literature

Children's Literature

Classics and Ancient Literature

Colonial Literature

Eastern Literature

European Literature

History

Medieval Literature

Oxford English Drama

Poetry

Philosophy

Politics

Religion

The Oxford Shakespeare

A complete list of Oxford World's Classics, including Authors in Context, Oxford English Drama, and the Oxford Shakespeare, is available in the UK from the Marketing Services Department, Oxford University Press, Great Clarendon Street, Oxford OX2 6DP, or visit the website at www.oup.com/uk/worldsclassics.

In the USA, visit www.oup.com/us/owc for a complete title list.

Oxford World's Classics are available from all good bookshops. In case of difficulty, customers in the UK should contact Oxford University Press Bookshop, 116 High Street, Oxford OX1 4BR.